A military history of Ireland

This is a major, collaborative study of organised military activity and its broad impact on Ireland over the last thousand years or so, from the middle of the first millennium AD to modern time. It integrates the best recent scholarship in military history into its social and political context to provide a comprehensive treatment of the Irish military experience.

The eighteen chronologically organised chapters are written by leading scholars each of whom is an authority on the period in question. Drawing the whole work together is a wide-ranging introductory essay on the 'Irish military tradition' which explores the relationship of Irish society and politics with militarism and military affairs. The text is illustrated throughout by over 120 pictures and maps.

A military history of
IRELAND

Edited by

Thomas Bartlett
University College, Dublin

and

Keith Jeffery
University of Ulster at Jordanstown

Published by the Press Syndicate of the University of Cambridge
The Pitt Building, Trumpington Street, Cambridge CB2 1RP
40 West 20th Street, New York, NY 10011-4211, USA
10 Stamford Road, Oakleigh, Melbourne 3166, Australia

First published 1996

Reprinted 1996

First paperback edition published 1997

Printed in Great Britain at the University Press, Cambridge

A catalogue record for this book is available from the British Library

Library of Congress cataloguing in publication data

A military history of Ireland / edited by Thomas Bartlett
and Keith Jeffery.
p. cm.
Includes bibliographical references and index.
ISBN 0 521 41599 3 (hc)
1. Ireland – History, Miltary. I. Bartlett, Thomas.
II. Jeffery, Keith.
DA914.M55 1996
355′.009415 – dc20 95–6124 CIP

ISBN 0 521 41599 3 hardback
ISBN 0 521 62989 6 paperback

Dedicated to

Thomas Bartlett (1868–1918),
Royal Garrison Artillery (1914–18)

Thomas Bartlett (1901–56),
Belfast IRA (1918–21) and Óglaigh na hÉireann (1922–4)

Ernest Jeffery (1885–1962),
Durham Light Infantry (1915–19)

William Lumley Hackett (1888–1918),
Canadian Machine Gun Corps (1915–18)

Contents

Illustrations

Maps

Tables

Contributors

_____

Thomas Bartlett   *Professor of Modern Irish History, University College, Dublin*

Ciaran Brady   *Senior Lecturer in Modern History, Trinity College, Dublin*

T. M. Charles-Edwards   *Professor of Celtic Studies, University of Oxford*

John Childs   *Professor of Military History, University of Leeds*

S. J. Connolly   *Professor of Irish History, The Queen's University of Belfast*

Virginia Crossman   *Lecturer in History, University of Staffordshire*

Steven G. Ellis   *Associate Professor of History, University College, Galway*

David Fitzpatrick   *Associate Professor of History, Trinity College, Dublin*

Marie Therese Flanagan   *Senior Lecturer in Modern History, The Queen's University, Belfast*

Robin Frame   *Professor of History, University of Durham*

Alan J. Guy   *Assistant Director of the National Army Museum*

Keith Jeffery   *Professor of Modern History, University of Ulster at Jordanstown*

David W. Miller   *Professor of History, Carnegie-Mellon University, Pittsburgh*

Harman Murtagh   *Editor of the* Irish Sword

Eunan O'Halpin   *Associate Professor of Government, Dublin City University*

Jane H. Ohlmeyer   *Lecturer in History, University of Aberdeen*

Katharine Simms   *Senior Lecturer in Medieval History, Trinity College, Dublin*

Edward M. Spiers   *Professor of Strategic Studies, University of Leeds*

_____

Preface

This volume, which deals with organised military activity and its broad impact on Ireland over the last millennium or so, reflects with an Irish dimension the enormous growth in serious military history which has occurred in the last three decades. In the past, many academic historians tended to dismiss 'military history' as no more than the limited, frequently antiquarian and rather technical study of battles and combat generally. Confined within a circle of martial enthusiasts the military historian could afford to ignore wider historiographical developments. Academics, for their part herbivorous creatures with delicate scholarly sensibilities, were content to keep their distance from the rough-and-tumble carnivores who dealt in the blood and thunder of the battlefield. Thus two branches of historical endeavour advanced, mutually uncomprehending, if not mutually antagonistic. In fact, this is a caricature. The wonderful range of work published since its establishment in 1949 in the *Irish Sword*, the 'house journal' of the Military History Society of Ireland, testifies to the richness rather than the narrowness of Irish military history. But this work has never properly been integrated into the academic historical mainstream, and an emphasis on combat has perhaps led to the neglect, for example, of the social history of the military in Ireland. This collection of essays seeks to redress that balance and attempts to draw together in a single volume the best fruits of military history within the broad social and political context of Ireland as it has developed to the present day. Taking up the metaphor used above, we contend that the historian must be an omnivore, and will neglect the bloodier aspects of our history at his or her peril.

One theme which we have addressed from the start is that of the alleged Irish 'military tradition'. Given the conventional wisdom that the Irish, north and south, were (and are) a martial, not to say warlike nation, it is surprising that to date very little attention has been paid to this area of study. In drawing up our agenda we have urged the contributors – each of whom is an authority on the period in question – to consider the interaction of the military with society in general. We have for the most part limited our study to military affairs within the island of Ireland itself and have not attempted to follow exhaustively the exploits of Irish

---

soldiers throughout the world. The exceptions to this limitation, which occur in one complete chapter and parts of others, have been made on the grounds that an examination of the service of the Irish abroad can help us test the validity (or otherwise) of an Irish military tradition. Overseas service, too, has clearly influenced social and political attitudes back home.

It may be that this volume, with its emphasis on the social aspects of soldiering and warfare, will be characterised as part of the so-called 'new military history'. At its most extreme this becomes the manifestly absurd production of military history with the war left out. In our view this would be neither magnificent nor history. On the other hand, while we have aimed to include some account of the chief battles of Ireland's history, we have not dwelt on them, nor have we required our contributors to provide 'blow-by-blow' accounts of Irish military engagements. Such narratives are already widely available, for example in the admirable work of G. A. Hayes-McCoy and A. E. C. Bredin. We have sought to build on this work and begin to fill in the wider social and political background to the armed life-and-death struggles of Irishmen through the centuries.

We have deliberately chosen to call this volume *a* military history rather than *the* military history of Ireland since we are acutely aware of how much work has recently been done in this field, and how much more academic research is currently being pursued. In a way, like all historians, our findings and conclusions can only be interim and provisional, and it ill behoves us to be too definitive or dogmatic. Working in the two polities of modern Ireland, though both having roots in the north of the island, it may additionally be taken that we are well aware of the corrosive impact which war, violence and militarism has had, and continues to have, on Ireland. But unless we strive to understand these forces and to examine their effects on society in general, and over our whole history, we will never even be able to counteract their malignant power and fearsome attraction. Our hope is that this work may contribute something towards such understanding, and, as we write just a few weeks after cease-fires have been declared by both republican and loyalist paramilitary groups, we hope that the apparent timeliness of our volume's completion may not be undermined by any resumption of organised military action on the island of Ireland.

The editors dedicate this work to their own forebears who in the twentieth century served as soldiers for Ireland and Britain.

Thomas Bartlett and Keith Jeffery
Galway and Belfast
Armistice Day 1994

Acknowledgements

During the preparation of this volume the editors and contributors have incurred many debts for the generous assistance of fellow scholars, archivists, librarians and others. The editors would like specially to acknowledge the support and encouragement they have received from their own colleagues and institutions; they are also grateful for the admirable tolerance which their families have at times demonstrated towards the whole exercise. Thomas Bartlett owes a particular debt to University College, Galway. William Davies, at Cambridge University Press, has been constantly supportive and helpful from the very start. Sheila Kane has been an exemplary copy-editor.

We have received particular help with illustrations from the Military Archives, Dublin (especially Commandant Peter Young and Captain Victor Lang), the National Gallery of Ireland (Marie McFee), the National Library of Ireland (Elizabeth Kirwan), the National Museum of Ireland (Michael Kenny and Raghnall Ó Floinn), the Office of Public Works (John Scarry), the Public Record Office of Northern Ireland (Trevor Parkhill), the Ulster Museum (Tom Wylie), Tony Feenan of the University of Ulster at Jordanstown, Kevin Whelan of the Royal Irish Academy, and John Bradley, for advice on pre-1500 material. Marie Therese Flanagan, Alan Megahey and Dáibhí Ó Cróinín were most helpful when we were preparing the bibliography, and Lydia Bradley's sharp eye was invaluable with the proofs.

We are indebted to Her Majesty the Queen for her gracious permission to use materials from the Royal Archives at Windsor Castle, and to the Comptroller of Her Majesty's Stationery Office for the use of Crown Copyright records in the Public Record Office, the Environment Service Monuments and Buildings Record and the Public Record Office of Northern Ireland. We have made particular use of unpublished materials in the Bodleian Library; the British Library; the Imperial War Museum; the Library of Trinity College, Dublin; the Military Archives, Dublin; the National Archives, Dublin; the National Army Museum, London; the National Library of Ireland; University College, Dublin, Department of Archives; and the United States National Archives; to all of these institutions, and their staffs, we are most grateful.

Abbreviations

Citations of both published and unpublished secondary sources in the notes consist of author's surname(s) and short titles, with full information being provided in the bibliography. Citations for primary sources are generally given in full in the notes, apart from some abbreviated references to well-known printed editions of documents.

Add. MSS	Additional Manuscript
AFM	*Annala Rioghachta Eireann*
ALC	*Annals of Loch Cé*
Ann. Inisf.	*Annals of Inisfallen*
Ann. Tig.	*Annals of Tigernach*
AU	*Annals of Ulster*
Bk Rights	*Lebor na Cert*
BL	British Library
Bodl.	Bodleian Library, Oxford
Cal. S.P. Dom.	*Calendar of State Papers, Domestic Series*
Cal. S.P. Ire.	*Calendar of the State Papers relating to Ireland, 1509–1670* (20 vols., London, 1860–1912)
Cal. S.P. Spain	*Calendar of . . . State Papers relating to . . . Spain*
CCC	Caithréim Cellacháin Chaisil
CGG	Cogad Gáedel re Gallaib
Cog. Gaedhel	*Cogadh Gaedhel re Gallaibh*
Commons' Jn.	*Journals of the House of Commons*
CS	*Chronicum Scotorum*
Fiants Ire., Hen. VIII (etc.)	'Calendar to fiants of the reign of Henry VIII . . . ' (etc.)
Franciscan MSS	HMC, *Report on the Franciscan Manuscripts preserved at the Convent, Merchants Quay, Dublin* (Dublin, 1906)
Gir. Camb. op.	*Giraldi Cambrensis opera*
HC	House of Commons (Papers)

HMC	Historical Manuscripts Commission (Royal Commission on Historical Manuscripts)
IWM	Imperial War Museum (London)
L. & P. Hen. VIII	Letters and Papers, Foreign and Domestic, Henry VIII (21 vols., London, 1862–1932)
MA	Military Archives (Dublin)
NAI	National Archives of Ireland
NAM	National Army Museum (London)
NLI	National Library of Ireland
New Hist. Ire.	*New History of Ireland*
OED	*Oxford English Dictionary*
Ormonde MSS	HMC, *Report on the Manuscripts of the Duke of Ormonde*, new series (8 vols., London, 1902–1920)
PRO	Public Record Office (Kew)
PRONI	Public Record Office of Northern Ireland
RA	Royal Archives (Windsor Castle)
RIC	Royal Irish Constabulary
Rot. Pat. Hib.	*Rotulorum Patentium et Clausorum Cancellariae Hiberniae*
s.a.	sub anno
S.P. Hen. VIII	*State Papers, Henry VIII*
Stat. Ire., John–Hen. V	*Statutes and Ordinances . . . King John to Henry V*
TCD	Trinity College, Dublin
UCDA	University College Dublin Department of Archives
USNA	United States National Archives

Chapter 1

An Irish military tradition?

Thomas Bartlett and Keith Jeffery

1

In the *Field Day Anthology*, a massive three-volume, 1,500-page collection of Irish writing, the very first extract tells the story of Cú Chulainn, the legendary warrior of the Ulaidh or Ulstermen who in prehistoric times dominated the north of Ireland. In the *Táin Bó Cúailgne* (Cattle raid of Cuailgne), the centrepiece of Irish heroic literature, we learn that Cú Chulainn, on hearing that 'if a warrior took up arms on that day, his name for deeds of valour would be known throughout Ireland and his fame would last for ever' demanded weapons of his king, Conchobar Mac Nessa. Conchobar duly obliged, but of the fifteen spare sets of arms which he kept in his house, 'not one was left unbroken' by Cú Chulainn when he tried them out. He finally settled for Conchobar's own weapons. It was a similar story when it came to Cú Chulainn's request for a fitting chariot: we are told 'He smashed twelve chariots. So finally he was given Conchobar's chariot and it withstood the test.' Brushing aside the warning that his life would be short-lived – Cú Chulainn retorted, 'Provided I be famous, I am content to be only one day on earth' – the chariot-warrior was quickly into action, driving into enemy territory with a firm intention 'not to avoid danger', and he was soon engaged in desperate single-handed combat, with stunning success: 'In one hand he held nine heads, in the other ten, and these he brandished . . . Those were the trophies of one night's fighting by Cú Chulainn.'[1]

The story of Cú Chulainn, and other warrior sagas such as the *Fianaigheacht* or Fenian Cycle, date from the early medieval period. These story cycles merit attention on several counts. First, although classical writers had already made much of the Celts' love of battle and their martial characteristics ('war-mad', claimed one author),[2] these Irish sagas present us with a first clear sighting of those, later, hallowed characteristics of the Irish soldier – reckless daring, spectacular ferocity and indomitable courage. Second, the adventures of Cú Chulainn and others also illustrate some of those less flattering attributes which have dogged Irish soldiers through the centuries, and which had also been earlier identified by Roman writers among their Celtic adversaries: simplemindedness, guilelessness and even

1

witlessness. Third, the legendary Cú Chulainn has exerted a particular fascination for later generations. Those who, like Standish O'Grady, sought to rediscover an Irish national spirit amidst the humdrum, and anglicised, conformity of the late nineteenth century, found the adventures of Cú Chulainn serviceable and enabling; predictably perhaps, W. B. Yeats was moved to give his version, and reveal his aristocratic vision, of the warrior's adventures; and Patrick Pearse, the insurgent leader of 1916, consciously sought to model the regime at the school he founded on the story of Cú Chulainn, and other martial sagas. Latterly, the enduring vitality of the Cú Chulainn legend has been again emphasised through its adoption by certain elements within Ulster loyalism as a symbol of their determination to defend present-day Northern Ireland.[3]

With Cú Chulainn, we can see an embryonic Irish military tradition centring on apparently identifiable martial qualities peculiar to the Irish soldier – a tradition which has proved remarkably resilient over the centuries. To say as much is not to concede that the tradition has substance, or to claim that its elements are self-evident, or indeed to accept that there is only one, uniform tradition. We have recently been reminded that traditions can be, and frequently are, invented.[4] The validity, thus, of an Irish military tradition and its precise constitution remain matters for argument; they were not fundamental or commonly agreed assumptions held by the contributors to this volume. Far from it, for the notion of a coherent, specifically Irish, military tradition running through the past 1,500 years would seem at first glance inherently implausible: it is surely the discontinuities of the Irish military experience, the varieties of the Irish military tradition (including a respectable anti-war tradition),[5] rather than its continuities and uniformities that are striking. And yet, the notion of a broad Irish military tradition spanning the centuries has proved serviceable in seeking to make sense of the military history of this island.

Ireland is an island whose peoples, structures, society and politics have been for centuries shaped, where not determined, by war, the threat of war or, at least, by the absence of peace; a place where armed men in uniform (formal or informal) have ever been a constant (benign or malign) presence; a small country out of which vast armies of men have poured to do battle abroad. It would indeed be curious if these persistent martial themes had left little mark in Irish culture; and it may not in fact be so surprising if, on examination, an Irish military tradition turns out to be central to the Irish historical experience, and a key element in modern Irish identity.

2

In 1751, Voltaire published his history, *Le siècle de Louis XIV*, in the course of which he delivered himself of this verdict on the Irish soldier: '*Les Irlandais que nous avons vus de si bons soldats en France et en Espagne ont toujours mal combattus chez eux.*'[6] Voltaire was not of course a student of Irish history and his remarks ought

1.1   The death of Cuchulainn, as envisaged by Patrick Tuohy, from
Standish O'Grady, *History of Ireland* (1880).

perhaps to have been ignored. They were not, however, and in 1845 Mathew O'Conor published his *Military History of the Irish Nation* which took issue with Voltaire's scathing and sweeping judgement.[7] O'Conor recalled the Irish victory over the Vikings at Clontarf in 1014 (and contrasted it unfavourably with the French submission to Rollo), and while he admitted 'our subjugation' by the Anglo-Norman adherents of Diarmait MacMurchadha, he pointed out 'the greater conquest that the English themselves had endured at the hands of the invading Duke of Normandy'. And then, Voltaire refuted, O'Conor rapidly moved on to this main purpose. He briskly dismissed the military history of medieval Ireland. 'Prior to the sixteenth century', he wrote, 'the wars of the Irish were either petty intestine feuds not worthy of historical notice or uncombined efforts in resistance to Norse and Anglo-Norman invasion.' In his view, it was the earl of Tyrone who 'may be regarded as opening the school for that national military genius which afterwards rose to so noble a pitch of fame in all the most warlike services of Europe'. O'Conor, however, found the seventeenth century wearisome and confusing – shifting allegiances, endless desertion and wholesale pillaging were not his forte – and so it was, he wrote, 'with inexpressible relief, the author finds himself at length arrived at a period in the military history of his countrymen when, taking service in the most honourable manner with their ancient allies [the French], they began that series of brilliant exploits . . . which has rendered the name of Ireland illustrious in the military annals of Europe'. He concluded his narrative of the sieges, battles and campaigns of 1690–1710 with the reflection that 'viewed carelessly at a distance, their [Irish soldiers'] varied services' might seem 'evidence of an unprincipled Praetorian race'. But, he argued, this was not in fact the case: 'examined in detail . . . they only prove an amount of patriotism, piety, and valour, which, concentrated at home to national service, would have made Ireland all we could wish her'.[8]

Voltaire's stinging apothegm had, however, not yet run its course. In 1964, the doyen of Irish historians, G. A. Hayes-McCoy, returned to the charge in his slim volume of essays entitled *The Irish at War*, and attempted a further refutation.[9] To Voltaire's indictment, Hayes-McCoy now added that of General Richard Taylor of the Confederate States of America. 'Strange people, these Irish!' mused Taylor, 'Fighting everyone's battles and cheerfully taking the hot end of the poker, they are only to be found wanting when engaged in what they believe to be their national cause.' Hayes-McCoy, however, believed that 'that taunt of inferiority' had been already effectively rebutted – 'we have Pearse to thank for that' – and he maintained that bad leadership and a lack of training explained the comparative failure of the Irish at home. 'There is no such thing as a born soldier', he wrote, 'nor do courage and strength of body alone make one: training and experience are necessary.'[10]

O'Conor's remarks are now very dated; he died before he had completed his work and it was published posthumously, perhaps ill-advisedly. But Hayes-McCoy's remarks also appear curiously old-fashioned. His preoccupation with refuting

1.2   A loyalist mural in east Belfast (1993), using the Cuchulainn myth to
sustain the contemporary role of the illegal Ulster Defence Association in
defending Protestant Ulster. Ironically, the image of the legendary hero is
borrowed from Oliver Sheppard's statue which stands in the General Post
Office, Dublin, commemorating the republican heroes of 1916.

'taunts', and his view of military history as being essentially about campaigns and
battles, victories and defeats, belongs to an earlier, 'drum and trumpet', era. His *Irish
Battles: a Military History of Ireland*, published in 1969, confines itself to fourteen
engagements and ends with the battle of Arklow during the 1789 rebellion. The
nineteenth century is ignored because it witnessed 'much military activity in Ireland
but . . . no warfare'.[11] Equally, Hayes-McCoy's perception of Irish military history
solely in terms of 'nationalist' soldiering, whether at home or abroad is much too
restrictive. The *Irish at War* contains nothing on those Irish who fought in the
British army, and it could be argued (as did Patrick Pearse) that the setting-up,
organising, and arming of the anti-Home Rule Ulster Volunteer Force from 1912 to
1914 constituted the most robust riposte to the jibe that the Irish were always
militarily useless at home. That said, Hayes-McCoy's writings cannot be dismissed
as biassed, narrow in scope or outmoded. They merely reflected the then conventional and limited view of the proper province of military history. Hayes-McCoy's
meticulous scholarship, however, lifted them well above the routine, ensuring for
them a continuing readership (and a recent reprint for *Irish Battles*).[12] His concern,
moreover, with 'reputation', 'pride', 'respect', 'honour' and 'national character'
reminds us that the military history of Ireland has ever had both political and
cultural dimensions which must be addressed. Put simply: if the Irish were militarily
incompetent at home, then that proved the point that they were not fit to govern

themselves. Similarly, if, as Hayes-McCoy claimed, 'few peoples have served under so many alien flags', then that raised doubts about the legitimacy of the Irish state in the period 1690 to 1921 and indeed posed questions about the possibility of Irish loyalty to any Irish state.[13] In short, the military history of Ireland cannot concern itself only with battles and campaigns, army organisation and recruitment nor even about the relationships and interactions between the armed forces and society at various periods: all of these matters are important and they are dealt with fully in the essays that follow. However, the thorny issue of Irish identity should also be confronted and the role that the belief in an Irish military tradition has played in its formation should be examined.

3

'Irish history is full of battles and . . . Irishmen have always been attracted by military service so much so indeed that the type and figure of the historic Irishman might well be a man in uniform.'[14] There is much evidence to support this view and the historians of early medieval and medieval Ireland (c. 700 to c. 1500) have described a country in which violence and, latterly, warfare was endemic.[15] Indeed, such was Ireland's reputation for being a perennial war zone that the very name 'Ireland' was played upon by Elizabethan writers as uniquely a 'Land of Ire' or 'Country of Wrath'.[16] Later chroniclers and historians concurred: in 1691, Bishop Dopping of Meath surveyed Irish history and concluded that there had been 22 general and 44 local uprisings in Ireland since the year 1172, and G. A. Hayes-McCoy himself totted up 200 military engagements on Irish soil down to the battle of Arklow in 1798.[17] The large garrison maintained in Ireland during the eighteenth century, and continued throughout the nineteenth century, added to this bellicose reputation.[18] And it may be added that the events both of the first twenty-five years of this century[19] and, of course, the past twenty-five years[20] have done nothing to disturb this sombre view of Ireland as essentially a land of war in which peace occasionally and fitfully breaks out.

Such a picture of Ireland and Irish history is in large measure a caricature: there was scarcely a society in medieval Europe in which 'endemic warfare' was not a feature; Irish warfare tended to be generally episodic and localised in its impact; and the presence of large garrisons should not be assumed to mean the existence of constant lawlessness. The caricature, distorted as it is, has however proved to be one which both governed and governors were happy to collude in perpetuating. On the one hand, endemic Irish 'violence' legitimised the English civilising presence in Ireland; on the other, continual Irish 'resistance' was gratifying to Irish national pride. To the English indictment of savagery, incivility, barbarity and ineptitude, the Irish (or some of them) would cast up the battles of Clontarf (1014), the Yellow Ford (1598), Benburb (1646) and Fontenoy (1745) (an Irish battle fought on foreign soil), and add in for good measure the 'Boys of Wexford' of 1798 and the 'Bold Fenian

Men' of the 1860s. The stereotype of the 'fighting Irish' or the 'martial race' was one of the few acceptable to all shades of Irish nationalists.[21]

One consequence of this preoccupation on all sides with the 'endemic' warfare in Irish lands has been a strong tendency for the Irish, native or newcomer, Church of Ireland, Presbyterian or Catholic, to define themselves militarily. For many, perhaps most, Protestant families of gentry stock, a military career for at least one member per generation, sometimes many more, was the convention. Many achieved high command: indeed at times the higher echelons of the British army looked like a gathering of the Anglo-Irish;[22] and, over the generations, it was inevitable that the Ascendancy would be viewed, and possibly see itself, as a military caste.[23] Certainly, families such as the Lenox-Conynghams sent so many representatives to the British army over several generations that they could qualify as members of such a martial order; and there were many other families with similar military traditions. This propensity on the part of the Irish gentry to seek commissions in the British army – in 1780 they held one-third of them, and in 1878 they were still grossly over-represented in the officer ranks[24] – can be explained in terms of a shortage of other career options. If we leave aside praying and politicking, soldiering was the only generally recognised, socially acceptable, outlet for the younger sons of well-born families settled in underdeveloped economies. Major Pierce Butler from County Carlow recalled in 1794 that he had enlisted in the British army 'not by choice but as from that necessity which flows from the injustice of a feudal system, giving to the first-born all'.[25] Scotland, similarly underdeveloped, and with an equally regressive inheritance system was also disproportionately represented among the higher ranks of the British army.[26] And yet, besides an absence of alternative employment, there were other factors at work in Irish society that made a military life both acceptable and desirable.

In the first instance, there has been a persistent military flavour to Irish life, from medieval through to more modern times, that has undoubtedly made a military career seem 'normal'. Medieval historians of Ireland have highlighted the martial ethos of the societies they describe. In the medieval period, the Anglo-Norman settlers held their lands by providing knights for the royal service, and there was usually an Irish contingent in the royal army. The sixteenth and seventeenth centuries likewise witnessed the beginnings of large-scale warfare, complete with standing armies and local auxiliaries.[27] Early modern historians have charted the emergence of the 'new ruthlessness' in sixteenth-century Irish warfare, and have considered the impact of no fewer than four separate, occasionally antagonistic, but always predatory armies operating in Ireland in the 1640s. Again, the military campaigns of the 1690s, with their battles – the nation-defining Boyne and the wave-smashing Aughrim – inevitably cast a long shadow before them.[28]

From the early eighteenth century on, Ireland was home to a large proportion of the standing British army. For most of that century between 12,000 and 15,000 soldiers were stationed in Ireland (after 1793, many more), and throughout the

---

nineteenth century, there were usually between 20,000 and 25,000. These soldiers were quartered in some 100 barracks with around 400 military stations dotted around the country, thus constituting a hugely visible, sometimes reassuring and, on occasion, an intimidating presence. Moreover, in addition to the regular army, there were Militia and Yeomanry formations which in the later nineteenth century were supplemented by the Royal Irish Constabulary, an armed police force closer to the French gendarmerie rather than the English 'Bobbies'.[29] Not surprisingly, the complexities of military-civil relations – social and legal – constitute an important theme in some of the essays of this volume.[30] In short, it is incontestable that armed men in uniform were, to a degree unthinkable in England, everywhere in Ireland in the period 1600 to 1900 and after; that the military and the civil powers were tightly intertwined for most of the period; and that for the gentry, and those with gentry aspirations, military service must have seemed like a public duty, even a noble calling.[31]

Irish Protestants also believed that they owed much if not everything to their ancestors' military prowess. Since the mid-sixteenth century, a constant stream, swelling at times to a flood, of captains, servitors, convenanters and Cromwellian soldiers had poured into Ireland. These settlers, however they might like to divest themselves of their military origins (and they did aspire to rise above them), never managed (or were permitted) to do so: the whiff of grapeshot continued to hang about their armorial bearings. One of the La Touche family of Dublin bankers, for example, was laughed at for claiming in the 1820s that his forebears had been part of the Huguenot influx: everyone knew, sniffed the dowager Lady Moira, a terrific snob, that he had been merely 'a private common soldier' in King William's army.[32] Despite the social risks, however, Protestants in Ireland from the 1600s valued military training and they took a fierce and sometimes petulant pride in the military achievements of their forebears. In any case, though Ireland may have been conquered, and plantations got under way, no one could plausibly claim that the danger from Catholics was over. Protestants were pleased that they had 'far more soldiers and soldierlike men than Catholics',[33] but vigilance was still the price of security and military experience provided an added reassurance.

Gaelic society had placed a high value on the martial virtues;[34] settler society equally esteemed the soldier. One historian has highlighted the military colouring to settler society in Sligo in the early seventeenth century, claiming that military service proved a strong bond among the new landowners and tenants and arguing that 'military experience may have been an important qualification for the role of sheriff'.[35] Certainly, a military background was no disqualification when standing for election: Irish officers were better represented in the Irish parliament in Dublin than their English counterparts were in London: one in six Irish MPs held a commission in the 1760s compared to one in ten MPs at Westminster.[36]

It was expected, moreover, that when there was a military alarm or agrarian disturbances, the local Protestant gentry would take on a leadership role and that

1.3   Women were not exempt from the allure of militarism:
Constance, Countess Markievicz in Irish Volunteer uniform, c. 1915.

they and their tenants would join in posses to pursue wrongdoers. When the French commander, Thurot, landed at Carrickfergus, County Antrim in 1760, he was quickly opposed by local levies, and during the Whiteboy disturbances in Tipperary and elsewhere from the 1760s on, local magnates led out their tenants in pursuit of them.[37] Indeed, as noted below, the Volunteers of 1778–82, the Yeomen of 1796 and the Ulster Volunteer Force of 1912 and even the Ulster Defence Regiment from 1970 all drew, and the various loyalist paramilitary organisations of today continue to draw, on that Protestant tradition of independent paramilitary action in defence of their interests which has been a feature of Irish life since the seventeenth century.[38]

This rugged independence (or recalcitrance) can be seen in the military action which led to the seizure of Dublin Castle in 1659, and in the decision by the Apprentice Boys to close the gates of Londonderry in the face of King James's army in 1689. In the crisis of empire, Irish Presbyterians predominantly sided with their colonial cousins during the American War of Independence (1776–83), and showed themselves ready to turn out in 1798 to do battle with the king's forces at Antrim, Ballynahinch and elsewhere. Everywhere they were routed: but that tradition of independent military action, if necessary against the crown itself, was to prove inspirational when a hundred years later, at the time of the Home Rule crisis, Ulster Protestants found their interests threatened by the British government.

This Protestant military tradition stemmed from the needs of a vulnerable settler community, suspicious both of the 'natives' and of the home government; but it was also an unavoidable result of the type of settler – frequently a military veteran of one war or another – who made his home in Ireland. Arguably, it may also have drawn on an older, Gaelic, tradition of applauding the man in arms, the hero who displayed 'reckless bravery': Simms tells us that the Fianna were never permitted to retreat unless outnumbered by more than ten to one.[39] It should be noted, however, that while Gaelic society honoured the hero, the individual warrior fighting alone, settler society in contrast stressed rather the value of communal military action. But even with this caveat, it is clear that Gaelic Ireland had as much of a military ethos as settler society: and, as in Protestant Ireland, there were dedicated warrior families, such as the MacSweeneys of Sligo/Donegal, the MacQuillans of Antrim and the MacMurrays of Leitrim – these last described as 'hereditary cavalry to the O'Rourkes'.[40] But there was also an abundance of freelance fighters and mercenaries and these elements added to the general martial atmosphere of Gaelic Ireland.

4

From earliest times, Irish warriors, mercenaries and swordsmen found employment abroad.[41] There were Irish soldiers at Calais and Agincourt in the fourteenth century: and the well-known Dürer prints depict Irish mercenaries in Germany in the early sixteenth century. From the late sixteenth century on, with the collapse of the Gaelic order, thousands of swordsmen found employment in the Spanish, French

———

and other armies.[42] However, the tradition of military service and of military families persisted, and may even have been strengthened in the seventeenth and eighteenth centuries. Gráinne Henry in her study of the Irish in the Army of Flanders in the early seventeenth century has uncovered the strong family and kinship networks that supplied the recruits for that force. 'The number of uncles, brothers, and cousins serving together in the Irish military group is quite amazing', she writes, adding, 'family migration seems to have been . . . common amongst those in the service of the Army of Flanders'.[43] And R. A. Stradling, in his account of the later history of Irish soldiers in Spain, finds evidence of the same.[44]

It was a similar story with the Irish regiments in the service of France in the eighteenth century. A search through the regimental *contrôles* (or muster rolls) reveals a strong family and regional basis to recruitment. Recruits to the Irish regiments in the French service ran at around 1,000 men per annum in the period 1700 to 1730 and while all parts of Ireland were represented there was a preponderance of men from the heartland of Irish Jacobitism – counties Tipperary, Cork, Clare, Kerry and Kilkenny. Moreover, certain surnames – O'Brien, MacCarthy, Nugent, Roche, Ryan, Comerford – recurred again and again.[45] In addition, scrutiny of the muster lists reveals the existence, by the 1720s, of a sizeable Irish community settled in the garrison towns (Douai, Metz, Arras, Verdun, Dunkerque, St Omer and Salines) of France, from which was drawn perhaps 20 per cent of the recruits for the Irish regiments. Again, there was the regimental 'family' itself with many recruits to the Irish regiments simply listed as either *fils d'Irlandais* or as having been born to the regiment. The four sons of Captain John Bourck and Agnes Schuster all served with their father in Berwick's regiment in the 1770s: all were recorded as having been *né au régiment*.[46] Finally, the cross-generational tradition of military families is well represented in the regimental documents. Consider, for example, the case of 'Alexandre de Comerford' [sic] Captain of Grenadiers in Dillon's regiment, who in 1776 sought a military pension having served thirty-four years in the French service. In his application, he listed his campaigns, and then pointed to his family's record:

> Son grand-père était major du régiment de Bulkeley lorsqu'il passa en France; son grand oncle ancien capitaine au dit régiment fut tué à la bataille de Malplaquet; son père, ancien capitaine du même régiment mourut de ses blessures en Ecosse en 1746. Il a aujourd'hui deux de ses oncles ancient Chevaliers de St Louis qui vont retirer et son fils officier au régiment de Dillon qui fait la quatrième generation de père et fils au service du roi.[47]

The fall of the Gaelic order, it is clear, did not mean the end of a Gaelic or Catholic military tradition: rather it merely marked its transfer to foreign fields.

With the tentative removal of the prohibition on Catholic recruits into the British army around the middle of the eighteenth century, the number of Irish taking up arms in the French service diminished. The officers in the Irish regiments in the

----

French army were still overwhelmingly Irish but, increasingly, the men were drawn from the Low Countries and the eastern provinces of France.[48] On the other hand, by the 1770s a substantial Catholic Irish recruitment to the East India Company was under way; and there was a large enlistment into the Royal Marines. But it was only in the 1790s that Irish Catholics were actively (as opposed to surreptitiously) recruited, both as a defence force in Ireland (the Irish Militia) and as a major component within the regular army.[49] Thereafter, the Catholic Irish proportion within the British army rose dramatically: by the mid-nineteenth century, over 40 per cent of the army was Irish-born or the sons of emigrants.[50] And at the time of the Great War, the level of Irish soldiers in the British army, despite the ravages of the Famine and emigration to the New World, was still higher than Ireland's share of the United Kingdom's population warranted.[51]

What were the motives that prompted, or the reasons that compelled, the Irish to enlist in such numbers at home and abroad between 1600 and 1920? O'Callaghan in his *History of the Irish Brigades in the Service of France* explained the recruitment of the Irish in the eighteenth century into the French army as proceeding 'from the attachment of the mass of the Irish people, as Catholics, to the representative of the Stuart dynasty, as deriving his origin from the old monarchs of Erin, as also a Catholic'.[52] There may be something in this explanation: the fidelity of the Catholic Irish to the Stuart cause was remarkable; but even O'Callaghan recognised that there was more to it than this. He wrote that 'multitudes in Ireland' enlisted because they had 'no better means of escaping the fate of unemployed poverty at home than emigration to obtain a livelihood by military service abroad'.[53] This complex question of motivation is discussed below, with a general emphasis on the undeveloped nature of the Irish economy and with comparisons between Ireland and other prime recruiting areas (Scotland, the Low Countries, and eastern Europe) in this respect.[54] In both Scotland and Ireland, when their economies began to prosper in the 1750s, recruitment to their respective brigades in the Dutch and French service declined dramatically.

Interestingly, an examination of the *contrôles* of the Irish regiments in the French service shows that desertion rates in them were comparable with other, non-Irish regiments: a finding hardly compatible with principled enlistment in the Irish Brigade. In fact, desertion rates for the Irish in the French army in the early eighteenth century and for the Irish in the British army in the early nineteenth century appear to be little different. The general conclusion must be that the Catholic officer class enlisted in the French army because they were not permitted to enlist in the British army: when they were allowed to do so, they did so.[55] It was a similar story for the men: a French military career was a substitute for a British one: but with the onset of large-scale recruiting (first for John Company's army in India, then for the British army proper), the attractions of the French service dwindled, though up to and after the French Revolution Irishmen enlisted in the French, Spanish and Imperial Austrian service.

———

This is not to say that France's Irish regiments were filled solely with the desperate, the poverty-stricken and the unscrupulous, who when the opportunity arose promptly transferred their attention, and their allegiance, to the British army. Rather, it may be suggested that enlistment has always been a private matter, not at all susceptible to such crass reductionism. The proper weight to be accorded the prospect of adventure (and plunder), the urge to escape a humdrum existence, even the simple desire to emigrate, cannot now be determined but should not be ignored. The decision to 'go for a sojer' cannot merely be seen as either a flight from poverty or as a principled adherence to the Stuart cause, or to the British crown. In the end, a tradition of soldiering within the locality and within the kinship network – even the *tradition* of an Irish military tradition – may have had a vital role to play.

Certainly, governments have not scrupled to play on the Irishman's alleged martial qualities and to trumpet his so-called propensity for war. During the First World War the British government sought to put over the message that *traditionally* the Irish have enlisted in Irish regiments, especially to help France, and that the Irish, with their fighting qualities, have historically made good soldiers. In this respect, the *perception* of an Irish military tradition proved eminently serviceable.

5

'The Irish are a military people – strong, nimble and hardy, fond of adventure, irascible, brotherly and generous – they have all the qualities that tempt men to war and make them good soldiers': so, inevitably, Thomas Davis. But the tradition of the Irishman as a born soldier and as being naturally courageous, resourceful, cheerful and strong, was not invented by Davis, and it long survived him. In the medieval period, Irish mercenaries were in demand in Europe because of their ferocity and their willingness to put up with hardship: and this reputation persisted. In 1544, Lord Deputy St Leger recommended the Irish soldier as being 'of such hardiness that there is no men that ever I saw that will or can endure the pains and evil fare that they will sustain'.[56] In the 1640s their staying power was commended and throughout the seventeenth century and later Irish soldiers were much in demand in the Low Countries and France: in 1702 their stamina was particularly commented on in a French military report.[57] Later, in the 1790s, the members of the Irish Army Medical Board drew attention to the very high mortality rate among English and Scottish soldiers serving in Ireland: it was, they declared, five times that of the Irish soldier.[58] And in the mid-1830s, Surgeon Rutherford Alcock, inspecting soldiers embarking for Spain, was favourably impressed with the physical health of the Irish recruits.[59] Certainly, there is some empirical evidence that the average Irish recruit (at least in the period 1750 to 1850) was rather taller than his English or Scottish comrade in arms. This height advantage may be attributed to the excellence of the potato diet and the marked advantages of a rural over an urban upbringing.[60]

In addition to their ability to withstand hardship, Irish soldiers had a reputation

---

1.4   Men of the 'Irish Brigade' raised by Sir Roger Casement from prisoners-of-war in Germany, c. 1915.

for cheerfulness and informality that marked them apart from other regiments in the British army.[61] Kipling referred to the 'Celt's . . . curious and incommunicable humour', and Tom Johnstone in his study of the Irish regiments in the First World War has written of 'an irrepressible spontaneous humour, exemplified by the Belfast and Dublin "crack", that dry, understated, biting wit, which almost unconsciously sees humour in the most dreadful circumstances'.[62] There was too, it has been claimed, a more easy-going attitude between officers and men in an Irish regiment: English officers serving in Irish regiments often commented on the relative lack of class division to be found in them.

The Irish regiments were also distinguished by an open respect for religion. Fr Willie Doyle, chaplain in the 16th (Irish) Division, claimed that it was 'an admitted fact that the Irish Catholic soldier is the bravest and best man in a fight but few know that he draws his courage from the strong faith with which he is filled up and the help which comes from the exercises of his religion'.[63] Equally, in the 36th (Ulster) Division, whose men were largely drawn from the pre-war Ulster Volunteer Force, there was clear evidence of strong religious feeling: 'One thing that really impressed me', wrote a visiting Church of England chaplain, 'was the number of men who actually read their bibles.'[64]

However, while cheerfulness in adversity, a lack of formality and strong religious convictions were regarded as typical characteristics of the Irish soldier, these could easily be taken as simplemindedness, ill-discipline and credulity. And for a long period, hostile critics made great play with the alleged poor discipline, allied to a propensity to disaffection, of Irish soldiers. The Connaught Rangers were dubbed the 'Connaught Footpads' for their thieving ways. But while the regimental historian is not altogether convincing in their defence, none the less it seems clear that Irish soldiers were certainly no worse than others where petty crime (or wholesale looting) were concerned.[65]

At first glance, the allegation of unreliability seems much better founded: the first major Irish excursion abroad – that led by Lord Stanley to the Low Countries to fight for the Dutch in 1587 – ended with the wholesale defection of the men to the Spanish service; and further instances can be cited over the centuries. During the wars of the period 1690 to 1713 there were numerous desertions and defections; and in the 1790s about a score of Irish soldiers were shot for disaffection in Ireland following a number of courts-martial.[66] Throughout the nineteenth century there was a general rule that Irish soldiers could not be relied upon in civil disturbances in Ireland and that they were better deployed against English or Scottish trouble-makers. Such anxieties were almost certainly baseless. The Fenians made a big effort to infiltrate the British army but despite all the dire rumours (and bragging), their penetration achieved little. Casement's efforts in the First World War similarly proved unavailing – one recruit to Casement's Brigade subsequently turned spy for Dublin castle and was eventually shot by the IRA.[67] And Hitler's 'Irish Brigade' to be formed out of Irish prisoners in the Second World War remained more notional than real. In the Irish Civil War, six members of the National Army were executed for treachery, but in the whole of the 'Troubles' from 1916 to 1922, among the Irish in the British army, only Private James Daly of the Connaught Rangers was executed for a politically-inspired mutiny – in India.[68] Given the hundreds of thousands who served, it is the loyalty of the Irish soldiers which is impressive, not the disaffection of the few. Perhaps ironically, the largest 'politically motivated' defection of Irish-born soldiers was that by fifty or so Irish soldiers in the United States army who deserted to the Mexican army in the 1840s, most of whom were subsequently executed.

Apart from their lax discipline and their reputation for unreliability, without a doubt it has been the ferocity and aggression of Irish soldiers which over the centuries has attracted most attention. By Shakespeare's time these latter qualities were sufficiently recognised to be embodied in the person of MacMorris, the captain in *Henry V*. And in the later seventeenth, and throughout the eighteenth century, the theatrical portrayal of the Irish soldier almost invariably highlighted his pugnacity and bravery.[69] On the battlefield, as opposed to the stage, this view of the 'Fighting Irish' was equally uniform. In 1697, the maréchal de Vendôme, watching his Irish troops before Barcelona, remarked on 'this warlike action' and described them approvingly as 'the butchers of the army'.[70] Irish aggression and fighting qualities were in evidence at Cremona, Malplaquet (on both sides), Ramillies (ditto), Fontenoy and in the battles (and especially the storms) of the Peninsular War, and in the Crimea. Even Irish insurgents showed these qualities: at the battle of New Ross in the 1798 rebellion, Colonel Robert Craufurd, later to gain renown in Spain, declared that 'I never saw any troops attack with more enthusiasm and bravery than the rebels.'[71]

In the American Civil War, Irish units gained a reputation for their fighting qualities at desperate (and forlorn) struggles such as that at Marye's Heights, in Fredericksburg, where the Irish Brigade in the Union army took shattering casualties.[72] Indeed, the proven aggression of the Irish soldier has been used, curiously, to explain *Confederate* military collapse. In their controversial analysis of the reasons for Confederate defeat, McWhiney and Jamieson claim that it was Confederate battlefield tactics, primarily 'the Celtic charge' which 'bled the Confederacy to death'. Arguing that the people of the southern states were predominantly of 'Celtic' stock, while those of the northern states were mostly of English origin, the authors claim that the Confederates 'and their Celtic forebears' were 'more emotional, foolhardy, romantic and undisciplined than their opponents' who in their turn were 'more practical, more materialistic, more literate, more tenacious and more machinelike than the Celts they fought'. For McWhiney and Jamieson, 'Southerners lost the Civil War because they were too Celtic and their opponents too English.' The élan, dash, humour and religiosity of the 'Celtic' Confederate soldiers were crushed by the practical, sober, and materialist 'Anglo-Saxon' Yankees.[73]

In the First World War, Irish soldiers were described by the well-known military journalist, Charles à Court Repington, as 'the finest missile troops in the British army'.[74] They (allegedly) relished both the ferocity of hand-to-hand fighting in the 'raiding phase' of trench warfare, as well as the mass attack where they were frequently described as 'impetuous' and 'eager', storm-troopers whose 'ardour could not be restrained' and who attacked with 'traditional Irish dash'.[75] At Guillemont, after their colonel, Jack Lenox-Conyngham, was killed as he led his men forward carrying nothing more threatening than his cane, the Connaught Rangers were 'unleashed' and, 'like hounds upon a quarry, they dashed into the enemy lines'.[76] Then again, there is the story of the London Irish at Loos dribbling a football towards the enemy lines, leading Tom Kettle to remark that 'instantaneity has been a characteristic of Irish soldiers as it has been of Irish football forwards'.[77] Finally, in his affectionate account of his service with the Irish Brigade in the Second World War, Colin Gunner (an Englishman) chose to preface his remarks with the revealing epigraph:

> For it's always to be seen,
> The Shamrock and the Green,
> *In front of* the thin red line.[78]

And yet, besides much anecdote and allegation, what hard evidence is there that the Irish soldier's reputation for particular aggression, or for those other 'typical characteristics' is well founded?

That Irish recruits were much in demand cannot be denied; that there were Irish military families has been demonstrated; that there was a special atmosphere in an Irish regiment is accepted; that Irish soldiers almost invariably fought well is not contested. What, however, may legitimately be questioned is whether the performance of Irish soldiers was all that different from other units in the French, American (Union and Confederate) or, especially, the British armies.

Irish soldiers fought for both the Union and the Confederacy in the American Civil War (though they were underrepresented in the Union army at least); and battlefield tactics were basically the same on both sides. Indeed, it could be argued that *pace* McWhiney and Jamieson, the frontal assault, the 'Celtic charge', against an entrenched enemy remained more of a Union than a Confederate tactic. The Confederacy's military failure because of its adherence to 'Celtic' military tactics remains unproven. Moreover, in the case of the British army, it is noticeable that most of those alleged 'Irish' characteristics – good humour, lack of discipline, and especially, reckless daring – were to be found equally in Australian, Canadian and New Zealand units, who frequently (like the Irish) were deployed as storm troops.[79] Some Indian army regiments, too, it is claimed, had these attributes: and black soldiers in the French service were regarded in much the same way. In other words, it may be suggested that the so-called classic Irish fighting qualities were in fact to be found in most colonial formations – more, that their adumbration by admirers (unconsciously?) served a political purpose.

17

Irish recklessness, Irish impetuosity, Irish ferocity, Irish ill-discipline, Irish child-like cheerfulness, even Irish religiosity, all of which were highly prized in warfare, were not at all needed or even desirable in peacetime. In fact, taken together, they tended to confirm the view that the Irish, like colonial troops everywhere, apparently lacking tenacity, steadfastness, determination and resoluteness, were unfitted to govern themselves. These strictures were applied only to Catholic Irish soldiers. Irish officers, predominantly Protestant and firmly Unionist, readily embraced the stereotype and drew the appropriate political message from it. Moreover, it is noticeable that descriptions of the conduct of Irish Protestant soldiers in battle were rather different to those of Catholic soldiers. In their reports of the 36th (Ulster) Division at the Somme, some correspondents stressed the ordinariness or matter-of-factness evident among the battalions. 'When I saw the men emerge through the smoke and form up as if on parade', wrote one observer, 'I could scarcely believe my eyes'; and another recorded that when the Tyrone battalion moved forward, there was 'no fuss, no shouting, no running, everything orderly, solid and thorough, just like the men themselves'.[80] and such steadiness, of course, contrasted vividly with the headlong charge, the wild yell and the fighting frenzy, all of which appeared to characterise Irish Catholic combat.[81]

In short, it may be suggested that observers in wartime were conditioned to see (or at least to highlight) certain qualities in Irish soldiers that accorded with peace-time political perceptions of Irish (and other colonial) subjects. It may also be argued that it was the attitudes and the expectations of others that defined as much as anything the battlefield behaviour of Irish soldiers. How else can one explain the recurrent emphasis on the Battle of Fontenoy or the historical redolence of the title 'The Irish Brigade'?

6

At Fontenoy in 1745 the Irish Brigade in the service of France, with their fierce cry of *Cuimhnigí ar Luimneach agus feall na Sasanach!*[82] had carried the day against the soldiers of George II. But it was in succeeding wars that Fontenoy was invoked on all sides to exhort the Irish troops to deeds of valour. The former United Irishman, Miles Byrne, serving in Spain with Bonaparte's armies recalled how on the morning of Busaco, General Masséna had addressed his Irish troops and 'reminded them of all the wrongs of unfortunate Ireland and called also to their recollection Fontenoy where the Irish Brigade in the service of France had decided the battle'.[83] In the American Civil War, General Thomas Francis Meagher tried to rally his Irish troops at Bull Run by urging them to remember 'Ireland and Fontenoy!'[84] Throughout the later nineteenth century, Fontenoy and the Irish Brigade were kept to the forefront of nationalist memory through the production of patriotic ballads and poems, by the reissue of such books at the Abbé MacGeoghegan's *History of Ireland* and the publication of the more scholarly J. C. O'Callaghan's *History of the*

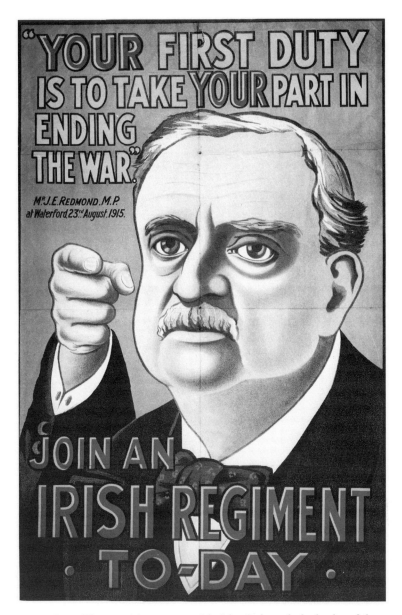

1.5 Great War recruiting poster, with John Redmond, the leader of the
Irish Parliamentary Party, urging Irishmen to join up.

Irish Brigade in the Service of France. In addition, and probably more accessible,
there was the engraving and distribution of highly stylised prints depicting Irish
martial valour in the service of France. No wonder then, that when in 1915, Miles
Emmet Byrne, colonel of the First Battalion, Tyneside Irish Brigade, spoke to his

troops before their departure for the Front, he asked them to 'remember how the Irish Brigade of France lightened the darkness of the seventeenth century and changed the history of Europe'.[85] This sentiment was captured by Kipling in his ditty to the Irish Guards:[86]

> We're not so old in the Army list,
> But we're not so new in the ring,
> For we carried our packs with Marshal Saxe
> When Louis was our King.
> But Douglas Haig's our Marshal now
> and we're King George's men.
> And after one hundred and seventy years
> We're fighting for France again!
> . . .
> Old Days! The Wild Geese are flighting,
> Head to the storm as they faced it before!
> For where there are Irish there's loving and fighting,
> And when we stop either, it's Ireland no more!
> *Ireland no more!*[87]

By a startling coincidence, the soldiers of the 16th (Irish) Division were occupying the historic battlefield of Fontenoy when the guns fell silent on 11 November 1918.

As much as the magic of Fontenoy, the title 'The Irish Brigade' was invoked for its talismanic qualities. According to Stephen Gwynn, formerly of the Connaught Rangers and editor of Miles Byrne's *Memoirs*, 'the first Irish Brigade of which there is record was in the Roman service'.[88] In the modern period, the Bourbons (French and Spanish) had had an Irish Brigade, so too had Bonaparte, and so too had his British opponents.[89] In the 1860s an 'Irish Brigade' went to the aid of the Pope and another to the French in their war with Germany, and there was an Irish brigade in the service of both the Union and the Confederacy in the American Civil War (1861–5). In the South African War (1899–1902), Major John McBride commanded a small pro-Boer 'Irish Brigade'. There were a number of Irish brigades in the First World War (the motto of one was 'Everywhere and always faithful' – the same as that of the Brigade of Louis XVIII), and Roger Casement attempted to form one out of Irish prisoners-of-war. So impressed was Winston Churchill with the historic resonance of the title that he sought to set up an Irish Brigade in the early days of the Second World War. Unionist opinion was predictably less than enthusiastic: John Andrews, prime minister of Northern Ireland, protested that an Irish brigade 'would inevitably be associated with the Irish who fought against England in the days of Marlborough and the Irish Brigade which fought against Britain in the Boer War'. Churchill, the biographer (and descendant) of Marlborough, overruled him, however, and went ahead with the formation of his Irish brigade; indeed, he even toyed with the notion of a separate Irish wing in the Royal Air Force, to be called the 'Shamrock Wing'. These 'Wild Geese', however, did not fly.[90]

1.6   Sinn Féin anti-recruiting cartoon, lampooning the Redmond recruiting poster.

Churchill and those others who sought to create an 'Irish brigade' valued above all the historical weight attached to the name. It mattered not that 'Irish Brigades' historically had fought against Britain, and had constituted in theory 'a cloud hanging in the sky, prepared to break forth upon this realm'.[91] These considerations were set aside, and by the early twentieth century it was claimed that 'the Irish regiments in the British service were the true successors to the Irish Brigades of continental fame'.[92] The title, 'The Irish Brigade', had come to embody a military tradition of overseas service, selfless daring, reckless courage, cheerful endurance (and robust recruitment): wartime governments appreciated all of these.

Consideration of the history of the Irish brigades and the romantic tradition which they enshrined, prompts also a more sombre reflection on the ambiguities of the Irish military tradition. These 'tragic complexities'[93] stemmed directly from Ireland's uncertain constitutional position as part English colony, part sister kingdom and even in the early years of this century, part imperial dominion. They most clearly revealed themselves in the numerous battles, both on the island itself and in contests abroad, in which Irishman confronted Irishman. The bitter ironies of Irish history are nowhere more piquantly revealed than in the spectacle of Irishmen locked in mortal combat with each other at such battles as Clontarf, Kinsale, Aughrim and Castlebar in Ireland and at Cremona, Malplaquet, Ramillies, Fontenoy and Dettingen in continental Europe. Throughout the Peninsular War, Irish soldiers were to be found on both sides, though predominantly in Wellington's army. At the battle of Wandewash in India, the opposing commanders, Lally-Tollendal and Eyre Coote, were both Galway men. In North America too, Irishmen and Irish generals (Moira and Montgomery) fought each other in the War of Independence, and in the War of 1812. Later in the American Civil War, Irish-born generals such as Claiborne and Meagher and over 150,000 Irish recruits took opposing sides. In 1916, the Easter Rebellion was put down partly by men from the Royal Dublin Fusiliers; ironically, in the Boer War, the Dublin Fusiliers had confronted the 'Irish Brigade' of the Easter Week leader, Major John MacBride.[94] John Dillon in his impassioned speech on the Rising declared that 'one of the most horrible tragedies of this fighting was that brother met brother on the streets of Dublin'.[95] But, with the appropriate change of location, he could have said the same about any of the major conflicts in the Atlantic world since the twelfth century.

The Easter rising appears to be outside the recognised Irish military tradition. It was well conceived, and in the circumstances, reasonably well planned and well executed.[96] The rebels fought bravely, putting up a stern resistance: but there were no futile heroics, no rash charges, and there was little evidence of dash, élan or cheerful good humour: no football was dribbled down Sackville Street. Here may be seen the beginnings of a 'new' military tradition, one in which tenacity was valued more than spontaneity, determination more than jocularity, and resoluteness more than impetuosity. None of these qualities was in fact new: the conduct of the Munsters in the retreat from Mons, of Irish regiments in the South African War, and

1.7 Men from the 1,400-strong Irish battalion of St Patrick, who served in
the papal army in 1860; one of several Irish *émigré* military formations
in the nineteenth century.

of Irish soldiers in numberless campaigns in other military theatres over the
centuries had revealed that they possessed in abundance these 'Anglo-Saxon'
characteristics. The Easter rising plainly showed that Irish rebels, perfunctorily
trained but highly motivated, could fight like English soldiers. This is surely what
John Dillon, an indefatigable recruiter for the British army, was getting at in his
speech in the House of Commons in the aftermath of the rising. 'I admit they [the
rebels] were wrong; I know they were wrong,' he confessed, and then he continued,
'but they fought with superb bravery and skill'. When there was audible dissent at
these remarks, he rounded fiercely on his critics: 'And . . . it would be a damned
good thing for you if your soldiers were able to put up as good a fight as did these
men in Dublin.'[97]

The Rising redefined the Irish military tradition; and the subsequent War of
Independence, followed by Civil War, with their assassinations, skirmishes,
ambushes and reprisals, further refashioned it. The Irish contribution in the First
World War faded from popular memory;[98] and with partition those regiments which
recruited primarily in the south of Ireland were disbanded. The traditions of such
regiments as the Connaught Rangers, the Royal Dublin Fusiliers and the Royal
Munster Fusiliers were largely forgotten, though there has continued to be a high

1.8   An American–Irish poster celebrating the patriots of Easter 1916,
featuring twelve of the fifteen nationalist leaders executed in the aftermath
of the fighting, together with The O'Rahilly and Francis Sheehy-
Skeffington, who were killed during the Rising (the latter murdered by a
British army officer), Roger Casement (hanged in August 1916) and
Countess Markievicz, who survived until 1927.

proportion of southern Irish recruits into the remaining Irish regiments in the British army. A recent history of the Irish army, however, traces its origins no further back than the setting up of the Irish Volunteers in November 1913, even though substantial numbers of this force in fact joined the British army in 1914.[99] With statehood, north and south, the Irish military tradition has largely retreated from the public view. However, the British army in Northern Ireland has been most reluctant to abandon its all-Ireland recruiting area, and Irish 'traditions' have been kept up. As for the Irish army, it most certainly did not win the peace in the years after independence and soon found itself a part of 'an emaciated and grievously under-equipped defence establishment'.[100] In fact, since the 1920s it has been the Irish *paramilitary* tradition which has prevailed, with the twenty-five years of armed conflict in Northern Ireland from 1969 rendering it dominant.

This paramilitary tradition undoubtedly merits a separate volume on its own and we can only touch on some of its characteristics here. Its endurance and resilience have been altogether remarkable and while its origins may be traced to the frontier-like conditions that prevailed in Ireland for most of the medieval period, its persistence thereafter can be attributed to a widespread disbelief in the legitimacy of the state and equally to a conviction of the relative powerlessness of the state. The tradition, dormant for most of the nineteenth century, was revived in 1912 by the formation of the (Protestant) Ulster Volunteer Force, followed a year later by the (largely Catholic) Irish Volunteers. In the last twenty-five years in Northern Ireland this paramilitary tradition has been responsible for a return to that situation identified by Charles-Edwards at the very start of our collective volume: 'little warfare but much violence'. With the announcement of ceasefires in 1994, para-militarism may become dormant once again, but it will not become extinct.

Undoubtedly, this paramilitary tradition has caught the world's attention since 1969; but there are still echoes of that older military tradition – the Irish recruits to Spain in 1937, those Irishmen who joined the British armed forces in the Second World War, those who fought in American or Australian units in Vietnam, those Irish soldiers serving on UN peace-keeping or relief missions – and it may not be entirely redundant still.[101] Even the Irish army, despite its (official) modern origins, is happy to look back to the 'legendary standing army of Ireland' and makes use of *Fianna* symbolism in its uniform and accoutrements.[102] 'We have had an extra-ordinary military history', wrote Hayes-McCoy: the chapters which follow confirm this.[103]

Chapter 2

Irish warfare before 1100

T. M. Charles-Edwards

From a modern standpoint, there was little warfare but much violence in early medieval Ireland.[1] We usually make a clear distinction between war and other forms of violence: war, as opposed to peace, is a condition of affairs in which large-scale violence is sanctioned by a state – a condition of affairs, moreover, in which state violence is deployed by soldiers as opposed to civilians. Normally, the enemy is also a state. In addition, the state which wages war is perceived, along the lines suggested by Weber, as successfully claiming a monopoly of legitimate violence within its territory. Such a perception involves two characteristic contrasts: first, between the violence of the state and the violence of the criminal, the bandit and the terrorist; secondly, between armies and civilian populations. It applies only to states, such as the Roman Empire, which could tax their subjects effectively enough to be able to pay for an army. It therefore does not apply to early medieval Ireland where kings did indeed exact tribute, but only to the point at which they could support a small group of household warriors.[2]

In the early Middle Ages, to fight was an obligation of status not the job of a profession. If someone was a layman and free – still more if he was noble – he was expected to fight. Only clerics, women and slaves could hope to remain civilians.[3] Also, because there was no sharp distinction between the wars of kings and the armed struggles of individuals, kindreds and noble retinues, there was nothing quite like the modern distinction between peace and war. What struck contemporaries was not war as a condition and period of hostility, but individual battles and feuds. Admittedly peace might be constructed between kingdoms, and royal authority might ensure some peace within a kingdom; but such peace was relative. It was sometimes clear that royal authority had broken down, and peace then went with it. After Conaire Mór, a legendary king of Tara, had passed Uisnech on his way eastwards across the midlands, he and his household saw 'the land of the Uí Néill' being harried from all sides so that the land was a blaze of fire about them. To Conaire's question, 'What is this?' his household replied, 'It is not hard to see that it is the royal authority which has broken down when people have set about burning the land.'[4] The saga could contrast a state of peace, such that, under Conaire's authority, no man struck another in Ireland, with the state of utter disorder and violence which prevailed as both his reign and his life approached their end. The annals, however, show that, in reality, the contrast was much less sharp.

If we take the long period between the fall of the Roman Empire in the West and the end of the eleventh century, there are three principal stages in the history of Irish warfare. The first is that of the late-Roman and immediately post-Roman period, an era in which the Irish Sea belonged to the Irish, and so did the Hebrides; from these waters, in Gildas's words, 'there eagerly emerged from the coracles that carried them across the sea-valleys the foul hordes of Irish and Picts, like dark throngs of worms who wriggle out of narrow fissures in the rock when the sun is high'.[5] This was the period of the great raids on Britain and of the creation of Irish settlements overseas: in Argyll, on the Isle of Man, in Dyfed in south-west Wales, and even in Cornwall. Sea power was, therefore, central to this first period. The subsequent period stretches up to the beginning of the Viking attacks on Ireland. The Irish Sea was no longer dominated by Irish fleets, and the Picts were now dangerous enemies rather than allies in Scotland. The warring Irish turned away from their neighbours across the water; there was even one year, 684, in which an English fleet attacked Brega, the kingdom north of the Liffey which was the pre-eminent power for much of the seventh century. Usually, however, war was now a business of limited political struggles within Ireland, carried out by armies that kept firmly to dry land. From the start of the Viking period, especially from the 830s when the intensity of the attacks increased markedly, sea power again became a dominant element in Irish warfare. From one point of view, this was a further extension of the previous period, in which Ireland had been subject to occasional attacks from Britons and English across the Irish Sea. It is not unfair to see the ninth century as a period in which the Irish, limited to land warfare, remained vulnerable to attack from the sea; but as soon as Irish kings came to control Viking settlements, they had sea power at their disposal. Some Irish rulers even mounted naval expeditions by themselves, both on the Irish Sea and on rivers and loughs.[6] Fleets controlled by Irish kings could carry exiled Welsh kings back to Wales and English noblemen back to England. They could also carry armies to attack other Irish kings. Moreover, the Vikings had not just reminded the Irish, in the most forceful way possible, of the importance of sea power, they had done the same for the great rivers and loughs of Ireland. The Irish were no longer so wedded to dry land as they had been since the sixth century.

These three periods are distinguished more by the strategies adopted by the principal rulers than by the technology of war. The normal Irish fighting man had a spear and a shield at the beginning of our period and also at the end.[7] Even the heroic Cú Chulainn received the usual *gaisced* (*gaí* 'spear' + *sciath* 'shield') when he 'took arms' from his lord and king, Conchobar. Nobles probably usually had swords as well; but even nobles went into battle without helmets or mail-shirts.[8] Horses were used by rapid raiding parties, but probably not in battle. The most important technological changes affecting Irish warfare were in shipbuilding, since it was their

27

superiority in this department that enabled the Vikings to rule the seas around Ireland.[9]

I shall first investigate the second period – that between 600 and 800. This is not because it was typical of the pre-Norman period as a whole (it was not, as we have seen already), but because it was more circumscribed and so easier to describe. It is better to begin by gaining some impression of what the Irish did in war when they were left to themselves, rather than when they formed a small part of a pattern of events covering all of northern and western Europe, as in the fourth and fifth centuries and again in the ninth and tenth.

Irish warfare in the seventh and eighth centuries

The annals are full of violence, most of it the violence of kings, much of it against other kings. This offers a preliminary working definition of war, *cocad*, for our period – namely as a series of acts of violence deployed by kings and their peoples against other kings and their peoples. Yet it is as well to realise at the outset that this is a brutal oversimplification. The annals hardly ever use a term which we could translate as 'war', and yet they contain a bewildering variety of acts of violence. There is violence against a people and its territory, but this may be territorial conquest, enforcement of hegemony and of tribute, or plundering carried out to destabilise a rival kingdom. There is also violence directed at a particular person rather than at a people or territory. Much of the violence in the annals consists of the feuds and dynastic rivalries of kings. These still count by our preliminary definition as acts of war, but they are not separated by any great divide from feuds within a single dynasty – from the violence, not just of kings, but also of those who desired to be kings. Even more seriously, the pressures which gave rise to the wars of kings were mainly internal rivalries. The structure of authority was not so stable that kings could leave war to others; to defeat, in person, external enemies was to disarm internal rivals;[10] conversely, attack from outside a kingdom was usually timed to coincide with internal dynastic conflict.

The character of war in all periods is determined in part by the nature of politics. In Ireland politics was pre-eminently dynastic, a jockeying for power both within and between royal lineages. The dynastic character of Irish warfare needs, therefore, to be explored, in particular the way that strictly dynastic objectives interacted with others. The first illustration of the way one form of violence was usually combined with another is the conquest by Cenél nEógain of the territory of Mag nÍtha, the valley of the River Finn in Donegal. In the *Tripartite Life of St Patrick*, reflecting ninth-century conditions, Mag nÍtha was a territory ruled by the then dominant Uí Néill dynasty of the North, Cenél nEógain.[11] It had only been conquered, however, in the eighth century by hard fighting against the rival northern Uí Néill dynasty of Cenél Conaill. The Annals of Ulster record fighting between the two dynasties in Mag nÍtha in 732, 733 and 734 – fighting in which Cenél Conaill was

2.1   Irish spearman: a detail from the late-eighth-century *Book of Kells*.

evidently on the losing side. The kingdom may, however, have passed back to Cenél Conaill after the death of Áed Allán of Cenél nEógain in 743, for Cenél Conaill appears to have been defending it when it was conclusively defeated in 789 at Clady.[12]

This conquest was crucial in the development of Cenél nEógain as the dominant power in north-western Ireland. The remaining territories of the ruling branch of Cenél Conaill lay partly to the south-west of Mag nÍtha, over the Barnesmore Gap, in Tír nÁeda (Tirhugh, around the modern town of Donegal), but also to the north in the Fanad peninsula on the west side of Lough Swilly. In the years around 700 Cenél Conaill probably dominated Cenél nÉndai whose small kingdom lay in the district of Raphoe immediately to the north of Mag nÍtha. The best communications between Tír nÁeda in the south and Fanad in the north lay through Mag nÍtha and the lands of Cenél nÉndai. Once Cenél nEógain had completed the conquest of Mag nÍtha, therefore, they had permanently weakened the Cenél Conaill over-kingdom, since the latter needed to be on good terms with Cenél nEógain in order to maintain communications through the Foyle basin between its northern and southern extremities. This seems, therefore, to be a good example of precisely the kind of territorial aggrandisement characteristic of so many modern wars, a conquest which gave not only extra territory but a strategic advantage. Yet it was also a dynastic struggle between two branches of the Northern Uí Néill. Moreover, within Cenél nEógain, the success of Áed Allán and Áed Oirdnide confirmed the power of the branch descended from Áed Uaridnach; while the failure of Cenél Conaill ensured that the line established in Fanad declined. Internal and external conflict were intertwined.

More often, war was designed to enforce hegemony rather than to gain territory; territory was sometimes gained by gradual pressure on vassal kingdoms rather than by outright war. Some time between 702 and 742 the Uí Chonaing kings of North Brega split the vassal kingdom of Ciannacht Breg between a rump to the north of the Boyne, Fir Airde Ciannachtae, and the southern part of the kingdom, which they ruled themselves as kings of Ciannacht Breg. As far as the annals go, this annexation seems to have occurred without any great defeat of the Ciannacht Breg; indeed, it occurred in a period in which the Uí Néill rulers of Brega were engaged in incessant internal feuding, which allowed supremacy within the Uí Néill to pass from Síl nÁeda Sláine, in Brega, to their rivals to the west in Mide, Cland Cholmáin, and to the north, Cenél nEógain. Both the feuding and the activities of the Uí Néill over-king are well illustrated by the battle of Kells in 718 and its aftermath. This battle saw the victory of one branch of Síl nÁeda Sláine, the Uí Chernaig of southern Brega, to the south of Tara, over their rivals, the Uí Chonaing and the Síl nDlúthaig in the valleys of the Boyne and the Blackwater. The battle was evidently the result of an attack by the Uí Chernaig since the kingdom of Síl nDlúthaig was in the vicinity of Kells, the site of the battle. The victor, Conall Grant, was himself, however, killed by the over-king, Fergal mac Máele Dúin, only two months after the battle. This is a striking example of the capacity of an Uí Néill king of Tara to discipline his kinsmen and potential rivals, even though Fergal, as king of Cenél nEógain, was based far to the north-west, in Inishowen.

Fergal's capacity to strike so far from his own kingdom was based on the support of the Airgialla, a group of peoples between the north of Meath and Lough Foyle. In the eighth and ninth centuries the Airgialla provided a major part of the armies of those kings of Tara who were of the Cenél nEógain.[13] They acknowledged their obligations to their Uí Néill overlords, which included six weeks of military service, although they wished to see this confined to once every three years.[14] One may compare the similar periods of military service demanded from feudal vassals throughout western Europe at a later period. The Airgialla settled furthest to the south-east were little more than 10 miles to the north of Kells. They could thus provide logistical support for a northern army making for Brega.

For a Cenél nEógain over-king to impose his authority further south was, however, a difficult undertaking, as the last years of the same Fergal mac Máele Dúin demonstrate. In 721, three years after the battle of Kells, Brega was harried by an unusual alliance between a king of Leinster, Murchad mac Brain, and a king of Munster, Cathal mac Finnguine. This stimulated an immediate riposte by Fergal, who invaded Leinster and imposed a tribute of cattle and a formal subjection of the Leinstermen as his clients.[15] At the very end of the next year, however, he had to

2.2   Crannóg – a defensible artificial island dwelling characteristic of
Gaelic Ireland – at Lough Owel, Westmeath.

invade Leinster yet again, and this time he was decisively defeated, and himself killed, in the battle of Allen (Allen, Almu, is the Hill of Allen, roughly 5 miles NNE of Kildare at N 76 20). The list of dead kings included rulers of the Ciannachta and the Airgialla.[16]

An easier form of imposition of hegemony occurred when the authority of a previous king of Tara was in decline and the new claimant was establishing his position. By the second half of the eighth century it was established that the kingship of Tara – and thus supremacy not just among the Uí Néill but also among all their vassal peoples, such as the Airgialla – was likely to alternate between the Cland Cholmáin kings of Meath and Cenél nEógain. This was not a fixed principle; successors therefore had to establish their position by force. A good example of the way this could proceed in the case of a particularly energetic and ruthless claimant is provided by the later years of Niall Frossach of Cenél nEógain. His power had reached its height with the proclamation of 'the Law of Patrick' in 767. In 769, however, Donnchad of Cland Cholmáin drove a southern Brega rival into exile; and in 770, exploiting dynastic struggles, he led an army of the Uí Néill into Leinster where it plundered widely. In 771 he led an army north into the inner sphere of Cenél nEógain power.[17] In 775 Donnchad attacked Munster; and he also established his authority, not without violence, in the major monastery of Clonard close to the boundary with Leinster. In 776 he used the dependants of another major monastery, Durrow, in a further attack on Munster. Switching east again in 777, he showed his power over Leinster by bringing an army from Leinster north, across the Liffey and the Rye, to attack Brega; this attack was followed up by further offensives against Brega in the same and the following year. The promulgation of 778 of 'the Law of Colum Cille' by Donnchad and by Bresal, abbot of Iona, demonstrated that Donnchad was now king of Tara even before Niall Frossach, aged about sixty, duly died the same year. Donnchad, therefore, had amply demonstrated, well before the death of Niall Frossach, that he disposed of sufficient power to demolish all rivals. He had shown an ability to campaign on all fronts except for the Shannon boundary with the Connachta, and yet had avoided having to campaign on more than one frontier at a time. The way he used a Leinster army to discipline Brega indicated that he could employ one of his military problems to solve another. Opposition to his ascent to hegemony among the Uí Néill came not so much from Cenél nEógain as from the rival southern Uí Néill of Brega – not surprisingly since it was only a generation since they had been among the leading contenders for a kingship itself associated with sites within their kingdoms, Tailtiu and Tara. Cenél nEógain could afford to bide its time, Síl nÁeda Sláine could not.

A common element in much Irish warfare of the early medieval period was harrying – *uastatio, indred*. It is tempting to regard such activities as a matter of a little gentlemanly reiving, removing a few cows, which, if the victims showed any proper spirit, they could regain by the same method the next year – hard work for the cows but good sport for the humans. The succinct style of the annals does not permit any definite conclusions about the severity of the plundering activities of kings and their armies; but anyone inclined to dismiss them should reflect that William the Conqueror's 'Harrying of the North' in 1069 left whole tracts of territory still waste nearly twenty years later in 1086.[18] Domesday Book also demonstrates, on a much smaller scale, the lasting effects of the harrying by an Irish fleet supplied to the sons of Harold in 1069 by Diarmait mac Maíl na mBó.[19] It is an assumption of the Irish saga writer and the Irish lawyer alike that such harrying will bring killing and burning, and that this will gravely disrupt society.[20] This assumption was made at least 200 years before the Dublin army led by Gothfrith ua Ímair, 'the most cruel king of the Northmen', killed 1,000 people in a single raid in Osraige.[21]

Sometimes the mere threat of harrying might be sufficient to bring an enemy to heel, but this was usually when the victim had recently suffered from threats carried out to the full. One of the recognised forms of *slógad*, 'hosting', was for a king to bring an army up to the frontier of another kingdom to demand his rights, 'so that he [the king] may have either battle or peace treaty'.[22] Thus Áed Oirdnide, a Cenél nEógain king of Tara, brought an army to Dún Cuair (probably Rathcore in County Meath) in 805, close to the northern frontier of Leinster. From there, apparently, he enforced a division of Leinster between two kings, weakening both and making them less able to resist Uí Néill pressure. This campaign had, however, been preceded in 804 by, first, 'the harrying of Leinster by the son of Niall [Áed

Oirdnide] twice in one month', then by 'a meeting of the synods of the Uí Néill', presided over by the ecclesiastical ally of the Cenél nEógain, the abbot of Armagh, also at Dún Cuair,[23] and finally by another campaign, also in 804, which compelled the king of Leinster to submit.

When a king went to war in order to dispose of the dynastic succession in a rival kingdom, and did so without more than the threat of force, he was gaining considerable benefit at minimum risk. But by the same token, a dynastic change within one kingdom could in effect be an act of war. The king removed from power by Áed Oirdnide in 805 had been responsible for killing Bran mac Muiredaig in 795, a king, moreover, who had been closely allied by marriage and by politics to the Uí Néill. One of the symptoms of the declining power of Donnchad mac Domnaill of Cland Cholmáin had been the killing of this same Bran, his brother-in-law and king of Leinster, together with the latter's queen, Donnchad's sister.

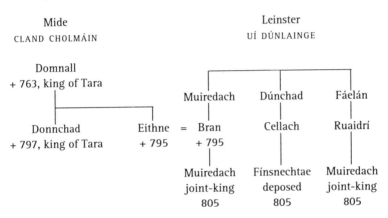

As these examples show, harrying of territory, interference in dynastic succession, feuding within a royal lineage, the deployment of the authority of ecclesiastical synods were all part of a complex pattern of political rivalry. Violence directed against a people and its territory was not clearly separate from violence directed against individuals.

The examples used hitherto have been of the Uí Néill and their rivals. This is inescapable for the pre-Viking period, for the annals are largely a record of the deeds of the Uí Néill combined with a great number of ecclesiastical and lay obits. For other kings we usually know only when they died; for the Uí Néill the evidence is sufficiently plentiful to permit some kind of connected account. If we look at the military activities of the Uí Néill in the eighth century as a whole, a striking contrast appears. After the battle of Corann in 703 between the Cenél Conaill king of Tara, Loingsech mac Óengussa, and the Connachta, hardly any hostilities were directed by the principal rulers of the Uí Néill west of the Shannon. In the same period, there was also very little Uí Néill activity directed against the Ulaid (the Ulstermen) in the north-east. There was rather more against Munster, but even this was usually connected with Leinster until we get to the reign of Donnchad mac Domnaill. In other words, the Uí Néill habitually fought the Leinstermen, but did not habitually fight anyone else apart from themselves. Of internal Uí Néill conflict there was plenty; but external violence was directed almost always against Leinster.

The one important exception to the general lack of Uí Néill activity against the Ulaid was the battle of Fochart in 735 at which Áed Allán defeated the king of the Ulstermen in the territory of Muirthemne (now in County Louth). Yet this victory seems not to have been intended primarily as a means to assert Uí Néill hegemony over the Ulstermen, but rather to give Cenél nEógain in particular an enduring foothold on the east coast making it easier for them to move armies into Brega and Leinster. In this way they could surmount the problem of the peripheral position of their own kingdoms in the north-west. The significance of Cenél nEógain's foothold in Muirthemne is neatly revealed by an entry in the Annals of Ulster for 756, according to which Domnall mac Murchada, then Cland Cholmáin king of Tara, brought a Leinster army up the east coast to Muirthemne to oppose the Cenél nEógain king, Niall Frossach.[24] The campaign served both the interests of Cland Cholmáin, by holding off the threat posed by their principal Uí Néill rivals, and also those of the Leinstermen, since the Muirthemne base was admirably suited to facilitate Cenél nEógain's attacks on Leinster. After that battle there were no Uí Néill attacks on the Ulstermen until 809, when Áed Oirdnide avenged the killing of Dúnchú, head of the church of Tulach Léis, 'beside the shrine of Patrick in the abbot's house at Tulach Léis'.[25] The Cenél nEógain king's defence of the honour of Patrick was probably required by the close alliance between his dynasty and the church of Armagh, itself an element in Cenél nEógain's drive towards the south-east.

There was then something which it is reasonable to call a strategy of the Uí Néill: peace on all fronts except one, the boundary with Leinster. Yet it is not obvious why this should have been the case. It raises the question of how, given the internal dynastic pressures leading towards external aggression, it was possible for peaceful relations to persist on a major frontier of direct Uí Néill power for an entire century. The laws (from the beginning of the eighth century) demonstrate that there were mechanisms available to support a peace truce once it had been made. Not surprisingly, the main problem was feud, which could cross the boundaries of kingdoms and so threaten to precipitate peoples towards war.

It has been acutely observed that Uí Néill attacks on Leinster usually occurred in periods of Cenél nEógain hegemony.[26] Cland Cholmáin kings of Tara, the centre of whose power lay in Mide close to the north-western frontier of Leinster, were more likely to pursue a peaceable policy towards their non-Uí Néill neighbours. They frequently attacked their Uí Néill neighbours to the east, Síl nÁeda Sláine, occasionally also Cenél nEógain and the Airgialla to the north; but, until the reign of Donnchad mac Domnaill, in the last decades of the eighth century, they were

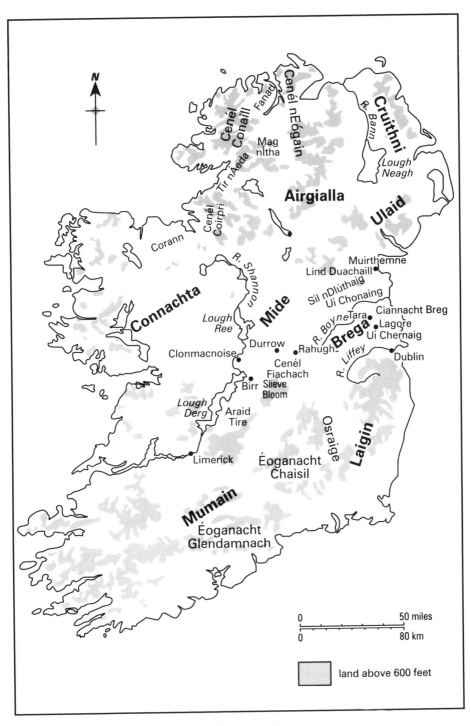

2.1   Ireland c. 750

much less likely to invade their neighbours to the south-east, south and west, in Leinster, Munster and Connacht. The distinction between the policies of Cenél nEógain and of Cland Cholmáin is borne out by Cenél nEógain's acquisition of lordship in Muirthemne: as we have seen, this was a preliminary to campaigns, not against the Ulaid (defeated in the battle of Fochart which gave Cenél nEógain this new base), but against Leinster. The reason for the difference is, however, unclear. Why should it be the case that Cland Cholmáin, apparently in much the best position to acquire new territory at the expense of Leinster, was much less aggressive in its policy towards its south-eastern neighbour than was Cenél nEógain?

The problem can be defined a little further, however, if we notice that the main Cenél nEógain attacks on Leinster occurred in the first half of the eighth century, in the reigns of Fergal mac Máele Dúin and his elder son, Áed Allán. This was the period when Cenél nEógain was establishing its primacy among the dynasties of the northern Uí Néill at the expense of Cenél Conaill. After the death of Áed Allán in 743, in battle against Cland Cholmáin, there was a period of relative peace embracing not only the reign of Domnall mac Murchada, the Cland Cholmáin king who defeated and slew Áed Allán, but also that of Áed's younger brother, Niall Frossach. Only when Niall's grip on power slackened, c. 770, and the Cland Cholmáin king, Donnchad mac Domnaill, began to demonstrate his military power, did the frontiers of the Uí Néill again see major military activity. Yet this time it was Donnchad, the king of Meath, who led an army of the southern Uí Néill against the Leinstermen.[27] The distinction between the policies of Cenél nEógain and Cland Cholmáin is most true, therefore, of the eighth century up to 770.

Peace with the Connachta west of the Shannon was a central element of Uí Néill policy during the eighth century, both for Cland Cholmáin and for Cenél nEógain. The policy was associated with the close kinship claimed between the Uí Néill and the Connachta. The latter had, so it was asserted, participated, together with the Airgialla, in the rise of the Uí Néill to hegemony, and had even, unlike the Airgialla, taken a share of the kingship of Tara.[28] Before Cenél nEógain's conquest of Mag nÍtha, however, at a period when Cenél Conaill was the pre-eminent Uí Néill dynasty in the north, relations with the Connachta were much more hostile. The area of the modern County Sligo was then the scene of attempts by Cenél Coirpri, Uí Néill clients of Cenél Conaill, to expand into northern Connacht.[29] This came to a dramatic conclusion with the deaths of Loingsech mac Óengussa, *rex Hibernie*, three of his sons and several other rulers in the battle of Corann in 703. The site of the battle, well within Connacht, shows that the Uí Néill were the aggressors.[30] In the reign of the next Cenél Conaill king of Tara, Congal mac Fergusa, limited aggression was resumed,[31] but Cenél Conaill was now under too much pressure elsewhere to be in any position to attack the Connachta. Once Cenél nEógain had gained the upper hand in the north, peace in the Sligo area was in prospect: Cenél nEógain was unlikely to expend any force in advancing the territorial interests of

2.3 The Grianan of Aileach, a massive royal fortification 4 miles west of
Derry, built by the northern Uí Néill in the sixth or seventh century.

Cenél Conaill and Cenél Coirpri. The decline of Cenél Conaill, therefore, prompted
an enduring peace between the Uí Néill and the Connachta.

The relative peace between the Uí Néill and Munster is less easy to explain. Cathal
mac Finnguine, king of Munster, became involved in the struggle between Fergal
mac Máele Dúin and Murchad mac Brain, king of Leinster, and again in that
between Fergal's son Áed Allán and Murchad's son, Fáelán. The involvement
began at the very beginning of Murchad's reign in Leinster and consisted of direct
aggression by the Leinster king. Murchad's predecessor, Cellach Cúalann, died in
715. In the same year Murchad assembled an army and marched it to the traditional
capital of Munster at Cashel.[32] There had also been a recent change of ruler in
Munster: Cormac mac Ailella of Eóganacht Chaisil had died in 713 to be succeeded
by Cathal mac Finnguine of the Eóganacht Glendamnach, based further south in the
valley of the Blackwater, north-west of Fermoy.[33] Cathal, therefore, may not yet
have fully established his control over Cashel. Six years later, however, he must
have been firmly in the saddle when he participated, together with Murchad mac
Brain, in the harrying of Brega in 721. We have seen part of the context already:
the raid on Brega provoked immediate retaliation by Fergal directed against
Leinster, not Munster. In the next year Munster was not involved in the defeat and
death of Fergal at the battle of Allen. One possible interpretation is that Murchad's

expedition to Cashel in 715 had induced Cathal to offer military aid to Leinster – an offer which was already discharged in 721 so that Munster forces took no part in the crucial battle in 722. Another explanation is that disunity among the Uí Néill of Brega occasioned not just the intervention of Fergal after the battle of Kells in 718, but the expedition of 721. This is more probable since Cathal is placed before Murchad in the annal entry in 721 making it less likely that he was in any way subordinated to Murchad. The context is better understood if one avoids the danger of hindsight: the Uí Néill of Brega, Síl nÁeda Sláine, had been the dominant Irish royal dynasty as recently as 690. The decline of their power, brought about by internal feuding, was allowing intervention from all sides in a highly unstable situation in which the Uí Néill monopoly of the kingship of Tara was at risk. In particular, the Leinstermen might entertain hopes of recovering territory north of the Liffey and the Rye lost since the early sixth century.

In the 730s, however, Munster's involvement in the wars of the Uí Néill and the Leinstermen was both secondary in importance and favourable to the Uí Néill. In 735 Cathal mac Finnguine was defeated by the Leinstermen. Two years later, in 737, Cathal and Áed Allán met at the monastery of Terryglas, within a Munster client kingdom but only about 10 miles from the frontier. The meeting was satisfactory to the Cenél nEógain king of Tara since it immediately resulted in the proclamation of the Law of Patrick within Munster: Armagh was already the ecclesiastical ally of Cenél nEógain. The annalistic evidence is not entirely above suspicion, but the likely sequence of events is as follows: an alliance between the Uí Néill and Munster having been concerted at Terryglas in 737, Cathal attacked Leinster very early in 738; this was followed by the death of Fáelán, king of Leinster, leaving his province divided between two kings; Áed Allán then took full advantage of the situation to achieve the great victory of Áth Senaig.[34] What we have then is the appearance, at least, of large-scale operations concerted at a *rígdál* in north-west Munster and prosecuted at a most opportune time, the last months of one reign and the first months of another. The king of Munster, previously defeated by the Leinstermen in 735, was able to compel Fáelán's submission shortly before his death; this agreement was undone by Fáelán's death, his successors not being bound by his promises, but Áed Allán then secured the decisive victory at Áth Senaig.

The relative uncertainty of relations between the Uí Néill and Munster, compared with the peace that reigned between the Uí Néill and the Connachta after 703, is to be explained, therefore, by Munster involvement in wars against Leinster, sometimes as an Uí Néill ally, sometimes on its own account, as in 794 when Donnchad mac Domnaill led an army of the Uí Néill to defend Leinster (then ruled by his brother-in-law) against the Munstermen. If we take the frontiers of the Uí Néill in turn – leaving aside those with fellow Uí Néill and the Airgialla – we can see the differences. The Shannon frontier with the Connachta was the most peaceable. This is so striking in the annals that we can infer the existence of an enduring *cairde*, formal peace treaty; the mechanics of such an arrangement were carefully set out by the lawyers.[35] Relations between the Uí Néill and the Connachta between the battle of Corann in 703 and the Viking attacks of the ninth century indicate how effective the peace-keeping devices of the lawyers could be in favourable circumstances.

The frontier with Munster lay across Slieve Bloom and along the Camcor and Little Brosna rivers until the latter's confluence with the Shannon.[36] This area, around Slieve Bloom, contained one of the greatest concentrations of monastic land in the whole of Ireland. On the Uí Néill side the kingdom of Cenél Fiachach contained Durrow, Rahugh, Lynally and Kinnitty and thus came to be known as *Fir Chell*, 'the men belonging to churches';[37] Delbnae Bethra was overshadowed by the great monastery of Clonmacnoise and its lesser neighbour Lemanaghan. Birr and Seirkieran lay very close to the frontier; further into Munster were Aghaboe, Clonfertmulloe, Lorrha, Roscrea and Terryglas. The western borderlands of Leinster made their contribution with Clonennagh and Killeigh. In part by these means – the transformation of the borderlands into sacred precincts – the frontier between Slieve Bloom and the Shannon was sealed off until the reign of Donnchad mac Domnaill in the last quarter of the eighth century. Already by the mid-eighth century, however, the great monasteries had acquired numerous tenants and clients: the *familia* or *muinter* of a saint was far from being confined to monks; moreover its leadership was sometimes in lay hands. Hence the succession struggle within Cland Cholmáin after the death in 763 of Donnchad's father, Domnall mac Murchada, was largely prosecuted with the aid of monastic forces: Domnall's brother, Bresal mac Murchada, led an army recruited from the *familia* of Clonmacnoise to victory against another army consisting of 200 men from the *familia* of Durrow. Instead of a sacred, demilitarised frontier zone, this was now a borderland fought over by rival *familiae* even without the stimulus of dynastic conflict within Cland Cholmáin. In 760, three years before Domnall mac Murchada's death, the *familiae* of Clonmacnoise and Birr had fought a battle in the boglands east of the Shannon. It is not surprising that, given this rising level of military activity, the reign of Donnchad mac Domnaill saw increasing hostility on the Munster border. In 775 Donnchad defeated the Munstermen and laid waste their borderlands; in 776 there was another Uí Néill victory in which the *familia* of Durrow took part. The norm, however, remained peace, and this again may suggest a formal *cairde*. Indeed, if there was a treaty between Munster and the Uí Néill over-king – in 775 still Niall Frossach of Cenél nEógain – it might explain why Donnchad, then challenging Niall Frossach's authority, attacked Munster.

The remaining frontier was that with Leinster. Here we should distinguish between the section of the frontier which lay on the lower Liffey as it ran eastwards towards Dublin Bay and the section which lay along the River Rye which joins the Liffey at Leixlip. After Kilcock, nearly 20 miles west of Dublin, the frontier turned west-south-west along a line of bogs running towards Slieve Bloom. There was some military activity on the lower Liffey, but here again there was a concentration of church land. Moreover, in this area the monasteries seem to have retained a more religious character than did the great houses further west. Finglas, Glasnevin, Clondalkin and Tallaght, on either side of the Liffey, offered much more support for the *Céli Dé* movement than did Clonard, Durrow, Rahan, Rahugh and Clonmacnoise, monasteries which were increasingly being drawn into the political orbit of Cland Cholmáin.[38] The main Uí Néill attacks on Leinster were therefore further west where Dún Cuair as well as one of the Uí Néill vassal kingdoms of Cenél Coirpri (which gave its name to the modern Carbury in the north-west corner of County Kildare)[39] provided possible advance bases. Once an Uí Néill army was across the boglands, usually roughly along what is now the L 181 road towards Clane, it was in the heart of northern Leinster, close to the major Uí Dúnlainge centres of Naas and Kildare.[40] One reason for Uí Néill interest in Leinster, therefore, was its accessibility, in spite of the defending boglands. The kingship of Leinster was usually held by the Uí Dúnlainge and their lands lay close to the frontier. Indeed, there is something to be said for seeing the whole of the eastern midlands in the eighth century, from County Louth southwards as far as the hills around Baltinglass, as a single rich agricultural zone exposed by political weakness to invasion from outside. Both the Síl nÁeda Sláne of Brega, north of the Liffey, and the Uí Dúnlainge of County Kildare were attacked by the dominant dynasties among the Uí Néill, Leinster mainly by Cenél nEógain, Brega mainly by Cland Cholmáin. The Eóganachta of Munster, however, were based many miles to the south of their frontier with the Uí Néill. Attack on them posed much more severe logistical problems.

The Uí Néill retained the military initiative as much by making peace as by making war. In the eighth century they had the good sense to remain content with limited objectives. This was to change in the Viking era, but how far this was due to the new invaders is a major problem.

The Irish Sea in the post-Roman period

In the late-Roman and post-Roman periods, and again in the Viking era, sea power dominated the military affairs of Ireland. In the early period, the power was normally deployed by the Irish; in the later period, it was usually deployed against them. In both periods, sea power led to overseas settlement, so that the Irish Sea, together with the arm of the Atlantic which comes in between the Hebrides and the north coast of Ireland, became a bridge between peoples of the same language. In the early period, it was a bridge between Irish speakers; in the later, it was initially the link between the overseas speakers of Scandinavian in the *vestr haf*, 'the western ocean'; yet, in the end, even such a Viking stronghold as the Isle of Man would become Irish in speech.

The Irish were one of the many peoples across the frontier who destroyed the Roman Empire in the West. Their contribution was a minor one, yet it is right to remember that the empire was not simply the victim of Germanic peoples. In the

---

north, the onslaughts took two principal forms: attacks by land armies across the Rhine frontier and smaller-scale raids using the seas around the British Isles. It is easy to assume that the land attacks on the Rhine, such as the famous crossing of the Vandals, Alans and Suebi over the frozen river in the winter of 406–7 must have been the most damaging to the empire. Yet the territory which was to fall most completely out of the Roman orbit, Britain, was conquered by sea power.

The attacks of the Irish on Britain are not likely to have been caused simply by the military weakness of the empire. The armies of Rome were no less effective in the fourth century than they had been in the first. On the other hand, it is evident that the Roman authorities in Britain did not control the Irish Sea, while a largely land-based defence was inevitably at a disadvantage against the mobility and secrecy of maritime raiders. Yet there is no reason to believe that Rome had controlled the Irish Sea in the first and second centuries, in spite of the achievements of Agricola's fleet in circumnavigating the north of Britain. What probably made the difference was, first, the relative wealth of Britain and, secondly, the demand for manpower both in the empire and in Ireland. The material culture of Ireland was surprisingly little affected by proximity to Rome; most of the Roman artefacts which have been uncovered come from the south-east of the island. It follows that trade between Ireland, on the one side, and Britain and Gaul, on the other, was either little developed or depended on importing non-durable commodities into Ireland. Irish kings in the late Iron Age may have drunk Roman wine, but they did not drink it out of Roman cups. There may, therefore, have been relatively little advantage for the Irish in preserving peaceful relations with the empire for the sake of trade.

Britain, however, in the fourth century was relatively rich, and some of the richest parts were easily accessible to Irish raiders coming up the Bristol Channel. Whereas, under the early empire, distant provinces were probably exploited by the core of the Empire, by the fourth century Italy was in decline while Britain flourished. The imperial authorities, now themselves usually based close to the frontier, in such cities as Trier or Sirmium, were far more concerned than they had been with the economic capacity of frontier provinces to provide logistical support for the army. Yet, because such towns as Trier were now among the grandest expressions of *Romanitas*, the contrast with the material culture of, for example, the Alamans, not many miles away across the Rhine – a culture still obstinately barbarian – was far greater than it had been under the early empire. While the barbarians preferred to remain barbarian – and for a long time that is what most did prefer – Rome remained fairly safe; but when their rulers decided that they would like to be equal to the Romans in material as well as in military terms, and that such an agreeable state of comfort was best attained on the Roman side of the frontier, then the empire was in grave peril.

Irish control of the sea was a means to such settlement within the empire. When Irishmen had made themselves rulers of Dyfed – the *civitas* of the Demetae in south-west Wales – they had themselves commemorated in stone inscriptions. Many of

---

41

these inscriptions were bilingual, both Latin and Irish; in this way Irish noblemen of the diaspora recorded both their determination to be grand in the Roman manner – in stone and in Latin – and also their determination to assert the high status of the Irish language which united them with their kinsmen across the sea. Irish was to be worthy of appearing on stone monuments alongside Latin within a former province of the Empire. The Irish settlers in Wales and Cornwall appear to have come predominantly from the same south-east quarter of the island which shows most evidence for trading contacts. The distribution of ogam inscriptions on stone in Ireland is also predominantly southern, though in this case it extends further to the south-west.

Yet the explanation of Irish aggression against Britain cannot be merely in terms of the desire of the relatively Romanised Irish of the south-east to enjoy the benefits of living within a Roman province. Another reason was the shortage of manpower within the empire, and also, but probably in a different form, in Ireland. The late empire was chronically short of manpower – hence the far-reaching restrictions on mobility of labour – but so also, perhaps, was Ireland. Whereas the empire attempted to cope with *agri deserti*, the Irish appear, in the period from the fourth to the seventh century, to have been expanding the scope of settlement and increasing the intensity of agriculture. This was achieved in spite of major outbreaks of plague brought to the West across the Mediterranean and over the western provinces. The engine behind Irish expansion in this period was perhaps not primarily an increase in population, but the universal desire in a highly stratified society to maintain or increase the material basis of status.[41] Men cleared land to protect their rank rather than simply to ensure an adequate food supply. The pressure therefore came more from the higher levels of society, with more to lose, than from the poor who were in danger of starvation. To clear the land, however, needed immense labour; yet the obligations of Irish freemen to do agricultural work for their lords were limited; in this context, it is hardly surprising that slave-raiding flourished. Patrick tells us that he was only one of thousands in his generation taken into slavery in Ireland.

An argument to show that the attractions, and indeed the weaknesses, of the empire cannot by themselves explain Irish expansion overseas is that settlement occurred both within and without the Roman province. The Irish colony in what is now Argyll appears to have been part of the same expansionary phase that took Irish settlers to Wales and to Cornwall, yet the reasons for its creation can have little to do with Rome.[42] The establishment of a kingdom of Dál Riata, which included both an Irish component in what is now County Antrim and a British component in Kintyre, Lorne, Cowal and the southern Hebrides, is a clear demonstration of the extent to which the sea was now a bridge between Ireland and Britain, a bridge travelled mainly by Irish settlers and raiders in one direction and British slaves and missionaries in the other. It is also a demonstration of the skill of Irish sailors. The waters between Fair Head at the north-east corner of Ireland and the Mull of Kintyre are among the most dangerous around the British Isles. The speed reached by the tidal flows as the Irish Sea fills and empties are at their highest point in this part of the North Channel – some 10 times the speed found west of Tory Island. For the early medieval navigator, the fearsome Corryvreckan (*Coire Breccáin*, 'the Cauldron of Breccán') was not situated between Jura and Scarba, as it is today, but off Rathlin Island, and thus in the very waters which bound the two parts of Dál Riata together.[43]

The seaways of Dál Riata remained under Irish control until the coming of the Vikings, but the Irish Sea further south seems to have passed into British hands in the sixth century. It was dominated by two islands, Man and Anglesey, called by Bede the Mevanian Islands.[44] For him both were British. Man, however, had been regarded by late Roman writers as Irish, and the extent of Irish control of the Irish Sea in the fourth and fifth centuries strongly suggests that they were correct. The British successor states of the fifth century had, however, been very rapidly militarised after the departure of the legions, to the point at which British kings and armies were recruited by Gallic provincials to fight their barbarian enemies.[45] The Britons were already beginning to dispute control of the Irish Sea in Patrick's lifetime, as shown by the slaving activities of Coroticus.[46] By the seventh century fleets were more likely to travel westwards rather than eastwards across the Irish Sea. The Northumbrian attack on Brega in 684 presupposes English exploitation of this British sea power; Bede was careful to point out that, earlier in the century, Edwin's *imperium* embraced even the Mevanian islands of the Britons. This shift in sea power is important for it partly explains the contrast between the fates of the southern and the northern Irish colonies in Britain. In the south, the seventh and eighth centuries would see assimilation of Irish rulers to their British subjects; in the north Dál Riata would become, in the Viking Age, a stepping-stone to a kingdom of the Scots, whose elite would remain Irish-speaking until the twelfth and thirteenth centuries, and sometimes even beyond.

Irish warfare in the Viking age

The long-term effect of the Vikings in the British Isles was fourfold: to destroy British control of the Irish Sea and so split the different British kingdoms further apart; to destroy Irish control of Hebridean waters and so divide the Irish of North Britain from the Irish of Ireland; to give southern Irish kings the opportunity of controlling the seaports created by their enemies and thus acquire indirect power over the Viking fleets which dominated the sea; and, finally, to destroy the core of early Anglo-Saxon England – the kingdoms of Mercia and Northumbria – to the benefit of the periphery, English Wessex in the south and the kingdom of the Scots in the north.

The Vikings thus transformed the British Isles as a whole; yet it is much more difficult to demonstrate the effect they had on the internal development of Ireland.[47]

43

The principal contemporary source – the Chronicle of Ireland which extends up to *c.* 911 – gives full attention to the nuisance value of the Vikings but seems to suggest that they had almost no idea of what to do with their military successes. Irish victories produced, at least temporarily, political control; Viking victories only destruction. This may be a misleading picture, but it is not easy to get behind it.

The development of the Viking military threat in Ireland proceeded according to much the same rhythm as elsewhere in north-western Europe. The main difference is that, whereas elsewhere Vikings both raided and attempted to gain control of the major *emporia*, specialised trading towns, in Ireland they created them. Viking attacks began from 794 with small-scale raids on the Hebrides and also on island monasteries off the Irish coast. The mainland of Ireland was first attacked in the years 811–13 by what may have been a single small fleet. There was then a pause from 814 to 820 coinciding with the period of the greatest power exerted by Áed Oirdnide, Cenél nEógain king of Tara. By now the Vikings probably had permanent advance posts in the Hebrides and thus sources of intelligence about political developments in Ireland. Áed Oirdnide's death in 819 was followed by an indecisive succession struggle and a renewal of Viking raids, mainly on the east coast from Ulster southwards as far as County Wicklow. The intensity of raiding activity increased *c.* 830 and again from 837 leading to the foundation of the permanent settlements of Dublin and Lind Duachaill in 841 (the latter site – the name survives in Linns, County Louth, O 07 94 – was between the sea and the river just before its mouth at Annagassan);[48] as at Dublin, there was a church there before it was a Viking 'ship-port', *longphort*.[49] The pattern changed again in the 850s when there was the first clear evidence of military collaboration between an Irish king and the Vikings, the arrival of a royal prince from Norway who claimed authority over all the Scandinavian settlers, and also a conflict among 'the heathens' setting 'fair heathens' against 'dark heathens'. The first royal figure from Scandinavia, Amlaíb (Óláfr), was soon followed by a second, Ímar (Ívarr, perhaps Ívarr inn beinlausi, 'Ivar the Boneless').[50] He was to found the principal royal lineage of the Vikings in Ireland, Uí Ímair, 'the descendants of Ímar'. They were initially based in Dublin, but later sent out a cadet branch to Waterford. Ímar and his descendants also became deeply embroiled in the affairs of England, Strathclyde and the kingdom of the Scots. In particular, they supplied several rulers to the kingdom of York until its incorporation into a united England in 954.

The diversion of the main Viking activities to Britain appears to have secured a relative peace for Ireland between *c.* 870 and 914. In the latter year, however, the Vikings founded a new permanent settlement at Waterford. Not long afterwards, another was founded, or refounded, at Limerick.[51] The twenty-five years from 915 to 940 were perhaps the highpoint of Viking aggression, with relatively permanent settlements not just on the east coast of the midlands, at Dublin and Lind Duachaill, but also further north at Carlingford Lough and Strangford Lough, and in Munster, at Waterford and Limerick.[52] The Irish were initially unable to counter these threats,

2.4 Cross of Muiredach, Monasterboice, where the soldiers seizing Christ
are using swords of a Viking type.

Niall Glúndub, the Cenél nEogain king of Tara, being killed in battle at Dublin in
919. Yet during the 940s the threat gradually receded again. There were occasional
dramatic plundering raids; but the Viking rulers were drawn into the Irish political
order, so that their military power usually served Irish political ends. After Máel
Sechnaill II's defeat of Óláfr Cuarán at the battle of Tara in 980, the Vikings were
never a major threat. The great battle of Clontarf in 1014, at which Brian Bóruma
was killed although his army was victorious, was brought about by a standard event
of Irish politics: Máel Mórda, king of Leinster, in alliance with the Vikings of Dublin
and elsewhere, rebelled against the ageing king of Ireland. Clontarf was unusual for
the degree of participation by Vikings from outside Ireland and for the number of
casualties, not for any difference it made to the position of the Vikings within
Ireland.[53]

Clontarf is, however, interesting in another way, for it offers an emphatic
illustration of how far the structure of power within Ireland had changed since 794,
when the annalist recorded the first raids of Vikings on 'the islands of Britain'.
Brian was king of Ireland, although he recognised the position of his ally Máel

Sechnaill II as king of Tara. Yet Brian came, not of the Uí Néill, but from Dál Cais, an upstart Munster dynasty from the lower Shannon valley.[54] Munster was now central to Irish politics, whereas in the eighth century it had been isolated. The old confederation of royal dynasties controlling Munster, the Eóganachta, had been elbowed aside by the new upstart. Likewise, Uí Néill control of Irish politics through their judicious mixture of alliance and aggression had been permanently shattered. The Irish political world in 1014 was, therefore, very different from that in 794, at the outset of the Viking attacks in the last years of the reign of Donnchad mac Domnaill as king of Tara. Yet it is not easy to see how far these great changes were the result of Viking aggression.

In order to clarify the nature and effects of Viking military activity within Ireland, I shall look at a single reign, that of Máel Sechnaill mac Ruanaid (Máel Sechnaill I, who died in 862).[55] Máel Sechnaill's reign as king of Mide, before succeeding Niall Caille as king of Tara, began immediately after the establishment of the *longphoirt* at Dublin and Lind Duachaill in 841. The important thing to notice about these particular *longphoirt* is that they differed from the usual wintering stations of Viking armies in Francia. The latter were normally occupied only for a single winter. The great Viking fleet of the 880s used all the major rivers draining into the English Channel and the adjacent part of the North Sea, the Rhine, Meuse, Scheldt, Somme and Seine; they therefore adopted a new fortified camp every winter as they shifted from one area of plunder and tribute-taking to another. The chroniclers could follow the movement of an army by noting its wintering stations. There were Viking bases of this kind in Ireland, as on Lough Neagh in 839 or Lough Erne in 924–5; but Dublin became the principal permanent base of the Vikings in Ireland, comparable with Kiev on the Dnieper,[56] while Lind Duachaill in County Louth was occupied until 927. If we compare Viking campaigning in England and in Ireland, it becomes evident that in this distinction between a temporary and a permanent settlement there lies a significant difference between the experience of the countries of Western Europe in the Viking period. The Vikings in England eventually acquired permanent settlements after the conquests of 'the Great Army' in the 860s and 870s – so that one could then speak, for example, of 'the army of Derby'[57] as an enduring part of the political landscape, just as one spoke of 'the fleet of Limerick'[58] – but these settlements in England were founded a generation later than their first counterparts in Ireland, Dublin and Lind Duachaill.

There is a further major difference. When the Vikings eventually acquired a permanent base in northern France, at Rouen near the mouth of the Seine, it became the capital of a territorial lordship; York was already the centre of a kingdom and an archdiocese before the Vikings made it the capital of their kingdom of York. The territory which eventually became subject to Dublin was very much smaller than its counterparts in other countries; and this may imply that the nature of the power enjoyed by Viking rulers of Dublin was not the same as that exercised by rulers of Rouen or York.

The situation of the two early *longphoirt* of Dublin and Lind Duachaill – astride the low-lying eastern coastlands between the Mourne and Wicklow Mountains – posed a direct threat to the kingdom of Máel Sechnaill. In 841, two years before Máel Sechnaill succeeded his father as king of Mide, the Vikings of Lind Duachaill marched right across the midlands to the kingdoms of Tethbae, approximately the modern County Longford, immediately to the east of the Shannon. Tethbae, however, was perhaps the most important of the Uí Néill client territories which had to be controlled by Cland Cholmáin, whose own lands lay further east around Lough Ennell. The capacity of the Vikings to strike so far threatened the authority of the king of Mide by revealing his inability to defend his principal clients. In the same year, the Vikings of Dublin ravaged the districts on either side of the frontier between Leinster and the Uí Néill as far as Slieve Bloom. In the next year, 842, 'the heathens from Lind Duachaill' plundered Clonmacnoise on the Shannon, as well as capturing the abbot of Clogher, one of the principal churches of the Airgialla; Vikings, perhaps from Dublin, also captured another of the client kings of Mide. Moreover, Mide was not the only leading Uí Néill kingdom to be threatened. The *longphort* at Lind Duachaill was immediately adjacent to Cenél nEogain's advance post in Mag Muirthemne.

Under such severe pressure, the political framework established by the Uí Néill proved remarkably resilient. One of their number, Cináed mac Conaing, king of Ciannacht Breg, 'rebelled against Máel Sechnaill by virtue of the power of the Foreigners' in 850, 'and plundered the Uí Néill from the Shannon to the sea'. He took particular care to sack the crannóg of the rival Síl nÁeda Sláine king of South Brega at Lagore (to the east of Dunshaughlin, County Meath) and to burn the adjacent church of Trevet. If Síl nÁeda Sláine as a whole had defied the authority of the Cland Cholmáin over-king and had sought an alliance with the Dublin Vikings, Máel Sechnaill might have been in severe difficulties, but, as usual, the internal rivalries of the Uí Néill of Brega – shown by the sacking of Lagore and the burning of Trevet – came to his rescue. This event shows how easy it was for the Vikings to find some Irish allies, but how difficult it was to make any progress beyond that point in the direction of a settled structure of authority. One Irish king as an ally inevitably entailed another Irish king as an enemy. In the very next year, 851, the power of the 'Foreigners', the *Gaill*, in which Cináed mac Conaing had trusted, was not enough to prevent him from being executed by drowning at the command of Máel Sechnaill and Tigernach mac Fócartai, king of Lagore. The inability of the Vikings to protect Cináed may have been due to their own divisions. Under the year 851 the annals record the arrival of 'the dark heathens' in Dublin, where 'they made a great slaughter of the fair foreigners' and plundered the *longphort*. They also attacked Lind Duachaill in the same year, but with less success. The identity of 'the dark heathens' and 'the fair heathens' has been a matter of uncertainty since the eleventh century. What is clear is that the division originated outside Ireland, that it caused some disarray among the Vikings for a few years, but that it was soon

47

rendered ineffective by the Scandinavian royal leaders who entered Ireland from 853.

The first of these leaders, Amlaíb (Óláfr), is described by the Annals of Ulster as 'the son of the king of Laithlind'. The annals add that 'the foreigners of Ireland gave hostages to him and tribute was paid by the Irish'.[59] What this ought to mean, given the usual conventions of Irish political vocabulary, is that the Vikings were treated as relatively privileged clients of Amlaíb, who was behaving as if he were the new over-king of Ireland, while the Irish kings were 'base clients', obliged to pay tribute.[60] It implies, therefore, a distinction in political status between, for example, the Vikings of Lind Duachaill and the neighbouring Irish peoples, the Conailli Muirthemne and the Fir Airde Ciannachtae. The Vikings were aspiring to impose themselves as a new ruling people within a political system which remained Irish.

Yet in the very next year, 854, Máel Sechnaill led an army into Munster and took the hostages of the Munstermen, a clear demonstration, apparently, that he was not merely still king of Tara, in spite of the hostages given to Amlaíb, but also that he proposed to make that kingship into an effective monarchy of Ireland by means of military power. He made another expedition to Munster in 856 in the very year in which the annals record 'a major war between the heathens and Máel Sechnaill who was supported by Norse-Irish (*Gallgoídil*)'.[61] These 'Norse-Irish' appear in the annals for the first time in this year. The scale of their operations is remarkable: one band was defeated by Áed Findliath, king of Cenél nÉogain, also in 856; another band was defeated by the Viking kings, Amlaíb and Ímar, in Munster in the next year. Even if these defeated Gallgoídil were his allies, Máel Sechnaill was not deflected from his drive to obtain a lasting submission from the Munstermen. Moreover, he had considerable success. In 858, he 'came with the men of Ireland to the lands of Munster', and, after defeating the kings of the Munstermen, 'he took their hostages from Belat Gabráin in the east to the Bull Island in the west, and from the Old Head of Kinsale in the south to Inisheer in the north'.

The annalist, almost certainly writing in the territories of the southern Uí Néill, was not disposed to minimise Máel Sechnaill's achievement. Yet it is worth examining what he says carefully. He suggests that the victory was not won over the king of Munster, but over 'their kings', one of whom was left dead on the battlefield. Moreover, even if we make due allowance for rhetorical exuberance, the point of saying that hostages were given from the four quarters of Munster must be that the client kings of Munster, not just their provincial king, had been made to submit personally to the king of Tara. In effect, Máel Sechnaill was bypassing the political authority of the king of Munster, just as Amlaíb, in taking the hostages of the Irish, had bypassed the authority of the king of Tara.

This impression of parallel and competing systems of authority is strengthened by a notice in the *Chronicum Scotorum* for the same year as Máel Sechnaill's victorious campaign in Munster: 'Cenél Fiachach, together with the Gallgoídil of Leth Cuinn, were defeated by Cerball and by Ímar in the territory of Araid Tíre; and the number of the Gallgoídil was 6,400.'[62] Cenél Fiachach was an Uí Néill client kingdom on the north side of Slieve Bloom. Cerball mac Dúnlainge, was king of Osraige (then part of Munster) on the south side of the same mountain range. The kingdom, Araid Tíre, in which they fought, was another Munster client kingdom, south-west of Cenél Fiachach and on the east side of the Shannon. What we may have here is a much shorter-range expedition by Cerball and Ímar, later in the same year as Máel Sechnaill's major campaign – an expedition on which the Gallgoídil, often Máel Sechnaill's allies, were, as usual, defeated. Máel Sechnaill responded directly, and in an unprecedented way, to this continued defiance from the king of Osraige. In 859 he held a royal meeting at Rahugh (N 37 31, in Westmeath but close to the border with Offaly), a church within the kingdom of Cenél Fiachach; here the king of Munster, Máel Guala, entered into a formal contract, for which he appointed sureties. The terms of this contract were that Osraige was to be permanently alienated to Leth Cuinn (the northern half of Ireland) and so come under the direct authority of Máel Sechnaill. Cerball himself made his own formal acknowledgement of the authority of Patrick's heir and the community of Armagh. Yet even this exceptional display of authority had its discordant accompaniment: the next entry in that year's annal reads simply: 'Máel Guala, king of Munster, was killed by the Northmen.'

The royal assembly at Rahugh in 859 was the highpoint of Máel Sechnaill's reign as king of Tara. He was to die in 862; and, as often in the history of the Uí Néill, an ageing king of Tara was challenged by his successor. In this instance, the challenger was Áed Findliath of Cenél nEógain. The habitual alternation between Cland Cholmáin and Cenél nEógain was maintained, with its usual warlike flurries as one reign ended and another began. What was significant on this occasion, however, was the inability of the Vikings to use the growing weakness of Máel Sechnaill to offer their own challenge. There was no question of Amlaíb or Ímar becoming the next king of Tara. Instead, Vikings became part of a distinctively Irish pattern of military and political activity. Moreover, because they became part of that Irish pattern, their military power served the purposes of an Irish king.

In 859, at the great meeting at Rahugh, the ecclesiastical supremacy of Armagh echoed the political supremacy of Máel Sechnaill. Armagh, however, was the traditional ally of Cenél nEógain rather than Cland Cholmáin. It looks as though Áed Findliath must subsequently have put pressure on Armagh to revert to its customary allegiance. In 860 Máel Sechnaill mounted the last of his great campaigns. He was able to secure contingents from Leinster, Munster and Connacht as well as from his own southern Uí Néill. With them he marched north towards Armagh. Close to his destination he was attacked during the night by Áed Findliath in alliance with Flann mac Conaing, king of Ciannacht Breg. Máel Sechnaill, however, defeated the attackers. In 861 Áed went further and harried Mide, Máel Sechnaill's own kingdom, in company with Vikings. In this instance, later in the year, Máel Sechnaill responded to this intervention on behalf of his rival by defeating 'the Foreigners of Dublin' in a battle fought on the north-western frontier of Leinster. In 862, with Máel Sechnaill only a few months away from his death, Áed Findliath again invaded Mide with the aid of Flann mac Conaing and of the Vikings of Dublin. This ability to know when a rival king's health was beginning to fail suggests that the principal Irish kings had access to good intelligence about their rivals. It is likely to have come, as among the Franks, from churchmen, able to move from one kingdom to another, or from poets who enjoyed similar privileges and were later suspected by English administrations in Ireland of being spies. It may be that the Vikings were not quite so well informed.

During Máel Sechnaill's reign, the Vikings were undoubtedly a major threat. Yet it is already clear that to make any real impact, they had to act in alliance with Irish kings. Very often this meant that their purposes were subordinated to those of their allies. Even at their moments of greatest military power, the best they could do in opposition to the Uí Néill was to create a parallel, and even more brittle, structure of authority. Sometimes client kingdoms must have been paying tribute both to Vikings and to the king of Tara. While such client kingdoms could still pay tribute to both overlords, the Vikings were not seriously disrupting the political framework created by the Uí Néill. Political discipline among the Uí Néill was occasionally broken, but the danger of allying oneself with the Vikings was great, as shown by the execution of Cináed mac Conaing for rebelling against Máel Sechnaill with the aid of the Vikings. Viking leaders had high political ambitions in Ireland, as shown by Amlaíb's success in 853 in making the Irish pay tribute to him. In the end, however, it was simply too difficult for the men whom the Irish continued to call 'the Foreigners' to make the Irish political culture serve these far-reaching aspirations. They were confronted by a pattern of loyalties inherited from, and validated by, the past. It would have required quite extraordinary resources to have created a new political order with themselves at the top. They never had the ready-made access to control of major tracts of territory which was offered to the Normans by Diarmait mac Murchada.

The Viking rulers appear to have made repeated efforts to create a structure of authority and tribute-taking. In the defeat of Óláfr Cuarán at the hands of Máel Sechnaill II in 980, one of the casualties on the Dublin side was a certain Conamhal *m. airri Gall*, 'son of a viceroy of the foreigners'.[63] In the years immediately before his decisive defeat in 980, Óláfr Cuarán had been attempting to assert the military power of Dublin; the appearance of an *airrí Gall* may be a consequence of his temporary success.

Among Máel Sechnaill I's military achievements, what mattered most for the future, and apparently mattered most to Máel Sechnaill himself, was not so much his wars with the Vikings, but rather his repeated invasions of Munster. Uí Néill aggression in the ninth century, followed by the renewed Viking threat between 914 and 940, itself concentrated in the south, compelled the kings of Munster to devote more resources to war. Yet in his aggression against Munster Máel Sechnaill was following the lead given by his grandfather, Donnchad mac Domnaill, in the eighth century. That policy was a major, and in the long run, disastrous break with the traditional strategy of the Uí Néill, but it was initiated before the Vikings and pursued by Máel Sechnaill almost as if there were no threat from 'the Foreigners'. Cland Cholmáin of Mide were now confronted by enemies on all sides except their western border with Connacht on the Shannon. They therefore had to win outright or their power would be undermined by their enemies. The Vikings might have better arms and armour, as they certainly had better ships.[64] Yet these technical advantages could soon be imitated or hired. What was not so easy to ensure was that the new Irish enemies of the Uí Néill, the Munstermen, would not learn the same lessons and attack Mide from the south at a time when Cland Cholmáin already had to defeat Cenél nEógain in the north and the kings of Brega in the east. Brian Bóruma, for example, was a notable builder of forts.[65] The peaceable policies of Domnall mac Murchada in the mid-eighth century might have brought less dazzling successes, but they were much more prudent. Cland Cholmáin were both the principal exponents of Uí Néill expansionism in the late eighth and ninth centuries and, in the end, its principal victims. A dominant military power was not to return to the midlands between the Irish Sea and the Shannon and between the Liffey and the Mourne Mountains until the arrival of the Normans.

Chapter 3

Irish and Anglo-Norman warfare in twelfth-century Ireland

Marie Therese Flanagan

Anglo-Norman intervention in the late twelfth century has been perceived as an important new departure in the military history of Ireland: military superiority has been highlighted as a major, if not the most significant, factor contributing to the establishment of an Anglo-Norman colony in Ireland and to its expansion and consolidation; emphasis has been placed on the professional military training of the Anglo-Normans and on their use of heavy cavalry, defensive armour and castles.[1] In contrast, Irish techniques of warfare have been characterised as little more than plundering and cattle-raiding, and have been deemed inadequate in the face of more advanced Anglo-Norman military skills.[2] The contrast between Irish and Anglo-Norman warfare does not depend, however, on any detailed studies of Irish warfare in the immediate pre-Norman period. It is an assumption derived in the first instance from the contemporary Anglo-Norman apologist, Giraldus, archdeacon of Brecon, more popularly known as Gerald of Wales, who drew an unfavourable contrast between Irish and Anglo-Norman methods of warfare. Giraldus did so explicitly by asserting that the Irish went 'naked and unarmed into battle', that they regarded weapons as a hindrance, and that they did not build castles, and implicitly by emphasising the successful military exploits of the first Anglo-Normans in Ireland, more particularly his own immediate relatives.[3]

In order to assess how far Giraldus is a reliable authority, Anglo-Norman warfare should be set in a wider context of military activity in pre-Norman twelfth-century Ireland. Only then can an estimation be made of the extent to which Anglo-Norman intervention marked a new departure and the degree to which military superiority was a significant factor in the establishment of an Anglo-Norman colony in Ireland.

The major source for warfare in pre-Norman Ireland is the Irish annals. These terse notices of events, devoid of sustained narrative content, rarely give detailed accounts of battles or campaigns, merely record their outcome, making it difficult to reconstruct details of strategy, tactics and military organisation.[4] For elaborative detail the annals have to be augmented with literary sources. Two twelfth-century dynastic propaganda texts, *Cogad Gaedel re Gallaib*, 'The war of the Irish against the Foreigners', and the so-called *Caithréim Cellacháin Chaisil*, 'The Battle Career of

Cellachán, king of Cashel', contain quite detailed descriptions of warfare.[5] While bearing in mind their propagandistic and encomiastic nature, it is nevertheless possible to compare the imaginative reconstructions of warfare in these texts with notices of actual military engagements recorded in the more laconic annals and, by combining these admittedly different kinds of sources, to try and assess Irish military capabilities on the eve of Anglo-Norman intervention.

Cogad Gaedel re Gallaib purports to be an account of the military exploits of the Irish against Vikings in the course of the ninth, tenth and eleventh centuries, the main emphasis being on campaigns waged by Brian Bóruma from 968 until his death at the battle of Clontarf in 1014, which forms the climax of the text. This narrative of warfare between Irish and Norse during the tenth and early eleventh centuries was written during the reign of Muirchertach Ua Briain, king of Munster (1086–1119), and great grandson of Brian Bóruma, in order to justify Muirchertach's bid for the high-kingship of Ireland. Although it drew on factual entries derived from annals recording Viking activity from the late eighth century onwards, the annalistic entries were augmented and amplified by the twelfth-century author's imaginative reconstructions of Brian's military exploits. The accuracy of the author's reconstructions of military engagements which took place a hundred and more years before he was writing, including the detailed account of the battle of Clontarf, 1014, cannot be relied upon. What may be suggested with due caution is that his descriptions, although doubtless exaggerated, should not be too far removed from the reality of warfare in the twelfth century, if the account was to be at all credible for the contemporary audience for whom it was intended.

The mode and scale of military activity depicted in *Cogad Gaedel re Gallaib* goes beyond the cattle raids so often considered as the typical military activity of pre-Norman Ireland. While harrying and plundering expeditions are undertaken, and spoils, including cattle, captured, there are also descriptions of pitched battles fought on open plains, and of the capture of the Hiberno-Norse towns of Limerick and Dublin.[6] Military campaigns are preceded by consultation between Brian and his nobles, in which a decision to go to war is taken and strategy and the logistics of assembling a force discussed. A muster (*mórtinól*, or *mórshlúagad*) is arranged for an appointed time and place.[7] Individual units (*cath*) assemble under leaders who acknowledge Brian's overlordship. A decision is made to march to a particular place to meet the enemy, so 'that they might ascertain if they were able to give them battle, and if not to make a wood and camp assault on them'. A distinction is drawn between a battle 'on the open part of the plain' and 'a wood or camp assault'. The battle of Sulchóit (Sologhead, County Tipperary), 967 AD, is fought on open ground from sun-rise until midday when the foreigners are routed, pursued across the great plain and 'beheaded from mid-day until evening'. The author is at pains to emphasise the extended duration of battles.[8] Brian Bóruma is depicted capturing the cities of Limerick and Dublin. In 999 Brian musters a Munster army to besiege Dublin. In response to the threat, the families and cattle of Leinster are removed to the 'angle of territory' controlled by the Hiberno-Norse. The men of Leinster and of Dublin then go beyond their families and advance to face Brian's army and a pitched battle is fought at Glen Máma (near Saggart, County Dublin) with heavy casualties on both sides, Brian's opponents losing 4,000 men. Brian wins the battle, the Foreigners are put to flight, and pursued until they reach the city of Dublin which capitulates. Brian then maintains an encampment (*longphort*), within the city of Dublin from Christmas until 1 February. During this time he also clears the passes (*beilge*) and fortresses (*daingne*) in Leinster. The implication is that a successful campaign against an enemy does not stop with victory in the field, but includes the dismantling of fortresses and the clearing of strategic passes. In 1013 Brian Bóruma is depicted again laying siege to and blockading Dublin for two months (*forbais* and *forcomét*), but being obliged to withdraw because of exhaustion of provisions.[9]

In addition to mustering large armies Brian also summons naval forces, such as the *mórcoblach* of 300 ships which he sails up the River Shannon as far as Loch Ree, plundering the kingdoms of Mide and Bréifne, while 520 men raid in Connacht at the same time.[10] Land and naval forces are summoned as part of a coordinated strategy of attack. In 1002 Brian Bóruma assembles a *mórcoblach* to sail to Athlone while his army goes by land through Connacht, the outcome of this joint expedition being that he secures hostages from the king of Connacht and the king of Mide.[11]

Brian challenges his rivals to fight him in pitched battle. In 1002 Brian offers Máel Sechnaill, king of Tara, the option of giving hostages, or doing battle, affording him a month's truce 'during which no plunder or ravage, no destruction or trespass, or burning, was to be inflicted upon him'. Brian offers Áed mac Néill, king of Cenél nEógain, and Eochaid, king of Ulaid, the same choice, allowing a year's truce, at the end of which Brian takes Áed's hostages 'since Áed failed to give him battle'.[12] The climax of *Cogad Gaedel re Gallaib* is a detailed account of the pitched battle of Clontarf in 1014, of the array and tactical disposition of the various units on the battlefield, together with descriptions of weaponry and armour and battle standards. The army opposed to Brian wields swords and Lochlann axes, spears and bows and arrows, and their bodies 'are encased from head to foot', though the only piece of protective armour mentioned specifically is the *lúirech* (Latin *lorica*, breastplate). Brian's army has swords and axes, spears and darts, and although his forces wear 'crested golden helmets' and carry bossed shields, more emphasis is placed on descriptions of clothing.[13] The inference is that the opposing army has more protective armour than Brian's army, which fights the more bravely. A contrast between Irish forces and better bodily protected Vikings is even more explicit in *Caithréim Cellacháin Chaisil* which depicts the Vikings wearing armour while the Irish had neither helmets, nor *lúirecha*, 'but only elegant tunics with smooth fringes, shields, and beautiful finely wrought collars to protect bodies and necks and gentle heads'.[14] The descriptions of battle dress ought not be taken at face value as evidence that the Irish did not use any protective armour by the twelfth century.

———

At the very least, they indicate Irish awareness by the twelfth century of the advantages of protective armour. Another twelfth-century pseudo-historical text, the *Book of Rights*, which, like *Cogad Gaedel re Gallaib*, emanates from the court circle of Muirchertach Ua Briain, depicts over-kings proffering *lúirecha* 'to ward off spears' as stipend to subordinates who are expected to reciprocate with military service.[15] Other proffers in the *Book of Rights* include swords, shields, and spears, horses and ships, with the implication that all these items would be employed on military service.

Cogad Gaedel re Gallaib formed the starting point of a pseudo-historical tradition about the battle of Clontarf, still undergoing accretion in the eighteenth century, which attributed to Clontarf an ever greater significance as a battle which prevented a Scandinavian take-over of Ireland, coupled with elaboration of details of the battle and participants. In reality, the battle of Clontarf was not a struggle of the Irish against the Vikings for the sovereignty of Ireland: by 1014 the Vikings posed no such threat. It was occasioned by a revolt of the provincial king of Leinster against the overrule of Brian Bóruma. A Munster army under Brian, which included two contingents from Connacht and the Hiberno-Norse of Limerick and Waterford, confronted the army of the king of Leinster, accompanied by the Hiberno-Norse king of Dublin plus mercenaries which the latter had raised in the Scottish isles and Man.[16]

Caithréim Cellacháin Chaisil, also depicts Ireland facing a threat of a Scandinavian take-over. It was written during the reign of Cormac Mac Carthaig (1123–38), king of Desmond, was directly modelled on *Cogad Gaedel re Gallaib*, and was intended to justify his taking of the kingship of Munster from descendants of Brian Bóruma. The aim of the author was to depict Cellachán, king of Cashel (c. 940–954) fighting a series of military campaigns against the Vikings accompanied by a tenth-century ancestor of families which were politically prominent in twelfth-century Munster.

Before taking up arms Cellachán spends a year and a half on military reconnaissance of geographical features and habitations 'in order that he might know the name of every settlement (*baile*) and *tuath* and have knowledge of every lord of an estate' while his mother collects arms and retains companies of fighting men (*ceithern*) and household troops (*caemteglaig*), to the number of 500 on his behalf.[17] Having completed his preparations, Cellachán embarks on a series of successful military campaigns against the Vikings in Munster, including the capture from them of Limerick, Cork and Waterford. However, he falls victim to a ruse, is taken prisoner by Vikings, and removed firstly to Armagh, and then to Dundalk. A detailed account is given of the land and naval muster summoned to effect his release. Kings of border areas of Munster are directed to remain and defend its frontiers, while the main Munster army proceeds to Armagh to effect Cellachán's release. The maritime kingdoms of Corcu Laígde, Uí Echach, Corcu Duibne, Ciarraige Luachra, Corcu Baiscinn, and Corcu Mruad make up the Munster fleet. The land

3.1 Nineteenth-century depiction of the battle of Clontarf, 1014, which was portrayed as an heroic Irish victory over the threat of Viking domination.

forces march to Armagh camping overnight on the way for which purpose they erect huts and open sheds.[18] The Munster army makes a four-pronged attack on the city of Armagh, which serves not only a strategic purpose but also the author's scheme to divide the forces in order of genealogical importance with those dynasts most closely related to Cellachán assuming the chief roles.

Armagh is taken, but Cellachán, in the meantime, is removed by the Vikings by ship to Dundalk. The sole purpose of this manoeuvre is to enable the author to stage a fictitious sea battle between a Viking and Munster fleet off the coast of Dundalk. The Irish 'fling tough ropes of hemp over the long prows of the Viking ships in order that they might not be separated from each other', and the Norsemen respond by throwing chains over the prows of the Irish vessels, so that they could fight at close quarters.[19] As in the descriptions of armour, the implication is that the Norse have superiority in metalwork. And, like the siege of Armagh, the sea battle has both a strategic and genealogical arrangement. Of twelve dynasts named as leaders of Munster naval contingents at the battle of Dundalk all are eponymous ancestors of prominent twelfth-century families which can be shown on annalistic evidence to have taken part in actual naval campaigns in the twelfth century. Dub dá Bairenn mac Domnaill, king of Uí Echach, for example, is accorded so prominent a role that he is actually killed at the battle of Dundalk. Not only was Dub dá Bairenn not killed at Dundalk, he was to succeed Cellachán as king of Cashel in 957. The author appears to have been attracted to Dub dá Bairenn because of his name element Domnall. Twelfth-century annals reveal an Ua Domnaill family active as leaders of Uí Echach naval forces: in 1127 Cathal Ua Domnaill, son of the king of Uí Echach, was captured during a naval encounter in which Ua Muirchertaig, king of Locha Léin, Mathgamain Ua Conchobair, king of Ciarraige, and Ua Conchobair, king of Corcu Mruad, also participated (*Ann. Inisf.*). Tenth-century ancestors of each of these kings are depicted in *Caithréim Cellacháin Chaisil* taking part in the naval battle of Dundalk. Captured in 1127 along with Cathal Ua Domnaill was his 'stirasmund' S[?en]an son of Gollsci; his patronymic and title steersman is suggestive of Hiberno-Norse influence in the naval forces of twelfth-century Irish kings. In 1128 the son of An Findshúilech Ua Domnaill is named in the fleet of MacCarthaig, king of Desmond (MacCarthaig's book = *Misc. Ir. Annals*, 1128).

There is no warrant for placing any trust in *Cogad Gaedel re Gallaib* or *Caithréim Chellacháin Chasil* as sources for the tenth century, but they do contain information both on twelfth-century politics and on techniques of warfare. Their composition, which must have been aimed at a contemporary lay aristocratic audience, suggests the importance of warfare for this class in the twelfth century. This is borne out by annalistic entries, where aristocratic military engagements predominate, although described with much less circumstantial detail than in the pseudo-historical texts. The annalistic entries, brief as many are, complement the descriptions of warfare in the literary texts. That twelfth-century Irish kings did maintain select retinues of household troops is corroborated by entries referring to the *lucht tige*, or *lucht teglaig*, of individual kings.[20] Annalists recorded protracted battles, which resulted in heavy casualties. They identified individual units within larger armies. At the battle of Móin Mór in 1151 (not a pitched battle, but one fought on the march) when Toirdelbach Ua Briain, king of Thomond, was defeated by the combined armies of Toirdelbach Ua Conchobair, king of Connacht, and Diarmait Mac Murchada, king of Leinster, Toirdelbach Ua Briain's losses were given as between 3,000 and 5,000 men (Mac Carthaig's Book = *Misc. Ir. Annals, AFM*), while the Annals of Tigernach adopted the biblical description that the slain were 'as many as the sands of the sea and the stars of the sky'. Medieval estimates of participants and casualties are notoriously impressionistic, and none of the figures given in the annals can be relied upon in detail, but there is no doubt of the heavy casualties incurred by Toirdelbach Ua Briain's army. Eighty-three of the more important dead, who fell on the side of Toirdelbach Ua Briain are named (*Ann. Tig.*; in *AFM* the number is 73) and with only one exception (Ua Loingsig of Uaithne), all belonged to Dál Cais lineages, that is were genealogically related to Toirdelbach Ua Briain. An indication of the impact of the battle of Móin Mór is the collapse of Ua Briain overlordship in north Munster after 1151 which was not to be reconstituted until the reign of Domnall Ua Briain (1168–94).[21] At Móin Mór, Toirdelbach Ua Conchobair, king of Connacht, although on the victorious side, suffered losses on a scale which persuaded him almost immediately afterwards to offer hostages to Muirchertach Mac Lochlainn, king of Cenél nEógain, his rival for the high-kingship, to avoid further military engagement. The Four Masters ended their account of the year 1152 thus: 'Munster was much injured, both church and state in consequence of the war between the Síl Briain and Clann Carthaig, so that great dearth prevailed in Munster from that war and their peasantry (*fodhaoine*) were dispersed in Leth Cuinn (northern half of Ireland) and many others of them perished from famine.'

The deployment of large armies, as described in *Cogad Gaedel re Gallaib* and *Caithréim Cellacháin Chaisil*, with individual battalions being assigned different offensive and defensive roles, is borne out by the twelfth-century annals, though inevitably with less detail. How much overall coordination and strategy there may have been between dynasts who led battalions as part of a larger army is difficult to say. The annals record how in 1103 Muirchertach Ua Briain, king of Munster and high-king of Ireland, mustered an army against the king of Cenél nEógain which comprised, in addition to the men of Munster, contingents from Leinster, Osraige, Connacht and Mide. It proceeded to Armagh and spent a week in beleaguerment (*forbais*), inflicting destruction and damage. The fictitious siege of Armagh in *Caithréim Chellacháin Chaisil* was probably inspired by Muirchertach's siege of 1103. His opponent, Domnall Ua Lochlainn, king of Cenél nEógain, 'faced' Muirchertach's army for a week on the plain of Uí Bresail Macha (*AU*, cf. *Ann. Tig.*, *Ann. Inisf.*, *Chron. Scot.*, *AFM*). No engagement having taken place, Muirchertach then moved on into Mag Coba (County Down), 'divided the army' (*Ann. Tig.*) and

---

left the forces from Leinster and Dublin and a detachment from Munster there. With the remainder of the army he proceeded to raid in Dál nAraide. Domnall Ua Lochlainn, in the meanwhile, followed into Mag Coba to attack the forces which Muirchertach had left there and 'he met them just as they were and gave battle'. The annalists named sixteen prominent dynasts from Leinster, Osraige, Munster and Dublin who were killed in the battle (actually a surprise attack) of Mag Coba, passing over many others 'for the sake of concision' (*AU*). Domnall Ua Lochlainn captured the royal tent (*pupall*) of Muirchertach Ua Briain as well as a battle standard (*camlinne*) and many other valuables, indicating that the main camp had remained at Mag Coba. The Bayeux tapestry depicts the Anglo-Saxons at Hastings with standards emblazoned with figures of dragons, birds or other creatures. One of those English standards found its way to the court of Diarmait mac Máel na mBó, king of Leinster (1042–72), when the sons of the defeated King Harold sought refuge at Diarmait's court after the battle of Hastings in 1066. In 1068 Diarmait mac Máel na mBó bestowed 'the battle standard (*meirge*) of the king of Saxons' as a ceremonial gift on Toirdelbach Ua Briain, king of Thomond (*Ann. Inisf.*). *Meirge* derived from Norse *merrke* which suggests that the practice of using battle standards was taken over by the Irish from the Vikings. Twelfth-century annalists provided increasing detail about individual contingents within an army. In 1159 Muirchertach Mac Lochlainn, king of Cenél nEógain and high-king of Ireland, hosted to Ardee, where he was met by an opposing army of Ruaidrí Ua Conchobair, comprising eight units from Connacht, Bréifne and Conmaicne, and a unit from Munster. Muirchertach inflicted a defeat on Ruaidrí's army which the annalist recorded as the slaughter of the men of Connacht around seven named royal dynasts, and of the men of Bréifne around six named leaders and of Munstermen around one named leader (*AU, Ann. Tig.*).

Some annal entries recorded not only the large numbers and individual contingents involved in, but the extended duration of, individual military campaigns. In 1113 Muirchertach Ua Briain, king of Munster and high-king of Ireland, is said to have brought an army to Grenóc (near Ratoath, County Meath) to halt the southward progress of an army of Domnall Ua Lochlainn, king of Cenél nEógain. Both armies 'were confronting each other for the duration of a month', until the stalemate was resolved by the negotiation of a year's truce under the auspices of Cellach, bishop of Armagh (*AU*). Extended military campaigns necessitated the acquisition of provisions such as food and fodder in the locality. In 1121 Toirdelbach Ua Conchobair, king of Connacht, took a *mórsluagad* into the plain around Birr in County Offaly where the annalist described him as 'consuming Ormond for the duration of the three months of winter' (*Ann. Tig.*). An idea of what impact 'consuming Ormond' may have had for the local inhabitants can be gained from *Cogad Gaedel re Gallaib*, which, by way of illustration of Viking oppression in tenth- and eleventh-century Ireland, described a Viking soldier billeted in every Irish household, with the consequence that none of the men of Ireland had power to give even the milk of his cow, nor as much as the clutch of eggs of one hen in succour or in kindness to an aged man, or to a friend, but was forced to preserve them for the foreign steward or soldier. And though there were but one milk-giving cow in the house she durst not be milked for an infant of one night nor for a sick person, but must be kept for the steward or bailiff or soldier of the foreigners. And however long he might be absent from the house, his share of his supply durst not be lessened.[22]

The billeting of troops on the civilian population is also attested in a number of twelfth-century charters issues by Irish kings to individual churches in which immunity from billeting on church lands was granted.[23]

Annals record the setting up of military camps (*longphoirt*) in the course of campaigns of extended duration, such as *Cogad Gaedel re Gallaib* described Brian Bóruma maintaining at Dublin in 1013. In 1124 Toirdelbach Ua Conchobair, king of Connacht, maintained a *mórlongphort* at Áth Caille (beside Limerick) from November until May 'and the foreigners of Limerick joined him' (*Ann. Tig.*). In 1126 the burning by Toirdelbach Ua Conchobair of a *longphort* set up by Cormac Mac Carthaig, king of Desmond, at Sliab an Caitlig (near Kilkenny city) is recorded (*Ann. Tig.*). Toirdelbach then set up his own *mórlongphort* in Ormond from August 1126 until February 1127. From that camp he plundered on different occasions in the vicinity of Limerick but also further afield to Glanmire (County Cork) and into Osraige (County Kilkenny) and as far as Dublin 'and not once was the camp emptied thereby' (*Ann. Tig.*). These encampments might contain large numbers of fighting men. In 1153 Tadg Ua Briain, one of two rival claimants for the kingship of Thomond, was surprised in camp at Áth Maigne (near Ardnurcher, County Westmeath), by a northern army supporting his dynastic rival Toirdelbach Ua Briain. The forces of Tadg Ua Briain were ejected out of their three *longphoirt* and 900 are said to have been killed (Mac Carthaig's book = *Misc. Ir. annals*, 1153, cf. *AFM*).

Annalistic entries relating to encampments and billetings serve to highlight another feature of twelfth-century Irish warfare, namely that kings were able to carry war far beyond the frontiers of their kingdoms. No indication is given of the method of construction of the twelfth-century *longphort*, but *Cogad Gaedel re Gallaib* depicts Brian Bóruma, before he embarks on his public battle career, gathering the young champions of Munster around him secretly in the woods and forests and setting up 'rude huts (*fianbotha folachta*), instead of *longphoirt*', the implication being that the *longphort* was a more elaborate construction.[24] The Vikings, in the meantime, raise a fortifying bank (*dúnclod*), around the district of Tradraige (in County Clare) with the intention of making of the entire district one *dúnárus*, or fortified dwelling place. The *dún* is depicted as a yet stronger fortified structure than the *longphort*. After his triumphal circuit of Ireland in 1105 Brian Bóruma is depicted erecting a series of royal fortresses (*dúin 7 daingni*) in Munster.[25] The Annals of Inisfallen record the construction of fortifications by Brian Bóruma in 995 and in 1012 (*daingne* and *cathir*). A distinction between the *longphort* and the *dún* may have been that the former was a temporary campaign fortification whereas the *dún* was characterised by a permanent garrison: in 1031 the keeper (*rechtaire*) of Donnchad mac Briain's fortress of Dún na Sciath (County Tipperary) was slain in the course of an attack mounted by Mac Gilla Pátraic, king of Osraige (*Ann. Inisf.*).

Thirteen fortified structures are named in the annals as having been built by the twelfth-century kings of Connacht, described as either *dún, caistél* or *caislén*.[26] *Caistél* (a loanword borrowed either from Latin *castellum*, or French *chastel*) is first attested in the annals of Tigernach in 1124 in respect of Gaillim (Galway), Cúl Máile (Colloony), and Caistél Dúin Leódha (Dunlo), erected by Toirdelbach Ua Conchobair, king of Connacht, prior to his undertaking a campaign in Munster. The variant form *caislén* appears from 1136 onwards. These word-forms were used subsequently by the annalists to refer to Anglo-Norman fortifications, which suggests that the annalists saw little difference between the Irish and Anglo-Norman constructions. The loanword implies the adoption of new techniques of construction and/or new functions. While the majority of these structures may be expected to have been of earth and wood some permanent fortifications may have been built partly of stone. Certainly the expertise to do so would have been available in Ireland by the twelfth century, bearing in mind contemporary ecclesiastical stone buildings such as Cormac's Chapel at Cashel, which was consecrated in 1134, or Mellifont Abbey which was begun in 1142. In 1118 Toirdelbach Ua Conchobair, king of Connacht, dismantled the Ua Briain fortress of Kincora, 'both stone and wood', which was hurled into the Shannon (*Ann. Tig.*). In 1166 Diarmait Mac Murchada's enemies are said to have demolished his stone house at Ferns and burnt his *longphort* (*Ann. Tig.*). Excavation of the early thirteenth-century castle at Ferns revealed a rock-cut fosse which may date back to Diarmait Mac Murchada's construction.[27]

Giraldus emphasised the construction of castles by the Anglo-Normans in Ireland as a means of conquest, but Giraldus's *castellum* can too easily conjure up a stone castle instead of a more flimsy earthwork, which may not have differed morpho-logically from the 'castles' that Toirdelbach Ua Conchobair erected in the twelfth century. In an Anglo-Norman context a castle functioned not only as a defensive structure but also as a fortified seigneurial residence, and, additionally in certain instances, as an administrative centre. In 1173, when Domnall son of Annach Ua Ruairc was slain by the *aes gráda* of Tigernán Ua Ruairc for abetting an Anglo-Norman party in the treacherous killing of Tigernán on the hill of Tlachtga in 1172, Domnall's hand was sent to Ruaidrí Ua Conchobair who nailed it to the top of the *caislén* of Tuam, which would indicate that Tuam was not just a garrisoned fortress, but also a royal residence and administrative centre (*Ann. Tig.*).

Garrisoned strongholds certainly played a role in twelfth-century Irish warfare, as illustrated by a series of campaigns waged by Cormac Mac Carthaig, king of Desmond, against Toirdelbach Ua Conchobair, king of Connacht, and claimant to the high-kingship, during 1132 and 1133. In 1132 Cormac Mac Carthaig allied with

Conchobar Ua Briain, king of Thomond, Tigernán Ua Ruairc, king of Bréifne, and Ua Máel Sechlainn, king of Mide, to launch a coordinated offensive against the king of Connacht, in effect, challenging him for the high-kingship. The Munster fleet, which included contingents from the coastal kingdoms of Uí Echach, Corco Laígde and Corco Mruad, sailed to Galway Bay where it met with an army led by Cormac Mac Carthaig; the *caislén* of Gaillim was demolished and the *baile* burnt (*Ann. Tig.*, Mac Carthaig's book = *Misc. Ir. annals*). The Munster ships were engaged on the following day by a Connacht fleet under Flaithbertach Ua Flaithbertaig, 'leader of the fleet', and suffered the loss of Lochlann, son of Amlaib Ua Lochlainn, king of Corco Mruad (*Ann. Tig.*, *AFM*). Ua Ruairc and Ua Máel Sechlainn, meanwhile, attacked Ua Conchobair's *caistél* at Athlone, which held out against them. Conchobar Ua Briain, king of Thomond, forced a crossing of the Shannon at another point and harried deep into Connacht. Cormac Mac Carthaig then sailed the Munster fleet up the Shannon to join Ua Briain for a second attack on Athlone, which still held out. Their forces were obliged to withdraw but early in the following year, 1133, Cormac Mac Carthaig resumed the offensive. Accompanied by Conchobar Ua Briain, he led a large army into Connacht and burnt Dún Mór (Dunmore) and Dún Mugdorn (Doon). Simultaneously, Ua Máel Sechlainn and Ua Ruairc succeeded in capturing and demolishing the *caistél* of Athlone. Even so, the allies failed to force Ua Conchobair to a decisive engagement and had to withdraw without securing hostages. Mac Carthaig reassembled an army comprising forces of Munster, Mide and Bréifne, to which was added Leinster, while a fleet of ships was drawn from Cork, Waterford, Wexford, Dublin and the Munster coastal kingdoms of Uí Echach and Corca Laigde. In the face of this formidable opposition Toirdelbach Ua Conchobair elected to negotiate: Muiredach Ua Dubhtaig (arch)bishop of Tuam, concluded a peace on his behalf with Cormac Mac Carthaig at Aball Ceternaig (County Westmeath, Mac Carthaig's book = *Misc. Ir. annals*).

The campaigns of 1132–3 against Toirdelbach Ua Conchobair, as recorded in the annals, substantiate another element of the literary texts, namely combined land and naval forces, which is a feature of *Cogad Gaedel re Gallaib* and, even more so, of *Caithréim Chellacháin Chaisil*. In Connacht, as in Munster, there is annalistic evidence of certain families being associated with the conduct of naval warfare, such as the Uí Dubda of Uí Fiachrach (*AU*, 1126, *AFM*, 1126, 1220), the Uí Flaithbertaig of Uí Briúin Seola (*Ann. Tig.*, 1132) and the Uí Máille of Fir Umaill (*Ann. Tig.*, *AFM*, 1123). In a late twelfth- early thirteenth-century tract on the inauguration of Ua Conchobair as king of Connacht, Ua Flaithbertaig and Ua Máille are said to command the fleet of Ua Conchobair at sea.[28] The early twelfth-century *Book of Rights* depicts ships being bestowed as stipend by the king of Connacht on subordinates in coastal kingdoms. Ua Dubda, king of Umall, for example is said to receive five ships from the king of Connacht; and it was 'lucky for the king of Connacht to have a fleet on Loch Ree', and 'for the king of Cashel to have a fleet on the Shannon'.[29] Naval engagements might be conducted on rivers, particularly the

Shannon, or at sea, as in the case of a battle 'at sea' in 1127 between the Munster and Connacht fleets in which the Munster fleet was defeated (*Ann. Tig.*). Such was the importance of ships in twelfth-century campaigns that they might be hauled overland by portage manoeuvres. In 1124 Toirdelbach Ua Conchobair, king of Connacht, hosted with his fleet from Lough Derg into Munster and at Dunass Rapids the vessels were taken out of the water and transported overland. A consequence of this expedition was that Toirdelbach Ua Conchobair seized the enemy fleet of Desmond (*Ann. Tig.*). In 1151 Diarmait Ua Conchobair, king of Ciarraige, whose naval forces were at the disposal of Toirdelbach Ua Briain, transported seven ships on wheels from Ess Duibe (Asdee, near Ballylongford) to Locha Léin (Killarney), (Mac Carthaig's book = *Misc. Ir. annals*). In 1159 Ruaidrí Ua Conchobair dragged eight ships overland in order to attack the Ua Máel Sechlainn royal residence in Lough Sewdy (*Ann. Tig.*).

The construction of fortified river crossings, bridges and blockades on the river Shannon by the kings of Connacht, Mide and Thomond to prevent the passage of enemy ships also attests to the strategic importance of ships. In 1089, when a Munster fleet sailed up the Shannon as far as Athlone, Ruaidrí Ua Conchobair, king of Connacht, blocked its return, whereupon the crew of the fleet placed itself under the protection of Ua Máel Sechlainn, king of Mide, and left its ships with him (*Chron. Scot.*, 1085 = 1089; cf. *AFM*), but Ua Conchobair nonetheless gained possession of the Munster ships and then used them to plunder in Munster. In 1071 Toirdelbach Ua Briain, king of Munster, summoned a muster (*tinól*) which spent a fortnight building bridges across the Shannon at Killaloe and Áth Caille (probably Athlunkard) (*Ann. Inisf.*). In 1120 Toirdelbach Ua Conchobair constructed bridges at Athlone, Áth Crocha (probably Ballinasloe) on the Shannon and at Dún Leóda on the Suck (*Ann. Tig.*). The men of Mide destroyed the bridges of Athlone and Áth Crocha in 1125 (*AFM*). In 1146 the rear of Toirdelbach Ua Conchobair's army was attacked on the wicker bridge of Athlone which collapsed 'and many men of low rank were drowned and killed there' (*Ann. Tig.*). The wicker bridge and fortress (*daingen*) of Athlone was destroyed and burnt by the king of Mide in 1153, but another wicker bridge was immediately built by Toirdelbach Ua Conchobair at Athleague (*AFM*). From the frequency with which rival forces attempted to dismantle bridges erected by their enemies, they were clearly of strategic importance. Some bridges at least may be identified as fortified river crossings. The location of both a fortification and a bridge at Athlone, Dún Leoda and Killaloe is noteworthy. It bears analogy with the series of defensive bridges, partly stone, partly wood, constructed by the Carolingian king, Charles the Bald (823–77), on the river Seine at Pont de l'Arche and other locations in order to deny access to Viking ships. Charles the Bald's structures had stone bridgeheads with a wooden span and the bridgeheads were protected by ramparted strongholds in which permanent garrisons were stationed.[30]

A feature of warfare recorded in the twelfth-century annals, which is not accorded prominence in *Cogad Gaedel re Gallaib* or *Caithréim Chellacháin Chaisil*, is mounted combatants as a distinctive element within the large armies fielded in that century. This may suggest that mounted soldiers became more important as the century progressed. In 1167 at the convention of Athboy which was summoned to confirm Ruaidrí Ua Conchobair, king of Connacht, in the high-kingship of Ireland following the expulsion of Diarmait Mac Murchada from the kingship of Leinster, 19,000 horsemen, of which 6,000 were from Connacht, 4,000 from Bréifne, 2,000 from Mide, 4,000 from Airgialla and Ulaid, 2,000 from north Leinster and 1,000 from the city of Dublin, reputedly were present (*AFM*). Later in the same year, Ruaidrí Ua Conchobair mustered thirteen battalions of foot soldiers (*cath da cois*) and seven battalions of horse soldiers (*marcshlúag*) with contingents drawn from almost every part of Ireland, including Thomond and Desmond, to campaign in the north as well as a naval fleet which met up with the land forces in the Lough Foyle estuary (*Ann. Tig.*). The expedition effected the division of Cenél nEógain between Niall Mac Lochlainn and Áed Ua Néill, and pre-empted a Cenél nEógain challenge to Ua Conchobair's high-kingship, and may, indeed, have been effective in removing Cenél nEógain from the national stage until the mid-thirteenth century. Horses figure as stipend proffered by a superior king to a subordinate in the early twelfth-century *Book of Rights*. The text distinguishes between different kinds of horses, horses for the road, horses for racing, horses for hosting, and in at least three instances horses proffered are described as imported or 'overseas horses', and in two other instances are specified as horses from France, and horses from Scotland.[31] An encounter between the *marcshlúag* of Connacht and of Conchobar Ua Briain, king of Munster, is recorded in 1131 in Mide (*AU*) in which the horsemen of Connacht were defeated. In 1170 the killing of Diarmait Ua hAinbheith, king of Uí Meith, also styled 'leader of the horse soldiers of the king of Cenél nEógain', is recorded (*AU*). A distinction between foot and horse soldiers is also apparent in the poem on the inauguration of the king of Connacht, where Ua Flainn of Síl Máel Ruain is described as having the stewardship of Ua Conchobair's horses and Ua hAinlide as commanding his foot soldiers.[32]

The mobilisation of large forces in the field, such as Ruaidrí Ua Conchobair mustered in 1167, presupposes some form of procedure which could be used to summon those eligible, or obliged, to fight. In *Caithréim Chellacháin Chaisil*, when detailing the muster of the Munster fleet, ten ships were to be supplied from each cantred of the coastal kingdoms, which implies that the cantred was used as a unit of assessment for military service.[33] It may be envisaged that any existing method for assessing taxes, or labour services, might be used also for military levies. That there must have been some procedure for the organisation of labour forces and materials is suggested by the muster (*tinól*) of Toirdelbach Ua Briain which was engaged for a fortnight in the construction of two bridges on the Shannon (*Ann. Inisf.*), or the muster in 1139 of Toirdelbach Ua Conchobair, king of Connacht, which dug a canal so as to link the river Suck and the Shannon (*Ann. Tig.*). A

3.2   Stirrup from tenth-century stratum at Fishamble Street excavations, Dublin.
Stirrups permitted the use of mounted troops in battle.

twelfth-century Irish king apparently could demand labour services from his subjects for military purposes in much the same way as Anglo-Saxon kings had summoned labour forces to construct fortifications, or repair bridges.[34] Toirdelbach Ua Conchobair's construction of a canal in 1139 required a degree of planning and organisation. The methods of assessing and exacting labour services and military service may have been similar. It may be postulated that the mobilisation of work-forces derived from two sources, military obligations and traditional labour services, that the military obligations of the aristocracy were rendered in the form of personal military service, more especially offensive warfare, while military service from all inhabitants may have been demanded for defensive purposes and in the case of the lower ranks of society was rendered in the form of labour services. How far stipendiary forces may have been used by twelfth-century Irish kings to make up a field army and whether these should be viewed as fighting as mercenaries is an open question. Stipend and/or maintenance cannot automatically be equated with a mercenary wage. Stipend was a resource which may have facilitated service; its provision and acceptance does not necessarily, however, explain why the service was sought or given; this may have been determined by overriding rights of lordship or ties of loyalty.

Taking the evidence from the annals, and fleshing it out with twelfth-century literary depictions of warfare, it is clear that there were more elaborate forms of warfare in use than simply cattle-raiding in twelfth-century Ireland. Siege warfare was not unknown before Anglo-Norman intervention. *Cogad Gaedel re Gallaib* and *Caithréim Cellacháin Chaisil* together provide incidences of Irish kings besieging Limerick, Dublin, Cork, Waterford and Armagh against the Vikings. On the evidence of the annals each of these settlements was actually under siege on occasion in the twelfth century. Muirchertach Ua Briain, king of Munster and claimant to the high-kingship, camped at Armagh in 1103 (*AU*). Limerick, which served as a royal stronghold of the Ua Briain kings, was besieged and captured by Toirdelbach Ua Conchobair, king of Connacht, in 1124 (*Ann. Tig.*, *AU*). It was taken in 1125 by Toirdelbach Ua Briain, king of Thomond, who was ejected later in the same year by Cormac Mac Carthaig, king of Desmond. Cork, which was being used as a royal residence of Cormac Mac Carthaig, was attacked by Toirdelbach Ua Conchobair, king of Connacht, with land and naval forces in 1127 (*Ann. Tig.*, *AU*). Diarmait Mac Murchada, with the support of Conchobar Ua Briain, king of Thomond, and the Hiberno-Norse of Dublin and Wexford, besieged Waterford in 1137 with a fleet of 200 ships (*AFM*).

The fictitious four-pronged attack on Armagh by the Munster forces in *Caithréim Cellacháin Chaisil* is paralleled in the description in the so-called *Song of Dermot and the earl* of Ruaidrí Ua Conchobair's siege of the Anglo-Norman garrison in Dublin in 1171 following the death of Diarmait Mac Murchada, king of Leinster. According to the *Song*, Ua Conchobair was positioned at Castleknock on the west side of Dublin, the king of Ulaid was on the north side at Clontarf, the king of Munster was on the south side at Kilmainham and Muirchertach Mac Murchada, king of Uí Chennselaig, was on the east side near Dalkey.[35] It is true that Ruaidrí Ua Conchobair failed to take Dublin from the Anglo-Norman garrison in 1171, but the lifting of Ruaidrí's two-month siege by an Anglo-Norman party which managed to get out of the city owed more to tactical surprise than inherent superiority in weapons, armour or techniques; as a surprise attack on a decamped army, it can hardly be dignified with the title 'battle of Dublin'.[36] In 1176 Domnall Ua Briain, king of Thomond, was to force the Anglo-Norman garrison in Limerick to abandon that city, and it was not to be retaken by Anglo-Normans until after his death in 1194 (*ALC*). Ruaidrí's failure to take Dublin in 1171 should not deflect attention from other military successes against Anglo-Norman forces. In 1173 Strongbow was forced to abandon the *caislén* of Cill Cainnig (Kilkenny) in the face of a siege (*forbais*), conducted by Domnall Ua Briain, king of Thomond, accompanied by a unit from west Connacht sent by Ruaidrí Ua Conchobair under the leadership of his son Conchobar (*Ann. Tig.*). In 1174 Ruaidrí Ua Conchobair, in alliance with Domnall Ua Briain, inflicted a defeat on an Anglo-Norman force at Thurles at which 1700

Anglo-Normans reputedly were slain (*Ann. Tig.*). While no credence can be afforded to this figure it may be compared with the annalists' assessments of between 4,000 and 7,000 casualties at the battle of Móin Mór in 1151, which afford a rough comparison of contemporary perceptions of the scale and significance of the engagement at Thurles. Strongbow was on a harrying expedition (*sluagad*) in northeast Munster when Ruaidrí Ua Conchobair, in support of Domnall Ua Briain, marched into Munster 'to seek battle'. Strongbow summoned the Anglo-Norman garrison of Dublin to augment his numbers, but was defeated nonetheless. An expedition mounted by Ruaidrí Ua Conchobair into Mide in the same year forced Hugh Tyrell to abandon an Anglo-Norman earthwork at Trim before Ruaidrí Ua Conchobair even reached it. In the *Song of Dermot* Ruaidrí is said to have burnt the *maison* and levelled the *motte* to the ground, so that when Strongbow arrived at Trim, having come to Hugh Tyrell's assistance, there was nothing left, 'neither house nor hut', where he could take shelter for the night.[37] While this Connacht expedition into Mide is described in some detail in the *Song of Dermot*, it does not appear to be recorded in the Irish annals, and it may be that from an Irish perspective it was not considered all that notable. In 1176 the castle of Slane was destroyed by Máel Sechlainn Mac Lochlainn, king of Cenél nEógain, with the capture of men, women, children and horses, and three other castles were then immediately abandoned for fear of Mac Lochlainn (*ALC, Ann. Tig.*).

A feature which certainly deserves more emphasis than it has received is the participation of Irish forces in most, if not all, the early Anglo-Norman field armies.[38] Strongbow, as Diarmait Mac Murchada's successor in Leinster, never fought without Irish troops. While Irish participation is obscured in Giraldus, the *Song of Dermot* generally lists those Irish who fought alongside Strongbow. When Tigernán Ua Ruairc, king of Bréifne, was killed at Tlachtga (Hill of Ward, County Meath) in 1171 by an Anglo-Norman party, a rival Ua Ruairc dynast, Domnall son of Annach Ua Ruairc, on the evidence of the annals, but not Giraldus, accompanied the Anglo-Normans (*Ann. Tig., ALC*). The Anglo-Norman expedition to take Limerick in 1175 was escorted by Mac Gilla Pátraic, king of Osraige, though, again, it is not Giraldus but the annals and the *Song of Dermot* which provide that information. When John de Courcy set out from Dublin in 1177 to undertake the conquest of Ulaid he was accompanied according to Roger of Howden by a party of Irishmen, again not mentioned by Giraldus.[39] It is Giraldus who portrays the early Anglo-Norman engagements as Anglo-Norman versus Irish encounters. It did not suit his purpose, which was to highlight the important role played by his relatives to acknowledge Irish participation in so many of the early Anglo-Norman campaigns. The Irish annals offer a different perspective: the first Anglo-Norman adventurers figure there as mercenaries in the employ of Irish king. What are presented as exclusively Anglo-Norman campaigns in the pages of Giraldus are recorded in the annals as Irish campaigns with an Anglo-Norman mercenary element. None of the early Anglo-Norman forces, with the possible exception of

Henry II's expedition in 1171–72, was a self-sufficient military force.[40] Anglo-Normans employed Irish as guides and fought alongside Irish units. Giraldus deliberately emphasised Anglo-Norman military prowess and sought to highlight Anglo-Norman military superiority, playing down, if not entirely suppressing, Irish involvement. The *Song of Dermot*, by contrast, is more frank in detailing the participation of Irish forces. The Anglo-Norman role as hired mercenaries in the employ of Irish kings is well illustrated in the case of Maurice de Prendergast, originally recruited by Diarmait Mac Murchada, but subsequently offering his services to Domnall Mac Gilla Pátraic, king of Osraige.

War could be, and was waged, on a large scale in twelfth-century pre-Norman Ireland, and in many ways which did not always differ markedly from Anglo-Norman warfare. This may at least partly explain why contemporary Irish annalists failed to recognise Anglo-Norman intervention as the major military turning point that historians have considered it to be. Annalists passed little remark on either the scale or techniques of Anglo-Norman forces. The annals of Ulster recorded King Henry II's expedition in 1171-2 as comprising 240 ships. The English court chronicler Roger of Howden put the number at 400.[41] King Henry's supposed 240 ships in the annals of Ulster is no more reliable than the figures offered by the Anglo-Norman chroniclers, but it serves as an impressionistic indication of how the Irish annalist assessed the scale of Henry's expedition. It may be compared with the 190 vessels attributed to Toirdelbach Ua Conchobair in 1127 (*Ann. Tig.*), or the fleet, variously assessed at 140 vessels (*Ann. Tig.*) and 200 vessels (*AFM*), assembled in 1137 by Murchad Ua Máel Sechlainn, king of Mide, and Tigernán Ua Ruairc, king of Bréifne, which was to no avail against Toirdelbach Ua Conchobair's *coblach mór*, or the combined fleet of 200 ships raised by Diarmait Mac Murchada to besiege Waterford in 1137 (*AFM*). Nor was Henry II's army in Ireland without its difficulties: the Anglo-Norman chronicler, Ralph of Diss, recorded that Henry's army faced problems with provisions, and that many suffered diarrhoea through lack of bread and the consumption of unaccustomed water and fresh meat.[42]

Twelfth-century Ireland was a militarised society, and all too frequently 'a trembling sod', in the picturesque phrase of the Four Masters describing the level of warfare in 1145. This militarisation, while it most directly involved the aristocracy as the main combatants, affected all classes of society. Bishop Gilbert of Limerick in his *De statu ecclesiae*, written about 1111, considered the standard medieval division of society into three orders, those who fight (*bellatores*), those who plough (*aratores*) and those who pray (*oratores*), as appropriate to twelfth-century Ireland.[43] It was the duty of the *oratores* to pray for those who fought 'to defend their fellows against bodily enemies'. That the Irish clergy did so is reflected in a liturgical missal of twelfth-century date, which was probably in use in the church of Armagh, which includes a prayer for 'the king of the Irish and his army' in a litany to be sung on Easter Eve.[44] In the *Book of Rights* a 'blessing of weapons' is included in a list of blessings bestowed by Patrick on the inhabitants of Ireland.[45] One index of the far-reaching effects of large-scale military activity in twelfth-century Ireland is the frequent record in the annals of negotiations, truces and peace concords agreed to by kings in the face of invading armies, usually arranged by ecclesiastics, and especially by the head of the church of Armagh.

If twelfth-century Irish military capability may have been underrated, Anglo-Norman military capability may have been exaggerated and undue emphasis attributed to certain techniques of warfare without any very detailed analysis of their deployment. Heavily armed knightly cavalry capable of charging the enemy in close formation has been presumed to have afforded a critical tactical advantage to the Anglo-Normans. The deployment of heavy cavalry was not, however, the chief strategy of Anglo-Norman warfare in Ireland. Forays, raids, skirmishes and burnings, and the capture of fortified positions were far more common occurrences than pitched battles. Nor were such tactics determined either by Irish circumstances or the Cambro-Norman background of the earliest adventurers into Ireland. In fact, battle charges deploying heavy cavalry were atypical of Anglo-Norman warfare, whether waged in Ireland, Wales, England, Normandy or France.[46] In a long reign of thirty-five years, including a six-month sojourn in Ireland, King Henry II (1154–89) never fought a single pitched battle. Battles were rare events, and the adoption of a battle-seeking strategy unusual. Campaigns without battle were far more usual modes of warfare, and typically took the form of harrying and ravaging the countryside in order to deprive the opponent of supplies, and, if possible, to acquire provisions, which was an overriding preoccupation of medieval military commanders.[47] In essence, this was also the main purpose of Irish raiding activity in the twelfth century.

After harrying and plundering, the most frequently deployed strategy was the capture of fortified strongpoints. The soldiers best suited to that kind of warfare were garrison troops and bowmen. Mounted soldiers played a role, particularly when out on reconnaissance patrol, or escorting and guarding foraging parties, but this was essentially the same role as that which may be presumed to have been played by the *marcshlúag* in pre-Norman Irish warfare. Undue emphasis has been placed on the battle charge of the heavily armed knight as the most important element of Anglo-Norman knightly warfare. The military career of William Marshal serves to illustrate the principal techniques of Anglo-Norman warfare. Marshal's career has been regarded as typical of the Anglo-Norman chivalric knight, who trained for war by participating in jousts and tournaments, and, by then using that training in actual war, converted himself from a landless knight into one of the most prominent landholders in the Angevin realm. In 1189 King Henry II granted William Marshal the marriage of the heiress Isabella, daughter of Strongbow and grand-daughter of Diarmait Mac Murchada, and, in right of his wife, William secured the lordships of Strigoil, Leinster and Pembroke. William Marshal is exceptional in having a vernacular biography, the *Histoire de Guillaume le Maréchal*, which bears comparison with *Cogad Gaedel re Gallaib* or *Caithréim Cellacháin Chaisil* in its descriptive detail of military campaigns. The characteristic of warfare, as waged in the campaigns in which William Marshal fought, and as described by the author of the *Histoire*, was, as John Gillingham has highlighted, ravaging and destruction, undercover musters and sudden attacks.[48] So rare an event was the battle charge of the heavily armoured knight that William Marshal in a remarkably long military career participated in only two, one in 1167 and another in 1217. The author of the *Histoire* regarded ravaging expeditions as the normal activity of war.

> The kind of war William fought – and by definition this was the kind of war the best knights fought – was a war full of ravaging, punctuated quite often by attacks on strong-points but only rarely by pitched battles. If you had to fight then you fought hard, but always before you fought you tried to catch your enemy offguard, and often you preferred not to fight at all.[49]

The Irish annalists described Anglo-Norman warfare in the same terms as they used for pre-Norman Irish activity: Anglo-Normans engaged in preys or plundering expeditions, termed a *crech*, or *sluagad*, just as Irish forces did. The annalistic evidence is not contradicted by Giraldus's accounts of actual Anglo-Norman campaigns in his *Expugnatio Hibernica* in the period between 1167 and 1185, for, although he asserted the general superiority of Anglo-Norman military techniques in the use of armour and castles, nevertheless his descriptions of actual military campaigns consisted chiefly of plundering expeditions and surprise attacks. Small-scale warfare characterised Anglo-Norman military activity in Ireland in the late twelfth century, which must be one reason why the Irish annalists did not identify Anglo-Norman warfare as significantly different. The Four Masters could remark in retrospect in the seventeenth century that 'the Gaels had set little store by the Flemings' (*AFM*, 1169). Anglo-Norman reluctance to fight pitched battles 'on open plains' may also have been a reason why contemporary Irish annalists did not present Anglo-Norman intervention as a significant military turning point. The admittedly partisan annals of Tigernach described Ruaidrí Ua Conchobair's army taking up position at Dublin in 1170 for three days and nights and seeking to engage the forces of Diarmait Mac Murchada and his Anglo-Norman allies, but, after the city had been struck accidentally by lightning and then fired deliberately from within, Ruaidrí returned to Connacht, as the annalist put it, 'with his army unhurt after Mac Murchada and the Foreigners (= Hiberno-Norse) had refused to give him battle'.

Protective armour was identified by Giraldus as a tactical advantage which the Anglo-Normans enjoyed over Irish forces. Giraldus notwithstanding, certain classes of Irish combatants may be presumed to have worn some form of protective armour by the twelfth century. *Lúirecha* figure prominently in the *Book of Rights* as stipend proffered by a superior king; so also do shields, including 'shields from across the sea', swords and spears.[50] The fact that the loss of horses, arms and armour of a section of a northern army attacked by a Connacht army is recorded in 1131,

3.3 Sword hilt (made of iron, copper alloy and silver niello) of *c.* 1100,
recovered from Lough Derg, near Curraghmore, County Tipperary.
One of the few finely wrought secular metalwork objects extant
from the twelfth century.

indicates the importance of weaponry (*Ann. Tig.*). The axes which Giraldus stresses
as the chief weapon of the Irish, are not mentioned in the *Book of Rights*, which lists
the same assemblage of equipment as was common to the noble classes in twelfth-
century England or the continent, namely a horse with saddle and bridle, a shield
and spear/lance, a sword, a helmet and corselet.[51] The sword was the weapon of the
nobility. Not without justification, Geoffrey Keating castigated Giraldus for 'taking
notice of the ways of inferiors and wretched little hags', while ignoring the lifestyle
and practices of the Irish nobility.[52] In 1068 Diarmait mac Máel na mBó, king of
Leinster, returned to Toirdelbach Ua Briain, king of Thomond, the sword of his
grandfather Brian Bóruma as a ceremonial gift. In 1167 Ruaidrí Ua Conchobair as
high-king returned to Diarmait Mac Carthaig, king of Desmond, the sword of his
father Cormac as a ceremonial gift. A particularly fine decorated sword of early
twelfth-century date was recovered from Lough Derg (near Curraghmore, County
Tipperary) in 1988.[53] More problematical is the use of bows. Since in *Cogad Gaedel*

3.4   Irish axemen fighting; a detail from a manuscript of Giraldus,
Topographia Hibernica (c. 1200).

re Gallaib the Vikings are depicted using bows at the battle of Clontarf it is possible, and, perhaps one may put it even more strongly, it is probable that bows may have been in use in twelfth-century Ireland (Irish *boga* is a loanword from Old Norse). The tympanum of the north door of Cormac's chapel on the rock of Cashel, which was dedicated in 1134, depicts a centaur with a bow and arrow. The centaur is also wearing a conical helmet of standard European type. Toirdelbach Ua Conchobair, king of Connacht, is recorded on his deathbed in 1156 to have distributed his movable wealth among the churches of Ireland, excepting his *bogha 7 bolgshaighid 7 stábuill*, his 'bows, quivers and slings' (*Ann. Tig.*). It is probable that these were his hunting rather than combat weapons, but stone-slings are attested both in Giraldus and in the *Song of Dermot* as a form of missile fire used by Irish forces.[54] Giraldus also asserted that the Irish did not use saddles, but saddles accompany horses granted as stipend in the early twelfth-century *Book of Rights*. The *Book of Rights* indicates that a certain amount of prestige equipment was available in or imported into Ireland for use among the highest ranks of the aristocracy; more critical, however, is whether the economic or technological

3.5 Tympanum of north door, King Cormac's Chapel, Rock of Cashel,
showing a centaur wearing a contemporary style conical helmet
and armed with a bow and arrow.

resources for mass production of weapons and armour were available in twelfth-century Ireland. That notwithstanding, on Giraldus's own testimony, Anglo-Norman forces were able to derive advantage from the capture of Irish arms and horses.

As for the tactical advantage afforded the Anglo-Normans by castles, this too may have been exaggerated since it is certain that garrisoned fortifications played a role in twelfth-century Irish warfare. It might be argued that the 'castles' constructed by Ruaidrí Ua Conchobair ought not to be compared with an Anglo-Norman motte in that the former were part of a series of royal fortifications, while the Anglo-Norman motte was essentially a private fortified residence. Some Anglo-Norman mottes at least were located at sites which can be described as the seigneurial centre of a pre-Norman Irish lord/king and may already have had elevated earthworks *in situ* in the pre-Norman period. Early charters of Gilbert de Nugent, who was granted the fee of Delbna by Hugh de Lacy, refer to Gilbert's castle at Telach Cáil; Telach Cáil was the *caput* of the pre-Norman kings of Delbna.[55] The Anglo-Norman motte at Tullow, County Carlow, was located at the *caput* of the kings of Uí Felmeda.[56] Telach/Tulach denotes a mound or hillock. In a recent study of mottes in Anglo-Norman Leinster, T. E. McNeill concluded that their distribution

73

3.6 Trim Castle, County Meath, the most impressive of the Anglo-Norman fortresses in Ireland, elaborately constructed more for prestige purposes than its strategic value.

pattern did not indicate a defensive strategy against either external attack or internal revolt, and that they were built more for reasons of social status than military defence.[57] Coincidentally, Roger Stalley has argued in respect of the de Lacy stone castle at Trim that its very unusual design, which had such serious limitations from a defensive standpoint, since it provided no less than twelve potential points of attack, suggests that it was built primarily as a status symbol, not as a defensive structure.[58] Anglo-Norman mottes and stone castles in certain parts of Ireland at least can be viewed as the fruits rather than the means of conquest.

A survey of pre-Norman Irish warfare suggests that too sharp a contrast has been drawn between Irish and Anglo-Norman warfare and that Anglo-Norman military superiority has been overemphasised at the expense of other factors such as Irish involvement and cooperation with Anglo-Norman forces. The odium for involving Anglo-Normans in Ireland has fallen almost exclusively on Diarmait Mac Murchada. He has been branded as an 'arch-quisling' in nationalist historiography, unfairly so if the assertions of the Anglo-Norman chronicler, Gervase of Canterbury, may be relied upon, that King Henry II's personal intervention in Ireland in 1171 was sought by a number of other Irish kings.[59] During Henry's six-month stay in Ireland his army is not known to have been engaged militarily. While it could be argued that this indicates the superiority of his forces and the latent threat which they posed, it is an assumption which presumes that Irish kings would have wished to engage

Henry's army. Evidence that Henry II's intervention was a military turning point is inconclusive, although in hindsight, it was to be critical in initiating a constitutional relationship between the English crown and Ireland.

R. R. Davies has argued that English domination in medieval Ireland did not derive from, or rely exclusively on, military confrontation: 'conquest in the sense of a military act is only one of the routes to the domination of one society by another and not necessarily the most attractive, rewarding, or important of such routes'.[60] Political and marital alliances opened important avenues to domination, as did commercial dependence on and economic entrepreneurship by the conqueror. A conqueror's ideology of superiority, as expressed most trenchantly by Giraldus, was also an element. This was reinforced in Ireland by the late twelfth century by reforming Irish churchmen, who had become committed to an international code of conduct which distanced them to a degree from the cultural affiliations and even political links within their own society. Factors such as these were equally, if not more, important than military factors. Setting Anglo-Norman warfare in the context of twelfth-century Irish warfare suggests that there has been too much emphasis on Anglo-Norman intervention as a military turning point and supports R. R. Davies's view that 'domination is a much more subtle, rich-textured and many-faceted process than an overconcentration on the military story-line of conquest might suggest'.[61]

Chapter 4

The defence of the English lordship, 1250–1450

Robin Frame

During the greater part of this period western Europe was much affected by war, above all by the struggles between England and France which drew other disputes, from Scotland to Spain, into their vortex. Although the Anglo-Scottish war briefly intruded into Ireland in the form of the Bruce invasion of 1315–18, the island lay on the outer fringes of the bigger conflict. Lords from Ireland occasionally led contingents overseas. In 1297 John fitz Thomas, later first earl of Kildare, served Edward I in Flanders; his grandson, Earl Maurice, was at the siege of Calais in 1347 and was knighted by Edward III; the White Earl of Ormond took part in the 1418 siege of Rouen and other campaigns of Henry V and his brothers. But the main effect of the Hundred Years War was to delay and hinder English military responses to an erosion of royal authority in Ireland of which the crown was aware at least from the 1350s.[1] There was an inverse relation between activity on the Continent and the troops, money and commanders who could be spared for Ireland; it is no accident that the only royal visits to the lordship were by Richard II, a king with little military reputation who, to his political cost, pursued peace with France.

Ireland itself was a land of continual, small-scale war.[2] Conflict was regional and local, its chief motor the ceaseless competition for power and resources – represented by livestock and grazing and by control over men's allegiances and services – between lords of varied origin and rank. At the top the protagonists were Anglo-Irish nobles and descendants of native provincial dynasties; lower down, those involved were lesser settler lords and the successors of Irish sub-chiefs. Despite the application of national labels to individuals and groups by all the sources, these tussles for wealth and power were not primarily along ethnic lines. Many lords, especially those of lesser status, were of mixed descent. Gaelic society was highly segmented; often a native lord's main enemies were his Irish neighbours and rival members of his own kin, against whom he sought support wherever it might be found. Likewise the forces led by settler magnates included clients and allies from both nations. The shrinkage of the lordship in the late middle ages was thus not the product of a native war of reconquest; it mirrored the gradual spread of the economic and social patterns of the Gaelic and border regions into the more marginal areas of colonial settlement. As this took place, the proportion of Ireland amenable to rule through English institutions dwindled.

The main theme of this chapter is the way in which the agents of the crown responded to the problems caused by the expanding areas of war. The role of royal government should not be underestimated. Within the heavily settled parts of the east and south lay manors, towns and counties whose defence Dublin helped to organise, and to some extent provided. There English forms of military obligation and administration existed, through which the king's ministers mobilised the population to counter incursions from the Wicklow uplands or the midland woods and bogs. Even in the region of the future Pale there was no straight confrontation between settler and native. Defence demanded close involvement with leaders on and beyond the frontiers; ministers came to exercise power in a mixture of styles, including that of the cattle-raiding, hostage-taking overlord. Beyond these areas the crown operated less directly. In Ireland as in other medieval polities central authority was spread unevenly; government shaded off into diplomacy, and relations with regional lords were crucial. Nevertheless in more distant areas occasional intervention from Dublin was needed. A typical precipitant of such involvement was the failure of a local power structure to preserve the stability that was the crown's main concern – as when the succession of a minor or heiresses to a key lordship left a vacuum of control, or when a noble persistently obstructed the wishes of the king or his representatives.[3]

At the risk of oversimplification, therefore, the defence of the lordship may be viewed as two activities: routine management of borders in the south-east; and the effort to maintain influence over power centres further from Dublin. Map 4.1, which relates to a period that has been closely studied, shows the contrasting degrees of government action in the two zones. While the difference can be seen throughout the years 1250–1450, royal authority became more circumscribed and shallow as time went by, though shrinkage was not smooth or continuous. The presence of forces from England, especially in the decades after the arrival in 1361 of Edward III's son, Lionel of Antwerp, led to spasmodic revivals of royal authority. There were also regional differences, caused in part by accidents of survival and extinction among magnate families: in the first decade of the fourteenth century, when the government was already bogged down in defensive warfare in Leinster, Earl Richard of Ulster was expanding his influence beyond the Foyle. Conversely, the murder of his grandson, Earl William, in 1333, like the death in battle of Richard de Clare, lord of Thomond, in 1318, left a gap that was too large for ministers to fill. Nevertheless, the contraction was real enough, as Maps 4.2 and 4.3, which mark the places to which the feudal service of Ireland was summoned between 1252 and 1442, show. The settler elite held their lands by providing knights for royal armies, a duty that for the most part was commuted into a tax, known as 'scutage'.[4] Before the Bruce invasion a significant number of summonses were for Ulster, Connacht or west

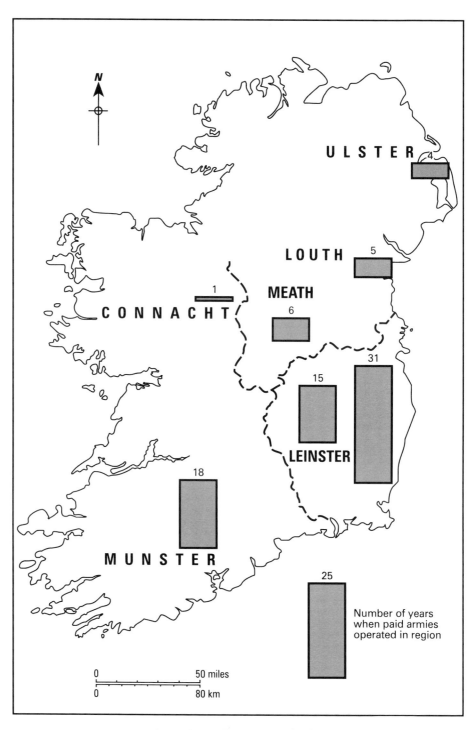

4.1 Expeditions by paid armies in Ireland, 1295–1360

Source: R. Bartlett and A. MacKay (ed.), *Medieval frontier societies*
(Oxford, 1989)

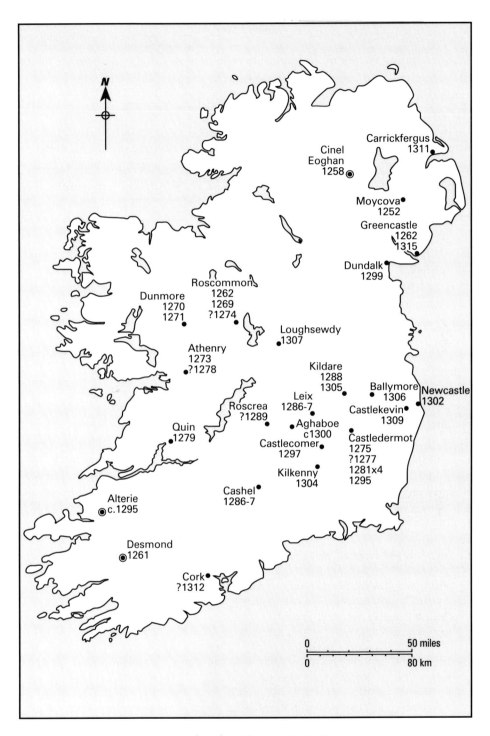

4.2 Royal services, 1252–1315

Munster. During the rest of the fourteenth century most scutages were for the future Pale counties, south Leinster or east Munster. By the early fifteenth century proclamations were limited almost entirely to the Pale region.

Legislation published in Irish parliaments and great councils affords a view of the defence arrangements that were at least partially effective within the regions the government monitored closely.[5] Alongside the quotas of knight service (amounting to some 425 knights in all) owed by direct tenants of the crown, there was a general obligation on adult males to serve in defence of their areas with the horses and arms appropriate to their wealth in land and goods. This was a version of the English obligation to arms which had been revised in the Statute of Winchester of 1285. The statute was not sent for observance in Ireland until 1308, but the duty to be equipped and ready for war was taken for granted before that. In 1297 an Irish statute laid down that everybody with land worth £20 a year was to have a barded (armoured) horse, the mount of a knight or other man-at-arms; those less wealthy were to keep 'hobbies' (the small horses of the hobelar or mounted lancer, who rode to war but fought on foot) or other unarmoured mounts.[6] The most detailed surviving schedule of horses and arms was drawn up for Geoffrey de Geneville, lord of Trim from 1252 to 1307. It shows that men worth as little as £3 6s 8d a year were expected to have a horse,[7] indicating the importance of small horses in the swift-moving raids in difficult country that were typical of Irish warfare: in England in 1285 the duty to have a horse fell only upon those worth £15 or more.

This pool of manpower was under the control of the sheriff of the county, who was increasingly aided by keepers (later justices) of the peace, chosen like himself from among the leading landholders. By the middle of the fourteenth century statutes assume that keepers of the peace existed in all counties.[8] Their military role is summed up in the Dublin peace commission of 1403:

> to assess and array all men . . . within that county to horses and arms, hobelars, archers and foot according to the quantity of their lands and tenements, goods and chattels; and when they are so assessed and arrayed, to group them in twenties, hundreds and thousands, and to lead them to border areas where hostile attacks by Irish or English, rebelling against us, our faithful people, and our peace, have occurred; and with God's help to fight and repulse such rebels.[9]

In 1392 John son of Nicholas Lombard had been rewarded with £20 upon petitioning the Irish parliament that he

> was charged and entrusted with the office of keeper of the peace in the county of Kilkenny, at a time when MacMurrough, O'Nolan, O'Ryan and other Irish of those districts were openly at war; and in discharging that office was so grievously wounded in an attack on MacMurrough in the marches there that he was in despair of his life – in which attack ten of the best men of MacMurrough were beheaded.[10]

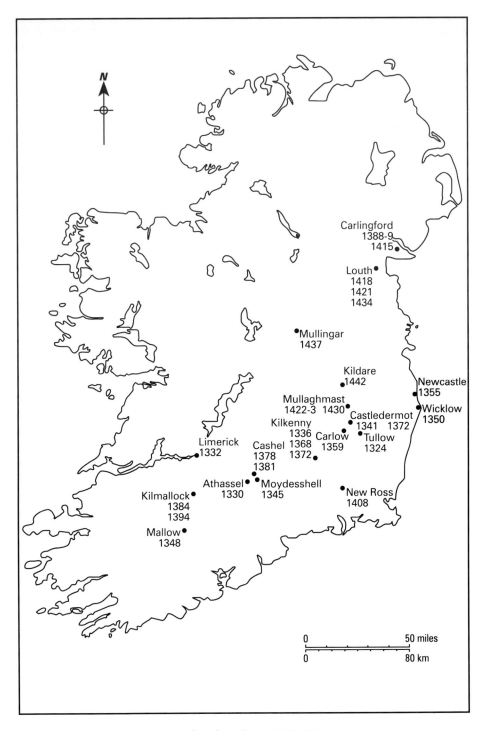

Carlingford
1388-9
1415

Louth
1418
1421
1434

Mullingar
1437

Kildare
1442

Newcastle
1355

Mullaghmast
1422-3 1430
Castledermot
1341   1372

Wicklow
1350

Kilkenny
1336   Carlow
Cashel 1368   1359
1378 1372
1381

Tullow
1324

Limerick
1332

Athassel   Moydesshell
1330   1345

New Ross
1408

Kilmallock
1384
1394

Mallow
1348

0   50 miles
0   80 km

4.3   Royal services, 1324–1442

These local officers were asked to enforce a variety of rules designed to discipline frontier relations. They might be ordered to make those with lands in the marches reside upon and defend them, or to prevent supplies, particularly of horses and arms, from reaching Irish outside the peace. Above all there was the matter of controlling the negotiations that, in a fragmented world, inevitably went on at local level. Legislation declared grandly that there should be 'one war and one peace' throughout Ireland; what this meant in practice was that adjacent counties and districts should maintain a common front and help one another, rather than making separate truces and (as a statute of 1297 put it) 'exulting in the damage and ruin of their neighbour'.[11] Once a settlement – which might include the payment of compensation to those who had been injured by raids – had been reached, Irish who had come within the peace were entitled to royal protection. In 1311 some English who seized a prey of cattle from O'Reilly escaped punishment only because the incident took place just before letters receiving him into the peace had been publicly proclaimed.[12]

The universal duty to provide defence often took a financial form. Men would be selected to guard strategic areas, the cost being spread across the community by means of a local tax. In 1332, when the justiciar was campaigning around Arklow and Clonmore, protection was arranged for the manors of south Dublin. A levy of 2s on the ploughland was imposed on the county 'for the sustenance of the men guarding Tallaght . . . to repress the malice and rebellion of the Irish of the mountains of Leinster, intending to invade the lands of the king's faithful people'. Exempted from assessment were those in the justiciar's army, those actually serving at Tallaght, and lands in the marches.[13] The idea that subsidies, whether charged on lands or on movable goods, should place most responsibility on the wealthiest was liable to fall foul of the realities of local power. In 1355 Thomas Rokeby, the justiciar, was exasperated to find that in Kildare assessments had been changed 'by favour and hatred, those having less land being assigned to the heavier burdens, and those having more to the lighter'.[14] But despite tensions, there was at root some concordance of interests between the crown, the greater lords, and the communities both had a duty to protect. Their interaction is symbolised in the fifteenth century by measures adopted to encourage the building of fortifications. In 1430 all land-holders in Dublin, Meath, Kildare and Louth who chose 'to build a castle or tower sufficiently crenellated and [fortified] within the next ten years – to wit, twenty feet in length, sixteen feet in breadth, and forty feet in height, or more' were to have £10 from the community of the county 'by way of subsidy, to help with the building'.[15]

In the south-east the constant local defence measures were backed by frequent central intervention. Virtually every year, and often more than once a year, the government raised paid armies. After 1337, when the new justiciar, John Charlton, brought 200 Welsh archers to Ireland with him, such armies might have a core of outsiders; these introduced into Irish warfare the mounted archers, equipped with

4.1 The Cantwell effigy at Kilfane, County Kilkenny,
showing chain-mail, tunic and shield.

4.2   Roscommon Castle, a royal castle, built or restored by
Robert d'Ufford, the justiciar, about 1280.

longbows, whose speed of deployment and fire-power had such an impact in France. When in 1420 Thomas Pettit contracted with the earl of Ormond to serve him with six archers, they were 'to be well armed, harnessed and mounted after the fashion of England'.[16] Later in the fifteenth century the Irish parliament was anxious to encourage the use of 'English bows' in the eastern counties. But English troops were present only now and then, and longbowmen remained in short supply. Most armies were made up of retinues of men-at-arms, hobelars and foot equipped with the short Irish bow, brought to the king's banner by magnates and lesser lords, including some native Irish leaders.[17] Certain commanders, such as the two Berminghams, William son of Andrew and Walter Carragh, who served in the 1350s with large contingents of kern, were professionals. When it came to raising armies ministers found themselves employing men of a type whose exactions and depredations were often condemned by Irish legislation. In 1302 the deputy justiciar, who was organising an expedition in the Leinster mountains, first went 'to the Meath districts . . . to seek Philip O'Reilly and other Irish felons', who had already fought for the king in Leinster in 1294–5.[18]

The force led by Thomas Rokeby against the O'Byrnes of Wicklow in 1353 (Table 4.1) is not untypical in its size and composition of the paid armies of the period.[19] It will strike the modern eye as tiny. By contemporary standards it was also small, but not ridiculously so. Edward III's major Scottish campaign of 1334–5 involved some 6,200 men, his forays of 1336 perhaps as few as 800.[20] We should remember, too, that Irish armies were augmented by local men serving in their own district

Table 4.1. *Forces serving in Leinster 27 September–15 October 1353*

leader	men-at-arms	hobelars	mounted archers	foot
Earl of Ormond	9	71	0	130
John de Carew	6	2	8	0
John Cusack	7	11	8	0
William son of Andrew Bermingham	13	168	0	278
Rory O'More	4	68	0	108
Odo [Aedh] O'Toole	2	15	0	4
McCraygh O'Kennedy	0	14	0	84
John Lykin and Roger Beveryk, hobelars	0	2	0	0
totals	41	351	16	604

without pay. The scale of paid contingents was determined partly by the government's finances. In 1306, when an exceptionally large army was deployed in Leinster over many weeks, the cost was £2,114 – about half the annual revenue.[21] After the Bruce invasion revenues rarely rose much above £2,000 a year, of which salaries and routine expenses ate up more than half: the £163 spent on the short campaign of 1353 was in this context not a trifling sum.[22]

The small size of armies and the limitations on the time they could be kept in the field helped to determine the nature of the tasks they undertook; equally, of course, the armies themselves reflected the low-intensity, short-winded character of most Irish warfare. While we are well informed about the make-up of forces and financing of campaigns, there is a frustrating lack of information about what armies did once they were assembled. The earl of Ormond's, probably disingenuous, comment on a failure against Brian Bán O'Brien near Thurles in 1330 strikes a rare human note: the campaign collapsed 'because the weather was so wet and windy, and on account of the great difficulty of the mountains, bogs and woods'.[23] To judge the success of campaigns we need to grasp what was attempted. In 1350 ministers newly arrived from England voiced frustration at the nature of warfare in Ireland, saying that it incurred costs without concrete results in the form of the conquest of land; they recommended that territory should be recaptured from the Irish, and repopulated.[24] This idea was revived in 1399 when Richard II's lieutenant, Thomas Holland, duke of Surrey, asked to have 'a man and his wife from every parish in England, or from every second parish . . . to inhabit the land where it is destroyed along the marches'.[25] The Irish government was well aware that defence depended on the presence of people. It offered financial inducements to men willing to take lands in exposed frontier districts of Leinster and build fortified houses: in 1334 Geoffrey Cromp was given lands at Bray for two years rent free, in order that he could repair a castle; his immunity from rent was later extended for two periods of

---

seven years.[26] But successive outbreaks of plague in the later fourteenth century brought a steep decline in population in Britain and Ireland which was all against the colonising entrepreneur. War remained a matter of punishing raiders and exacting submissions from their leaders.

This was achieved in various ways. Some royal expeditions were in essence retributive cattle-raids. In 1340 the Dublin annals remark that 'a great prey, the like of which had not been seen in the parts of Leinster, composed of various sorts of animals, was taken by the lord Thomas [Charlton], bishop of Hereford, the justiciar of Ireland, from the Irish in the area of Idrone, with the aid of the English of that district'.[27] A year later the bishop's successor, John Morice, hired Philip MacNeill, as a 'spy of the lord king'; Philip's activities allowed Morice to pinpoint and seize a prey of cattle from some Meath Irish.[28] This form of pressure could be accompanied by destruction of crops. Friar John Clyn of Kilkenny, the only other annalist writing in the heartlands of the lordship, describes how in the late summer of 1344 the next justiciar, Ralph Ufford, 'burnt the lands of MacMurrough in Uí Cheinnsealaigh, together with the corn of the Irish of the vicinity, and made them give hostages for the peace'.[29] Ufford commented laconically in a letter to Edward III that the Irish of Leinster 'do not walk so tall now as they did'.[30] Actions of this sort lay at the heart of medieval war; they enabled objects to be achieved without the lottery of battle, which sensible commanders did their best to avoid. The infliction of damage and terror weakened the ability of the enemy to resist, while plunder of course transferred their resources to their opponents; their leaders might be persuaded to switch allegiance to those who could, by implication, protect them.[31]

Occasionally we hear of more substantial engagements.[32] In 1359, when the retreat of settlement in south Leinster was offering more freedom of manoeuvre to Gaelic lords, MacMurrough, O'More and others were confronted by the justiciar, the earl of Ormond, near Athy in Leix. Ormond, who had the earls of Kildare and Desmond with him, describes how, lacking money, 'he rode all the English country close to that march and took the animals and other foodstuffs that could be found . . . [and] delivered those animals and victuals to his army instead of wages'.[33] Circumstantial evidence confirms that there was a battle: Nicholas Power of Kilmeadan and thirty-two of his men were wounded, and Ormond claimed that many Irish fell 'through God's providence'.[34] His victory stuck in men's minds. Some sixty years later James Yonge of Dublin composed a book of advice and instruction for the White Earl. Among the *exempla* he selected for the earl's edification was his grandfather:

> but victori in battail Pryncipal is in god. That Sheweth wel the deddis of the nobylle victorius Erle, Syr Iamys, yowre gravndeSyre, whych in al his tyme lechury hatid: And ther-for god in al his tyme granted hym mervellous victori up his enemys with fewe Pepill, Namly up the morthes, of whyche he slew huge Pepill in the red more of athy, a litil afore the Sone goynge downe, stondynge the Sone mervelosly still till the slaght was done.[35]

When faced by prolonged disorder, the government adopted a more complex strategy, which was as characteristic of the warfare of the period as the cattle-raid. It set up chains of 'wards', placing troops at strategic points to defend stretches of countryside and, when appropriate, take retaliatory action. Operations of this sort could protect arable areas on the fringes of the Wicklow mountains, defend the Barrow route between Dublin and the south, or police the marches of Leix and Offaly. They tended to bring into a single focus the various forms of military obligation which have already been described. In the early summer of 1355 Thomas Rokeby led an army into Wicklow, for which the knight service was summoned to Newcastle McKynegan. This was accompanied by royal pressure on County Dublin to assume responsibility for wards at Bray and Tallaght, and on the landholders of Kildare for those at Ballymore Eustace, Kilteel, Rathmore and Graney.[36] At the same time the government placed paid forces, mostly recruited from the settler lineages of Wicklow, such as the Lawlesses, Harolds and Archbolds, at key points south of the city of Dublin and along the coast from Bray and Killiney to Wicklow.[37] Typically, the role of these wards was not wholly defensive: the paymasters' accounts show that from them spying missions were organised, leading to nocturnal burning of the crops of the Irish. In this strategy castles and fortified houses found a natural place. Castles such as Wicklow, Balyteny [?Powerscourt] and Newcastle were repaired and garrisoned. Wicklow castle was used as a base to which supplies were shipped. Laurence Danyell had sixteen foot soldiers within his 'stone house' nearby. Donald son of Paul Lawless was paid for the repair of the 'fortalice' (probably a tower) at Kilmartin, between Bray and Wicklow. Stone, timber, iron, lead and lime were bought for the purposes of fortification. Further expeditions in the late 1350s took place within the context of these wards centred on carefully maintained strong-points. Such royal works were small beer compared to the vast effort that had gone into the building of a great castle such as Roscommon in the later thirteenth century, when the crown was still trying to maintain a presence west of the Shannon; but, when set alongside other evidence (for instance, of the reconstruction of Arklow, Clonmore and Balyteny during the 1330s) they support the recent conclusions of archaeologists who have questioned the traditional view that there was virtually no castle building in Ireland during the fourteenth century.[38]

This background enables better sense to be made of the approach adopted by Richard II on his Irish expedition of 1394–5. Richard's main military success was a campaign that rapidly got submissions from MacMurrough, O'Byrne, O'Nolan and other Irish of eastern Leinster; this encouraged native leaders in more distant parts of Ireland to submit with little further fighting.[39] A letter from an anonymous lord in the king's company described his campaign in admiring terms, explaining how 'our very redoubted lord and king did set certain wards ('gardes'), very cunningly as it seemed to me . . . round about the Irish enemies'.[40] Since Richard's forces, even before they were augmented by the magnates of Ireland, were several times larger than any governor could hope to muster, those stationed in the wards no doubt took a more aggressive stance than normal: the writer claims, with pardonable exaggeration, that 'the earl marshal [Thomas Mowbray, earl of Nottingham] . . . slew many of the people of MacMurrough, and burned . . . nine townlands, and preyed of his cattle up to the number of 8,000'. The campaign may be seen as a development of established practice. After he returned to England in May 1395, Richard left wards in place to guarantee the fragile peace he had established in Leinster; it was when lack of money led to the watering down of these measures that the province returned to its usual instability.[41]

Military operations cannot be isolated from politics and diplomacy; force was merely one ingredient in a form of management that had much in common with the overlordship wielded by colonial magnates or Gaelic lords in their own spheres.[42] Since the original occupation of Ireland had been achieved by forces in which newcomers and natives fought side by side, it is hardly surprising that from the moment we have details of royal armies they include Irish contingents. The exploiting of segmentary discord, the attachment of individual lords to the crown, and the building of favourable coalitions was a conscious policy. In 1307 John Wogan, the justiciar, granted Glenealy, which had been held by the O'Tooles, to the O'Byrnes, with the remark, 'this gift is made that . . . dissension may be moved between the said families'.[43] When Piers Gaveston, as Edward II's lieutenant in Ireland, led an army against the O'Byrnes in 1309, he gave £6 to Henry O'Toole 'for certain business done'.[44] In 1312 Muircheartach MacMurrough, head of the former ruling dynasty of Leinster, was getting a regular fee from the exchequer, together with the custody of the manor of Courtown on the Wexford coast, in return for service against the O'Byrnes. A century later, when a letter was sent to England in support of Henry V's lieutenant, John Talbot, its authors picked out for special praise the fact that he had defeated a series of Irish lords, compelling them as he did so to enlist against his next opponent, so causing 'in many places every Irish enemy to serve upon the other'.[45]

One object of military expeditions was to remind native lords of their allegiance to the crown and to use them in the stabilising of the marches. This goal is clear in documents recording submissions. In 1335, at a session of the court of the justiciar at Newcastle McKynegan, attended by Gerailt O'Byrne (who had a long history of serving in royal armies), Murchadh O'Byrne, the head of the lineage, accepted terms:

> Murchadh [sought] the grace and mercy of the lord king, undertaking that he would, with his wife, children and adherents, stay at Kilmartin or Wicklow at the command of the justiciar; and that he and Gerailt would answer for all trespasses against the English of the march perpetrated by the rest of their lineage from Wicklow to Dublin; and they would daily fight those rebels until they came wholly within the king's peace; and they would obey the king and his ministers as is fitting; and from each of their lineage having a family they would take one hostage.[46]

4.3 Dalkey Tower House, an example of a very common type
of relatively modest fortified dwelling.

In a more elaborate submission at Athy in 1347, O'More agreed to pay reparations
in the form of 1,000 cattle, of which 200 were to be handed over quarterly in batches
of 50, while exaction of the remaining 800 was suspended so long as he behaved
himself; he was to serve the justiciar in war at his own expense in his own area
but at the king's wages beyond it; he also undertook to compensate the English
damaged by his raids, to keep his military followers under control, and to surrender
hostages for himself, his brother and other leading members of the lineage.[47] In
applying force the government sought to harness Irish political structures rather
than to destroy them. By exacting hostages, who were usually housed in Dublin
Castle or given into the keeping of reliable magnates, it laid hands on a key symbol
of lordship. The centrality of the hostage is shown by examples of bargaining about
who was to be surrendered. In 1325 Murchadh O'Byrne had captured three members
of the Lawless family and used them as counters to obtain the release of a son
who was held in the Castle: but he was willing to give up another son, who was
presumably younger or born of a woman of lesser status, in return.[48]

In the middle of the fourteenth century, when pressure from the Irish was
growing in Leinster, relations between ministers and Gaelic lords quickened.
Thomas Rokeby parleyed intensively and expanded the practice of paying retainers.
In 1354 he explained to the English exchequer, which challenged these gratuities to

unknown men with strange names, that he had 'by advice of the council . . . and of the magnates and marchers of Ireland, and in order to obviate greater costs, retained certain Irish who were within the peace to make war upon and injure other Irish, who were enemies'; and that 'a certain small fee was given and granted them by the same advice'.[49] Among those retained in 1351–3 were O'More and O'Toole, who led troops to the royal army in 1353 (Table 4.1).[50] The benefits of Rokeby's diplomacy are apparent in a reward to O'More when he 'took from O'Connor, a powerful Irishman, formerly enemy and rebel of the king, a hostage valid for the peace of the land of Ireland, and delivered him to the justiciar of Ireland in the king's name'.[51] O'Connor Faly had remained outside the network of favour.

The government passed beyond tying native leaders to the king by submissions and fees, and began formally to confirm their position within their own society, bestowing titles acceptable to Dublin. In 1350 Rokeby presided at sessions where the O'Byrnes, along with settler lineages of Wicklow, chose their leaders.[52] In 1357 a payment to Art MacMuircheartach Caomhánach was made

> because Art has been created 'MacMurrough' by the justiciar and council of Ireland, and through indentures drawn up between the lord king and his court and MacMurrough [has promised] that he will serve the king well and faithfully against all those Irish or English who are disobedient to the king, with his whole power at the disposal of the king, having touched the Holy Gospels in the presence of a public notary; and because MacMurrough has set aside his action concerning the 40 marks that he seeks annually from the council of the king, which he asserts to have been customarily paid from the treasury of the king to his ancestors.[53]

A chiefly style, expressing recognition of a lord as 'captain of his nation', was infinitely preferable in official eyes to the ancient title 'king of Leinster', which implied a rejection of the crown's authority. The royal style had been briefly resumed by the MacMurroughs in 1328, but it was from the 1350s that it began to be used frequently and given meaning. This coincided with the emergence of more widespread Irish coalitions, such as the one that led to the battle near Athy in 1359. Governors might almost be seen as competing with the MacMurroughs for lordship, since a scheme of allegiances along the lines of that created by Rokeby could also be built up by a native leader. When Richard II arrived in 1394, Art MacMurrough (son of the Art of 1357) was a figure of weight, with whom the king had no choice but to deal. Art had grown rich on exchequer fees and on black rents extorted from weakened English communities in the Barrow valley; he made allies in western Leinster and Munster, and added the words 'by the grace of God' to his title.[54]

By the early 1400s the position in south-east Ireland differed from that of a century earlier. The military and diplomatic efforts of governors had not prevented the colonised areas from shrinking. The Irish who menaced them were led by substantial and, in some cases, enduring figures (Art MacMurrough ruled from 1375 to 1416) who were important enough to be known in England. Art's son, Gerailt, had a safe-conduct to do fealty to Henry V in 1415; Gerailt's son Donnchad was captured by John Talbot and spent a period, not in Dublin Castle like his forbears, but in the Tower of London. Yet these developments had their compensations. The settled zones had shrunk to their defensible cores and would contract little more, while ministers had found ways of living with larger Irish powers. The situation may have been more manageable than when the Dublin government had struggled to protect a larger area against a more splintered opposition.

Further away from Dublin defence depended on the capacity of magnates to organise their regions.[55] There is nothing strange in this. Governors could not be everywhere at once, and in any case the lordship had been largely the creation of baronial enterprise in the first place. Aristocratic control of the localities might be formalised through liberty jurisdictions or by giving magnates peace commissions covering several counties. But, in essence, like the authority of lords in the Welsh marches in the century after the Norman Conquest, it rested less on law or theory than on military exigencies and the facts of power.[56] When magnates found their actions challenged, they fell back on common sense, which they presented as ancient custom. In 1330 the earl of Desmond defended himself against the charge that he had received Brian Bán O'Brien after Brian had committed felonies, by saying that 'it was permitted to him and to all other lords of Ireland, for the betterment of the peace, to treat with any felons of their own marches, and to receive them, according to the custom of the land of Ireland, without seeking or receiving the lord king's licence'.[57]

Regional power centres were vital even in the south-east. As well as imposing military assessments on his tenants, Geoffrey de Geneville claimed the right to have truces with Irishmen who were outside the king's peace, and agreed with the barons of Trim local rules for the division of the spoils of war.[58] In 1360–1, when Trim was in the king's hand, the royal records preserve details of war and diplomacy of a sort that are usually lost. A force of 200 horse was raised to impose peace among the Tyrells, De La Mares, Tuyts and Pettits at Mullingar and Taghmon. Defences were maintained near Trim against 'the evildoers of Carbury and Offaly'. Parleys were held with the O'Farrells at Fore. The De La Mares seized a hostage from the O'Farrell leader and deposited him in the castle at Trim.[59] Evidence from the orbits of the earl of Kildare and of the seneschals of the absentee lords of Kilkenny reveals similar patterns.

In more distant regions the power of great lords such as the earls of Ulster (while they lasted), Ormond and Desmond was crucial. As well as acting as direct rulers of the settled heartlands of their lordships, they bound lesser lords into political and military relationships, creating webs of clientage that could normally be made to work for rather than against the interests of the crown. In 1356 the second earl of Ormond entered into written contracts involving service in war with Oliver Howell,

Richard de Burgh, Geoffrey le Poer, Mahon O'Kennedy and Donough son of MacNamara.[60] These links reinforced his influence in north Tipperary, Limerick and Thomond. Such networks could be of use to the central authorities in one very practical way. When, as in 1353, the earl took part in campaigns in the south-east he mobilised in the government's service, in his own retinue and those of his client lords, manpower from far afield (Table 4.1). Even the more distant and difficult earls of Desmond brought troops into Leinster on occasion. When such lords were themselves governors of Ireland, their personal contacts were invaluable: in the fifteenth century, when the Dublin government was virtually bankrupt, the White Earl of Ormond was able to give it an authority and a range of influence that could otherwise be achieved only by an English noble backed by troops and funds that the king could ill afford.[61]

The most impressive military operations organised by the Dublin government took place when it became necessary to intervene in the remoter parts of the lordship. Map 4.4 shows the campaigns undertaken by Ralph Ufford in 1345.[62] Ufford was a banneret of Edward III's military household who brought with him to Ireland forty knights and other men-at-arms and 200 mounted and foot archers. He had married the king's cousin, Matilda of Lancaster, widow of the earl of Ulster killed in 1333. Her daughter, the heiress of Ulster and Connacht, was already betrothed to Edward's second son, Lionel. Early in 1345 Ufford moved into Ulster. He was intercepted in the Moiry Pass near Newry by MacCartan of Iveagh, losing twenty-nine war horses and a number of pack-animals and carts. Overcoming this setback, he left troops to clear and guard the pass; they soon succeeded in capturing MacCartan. Within Ulster he removed Henry O'Neill (of Clan Aodha Buidhe) from power, replacing him with Aedh O'Neill, from whom he took a hostage.

This swift coup was followed by intervention in the opposite corner of the island. Soon after Ufford's return from the north, relations with the earl of Desmond broke down. Despite the turbulence of Ireland, military confrontations between the crown and Anglo-Irish earls were rare. Juries accused Desmond of plotting to make himself king of Ireland; but these extravagant claims obscure the real reason for the crisis, which lay in the tactless actions Ufford had taken to promote the interests of absentee landholders (such as the heirs of the de Clare lords of Thomond) into whose notional spheres of influence Desmond had intruded. The justiciar moved south in the early summer. By 7 July he had some 900 troops in pay in addition to his remaining English retinue of 40 men-at-arms and 74 archers. As he swept westwards into Limerick, Cork and Kerry his army grew; by October the total force had doubled to over 2,000 men. He was joined by Butlers and de Burghs who had no love for the Geraldine earl. Native Irish retinues provided about one-third of the army. MacMurrough and O'More had gone with him from Leinster, while O'Brien and MacNamara, no doubt sensing the way the wind was blowing, joined him near Askeaton, swelling the Irish-led element in the army to 8 men-at-arms, 176 hobelars

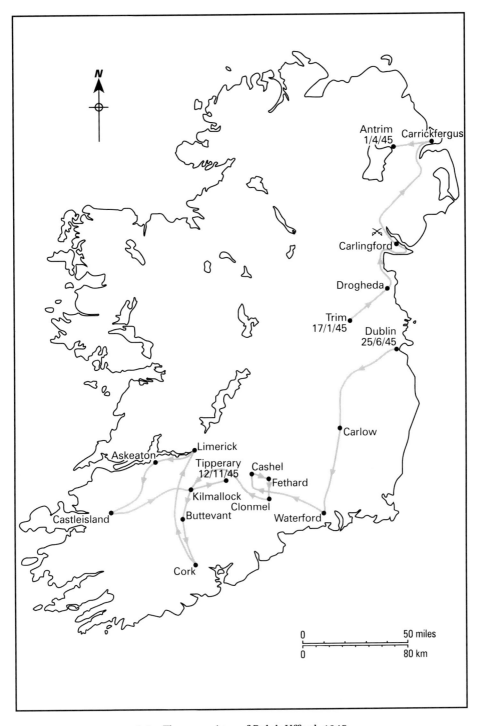

4.4 The campaigns of Ralph Ufford, 1345

and 484 foot.[63] In the face of this onslaught support for Desmond crumbled; his castles of Askeaton and Castleisland fell without prolonged sieges, and he went into hiding.

Yet these events show the limits as well as the strength of central authority: it was one thing to promote the fortunes of a Gaelic dynastic segment or to demolish an earl's power base, and another to control what happened afterwards or replace what had been destroyed. In Ulster Ufford may in the longer term have strengthened the position of the alternative branch of the O'Neills, thereby helping to create the power with which Richard II, successive Mortimer earls of Ulster, and Richard, duke of York had to deal. In the south-west the earl of Desmond had been restored by 1351; by 1355 he was justiciar of Ireland. This is not really surprising; the expropriation of noble houses was not undertaken lightly, especially by Edward III whose strength lay in his ability to cultivate and harness them. But documents passing between Dublin and the council in England show that there was an additional reason for leniency: the inability of ministers in Ireland to exploit the former Desmond lands, or to fill the gap his removal had left. A marcher society could not be defended and managed except through reliable magnates who gave political shape to the regions. Their role is symbolised by the 'Statutes and "Corrections"' issued by the earl of Ormond in Tipperary in the late 1440s which, mimicking the legislation of the Irish parliament, sought to check raids on adjacent communities and to limit the exactions of heads of lineages and troops of kern.[64] The survival of regional powers was necessary if the lordship of Ireland were not to contract to the counties around Dublin, and the immediate hinterlands of the royal towns of the south. Continued interaction between the government and local centres of authority, not least in the military sphere, meant that the lordship, while shrunken and fragmented, remained more than the sum of its parts.

It was this decentralised, competitive world, where government was thinly stretched, that Scottish forces under Edward Bruce invaded in 1315. There were, of course, age-old links between western Scotland and the north of Ireland. From the mid-thirteenth century Gaelic lords in Ulster and Connacht had been bringing in Scots mercenary troops. Once war broke out between Edward I and the Scots in 1296 Ireland was in the eye of the storm and interactions across the North Channel took a novel form. Ireland was an obvious point from which to put pressure on western Scotland and the Isles. The crown called upon treasure, foodstuffs and other supplies which could be conveniently shipped from Dublin or Drogheda to the hinterland of Carlisle. Armies sailed from Ireland to take part in campaigns between 1296 and 1335.[65] Irish forces also added something to the English tactical repertoire. Edward I was struck by the value of the hobelar in Scottish terrain. In the early fourteenth century steps were taken to have men of the English shires equipped and mounted as hobelars; these played a major part in English campaigns until they were displaced by mounted archers in the early part of the Hundred Years War.[66] It

4.4 Effigy of knight with plate armour and helmet at 'Hospital Church', Barrysfarm, County Limerick.

is scarcely surprising that the Scots should seize any opportunity to strike back on the Irish front. Their chance came when Edward II's regime faltered in the wake of Robert Bruce's victory at Bannockburn in 1314.

Edward Bruce, Robert's brother, landed in Ulster in May 1315; from there he launched campaigns in Meath, Leinster and Munster until his defeat and death in the battle of Fochart in October 1318. The aims of the invasion have been much disputed, but recent writers seem agreed on two points: that Edward was engaged in a serious attempt to make himself king of Ireland by mobilising Gaelic and (where possible) Anglo-Irish support against the Dublin government and settler lords; and that his ambitions had sustained support from King Robert, who himself campaigned in Ireland between January and May 1317.[67] From Robert's point of view the venture might have value, in putting pressure on the English, even if Edward's ultimate ambition was not achieved.

Historians writing in the early part of the century had little good to say of Scottish tactics: outside Ulster the Scots had engaged in wanton plunder and destruction without taking an effective grip on the land they were supposedly trying to conquer. The reputation of the Dublin government and Anglo-Irish lords stood little higher: their resistance was ill-organised and they failed for three and a half years to defeat the Scots in battle and expel them from Ireland. In the context of the economic and political conditions of Edward II's reign such judgements appear unduly harsh. The years 1315–17 were ones of severe famine, making it exceptionally difficult to keep armies supplied and disciplined. In England factional struggles meant that little help was given to the northern counties, let alone Ireland; indeed resistance to the Scots by the king's subjects in Ireland was probably more effective than that mounted in the north of England. The activities of the Scots and their opponents also make better sense in the light of modern work on the conventions and practice of medieval warfare.

In Ulster, with the help of Domhnall O'Neill, the Scots succeeded in expelling the earl and establishing a base. Their power on sea and land enabled them to mount a successful year-long siege of Carrickfergus castle; its fall in September 1316 symbolised the passing of the earldom into Edward Bruce's hands.[68] Beyond Ulster they lacked the capacity to take fortified centres, but their campaigns were not mindlessly destructive; they moved through the countryside, seeking to pick up native Irish support and inflicting damage in order to advertise their mastery and persuade members of the settler elite to throw in their lot with them. Famine conditions added an extra edge to their activities. Resistance on the part of the government and the magnates was hampered by shortage of funds, and by the difficulty of keeping together for any length of time lords from many parts of Ireland who had worries about Irish assaults on their own lands. None the less each movement of the Scots beyond Ulster was countered. In February–March 1316 and again in April–May 1317 they retreated north, starving. At length in 1318 a group of lords from Meath and Louth won the only conclusive victory that Edward II could celebrate anywhere in the British Isles during the twenty miserable years of his reign.

The campaign of 1317, when Robert Bruce was in attendance, shows what was possible and what was not for both sides.[69] Having come south, the Scots raided Castleknock and threatened Dublin, where the citizens fired part of the suburb and demolished buildings in order to reinforce the city walls. Just before this the Bruces had been in touch with disaffected elements in Wales;[70] it is conceivable that they hoped that panic might deliver Dublin into their hands and enable a real military alliance to emerge in a region where in the eleventh century Welsh and Irish leaders had often cooperated. But there was no way in which a siege could be mounted. The Scots did not control the countryside and would have been sitting targets for a relieving army; they did not have a fleet sufficient to invest the city by sea; the famine made it hard to remain in one place for long. Instead they withdrew south and west, ravaging the manors of Kildare, Kilkenny and Tipperary. Their goal had now become Thomond, where they had struck up an alliance with an excluded segment of the O'Briens. Their campaign displays many of the classic features of medieval warfare – in its tentative, probing character; in the avoidance of battles; in the infliction of damage on the opposing countryside; and in its ultimate dependence on the ability to exploit alliances.

The response of the Dublin government also falls into recognisable patterns. Edmund Butler, the justiciar, did not confront the Scots at an early stage, and seems to have assumed that Dublin could look after itself. Instead he headed for Cork and raised the southern counties where his own connections and a reservoir of military strength lay. Among the lords who became involved in the resistance were Maurice fitz Thomas, the future earl of Desmond, Richard de Clare, lord of Thomond, and Muircheartach O'Brien, who was actually in possession of Gaelic Thomond. The paymaster's account of the daily wages of the troops Butler hired enables us to track their movements. During March the Scots moved from Castledermot to Callan and then Cashel. The royal army dogged their footsteps: at one point Thomas Butler, the justiciar's brother, was sent with a detachment 'to shadow and harass' them. Towards the end of March the Bruces moved north towards Nenagh; the justiciar then rapidly rode into County Limerick, making his lordship of Caherconlish to the south of the city the centre of his operations, while the Scots camped at Castle-connell to the north. For some days the armies confronted each other, apparently without striking a blow. By mid-April the Scots were withdrawing, eventually reaching Ulster gravely weakened by hunger. The Dublin annals imply that the justiciar and magnates had shamefully failed to defeat the Bruces. The record of events indicates, rather, that Butler had been successful in mobilising the south of Ireland against the Scots, leaving them without options.

The withdrawal of Robert Bruce to Scotland in May 1317 was, with hindsight, the beginning of the end of the only focused challenge to the existence of the English lordship in these centuries. The Scottish invasion highlights many of the features that shaped warfare in Ireland: the regional character of the country, which made it easy to penetrate but difficult to control; the segmentation of Gaelic society, which rendered attempts to build a common front abortive; and the capacity of the crown to defend not merely the south-east but the whole area south of a line running from Dundalk to Limerick, Tralee and Cork. Dublin's authority weakened in the late fourteenth and early fifteenth centuries, and the dynamics of local politics and war grew increasingly autonomous. But even in 1450 its lines of command and influence, indirect as they often were, had not contracted to an embattled Pale.

Chapter 5

Gaelic warfare in
the Middle Ages

Katharine Simms

During the high middle ages in Ireland the single most important development in warfare was a constantly increasing reliance on mercenaries, men who made soldiering their sole occupation in life. With their more widespread employment came social acceptance and integration, so that the upper ranks of the professional soldiery became influential hereditary members of the Gaelic aristocracy.

Already from the eleventh century onwards we hear of one permanent fighting force at an Irish king's disposal that was recruited at least in part from his own vassal nobility, that is, the troops of his 'household' (*teaghlach, lucht tighe*). The annals show them as a formidable elite force always at hand to respond to unexpected raids, or in the case of a full-scale hosting, or general summons calling on the free landowning families to send men to the fight, the household could spearhead the attack of the less trained troops. The 'household' of a high-king might include a number of reigning sub-chiefs, and in the province of Connacht the title 'captain of the household' (*dux luchta tighe, taoiseach teaghlaigh*) was an important office hereditary in the Ó Taidhg family. There are grounds for comparing these aristocratic warriors with the knights found serving great lords elsewhere in Europe, particularly when we find the Annals of Connacht describing Stephen D'Exeter, of an Anglo-Irish baronial family, as fighting in the 'household' (*lucht tighe*) of Edmund Albanach Burke, lord of Mayo, in 1355. It is even possible that military service in an Irish king's household was linked to tenure of estates on the king's mensal lands since the word *lucht tighe* altered in meaning during the course of the fifteenth century from 'household troops' to 'mensal lands', and in the early seventeenth century the chieftains who occupied the *lucht tighe* or mensal lands of the Great O'Neill are described as his 'horsemen'.[1] Earlier in 1397 Count Ramon de Perellós, a Catalan pilgrim to Lough Derg, observed that the Great O'Neill had 'forty horsemen. They ride without a saddle on a cushion and each wears a cloak according to his rank. They are armed with coats of mail, and round iron helmets like the Moors and Saracens. Some of them are like the Bernese. They have swords and very long knives and long lances.'[2]

We need not assume that such a retinue was entirely made up of a king's 'natural subjects'. At the end of the sixteenth century Richard Stanihurst, the Dublin writer, tells us that horsemen who have no private means of subsistence 'gad and range from house to house like arrant knights of the round table'.[3] Already in the Middle Irish period (900–1200 AD) the legal commentaries have a phrase *carpat ar imram*, 'a wandering chariot', to describe a person who seems to be part of a new class in Irish society, freemen with cattle but no land, categorised in a tract of *c.* 1300 as 'chieftains without lordship, wealth or patrimony . . . the son and heir of a military vassal who possesses a herd, the kinsman of a sub-king or a chieftain who possesses nothing but a herd . . . they have jurisdiction over their own followers'. At least two such landless gentlemen, 'Doneghuth Orailly' and 'Donneghuth Ocoghegan', each with a military following, and certainly in 'Orailly's' case, a herd of cattle also, turn up in the records of the justiciar's court in the opening years of the fourteenth century. At different times each had entered the service or 'resided under the avowry' of an Irish chieftain and later an Anglo-Irish lord, grazing their cattle on the land of their protector for the time being. Under his Anglo-Irish patron 'Orailly' is said to have had the function of maintaining local order, being 'wont to repress the felons of his parts for the good of the peace'.[4] Such miscellaneous followers or adherents recruited at least in part from beyond the borders of the chief's own territory may be intended by the Latin expression *satellites*, 'followers, retinue' which is very commonly used in association with one of the variant terms *turbe, turbarii, turbales*, 'troops, troopers, kerne', to describe in Latin sources the forces of Irish chiefs and Anglo-Irish barons from the thirteenth to the fifteenth centuries.

The word *cethern*, 'a warband', appears already in Cormac's Glossary (*c.* 900 AD), where it is derived from words signifying 'battle' and 'slaughter'.[5] Early annal references may apply to war-parties composed of the fighting men of particular territories, as when the Annals of Tigernach record under the year 1101, 'The conflict in Clonmacnois of two bodies of footsoldiers (two *ceithernn*), namely, the Munter Thadgain and the Munter Chinaetha'. However by the opening years of the thirteenth century we are clearly dealing with bands of native Irish mercenaries, sometimes called *ceithirne congbhála*, 'retained bands'. The Anglo-Irish term 'kernes' was used to signify either the bands themselves, or individual members of such bands, the *ceithearnaigh*, a word that could almost be rendered 'bandits' rather than 'troopers', such was the horror and revulsion they seemed to inspire in the church and the learned classes. By the end of the sixteenth century the word *ceithearn* was popularly etymologised *cioth Ifrinn*, 'a shower of Hell'.[6]

Part of the explanation for this horror lay in the fact that at least during the thirteenth century such bands both in their behaviour and perhaps even in their physical appearance resembled the Old Irish *díberga* and *fianna*. In Old Irish sagas, saints' lives, homilies and legal material of the seventh and eighth centuries these two words are used interchangeably to describe an institution of pagan origins, whereby young unmarried nobles spent the years between the end of fosterage and the inheritance of their father's lands as devotees of a warrior cult, roaming the hills and woods, living by hunting and looting. They are described as wearing devilish tokens on their heads as signs that they had bound themselves by oath to kill a particular person or persons. Moreover, they engaged in noisy jubilation over the bodies of the slain, and they were notorious for raping any women they might come across. Such bands of youthful warriors could provide an elite back-up to the ordinary military hosting of a territory, and while most members eventually inherited land, married and settled down, some passed their lives as professional champions, employed by the rest of the population to avenge their wrongs, collect debts, enforce order at feasts and so forth. They were naturally abhorred by churchmen, who anathematised them as excommunicates, *maicc báis*, 'sons of death', or *latrones*, the Latin for 'brigands'. Perhaps as a result of this rejection by Christian authorities, the seventh-century warrior cults were associated with the last surviving druids.[7] More relevant to the present subject however is the question of their hairstyle, since they are described both as having a form of tonsure (*cendgelt*) and as wearing their back-hair long and plaited.[8]

In the year 1297 the Anglo-Irish parliament complained that in recent times degenerate Englishmen had taken to wearing Irish costume and that having their heads half-shaved, they grew their back-hairs long and called them 'culan'. Since they thus resembled Irishmen in both face and clothes they were often killed as such, although there were differing penalties for causing the death of Irishmen and Englishmen. As these misapprehensions often gave rise to feuds between the families of the slayer and the slain, the justiciar, sheriffs or local lords of such degenerate Englishmen were to compel them by confiscation of their goods or if necessary imprisonment to abandon Irish dress, or at least that they should no longer presume to turn back their hair in the culan.[9] Some modern writers have concluded that this legislation represented an intolerant attitude to the ordinary hairstyle of the native Irish and a hint that wild Irishmen found in the land of peace were liable to be attacked on sight without further parley.[10] However the Irish form of the mysterious term 'culan' or 'colan' was *cúlán*, as is attested by the nickname of a contemporary king, Niall *Cúlánach* O'Neill (d. 1291), and the fact that his hairstyle earned Niall this distinctive nickname suggests strongly that it was not a universal fashion for Irishmen in his time. If we conclude on the contrary that partially shaving the scalp and growing the back-hair long was a traditional quasi-berserker hairstyle affected by those whose lives were dedicated to rapine and murder, the high incidence of violent death among Englishmen who affected the style becomes self-explanatory, and also perhaps the anticipated difficulty for sheriff or overlord wishing to compel them to adopt a more civilised appearance.

Of course the actual pagan warrior cult of *díberg* had been extinct for centuries – there is a possible late reference to the practice in the Annals of Ulster under the year 847, but by the twelfth century the term *díbergach* could be applied as a general term of abuse to any conscienceless freebooter, and in 1176 the Annals of

---

Tigernach bracket both the Viking Turgesius and the Norman leader Strongbow under this heading. It was because memories of the real institution had grown so dim that men were able to transform the literature based on it to serve the aspirations of a new age. Before the tenth century *fiannaigecht*, legends about the *fian*-bands, centred around a number of heroic bands and Finn mac Cumaill was not yet represented as a national figure dominating the cycle of tales like a second King Arthur of Britain. In this early period the *fianna* are shown as roaming hunter-warriors, pagan and magical elements abound and the term *fianna* can be used interchangeably with *díberga*, the ritual brigands anathematised by the church. During the Middle Irish period (c. 900–1200), however, Finn and his companions begin to predominate, the *fianna* are unhistorically distinguished from the *díbergaig* and acquire steady employment as professional soldiers in the service of the high-kings.[11] *Tochmarc Ailbe*, one of the earliest of the *fiannaigecht* romances to be admitted to the official tale-lists of scholarly poets, typifies this transition. In the long poems it contains, which are of perhaps tenth-century date, Finn woos the high-king's daughter by promising her a roving, gypsy life, eating wild game by the blazing camp-fire, sleeping on a pile of birch leaves. In the accompanying prose narrative, somewhat later in date, we are told that Finn mac Cumaill's *fianna* were the kernes and household (troop) of the high-king, Cormac mac Airt. During a period of estrangement from Cormac, Finn had recruited his men from deserters and *díbergaig* outlawed by the king, and at the feast held after their reconciliation *fianna* and *díbergaig* were entertained together with their female companions in one group, being distinguished from kings and nobles on the one hand, and the ordinary non-combatants – hospitallers, youths and 'cowards' (*midlaig*) on the other. In the previous generation, we are told, Finn had served as *taísech cethirne*, 'captain of the kerne' to Cormac's father Art.[12] In another text of perhaps twelfth-century date Finn is described as Cormac's captain of the household, of the mercenaries and of the huntsmen (*táisech teglaig 7 amus 7 gilla con*).[13]

Georges Duby has spoken of the landless young knights of northern France in the twelfth century as an important part of the audience for the chivalric romances of the time which glorified their life-style and values.[14] It seems probable that the increased respectability and professionalism of Finn MacCumaill's image in high medieval romances reflects the ideals and aspirations of a rising class of landless nobles in military service to the Irish kings, men who are termed 'knights' in French or Latin ecclesiastical sources, as for instance the 'knight Owein', apparently in the service of King Diarmait MacMurrough, who acted as interpreter to Abbot Gilbert of Basingwerk c. 1151,[15] or the 'knight' Tnugdal of Cashel (fl. 1149) who

> was of a young age, of noble lineage, had a happy face and an elegant appearance; he had been brought up in the manner of the court, was carefully dressed, arrogant in spirit and not ill-trained in martial arts . . . He did not care about God's Church and did not even want to see Christ's poor. He gave away whatever he had to jesters, players and jugglers.[16]

———————

5.1   Gaelic soldiers, from Derricke's *Image of Ireland*, 1581.

It seems clear that this literature was not primarily aimed at the ordinary kerne. Like the kerne themselves, the original cultic warriors of the *fianna* were unambiguously foot-soldiers – when Finn woos Ailbe to join his roving life in the tenth-century poem, he promises her 'neither steeds nor chariots' and she opts for the fleet-footed creatures of the wild as against her father's race-horses[17] – but in a Fenian lay dated by Murphy to the late twelfth century, Ailbe arbitrates a dispute among the *fianna* by citing the principle 'to every warrior is due his good horse'.[18]

Chivalric literature on the continent of Europe evolved between about the years 1000 and 1200 with the changing status of the early feudal knights, from hired hands criticised by churchmen as 'pillagers without prowess'[19] into minor nobility. As a side effect of the eleventh-century religious revival bands of knights were assembled before bishops and made to swear oaths to observe the Peace of God, which would preserve church property, unarmed clergy and law-abiding peasants immune from the violence of their wars and feuds, and the Truce of God, binding participants not to make war on Sundays, and an ever increasing list of holy days and seasons throughout the church's year. Such cooperative knights might receive their arms with a ceremonial church blessing, and were encouraged especially by

103

the influential monks of Cluny to see themselves as bearing weapons in Christ's service, as *milites Christi*, 'warriors of Christ' in the practical sense as the monks themselves were in the spiritual sense.[20] A new image of knighthood as a vocation to bear arms in the service of God and in defence of the weak gradually penetrated the chivalric literature of the day as the lays and prose tales of strolling 'Breton' minstrels were superseded during the twelfth century by the more elaborate written compositions of secular clerics. By the thirteenth century some versions even show monastic influence and a pointed moral, as when in the case of Sir Galahad we find chastity represented as one of the prerequisites for perfect knighthood.[21]

Over the same period the transmission of *fiannaigecht* literature in Ireland came increasingly into the hands of clerical scholars, and the texts acquired a new moral dimension. There is a marked contrast between the early eleventh-century preface to the *Amra Choluim Chille* which mentions the composition of lying *fian*-stories among the sins of poets deplored by the church[22] and the full clerical acceptance of *fiannaigecht* symbolised in the major prose compendium *Accallam na Senórach*, 'the Colloquy of the Ancients' (?*c.* 12–13th century), by an opening scene where a few miraculously surviving heroes of the *fianna* are received and baptised by St Patrick. The 'thousand legions of demons' floating over their heads until that day were exorcised, and two angels commissioned Patrick to write down such tales of their adventures as the old men could still remember, 'for to the companies and nobles of the latter time to give ear to these stories will be for a pastime'.[23] The way was now open for *fiannaigecht* ballads and prose narratives to compete successfully against the romances of King Arthur and his Knights of the Round Table during the fourteenth, fifteenth and sixteenth centuries not only in the courts of the Gaelic chieftains but among the Anglo-Irish barons and earls as well,[24] incidentally setting a standard for chivalrous behaviour rather less demanding than that posed by Sir Galahad.

A code of honour there had to be, because clerical approval was only made possible by insistence on an unhistorical distinction between the heroic *fianna* and the execrated, anti-christian *díbergaig*, as set forth in O'Mulconry's Glossary: 'díberg, i.e. dí-bí-argg "non-be-hero", for he is not reckoned with heroism like the hero of the *fianna*, for denial of God and clientship of the Devil is not proper heroism'.[25] 'The Enumeration of Finn's Household', a text ascribed by Meyer to the twelfth century, states that it was a condition of admission to Finn's service, *as it was for Cúchulainn in his day*, not to engage in cattle-rustling, or violation (*sárugud* = violation of women, sanctuaries or guarantees), to refuse no one (his petition) for food or valuables, and not to flee before odds of less than ten to one.[26] Reckless bravery and inexhaustible generosity had long been, and were to remain indispensable ideals for the Gaelic nobility reflected not only in the literature of the later middle ages, but in historic chieftains' disregard for their personal safety in battle, in their lavish feasts and gift-giving.[27] On the other hand, the rape of women and the plundering of churches were both regarded as typical activities of the aristocratic *díbergaig* of yore[28] and it is significant that the bard lamenting the defeat and death of Brian O'Neill at the battle of Down in 1260 is careful to emphasise that his master conducted his warfare by the church's rules, making heaven's degree that he should meet with defeat and death doubly inexplicable:

> A poor man's cow was not brought to his house, he did not violate a priest's relic; what did he violate that the battle was routed? There is no church against which he was guilty.
>
> A horse with its ornate harness about its head, if it had come the length of Ireland, would have passed without a hand laid on its harness across Inis Fáil to Brian of Breagha.
>
> Under Brian's rule a woman would have walked from Sliabh Callainn to Coirrshliabh; travelling amongst the Irish is horrible to me since the hero of Ireland has departed.
>
> Ó Néill did not violate church privileges, he did not disobey the church; Brian's prosperity was swamped by heaven; to be religious after his death is difficult.[29]

This theme was not a mere poetic conceit. In 1233 the Annals of Connacht record the defeat and death of Áed, king of Connacht, and his brother Áed Muimnech with the words

> Aed Muimnech had violated the sanctuary of Tibohine and plundered it, and many other churches and sacred buildings had been plundered by them, so that they fell [by the hand of their enemies] to avenge the honour of the saints and churches of Connacht . . . Owen Guer and many other Galls [foreigners] were also killed there, all of whom had been cursed and excommunicated by the churchmen of Connacht.

This passage is part of a detailed narrative of the Norman conquest of Connacht emanating from the Premonstratensian Abbey of Loch Cé which shows little in the way of local patriotism, but a consistent condemnation of the horrors of a warfare which entailed not only attacks on churches, but the killing of women, children and unarmed peasants, the devastation of a once prosperous countryside and ensuing famine and plague. Much of the blame for atrocities is laid on the kernes and foreign mercenaries employed by all sides in the conflict, but the Norman leaders are singled out for due credit because they declared churches immune, and paid compensation or restored plunder when their underlings committed sacrilege, besides refraining from warfare on holy days.[30]

The fact that the Connacht chronicle twice refers to the early thirteenth-century warbands as 'kernes and sons of malediction' (*cetherna ⁊ meic mallachtan*) recalls the grouping of druid, *díberg* and *mac mallachta* as the three sinners said to be beyond salvation in the twelfth-century Life of Colmán son of Luachan. Moreover in Oirghialla, where Niall McMahon had recently replaced the O'Carroll dynasty presumably by military force, the statement that in 1206 the monastery of St Peter and Paul (?Knock, County Louth) was plundered by MacMahon's *latrones*

(*ladrannaib*), his 'bandits', also echoes ecclesiastical censures of the semi-pagan warrior cults of earlier times.[31]

This emphasis, however, on the miseries of warfare and the evil reputation of kernes in particular is not found in later years. One reason for this may be that Dominican and Franciscan friars had made a determined and largely successful effort to eliminate any actual paganism that may have lingered on in Irish society by the mid-thirteenth century.[32] At the same time Irish literature passed out of the hands of churchmen to the laity, to bardic poets and historians whose values reflected those of their patrons. Not a trace of outrage is shown by the poet-historian Seán Magrath in chronicling the 'Carnage of Clare' (c. 1278) in which the O'Brien and MacNamara victors: 'having taken so many as they got of [Cineál Dúnghaile's] men, their fair-haired women, their little boys and other members of their families, of their servants, kerne, horseboys and herdsmen, they made of them one universal litter of slaughter'.[33] In a later passage a band of kerne are presented in a heroic and selfless light. Having been trapped against the banks of the Shannon as they tried to escape with their prey, deserted by the Anglo-Norman auxiliaries, the 'household' troop slain, the chief himself, Maccon MacNamara, having escaped across the water in a small boat, the leaderless footsoldiers:

> elected a commanding officer (*tigerna*) and devoted themselves to giving and taking hurt; they made incredible slaughter of the enemy, and their main discontent was that he would not grapple, but from afar off picked them off with missiles. Each one of them according as he felt death upon him would in either hand carry to the Shannon's brink a head to hold up and show to his noble lords, then heave them from him to sink in the abyss, and on the bank undismayed breathe out his own life afterwards. One after another perpetually they appointed over themselves a 'master of the pack' (*taisech cuanairte*) to head them, until at last it was a commander of but six good men that handled them.[34]

'The Triumphs of Turlough', the mid-fourteenth-century text from which these extracts are taken, recounts the wars of King Toirdhealbhach Mór O'Brien (d. 1306) and his sons against rival kinsmen and against the Anglo-Norman lords of Thomond in the same vein of mixed history, entertainment and panegyric in which Jean Froissart chronicled the campaigns of the Hundred Years War. However the Irish author's treatment is distinguished not only by heroic visions and portents that appear to the chief protagonists, such as the loathsome hag washing bloodstained armour in a stream, that foretold imminent defeat and death to de Clare before the Battle of Dysert O'Dea, but also by the ferocity of his battle scenes which include dying warriors, with both arms lopped off, attempting to chew off their opponents' noses, and the routine stacking and counting of decapitated heads after each conflict. Magrath found native Irish models for his undertaking in the Brian Boru saga, *Cogad Gaedel re Gallaib* and in the *Cath Cathardha*, the Irish version of Lucan's *Bellum Civile*. This use of literary models presents certain problems for the historian. Potentially the 'Triumphs of Turlough' is a mine of information on tactics

---

and strategy, but when it tells us that an early fourteenth-century Irish chief prepared for pitched battle by grouping the main force under his own command in the centre, with a wing (*sciathán*) extending forwards on either side to attack the enemy's flanks, are we to see in this merely an echo of Pompey's division of his army into three parts in the *Cath Cathardha*, with a large group under his personal command in the rear and two cavalry divisions forming a right and left wing (*eiti*) in front?[35]

Other details given, however, inspire greater confidence since they correspond with what is recorded elsewhere of Irish warfare. The units of command both on the battlefield and when marshalling trains of migrants displaced by the fighting were the *airechta*, the territorial councils formed of the noble landowners in each sub-chieftaincy, under the leadership of their dynastic heads. Such territorial levies are described as composed of chieftains, non-noble landowners (*brughadha*), youths and more generally, 'kindreds' (*cineadha*),[36] but they were reinforced by specialists. The chiefs' 'households' play a prominent part at all times, and while the ordinary footsoldiers, as in the first days of the Norman invasion, used throwing-darts and sling-stones, the horsemen were clearly equipped with coats of mail, helmets, swords and spears in the manner of the Great O'Neill's cavalry mentioned earlier.[37] There are interesting indications that when engaged in a pitched battle the horsemen might dismount, as had been the practice in Viking warfare. In 1309, we are told, the Irish nobles serving Donnchadh O'Brien 'handed over to their horseboys their horses to lead them to the rear, pursuant to their resolve that never would they desert their chief', and later on the narrative refers incidentally to Mathghamhain O'Brien 'who on this occasion had not dismounted from his horse to take part in the fight'.[38]

However most campaigns took the form of plundering and harrying raids, and here horsemen had a key role to play, either escorting the trains of fugitives out of the combat zone, or covering the rear of a successful preying party. In each case the lightly armed kerne were chiefly used to herd the cattle which constituted the main source of wealth in this society, while the real fighting fell to the share of the comparatively small numbers of cavalry. Just how small a number might bear the brunt of the battle in such cases is well illustrated by this account of a campaign by Toirdhealbhach Mór O'Brien in 1281:

> Lustily his people shouted round about, bringing dismay upon homesteads, harshly giving to their enemies a chilly rousing out. From the westernmost side of the country they drove its cattle to meet that of the eastern; on the flanks of the massed droves they formed a prickly palisade of spears, and to cover them in the rear had a clump of red ensigns with a troop of horsemen; their common kerne and camp-followers they assigned to drive them as hard as might be . . . In all directions the gentlemen of the neighbouring coasts rose out to attack them; and so before long the pursuers in number became more than the pursued . . . Then it was that Cumea MacConmara, as he brought up the rear of the close-packed prey, delivered himself

thus boldly: that he had with him but nine riders, and nevertheless in all open ground would so fend the pursuit from off his people, as that neither servitor nor kern nor gentlemen of descent should be killed, wounded or taken, if they for their part would but see him safe over broken land and through the strait places. Their clause of the contract the others took on them to perform, and into Echtge thus they brought the multitudinous droves in safety.[39]

Sometimes these bands of cavalry were reinforced by armoured footsoldiers. Since the campaigns described in the 'Triumphs of Turlough' took place in Munster during the late thirteenth and early fourteenth centuries, there is no mention here of the Scottish galloglass who were already playing an important military role in north Connacht and Ulster by this date, but a very similar function was fulfilled by regiments of Anglo-Norman or Welsh auxiliaries serving with the Irish kings as political allies or simple mercenaries. Such a regiment was termed by the Irish a *rúta* (from the French *route*) and an individual Welsh or English mercenary a *seirseanach* (perhaps from the French *sergent*). Like the galloglass these men are referred to as wearing armour and wielding battle-axes.[40]

In 1313, according to 'The Triumphs of Turlough', King Muircheartach O'Brien was assisted by 'William Burke's route'.[41] This could be an early reference to MacQuillin's Route, a band of mercenaries about whom we know or can reconstruct rather more than usual. The 'William Burke' in question was certainly Sir William *Liath* de Burgh, cousin to Richard de Burgh the 'Red Earl' of Ulster. The *rúta* may well have been the troop of 200 *seirseanaigh*, also described as a retained band (*cethern*) or billeted soldiers or 'bonaghts' (*buannaidhe*) under the command of Johnock (Seonac) MacQuillin, who took service with Sir William de Burgh in 1310, having been bribed to assassinate their former employer, Aodh Breifneach O'Conor. Thereafter, the annals tell us, William de Burgh billeted these 200 men on the Irish of Roscommon, and there was a 'bonaght' quartered on every townland as long as he retained control of the area. If this Johnock MacQuillin is to be identified with 'John Howelin' one of the military commanders brought from Connacht by Sir William de Burgh to serve against the Leinster Irish in 1310,[42] he was probably of Welsh extraction. Johnock was killed with his own axe in 1311, but subsequently Richard de Burgh, the Red Earl, appointed William MacQuillin as commander of his 'bonaght' or troop of billeted soldiers in Ulster. In 1323 hereditary command of these men was conferred on the seneschal of Ulster, Sir Henry de Mandeville, but later on in November 1331, after de Mandeville was found to be involved in treasonable conspiracy against the Red Earl's grandson, Earl William de Burgh, Stephen MacQuillin bound himself to the earl in the sum of £200 for the office of 'constable of the bonaght'. Because the grant to Henry de Mandeville had been hereditary, the historian Edmund Curtis concluded that the MacQuillins were a branch of the de Mandeville family,[43] but there is no real evidence to support this theory.

Two years later Earl William's worst fears were realised when he was assassinated by the de Mandevilles. The royal inquisition as to the extent of the earl's lands and

5.2 Harry Avery's Castle, County Tyrone, a pre-plantation castle said to
be named after Énri Aimhréidh Ó Néill who died in 1392. This widely
accepted late fourteenth century date makes it
one of the earliest castles built by a native Irish chief.

rights on the day of his death showed that the 'bonaght of Ulster' now amounted to
345 soldiers, billeted on the Irish chiefs of Ulster in peacetime at a cost of about £1
a year each for food and wages, but permanently available to serve the earl's needs
in time of war, so that MacQuillin's Route could be described as Ireland's first
approximation to a regiment or brigade in the modern sense. The inquisition states
that the former rights of 'bonaght' had become unenforceable as a result of the
rebellion and war that broke out at the earl's death, and this institution was never
to be revived in its original form, but the constable Stephen MacQuillin and his
soldiers did not vanish overnight. Apparently he hired himself out to the Great
O'Neill of Tyrone, who took over the earl's practice of forcing the Irish chiefs of
Ulster to maintain his 'bonaght'. A part of the evidence pointing to this conclusion
is that in 1350 MacQuillin is listed as one of the king's enemies and rebels,
attacking the county of Louth in company with the Great O'Neill; also the annals
still describe Stephen MacQuillin as 'constable of the province of Ulster' at the time
of his death in 1368; and in a treaty made with the Anglo-Irish government in 1390,
the chief Niall Mór O'Neill undertook to 'yield back and not to intermeddle with the
bonnaughe of Ulster'.[44] Within five years of this latter date, however, Seinicín Mór,

the new head of the MacQuillin family, is referred to as the 'man' of Edmund Savage, the seneschal of Ulster, warring against Magennis and O'Cahan, the Irish chiefs on the frontier of the earldom. It may have been as vassals of the Savage family that the MacQuillins were first given estates in north county Antrim, where the new lordship they founded here acquired the name 'MacQuillin's Route', presumably because it was colonised by the mercenaries under MacQuillin's command.[45] The genealogies of MacFirbhisigh describe this Seinicín Mór as the first of his family to use the name 'MacQuillin' as a title, signifying chieftainship, and from the fifteenth century onwards the MacQuillins figure as political rulers rather than mercenaries. The Great O'Neill continued meanwhile to exact the 'Bonaght of Ulster', but by this time it had become known as 'MacDonnell's bonaght', and the office of 'High Constable of the Province of Ulster' was held by Scottish galloglass captains, members of the Clann Alexander MacDonnell, from the 1360s.

Already in the eleventh and twelfth centuries the most powerful Irish kings imported Hebridean-Norse mercenaries from the Western Isles of Scotland, whether in regiments to serve in a particular campaign, or in smaller numbers to act as king's bodyguard. Such men enjoyed a privileged status in Irish society; an insult or offence against a king's foreign mercenary incurred the same fines as an attack on the king himself.[46] Diarmait MacMurrough's decision to switch to employing Cambro-Norman knights precipitated the Norman invasion, discussed elsewhere in this volume, and for a brief period in the early thirteenth century men from the Western Isles seemed about to join in the conquest and colonisation of Ireland. During his quarrel (c. 1210–26) with Hugh de Lacy the younger, first earl of Ulster, King John granted away the northern coast of Ireland from Derry to the Glens of Antrim to Thomas, earl of Athol, and his brother Alan of Galloway. In 1211–12 when one of the famous 'sons of Somhairle' from whom the MacDougalls, MacDonnells and MacRorys descend assisted Thomas of Athol in raiding Derry and Inishowen with a view to conquest, Domhnall Mór O'Donnell, the king of Tír Conaill, joined forces with them,[47] presumably to forward his own long-term ambition to annex Inishowen. The plantation project was aborted by the earl of Ulster's restoration to favour, but when in 1247 Domhnall Mór's son Maoileachlainn O'Donnell was killed in the Battle of Ballyshannon vainly defending his kingdom from invading Anglo-Normans, the annals tells us that 'Mac Somhairle, king of Argyle' died fighting at his side.

For the rest of the thirteenth century military cooperation between the Irish chiefs and the islanders retained this aspect of political alliance in addition to mercenary service. In 1259 the Connacht prince, Aodh son of Feidhlim O'Conor, acquired a troop of 160 fighting men as dowry with the daughter of Dubhghall MacRory, king of the Hebrides. Similarly Domhnall Óg O'Donnell (d. 1281) contracted marriage alliances with MacSweeny of Castle Sween and MacDonnell of the Isles whose kinsmen and followers were the main source of galloglass (*gallóglaigh* = 'foreign warriors') in Ireland at that time. From the point of view of the Ulster kinglets,

5.3 Three gallowglasses, with swords and chainmail, on the O'Connor
tomb, Roscommon Abbey (late fifteenth century).

strenuously defending their patrimonies against the expanding power of Richard de
Burgh, the Red Earl, the arrival of Edward Bruce and his army of Scots at Larne in
1315 was a logical extension of their political alliances with the men of the Isles.
However by this date independent bands of Scottish mercenaries were being widely
employed by the northern chiefs on a purely professional basis. O'Neill, MacMahon,
Maguire and O'Reilly are all recorded as using their services, and during the Bruce
invasion itself we know of the activities of at least one galloglass troop serving
O'Donnell's wife which was quite unconnected to the main Scots army.[48] Indeed,
King Robert the Bruce's victory in the Scottish war of independence, which was also
a civil war, created many landless nobles among the losers, and as pointed out
earlier, landless nobles were pre-eminently the class from which elite armoured
retainers were recruited. It was as political exiles that the Clan Alexander
MacDonnells came to serve the Great O'Neill in the mid-fourteenth century.[49]

The traditional history of the MacSweeny family insists that they like the other galloglass originally operated as free-lances: 'no lord had a claim on them for a rising-out or a hosting, but they might serve whomsoever they wished. It was the Scottish habit (of military service) they had observed . . . namely each man according as he was employed.'[50] During the course of the fourteenth century, however, the various families of galloglass leaders became associated with particular lordships, and acquired an honourable and financially secure position within Irish society. MacDonnell Gallóglach was not merely supported by O'Neill's exaction of 'bonaght' from the other Ulster chiefs, but received estates of land in north Armagh and south Tyrone; MacCabe received tax-free lands from Maguire in Fermanagh, and was also employed by McMahon and O'Rourke. Between the fourteenth and the sixteenth centuries the MacSweenys rose to occupy three sub-chieftaincies within O'Donnell's lordship of Tír Conaill and had also spread to Connacht and Munster, where they were joined in the fifteenth century by the MacSheehys. By the late fifteenth century the earl of Kildare was quartering galloglass in the Dublin Pale,[51] though how many of the rank and file of such troops were still of Scottish extraction must remain a matter for speculation.

In principle, however, the galloglass were officered by their own chieftains and nobles. This may be one reason why they seem to have enjoyed a better reputation for discipline than the kerne. They are described by Richard Stanihurst as 'commonly wayward rather by profession than by nature, grim of countenance, tall of stature, big of limme, burly of body, wel and strongly timbered, chiefly feeding on beefe, porke and butter'.[52] Medieval tomb sculptures show them armoured like the horse-men with round helmets, collar-pieces and coats of mail or padded leather jacks, wielding pole-axes or lances and great two-handed swords.[53] Like the horsemen, they were commonly stationed at the rear of a plundering party to beat off the pursuit, but since they were slower moving than the cavalry, it seems they might be placed in ambush at some point along a prearranged route by which the marauders proposed to withdraw with their plunder, so that they could step in and block the way when the cavalry found themselves hard-pressed. Thus in 1416 the Annals of Connacht report: 'O Ruairc's sons were in great distress until they reached their gallowglasses . . . But when they reached them both parties turned upon the pursuers and killed . . . forty-eight of the Fir Manach.'[54] Similarly in 1419, according to the same source, the galloglass's function was to provide a defensive shelter for the retreating nobility: 'The Connacht horsemen were hurled back towards their gallowglasses, but these held their ground and fought on.'[55]

Apart from their tactical deployment in the battlefield, the long-term main-tenance of substantial retinues of heavily-armed soldiers by the major chieftains led in the second half of the fourteenth century to the garrisoning of castles by the Irish. At first these were castles leased or captured from the shrinking Anglo-Irish colony, but soon the chieftains were building their own. For instance, Niall Garbh O'Donnell (d. 1439) erected the castle of Ballyshannon in the year 1423 to guard the ford over the river Erne which had hitherto been used by the O'Conors Sligo when

---

Two types of body-armour worn by native Irish

5.4   Padded leather jack on effigy of
O'Cahan at St Mary's Abbey,
Dungiven (late fifteenth century).

5.5   Plate armour on effigy of Malachy
MacOwny O'More (1502),
Abbey Leix House, County Laois.

5.6 Two gallowglasses, with sword, axe and chainmail, on the O'Connor tomb, Roscommon Abbey (late fifteenth century).

invading his kingdom of Tír Conaill, and a bardic poet celebrates the wisdom of this measure: 'Till the hawk of Srubh Broin had built this tower opposite Áth Seanaigh, he kept busy at the work all the while, fighting for his province.' As ambitious as any of his sixteenth-century descendants, in 1428 Niall Garbh even planned to besiege and capture Carrickfergus castle, the last bastion of English power in Ulster, and for this purpose imported 'a great multitude of Scots' in addition to his own forces. This appears to be the first recorded use of seasonal Scots mercenaries or 'redshanks' who, because they did not need to be provided with long-term maintenance like the hereditary gallóglass captains, could be brought over for short periods in much larger numbers, in thousands rather than hundreds. They were to transform the scale of Irish warfare during the Tudor reconquest, but there was a price to be paid for their services, both literally and politically, a price paid at the expense of the subjects rather than their lords. An unusual bardic poem addressed to this same Niall Garbh reveals that there was resentment within his kingdom at the heavy taxation levied in support of his military establishment, and the expenditure is justified not only as ensuring the country's defence against external enemies, but also as guaranteeing internal law and order:

> Though the son of Toirrdhealbhach seems oppressive to you, his country is the better for the restraining of its evil-doers. Anything that does not please the descendant of Eochu, he has only to say 'Avoid that'.

> Peace has been made with the Irish host, the threat of plunder by the English is far removed; if a cow were left out in the open for a year, it is only necessary to search for her (and she will be found).[56]

The implication that importing mercenary armies increased the control exercised by a prince over his own people foreshadows Sir Nicholas Malby's comment in sixteenth-century Connacht: 'If any principal lord or chief of a country be ill dealt withal by his own freeholders and such as dwell under him . . . the said lords were wont for suppressing such to entertain Scots and kerne and galloglas.'[57] Subjects felt dominated not merely by the arbitrary power of the lord himself, but by the individual mercenary soldiers billeted in their houses, as may be deduced from the fact that the Irish word *ceithearnach* or 'kerne' came to mean 'a bully', 'a tyrant' or even 'a yeoman (of 1798)' in later language.[58] The hostility felt by the peasantry seems to have been returned. With the end of the Nine Years War (1603) and the general imposition of Common Law throughout Ireland under King James, private armies and private wars were banned. Freed at last from the burdensome imposition of military billeting, the peasants aspired to independence, prosperity and education for their children, whereas the kernes and the bardic poets who had celebrated their warlike deeds found themselves unemployed, even social outcasts. It was against this background that a disgruntled Munster author wrote in the early seventeenth century that peasants 'are known as the infernal shower, and not the company of kerns; for a company of kerns', he added nostalgically, 'is so called by reason of its edges of prowess and encounter and of razor-sharp weapons'.[59]

Chapter 6

The Tudors and the origins of the modern
Irish states: a standing army

Steven G. Ellis

On the eve of the Tudor conquest, the character of warfare in Ireland was still to a large extent shaped by the geographical and cultural divisions created by the earlier, medieval phase of English settlement there. The Norman invasion had failed to turn the whole island into 'a smaller England across the Channel'.[1] Yet in the southern and eastern lowlands the introduction by the Norman barons of large numbers of English tenants to underpin their military conquest had led to the creation of a viable English lordship in those areas. When in turn the tide of Gaelic revival had enveloped the outlying tentacles of English settlement and swept away English claims to feudal overlordship, there still remained in the fertile river valleys of Leinster and south Munster a recognisably English society whose traditions and values were those of the motherland. The very existence of the English of Ireland was of course a major reason for the border warfare which typified later medieval Ireland, and their loyalties and outlook were to alter considerably under the strains of the Tudor conquest. Nonetheless it was chiefly these Englishmen and their Tudor successors, rather than the Gaelic peoples, who built up in the island the traditions of military service to the state which are now exemplified in such units as An Fórsa Cosanta Áitiúil in the Republic of Ireland and the Royal Irish Regiment in Northern Ireland.

After the French conquest of Gascony and Normandy (1449–53), the lordship of Ireland and the far north of England shared the distinction of being the only regions of the English state with extended land frontiers. By about 1500, the lordship stretched over about a third of Ireland, and comprised two substantial blocks of territory, plus a number of outlying seaport towns like Carrickfergus and Galway. In the east, there were the four shires of the English Pale – Louth, Meath, Dublin and Kildare – over which the Dublin government exercised a fairly close control; whilst in the south, and linked to the Pale by the narrow corridor of the king's highway down the Barrow valley through County Carlow, lay seven more shires – Kilkenny, Wexford, Waterford, Tipperary, Cork, Limerick and Kerry – over which the supervision of the Dublin government was less effective. Thus few parts of the Englishry lay very far from the Irishry, and even Dublin was vulnerable to Gaelic raids.

English Ireland was indeed 'a highly regional land, of many marches'.[2] Although the boundaries between English and Gaelic Ireland were very different from the present border between the two Irish states, and were indeed quite fluid, the proximity of the frontier influenced medieval society in a similar way as 'the loyal English lieges' struggled to protect their embattled communities from constant Gaelic raids.

Not surprisingly, people thought easily in military terms, and tall men were at a premium. Asked if he had known Nicholas Travers of Corkelagh (d. 1486), Sir William Darcy of Platten remembered in 1517 that he had been invited to his wedding thirty-five years earlier, 'at the which time, the said Nicholas was as tall a man as ever he was and the best & strongest archer that was at that marriage. And at the least, to the said Sir William's remembrance, there was xl [forty] good bows there.'[3] As in England, the king's subjects were required to keep weapons appropriate to their status and degree, and all able-bodied men between the ages of 16 and 60 were obliged to do military service for the defence of their country. The conditions of this service were laid down in a series of increasingly detailed regulations.

> Every man, having goods to the value of 10 li. [£10] shall have an English bow & sheaf of arrows . . . Every lord, knight & squire shall have for every yeoman in his house, jack [= leather coat], sallet [= helmet], bow & arrows . . . And who that cannot shoot, shall have such weapon as he can handle or occupy.

The leading gentry and nobles of each county were appointed keepers of the peace and commissioners of array to make regular musters of the king's subjects and to take command of those with horse and harness 'at every great need, when any of the king's enemies shall enter or invade the country'.[4] In Ireland, moreover, landlords were required by statute to maintain at least one mounted archer with an English longbow for every £20 worth of land which they held.[5] And in some parts, such as the Dublin marches in 1461, a local tax called Smokesilver was levied 'to defray the charge of the watchmen or ward' maintained 'for the better preservation & custody of the country & to resist the king's Irish enemies & rebels thereof'.[6] At need, the governor could raise a substantial force of 1,000 men or more by proclaiming a hosting. General hostings against particular Gaelic chiefs were usually proclaimed once or twice a year and lasted for a maximum of forty days, but the power of a particular shire might also be assembled for 'sudden roads and journeys' lasting a week or less. And until the 1530s, those feudal tenants who held their land by knight service were sometimes called upon to pay scutage, no doubt in order to hire additional troops.

Thus, the English lordship was a society organised for war and accordingly the local community took great pride in its military traditions. Its armies invoked the assistance of St George, whose feast day provided the occasion for one of Dublin's two main annual pageants – the other was on Corpus Christi Day – and in 1474, when a small standing force of 160 men known as the Brotherhood of Arms was established, it seemed natural that the Brotherhood should likewise be dedicated to the patron saint of England. At the battle of Knockdoe in 1504, when the earl of Kildare wished to place the galloglass in the vanguard of his army on the grounds that 'it is less force of their losses than it is of our young men', Lord Howth counselled against this: 'we will not hazard our English goods upon Irish blood'.[7] In encounters with Gaelic troops, moreover, this pride seemed more than justified. English bills and bows still enjoyed a formidable reputation in Europe, where the lordship had played some role in the final stages of the Hundred Years War with France (1337–1453): Thomas Butler, prior of Kilmainham, and John Talbot, earl of Shrewsbury and Waterford ('the English Achilles') had died there. By contrast, Gaelic weapons and tactics were outmoded. They lacked the equipment to conduct a successful siege of a major Norman castle like Trim or Carrickfergus, although they were responsible for building or razing many of the small peles, or tower-houses, which were characteristic of the military architecture of this period. Their horsemen rode without stirrups and were therefore unable to couch a lance: instead they carried javelins overarm. Their kerne wore no armour, and the bows they carried were only half the length of English longbows and correspondingly less penetrative. Only the professional galloglass enjoyed any kind of reputation. Not surprisingly, the Book of Howth observed laconically of the kerne shipped to England and slaughtered at the battle of Stoke in 1487 that 'the Irish men did as well as any naked men would do'; forty years later Chief Baron Finglas boasted that 'in all my days, I never heard that a hundred footmen n[or] horsemen of Irishmen would abide to fight so many Englishmen'.[8]

Thus in a pitched battle English troops had all the advantages, but in practice the military balance in late medieval Ireland came close to stalemate. The reason for this was the topography of the respective English and Gaelic districts, and the fact that the government gave the Irish theatre of operations such a low priority. The heavily wooded, marshy or mountainous country which typified Gaelic Ireland was much less suitable for English troops than the coastal plains and river valleys which constituted the heart of the lordship. The longbow was better suited to open country. In Ireland English armies relied chiefly on light cavalry, especially hobelars – 'small light horses after the use off the middle marches foranempst Scotland, for the ground is soft and all mosses so that great horses will not serve'.[9] Mounted archers and spearmen were thus preferred to the demi-lances of continental campaigns, and even then they could not always follow the small native horses. These problems had long been recognised by the government, which regularly employed contingents of Gaelic troops, but many governors got into difficulties because of their unfamiliarity with the difficult terrain of Gaelic parts. Gaelic chiefs were very adept at exploiting the local terrain: large armies found no-one to fight, or faced a series of ambushes, and small armies were beaten. As with the border surnames of the Anglo-Scottish marches, the Dublin government found it hard to penetrate the fastnesses of the clansmen and defeat them militarily, although their

---

6.1   Successful return of English force after the defeat of the Irish kerne,
from Derricke's *Image of Ireland*, 1581.

frequent but petty raiding rarely challenged English rule and was mostly confined
to a campaigning season which lasted from Easter to Michaelmas. In fact most of
the border chieftaincies were poor and weak, and raiding was an important source
of income to them: some clans like the O'Tooles probably survived largely by
preying on their wealthier lowland neighbours.

   Until 1534, most of the armies raised for the defence of the lordship were
scratch levies diverted from their usual occupations for a few days or weeks of
campaigning. In consequence, when a major military effort was mounted, other
business was neglected. In June 1495, for instance, no business was transacted at
the quarterly assembly of the citizens of Dublin 'because the mayor, bailiffs, and
many of the citizens and commons were at Waterford, in Munster, on a hostile
expedition with Sir Edward Poynings, the king's deputy'.[10] And throughout July
1521 Undertreasurer Stile was unable to supply the king with urgent information
about the state of the Irish revenues because 'the officers and clerks be so occupied
in the hosting gone forth' with Lord Lieutenant Surrey against O'Carroll and
O'Connor 'that almost no man is left at home'.[11] Governors were obliged by the
terms of their commission to maintain a small bodyguard: the minimum was
traditionally twenty men-at-arms to be paid for out of a salary of £500 per annum,
but particularly in the period 1361–1478, and occasionally thereafter, governors
often maintained much larger retinues, for which they were paid correspondingly
more. On his return to Ireland as deputy-lieutenant in 1479, for instance, the earl of
Kildare undertook to 'have continually during the said time with him, and for the
safeguard and keeping of the same, iiij^{xx} [80] yeomen abled archers and xl [40]

other horsemen called spears', to be paid for out of his salary of £600 a year.[12] Forces of 200 or 300 archers were not unusual, and three governors brought small armies with them from England – Sir John Tiptoft, earl of Worcester (1467–70), 700 archers; Sir Edward Poynings (1494–5), 653 archers and gunners; and Thomas Howard, earl of Surrey (1520–2), 500 horsemen and yeomen. The governor's retinue thus formed a professional nucleus for many of the hostings against the Irish. Kerne and galloglass were often hired for these campaigns too, such as the 100 kerne and the galloglass retained by Sir James Ormond in 1496 after the departure of Sir Edward Poynings. And from c. 1500 Kildare maintained a permanent retinue of 120 galloglass and 120 kerne for the defence of his estates and in connection with his military duties as governor. Yet in all these cases, the retinue or army was associated with a particular governor, and when the governor was recalled the troops were disbanded.

Hostings against the Irish were a recurrent feature of life in the lordship. Most were organised in connection with the defence of the English Pale, but sometimes more distant parts were visited: between 1495 and 1510, for instance, the governor visited Carlow, Carrickfergus, Cork, Galway and Athenry, Kilkenny, Limerick and Waterford in connection with hostings. Moreover, in addition to military operations against the Irish, the exigencies of English politics prompted a number of important military expeditions to and from England during the period. During the so-called Wars of the Roses (c. 1455–97), the Yorkists and Lancastrians regarded control of Ireland as a valuable prize because of its strategic location and ready supply of troops. The founder of the Yorkist dynasty, Richard duke of York, was also lieutenant of Ireland (1447–60) and the most powerful Irish landowner. The lordship was thus heavily involved in York's invasions of England in 1450 and 1460. And in 1487, after the coronation of Lambert Simnel as King Edward VI in Christ Church cathedral, Dublin, the Yorkist army which landed near Furness in Lancashire included 2,000 German mercenaries and large numbers of Gaelic kerne. Conversely, the attempts to seize and control the lordship on behalf of the Lancastrian and, later, Tudor interest led to expeditions to Ireland in 1462, 1488 and 1491–4. Unlike the period after 1361, however, when expeditions to Ireland had aimed primarily at consolidating English control against the resurgent Gaelic lordships, the military expeditions of the later fifteenth century were directed chiefly at restoring royal authority within the lordship. By the Yorkist period, indeed, the lordship was militarily self-sufficient, and this situation continued effectively down to 1534.

In 1534, however, there occurred a major rebellion which shook English rule in Ireland to its foundations and which can be seen, in retrospect, as prompting the establishment there of a standing royal army and, with it, the further development of a distinct Irish military tradition. Henry VIII responded to the revolt by dispatching the largest expedition to Ireland since the visit of Richard II in 1399. And in many ways the campaign of 1534–5 set the pattern for later campaigns prompted by growing unrest and rebellion in Ireland as the Tudors struggled to extend their authority throughout the island. In addition, the changed political circumstances in the aftermath of the revolt led to the consolidation in power of a new group of military men, known to historians as the New English, whose influence in military administration laid the foundations for their later emergence as a landowning elite in Ireland. Since so many of the problems which emerged in the expedition and campaign of 1534–5 were to be repeated in the campaigning later in the century, the episode is perhaps worth more extended consideration than it has yet received from historians.

The lack of a standing army was a notorious weakness in the machinery for policy enforcement available to Tudor governments. It rendered the regime more vulnerable to popular uprisings, made it more dependent on great regional magnates like Kildare for raising levies of their tenants, and forced it to rely more on *ad hoc* administrative arrangements in equipping and supplying such armies as it put in the field. Not surprisingly, therefore, there remained in this sphere a particularly wide gap between planning and enforcement. Most notably, the difficulties of communication, of arranging adequate victualling, and of ensuring adequate training and equipment for the scratch levies commonly recruited meant that sickness, desertion, and demoralisation were frequently more formidable foes than the enemy in the field. In consequence, Tudor armies functioned less than efficiently, although probably no less so than their continental counterparts.

These remarks apply most immediately of course to the well-known campaigns of the period, in France and Scotland; the major internal disturbances, when royal armies were needed to crush rebellions like those in Norfolk and the West Country in 1549, rarely lasted long enough to expose the shortcomings of the administrative arrangements for transport and the supply of food and weapons. Yet neither expeditions to France nor to Scotland exposed the full range of the government's problems – in the one theatre because campaigns there were a prestige event, attracting leading courtiers and willing cooperation against the ancient adversary; in the other because invasions of Scotland were commonly extended border raids which could draw on standing arrangements for border defence. Technically, the 1534–5 campaign in Ireland was a response to an internal rebellion within the Tudor state. Yet the revolt took fourteen months to suppress, in part because the lordship was geographically separate from England and because the rebels also won considerable support in Gaelic Ireland. What in 1534 was an unusual range of problems was to become a recurring feature of Tudor campaigns in Ireland.

The lordship had always been a distinctly secondary concern to the Tudors, and such problems as arose were usually delegated to a local noble. Yet the 1534 rebellion was engineered by Gerald Fitzgerald, ninth earl of Kildare, the very lord who normally represented the crown as governor, and it was centred on the heart of the English interest in Ireland, the Pale. In addition, its leader, Thomas Lord Offaly (who succeeded his father as tenth earl of Kildare in September) astutely represented the rising as a response to Henry VIII's ecclesiastical policies rather than the political reaction of a discontented noble which it actually was. Ireland was of course too far from the centre of power to pose a serious direct challenge to the government, but there was a danger that some politically more important area might be encouraged to follow the lordship's lead. Thus the circumstances of the rebellion, occurring from an unexpected quarter at a critical time for general acceptance of the revolutionary changes associated with the Tudor Reformation, ruled out compromise and demanded a vigorous and speedy response. In other respects, however, the difficulties involved in organising a relief army for Ireland did not appear too formidable. By 1534 the government was well aware that its religious policies were provoking widespread discontent, and it had already taken appropriate steps to guard against popular rebellion or foreign invasion. *Inter alia*, these included orders for repairing and putting in order the king's ships, ordnance and munitions, coastal fortresses and beacons, while measures had been taken for the defence of the far north, Wales and Ireland.[13] Thus although the government was heavily committed in other respects, the Irish campaign was in fact a very fair test of the regime's military capacity and preparedness.

In the event, Lord Offaly's resignation as vice-deputy and formal defiance of the king at a meeting of the Irish council on 11 June 1534 marked the first act of rebellion. Yet it was only from mid-July, following the news of Earl Gerald's arrest in London on 29 June, that the rebels made serious efforts to win control of the Pale. These efforts culminated in the murder of Archbishop Alen of Dublin on 27 July and the siege of the city. In response to the first reports of the rising, the government complacently continued its preparations for the dispatch of Sir William Skeffington, the governor designate, with a retinue of 150 men. The imperial ambassador, Eustace Chapuys, reported that it showed little urgency in the matter. Skeffington's retinue of 100 mounted archers and 50 foot, although now grossly inadequate, was taken into pay from 19 July, and his ordnance was ready in London awaiting transport to Chester.[14] Yet before the end of the month, the king had changed his mind and the government began to exhibit signs of panic. Skeffington was appointed lord deputy of Ireland for life on 30 July – an extraordinary departure from early Tudor policy of curbing the autonomy of its officials in outlying parts – and a relief army of 1,500 men was decided on. Soon after, Skeffington departed for Wales to recruit troops.[15]

Following its belated recognition of the seriousness of the Irish situation, the government now faced further headaches. The rebels' establishment of military supremacy in the Pale and their seizure of the king's ordnance raised the question of whether the relief army would be able to land near Dublin, and therefore whether Chester or north Wales were convenient points of embarkation. Moreover, Skeffington's suitability as commander of the expedition was called in question. There was no doubt about his qualifications: he had already spent two years as deputy-lieutenant of Ireland (1530–2), and his office as master of the ordnance and his previous work on the fortifications of the English Pale at Calais certainly

6.2   Dublin Castle under siege in 1534, from Holinshed's *Irish Chronicle*, 1577.

equipped him well for the post. Nor was there much competition from other military men to lead an expedition to an impoverished borderland from which, as Chapuys expressed it, 'il ny a que gaigner que cops de bastons'. Skeffington probably owed his appointment to his lack of rivals as much as anything else, for he was 'scantily beloved' at court and over 70 years old. Chapuys reported that he was 'the most unfit for the command of that country that could be chosen', an assessment which subsequently proved accurate when his health broke down.[16]

Likewise, the selection of a suitable port of embarkation led to an unfortunate compromise. The original intention seems to have been that Skeffington's retinue should sail from Bristol for Waterford, and indeed a force assembling in the West Country was soon reinforced in response to appeals from the earl of Ossory for assistance in holding the south-east against the rebels.[17] Yet the need for additional troops prompted the recruitment of northern and Welsh troops who were more conveniently embarked at Chester, as was the ordnance since this could not easily be transported from Waterford to Dublin. Thus the relief army sailed in two parts, and this adversely affected its efficiency. Meanwhile the original complement of artillery was shipped independently to Waterford, leaving London on 23 August.[18]

The Bristol contingent had apparently been envisaged primarily as a garrison force; but as augmented it was in fact too large for this. It comprised 900 troops: 600 foot from the West Country commanded by Sir John Saintlow and his brother, plus 200 Welsh foot raised by Sir Rhys Maunsell, a member of the council in the marches of Wales, and 100 horse under a Devonshire gentleman, John Kelway.[19] At Bristol, the main problem was the shortage of ships for transport. Chapuys reported in late July that in the Thames the king had only six seaworthy ships, but by mid-September ten ships, including embargoed Spanish and Flemish merchantmen, had been made ready at Bristol. Ships being prepared elsewhere were countermanded because of the difficulty, through contrary winds, of getting them to Bristol. The king then intervened to change two captains because he found others offering to sail within six days, weather permitting, with an increased complement of troops. The force sailed at the end of the month and reached Waterford without difficulty. Yet once the Chester contingent had arrived, most of the Waterford garrison were needed in the Pale, but could not be moved until December when cavalry was sent down to escort them north.[20] As a fighting force, therefore, the army was rather less formidable than its actual numbers suggested.

At Chester, the problems were more serious. Skeffington's force eventually comprised 1,600 men: 250 Cheshire foot under Sir William Brereton; 250 Welsh foot, led by John Salisbury, esquire for the body and steward of the lordship of Denbigh; and 466 northern horse, under four Cumberland gentlemen. The remainder consisted of Skeffington's original retinue, plus 100 horse under Edward Sutton, son of Lord Dudley, and a hastily recruited Welsh force of 220 horse and 150 foot.[21] Of these troops, the company about whom most is known were the northerners. They were clearly the elite of the relief army, and consisted mainly of spearmen, recruited from the west marches, who were well accustomed to the kind of border warfare they would encounter in Ireland. Of their captains, Leonard Musgrave was constable of the royal castle of Penrith, and had served in Ireland twice before, under the earl of Surrey (1520–2) and during Skeffington's previous deputyship (1530–2).[22] Edward Aglionby was a gentleman of William Lord Dacre's household, with modest possessions around Carlisle, who had been licensed by the king in 1524 to retain 100 men 'of your own tenants and servants', or of Dacre's tenants, for the defence of the west marches.[23] He too had served in Ireland under Skeffington in 1530–1. When Dacre was arrested and indicted for high treason in June 1534, Aglionby immediately wrote to Cromwell begging to be remembered for a lease of Dacre's lands if they were forfeited.[24] It was no doubt this letter which ensured his return to Ireland four months later, along with Captain Thomas Dacre, Dacre's illegitimate half-brother, and Captain Laurence Hamerton.[25] Serving under them, presumably as petty captains, were Thomas Aglionby, perhaps a younger brother of Edward, and Richard Dacre, who was Lord Dacre's cousin.[26] Finally, there was John Musgrave, an illegitimate son of Dacre's erstwhile retainer and principal accuser in 1534, Sir William Musgrave, who acted as his deputy-keeper of the royal outpost of Bewcastle. Thomas Dacre and John Musgrave had clashed with each other during the recent Anglo-Scottish war, and Cromwell presumably thought the west marches would be quieter if their services were employed elsewhere.[27]

Thus the captains included some experienced men, but few courtiers, and some like John Kelway who lacked both experience and connections. The account of the treasurer-at-war suggests that the total number of troops landed in the two forces was 2,502 men.[28] No doubt few of these troops had experience of Ireland, but Welsh and northern men had formed the backbone of the English forces serving there under Surrey and Skeffington.[29] More disconcerting was the fact that for an Irish campaign, with mobility at a premium and few opportunities for a set-piece battle, the army was not a balanced force. In particular, the delays in sailing meant a winter campaign, in which the footmen could not be effectively deployed. In December, a further 200 northern spearmen and 100 Welsh spearmen were requested and the Welsh foot to be discharged. The government later found horses for eighty of the footmen in order to use them as mounted archers, but the cavalry already included too large a proportion of mounted archers and not enough of the highly prized northern spears. In effect, the government was repeating the mistakes of Surrey's expedition in 1520 when the decorative but largely ineffective yeomen of the guard had been sent over.[30]

Nevertheless, the army had grown considerably from the 1,500 men envisaged in late July, partly no doubt because, with the splitting of the army into two forces, the Chester contingent was now deemed too small to operate as a field army. By the end of August, Skeffington, his retinue, and the bulk of the ordnance were at Chester awaiting the arrival of shipping and money. But as the news from Ireland grew gloomier, the deputy sent his son back to London to plead for reinforcements, and then departed into Wales to raise more troops.[31] The king appointed William Brabazon, servant of his secretary, Thomas Cromwell, as undertreasurer and treasurer-at-war (26 August) to pay the augmented force, in which the levy of 450 northern horse was now included. Chapuys reported that the mounting of a major expedition under the duke of Suffolk or Norfolk was also canvassed at court, and inquiries were made about the possibility of recruiting 300 foreign mercenaries as arquebusiers.[32] Yet by the time the northerners were ready, the deputy's retinue had been depleted by desertions, horses were lacking, and Skeffington himself was still in Wales.[33] Moreover, the rebels had intercepted a ship laden with horses for the deputy and another had been stolen out of the Thames.[34] These losses followed a rebel decision to fit out ships to harass the invasion fleet, and in reaction the king was forced to mount coastal patrols.[35]

At Chester, Brabazon was now in charge and still awaiting the money which, contrary to Skeffington's instructions, had been sent to Bristol. A favourable wind had blown for over a week, and following receipt on 23 September of Cromwell's instructions to embark the troops, Brabazon had ordered the northern men aboard ship, intending to collect Skeffington's force at Holyhead. John Alen, master of the rolls in Ireland (unrelated to the archbishop), was detailed to remain at Chester to receive the money and pay the ships for Brereton and Salisbury's retinues.[36] The deputy, however, was still at Beaumaris waiting for additional guns and artillery being transported from Conway castle, and on 4 October the northerners were still on board ship at Chester, now awaiting wind and weather, although Brereton's company had since arrived.[37] In excuse, Skeffington alleged the danger of sailing without an adequate force, but at the end of September the king, increasingly exasperated at the delays, sent his peremptory orders to sail by the first wind. Cromwell's agent, Stephen Vaughan, was also sent down to Chester to speed the preparations.[38] The fleet sailed up from Chester, and eventually left Graycourt Harbour for Ireland on 14 October, arriving off Lambay Island on the 15th.[39] Altogether, it had taken nearly three months to raise, equip and transport a relatively small army to Ireland. And the operation, although occupying much of Cromwell's time, was apparently characterised more by improvisation than by proper planning.[40]

Even so, the government's problems were far from over after Skeffington's force had landed, with difficulty, near Dublin over the period from 16 to 24 October. Upon arrival, it soon became apparent that the army was seriously short of weapons. Councillors later reported from Dublin that 'of 1,600 men being here at the landing of the same, there were not 400 of them furnished with weapon'. The livery supplied from the Tower of London sufficed only for Skeffington's original retinue of 150 men, while the bows which came from Ludlow castle were useless, 'for many of them would not hold the bending'.[41] Longbows could not be obtained in Ireland – supplies were normally imported from England – and from Waterford Sir John Saintlow reported a great shortage of handguns.[42] Moreover, many of the horses had died in passage because of the delays in sailing.[43] As late as the following February, John Alen was complaining that 'this army want bows and arrows and strings, and many other hablements of war'.[44] In fact supplies of weapons had frequently not been increased from early estimates prepared in the ordnance office in late July, viz. 500 bows and 300 northern spears. An important exception were the very substantial pieces of artillery sent – notably two demi-cannon and two demi-culverins, as well as some smaller pieces – because of reports (only partially correct) that the king's ordnance in Dublin Castle had fallen into rebel hands. Indeed the 1534–5 campaign witnessed much the largest deployment of artillery in Ireland since its first introduction a half-century earlier, and the demi-cannons, firing 30 lb shot, were three times the size of any field piece available later to Elizabeth's army there. Ironically, however, the other difficulties besetting the army meant that there was little opportunity to use them before the siege of Maynooth the following March.[45]

As with campaigns in Scotland and for similar reasons, food was in short supply. Even without the additional burden of the army, the lordship commonly imported grain in years of poor harvest. Moreover, the rebels adopted a scorched-earth policy.[46] Yet in this instance the supply arrangements were apparently adequate. The deputy was authorised to appoint victuallers to purvey grain in England and there were no complaints about shortages of food.[47] Another perennial problem facing armies was sickness and disease. The 'death' (plague) had ravaged the English Pale shortly after Surrey's arrival in 1520, causing serious billeting difficulties, but the 'sickness' (sweating sickness, a viral disease) which affected the army between

November 1534 and February 1535 was disruptive for different reasons, and during summer 1535 there was a resurgence of plague in the Pale. Forty men died in Salisbury's retinue from the 'sickness': altogether only 100 men were affected, but these included Salisbury and Skeffington himself who lay ill and incapacitated for twelve weeks.[48] The deputy had recovered sufficiently by March to take the field, but his health was gone and he eventually died in December. In August, while sitting in council, he was said to be 'almost dead among them' and 'if he rise before 10 or 11 of the clock, he is almost dead or [= before] noon'.[49] During winter 1534–5 Skeffington's incapacity was a serious hindrance because there was no-one else of sufficient seniority and experience to whom he dared to delegate command of a major expedition.[50]

The army's financial situation was also unsatisfactory. The lordship's internal revenues normally just covered administrative costs, and little money could be raised there by way of loans.[51] Once again, the initial delays set the pattern. Between July and October 1534 Cromwell disbursed £9,499 14s 8d from the Jewel House for the war in Ireland, but over £2,500 of this had been spent before the deputy had even sailed.[52] By dint of leading a force of 300 cavalry to Waterford, Brabazon was able to bring the rest of the money (and incidentally to escort back 500 footmen), and so had enough money for the army's pay-day in December. He scraped up sufficient in loans to pay most companies again in January, but from February army pay was usually in arrears.[53] Indeed, until new revenue began to come in from first fruits and tenths, the English government was itself pressed for money. A further £5,166 13s 4d was sent in late January, but it took a month to arrive because the ship conveying it was 'with contrary wind & evil weathering brought hither to the Holyhead again'.[54] In May a further £3,000 was dispatched, and £3,000 more in July, but the army was still a month in arrears after the July payment.[55] And by summer 1536, their pay was so far in arrears that the army mutinied.[56]

The cumulative effect was a serious deterioration in army discipline, and consequently in military effectiveness. In default of a vigorous commander, the army spent much of November and December uselessly garrisoning Dublin and Drogheda, whilst the captains, who had been appointed to the privy council, democratically decided whether or not they would assent to any journey.[57] The army was not mustered before payment as required, and the captains enlisted others without licence to fill vacancies. Some troops had gone missing, notably the northern men whose numbers were 'sore diminished, and without them no notable exploit can be done'. Few had actually deserted to the rebels, although some of the captains were related to leading rebels and were reluctant to prosecute the war against them.[58] The wardens of the marches were required to search for soldiers absent without licence, and Alen vainly recommended the recruitment of 200 more northern horse 'with some hardy captain' and to discharge some Welsh horse and foot.[59] Perhaps because they had been hurriedly raised by an outsider who had no natural ties with their region, the Welsh troops were particularly indisciplined, and Salisbury and

---

Brereton were lax in controlling their men. Alen urged the appointment of a marshal 'which may be no Welshman', for 'there was never army further out of order'. Lacking pay, 'they rob both friend and foe, and smally regard the deputy, and much less any of the council'.[60] The appointment in January of William Pole, a protégé of Cromwell, as provost-marshal and Thomas Paulet as special commissioner temporarily checked this indiscipline. Paulet brought instructions and a royal proclamation for reordering the army, and also a commission for Sir John Saintlow as chief marshal.[61] Yet Saintlow remained in Waterford until mid-April, delayed first by the non-payment of his troops and then by the military situation; so Paulet stayed on to keep order, taking musters of troops, forcing the captains to follow orders and accept lower rates of pay, and restraining the soldiers from robbery.[62]

Nevertheless, by June army discipline was worse than ever. Everywhere there were complaints that the army 'pill [= rob] and extort the people'. The footmen stayed in Dublin and 'snarl us with lack of money and weapon', while the horsemen would 'pay in manner neither for horsemeat nor man's meat, and the country ready to flee from us'. Not even the lands of loyalists were safe from them: they pillaged three of the earl of Wiltshire's manors in County Kildare and robbed his bailiff of a County Dublin manor. In particular, the Welsh cavalry were almost uncontrollable and were discharged in August.[63] Skeffington's debility was no doubt partly responsible for the situation, but Saintlow was also sick at this time, and in July the king superseded his deputy as army commander, appointing instead a lord marshal to take charge of the campaign – Lord Leonard Grey, son of the marquis of Dorset and brother to the ninth earl of Kildare's second wife.[64] Thus, overall, it was the inadequacies in military administration as much as rebel strength which hindered the quelling of the revolt.

The story of the campaign itself may be told more briefly. When Offaly went to Dublin on 11 June to resign the governorship, he brought with him a force of about 1,000 retainers. Leaving the bulk of his troops outside the city, he rode through the city to St Mary's abbey, where the council was meeting. He was accompanied by a strong company of horsemen who wore the silken fringes on their head-pieces from which he received his name.[65] After news of Kildare's arrest, however, Offaly moved to seize military control of the Pale. The Pale gentry were forcibly sworn to him, while leading loyalists had their lands wasted or were imprisoned in Maynooth castle.[66] According to the Annals of Connacht, 'mac an Iarla .i. Tomás do milled muinter Righ Saxa a ndigail a athar in gac ait a rabadar a nErinn' (the son of the earl i.e. Thomas destroyed the people of the king of England everywhere they were in Ireland in revenge for his father). Anyone born in England who fell into rebel hands – of whom Archbishop Alen was the most prominent – was summarily executed. At court, news circulated that Offaly 'spareth not to put to death man, woman or child which be born in England, & so continueth in as well tyranny & murdering the king's subjects'.[67]

By late July resistance within the Englishry was confined to the County Louth border, where Sir Walter Bellew of Roche held out against him, the city of Dublin and Finglas to the north, and the Butler territories of the south-east. Leaving Sir John Burnell to watch the city, Offaly moved north with 2,000 men in late July to crush Bellew and to parley with O'Neill whose support he secured by ceding custody of Greencastle, County Down. Meanwhile, the citizens of Dublin were defeated by Burnell and the O'Tooles at Salcock Wood on 4 August while trying to defend Finglas, the city's granary. And on his return Offaly was able to negotiate a favourable truce which allowed him to lay siege to the king's castle from the city.[68] Leaving a small force to besiege the castle, Offaly then marched south to attack the Butlers who had been raiding the Kildare estates in Counties Carlow and Kildare. He took Tullow castle after a five-day siege and then advanced down the Barrow valley as far as Great Island, where there was a skirmish with Ossory in mid-August, followed by a brief truce. The arrival of O'Neill with reinforcements allowed Offaly to resume the offensive, and the Butler estates were wasted as far south as Thomastown, where Ossory was heavily defeated and Lord James Butler severely wounded. Ossory retired to Waterford and Butler was besieged in Kilkenny. In early September, Offaly retained MacMurrough, O'More, O'Connor and O'Byrne and left them and the Kildare gentry to deal with the Butlers while he returned to Dublin where, on the king's orders, the citizens had broken the truce and captured many of his men.[69]

As lord deputy, Kildare had had control of the king's ordnance in Ireland, and many of the artillery pieces had been removed from Dublin Castle in the months before the revolt, and so passed into rebel hands. With these, Offaly had laid siege to Dublin, which was a vital objective – politically because it was the lordship's capital, but more importantly because the castle contained the chief store of powder and shot which he needed for his artillery. John Alen, writing from Chester warned Cromwell that

> the loss of that city and the castle were a plain subversion of the land. Also the rebel, which chiefly trusteth in his ordnance, which he hath of the king's, hath in effect consumed all his shoot; and except he winneth the castle of Dublin, he is destitute of shoot which is a great comfort and advantage for the king's army.[70]

To this end, Offaly now called up all the troops at his disposal, and the city was besieged by 15,000 men. Stanyhurst records that many of the Pale gentry, although forced to take part with their tenants in the siege, simply shot headless arrows or messages into the city. Thus the rebel army was nothing like so formidable as it seemed. Even though the rebels broke into the city and did considerable damage, they were driven out again. The castle was also damaged, but the garrison of fifty gunners held out against the increasingly desperate attacks: one soldier, Francis Herbert, who had brought the king's orders to break truce, was said to have killed twenty-four rebels, twenty on one day.[71]

The failure to capture Dublin marked a turning point in the campaign. Realising that his artillery was inadequate to breach the walls and that he lacked the time to starve the city into surrender, Kildare (as Offaly now was since his father's death on 3 September) again took truce with the citizens and shifted his ordnance to Howth Head to try to oppose Skeffington's landing. Initially, he had some success. The deputy was caught as he disembarked some Cumberland spearmen; the fleet was driven off by his ordnance, and a transport conveying horses captured by the Geraldine navy. The spearmen made for Dublin but were intercepted by 200 rebel cavalry at a bridge near Clontarf and 22 men, including Captains Leonard Musgrave and Laurence Hamerton, were killed and 18 taken prisoner. This, however, was Kildare's last major success. The following day Skeffington landed two forces at Skerries and Dublin (17 October), and a week later he disembarked with the rest of the troops at Dublin.[72]

Thereafter, Kildare withdrew to Maynooth, his principal castle, which had been prepared against a siege, and began a scorched earth policy in the Pale, 'whereby he thinks to enforce this army to depart'.[73] Yet most of his supporters within the Englishry defected to the lord deputy after the army's arrival and his proclamation as a traitor from the High Cross at Drogheda. Although Kildare had commanded the support of the Palesmen as the king's deputy, after Skeffington's arrival only a small minority were willing to bear arms against their sovereign lord. Thus the earl was quickly reduced to reliance on the few hundred Gaelic horsemen, galloglass and kerne he normally retained.[74] During the winter Skeffington's illness, and the army's own inactivity and inadequacies, allowed the rebels to hold out, but in March the deputy invested Maynooth, which fell after a ten-day siege. The army took the basecourt by assault after an artillery bombardment, but the constable was tricked into surrendering the great castle for a bribe. The summary trial and execution of the garrison which followed was widely seen in Ireland as a major breach of trust. And subsequently, during the Tudor conquest, 'the pardon of Maynooth', as it was called, long served as a reminder to those in arms against the crown of what they might expect if they refused to surrender castles when summoned to do so.[75] After the fall of Maynooth, Kildare took refuge among the Irishry, from where he initiated a series of raids on the Pale. Yet although these raids were of little military significance, politically Kildare's continued activity was a major embarrassment to the government, and the army proved ill-suited to the task of hunting down rebels in the independent Gaelic regions. Accordingly, Kildare was induced to surrender (24 August 1535) by a promise that his life would be spared. In the event, however, he was sent to the Tower, and subsequently executed for treason at Tyburn (3 February 1537) after an interval which the government used to restore royal authority in the lordship.[76]

The conduct of warfare by both sides in the 1534–5 campaign had exhibited a ruthlessness which was seldom seen in English revolts and which certainly departed from 'the rules of war' as practised in Anglo-French campaigns. In part this was

6.3 The massive Geraldine castle at Maynooth, which fell to English
forces during the revolt of 'Silken Thomas' (the tenth earl of Kildare)
following a ten-day siege in March 1535.

because warfare as practised by Gaelic forces differed from English perceptions of
what was permissible, but there is little doubt that the events of 1534–5 set the tone
for the atrocities of Elizabethan Ireland. Indeed, following experiments with the use
of Gaelic kerne in France and Scotland in 1544, where their conduct distressed the
French and appalled the Scots, Henry VIII decided to employ 2,000 of them in
Scotland the following year, and gave instructions that they were to be recruited
'out of the most wild and savage sort of them there, whose absence should rather do
good than hurt'.[77]

   The Kildare rebellion also had a major impact on the overall conduct of government in the lordship. With the attainder of the magnate best placed to defend the
English interest in Ireland, the crown was forced to fall back on the expensive
strategy of appointing an outsider as governor, backed by a standing garrison to
uphold royal authority. Hitherto, this strategy had only been followed for two short
periods of two or three years, particularly when some special effort was
contemplated; but from 1534 the king's choice as governor of Ireland was almost
invariably an English-born outsider. Similarly, although the army was paid off
immediately after Kildare's surrender, save for a garrison of 700 men which
was reduced again to only 340 two years later, the government soon learned that,

without Kildare to control the Gaelic lordships bordering the Pale, some kind of standing army was essential to defend the Englishry. Kildare's galloglass and kerne eventually passed into the crown's service, it being argued that they had been recruited by the earl in his capacity as the king's deputy. This certainly made the army a more versatile force, but 500 English troops came to be regarded as an absolute minimum for defence; and after Henry VIII's death, when the government attempted to extend Tudor rule into Gaelic Ireland by more coercive methods, the garrison normally numbered at least 1,500 men.[78]

In turn, the provision of a standing army for Ireland came to have a major impact on the character of royal government there. Traditionally, English administration had encountered many obstacles in the lordship, and the power of the central government had been weak. Yet the crushing of the Kildare rebellion did little to alter the essential problems of ruling a half-conquered borderland; and as unrest and rebellion escalated, the government came increasingly to rely on the army to assist local officials in the execution of their duties. Thus began the practice of using the army in support of the civil power which has remained a characteristically Irish contribution to the development of English administrative structures down to the present day.

More immediately, the establishment of a standing army also led to the growth of a distinct group of soldiers and military administrators who depended chiefly on the army for their living. True, after a few years' service in Ireland, most of these soldier-administrators departed to serve the king elsewhere, but for two main reasons a significant minority stayed on in Ireland, and some of them eventually came to establish themselves as part of the Irish landowning elite. In the first place, apart from the garrisons at Berwick-on-Tweed, Carlisle and – until its loss in 1558 – Calais, service in Ireland constituted almost the only regular source of employment to military men within the Tudor state. The intermittent wars with France and Scotland certainly offered more promising opportunities for fame and fortune while they lasted, but, under Elizabeth, England enjoyed an unwonted period of peace until 1585, whereas the gradual escalation of the wars in Ireland provided steady and profitable, if unspectacular, employment to Tudor adventurers. Second, many of these adventurers were younger sons of established gentry families, who inherited their family's aristocratic outlook but not the estates to support it. Not only did Ireland offer an outlet for military talents, but beginning with the estates of the earl of Kildare and the monasteries, the periodic confiscation of land by the crown and its leasing or regranting on favourable terms also provided the opportunity to build up a landed inheritance. The final part of this chapter briefly considers the subsequent careers of some of the men who served in Ireland in the 1530s.

Among those who came to Ireland with the army in 1534 were Sir William Brereton, captain of 250 footmen, and Thomas Agard, treasurer's clerk. Francis Herbert was made captain of twenty horsemen for his exploits in the siege. Other military men who arrived within the next few years included the soldiers, Francis

---

6.4 Execution of rebels by Lord Deputy Sidney,
from Holinshed's *Irish Chronicle*, 1577.

Cosby, and Lord Leonard Grey's servant, Mathew King, Edward Basnet, receiver to
Captain John Musgrave, who was appointed dean of St Patrick's in 1536, Henry
Draycott, and Osborne Etchingham, marshal of the army in 1540. In each case,
they were able, within a few years, to secure leases of confiscated lands, and
subsequently to convert these into, or exchange them for, land in freehold. And in
the case of Brereton, Cosby, Draycott, Etchingham and King, their descendants
appear as landed gentry at the time of the Ulster rising of 1641.[79] Brereton was,
unusually, already one of the Cheshire county gentry, and returned there when the
army was disbanded. Yet in 1539 he returned to Ireland with military reinforcements, was briefly appointed governor there; and the family's Irish branch was
founded, apparently, by his two sons, John Brereton, seneschal of Wexford, and
Captain Andrew Brereton, who received leases of land in Wexford and Lecale
respectively. Allegedly, Cromwell told Herbert on his return to Ireland during the
siege that if he died in his prince's service, he died in the service of God; and if he
lived doing him service, he should undoubtedly be made a man thereby.[80] Herbert
was knighted for his services, secured a lease of the border manor of Portlester,
married into Pale society, and died about 1570.[81] Agard got leases of monastic land
in Meath, and his son, Captain Francis Agard, was seneschal of Wicklow under Lord
Deputy Sidney (1565–76). Perhaps the most unusual member of this group was Dean
Edward Basnet, a married priest, who was described in 1551 as 'a man experimented
in the wars of this country', and who acquired lands for his two brothers in the
Dublin–Wicklow marches.[82]

Alongside these New English, members of the local Englishry also profited from the army's presence. Two notable examples were David Sutton, a younger son of a Kildare marcher family, who was appointed to the council, and John Travers, who became master of the ordnance. Both secured favourable leases of monastic land. Yet although local men joined the army, the more important posts mostly went to outsiders, so that the garrison was seen as predominantly New English. The ambitions and outlook of these military men are in part illustrated by a letter to the king written by Marshal Etchingham in 1545. Etchingham observed that he had served in the king's wars for the best part of his life, and had come to Ireland because the land was then in rebellion and the king was at peace with other realms. Now, however, Ireland was peaceful and the king at war with France, and he asked therefore that, since he was growing old, if the king wished him to stay in Ireland, he would grant him the lordship of Dunbrody, County Wexford, in exchange for a life interest in a manor in Norfolk. His request was granted, and within eighteen months he was dead.[83]

Yet the vast majority of the soldiers and captains who went to Ireland in 1534 failed, or did not choose, to make a career there. In most cases we know very little about them, but something can be said about the northerners. Despite their obvious suitability for service in Ireland, and the recognition they achieved there, the northerners probably judged that service to the crown in the similar conditions of the west march, among their own countrymen, offered more promising opportunities of advancement. After the death of Captains Hamerton and Musgrave in the abortive landing at Howth, Thomas Aglionby and John Musgrave were promoted captains, and Edward Aglionby was appointed to Musgrave's old office as constable of Penrith castle. Yet their companies remained, respectively, twenty and thirty-one men short.[84] Indeed, Thomas Aglionby's company – by then little more than half strength – was disbanded after only five months, and the men were transferred to bring Musgrave's company up to full strength.

Edward Aglionby's company was disbanded in September 1535, and he returned to Cumberland to take up his office as constable of Penrith. At the time, there was a proposal to settle 300 of the northern men in the recently recaptured County Kildare under one of their captains, and to send over 500 more northerners to make the land peaceful and profitable.[85] Yet with hindsight, Aglionby's departure appeared a wise move, because his patron had already been superseded as military commander, and in fact died in December. The Dacres and Skeffington's son-in-law, Captain Anthony Colley, soon found themselves in trouble with Lord Leonard Grey, who allegedly bore them no good will. Thomas Dacre was committed to the Marshalsea for eight days during autumn 1535 pending examination by the council, and Richard Dacre, who was committed at the same time, languished there for seven weeks.[86] In June 1536, the northern men mutinied for lack of pay, and threatened to send a deputation to the king.[87] They were discharged soon after, just in time to participate in the second major rebellion of the reign, the Pilgrimage of

Grace, which spread throughout the north in October and November 1536. Richard Dacre had himself proclaimed grand captain of all Cumberland and later brought some of Lord Dacre's Gilsland tenants into Carlisle to create trouble. Trouble was appeased by Edward Aglionby who, together with John Musgrave remained loyal during the insurrection.[88] Aglionby was subsequently appointed to the commission of the peace for Cumberland, and served as sheriff in 1546. And in the reorganisation of the north which followed the Pilgrimage, Aglionby, Musgrave and Thomas Dacre were all fee'd by the king as assistants to the deputy-warden of the west marches.[89] Interestingly, in 1540 a similar scheme for royal pensioners in Leinster envisaged appointing Thomas Dacre as second pensioner 'if he come to inhabit in Ireland'.[90]

In one sense, the outcome of the 1534–5 campaign was entirely predictable. It demonstrated in an Irish context what had long been apparent to Tudor magnates elsewhere. It showed that not even the strongest and most heavily defended medieval castle was proof against the heavy artillery now available to the crown, and that the administrative resources of the Tudor monarchy far outstripped anything available to even the most 'overmighty' of their subjects. Yet with the establishment of a standing army in Ireland, and the related administrative reforms centring on the replacement of a locally born viceroy by an outsider, the Tudors demonstrated a commitment to the government of Ireland which had hitherto been lacking. It is a fallacy to see the assimilation of Gaelic Ireland into the Tudor state as an inevitable consequence of these changes. Yet in retrospect the transformation of Tudor rule in Ireland which accompanied the 1534–5 campaign did mark a major step towards the ending of Ireland's medieval partition and the establishment of Dublin castle as the headquarters of a united Ireland within a United Kingdom.

Chapter 7

The captains' games: army and society in Elizabethan Ireland

Ciaran Brady

The general history of Ireland in the later sixteenth century has commonly been understood to be especially suitable for treatment by the methods and perspectives of the military historian. Though the importance of military orders in the social structure of earlier periods has been fully recognised, and though it has always been acknowledged that wars and individual battles exercised a decisive effect in the course of subsequent centuries, the assumption that the essential story of the era could be summed up in a list of military confrontations, of rebellions and conquests, has remained peculiar to Eizabethan Ireland. Thus it is not surprising that for many decades the most frequently cited single volume survey of the period was Cyril Falls's *Elizabeth's Irish Wars*, a straight military history written by a distinguished soldier-scholar, nor that the editors of *A New History of Ireland* should have commissioned a leading military historian, G. A. Hayes McCoy, to write the main narrative chapters of the sixteenth century.[1]

1

The assumption that the military history and general history of the Elizabethan era are effectively coterminous is, on the surface at least, quite plausible: for the successive decades of the reign seem each to have been dominated by one of a series of increasingly violent confrontations between the forces of the crown and the private armies of the native lords. By 1558, at the very beginning of Elizabeth's reign, the Dublin government had already become embroiled in a bitter struggle to assert its authority in Ulster against first the defiance and later the overreaching expansionism of the lord of Tyrone, Shane O'Neill. The conflict ended only with the assassination of O'Neill in 1567. Yet within a year the government faced an equally dangerous challenge in Munster, as James Fitzmaurice Fitzgerald, the *major domo* of the earl of Desmond rose up in revolt and succeeded in securing the support of some of the most powerful families in the province, including for a time his ancient Butler rivals. The rebellion was suppressed in 1573 when Fitzmaurice surrendered to Sir John Perrot, the recently appointed president of the province. But trouble continued to smoulder throughout the decade; and in 1579, when Fitzmaurice returned from abroad with a small force, the province again broke out in a rebellion that resulted after much bloodshed in the complete annihilation of the Desmond lordship four years later.[2]

Seen against this background, the closing years of the 1580s constituted a period of relative peace. Yet even then a localised but extremely vicious war was taking place between Sir Richard Bingham, the English provincial president of Connacht, and the principal families of Mayo, while an anxious expectation that an imminent Spanish landing would precipitate general rebellion throughout the island was pervasive.[3] In the following decade such fears and hopes of a general uprising were finally realised. Beginning in the early 1590s an unprecedented alliance of the great Ulster lords of O'Donnell, O'Neill and Maguire first drove the English from Ulster and, after astonishing victories at Clontibret (1595) and at the Yellow Ford (1598), gradually spread insurrection into every province in the island. The rebellion, conveniently but (given the halting manner in which it was conducted between 1594 and 1603) misleadingly labelled by historians as the Nine Years War, constituted the most dangerous and most expensive challenge ever posed to Tudor government in Ireland, and might well have proved fatal to English claims to the country had it not been for the débâcle at Kinsale in 1601 which ended at once all Spanish interest in exploiting Irish unrest and broke the spirit of the Ulster lords' resistance.[4]

The brief catalogue of events outlines a simple and compelling story. Yet it is seriously misleading on a number of levels. It obscures, in the first place, the extent to which – even in the midst of most of these conflicts – the bulk of the island remained at peace. Thus during the wars against Shane O'Neill, though guerrilla activities arose in the midlands and though the earls of Ormond and Desmond intermittently revived their perennial feud, the vast majority of the Irish lordships either remained at peace, as in Munster and Connacht, or, as in Ulster, actively lent support to the forces of the crown. Again, when Munster was out with Fitzmaurice in the late 1560s and early 1570s, Ulster, despite some posturings from Turlough Luineach O'Neill, offered no support while in Connacht the Clanrickard Burkes returned to peace once Sir Edward Fitton, the English official appointed as regional governor in the province, had been withdrawn. When Desmond rose for a second time both provinces remained quiet, and several lords from both regions actually sent forces to aid the crown against the rebels. Finally, the troubles in Ulster in the early 1590s, like those in Connacht in the previous decade, remained for a long period relatively local. It was indeed only for three years between 1598 and 1601 that something like the grand nation-wide revolt much feared by the English and regarded thereafter as inevitable by historians actually materialised.[5]

Most of these well-known conflicts, moreover, could hardly be characterised as periods of continuous war. The crown's struggle with Shane O'Neill took the form merely of a series of punitive campaigns lasting no more than a season and separated on occasion by more than a year. The great set-piece battles of Shane's career were fought not against the Dublin government but against the Scots at Glenshesk (1565) and the O'Donnells at Farset More (1567); and, as is well known, he was finally destroyed not in battle, but as the result of a sordid intrigue by which the government bribed the Scots to murder him, on the basis of a false promise to recognise their settlement in Antrim.[6] The first Munster revolt was likewise a rather discontinuous affair. It flared at its most dangerous only in the months between June 1569 when Fitzmaurice was joined by the Butlers and the following December when he was deserted both by the Butlers and his chief Gaelic allies MacCarthy More and McDonough.[7] Thereafter, while he was still able to stage damaging surprise attacks on enemy positions, Fitzmaurice resorted to guerrilla methods, launching his raids only intermittently and with a steadily diminishing force until his surrender early in 1573. The second Desmond rebellion likewise underwent distinct phases. Far more serious than its predecessor in its earliest days, the revolt, which had tied down more government troops than any previous disorders and seemed for a while to endanger the entire province, steadily lost momentum under the vigorous campaigning of Sir William Pelham and the earl of Ormond in Limerick and Kerry and especially following Lord Deputy Grey's and Sir William Winter's ruthless dispatch of a garrison of more than 600 Italian and Spanish troops at Smerwick in November 1580.[8] Ironically, the revolt was resuscitated only as a result of the crown's hasty decision simultaneously to grant pardons on a selective basis and to withdraw the bulk of its troops from the province in the winter of 1581.[9] But even then the revival was short lived: for after a year of minor skirmishing and general inaction, the earl of Ormond within six months of his appointment as lord general of Munster in 1583 hunted the unfortunate earl of Desmond to death and put an end to the last pockets of resistance.[10] Finally, in relation to the Ulster rebellion of the 1590s, it should be observed that notwithstanding the rebels' spectacular individual successes in the field and the long-term investment of strategic positions at Enniskillen and the Blackwater fort, the Nine Years War retained until its final three years the discontinuous character of earlier conflicts, as military actions alternated regularly with protracted negotiations and lengthy truces.[11]

Such observations are not, of course, intended to suggest that for most of the Elizabethan era Ireland was a land at peace. On the contrary, low-level conflict – 'stealths', 'borderages', cattle raids, personal and dynastic feuds – were endemic throughout the island; and the evidence indicates that they were a good deal more common than was actually reported in the official correspondence of state. On the borders of the Pale, for instance, the Wicklow septs of the O'Byrnes and O'Tooles carried out regular raids on the farms of Palesmen and the English forts meant to protect them. Heavily armed gangs such as those of Piers Grace in Kilkenny and the notorious 'Bastard Geraldines' of Kildare frequently disrupted the peace in their respective territories. Toward the north, the Nugents and the Plunketts persisted in

---

7.1 Narrative sequence of illustrations from Derricke's *Image of Ireland*, 1581: (i) departure of Sir Henry Sidney from Dublin Castle.

their traditional feuds with such lesser Ulster families as the O'Reillys and the Mac Mahons. And in the west and south, conflicts between the Clanrickard Burkes and the O'Briens or between MacCarthy More, Mac Carthy Reagh and O'Sullivan Beare frequently produced petitions for the intervention of the crown. But the English government's involvement in such little wars, despite appeals from one or other of the parties, was intermittent and certainly did not form part of a predetermined and systematic campaign of conquest. They were, for the most part, regarded as holding operations, defending positions already established, upholding old allies or agreed arrangements, or punishing would-be disturbers or those who plotted to unsettle the existing balance of power. The cumulative effect of these local conflicts, as they increased over the period both in their frequency and ferocity, was indeed decisive. But for the present it is sufficient to observe that they were understood to play no significant role in the grand strategy of the Elizabethan governors in Ireland.[12]

2

That strategy, in so far as there was one, proved to be remarkably conservative and surprisingly resistant to reform. For during most of the reign it rejected or at least subordinated the two most obvious – and most frequently canvassed – tactical options for a successful military conquest in favour of a third, and apparently wholly ineffective one. The first of these purely military proposals was total war by means of scorched earth and territorial clearance. Often identified with the ruthless campaigns of Mountjoy and Carew in Munster and Ulster at the close of the century, and with the blood-thirsty writings of men like Spenser which immediately preceded them, the idea of reducing Ireland by means of relentless and uncompromising war had been openly promoted by commentators in the 1520s and 1530s.[13] And it continued to be advocated, if only as an ideal, by commentators as diverse as Archbishop Dowdall and Sir Walter Raleigh, throughout the next half-century.[14] In times of crisis it was, moreover, put into practice by Elizabethan commanders without much compunction. It was applied on a limited scale both by Humphrey Gilbert and Sir John Perrot in Munster during the first Desmond rebellion when Gilbert alone could claim credit for the surrender of more than thirty Desmond castles through the destruction of all the corn and the slaughter of all the cattle in the territories surrounding them.[15] Notoriously, the tactic was extensively deployed during the second Desmond rebellion by most of the English commanders who formally commissioned their subordinates to 'burn the . . . corn, spoil the . . . harvest, kill and drive the . . . cattle' of the rebel territories.[16] In Connacht President Malby reported in 1578, a little nervously, that he had employed it to great effect, while his successor Bingham unabashedly proclaimed its exemplary success: his rapid suppression of the rebellion raised by the Burkes in Mayo, he boasted to Perrot, had been achieved by the unrestrained use of the tactic until the rebels at last submitted, 'so pined away for want of food and so ghasted with fear . . . by reason they were so roundly followed without any interim of rest that they looked rather loke to ghosts than men'.[17]

But despite its attractions and its apparent efficacy, scorched earth was never endorsed by the principal Elizabethan governors in Ireland as a general strategy. Though they occasionally made resort to the use of unrestrained force in particular circumstances, neither Sussex, Sidney nor Fitzwilliam were prepared to advocate general extermination, and the latter, despite his choleric temperament, condemned and eventually proscribed Bingham's tactics in Connacht.[18] Most significantly, Perrot, despite his experiences as president in Munster, formally renounced the use of open war in his programme for government in the 1580s.[19] Until the very close of the century 'scorched earth' was regarded as an emergency measure to be used only in restricted circumstances and for a limited period of time. And despite a very clear experience of what it might achieve, it was never advanced by governors as either a desirable or a necessary means of imposing English authority in Ireland.

A second obvious military solution was sometimes promoted in tandem by the more advanced advocates of scorched earth, but was generally seen as an alternative to open war. This was the idea of establishing an elaborate network of garrisons throughout the island as a means of enforcing a rigorous policing over all of the native lordships. Intensive national garrisoning was a strategy that came to be urged with especial vigour in the several military tracts and memoranda produced in the 1580s and 1590s and the appropriate *exempla* from antiquity – particularly Roman history – were commonly adduced as though to lend special authority to the case.[20] But again, like scorched earth, it had a far longer Irish genealogy. Unlike the latter,

---

7.2   (ii) Sir Henry Sidney in the field delivering a message.

however, it commanded far wider currency and acquired something of an orthodoxy of aspiration as the century progressed. But despite a general agreement that a garrison grid was a desirable thing in itself, the policy was in practice pursued only fitfully by successive administrations.

In the 1530s and 1540s the old crown forts on the southern borders of the Pale at Ferns and Leighlin Bridge were reoccupied and refurbished; while in the early 1550s, under the enthusiastic supervision of Protector Somerset, the coastal forts at Waterford, Youghal and Kinsale were strengthened and extended and the first new garrison of the century, Fort Protector, was constructed by Lord Deputy Bellingham in Laois.[21] In the later 1550s and early 1560s the earl of Sussex built major fortifications to defend the midlands plantations at Maryborough (Portlaoise) and Phillipstown (An Daingean), and both he and his successor Sidney repaired and extended the old castles at Athlone and Carrickfergus.[22]

But thereafter the extent of further fortification was strictly limited. Sir Henry Sidney's bold initiative in constructing a new fort at the Derry in 1566 proved to be an expensive failure. Already worn down by lack of supplies, malnutrition, sickness and the loss of its commander in battle, the garrison was finally destroyed by a massive, though accidental explosion just nine months after its foundation.[23] The disaster at the Derry, a fort which was originally intended to serve as the flagship of Sidney's new Ulster policy, firmly dissuaded that governor from any other costly investments in garrisoning. No further attempt was again made on Lough Foyle until Sir Henry Dowcra established his position there in 1600.[24] And, in the meantime, the only English outposts to remain in Gaelic Ulster were the products of private enterprise: Sir Nicholas Bagenal's fiefdom at Newry and the rather less

141

successful and only intermittently occupied Blackwater fort built at his own expense by the earl of Essex in the mid-1570s.[25] The official attitude towards garrisoning in the equally turbulent province of Munster was almost identical. Though during the troubles of the late 1560s and 1570s English forces occupied or destroyed several Desmond castles, no effort was then made to erect a permanent English garrison in any strategic site beyond the walls of Limerick. Even after the confiscation of Desmond's lands and the establishment of the plantation in 1586, the government remained diffident. Despite frequent assurances to the undertakers that their holdings would be fully protected, and despite the urgent demands of planters, like Sir William Herbert, who plied the government with detailed schedules as to where new forts might most effectively be placed, the crown did little more than place some small bands in a handful of old Desmond castles, Castlemaine, Askeaton and Dingle.[26] For the rest, the planters were left to themselves; as in Ulster, private enterprise was the government's solution to the problem of providing fortifications. Such privatisation was, in any case, hardly regarded as a scandal; for this was a process that had already taken root in the older crown forts of Leighlin, Ferns, Duncannon and Carrickfergus which were under the control of constables who held office with virtually no interference from the government for long periods of tenure, usually for life.[27]

Garrisoning, then, despite a clear recognition of its strategic value and the many opportunities that arose to develop it throughout the second half of the century, remained in practice of secondary value in the plans of the Tudor viceroys: a policy where maintenance took priority over innovation and where the expenditure of private monies as opposed to government funds was to be preferred wherever possible. Finance – the sheer cost of constructing the forts – accounts in part for the government's lack of enthusiasm, though it should be said that in recognising costs as an inevitable constraint, the policy's advocates went to great lengths to show how economies might be made, and how the network should be constructed gradually in carefully costed stages. But their advice had little influence.[28]

It was therefore curious and, to some late Elizabethan critics, inexplicable, that the strategy most consistently favoured by the Irish viceroys above the alternatives of total war and garrisoning was, from a strictly military point of view, the least cost-effective of all. This was the practice of collecting relatively large campaign armies with an eye to confronting the enemies of state directly or forcing them to surrender or retreat from the field of battle. The tactical weaknesses of the general hosting as a military instrument were fully exposed by a number of Elizabethan soldier critics in the 1580s and 1590s like Barnaby Rich and Nicholas Dawtrey, and their observations have been duly followed by military historians ever since.[29] Its deficiencies were indeed manifest. As it wended its way through the boggy soils, narrow passes and exposed plains of the Irish countryside, the thinly spread army with its awkward supply train and innumerable followers was notoriously vulnerable to guerrilla tactics: to simple ambushes, or to more complicated

7.3 (iii) Sir Henry Sidney's army on the march.

diversions which severed the van from the rear, or the cavalry from the foot, or
rendered the drawing up and use of heavy ordnance impossible. Even when it was
successful, and the commanders succeeded in rasing a strong castle, clearing a
territory of rebels or, most infrequently, actually defeating an enemy in the field,
the achievement was rarely enduring. The enemy regrouped, the castles were
restored or new ones built elsewhere.

This unwieldy strategy occasionally led to calamity or near disaster on several
occasions. One such was Sussex's near rout at the hands of Shane O'Neill in 1562
when a sudden attack from the rear threw his army into disarray and precipitated a
general retreat.[30] Another was Fiach MacHugh O'Byrne's mauling of Lord Grey in
the death trap of Glenmalure in 1580.[31] And the most famous was Sir Henry
Bagenal's fate at the Yellow Ford when a sustained attack on the flanks of
the dangerously attenuated column, followed by a vigorous direct assault on the
confused and frightened infantry led to the loss of more than 2,000 men.[32] But
more frequently the effect of the long campaign marches was simply to induce
exhaustion among the crown forces and to persuade their enemies to withdraw
temporarily from the theatre of war until the force of the grand army had been
spent.

The ineffectiveness of the general hosting as a military strategy was so glaring
that it seems obvious to ask why those governors, like Sussex, Sidney and Perrot,
who had had ample opportunity to appreciate its dangers, should have persisted in
employing it. As before, financial constraint would appear to supply the simplest
explanation for this strategic conservatism. That the English crown was unwilling
to invest anything like the amount of treasure required to establish its authority in

Ireland by force had long been evident. Yet this simple and irreducible fact cannot alone supply an adequate explanation of all that happened in the later sixteenth century. As an immovable sanction, it clearly determined what could not be attempted, and profoundly influenced the range of alternative strategic options which could be devised, but it did not determine the actual selection among choices, nor indeed how, working within its constraints, the Elizabethan governors in Ireland sought to achieve the objectives for which force could not be employed.

3

The best indexes of the Elizabethan government's extremely limited commitment to the enforcement of its authority by means of military force alone are provided by the volume of expenditure of royal treasure on Irish affairs in the period and by the size of the standing army which such spending was intended to sustain. Over Elizabeth's reign Treasury disbursements to Ireland, intended primarily to subvent the military establishment, rose steadily; yet until the very end of the century the increase of investment in the crown's Irish army was never spectacular. The crown spent on average a sum of £21,200 stg. on the Irish establishment in the 1560s. In the following decade it was spending a little over £30,000 stg. per annum. Expenditure increased to over £40,700 stg. in the 1580s, though the high expenditure of the first half of the decade obscures a rapid return to the more modest levels of the 1570s in the second half. In the first half of the 1590s, average spending actually fell back to the levels of the later 1560s (around £27,000 stg. per annum); and it was only in the years 1595–1601 that the crown's outlay really exploded to an average of over £120,000 stg. a year. In the last two years of the period the treasury was compelled to pour almost £200,000 stg. per annum into the Irish war.[33]

These figures are a direct but by no means an accurate reflection of the second major index of England's military commitment to Ireland, the size of the garrison. A clear estimate of the strength of the English army in Ireland is extremely difficult to essay. Numbers shifted constantly from year to year as companies were enlisted and disbanded. The government depended heavily on semi-private operators – pension holders, local magnates and kerne, those professional Irish mercenaries – who sometimes were and sometimes were not included as part of the establishment. But most importantly the figures themselves were seriously inflated, in part officially – through the crown's overt acceptance that the bands should be 10 per cent below strength and that the captains should pocket the 'dead pays' that consequently accrued – but in greater part unofficially, through the widespread falsification of service rolls which was a persistent scandal throughout the period. Recorded estimates of soldiers in pay are then little more than an expression of the degree to which the crown was prepared to make an official commitment to

7.4 (iv) Sir Henry Sidney's army in battle with an Irish force.

maintaining a military presence in Ireland; and even then they supply a seriously exaggerated impression of what that commitment actually was in practice.[34]

Such qualifications notwithstanding, the figures are themselves instructive. For they reveal the very modest power that, for the most part, was expected to serve as the enforcer of Tudor rule in Ireland. Excluding for the present the Irish kerne, the pensioners and ancillary numbers in the office of ordnance, the standing army in Ireland at the beginning of Elizabeth's reign was something in the region of 1,200 fighting men. Numbers fluctuated during the earl of Sussex's term as viceroy – in 1561 there were some 2,500 men in service – but by the middle of the decade the garrison had actually shrunk to little more than 1,000. At the height of the struggle with O'Neill, Sir Henry Sidney had charge of over 3,000 men. But following Shane's death the garrison was again reduced by half. Even in the midst of the first Munster rebellion the establishment did not exceed 2,000; for the remainder of the 1570s it fluctuated between 1,500 and 1,000 and on Sidney's departure in 1578 it fell to even less.

Upon the outbreak of the Desmond rebellion, the army was steadily and substantially reinforced. By the middle of 1581 there were some 6,000 men in arms. But as the rebellion waned, the garrison contracted sharply to 2,500 and eventually to less than 2,000. In the second half of the 1580s it again oscillated between 1,500 and 2,000, and in the early 1590s, despite some very brief reinforcement occasioned by fear of a Spanish invasion it continued to hover between these figures. In 1593, on the eve of the Nine Years War, it stood at a mere 1,500.

The outbreak of rebellion in Ulster produced major reinforcements. By the end of 1595 the garrison had regained the strength it possessed in 1581. But it was only after the Yellow Ford that it grew to exceed 10,000. Thereafter growth was exponential: by the time of the battle of Kinsale, the garrison had doubled to over 20,000. Yet for most of the second half of the century the official – and therefore overstated – strength of the English army stood at something less than 2,500.[35]

The weakness of the English army as a national force contrasts markedly with the size of the private armies maintained by the island's provincial and sub-provincial lords. At the close of the reign of Henry VIII a detailed account of the forces of the leading lords estimated quite conservatively that there were at least 24,000 armed retainers in the country. At that time, relatively modest powers, like MacMorrogh Kavanagh in Leinster or O'Connor Sligo were reported to maintain 580 men apiece; while the powerful and distant MacCarthy More was said to have retained more than 2,000.[36] In the reign of Elizabeth the earl of Desmond also commanded a fighting force of 2,000 and his rival, the earl of Ormond, was able to match this number with ease.[37] At the height of his power in the mid-1560s Shane O'Neill led an army of 5,000, while his successor Turlough Luineach even when at peace maintained a native army of 1,800 which could be quadrupled at will by the Scottish mercenaries which he could call upon through the offices of his wife Agnes Campbell.[38] The MacDonnells of Antrim regularly raised a force of over 2,000 men both as a means of defending their settlements in the Glens and of intimidating their Ulster neighbours.[39] In Ulster lesser lords like O'Reilly and Maguire maintained armies of between 500 and 600 men.[40] In West Breifne, one of the poorest lordships in Ireland, O'Rourke boasted a force of 600 while MacWilliam Burke in Mayo had a force of around 680.[41]

Confronted thus by a panoply of independent private armies, the English garrison in Ireland can hardly be represented as a particularly intimidating force, still less as a machine of conquest. Moreover, its usefulness as an instrument of government seems even less impressive when its command structure and administration are examined. The Elizabethan viceroys were formally the commanders-in-chief of the army. But until the later 1590s the vast majority of the men who held the office were principally courtiers with administrative, diplomatic and political backgrounds, rather than figures with substantial military experience or expertise. Once in Ireland, several of them, to be sure, demonstrated a taste for combat and some showed considerable talent in the field: but throughout they regarded the army as a subordinate instrument of support for policy rather than as a institution of first importance. Thus they elected to delegate responsibility for the administration, training and even the deployment of the army to lesser officers. The officer corps of the Irish army was an extremely small group. The offices of general or lieutenant-general, or general of the horse, all standard in the command structure in England were not established by patent in Ireland until the next century.[42] The title of colonel was granted briefly to Humphrey Gilbert in 1568 but the genuine office with its responsibility over a group of bands gathered together in a regiment did not appear in Ireland until the end of the 1590s.[43] The effective head

7.5 (v) The submission of Turlogh O Neill to Sir Henry Sidney.

of the army was not as in England, a lord high marshal, but a knight marshal, and his executive officer, the provost marshal was not appointed in Ireland until the mid-1570s and not confirmed by patent until 1583.[44]

The marshalship itself was for the half-century between 1547 and 1598 held almost as a family fief by the Bagenals who, with the exception of the years between 1556 and 1565, were in continuous occupation of the post. Sir Nicholas's patent was granted at pleasure only but he secured a reversion for his son Henry without difficulty in the early 1580s and had smoothly passed over the office to him by the end of the decade. The Bagenals were not enthusiasts in the office. Preoccupied with the defence and development of their estate in Newry they were content in the main to allow operations in the provinces outside of Ulster to be conducted by other commanders. And it is significant that while both were authors of substantial official memoranda on political matters, neither had anything material to say concerning the administration, reform or even in defence of the army.[45]

Thus between the marshal, who rarely assumed the conventional responsibilities of the office, and the ordinary soldiers on the ground only one level of authority existed where all the routine but crucial decisions concerning the maintenance, discipline and deployment of the English army in Ireland were made: the captains of the bands. It was the captains who from the outset assumed the responsibility and the power for the recruitment of the volunteers and levied troops who were to serve in Ireland, and for their training and transportation. It was they who took charge of the supply of the soldiers' needs, of food, clothes and munitions; it was they who exercised complete control over both the distribution and the actual extent of the soldiers' pay.

4

The virtual autonomy of the captains in relation to the Irish administration and even the Irish viceroy himself was established from the outset by the manner in which they were appointed to serve in Ireland. Commissions to levy troops or to enlist them in service in Ireland were in general issued by the English privy council, sometimes by the council in Wales and only infrequently by the Irish council.[46] The Irish governor, of course, normally exerted considerable influence over the nomination of those who were granted such commissions, and relatives, clients and dependants of the viceroys featured regularly in the lists of the captains in service in Ireland. But this influence was informal and never absolute: and governors were frequently compelled to accept the continuance of their predecessors' nominees in office while having their own preferred nominations queried or deferred, or discharged from commission in times of retrenchment.[47]

The captains' independence of Irish government was established, however, in a much more certain manner by the weakness, ineffectualness and virtual absence in Ireland of the conventional administrative offices responsible for monitoring their conduct during the time of their commissions. An office of ordnance with responsibility for the acquisition, maintenance and disbursement of artillery, firearms and other heavy weaponry, and for the training of the soldiers in the use of the same had been established in Ireland in the 1530s. But from the beginning its operations were marred through the granting of a life interest to the first two masters of ordnance, John Travers and Jacques Wingfield which allowed them to treat the post as almost a personal sinecure.[48] Wingfield's grip on the office between 1558 and 1587 was so firm that it withstood both his well-known recusancy and more notoriously, his display of cowardice in the field; and indeed by the close of his career, he was so secure in the post that he was able to arrange the reversion of his office after his death to his fellow recusant, Sir William Stanley, whose succession was prevented only by his treason while serving with the English expeditionary force in the Netherlands.[49]

Under Wingfield the office had been managed with gross inefficiency. A frequent absentee, he delegated the routine administration of affairs to the clerk of ordnance, Richard Hopwood, who in turn sub-let his interest to a series of deputies over a period of twenty years, while he pursued a more profitable career as a victualler. In these circumstances neglect was chronic. No regular records of acquisitions and disbursements were kept, inventories were only rarely and infrequently drawn up, equipment was allowed to decay, and most seriously of all the failure to keep an adequate tally of the captains' receipts for munitions and arms received over many decades rendered a proper audit of both the offices' and the captains' accounts quite improbable.[50] Yet despite the exposure of these abuses on Wingfield's death, the mastership was again granted away on life tenure, to George Carew in the first instance and then to George Bourchier, who had been Carew's deputy and the neglect and mismanagement of accounts continued to the end of the century.[51]

Concerning the other aspect of the office's role, the training of the soldiers in the use of arms, little further may be said. A post of master gunner had been established in Ireland since the 1530s and was formally instituted by patent in 1551. But once again it was granted for life to one Thomas Eliot the original holder, and though Eliot is known to have distinguished himself in the field on some occasions, he seems never during his fifty years tenure to have discharged any of the specific duties attached to the office, but busied himself instead in becoming a substantial landowner in County Meath.[52] Similarly, one Christopher Mortimer is described in a single document of the 1580s as holding the position of chief engineer in the office, but no patent for such a post was issued and Mortimer never again found mention in the records of state.[53] Thus, as in the case of recruitment and replacement, the military supply and training of the bands was to a very large degree left to the discretion of the captains.

What was true of the soldiers' military needs was equally and more urgently true of their subsistence. A central office of surveyor-general of the victuals with responsibility for organising supply to the whole of the garrison was created only in 1583 with the granting of a patent to George Beverley.[54] But the terms of Beverley's appointment suggest that his function was less administrative than commercial. Allowed an apparently handsome stipend of 10s a day in return for his agreement to supply all the army's needs, Beverley's position was in fact nothing other than a more official version of the contracts entered into by private entrepreneurs like Thomas Might and Thomas Sackford who had assumed similarly wide commitments for limited periods in the past. Like them Beverley was understood to bear all financial responsibility for losses and like them also, his losses were heavy.[55]

But such general contracts, whether private or semi-official, were in any case of secondary importance. The routine business of supplying the army was carried out throughout the century in a much more dispersed manner. Drawing their sustenance from the country through the onerous and hotly disputed 'cess' (the feudal right claimed by the royal army to take up food, carts, horses etc., at prices fixed well below the market), the bands were supplied by a host of smaller victuallers, 'cators', serving directly the needs of the captains in local garrisons or by the captains themselves acting as independent victuallers in their own right. Here again the cost, quantity and quality of the supplies provided to the soldiers was left almost entirely to the captains' discretion.[56]

The freedom enjoyed by the captains in all these matters of recruitment, training and supply was underpinned and enhanced by their greatest discretionary power of all: their right to determine their soldiers' pay. In principle the method of paying the troops in Ireland followed the traditional, elaborate and astonishingly unwieldy procedures practised in England. The soldiers' pay was fixed at a certain rate per diem (e.g. 9d for horsemen, 8d for arquebusiers, 6d for archers and pikemen at the beginning of the reign of Elizabeth; 12d for horse, 10d for arquebusiers, 8d for archers and pikes at the close).[57] Following a period in service, supposedly fixed, but determined in practice by the capacity of the royal treasury, a full pay would be announced. The gross pay of the soldier was then calculated, and deductions were made for supplies of munitions, uniform, lodging, food and prest payments (occasional payments on account) in order to arrive at the net entitlement of the soldier. This was a system which called for the maintenance of an elaborate record of separate interim accounts concerning each of these 'defalcations' between the soldier's date of enlistment and the time of the full pay. The captains were required to keep such accounts and it was the task of an independent auditor – the muster-master – to check their records against the receipts of victuallers, suppliers, ordnance officials and the soldiers themselves.[58]

Even in England such a highly complicated procedure (whose only merit seems to have been to deprive the ordinary soldier of the chance of getting more than a minimum wage from the crown) never succeeded in practice. But in Ireland for most of the sixteenth century it hardly operated at all. Though its introduction had long been urged by several reformers, the office of muster-master was not established in Ireland until the 1590s.[59] Until then the crucial task of auditing the captains' accounts was left in the hands of men of lesser official and social standing who had not the influence or perhaps the desire to challenge the captains' word, the clerks of check.[60] Nevertheless the crown immediately forfeited whatever countervailing power it might exercise over these figures by granting the office on life tenure. Thus Mathew King, clerk of check for over thirty years after 1540, readily made his decision to side with the captains. In the 1560s, investigations carried out by William Bermingham and Sir Nicholas Arnold exposed his incompetence and strongly suggested corruption. King was shown not to have held regular musters, to have accepted the captains' records without accompanying certification and to have ignored the counter-claims of the countrymen and the soldiers themselves.[61] But in face of his and the captains' blanket denials, allegations of outright malfeasance could not be proved and he held on, suspect always and regularly criticised for misconduct, but still in full enjoyment of his stipend until his death in 1575.[62] His successor, Owen Moore, seemed to herald an improvement. Kinsman both to Lord Deputy Sidney and Secretary Walsingham, his early intensive musters indicated that he would be little intimidated by the captains. But after Sidney's departure, enthusiasm waned. He delegated the office to a deputy, the unpatented Thomas Mynne, while he himself, with scant regard for a conflict of interest, joined the ranks of the captains.[63] His two successors in the post, Thomas Williams and Ralf Lane, each followed his example in exposing the faults of their predecessors and making an early show of reform. But whether or not their early efforts were merely cosmetic they soon foundered on the twin obstacles to efficient musters, life tenure and a failure to challenge the captains' evidence with that of the soldiers.[64]

The abuses which this chronic lack of managerial and financial control

---

encouraged among the captains were multiple. They were especially placed to cheat everybody else in the system, and to a greater or lesser degree they did. They cheated, in the first instance, the crown, overstating the numbers actually in service in their bands and the length of service of each man, while understating the amount of dead pays they were allowing themselves and the number of Irish kerne (who were paid considerably less than English soldiers) that they employed in their companies. They cheated, of course, on their soldiers, giving false estimates of their length of service, and of the munitions and victuals supplied to them, with-holding such supplies, skimping on their food and even depriving them of a basic uniform, and confiscating the pay due to those who had died in service, or been discharged or deserted before a full pay. Most notoriously, they cheated the countrymen, commandeering far more than the official cess entitled them to, tolerating the soldiers' extortions, or entering into unofficial deals in order to secure cash payments in lieu of a threatened cess or quartering. Finally, though perhaps most indirectly, they cheated their own commander, the viceroy, offering a defence force that was far below his official requirement both in size and in quality, and creating for him a set of problems and tensions in relation both to the crown and the country which distracted them from the central concerns of government.[65]

Thus scattered in small garrisons throughout the country, or at the head of companies billeted in the Pale, or resident in Dublin Castle as commanders of units serving as bodyguards to the viceroy and other chief administrators, the captains determined the essential character of the Elizabethan army in Ireland. It was not a coherently organised efficient fighting force, an engine of conquest. It was constituted rather of a loosely connected series of franchises, conducting (or misconducting) their everyday affairs with only the minimum interference from their nominal superiors as semi-independent statelets in which the captains were kings.

5

It is doubtless easiest to explain the extraordinarily disjointed state of the Irish army simply as yet another instance of the venality, inefficiency and neglect which characterised Tudor administration in general. Here as elsewhere the crown's obsessive frugality, its determination only to expand the minimum of its revenues on the most necessary of issues, had encouraged a subversive privatisation in which the offices of state were converted into speculative opportunities for entre-preneurial investment. Thus given the Treasury's refusal to subvent the Irish administration in any realistic manner, the granting of commissions on terms which seemed formally quite unfavourable, but which nevertheless made available unofficial and highly lucrative opportunities to individuals prepared to exploit them appeared on balance to offer the best compromise available.

Such an explanation is partially true. Yet it fails to explain why successive viceroys could tolerate such an inefficient, unstable and highly attenuated structure as a medium of executing their major commitments in Ireland. That the viceroys rarely sought to reform their army, that they stoutly resisted indeed the constant complaints and reformist challenges that were raised, and finally, that so many of them regarded the captains as their closest and most dependable supporters in government all suggest that they looked upon their army with all its faults not regretfully as a necessary evil, but in a much more positive manner, as an instrument that was expressly tailored to the specific strategic needs of English policy in Ireland.[66]

The means by which this captains' army served the needs of the governor were several. Most obviously and perhaps least helpfully they provided the units that made up the core of the viceroy's general hosting. The weakness of the grand army as a military strategy has already been noted; but it is its success as an instrument of diplomacy that should more properly be stressed. Between the 1530s and the 1580s viceroys from Lord Leonard Grey to Sir John Perrot perambulated the country regularly, restoring order and enforcing settlements in lordships riven by internal strife. Sidney's great tour of Munster in 1566-7 and Perrot's annual visitations to Ulster in 1584-7 are among the best known of these circuits, but they are only the most publicised instances of a regular practice of government whose achievements have long been forgotten.[67] Frequently outnumbered and always understrength, the viceregal train passed through difficult terrain and dangerous situations with remarkable ease. It has sometimes been fashionable to stress the geographical ignorance and cartographical illiteracy of the Elizabethans in Ireland.[68] But the detailed and remarkably precise topographical information provided by these lengthy records is eloquent testimony to the success of the governors in their efforts to penetrate deep into the heart of Gaelic Ireland. The settlements made during these tours were often fragile and short lived. Yet the acknowledged ephemerality of the achievements should not detract entirely from their significance. For it was by these means that the English government succeeded in asserting its right to intervene in and arbitrate upon major dynastic disputes in the great lordships, in fashioning a substantial movement of alliance and support from within the lordships and in inculcating a gradual but accumulating respect for English legal and political processes throughout the island.

That they should have done so with a relatively small and loosely organised army is not altogether surprising. As a force at once too small to pose a deadly challenge to the independence of the lordship and yet large enough to intervene effectively in favour or against one disputing group or another, the touring army enabled the viceroy to assert his right to determine political issues in the territory without alienating large numbers of its inhabitants in a manner threatened by outright coercion. In this process the captains played a crucial role. The simple detachment of companies to the service of whatever disputant the governor chose to favour offered crucial additional strength during the period of settlement, and, over time captains, like Henry Davells, Francis Agard, Robert Pipho and Humphrey Warren, who had frequently been used in this way assumed the important diplomatic role of go-betweens able to represent the interests of the government and the local powers to each other. Long experience in Munster enabled Agard, for instance, to play a vital role in restoring order there in the early 1570s in the aftermath of the first Fitzmaurice rebellion.[69] Davells's attempt to enact a similar part on the return of Fitzmaurice in 1579 proved fatal; but the universal revulsion provoked by his murder during his diplomatic mission was a clear indication of the respect and trust which he had earned over the previous twenty years.[70]

Such a diplomatic function was served in a more overt and permanent manner by other captains who were appointed constables of certain forts or seneschals of particular territories. As constables of Dublin, Leighlin, Ferns, Athlone, Maryborough, Dungarvan, Limerick, Carrickfergus and several lesser sites, captains like Nicholas Heron, Francis Cosby, Francis Agard, Henry Harrington, Robert Hartpole and William Piers were expected to act as defenders of the crown's interests.[71] But they played also a much more positive role in the politics of the areas surrounding them, settling disputes and upholding the interests of those who had promised support for the government. William Piers's role in stemming the flow of Scots into the north-east and in defending his allies among the Clandeboye O'Neills from attack by both Irish and English interests was vital to the stability of the region. And though some senior officers, notably the first earl of Essex, were extremely critical of his influence, many others within the administration in Dublin fully acknowledged his role in shaping the politics of the north.[72]

Yet the responsibilities which the captains were expected to assume in this regard were more than simply conservative, the manipulation of the existing political forces in order to maintain peace. With few exceptions the Elizabethan viceroys attempted to use the captains as central agents in the advancement of a policy of gradual social and political reform by which, in the absence of any practical financial support for a full-scale conquest, they attempted to extend English rule in Ireland. Thus in determining their settlements and shaping their alliances the captains were expected to favour those who had accepted or supported the government's attempts to anglicise the social and political structures and processes in the lordships by means of the legal and diplomatic agreements known as surrender and regrant. Or more sensitively, the captains were required to investigate how such intricate and delicate agreements between the crown, the lords and their tenants and vassals should actually be drafted, and to discover why original or earlier agreements had failed to encompass the real distribution of power in the lordships. More routinely, as constables and seneschals, the captains were directed to extend the authority of English law in the lordships by holding informal judicial sessions which dispensed a blend of common law and local modes of arbitration, and by referring civil and criminal disputes to the courts in Dublin and to the Irish council. Finally it was envisaged that when the process of legal reform was well advanced, that certain captains would dispense with their ambiguous military/

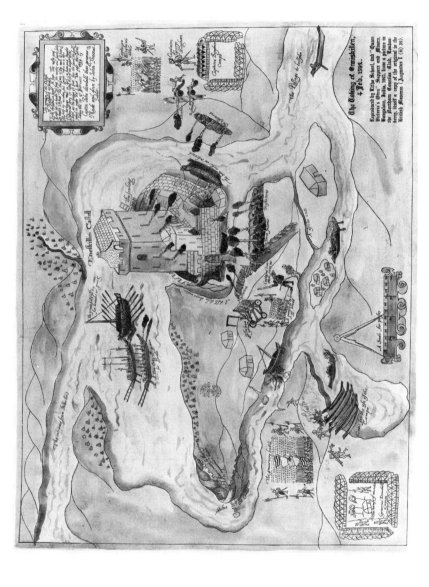

7.6 'The taking of Enniskillen, 4 Feb. 1592' [actually 1594], by John Thomas, a soldier participating in the English 'pacification' of Ulster.

political role and assume civil authority as the first sheriffs of the newly organised Irish shires.[73]

The effectiveness of the captains in their reformist role was, of course, determined by the consistency and force with which the policy was pursued at the centre. With the important exception of Sir William Fitzwilliam (lord deputy between 1571 and 1575 and again between 1588 and 1594), most of the viceroys who held office for any time in Elizabethan Ireland were strongly committed to reform. But equally most were compelled to concede that the record of their efforts to advance change had been extremely slow and uneven, that many lordships had hardly been affected, and that in many others significant early gains had been lost. In accounting for the disappointments of reform two reasons were commonly advanced. First, the unstable and short-term nature of the viceregal tenure of office had introduced discontinuities in policies and political alliances and disrupted processes of change that had been under way. But second and more important, it came to be recognised that the legal and diplomatic procedures of surrender and regrant had never succeeded in penetrating far enough into the actual power structures of the lordship or in confronting the challenge presented by the great private armies who were threatened with extinction by reform's advance.[74]

It was to meet these twin difficulties that two Elizabethan governors, Sir Henry Sidney and Sir John Perrot, adopted the policy of 'composition'. This was an ambitious, systemic strategy which sought to persuade the lords to accept a rapid commutation of their feudal and bastard feudal claims over their subjects by means of a powerfully reinforced resident English army which threatened to exact from the country even more than the lords' forces had done. Having enforced the commutation the army would then be withdrawn, and a much smaller force left to ensure that the sums agreed upon were collected for the lord. 'Composition' was a policy that seemed to address the outstanding problems of reform. Enforced intensely over a period of two or three years, the drive for commutation could be completed in the term of a single viceroy. It operated also at every level of the lordships' society, rapidly transforming social and economic relations, while making that most onerous and expensive of items, the private army, redundant, unwanted by either the lords or their subjects. In guaranteeing the success of this policy the role of the captains was central.[75]

Under Perrot, who developed the scheme to its greatest extent, regional command of the great composition armies was placed in the hands of provincial presidents in Munster and Connacht and in the case of Ulster, in the initial stages, under the viceroy himself. But at local levels, the task of quartering, of placing the most extortionate demands on the land, and then of negotiating appropriate compositions was to be carried out by the captains. The very methods which they had become so expert at practising in their own interests were now to be turned to serve the crown and the policy of reform: the captains' vices would yield public benefits. The commutations agreed, however, a select group of captains with their

---

155

slimmed-down companies were to be given charge of the collection of the composition rents and the arbitration of whatever disputes arose concerning them, while extracting a portion of the rent for their own maintenance. In this their identification with the lords and those of their subjects who accepted composition was complete. For they would emerge not simply as surrogates of the old private armies, but as the defenders of a new indigenous order in the lordships, representing and protecting the interests of those who had embraced the composition against both internal resistance and external interference.[76]

This, at any rate, was the theory, and the centrality of the captains to its success in practice accounts in large degree for why Sidney and Perrot were willing to tolerate their abuses and shield them from complaint. Thus Sidney was always prepared to defend as politically necessary the excesses and sudden changes in tactics which Malby and his subordinates in Connacht engaged in to better their positions; while Perrot openly acknowledged Henry Duke and William Mostyn, the captains appointed to negotiate composition settlements in Breifne and Tyrconnell respectively, as his clients to whom he was dispensing patronage.[77] Composition in fact simply made clear what had been an assumption inherent in all reform policies, that the independence and private ambitions of the captains gave them a flexibility and sensitivity to opportunity that was essential to the progress of gradually negotiated change. Handled in the right way, their susceptibility to seizing the main chance was not regrettable, it was positively beneficial.

But the captains' commitment to reform was never vouchsafed. It was conditional both upon the opportunities it offered them and upon the continuing authority of those driving the initiative from the centre. And when the latter faltered, the imperative of the former drove them in very different directions. Once the pursuit of reform was disrupted through the dismissal of a viceroy, his replacement by a rival, or his preoccupation with urgent matters elsewhere, the captains reacted in several ways. Some, like William Piers, became so identified with certain groups within the country in which they served, the Clandeboye O'Neills in this case, that they became hated by other groups (Turlough Luineach and his followers), mistrusted by some of their own colleagues in government, and so lost the ability to function as mediating agents at both local and national levels. Others so overestimated their ability to assess the underlying political currents amongst the people that they made disastrous misjudgements at critical times – fatally, for himself in the case of Henry Davells, and for many others in the wake of the bloody midlands rebellion precipitated in the late 1570s by Captain Cosby's tardy realisation that he had placed too much confidence in Rory Oge O'More.[78] For many more the response to the interruption of reform was simply to defend and consolidate their position by intensifying their military activities, enforcing a crude form of martial law or attacking those who appeared to threaten them once the lord deputy had lost interest in the region. Such, for instance was the response of Thomas Masterson and Robert Pipho, both seneschals in Leinster, and of Constable Sir

Edward More in the midlands. The effect of these different reactions, however, was simply to reinforce the existing modes of politics that already prevailed in the regions, and to confirm the impression that whatever its pretensions, the practical effects of reform were simply to compound existing problems.

Disappointment with the promise of reform occurred even while it was being presented at the most tentative and superficial stages of diplomatic negotiation. But when the policy had been developed into an intensive and thoroughgoing strategy, the consequences of its disruption for the captains and the people among whom they operated were far more serious. Such was the case of composition.

Though it had succeeded remarkably well in its early stages, Perrot's imposition of a composition settlement in Connacht and in Ulster was soon disrupted by a series of extraneous, unanticipated problems. Arguments with the Palesmen, with the Munster planters, with the archbishop of Dublin and with the majority of his own council led to his recall in the summer of 1588 and to his replacement by Fitzwilliam, the one viceroy who had explicitly rejected reform in general and reform by composition in particular. But in the provinces where composition had been initiated, it did not disappear with Perrot. Instead, at every level, those who had been charged to implement it by Perrot moved to exploit its private opportunities now that the constraining hand of central government had been removed.[79]

In Connacht, Sir Richard Bingham sought to renegotiate and extend the first agreements, increasing his own exactions denying the claims of certain lords and seeking to revise the freedoms granted and the settlements made with some lords, most notably O'Rourke. Bingham's activities immediately provoked violent reaction.[80] But below this captain-president a select group of ordinary captains, including John Mordaunt, John Newton, William Merriman and Bingham's own brother, George, set about enforcing extortion rackets of their own. Newton and Merriman, it was alleged, and Lord Deputy Fitzwilliam upheld the allegations, executed scores by martial law and appropriated their goods and lands; George used torture to extort money; all pillaged the country ruthlessly.[81] The atrocity perpetrated by these men on the Joyces' country in 1589, when they seized about 6,000 cattle and in one day alone slaughtered men, women and children out of hand on the pretence that they were sheltering rebels – and even murdered the guide who had brought them there – is perhaps the most notorious case of their efforts at extortion. But it is merely an extreme instance, and indeed was intended to serve as an exemplary model of their general *modus operandi*.[82]

In Ulster the attempts of Captains Willis, Mostyn, Connill and Herbert to maintain a private composition strategy of their own were more modest. But the consequences were more fateful. Without the control of a presidential commander, the pretensions of these small bands to function as an independent force in the province fuelled a common reaction among both the indigenous military leadership and the former supporters of composition in the lordships that took the government in Dublin wholly by surprise. For the professional swordsmen, just recently threatened with extinction by the implications of a successful composition scheme, the captains' conduct supplied an ideal opportunity to demonstrate to their people that their supposed liberators from the traditional extortions of coyne and livery represented merely another version – an alien, unstable and unprincipled one – of the old system. And so, under the leadership of Aodh Rua O'Domhnaill, the principal representative of those who had most to lose from the success of composition, they went to war, proclaiming that they were again offering the protection that legitimised their existence. For the sometime supporters of reform among the dynastic elites and freeholding groups in the Ulster lordships, the captains' freebooting constituted nothing less than betrayal; some, like Aodh Dubh O'Domhnaill, Aodh Rua's half-brother and rival contender for the lordship, went into hiding, some, like Sir John O'Reilly openly resisted, others, like Sir Donnell O'Domhnaill, were murdered. But most, sooner or later, made their peace with the swordsmen in revolt.[83]

The authentic attitude of Hugh O'Neill, recently created earl of Tyrone as part of Perrot's drive to erect a stable composition in the province, to all of these developments remains a matter of speculation. The greatest potential beneficiary both of a successful composition settlement and of a successful revolt; the greatest potential victim should he choose to resist the rebels, his responses to events for long remained ambivalent, the product both of uncertainty and duplicity.[84] But from the beginning of his carefully constructed career O'Neill had recognised that the creation of a distinctive private army, which was equal in its equipment and use of arms to any of the English bands, was equal also to any of the Irish armies in its tactical flexibility and loyalty to the aims of its leader. And when he chose to deploy it, it placed him at the head of the unprecedented rebellion with which the Tudor century closed.[85]

In the crisis of the 1590s, however, a similar ambivalence that had been characteristic of the captains throughout the rest of the century and which when deftly exploited by the governors had been such a support to the aims of reform at last disappeared. A few, like Thomas Lee and Humphrey Warren, continued throughout the later 1590s to play the mediating role which had so often helped to restore peace in decades past, and some, like Hugh Mostyn, determined at the end to throw in their lot with the rebels.[86] But these were the exceptions and the losers: Lee was executed as a traitor, Mostyn fled into exile, Warren narrowly escaped disgrace. Instead, from captains serving in the war both in Ulster and in Munster there arose a new and surprisingly articulated call for the abandonment of the strategies of persuasion that had hitherto characterised Tudor policy in Ireland, and the adoption of an unalloyed strategy of total war by scorched earth to be followed by intensive garrisoning and plantation. The pacification of Ulster, urged Captain William Mostyn, would not be achieved by the methods of reform, or even by the sword alone, but must also 'come by the cruelty of famine which must be by the taking away of their cattle in each part where the traitors inhabit . . . (so that) those not cut off by fire and sword will in a short time be despatched by famine'.[87] By the time he made this call (1598) Mostyn was by no means alone in urging total war; for this was now the common cry of English soldiers and captains in Munster and Leinster.[88] But that this veteran of thirty years service who had served in the composition schemes of Sidney and Perrot and whose own brother Hugh had become so compromised in his dealings with the Ulster lords that he had actually joined their rebellion, should openly reject the principles under which he had served during his entire career is testimony as to how superficial had been most of the captains' commitment to those principles in the first place.

Amidst the devastation and waste of a national war which the crown had long sought to avoid and its agents had inadvertently provoked, the captains at last found their *métier* in circumstances that promised far more direct opportunities for gain than the sober drifts and politic ways of reform. Their adherence to the process of reform had always been conditional and ambiguous, and when other more attractive, entrepreneurial prospects beckoned, the captains seized their chance first to subvert and then to destroy it.

Chapter 8

The wars of religion, 1603–1660

Jane H. Ohlmeyer

'This is a war' wrote one Irish Franciscan of the Irish conflict of the 1640s, 'waged solely for God and the defence of the Catholic Church, the kingdom and monarchy of Christ's Vicar on earth.'[1] Wars of religion were commonplace in early modern Europe, as the French Religious Wars, the Dutch Revolt, the Thirty Years War and the Bishops' Wars in Scotland demonstrate; and it is tempting to view the Irish civil wars as one more, for religion shaped much of Ireland's military history between the conclusion of the Nine Years War in 1603 and the restoration of the Stuart monarchy in 1660.

Military events during these years can be divided into two parts. The first (1603–41), a period of nearly forty years, was one of peace and relative prosperity interrupted by two national emergencies (in 1625–30 and 1638–40), the second (1641–60), a period of just under twenty years, was characterised by widespread war and then military occupation.

The Protestant Reformation which transformed the religious complexion of England in the 1530s turned Catholic Ireland into a strategic threat, for it ensured that from this point on the Catholic princes of Europe carefully monitored, and occasionally interfered in, Irish affairs. In 1579 a papal force of Italians and Spaniards landed at Smerwick in County Kerry in order to help Irish insurgents and in 1601 King Philip III of Spain sent another Spanish expeditionary force to Kinsale in County Cork to aid the rebels led by Hugh O'Neill during the Nine Years War. Determined not 'to have the Pope keeper of the keys of [our] back door',[2] the English administration in the early seventeenth century set about securing the country both from external attack and internal rebellion by constructing new artillery fortresses, which were surrounded by ramparts and bastions and could only be taken by prolonged blockade, in strategic locations throughout the country. Thus Sir Josias Bodley, assisted by Dutch engineers Levan de Rose and Josias Everard, built Elizabeth fort (near Cork) and St Augustine's fort (near Galway) according to the latest European specifications. Many other fortifications – for example Carrickfergus or Limerick castles, were remodelled with artillery bastions and earthworks in order to make the structure more resistant to attack and artillery fire.

This radical development in fortifications has been identified by some historians as the crux of the 'military revolution' which swept through early modern Europe.[3] However in Ireland an absence of resources, technology and manpower, especially trained and experienced gunners and military engineers hampered the spread of the 'military revolution'. Costs were particularly prohibitive. For instance, one estimate, drawn up in *c.* 1627, of the charges involved in fortifying and providing Derry, Coleraine and Culmore with earth ramparts and ditches came to £10,800.[4] As a result many of the country's forts were decayed and in poor repair and, on the eve of the 1641 rebellion, the only modern fortifications were located on the coastlines of Munster and Connacht, where the threat of external invasion was greatest, and in Ulster, where Gaelic unrest was more likely. By contrast the Leinster coastline remained relatively unprotected. In particular, Dublin's city walls remained old-fashioned and had 'no flankers on them nor places for men to fight on', while the castle itself was in poor shape 'having on it no modern fortifications'.[5]

If artillery fortresses were a first vital ingredient in the preservation of the Protestant interest, the maintenance of an English standing army in Ireland was a second. Once Hugh O'Neill's rebellion had been safely crushed in 1603, this consisted of merely 1,000 foot and 300 horse and these troops made short work of the O'Doherty rebellion in north-west Ulster (1608) and of a plot to attack the Ulster plantation settlements (1615). However the outbreak of war with Spain in 1625, quickly followed in 1627 by war with France, forced the Dublin government to bring over fresh recruits from England and to increase the standing army to 5,000 foot and 500 horse. Although the danger was real enough – Spain seriously considered invading Ireland in 1625 and, with French assistance, again in 1627 – the Irish administration was unable to find an additional £3,000 per month necessary for the support of the army and resorted to exacting loans, quartering soldiers on the towns and dispersing them throughout the countryside, much to the disgust of the local population. The government also overhauled the country's fortresses: the defences of Galway, Waterford and Cork were either amplified or rebuilt while the town defences of Derry and Coleraine were improved.

However these measures provoked a political crisis. In 1627 an Irish delegation left for England to present their complaints 'about the maintenance of the army in Ireland',[6] and the following year secured from Charles I the 'Graces' – religious, tenurial and other concessions promised by the king to his Catholic subjects. Although they were only partly implemented, and never confirmed by the Irish parliament, in return the agents agreed to provide the government with subsidies of £120,000 for the defence of Ireland.

The conclusion of peace in 1629–30 ended this emergency, but within a decade the king was faced with yet another, more sinister national crisis: rebellion in Scotland. In an effort to suppress the Bishops' Wars (as the Covenanters' insurrections was dubbed), he authorised in 1638–9 the second earl of Antrim, an influential courtier and a Gaelic warlord, to raise an army of 5,000 men from among

8.1 Portumna Castle, County Galway. Built c. 1618, the castle's outer buildings were defensive in character, while the inner stone house resembled an English manor house, demonstrating the 'civility' and 'Englishness' of the residents, the Burkes of Clanricarde.

his Catholic kin and followers in Ulster and in the Western Isles of Scotland. Lord Deputy Wentworth, who bitterly opposed arming 'as many Oe's and Mac's as would startle a whole council board' and 'in a great part the sons of habituated traitors', refused to support the design which, largely as a result, foundered. Antrim's army was never even mustered.[7]

Ironically, however, early in 1640 Wentworth enlisted many of these 'Oe's and Mac's' himself for an army of his own, also commissioned by Charles I, to quell the dissident Scots. The formation of Wentworth's 'New Army' (as it was known) of 8,000 foot and 1,000 horse marked a daring departure in that, unlike all previous forces of the Dublin government which had been raised in England, with the exception of the senior officers it was a predominantly Catholic body. Thanks to a rigorous training programme the New Army was fit for service within a relatively short period of time. According to their commanding officer: 'Thes are not . . . poor stinking rascally sneaks[;] thes are brave gallant fellows . . . there cloaths are better, theire persons [are] better and there mettell is better.' He later added, 'I doe not care whoe sees them . . . noe prince in the Christian world hath . . . better men, nor more orderly.'[8] However early in 1641, following Wentworth's trial and execution, the New Army disbanded with the result that the original Irish standing army (a Protestant force of 2,297 foot and 943 horse), poorly supplied, armed, paid and dispersed throughout the country, was all that remained to suppress the major insurrection which broke out late in 1641.[9]

The 1641 rebellion is a central military event in Irish history and played a crucial role in shaping the fate of the triple Stuart monarchy during the seventeenth century. Yet according to accounts left by Protestant contemporaries it came as a total surprise: Audley Mervin, for one, could hardly believe that it was 'conceived among us, and yet never felt to kick in the wombe, nor struggle in the birth'.[10] Nevertheless the rising, which began in Ulster on 22 October 1641, quickly 'diffused through the veines of the whole kingdome'[11] and the Irish insurgents, led by Sir Phelim O'Neill, succeeded in taking the key Ulster strongholds of Charlemont, Mountjoy Castle, Tandragee and Newry (only Derry, Coleraine, Enniskillen, Lisburn and Carrickfergus escaped capture). Inevitably bloodshed and unnecessary cruelty accompanied the insurrection but the extent of the 'massacre' of Protestants was exaggerated, especially in England where the wildest rumours were readily believed. For instance, a recent detailed study of the rising in County Armagh, where some of the worst atrocities occurred, suggests that between 600 and 1,300 people (or 10.5 and 25 per cent of a total settler population of 5,000) died as a result of the violence. In fact throughout Ireland as few as 4,000 Protestants may have been murdered during the early months of the rising; a far cry from the figure of 154,000 which the lords justice alleged had been butchered by 16 March 1642.

The political reverberations from the rising were quickly felt in Britain and the struggle between Charles I and his English parliament over who should control the army to be raised to put down the Irish rebellion ultimately resulted in

---

163

parliament taking up arms against its monarch. The 'Wars of the Three Kingdoms' had begun and throughout the 1640s Charles I remained acutely sensitive to the interrelations between his three dominions and, as in the Bishops' Wars, hoped to use Irish troops against his rebellious British subjects. Likewise the king's opponents in Britain – the English parliament and (before 1648) the Scottish Covenanters – vowed to prevent Ireland from becoming a royalist stronghold. As a result Ireland became sucked into the British political and military arena, and after 1648, and the outbreak of the second English Civil War, actually became an extension of it.

In addition, during the 1640s, Ireland became embroiled in the continental theatre of war, dominated by the rivalry between the Habsburgs and the Bourbons for European hegemony. In fact, according to a leading historian of the Confederate era, there were 'few periods in which Irish politics have been so much a part of the mainstream of European history'.[12] Certainly all of the combatants fighting in Ireland turned to the major European states for assistance while, for their part, the principal Catholic powers maintained an active diplomatic presence in Kilkenny. Papal interests were represented first by Pietro Francesco Scarampi and, after October 1645, by Giovanni Battista Rinuccini, archbishop of Fermo and papal nuncio; the Spanish and French crowns sent a series of envoys to Ireland, who were primarily responsible for recruiting Irish mercenaries for service abroad. As the 1640s progressed the desire to become Ireland's 'protector' and to interfere directly in Irish politics also became an aim of French, Spanish and papal diplomacy. Therefore in addition to the royalists, the English parliament and the Scots, Spain, France and the papacy endeavoured to manipulate Irish affairs to their own advantage. To some extent Ireland had become an international battleground, a minor sideshow in the all-embracing Thirty Years War then raging on the continent.[13]

Inevitably this external meddling further complicated an already complex domestic situation. Nevertheless the Irish civil wars fell into three reasonably well-defined, chronological phases: 1641–3, 1643–7 and 1647–53. The first phase began with the outbreak of the rebellion (October 1641) and ended with the conclusion of a ceasefire (September 1643) between the Irish Catholic Confederates and the predominantly Protestant, Irish royalist forces, under the command of the marquis of Ormond. During these months the protagonists struggled for control of the country's strategic towns and strongholds. By the summer of 1642 an anti-Catholic coalition – made up of Ormond's troops, the Scottish Covenanters (who had arrived in Ulster in April) and a host of regional commanders, such as Lord Inchiquin in Munster – which remained loosely obedient to the king, enjoyed a tactical and numerical advantage. As map 8.1 shows, the Irish royalists, as Ormond's force became known, dominated Dublin, much of the Pale, County Louth and parts of Counties Down and Cork together with numerous small enclaves in and around Carlow, Derry, Dungannon, Enniskillen, Loughrea and Portumna; while their Scottish allies, under the command of Major General Robert Monro, entrenched themselves in east Ulster. Even though the Catholic insurgents controlled the rest of

---

Territory controlled by the Irish confederates

Territory controlled by the Scots

Territory controlled by the Irish royalists

North Channel

Rathlin Island

L. Foyle

Dunluce

Culmore
Coleraine
Derry
Glenarm

R. Bann

LONDONDERRY

DONEGAL

ANTRIM

Lifford

Carrickfergus
Belfast

TYRONE

ULSTER

L. Neagh

Belfast

R. Lagan

Dungannon
Charlemont
Benburb

Lisnagarvey

DOWN

Enniskillen
Monaghan

Armagh

Manor Hamilton

FERMANAGH

Newry

Sligo

MONAGHAN

ARMAGH

LEITRIM

LOUTH

SLIGO

Greencastle

Carlingford

MAYO

Boyle
Jamestown

Cavan

ROSCOMMON

CAVAN

CONNAUGHT

LONGFORD

Slane
Drogheda

Ardmore
Castlecoote

Roscommon

Athboy
MEATH

R. Boyne

WESTMEATH

Trim

GALWAY

R. *Shannon*

KILDARE

DUBLIN

R. Liffey

Galway

KING'S COUNTY
(now OFFALY)

Dublin

Loughrea

Naas

Portumna

LEINSTER

Maryborough

WICKLOW

QUEEN'S
(now
Leix)

COUNTY

Wicklow

CLARE

L. Derg

CARLOW

TIPPERARY

KILKENNY

Carlow

Kilrush

Limerick

Kilkenny

WEXFORD

LIMERICK

Clonmel

Old
Ross

Wexford

MUNSTER

WATERFORD

Waterford

Duncannon
The Passage

KERRY

CORK

Lismore
Dungarvan

Ardmore

Cork

Youghal

ATLANTIC OCEAN

St. George's Channel

N

0   50 miles
0   80 km

8.1   Ireland on the eve of the cessation of arms, September 1643

165

the country, there can be little doubt that the Protestant coalition would have suppressed the rising had civil war not broken out in England in August 1642. The onset of cross-channel hostilities had an immediate and destabilising impact on Irish affairs. On the one hand, it reduced the amount of money and the quantity of supplies and soldiers available for the Irish war effort and put pressure on the uneasy Protestant alliance. On the other, it gave a welcome boost to the Catholic insurgents, now bonded by an oath of association, who organised themselves into a formal confederation, modelled on the English Parliament, with its 'capital' at Kilkenny.

The second phase of the war, between September 1643 and autumn 1647, characterised by tortuous peace negotiations between the royalists and the Confederates, was particularly complex. The ceasefire of 15 September 1643 – known as the 'cessation of arms ' – heralded a new departure in Anglo-Irish relations. After much haggling it was agreed that in return for troops, supplies and £20,000 in cash for the English war effort, the king would consider repealing the penal laws and granting the Confederates considerable political independence, freedom of worship and security of land tenure. Yet the cessation achieved nothing. Instead it immediately shattered the already strained anti-Catholic alliance because many Protestants could not stomach the king's concessions, and it intensified the war first in Ulster (by driving the Scots deep into the parliamentary camp) and then in Munster (by alienating, in July 1644, Inchiquin and his Protestant army from the royalist cause).

Nevertheless, military defeat in England, first at Marston Moor (July 1644) and then at Naseby (June 1645), strengthened Charles I's resolve to obtain immediate and substantial support from Ireland. In January 1645 he instructed the earl of Glamorgan, a prominent Catholic noble, to secure Irish troops for royalist service in return for religious concessions. The following August the Confederates and Glamorgan agreed upon a secret treaty which involved sending 10,000 Irish troops, arms and munitions to England; however, the extreme Catholics, led by Nuncio Rinuccini rejected this and a further agreement more favourable to Catholicism was finally concluded in December. In the event, this 'Glamorgan treaty' was quickly undermined by the First Ormond Peace of July–August 1646, this time between Ormond and the Confederates; but it too failed to secure Irish aid for the royalist war effort.

The inability of Ormond and Glamorgan to manipulate Confederate resources and manpower to their royal master's advantage provides a stark contrast to the record of the Catholic earl (and after 1645 marquis) of Antrim. Throughout the 1640s Antrim involved himself in seemingly endless plots with the king to send Irish troops to Scotland both to fight for the royalist cause and to continue his personal feud with his arch-enemy, the marquis of Argyll. In the event the only scheme to reach fruition occurred in the summer of 1644 when the arrival of 2,000 Irish veterans, raised by Antrim, armed, victualled and financed by the Confederates, and led by the marquis of Montrose, threw Scottish affairs into chaos for over a year and reduced to a bare minimum covenanting aid for the parliamentary war effort.[14]

In Ireland, too, Scottish fortunes reached a particularly low ebb and at the battle of Benburb (5 June 1646) the Confederate army of Ulster routed Monro's forces. But the failure to expel the Scottish army from Ulster quickly lost the Catholic party any advantage which their textbook victory might have brought them. Equally seriously Benburb wrought havoc on Kilkenny politics. Simply stated there were two principal factions within the Confederation throughout the 1640s. The first consisted of members of Old English families, many of whom were Ormond's clients and thus eager to conclude a peace with the king even if it jeopardised the future safety of the Catholic religion. This body dominated the Supreme Council, the Confederate executive body responsible for carrying out the orders of the General Assemblies and for supervising the Catholic war effort. The second faction, led after 1645 by Rinuccini, consisted of members of Gaelic families, predominantly from Ulster, of General Owen Roe O'Neill and of clerics. This Old Irish or 'clerical party', viewed freedom for the Catholic religion as the inevitable price of any compromise with the royalists and tended to predominate in the Confederate General Assemblies.

Tensions between the two sides reached a climax during the summer of 1646 when Rinuccini and the Old Irish faction, elated by the victory at Benburb, declared the First Ormond Peace unacceptable and first excommunicated and then exiled from Kilkenny those Confederates who favoured it. Defeat on the battlefield further exacerbated these factional divisions within the ranks of the Catholic party. In June 1647, after lengthy talks, Ormond abandoned the king's cause and handed Dublin over to a parliamentary army under the command of Colonel Michael Jones, and promptly withdrew to England and then France. Almost at once the Confederate army of Leinster, under Preston's command, launched an offensive against the parliamentarians only to be routed at the battle of Dungan's Hill (8 August). Three months later the Army of Munster met a similar, humiliating fate at the battle of Knockanauss, County Cork (13 November).

These twin débâcles brought the second phase of the Irish civil wars to an inglorious end. Throughout this four-year period the Confederates had been aware of the need to prevent the English parliament, their implacable enemy, from becoming so powerful that it could invade and destroy them. To achieve this two options had been open to them: either they could aid Charles I with all their might in return for the best political, religious and tenurial concessions they could extort, and hope for a royalist victory in Britain; or they could abandon the king altogether and make Catholic Ireland, with the aid of foreign powers, impregnable to invasion from England. By failing to decide between these equally viable but totally incompatible options, the Confederates failed to achieve their principal objective and thus safeguard their own survival.

As a result, the third phase of the conflict, between autumn 1647 and the completion of the Cromwellian conquest of Ireland in April 1653, witnessed the political and military dismemberment of both the Catholic and royalist armies at the hands of an army controlled by the English parliament. Despite losing the first English civil war, Charles I had refused to acquiesce to parliament's demands and instead had allied himself with the Scots and tried to rekindle his power base in Ireland. However his overwhelming defeat in the second English civil war in August 1648 meant that any hope of continuing the royalist war effort in Britain depended exclusively on Ormond's ability to unite Ireland's divided factions under the authority of the king. The marquis, who returned from his exile in France in September 1648, eventually managed to do this and the Second Ormond Peace, which finally merged the men and resources of the Irish royalists with those of the Confederates, took effect on 17 January 1649. However Irish aid came too late to save Charles I, who was executed by his parliamentary opponents on 30 January 1649, and instead merely served to increase parliament's resolve to deal with the 'Irish problem'.

Oliver Cromwell and his force of 12,000 veterans from the New Model Army, with a powerful siege train and a war chest of £100,000 landed at Dublin in August 1649. Within three months the royalist and former Confederate strongholds of Drogheda (11 September), Wexford (11 October), New Ross (19 October) and Carrickfergus (2 November) had either been taken by, or surrendered to, the English invaders. The capture of Kilkenny (27 March 1650), Clonmel (10 May), Carlow (24 July), Waterford (6 August), Charlemont (14 August), Limerick (27 October 1651) and finally Galway (12 April 1652) virtually completed the Cromwellian conquest of Ireland. Thanks to aggressive parliamentary leadership, a steady flow of supplies, money and men from England, continued divisions within the anti-English coalition in Ireland, and uninspired leadership by Ormond, who 'lacked the vision and experience' to capture Dublin prior to Cromwell's landing, the 'Wars of the Three Kingdoms' were over.[15]

In just under three years the parliamentary army succeeded in uniting Ireland under one ruler, something the royalist, Scottish and Confederate armies had failed to achieve over the previous nine years. This inability can be attributed partly to the conduct and character of the war. With the exception of seven battles there were few set-piece encounters; instead, uncoordinated 'small wars' or 'guerrilla tactics' dominated the military proceedings. For every major confrontation there were literally hundreds of skirmishes, ambushes and forays which revolved around the capture of key forts, towns or ports in the country and the destruction of the enemy's economic base. These 'wars of attrition', where all sides aimed 'to burn all the corn, and kill all the cattle, and to bring famine' to their enemy, dominated the seventeenth-century Irish military landscape.[16]

Sieges became another feature of Irish warfare as armies sought to reduce towns into submission by closely investing them. For instance, the Confederates eager to take Duncannon, which dominated the passage and shipping *en route* to Waterford, spent two months starving the garrison into surrender (January–March 1645); while

8.2   Randal MacDonnell, second earl and first marquis of Antrim
(1609–1683). As a Gaelic warlord of Scottish descent and a Caroline
courtier, MacDonnell played a leading role in rallying support for the king
in Ireland and Scotland.

Table 8.1. *Estimates (in ranges) of Protestant troop strength, 1642–1649*

Year	Leinster	Connacht & Munster	'British' in Ulster	Scots in Ulster	Total
1642	4–6,000[a]	2–6,000	6–?11,000	10,000	22–33,000
1643	4–7,000[a]	4–6,000	8–?12,000	c. 9–10,000	25–35,000
1644	3–5,000[a]	2–3,000	8–?10,000	6–7,000	19–25,000
1645	3–5,000[a]	2–5,000	8–9,000	5–6,000	18–25,000
1646	2–4,000[a]	4–5,000	5–9,000	5–6,000	16–24,000
1647	7–8,000[b]	5–9,000	5–8,500	2–3,500	18–26,500
1648	7–9,000[b]	4–6,000	5–8,000	c. 2,000	18–25,000
1649	16–24,000[c]	4–6,000	5–8,000	?	25–38,000

[a] Ormond's forces
[b] Jones's forces
[c] Cromwell's forces
Source: Wheeler, 'Four armies in Ireland', pp. 50–1.

six years later the Cromwellians adopted similar tactics against Limerick (June–October 1651). To take a fortified place by storm proved more difficult since this required heavy artillery which was in short supply, especially in Ulster, during the early years of the war. As a result, in March 1642 after five months the Confederates raised their siege of Drogheda, which had been strengthened by 'brestworks' at every gate and by 'platforms in such places where the walls were defective', and the royalists abandoned their siege of New Ross early in 1643.[17] However when heavy artillery manned by experienced gunners and skilled military engineers became available, Ireland's defences could be breached easily. This happened in the summer of 1645, when forces loyal to the English parliament managed to take Sligo 'after the batteringe of two houses'; in July 1646, when two Confederate cannon quickly breached Bunratty's extensive earthen outworks; and in September 1649, when Cromwell's superior artillery made short work of Drogheda's medieval walls.

By and large, though, any advantage gained by the capture of a fortified position was soon lost largely because neither the Confederates, the royalists, the Scots nor the parliamentarians (prior to 1649) appeared to have a 'grand strategy' for winning the war. On the contrary there was no cooperation between the various commanders. Thus the Confederate armies (of which there were four – one for each province) all acted as independent units, advancing, retreating and offering battle as the opinion of the commanders and local circumstances dictated. To make matters worse the leading Irish generals constantly feuded and bickered with one another over trivial, personal matters. The consequences were often profound: the feud in 1644 between Antrim and Castlehaven over who should be given supreme command of all of the Confederate armies ensured that the summer offensive

Table 8.2. *Estimates (in ranges) of Catholic troop strength, 1642-1649*

Year	Ulster (O'Neill)	Leinster (Preston)	Munster (Taaffe)	Connacht	Total
1642	3–8,000	4–8,000	2–5,000	c. 2,000	11–23,000
1643	3–6,000	5–7,000	4–7,000	c. 2,000	14–22,000
1644	5–7,000	6–7,000	5–8,000	c. 2,000	18–24,000
1645	3–5,000	5–7,000	4–6,000	c. 2,000	14–20,000
1646	5–7,000	4–7,000	4–6,000	2–3,000	15–23,000
1647	6–8,000	6–8,000	4–8,000	4–6,000	20–30,000
1648	7–8,000	3–5,000	5–7,000	3–4,000	18–24,000
1649	5–8,000	10–15,000[a]		3–5,000	18–28,000

[a] Confederate forces under Ormond's command.

against Ulster ended in a shambles; while the quarrel between O'Neill and Preston lost the Confederates the chance of taking Dublin in 1646. In fact one recent historian has concluded that 'A failure of Irish leadership, not "Cromwell's curse", dashed Catholic hopes for religious toleration and political autonomy.'[18] Prior to 1649 the same could be said for the armies raised to quell the Irish rebellion: no joint action against the Confederate foe was ever arranged between the various forces hostile to the Catholic cause. While the uneasy coalition of those troops loyal to the king and to the English parliament disintegrated after the conclusion of the 1643 ceasefire and from this point on the Scottish and parliamentary forces not only regarded their royalist coreligionists as the 'enemy' but remained intensely suspicious of and uncooperative towards each other. Under these circumstances, the military stalemate which existed for much of the decade hardly comes as a surprise.

The soldiers

At the height of the Irish civil wars of the 1640s four separate armies – the Scots, the Confederates, the royalists and the parliamentarians – took the field. The absence of reliable quantitative data makes it impossible to estimate accurately the size of these forces; but the survival of a few musters and of numerous qualitative sources such as letters, ambassadorial dispatches, intelligence reports, contemporary pamphlets and newsheets indicates that between 40,000 and 50,000 men bore arms throughout the decade.

Shortly after the outbreak of the rebellion between 33,000 and 60,000 men fought in the Confederate, royalist and Scottish armies; by 1649 this figure had risen to between 43,000 and 66,000 soldiers. These totals are striking, given that Ireland's population has been estimated at around 2.1 million people. If roughly 20 per cent (or 9,000 men) of this force of 45,000 were 'foreign' (largely English or Scots), one could argue that, prior to 1649, 17.1 Irish people out of every 1,000 inhabitants, or nearly 2 per cent of the total population, served in the armed forces. If accurate this would indicate that as many Irishmen, in relation to total population, bore arms in the 1640s as served in the armies of Louis XIV during the 1690s, where the military participation ratio stood at 17.6 for every 1,000 inhabitants and where society was much better prepared for lengthy and costly combat.[19]

Extant musters provide further information on the composition and strength of these forces and on how well they were armed.[20] On the Confederate side the four provincial armies theoretically consisted of 6,000 foot and 400 horse and of a 'running army' of 2,000 foot and 200 horse – a fairly typical ratio of infantry to cavalry for the war. However, muster extracts suggest that the Confederates failed to maintain these levels. The Army of Leinster, when mustered in May 1646, numbered just over 5,000 men (with an average of 84 men, instead of the specified 100, in each company); but by 1649 this figure had dropped to just under, 4,000 men (with an average of 75 men in each company). The Army of Munster, at a muster in 1649, contained roughly 3,500 men (with an average of 60 men in each company). In 1643 the 10,000-strong Scottish army in Ulster included roughly 98 soldiers in each company; while the average size of the royalist companies varied from 108 in May 1642 to 71 in November 1642.

Whatever the size of the unit, however, every effort was made to equip these troops with firearms and pikes. For instance during the First Bishops' War of 1638–9 Antrim proposed to organise his army according to the most up-to-date European specifications and ordered that his three regiments of foot were to consist of two parts 'shot' (musketeers), and one-third pike. So too during the 1640s the Irish Confederates decreed that in each company 'two parts [should be] armed with muskets well fixed and a third part with serviceable pike'.[21] An extant muster dating from 1649 suggests that these specifications were occasionally met, for nearly two-thirds of the Army of Leinster in that year were armed with muskets. And the ratio of musket to pike among both the royalist and Scottish forces appears to have hovered around 3 muskets to every 2 pikes. But the musket did not reign supreme throughout Ireland. Barely half of the Army of Ulster used firearms, while pikes predominated in the Army of Munster.

The musters further indicate the prevailing ratio of officers to the other ranks. For example, roughly 11 per cent of the Scottish army in 1642 were officers; the percentage of officers in the Irish royalist forces nearly doubled from 7 per cent in May 1642 to 13 per cent in 1644, while the percentage of officers in the confederate armies varied from 9 per cent to nearly 20 per cent. Many of these regimental commanders were the heads of Gaelic septs or prominent Irish and Scottish noblemen: Lords Taaffe and Dillon, together with the earls of Westmeath, Castlehaven and Antrim, all held Confederate commands; the marquis of Ormond, Sir Henry Tichbourne, Sir Francis Willoughby, Lord Inchiquin and Sir Charles Coote led royalist regiments; and the earls of Leven, Lothian, Glencairn, Eglinton, Lindsay and the marquis of Argyll raised Scottish regiments in which they served as titular colonels. By and large, the company officers and especially their deputies were all followers or kinsmen. For instance the commanders selected to fight in Antrim's expeditionary force to Scotland in 1644 – the majority of whom were named MacAllester, MacCormack, MacDonnell, MacDermot, MacHenry, MacQuillan, O'Cahan, O'Hare and O'Neill – appear to have originated, as one might expect, in Counties Antrim and Londonderry.

Alongside these inexperienced baronial commanders fought professional soldiers. Confederate Generals Owen Roe O'Neill ('a soldier since a boy, in the only martial academy of Christendom – Flanders'),[22] Thomas Preston and John Burke all distinguished themselves fighting in the Spanish Army of Flanders; Major General Robert Monro had served with the Scottish troops in Germany between 1627 and 1633 and in Scotland during the Bishops' Wars; and the commander of Drogheda in 1649, Sir Arthur Aston, had fought in the Russian, Polish and Swedish armies before joining the royalists. Many of their officers included career soldiers well versed in the ways of continental warfare: Lieutenant-Colonel George Monro and Major James Turner of the Scots Brigade in Ulster had both enlisted in the Swedish forces in Germany; Hugh Dubh O'Neill, Garret Wall, Con and Brian O'Neill and many others had considerable experience of active service in the French and Spanish armies.

So much for the chiefs: who made up the rank and file and how were they recruited? From the outset it seems that 'of men fit for warr there are certainly a sufficient number' in Ireland, though these human resources were not always tapped to optimum effect.[23] Initially, Irish grandees summoned their followers, tenants and kinsmen to arms in a time honoured fashion. Thus Antrim proposed to exploit his position as a Gaelic lord in both Ulster and the Western Isles to levy the 5,000 foot and 200 horse needed for the First Bishops' War; and again in 1644 he summoned the men of his own lordship and of neighbouring sublordships to volunteer for service in Scotland. Likewise leading Protestant landlords – the lord of the Ards, Sir James Montgomery, Sir Robert Stewart, Sir William Stewart, Sir William Cole and Sir Ralph Gore – raised 9,900 foot and 750 horse in Ulster by 1643; while the earl of Cork initially held Munster for the English by raising forces from among his tenants and relatives. A mixture of impressment and voluntary enlistment were also used. By the later 1640s the Confederates required each county to produce quotas of men for service and charged local power-brokers with drilling and maintaining 'trained bands' to be drawn upon in times of emergency.

The Confederates, in particular, also urged their compatriots serving in Germany, France, Flanders and Spain to fight in Ireland. The English ambassador in France noted early in 1642 that 'the common men come from their winter quarters by twenties and thirties . . . and hasten towards Ireland as fast as they can'.[24] The trickle soon turned into a flood. By 1645 only one Irish regiment remained in French service (there had been seven in 1641); between 1641 and 1643 an Irish regiment could not be mustered in Flanders; and by 1645 there was only one

Irish regiment serving in Spain. Medical personnel accompanied these veterans. For instance, Owen O'Sheil, originally from County Westmeath, who had studied medicine at Douai and practised at the military hospital of the Army of Flanders at Mechelen, in 1642 returned to Ireland where he served as physician general first to the Army of Leinster and then to the Army of Ulster. A number of foreign technicians skilled in the ways of war also moved to Ireland: John Vangyrish, a German engineer, enlisted in the Army of Connacht; while a Frenchman, Monsieur Laloe, was engineer general for the Confederates and used his 'bumboes and fire-workes' to great effect at the siege of Duncannon and elsewhere.[25] Thomas Harley became chief engineer in Munster and excelled in the destruction of strongholds, as did his counterpart in the Scottish army, Henry Jardine.

All sides recognised the advantages brought by these professional soldiers who 'spend their whole time in the exercises of military discipline, to whome fights, sieges, batteryes, approaches, and underminings were as familiar as were the wearing of their corsletts'.[26] For although a large number of ordinary native Irish soldiers had already received some military training in Stafford's New Army in 1640, most of the rank and file resembled those under Ormond's command during the early 1640s, who were 'onely a rable of disarmed freshwater souldiers, without armes, ammunition or souldier commander',[27] or those Catholic recruits, of whom Owen Roe O'Neill complained in 1642 that there was 'no obedience among the soldiers, if one call men soldiers who behave nothing better than the animals . . . I am killing myself bringing them to some order and discipline.'[28]

Nevertheless within a relatively short period of time the continental veterans had 'reduced many of the natives to a more civil deportment, and to a pretty good understanding of military discipline'.[29] They also introduced modern tactics, pioneered by Maurice of Nassau at the turn of the seventeenth century and continued during the Thirty Years War, whereby small tactical units fought in a linear formation 'in which the firepower of musketeers was coordinated with the shock strength of pikemen'.[30] The Irish victory of Benburb demonstrated the effectiveness of linear formation fighting and how, on occasion, the Irish soldier appears to have been blessed with remarkable stamina, courage and endurance. Certainly the Confederate general the earl of Castlehaven believed that though he only had 5,000 foot and 800 horse 'their contentment and couradge . . . does make them in my esteeme more than duble that number'.[31] By 1646 two leading royalists maintained that the Confederates 'have their men in a better order of war and better commanded by captains of experience and practice of warr then ever they were since the conquest'.[32]

Every effort was made to maintain discipline among the soldiers. All sides issued lengthy lists of regulations which forbade adultery, blasphemy, treachery, disobedience, pillage, theft, arson, murder, drunkenness, liaisons with the enemy, boys or women, or the sale of arms, and which promoted prayer, loyalty and self-discipline.[33] However lack of pay and other basic necessities meant that indiscriminate plunder and pillage occurred regularly, as indeed was the case with any army on the move in mid-seventeenth-century Europe. For example, in July 1647 parliamentary troops garrisoned in Dublin plundered the local market, shops and homes before breaking into and robbing the excise house; while the horrified citizens remonstrated at once to Westminster about 'the enemy abroad and the soldiers at home'.[34] An added threat came from renegade soldiers who terrorised the local populace, especially in remote regions, by becoming highwaymen, robbers and murderers. One leading Confederate complained to Ormond of 'the rapines, depredations, and disorder of the souldiers (which . . . eat into the bowels of the country)'.[35] As the war progressed lawlessness became endemic. In 1647 the Confederate General Assembly lamented that the 'frequent committal of murthers, thefts, robberies, forcible entries, extortions . . . do daily multiply and increase through the want of gaols in severall counties, the defect in gaolers . . . and other officers, to execute and perform their respective duties'.[36] Despite every effort to control the 'vice and disorder of theft, burglary and robbery' associated with the army, soldiers continued to exploit and to intimidate the civilian population.[37] Only regular pay and an efficient system of supply would have improved the discipline, morale and combat effectiveness of the soldiers fighting in Ireland. And this was sadly lacking.

Feeding Mars

War everywhere tested a society's capacity to provide logistical backing as much as its ability to mobilise soldiers. Money – the sinews of any war – was needed to pay, feed, clothe, arm and care for the troops; but costs often proved prohibitively high. To keep 6,000 Confederate foot and 800 horse and their officers in the field for six weeks amounted to just over £10,000, while £16,000 per month was needed to keep the 10,000 Scots in Ulster. The annual charge of Ormond's army exceeded £600,000, or seven times the income of Ireland in the 1640s.[38]

Paying these bills proved difficult and all sides resorted to similar fund-raising tactics. From the outset the Catholic party remained painfully aware that without substantial foreign aid their cause was almost hopeless: 'Our wants are money, arms and ammunition; these we have no way to provide for, the country being exceedingly exhausted unless we may be assisted by those who wish well unto our cause beyond the seas.'[39] In all they received in the region of £70,000 from 'beyond the seas': papal sources provided roughly £25,000 in cash and £31,000 in bills of exchange; France donated nearly £6,400; while Spain contributed a further £5,000 (most of it in gold coin). For their part, the parliamentarians solicited Dutch aid and over five years (1643–8) collected £31,218. In addition, by 1646 'voluntary' subscriptions 'toward the relief of His Majesty's distressed subjects of the kingdom of Ireland' brought in nearly £46,000 from London and the home counties. The various combatants also borrowed substantial amounts. Merchants in London,

Edinburgh and Antwerp lent the House of Commons vast sums of money (roughly £333,000) for the Irish war effort,[40] and leading Irish merchants also made funds available to royalists and Confederates alike: Patrick Archer of Kilkenny, for instance, provided the Catholics with cash and goods to the value of £5,000 in 1644–5 and at the Restoration claimed that Ormond owed him £10,000. Leading grandees also put their personal fortunes at the disposal of their respective governments: Ormond, for one, lent the crown nearly £162,000 over eight years; the earl of Cork initially funded the entire Protestant war effort in Munster; while the earl of Clanricard preserved 'the rights and interests of the Crown of England' in County Galway 'even to the ruin of my fortune'.[41]

Money was also raised through taxation. The Confederates controlled the disposable income derived from church lands (both Catholic and Protestant) and used 'the profit of the two parts of ecclesiastical tythes and church-livings' for the upkeep of the army. In addition they initially taxed 'thirds [of freehold] and tenths [of movable goods]' and ordered that 'e[a]ch man grants the fourth parte of his estate towards the maintenance of the warr'.[42] This system proved inefficient and impossible to administer effectively and it was replaced variously with 'assessments', 'contributions' and 'applottments' which were calculated according to a country's ability to pay. For instance in Leinster, out of every £1 10s (or 360 pence) raised, each county paid in the following proportion:

	pence	%		pence	%
Longford	27	(7.50)	Kildare	14	(3.88)
Wexford	65	(18.05)	Kilkenny	65	(18.05)
Kilkenny city	16	(4.40)	Westmeath	54	(15.00)
Wicklow	29	(8.05)	King's County	40	(11.10)
Meath	15	(4.16)	Queen's County	14	(4.16)
Carlow	20	(5.55)			

Thus the wealthier counties, especially Wexford and Kilkenny, which were least affected by the dislocation associated with armies on the move and military action, bore the greatest financial burden. In areas controlled by the royalists or the parliamentarians an assessment was laid upon a 'plough-land' (120 acres of arable land). Under the Cromwellians the contribution system reached its apogee. In 1651 the province of Ulster alone was expected to provide £5,430 towards the upkeep of the army for six months, and the following year the whole country was charged £24,770 in 'cess', with a further £6,495 5s 6d in 'forage'. In Britain, parliament levied assessments for the relief of the army in Ireland. Thus by the ordinance of 18 October 1644 weekly contributions of £3,740 for Ireland were exacted from those areas of England under parliament's control, which over twelve months yielded roughly £194,500 and over the remainder of the decade raised nearly £1 million.

Revenue from customs and excise duties was also tapped. The royalists charged excise on the sale of ale, beer, wine, whiskey, tobacco and cattle in Dublin, Trim, Drogheda and throughout Munster. Similarly in England the government earmarked £20,000 per annum from the excise for the war in Ireland, generating £110,000 over eight years. Anticipated revenue from customs and excise duties also served as security for further loans. For instance in March 1646, using as collateral 'the accruing profits of the excise in the cities of Waterford, Kilkenny and Limerick and in the towns of Galway, Wexford and Clonmel', the Confederates raised £3,000 in under a week 'by way of [a] loan on security of able merchants'.[43] Though customs and excise did yield some income for the Confederates (early in 1649 Irish customs allegedly brought in £100,000 annually),[44] the tenths, collected on all prizes brought into Irish harbours, proved much more lucrative. After January 1649 Ormond briefly exploited this resource and, using the revenue from tenths as security, borrowed £4,000 from Waterford, nearly £1,500 from Wexford and £750 from Ross.

All the combatants exploited the assets of their enemies. The English parliament collected in the region of £300,000 in London by confiscating 2½ million acres of Irish land belonging to 'papists' and 'rebels'; a further £140,000 came from the estates of delinquent royalists in England. In a similar fashion, the Confederates ordered that the estates and goods of those in arms against them, together with the king's 'customs, rents, revenues, arrears and dues', be collected and used for their war effort. Between Michaelmas 1646 and July 1647 the Confederates received £627 10s from 'the enemies' and 'neuters' [i.e. neutrals] rents in County Carlow alone; whilst the rents of those liable to sequestration in Counties Wexford, Carlow and Kildare in 1649 exceeded £2,700.

Although the Confederates enjoyed the advantage of controlling most of Ireland's taxable resources, they failed to exploit them to full effect. Contributions raised throughout Confederate quarters in the spring and summer of 1646 were expected to yield nearly £19,000; of this it was anticipated that 'a good parte . . . will be lost by desperate delinquencie, wastes, paieinge of garrisons, 6d per pound to the commissioners and receavers, and it is conceaved probable that £8,000 may be had cleere thereof for this harvest service'.[45] In an attempt to improve their crude and inefficient financial machinery the Confederates farmed out the excise, overhauled the collection of tithes and punished tax evaders, but to no avail: by August 1648 they were virtually bankrupt and had few prospects of raising money 'from a country so totally exhausted, and so lamentably ruined'.[46]

In addition to money, the Confederate armies of course needed cannon, muskets, powder, swords, bullets, barrels and locks, iron, steel and armour. In the early years of the war the Irish manufactured their own cannon out of 'pots and pans' but they burst when discharged; they also tried leather guns with predictably disastrous results. But from the summer of 1642 piecemeal shipments of arms and munitions began arriving in Ireland from overseas: in July 1642, 40,000 pounds of powder and

3,000 muskets were sent from Flanders; in October, 200 barrels of powder, muskets and three 'pieces of bronze' left Nieuport in Spanish Flanders; in March 1643, four small frigates laden with arms left northern Spain; and early in 1644 yet more arms and ammunition arrived in Wexford and Waterford. In fact so much military hardware arrived from the continent that by 1646 the Catholic party had succeeded in building up reserves of powder, match and bullets: a muster of the Army of Munster (taken early in 1649) suggests that, with the exception of a few companies, their regiments were reasonably well armed. By contrast the Irish royalists under Ormond's command remained poorly supplied with military equipment and turned to merchants and arms dealers in Amsterdam, Caen and Paris for assistance.

Providing food, quarters and clothing for thousands of men over a prolonged period of time proved far more difficult, especially for the royalists whose 'wants' throughout the 1640s were never entirely satisfied. Even the Confederates who controlled the greatest amount of profitable territory had similar problems. Though semi-nomadic 'creaghts', with their large herds of cows and flocks of sheep, partly maintained and victualled the Army of Ulster, the other Catholic armies were less fortunate. In an effort to spread evenly the burden of providing the soldiers with grain and meat, detailed targets were laid down for each country. But meeting these quotas proved almost impossible: for instance, of 10,000 barrels of corn applotted on the provinces of Leinster and Munster in the spring of 1650 fewer than a third were ever collected in Leinster and only a half in Munster. Another heavy burden was housing troops: up to seven infantry regiments were billeted in houses in and around Dublin during the 1640s and as many as 1,500 soldiers crammed into Kilkenny. By 1650 1,300 soldiers plus their camp followers had gathered in the unfortunate town of Clonmel; hardly surprising 'many of ye poore inhabitants have deserted ye town'.[47]

Inadequate shelter, a poor diet, a damp climate and the rigours associated with campaigning or with cramped living in unhygienic garrisons resulted in pneumonia, flu and consumption ('the looseness and the malignant fever', 'violent coughs', 'stopping of the breath') in winter, and in enteric fevers, bacillary dysentery, hepatitis and typhus (fluxes and agues) in summer. In a single year 300 men, or nearly a third, of Colonel Edward Conway's regiment died for want of quarter and provisions 'whereby ye souldiers fell into a disease taken by cold'.[48] Many of the royalist forces stationed in Dublin during the early 1640s became ill – 'so many of them being sick as much weakens all the companies'.[49] During the siege of Drogheda over the winter of 1641–2 one combatant noted how 'famine and fluxes with other diseases returned againe to their former dominion over us; death began to look more terrible within the walls then without'.[50] In the spring of 1642 an outbreak of fevers and fluxes (probably bacillary dysentery) reduced the royalist forces in Munster by two-thirds; while later that year in one Dublin regiment alone there were 300 foot and 30 officers sick.

To make matters worse, medical services were at best rudimentary. The absence

---

8.3 Soldiers, whether loyal to Charles I or parliament, lacked adequate supplies of food, shelter, clothing, arms and medicines for much of the war. This 'English–Irish soldier', who 'had rather Eate than Fight', is from a broad-side ballad of 1642.

of a doctor during the siege of Duncannon fort in 1645 meant that 'divers men perished of curable wounds'.[51] Medication was also in very short supply. The lords justice complained in April 1642 that 'the want of medicaments here for sick and wounded soldiers is so lamentable as many die daily here under the hands of physicians and chyrurgions by occasion of that want'.[52] When medical supplies finally arrived they were of poor quality and insufficient quantity. Extant musters indicate that the confederate troops enjoyed better health than their royalist or parliamentarian counterparts: less than 3 per cent of the Army of Leinster was listed as 'sick' in 1649; less than 6 per cent of the Army of Ulster in 1650. According to one account, the fact that the Irish troops were not confined to garrisons, were apparently better clothed and enjoyed superior food and quarter helps to explain their hardiness and better immunity to disease.[53]

The inability of the protagonists fighting in Ireland – especially the royalists, the Scots and the parliamentarians – to care for their soldiers either physically or financially had serious implications. Thus, even though by the summer of 1642 anti-Catholic coalition forces had a numerical advantage over the Confederates, they failed to use this to full effect due to a lack of money, food and equipment. The royalists attributed their military ineffectiveness during the early 1640s to logistical difficulties and in 1643 believed that they were 'equally in danger to be devoured through our wants, or to be destroyed by the rebels for want of needful habiliments of war'.[54] Little wonder they concluded a ceasefire with the Catholics later that year. The Scottish offensive in Ulster in 1642 ground to a halt due to lack of provisions, and logistical difficulties kept it on the defensive until 1646. Likewise in 1647 Ormond claimed that supply problems were one reason why he handed Dublin over to the parliamentarians. Despite the dispatch of over 2 million pounds for the Irish war effort (prior to 1649) the parliamentary forces remained so poorly supplied that they signed informal local truces with the Irish late in 1648 and again in May 1649.

By contrast, the Confederate victory at Benburb can be attributed as much to the ability of the Catholic party to pay and supply the Army of Ulster with victuals, arms and munitions as to O'Neill's abilities as a military commander. Similarly, Cromwell's Irish campaign proved to be a logistical triumph: his troops were well fed, well equipped and well paid – a feat which, between May 1649 and November 1656, cost the British government £3.8 million (or the equivalent of £37,000 per month).[55] One military historian has even suggested that, 'Without this increased financial efficiency, it is doubtful whether even Cromwell's military genius could have forced the decisive action he did in so short a time'.[56]

The impact of war on Irish society and the economy

> Who brings famine? The army
> Who brings the plague? The army
> Who the sword? The army

Who hinders trade? The army
Who confounds all? The army[57]

Ireland was no stranger to warfare: indeed until the beginning of the seventeenth century rebellion and long drawn out military struggles had seemed endemic. However during the thirty-eight years of peace prior to the outbreak of the 1641 rebellion the country slowly recovered from the devastation caused by the Nine Years War (1593–1603) and the economy began once more to prosper. Nevertheless economic considerations – especially poor harvests during the later 1630s, endemic indebtedness and loss of property through plantation, mortgage or through the practice of primogeniture – helped drive the Irish to take up arms in 1641. The lengthy war which ensued then sparked a series of devastating commercial crises which crippled Irish trade and drained an already weak economy of much needed specie.

Even though the extent of the destruction varied enormously from region to region, no Irish county or town was spared entirely. Property was destroyed throughout Ireland either by the enemy in offensive action (bombardment, punitive burning and plunder) or by 'friends' in order to deny quarter, fuel and cover to their opponents. Towns became overcrowded with war refugees: by 1642 the lords justice estimated that 4,000 Protestant refugees, or the equivalent of 10 per cent of the capital's pre-war population, had descended upon Dublin, half of whom were classified as 'destitute', and in the parish of St John the Evangelist alone 158 of them died between January and September 1643. Rural areas also suffered. For some the conflict proved a disaster; for others, at least until 1649, it meant little more than heavy taxation and temporary dislocation of the social order and hierarchy. Towards the end of 1647 Patrick Darcy, the Confederate lawyer, found 'nothing but grass, waters and ayre' in the Confederate quarters in Munster.[58] Yet only two years previously a papal visitor to Ireland had described the countryside on his trip from Kenmare Bay to Limerick in glowing terms. 'The country through which we passed, although mountainous, is picturesque and everywhere covered with all sorts of cattle browsing in rich pasture.' He added that the lowland areas appeared to be particularly prosperous 'abounding in herds, cattle and sheep from which fine wool is made'.[59] By 1646 four out of the six counties in Connacht were deemed 'wasted': yet County Mayo remained well endowed 'with a great abundance of cows, garrons, sheep, hogs'.[60]

The conflict hit the eastern provinces especially hard. By July 1643 much of Leinster was 'so wasted that scarce a cow, garron or man is to be seene in many miles together . . . the eares of the corne which is now growing in many of these parts, is so generally cut off now before it is ripe, by the hunger starved rebels, that very little will be reaped'.[61] Parts of Ulster were equally devastated. Late in 1642 General Owen Roe O'Neill reported back to Rome that County Donegal, 'not only looks like a desert, but like Hell, if there could be a Hell upon earth; for besides the

---

sterility, destruction, and bad condition it is in, the people are so rough and barbarous and miserable that many of them are little better in their ways than the most remote Indians'.[62]

The situation was exacerbated throughout the decade by marauding soldiers who stole, burned and plundered civilian property, goods and livestock, commandeered grain, horses and weapons and forced the populace to pay contributions, to feed and to quarter the troops. Lord Inchiquin, appropriately named 'Morrough of the burnings', and his men, were particularly destructive. In 1644 the gentry of County Cork complained that his forces had taken all of their corn, wasted estates by cutting down trees and orchards, stolen their horses and intimidated local farmers. Certainly during one foray into County Tipperary late in 1647, Inchiquin's forces burned £20,000 worth of corn around Cahir and reduced the inhabitants of Upper Ormond 'to eat their garrans and plough-horses'.[63]

From the perspective of the Irish landlord, this destruction of property and loss of livestock was compounded by the fact that it was difficult or, in most cases, impossible for tenants to pay their rents. Extant rent rolls for the County Fermanagh and Tyrone estates of the countess of Huntington record no income at all from her property during the 1640s and early 1650s: not until the later decades of the seventeenth century did her rental begin to reach its pre-1641 level. The earl of Antrim also suffered acute financial hardship, losing roughly £150,000 in rents due to the fact that the Scots occupied his extensive estates for most of the 1640s; his neighbours in Ulster, George Rawdon and Sir William Stewart, also lost their annual rentals of £300 and £2,000 respectively.

One of the greatest threats to both rural and urban communities was the destruction of local commerce and trade networks. Thus the conflict quickly wasted Dublin and merchants feared to bring merchandise into the city in case the army confiscated it, while the absence of 'native' commodities made it impossible to export goods. As a result Dublin's customs for 1644 to 1645 yielded less than £1,400 and by 1647 this figure had probably dropped to £600, just over a tenth of the value of the pre-war customs.[64] The same held true for Cork where the army exacerbated the problem by seizing corn reserves, levying extortionate fines on hides ready for export, and confiscating barrels of salt, wine and tallow.

A chronic shortage of specie made the already bleak economic landscape gloomier still. 'The want of money keeps us back from doing those things which are expected from us' the Supreme Council complained early in 1643 'for although the people contribute cheerfully what they have, yet, the stock of money now in the kingdom answers not their desires, our late greedy governors having drained our whole substance'.[65] Moreover the absence of coin drove up both rates of interest (to around 45 per cent during the early 1640s) and prices (between 1642 and 1645 the price of corn doubled and that of wheat nearly quadrupled). The establishment of a cash-oriented market economy, clearly progressing in the early seventeenth century, was set back for years as a result of the civil wars.[66]

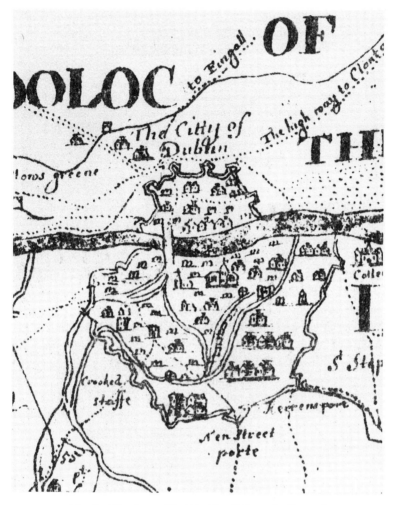

8.4   The fortifications of Dublin (detail from the Down Survey,
1655–1656). During the 1640s huge defensive earthworks transformed
Dublin into an artillery fortress.

However, war quickly became Ireland's major industry and within a relatively
short period of time the Irish economy became finely tuned to the needs of armed
conflict as enterprising individuals exploited to maximum advantage any opportunities which the discord created. With the notable exception of Dublin, commerce
between Irish and continental ports continued: Waterford and Wexford (and to a
lesser extent Carrickfergus, Belfast, Dungarvan, Cork, Limerick and Galway)
continued as centres of international and domestic trade, exporting wool, hides,
sheepskins, goatskins, tallow, herring and salmon to friendly ports in England and
to the continental ports of Nantes, St Malo, Bordeaux, La Rochelle, Brest, Dunkirk,

Bilbao, Amsterdam, Rotterdam and Hamburg, in return for all manner of guns, munitions and other commodities. The Spanish agent in Ireland even recommended that Spain improve commercial relations with Ireland since

> apart from a certain rudeness of the people . . . Ireland should be a good market for Spanish wine, olive oil and sugar and some munitions of war and weapons and you can get from here fish, wool, wax, hides, butter and corn. In all these things and in sheep raising this kingdom is as abundant as any land in Christendom. And if you could have ships in San Sebastian or Bilbao travelling every fortnight between Spain and Ireland, I do not doubt that it would be of great profit.[67]

Trading with Ireland was admittedly hazardous, with many merchantmen taken prize by enemy warships or privateers, but despite this, merchants, particularly arms-dealers, continued to do so largely because it was 'as profitable a voyage unto Ireland . . . as unto the East or West Indies'.[68] Consider the example of the Flemish money lender Antonio Nicholas Vanderkipp who managed one of the most successful privateering enterprises in the country, supplied arms, munitions and victuals to the highest bidder, and hired transport vessels at extortionate rates out to the Confederates, the royalists and the foreign powers operating in Ireland. His compatriot, Adrian Van Haute, ran similar enterprises; as did native merchants such as John Davis of Carrickfergus, James Maxwell of Strabane, John Stuart and Archibald Moore of Belfast, Francis Dormer of Ross and Patrick Archer of Kilkenny.

In some areas the war stimulated the local economy. During the 1640s Belfast, ideally situated for distributing military supplies to the Scottish army, laid its foundations for later expansion and by the 1650s the town's seaborne trade was six times that of its traditional rival Carrickfergus. Shipbuilding flourished in Wexford where both warships and merchantmen were built throughout the decade. The presence of large privateering communities also contributed to its prosperity, as well as some other Irish ports, and by the mid-1640s there were roughly fifty privateers operating out of Wexford and Waterford alone. They sold many of their prizes in Ireland and thereby supplied the country with a remarkable range of basic food products – fish, beef, pork, grain, beans, salt, vinegar, malt, wine and oil – together with luxury items such as sugar, raisins, tobacco, lemons, oranges, tar, cloth and whiskey. Certainly the towns and counties of Waterford and Wexford benefited immensely from this constant, though somewhat erratic, stream of goods. For instance, a contemporary observer noted that the 'cellars and storehouses at Waterford are full of Englishmen's goods, and the Irish there come and trade for them familiarly'.[69] By the later 1640s the only surplus of grain in the entire country was to be found in Waterford.

This shortage of grain was due to the famine which gripped Ireland during these years. Of course there had been famines, harvest crises and grain shortages in 1601–3, 1607–8, 1621–4, 1627–31 and 1639–41; but the subsistence crisis of the later 1640s was by far the worst both in Ireland and, indeed, throughout Europe.

Early in 1648 the Spanish agent in Kilkenny complained of the terrible food shortages which had pushed the cost of a loaf of bread up fivefold. By the summer of 1648, according to another source, there was 'so great a dearth of corne, as Ireland hath not seene in our memorie, and so cruell a famine, which hath alreadie killed thousands of the poorer sort'.[70] Outbreaks of plague, small-pox and dysentery which became endemic between 1649 and 1651, and in a single year claimed some 20,000 lives, accompanied the famine. In 1650 the plague allegedly killed a third of the population in Kilkenny and reduced the garrison there from 1,200 to 400 men; and a year later between 5,000 and 8,000 people died during the five-month siege of Limerick 'through the sword without, and the famine and plague within'.[71] According to one Cromwellian, in 1652 County Clare – where 'people die under every hedge' – was 'the saddest place (reported by all that are there) as ever was seen'.[72]

Estimating how many people died 'by War, Plague and Famine' is impossible. Sir William Petty suggested in 1672 that

> The number of British slain in eleven years was 112,000 souls of which I guess two thirds to have perished by War, Plague and Famine. So it follows that 37,000 were massacred in the first year of tumults . . . it follows also, that about 504,000 of the Irish perished, and were wasted by the sword, Plague, Famine, Hardship and Banishment, between the 23rd of October 1641, and the same day 1652.[73]

Petty's figures are little more than inspired guesses which suggest that the population of Ireland dropped by between one third and one quarter within a decade, a fall which would be extremely high considering that Germany's population is thought to have fallen by about 15 to 20 per cent during the entire Thirty Years War.[74]

A war of religion?

> The Gaels in arms shall triumph
>   Over the crafty, thieving, false sect of Calvin.
> Their nobles shall bear sway over unbelievers,
>   And scatter the brood of Luther.
> True faith shall be uncontrolled;
>   The people shall be rightly taught
> By friars, bishops, priests and clerics,
>   And everlasting peace shall dwell in Erin.[75]

During the early years of the 'holy war' (as one cleric termed the civil wars) the Confederates tried to turn their cause into a crusade by claiming that an international Protestant conspiracy led by English Puritans threatened to extirpate the Catholic religion. If Ireland fell, the Confederate Supreme Council reminded their agent in Flanders, 'heresy will not only prevaile but alsoe extinguish the orthodox faith [in] all the north partes of the world. The Hugonetts of France, Germany and

Holland, and their correspondents, are not to be forgotten; and . . . the disunion of Catholic princes is too well known.' They added that, if only the Catholic princes would support their cause, Ireland 'might from thenceforth be a great bulwarke against all the hereticks of the Northerne partes of Europe'.[76] For the Catholic party – many of whom had taken up arms 'for the honour of God; to obtain a free exercise of the ancient Catholick Romish faith'[77] – the presence of a papal nuncio, Rinuccini, in Ireland with instructions 'to restore and reestablish the public exercise of the Catholic religion in the island of Ireland' further underlined the religious character of the war.[78] Moreover the Confederate government functioned with the blessing of the church; while the bishops, who sat as spiritual peers in the General Assemblies and on the Supreme Councils, played a prominent role in governing the country.

Many Protestants also viewed the conflict as a religious struggle. The Ulster rebellion confirmed and inflamed fears that a great Catholic conspiracy was about to engulf Britain and to reduce it to popery. English parliamentary leaders quickly exploited this Protestant paranoia by blaming all England's misfortunes on the 'impious and wicked conspiracies and practices of many of the Popish profession' and delighted in reporting the latest 'massacre', 'conspiracy' and 'atrocity' from Ireland. For instance, one pamphlet, *Worse and worse newes from Ireland . . .* , published in London late in 1641, misleadingly asserted that the rebels tormented the 'poore Protestants, wheresoever they come; cutting off their privie members, ears, fingers, and hands, plucking out their eyes . . . ravishing wives before their husbands['] faces and virgines before the parentes faces, after they have abused their bodies, making them renounce their religion'.[79] Hardly surprisingly Lord Balmerino, a prominent Scottish nobleman and Covenanter, was not alone in believing that 'unlesse we doe fully vindicate these malicious papists [in Ireland], these two kingdomes both Scotland and England, cannot sleepe long in security'.[80] The English parliament, for its part, encouraged the Scots invasion of Ulster in defence of the Protestant cause.

Religious rancour on both sides also brutalised the struggle. One Protestant claimed in 1642 that the papists' cruelty was 'never used by the Turks to Christians . . . no quarter is given, no faith kept, all houses burnt and demolished, man, wife and child put to the sword'.[81] In the same year the Catholic General O'Neill noted that 'on both sides there is nothing but burning, robbery in cold blood, and cruelties such as are not usual even among the moors and Arabs'.[82] In England captured Irish soldiers faced immediate death; while in Ireland the royalist, Scots and parliamentarian armies killed their prisoners unless they could be easily ransomed or exchanged. For instance, early in 1644 one parliamentary commander in Ulster allegedly slaughtered 1,000 Irish soldiers and camp followers in a single raid and later boasted that 'the reason why our prisoners were so few was because . . . [we] had no stomacke to give such perfidious rogues any quarter'.[83]

Finally religion impinged disastrously upon the conduct of the war. This was

---

particularly true in September 1643 when the conclusion of a ceasefire between the king and the Confederates shattered the uneasy anti-Catholic alliance; and again in July–August 1646, when the First Ormond Peace further divided an already fragmented country into 'a woeful spectacle, cantonized into severall sundry factions, drawing all divers waies, and driveing on several interests'.[84] Throughout the 1640s religious differences remained the main stumbling block to any peace and ultimately led to the downfall of the Irish party. For a failure to agree over religion not only caused internal divisions but also prevented a lasting alliance with the royalists and thus frustrated any chance of defeating the English parliament. The myopia of the Irish baffled even well-informed Catholic observers. As the French ambassador in London wrote in 1648:

> What really surprises the majority of those who contemplate the affairs of Ireland is to see that people of the same nation and of the same religion – who are well aware that the resolution to exterminate them totally has already been taken – should differ so strongly in their private hostilities; that their zeal for religion, the preservation of their country and their own self-interest are not sufficient to make them lay down, at least for a short time, the passions which divide them one from the other.[85]

The civil conflict was therefore not the last war of religion in Ireland, only a beginning.

Chapter 9

The Williamite war, 1689–1691

John Childs

The Williamite or Jacobite War in Ireland was a civil war. Protestant Irishmen, assisted by troops from England, Denmark, the Netherlands and Germany, fought Catholic Irishmen who enjoyed the active support of France. Two regular armies represented the causes of King James and King William in addition to a number of unofficial and irregular bands. The Enniskillen and Londonderry forces were not regimented into the Williamite army until the summer of 1689 whilst Hugh Balldearg O'Donnell's army of Ulster or north Connacht Gaels, amounting to 10,000 men, operated as an independent if ineffective force in 1690 and 1691. On the Catholic side were the rapparees, or guerrillas. The war was also a part of the much wider Nine Years War (1688–97), in which a loose confederation, 'the Grand Alliance', led by the Netherlands and the Holy Roman Empire, fought against the France of Louis XIV. The resistance of the Jacobite forces in Ireland severely distracted the attentions and resources of William of Orange from the principal conflict in the Low Countries and Germany during which time the French won a major battle at Fleurus (1690) and captured the important fortress of Mons (1691).

Although politically connected, there was little operational similarity between the Williamite War in Ireland and the Nine Years War in Europe. Ireland was bereft of the multitude of fortified towns which dominated land warfare in Flanders and Germany and her small population and underdeveloped economy could not provide the infrastructure which supported war in the major continental theatres. In many respects, warfare in Ireland resembled operations in Spain, Poland and the Baltic regions. Geographical factors – mountain and marsh – and the frequently appalling weather were often predominant in a land where communications were primitive. Operations usually boiled down to series of small raids and ambushes rather than actions between large, regular forces. Sieges were relatively rare and, with the exception of Londonderry and Limerick, short-lived. Supply of food and fodder was vital, the Williamites accepting early in the proceedings that a modern army of 35,000 men could not be adequately fed from the resources of Ireland, especially after the Jacobites adopted a scorched-earth policy in the autumn of 1689. Meteorological conditions also played an important part; the sole substantial defeat of the Williamite forces, at Dundalk in 1689, resulted from a combination of poor weather and incompetence rather than direct enemy action. However, the numerically inferior and often poorly equipped Jacobite forces maintained the struggle against the professional troops of William III for three years. So stout was the Jacobite resistance that William was keen to conclude a compromise peace in the winter of 1690 in order to free his forces for employment in the Spanish Netherlands. Indeed, William had not been enthusiastic about commencing action in Ireland in 1689. If his negotiations through Richard Hamilton had been successful and if the French had not supported the cause of Tyrconnell and obliged James II to return to Dublin, it is conceivable that William would have concluded a settlement in the winter of 1688-9. However, although the outbreak of war in Ireland was viewed by William as a sideshow, an irritating and worrying distraction from the main business of thwarting Louis XIV in the Netherlands, it was the Irish situation which persuaded the English parliament to declare war on France and enter the Grand Alliance. Until James II arrived in Dublin on 24 March 1689, the Lords and Commons had not regarded English entry into the Grand Alliance and consequent involvement in a war against France as the corollary of their offer of the joint monarchy to William and Mary on 13 February. On the contrary, there were many in the parliament who thought that the invocation of the 1678 Anglo-Dutch Treaty was sufficient response. It took the Irish war and, particularly, overt French support for the Jacobite cause in Ireland, to convince the English parliament that a declaration of war on France was not a luxury but a necessity. For England, if not for King William, the war in Ireland was initially more important than the European conflict as the outcome of the Glorious Revolution and the survival of the new regime depended absolutely upon defeating the forces of ex-King James.[1]

In 1685, James II inherited an Irish army of 8,238 men. Both officers and men had to provide certificates stating that they received the sacrament according to the rites of the Church of England twice a year. Despite this precaution, a few native Catholics had crept into the ranks, especially after 1683. The officers all hailed from Anglican gentry families, many having served in the Cromwellian forces. By 1688, the army had grown slightly to 8,938; 2,820 soldiers from the Irish army, roughly one-third of the total, sailed to England in September 1688 to reinforce the English army in preparation for the expected invasion by Prince William III of Orange-Nassau. In the ensuing débâcle, the entirety of the Irish force in England was forfeited; some individuals made their way back to Ireland but 1,500 were disarmed and held on the Isle of Wight from whence they either deserted to Ireland and France or were sold into a mercenary regiment in the imperial service. Tyrconnell's purge of Protestant officers (see below, pp. 213-14) and men between 1685 and 1688 had already rendered the Irish army weak and undertrained but the loss of one-third of its strength on the eve of the Jacobite war further enfeebled the cadre around which expansion would have to take place.[2] In January 1689, Tyrconnell issued warrants for raising 40,000 new levies divided into forty regiments of foot, four of dragoons and two of horse. Despite the enthusiasm of the men, there were no uniforms and so few weapons that many recruits were armed with rusty muskets, rotten pikes or sticks tipped with nails. If the Jacobite army was to offer serious resistance to the armed Protestants of Ulster and the Williamite army, professional organisation was required.[3]

Many of the new regiments consisted of between thirty and forty-five companies as Catholic gentry realised the profits which might accrue from military service but a team of inspectors, amongst whom was Brigadier Patrick Sarsfield, rapidly reduced these to more manageable totals. Neither Tyrconnell's government nor the Irish economy could afford the arms and the officers for such forces and by the summer of 1689 most infantry regiments had settled into the standard pattern of a single battalion composed of twelve line companies and a grenadier company although the Foot Guards and a few other select regiments consisted of two or more battalions. A standard infantry battalion possessed an establishment of 771 officers and men whilst a cavalry regiment contained 527. However, the field strength of battalions and cavalry regiments was frequently well below the paper establishment. Battalions rarely numbered more than 300–400 privates and horse regiments averaged between 300 and 400 troopers. The final establishment for 1689 listed forty-five infantry regiments, eight of dragoons, seven of cavalry and a Life Guard; these figures altered little during the remainder of the war. Three foot regiments went to France in 1690 in partial exchange for six French regiments whilst six or seven infantry regiments were lost at the capture of Cork by Marlborough. However, these were replaced and there still appear to have been forty-five foot regiments in existence in 1691. The dragoons lost one regiment to Scotland in 1689 and there-after their establishment remained at seven. The cavalry regiments increased in number from seven in 1689 to nine in 1691. The six regiments from the army of Louis XIV which served during the campaign of 1690 amounted to 6,666 men – four French regiments, one German and one Walloon. At the opening of the campaigning season in 1689, the Jacobite army probably numbered 36,000 men. In November 1690, it was in the region of 28,400 and in the final year of the war it averaged 30,500.

One of the problems associated with the purge of Protestant officers followed by the rapid augmentation for war was that the Irish army was short of experienced field officers. During the reign of Charles II, Catholics had been barred from holding commissions in the Irish army with the result that the majority of Catholic soldiers had sought employment overseas. Tyrconnell's purge between 1685 and 1688 had brought the majority of qualified Catholic officers on foreign service back on to the Irish establishment. Finding a sufficient additional supply of experienced men to hold field rank after 1689 was a major problem and, as a result, a number of Jacobite colonels were new to military service and had to be supported by professional lieutenant-colonels and majors. Following the disintegration of the English army in November and December 1688, a considerable number of officers

9.1   King William III, by Jan Wyck.

from that establishment joined the Jacobite army in Ireland, particularly after the return of James II to Dublin. By the summer of 1690, a number of Frenchmen had also been drafted into commissions – 19 lieutenant-colonels, 18 majors, 138 captains, 65 lieutenants and an ensign. Not too much, however, should be concluded from these deficiencies. It did not take long to learn the martial trade in the later seventeenth century and many of the Jacobites who were novices in 1689 quickly acquired the rudiments of regimental drill, discipline and administration. Senior command of brigades, detachments and corps, however, called for different qualities and here the Jacobites were at a disadvantage throughout the war. James was a broken reed and, although Sarsfield proved an aggressive and successful commander, the Jacobites became reliant on generals sent from France – Rosen, Lauzun, Berwick and St Ruth. Out of twenty-five officers who reached the rank of major-general and above during the war, only six were Irish: Tyrconnell, his three Hamilton brothers-in-law, Mountcashel and Sarsfield. The rest came from France, England and Scotland.

Not only was the Jacobite army short of trained officers but it was equally short of trained men. Tyrconnell's purges had affected the rank and file as severely as the officer corps. Effectively, despite summer training camps at the Curragh in 1686 and 1687, the army in late 1688 was a regimented band of untrained raw recruits, the better soldiers having been shipped to England in September. Apart from emergency measures following the defeat at Aughrim in 1691, the Jacobite army remained a volunteer force. The French did their best to assist in the training of the Jacobite levies but it could never be claimed that the Jacobite infantry was trained to a truly professional standard. Part of the trouble was an acute shortage of arms. Despite convoys from France and some limited attempts at local manufacture, there were never sufficient muskets and Tyrconnell estimated that two-thirds of his army never fired a shot through want of powder. The muskets which the French did send were mostly obsolete matchlocks, often in poor condition. With inferior equipment and inadequate training, the Jacobite infantry, although individually brave, was never able to stand, manoeuvre and fight in the open field. It was capable of operating from behind fixed and field fortifications, as at Aughrim and during sieges, but it was unable to cope with open combat. The cavalry was much better. Well mounted, well led and well equipped, the 'priding cavalry' was the principal arm of the Jacobite army, distinguishing itself both in battle and on raids and ambushes. The artillery was weak. Only two heavy guns were brought into action against Londonderry, a major reason why the town was able to endure the siege, although 250 cannon were available in various garrisons. However, nothing was done to mount these on mobile carriages. By the end of 1689, the baron de Pointis had organised a field train of eleven pieces of cannon and the French expeditionary force of 1690 contained a train of twelve guns. At the Boyne, sixteen Jacobite cannon accompanied the army.

General army services were inadequate and poorly administered. A surgeon was attached to each regiment but the French thought little of their abilities. There was no field hospital and much of the equipment for base hospitals was lost at Drogheda and Dublin after the defeat at the Boyne. The Irish road network was primitive and its waterways undeveloped. Native Irish carts had restricted carrying capacity and Irish draught horses were physically small and of limited strength. By 1691, the Jacobite transport train comprised 170 wagons, 400 carts and 10 gun carriages. However, much use was made of pack animals and even of baskets carried on the human back.

In contrast to the Jacobite army, the Williamite forces were more professional, experienced, and better trained and organised. On 8 March 1689, William sought the approval of the House of Commons to send a force to Ireland sufficient to quell the rebellion within the year. The corps was fixed at 22,230 men. As the English army was but slowly recovering from the trauma of the Glorious Revolution and was dispatching 10,000 men to Flanders to join the Dutch army, the commitment to Ireland could only be met by raising new levies and by hiring mercenaries from Europe.[4] In the meantime, whilst waiting for these new forces to be raised and rented, the Ulster Protestants decided to look after themselves. An anonymous proposal had suggested that 6,000 'effective foot' and six troops of dragoons could be raised from amongst the 300,000 Protestants in Ireland, and this project came close to being put into execution until the emergencies at Londonderry and Enniskillen demanded more immediate measures.[5] The battalions of Solomon Richards and John Cunningham arrived off Londonderry on 15 April 1689 but, after a conference with Robert Lundy, they decided that the town was incapable of defence and brought their regiments back to England. On 31 May, Percy Kirke sailed for Lough Foyle with three battalions to relieve Londonderry but he was over-cautious and took six weeks before breaking the boom and lifting the siege. In the interim, the suggestion to regiment the forces of the Ulster Protestants was put into effect. The Enniskilleners were organised into three battalions of infantry, two regiments of dragoons and one of cavalry whilst the Londonderry soldiers were arranged into three battalions. They were officered by Ulster Protestants, many of whom had been cashiered during Tyrconnell's purge. To begin with, the Ulster forces were treated as a militia and not until the summer of 1690 did they receive the same pay as the English regular army. On 1 April, the Williamite forces in Ireland amounted to 9,030 men.[6]

After the relief of Londonderry, Kirke's three battalions and the Ulster troops secured western Ulster while, in England, Marshal Herman von Schomberg prepared to embark the main expeditionary force at Hoylake. He sailed on 12 August with 6,000 men and, by the end of 1689, nearly all of the promised 22,000 men had arrived. An establishment for 20 September 1689 lists the total Williamite forces in Ireland as 29,954, including the 6,000 troops from Londonderry and Enniskillen.[7] Schomberg's corps was composed of three experienced Huguenot battalions, a regiment of Huguenot cavalry, one Dutch battalion, and the remainder were either

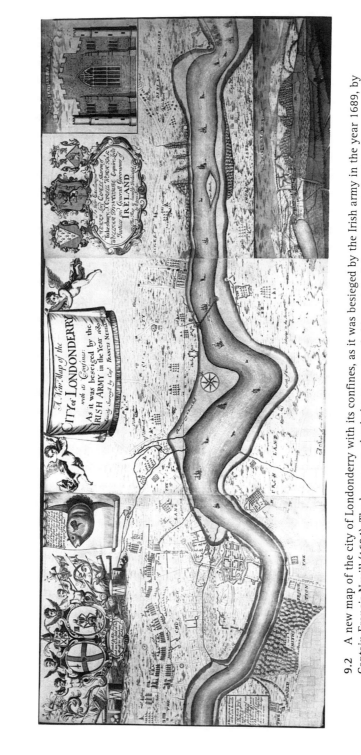

9.2   A new map of the city of Londonderry with its confines, as it was besieged by the Irish army in the year 1689, by Captain Francis Nevill (1694). The boom can clearly be seen, guarded by entrenchments, batteries and Charles Fort. The inset on the bottom shows 'the N.W. prospect of the city' and depicts the fire from the Jacobite batteries. The fish 'was taken on the N.W. side of the quay of Derry on the Lord's Day while the people were at Church by a ship-boy not long before shutting the gates. It was 4 foot long, 2 foot broad and 5 foot 3 inches from point to point of the fins.'

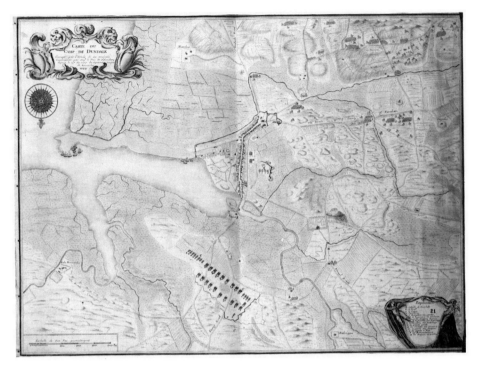

9.3 A French manuscript of Schomberg's encampment at Dundalk,
7 September to November 1689.

new raised English regiments or survivors from James II's English army which had seen little or no active service. Through lack of field craft, inexperience and weak command, 5,674 of these men died whilst the army was encamped at Dundalk between September and November. Most died from disease – dysentery, typhus or pneumonia – induced by a poorly chosen camp site on marshy ground, the huge majority of the casualties occurring amongst the English troops through a lack of common sense and hygiene.

Having failed to bring the Jacobite forces to battle in 1689, William III took personal command of the army in Ireland for the campaign of 1690. Schomberg had proved himself to be dilatory, over-cautious, unenterprising and, as the commander who had selected the camp-site at Dundalk and persisted in its occupation, directly responsible for the loss of one quarter of the British expeditionary force. Regardless of the situation in Flanders, William determined to commit the majority of the available British forces to Ireland in order to win the war in a single campaign. A total of 30,717 men was accordingly added to the corps already in Ireland. Three regiments of horse and eight battalions of foot had been hired from Denmark, 'all stout fine men, the best equip'd and disciplin'd of any that ever was seen'.[8] Nine Dutch cavalry regiments, one of dragoons and six battalions of foot were also sent

195

along with two troops of the English Life Guards, the Royal Horse Guards and six English battalions. Schomberg's original corps was also recruited to full strength.[9] At the opening of the 1690 campaign, the Williamite army had perhaps an effective strength of around 35,000 men. In September 1690, the earl of Marlborough captured Cork and Kinsale with a force of eleven battalions, nine of which remained in Ireland for the campaign of 1691. Having failed in his ambition to clear up the Irish situation in one year, William's army for 1691 was reduced by a total of three cavalry regiments and four battalions from the establishment of 1690.

During the winter of 1690–1, the Protestant militia was re-established and accordingly embodied in towns and regions which had been liberated by the Williamite army. By the spring of 1691, perhaps as many as 15,000 militiamen were ready to support the field army in various parts of Ireland. Their local knowledge made them an admirable force for opposing the Catholic rapparees.

One of the reasons for the poor showing of the British corps in 1689 had been the commissariat. After Schomberg's men had landed at Carrickfergus they found plentiful supplies of local standing corn but as they advanced south towards Dundalk they entered the region which the Jacobites had devastated. The only answer was supply from England. However, Schomberg's force was accompanied by neither wagons nor horses whilst the provision ships docked at Carrickfergus, County Antrim, instead of going forward to Carlingford, County Louth. On 13 September, Schomberg complained to Lord Portland that he had been unable to advance for four days because he lacked bread for his soldiers. No-one seemed to be in charge of the bread supply and the two or three commissaries who had come over with the expedition were useless, 'like children'. They had even crossed the sea without any money in their pockets.[10] John Shales, the commissary-general of the provisions, bore most of the blame but the real fault lay with William Harbord, the purveyor and paymaster of the forces in Ireland. 'Mr. Harbord', wrote Schomberg to William, 'makes great profit out of the musters, the hospital, the artillery and the payment of the troops.' At the time of his dismissal in 1690, Harbord's accounts showed a deficit of £406,000.[11] Shales was the scapegoat. He was arrested by Schomberg and all his books and papers seized. William Robinson and Bartholomew Vanhomrigh were sent to Ireland by the House of Commons to interrogate Shales and to act as caretaker commissaries-general of the provisions. In reality, a number of agencies and individuals were to blame for the failure of the commissariat in 1689: the Treasury for incompetence; the king for failing to exercise executive authority over the army; the army for its suspect and divided loyalties and its ignorance of field conditions; Schomberg for tactical passivity; the House of Commons for their ignorance of the demands of modern war and their reluctance to vote sufficient funds; and Harbord for greed and venality.[12]

For the campaign of 1690, William reverted to the practice of the Dutch army in Europe and entrusted the supply of bread to the troops in Ireland to civilian contractors. Isaac Pereira, a partner in the Sephardic Jewish army victualling firm of Machado and Pereira based in The Hague, accepted the Irish bread contract. He undertook to provide 36,000 one-and-a-half pound loaves to the army every day at a charge of 1¹/₄d per loaf. If there was no bread, then Pereira agreed to provide one pound of hard biscuit. The paymaster stopped 1¹/₄d a day from each soldier's wages and accounted with Pereira once a month. Although Pereira did not make a profit out of the contract, which ran until the end of the war, he did not fail in his obligations and the Williamite army did not again suffer the ravages of near famine.[13]

In an effort to maintain discipline and lessen the impact of the army on loyal and Protestant Ulster, the troops were forbidden to plunder and all camp followers were regarded as common robbers unless they were registered as servants or sutlers. A similar proclamation was repeated on 24 June 1690 demanding that soldiers pay for all provisions and did not rob the sutlers. Soldiers were barred from foraging without orders. In their winter quarters, the inhabitants were to provide each soldier with one hot meal a day 'and the remainder of the dinner' plus a bed for the night at the daily rate of 3d for the infantry, 3¹/₂d for the dragoons and 4d for cavalry troopers.[14] However, the discipline of the Williamite army was generally poor. The Ulster Protestants plundered the Catholics, the unpaid English stole from anybody whilst the Danes were likened to Tartars.[15]

Transport between England and Ireland was relatively easy to find even if discovering funds for the payment of the shipowners was less comfortable. The collier-masters from Whitehaven, who worked the Dublin–Whitehaven coal trade, found a general disruption in traffic between Liverpool, Chester, Ireland and Carlisle as a result of the war. Paid at the charter rate of 14s a ton with 4d a ton demurrage, the colliers rapidly converted to the new and potentially lucrative employment of military transportation. The overall responsibility for sea transport fell to the commissioners for transportation who were in charge of chartering and loading suitable shipping. Twenty-nine Whitehaven colliers were converted to horse transports and eighteen served as troop transports.[16] A further development for the 1690 campaign was the provision of improved medical arrangements, again based on the Dutch model. A base hospital and medical supply depôt was established in Dublin whilst a 'marching hospital' accompanied the army into the field. A third, or 'field' hospital, was created in the nearest town when a siege or an action threatened. One physician was attached to each hospital, together with master-surgeons. Eighteen additional surgeon's mates were allocated as required, either to assist in the hospitals or to help the regimental surgeons, and forty nurses, or 'tenders', were located as necessary. There was even the provision of fifteen 'washers'.[17]

As Protestant refugees pressed as much as 10s a head into the hands of Whitehaven collier-masters in return for a passage to England, Tyrconnell set about trying to exploit the Glorious Revolution for the advantage of Ireland. Fearing an attack from England, Tyrconnell issued warrants on 8 December 1688 to raise

20,000 men but he also entered into negotiations with both Ulster Protestants and the authorities in London. Already, on 7 December, Londonderry had shut its gates against the Catholic soldiers of the earl of Antrim's battalion and Protestants were migrating into Ulster as well as into England. Arriving with news of the conditions in London, Richard Hamilton persuaded Tyrconnell to resist rather than submit to Williamite England. Emphasising to James II in St Germain-en-Laye the need for French money and assistance, Tyrconnell set about augmenting his army and extending his control over all of Ireland. Having disarmed the Dublin Protestants in February, by the beginning of March 1689 Tyrconnell was in command of the country with the exception of Ulster. Londonderry and Enniskillen were the main hubs of organised Protestant resistance, the garrison of the latter under Gustavus Hamilton having driven off a small foray by Tyrconnell's forces. At another centre of Protestant defiance, in Hillsborough, County Down, the earl of Mount-Alexander's weak force of 500 men, commanded by Sir Arthur Rawdon, was routed by Richard Hamilton's 2,500 at the 'Break of Dromore' on 14 March. Hamilton then mopped up several more small Protestant garrisons, including that of Coleraine. By the end of March, Tyrconnell controlled the whole of Ireland except for the garrisons of Enniskillen and Londonderry.

When he reached France after his flight from England, James would have been content to remain at St Germain-en-Laye wallowing in self-pity but Louis XIV and his minister of marine, the marquis de Seignelay, had other ideas. An expeditionary force, complete with the person of King James, to support Tyrconnell in Ireland would oblige William to respond, diverting his attention from the main war in Flanders. Following a reconnaissance by Pointis, a French fleet of twenty-two ships landed James at Kinsale on 12 March. With him were French arms and money, some French officers under Lieutenant-General Conrad von Rosen, the diplomat the comte d'Avaux, and a number of Irish, Scottish and English volunteers, among them Patrick Sarsfield, the duke of Berwick and Roger MacElligott. James entered Dublin in triumph on 24 March. A second French convoy arrived off Kinsale on 29 April but the close attentions of Admiral Edward Herbert's Williamite fleet forced it into Bantry Bay where it unloaded stores, provisions and between 1,500 and 3,000 English, Scottish and Irish volunteers who had previously made their way into France. An indecisive naval action in Bantry Bay on 1 May left the French free to complete their unloading before sailing for Brest.

After summoning a parliament to Dublin to repeal the Act of Settlement and pass an Act of Attainder against all those who had joined the Williamite cause, James proceeded to assert his authority in rebellious Ulster. Richard Hamilton's small force, which had been briefly checked at Coleraine, was insufficient to take the walled town of Londonderry and there was intelligence from England that a relief force was due to sail from Liverpool. Londonderry was packed with 30,000 refugees and a garrison of Protestant soldiers from Mountjoy's regiment under Lieutenant-Colonel Robert Lundy. Hamilton and Rosen approached Londonderry driving in Lundy's

---

inexperienced outposts along the Rivers Finn and Foyle. As the Protestant soldiers filed back into the town, Cunningham's and Richards's battalions arrived in Lough Foyle to find morale so low that a council of war decided that Londonderry could not be defended and the two battalions departed for England in company with many of the leading officers and dignitaries from the town. The marquis de Maumont took charge of the 4,000 Jacobite siege forces with Richard Hamilton as second-in-command whilst James and Rosen returned to Dublin. In the town, the male inhabitants were organised into seven battalions of foot and one of horse, a total of 7,361 men, but Lundy, whose allegiance was suspect, refused to take part in these preparations and the driving force behind the defence came from the Reverend George Walker and Major Henry Baker.

The Jacobite siege corps, commanded by Rosen after the death of Maumont, was desperately short of equipment and cannon. Their only feasible tactic was to starve the garrison into submission, and the blockade was made more secure by the construction of a boom across the River Foyle by Pointis. Faced with a besieging corps which was roughly half its own size, both sides being relatively untrained, the garrison showed a remarkable lack of initiative and enterprise in remaining locked within the 2 square kilometres of the town. Major-General Percy Kirke's relief expedition arrived in Lough Foyle but decided not to attempt the boom. Instead, Kirke retired into Lough Swilly and occupied Inch Island, where he remained, largely inactive, for six weeks. Uncertain political loyalties may well have accounted for Kirke's seeming indecision; there was little about any aspect of the siege of Londonderry to impress the professionals. Eventually, at the end of July, the boom was smashed and on 31 July the Jacobites broke camp and retired towards Lifford. After a siege of 105 days, the wreckage of the town and its hinterland took years to recover. In purely military terms, the siege confirmed that the Jacobites were not strong enough to conquer all of Ireland. In emotional and psychological terms, the staunchness of Londonderry has endured as a Protestant totem for over 300 years.

The other base of Protestantism, Enniskillen, was very different. The Protestant forces were grouped around Enniskillen castle on an island between Upper and Lower Lough Erne and at Ballyshannon at the mouth of the River Erne. The whole of the Erne Valley effectively formed a Protestant enclave and posed a serious threat to Jacobite communications between the siege forces at Londonderry and Dublin. Tyrconnell dispatched Viscount Galmoy against Enniskillen in March 1689, but he was easily repulsed. Under the leadership of Thomas Lloyd and Gustavus Hamilton, the Enniskilleners launched guerrilla raids to within 40 miles of Dublin. Attempts by Sarsfield and Rosen to dislodge the Enniskillen raiders were comfortably resisted but, at the end of June, James ordered Berwick to join Sarsfield. Berwick was on the point of success when James called him away to face the challenge posed by Kirke's battalions around Lough Swilly. Towards the end of July, James sent Justin Macarthy, Viscount Mountcashel, with three regiments of foot, sixteen troops of horse and eight field guns to deal with Enniskillen. He was joined by Major-General

Anthony Hamilton commanding some dragoons and a number of Ulster Gaels under Cuconnacht Mor Maguire. If Mountcashel had been able to link up with Sarsfield and Berwick then Enniskillen would have been placed under heavy pressure. However, Kirke had sent Colonel William Wolseley with some arms and equipment to Enniskillen. On 30 July, Mountcashel attacked Crom castle on Upper Lough Erne, 15 miles south of Enniskillen. As Lieutenant-Colonel William Berry led reinforcements from Enniskillen towards Crom, he was attacked by Anthony Hamilton's dragoons. Berry withdrew leading Hamilton's pursuing troopers into an ambush where they were severely mauled. Wolseley joined Berry to make a combined force of 2,200 and they resolved to attack Mountcashel who stood to the south of Newtownbutler with over 4,000 men. In the ensuing rout, Mountcashel was badly wounded and his army lost 1,000 dead, 500 prisoners and all of its baggage and cannon.

In mid-July, Schomberg was appointed to command the major expedition to Ireland. He sailed from Hoylake on 12 August and rapidly occupied Belfast. By the end of August Schomberg had eighteen infantry battalions and he immediately set about the reduction of Carrickfergus where the regiments of MacCarthy More and Cormac O'Neill put up a stout resistance for a week. James and Rosen could put no more than 6,000 or 7,000 men into the field against Schomberg, and most of these were ill-trained and poorly equipped. The French advised James to burn Dublin, retreat to Athlone and defend the line of the Shannon until winter. Shortage of cash and the rocketing inflation caused by 'gun money' added to the woes of the Jacobites. Tyrconnell was more resolute and insisted that James stand firm and trust to the fortitude of the Irish and in a reorganisation of the army. For the last time in his life, James demonstrated both moral and physical courage and moved forward to Drogheda and then Ardee to oppose Schomberg who advanced south through Belfast and Newry to a position just to the north of Dundalk. Schomberg was beset by numerous difficulties. He distrusted the political loyalty of many of his officers, the majority of his English battalions were raw and poorly trained, his commissariat was inefficient and corrupt and he himself was old and indecisive. Instead of confronting the inferior Jacobite forces and attempting to win the war in 1689, he encamped on marshy ground close to Dundalk where, over the next two months, a quarter of his army succumbed to disease.[18] James marched his troops to a camp within cannon shot of Schomberg but he could not stir the German into action. On 6 October, James withdrew to Ardee, his own army much affected by sickness and the bad weather. Sarsfield further raised Jacobite morale by capturing Sligo from Thomas Lloyd. In mid-November, Schomberg fell back from Dundalk to Lisburn and dispersed his men into winter quarters throughout Ulster. The Williamites may not have won the war in 1689, much to William's annoyance, but Ulster had been brought firmly under Protestant control and a considerable Anglo-Irish army had been landed and established. With the king in personal command, there was every reason to expect the collapse of Jacobite resistance in 1690.

During the winter and spring of 1689–90, the Williamite army was substantially strengthened by new English regiments, the Danish corps under the duke of Württemberg-Neustadt and several Dutch regiments. William landed at Carrick-fergus on 14 June with 300 ships bearing 15,000 of the reinforcements, artillery, money and supplies. The Jacobites gained the French brigade of 6,666 men under the comte de Lauzun but lost 5,387 men, commanded by Mountcashel, to France in exchange. On arrival in France, Mountcashel's men were arranged into three foot regiments to form the original 'Irish Brigade'.[19] William was intent on capturing Dublin, an invaluable possession which James was equally determined to defend. On 16 June, James marched north from Dublin for Dundalk to meet William, probably with the intention of consuming the forage on the direct route to Dublin. As William advanced south from Belfast, James withdrew from Dundalk and took up a position to the south of the River Boyne, the only defensible barrier north of Dublin.

It was very much James's personal decision to fight on the Boyne. The French wanted to burn Dublin and withdraw behind the Shannon and even Tyrconnell was unenthusiastic about the prospects of the Boyne position; the river was fordable at numerous places. Also, there was no time for the Jacobites to raise field fortifications and make other preparations as William's army was only one day's march behind. James had about 25,000 men, less 1,300 in garrison in Drogheda, and William around 36,000. The key to the battle on 1 July 1690 was William's flank march. Holding two-thirds of his army to effect a crossing of the Boyne at Oldbridge, William sent the remainder of his force under Schomberg's son, Count Meinhard, to find a ford or bridge to the west and then attack the Jacobite positions around Oldbridge and Donore in the flank. James and Lauzun noticed the march of the younger Schomberg, wrongly assumed that it was the Williamite main body and sent the major part of the army to their left wing to counter the threat. As a result, at Oldbridge, two-thirds of William's army faced but one-third of that of King James. After a stiff fight, the Williamite infantry forced a passage whilst William himself led another force across a ford a short distance to the east. The Jacobites were now in danger of being trapped around Donore in the bend of the river by forces approaching from the centre, left and right. The Jacobite army gave way and headed for the bridge at Duleek over the River Nanny. The withdrawal never degenerated into a rout, the French retreating in excellent order, and the Williamite cavalry did not pursue far beyond Duleek. The Jacobites lost about 1,000 men and their opponents around 500. James reached Dublin on the night of 1 July but had fled by the following day, when the Williamite forces marched into the capital. James was escorted from Kinsale to France by a French fleet whilst his army retreated through Dublin to rendezvous at Limerick.[20]

Tyrconnell recognised the need to reach an accommodation with William whilst there was still an Irish army in being but there was an equally strong party, led by Sarsfield, which advocated continuing resistance. William took five weeks to travel

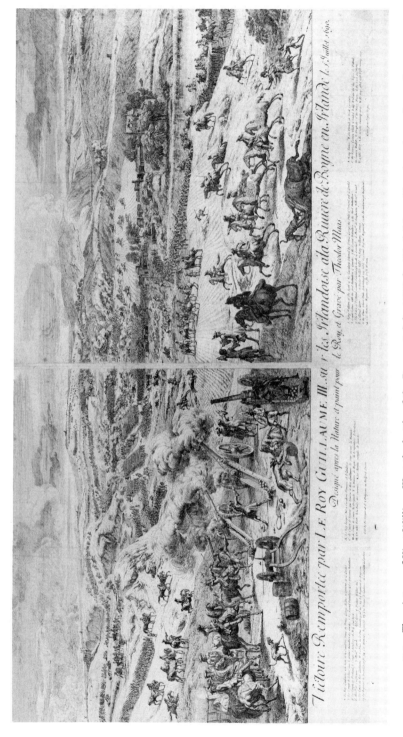

9.4 The victory of King William III at the battle of the Boyne, 1 July 1690, by Dirck Maas. The view shows the main crossing of the Boyne at Oldbridge and William's passage by the ford to the east.

to Limerick, during which time Lieutenant-General James Douglas had made an abortive attempt to seize Athlone. In an effort to extract political capital from his victory, William offered a pardon to all but the 'desperate leaders of the rebellion', a definition which seemed to include the majority of Jacobite officers. Rather than induce a Jacobite collapse, the declaration encouraged resistance. William's slow advance to Limerick was partly occasioned by the French naval victory off Beachy Head. With French ships commanding the Channel, there was every danger that the French might invade England and induce a Jacobite rebellion thus isolating William in Ireland. Partly in response, William took Waterford *en route* to Limerick in order to give himself an additional port but just as he was on the verge of departing for London came the news that the French had only burned Teignmouth village and the Anglo-Dutch losses at Beachy Head were not as serious as had been initially feared. William decided to remain in Ireland and undertake the siege of Limerick. Nevertheless, throughout the war, the French possessed almost unchallenged naval communications between their more westerly ports, especially Brest, and southern Ireland. Not until the victory by Edward Russell off Cape La Hogue in 1692 did the Anglo-Dutch navy achieve command of the English Channel and the Western Approaches. If the Royal Navy had been able to interrupt Franco-Irish sea communications then the Jacobite efforts would probably not have survived into 1691.

Although Lauzun had withdrawn the French troops to Galway, Limerick was placed under the marquis de Boisseleau who commanded a garrison of 1 regiment of cavalry, 1 of dragoons and 28 infantry battalions, a total strength of about 14,000 men. Considerable improvements had been made to the medieval fortifications of Limerick during the five weeks of grace permitted by William's slow march from the Boyne. Sarsfield commanded 2,500 cavalry in County Clare and Hugh Balldearg O'Donnell stood on the Shannon with a large force of Ulster Gaels. William approached Limerick with no more than 25,000 men, some regiments having been sent to England in the emergency after Beachy Head and others having been left to garrison Dublin, Waterford and some minor posts. Although William was close to Limerick on 7 August, another delay was caused by the tardy arrival of the siege cannon.

Early on the morning of 12 August, Sarsfield had intercepted the Williamite siege train at Ballyneety; many cannon and pontoons were wrecked and 100 waggons were destroyed along with 12,000 lbs of powder. Only six siege guns were retrieved from Ballyneety, arriving at Limerick on 16 August. Despite deteriorating weather, a breach had been effected in the ramparts by 27 August but the subsequent infantry assault was held by the garrison who inflicted 2,300 casualties. Artillery ammunition was now in short supply, thanks to Sarsfield's raid, and with more heavy rain falling the siege was raised by 29 August. Despite the Irish success at Limerick, Lauzun abided by his orders to evacuate the French brigade. This was achieved through Galway on 12 September. As far as Louis XIV was concerned, the

---

9.5 Prospect of Limerick, 1685, by the military engineer, Thomas Phillips. The English Town is in the centre with the Irish Town on the right; Thomond Bridge is on the left of the picture.

war in Ireland was as good as lost and no longer justified the commitment of French troops.

On 7 August 1690, the earl of Marlborough proposed to the English Privy Council a scheme to seize Cork and Kinsale, the two ports which provided the shortest and best communication between Ireland and France. It was very much Marlborough's own personal plan devised partly to assist the war in Ireland and partly to boost his own prestige both within the English army and in the eyes of King William. With the backing of the marquis of Carmarthen, the effective head of the government in England, and Admiral Edward Russell, the plan was shown to William two days after the disaster at Ballyneety. He approved, even though Marlborough's expedition was to take 5,000 troops from the skeleton garrison of England. Marlborough sailed on 17 September and disembarked close to Cork harbour on 21 September. By this time, William had returned to England leaving the Irish army under the command of Lieutenant-General Godard van Reede van Ginkel. Ginkel withdrew from the line of the Shannon and took up winter quarters, beating off a Jacobite attempt to seize Birr Castle. A weak effort to occupy Kilmallock was easily brushed aside. Ginkel's new dispositions diverted Jacobite attentions away from Cork and Kinsale which duly fell to Marlborough on 27 September and 15 October respectively. His highly personal mission accomplished, Marlborough returned to England.

A strip of no-man's land was created between the winter lines of the two armies. Ginkel's headquarters were at Kilkenny, Douglas commanded in Ulster at Legacurry between Omagh and Dungannon, and Württemberg was at Waterford supervising the Danish corps which was quartered over south-east Ireland. Both sides raided heavily into no-man's land which suffered severe depredations. The Jacobite troops were poorly paid and ill-supplied, living mainly by plundering, but the Williamite troops were in arrears of pay, particularly the Danish corps, and loosely disciplined. Throughout the latter stages of the war, the Catholic rapparees caused enormous damage through guerrilla action. The Ulster regiments were also particularly rapacious, treating the conflict as a religious civil war. During the winter, William re-established a civil government in Dublin under two lords justices, Sir Charles Porter and Thomas Coningsby. In counties which had been recaptured, the full panoply of Protestant English administration was re-established including the arrest of Jacobites for treason. Jacobite estates were confiscated and administered by commissioners.

With King James and the French departed, there were good prospects of a peace being negotiated during the winter of 1690–1. Ginkel and Willem Bentinck, earl of Portland, favoured a generous offer of terms to Catholic landlords but William wanted a settlement in which sufficient confiscated land was available to reward his political friends and associates. The Irish Protestants also pressed for confiscated lands as compensation. After the defeat of the Alliance army under Waldeck at Fleurus on 21 June 1690, the French had become dominant in the Low Countries and the Allied forces in Ireland were urgently required across the North Sea. Ginkel attempted to hasten the diplomacy with military pressure. The Danish major-general, Julius von Tettau, raided into Kerry and James Douglas made a half-hearted attempt against Sligo. Generally, though, Sarsfield maintained the line of the Shannon and prevented serious violations of Jacobite territory. Having sought French assistance and guidance during the winter, Tyrconnell returned to Ireland in January to take command of both the army and the civil government. Sarsfield and his supporters resented Tyrconnell's assumption of control over the army and the Jacobite command divided into feuding factions, made worse by Balldearg O'Donnell whose force of Ulster Gaels did not recognise any authority. The only solution was to impose a commander from outside; the Marquis de St Ruth was selected by Louis XIV.

The failure of the peace negotiations guaranteed a further campaign. In order to bridge the Shannon, Athlone was almost certain to be the initial target of the Williamite forces. During April and May, an artillery train of thirty-six cannon and six mortars, enough money for four months' pay and supplies of all varieties poured into Ireland to support Ginkel. On 9 May, St Ruth arrived at Limerick with two French lieutenant-generals, the comte de Tessé and François d'Usson, and large quantities of arms, ammunition, food and clothing but no money and no men. St Ruth found shortages of every description and his arrival failed to quell the dissension in the Jacobite ranks between the supporters of Sarsfield and those of Tyrconnell. Concentrating at Mullingar, Ginkel marched on 6 June and captured the fort at Ballymore on the following day. Instead of pressing on to Athlone, Ginkel delayed for a week awaiting his bridging train from Dublin. He left Ballymore on 18 June, joining with Württemberg's corps that same night, and the combined force of 18,000 advanced to Athlone on 19 June. Despite the arrival of St Ruth with the main Jacobite army of 16,000 infantry, 3,000 cavalry and 2,000 dragoons on 21 June, Ginkel took the English town of Athlone on 20 June but the Jacobites withdrew into the Irish town and broke down the bridge over the Shannon. After a week of heroic efforts to rebuild the bridge under heavy fire, the Williamites discovered a ford close to the bridge. An assault on 30 June via the ford carried Athlone. In the wake of this victory, Ginkel issued a proclamation offering pardon and restoration of estates to those who surrendered. It was not initially well received but it started a train of negotiation which was to lead to the eventual peace at Limerick.

St Ruth fell back to Ballinasloe, anxious to give battle after his failure at Athlone. Sarsfield thought the Jacobite army too weak to fight in the open field and advocated holding Galway and Limerick in strength whilst raiding heavily into Munster, Leinster and Ginkel's rear areas. His advice was ignored and although d'Usson was sent to garrison Galway, St Ruth selected a battleground behind a strip of marshland on the eastern slopes of Kilcommodon Hill, 5 miles south-west of Ballinasloe. Only two narrow causeways ran through the bog, the more northerly guarded by Aughrim Castle. St Ruth occupied the Aughrim position on 8 July enjoying four days to make preparations. To the rear of the bog the ground was covered by hedges and ditches, excellent field fortifications for the undertrained Jacobite infantry. His army contained around 20,000 men. Early on the morning of Sunday 12 July, Ginkel advanced from Ballinasloe with 20,000 men and drove the Jacobite outposts behind the bog. At 3.00 p.m., the main action opened, Ginkel attacking the Jacobite right to force them to draw forces from Aughrim castle on their left. Once the enemy had weakened their left at Aughrim, Ginkel intended to force the causeway. Despite fierce resistance from the Jacobite infantry, the battle went largely to plan although the causeway at Aughrim was not opened until St Ruth had been killed and Henry Luttrell had failed to act resolutely in its defence. In the following rout, much of the Jacobite army was massacred, perhaps as many as 7,000 men and 400 officers meeting their deaths.[21]

The Williamites attacked Galway on 19 July which almost immediately surrendered, Ginkel granting very favourable terms. It was hoped that this show of generosity towards the Jacobites would lead to the rapid capitulation of Limerick. Balldearg O'Donnell and his Ulster Gaels, who were no more than a marauding rabble, deserted the Jacobites after Aughrim and reached an accommodation with Ginkel. On 14 September, Sligo surrendered after a show of resistance by the governor, Sir Teague O'Regan, and one of incompetence by the Williamite commander, Colonel John Mitchelburne. The only place of military significance remaining to the Jacobites was Limerick. At Limerick were 18,000 Jacobite infantry, 3,000 cavalry and 2,500 dragoons but only half had arms and morale was low. Henry Luttrell was arrested for corresponding with the enemy, Tyrconnell died from a stroke on 14 August and the troops were beginning to desert.

Ginkel took a month to invest Limerick after the fall of Galway, a caution necessitated by difficulties in transporting his siege train and a reluctance to undertake a formal siege if another offer of generous terms might bring capitulation and peace. Ginkel arrived before Limerick on 25 August and his batteries opened fire on the English town on 8 September. On the night of 15/16 September, the Williamites built a bridge across the Shannon ready to invest Limerick on all sides. This was achieved on 22 September. The only hope for the defenders of Limerick was a promised French convoy from Brest laden with arms, ammunition and money. It was delayed, finally reaching the Shannon ten days after the surrender, but, in any event, an English naval squadron stood at the mouth of the river to bar its passage upstream. On 23 September, Sarsfield and Major-General John Wauchope asked Ginkel for a cease-fire; this was granted and Sarsfield took the leading role in the subsequent negotiations. The principal issue at stake was the fate of the Jacobite army. Sarsfield wanted it to go to France to continue the fight, and it was a measure of the desperation of the Alliance cause in Flanders after the loss of Mons that the Williamites were prepared to countenance this proposal even though it meant giving additional troops to their enemy. For William, the ending of the Irish

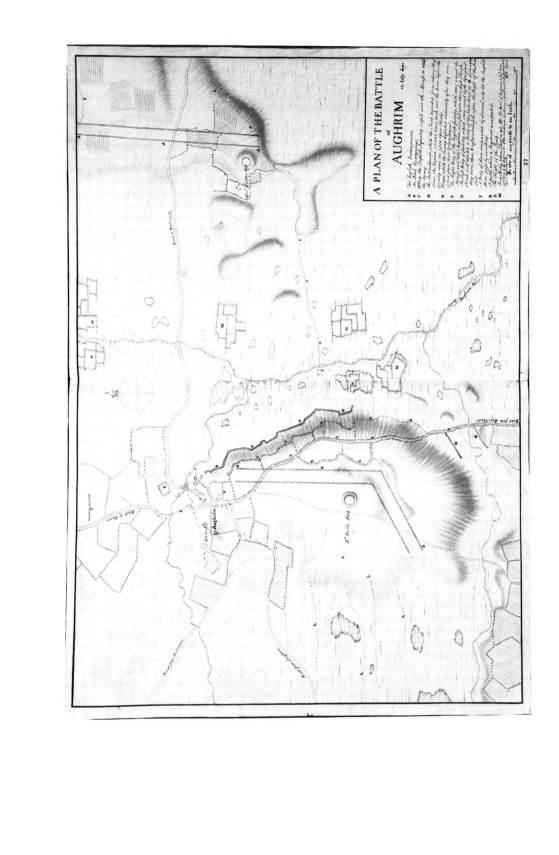

A PLAN OF THE BATTLE
of
AUGHRIM 12. July 1691

37

war was all that mattered. Serious negotiations commenced on 27 September and the Treaty of Limerick was signed on 3 October 1691.

Between October 1691 and January 1692, 19,000 Jacobite soldiers, the 'Wild Geese', sailed for France, complete with wives and children, on board French and English ships. They provided James II with a personal army which was paid by Louis XIV until 1697 when some regiments were disbanded and the remainder were absorbed into the French army.[22] Those Jacobite troops who did not wish to go to France were retained in William's service until 1692, when the majority were demobilised and 1,400 were sent to serve in the imperial army under Lord Iveagh. For the Jacobites who stayed, those who were in Limerick or were otherwise under the protection of the army were permitted to retain their property provided that they took an oath of allegiance to William. Freedom of worship was allowed to Catholics provided that it was 'consistent with the laws of Ireland or as they did enjoy in the reign of King Charles II', whatever that meant.[23] No sooner was the ink dry on the treaty than the Williamite regiments were shipped into England to face a possible invasion attempt by a Franco-Irish corps or straight into the Spanish Netherlands to reinforce the Grand Alliance army.

Prima facie the Jacobite wars fit the pattern of other Irish civil conflicts complicated by outside intervention and exploitation within the context of a general European war. However, their consequences were more profound and enduring than those of their predecessors and successors. In the first place, between

9.6   A plan of the battle of Aughrim, 12 July 1691.
A manuscript map by William Eyres. The legend reads:

A. The English Encampment.
B. The Irish Encampment.
C. Where the English infantry crossed over the morass to attack the enemy.
D. The entrenchments which the Irish defended from whence they drove the English several times back over the river before the cavalry came in upon their flanks.
E. Hedges, which the enemy defended obstinately after they were forced from their entrenchment.
F. The right wing of the English cavalry, which came round the morass, and through Aughrim, and fell upon their left flank.
G. The left wing of the cavalry, which came round by the Eyre-Court Road, and attacked a body of the Irish horse at H, from whence they drove them, and afterwards fell upon the right of the Irish foot.
I. A body of horse commanded by Lutterel [Luttrell], who let the English horse pass by unnoticed.
K. A castle [Aughrim Castle] where a regiment was posted.
L. The flight of the Irish.
M. Bog-holes where turf is cut. N.B. The march of the cavalry is laid down according to the information of the inhabitants, but history informs us that the greatest body passed at the castle.

1685 and 1688, Tyrconnell's purge of the Protestant establishment created a position in 1688–9 which seemed to offer Ireland the possibility of reaching an accommodation with William III. It is not inconceivable that some form of political and religious independence might have resulted. Even when this hope had evaporated, under the personal leadership of Tyrconnell and King James the whole country came close to complete conquest by the Catholics for perhaps the first time in modern Irish history. When the war was halted in 1691, the situation had been totally reversed; the Treaty of Limerick recognised the final and complete English conquest of Catholic Ireland and its subjection to a Protestant government administered from Dublin and directed from London. An Irish army ceased to exist to be replaced throughout the eighteenth century by an English army of occupation or, to be more exact, a collection of English regiments and battalions stationed in Ireland in order to relieve England of the cost, inconvenience and political and social embarrassment of maintaining its own troops. The short history of the Protestant Irish standing army, created in 1661, ended thirty years later.[24]

Chapter 10

The Irish military establishment, 1660–1776

Alan J. Guy

In an article written in 1949 for the inaugural number of the *Irish Sword*, Major
S. H. F. Johnston called for a commitment to research on both sides of the Irish Sea
to fill the gap in the history of the military 'old régime' in Ireland caused by the
disastrous Four Courts fire of June 1922.[1] Pioneering work by recent historians,
most notably John Childs, Kenneth Ferguson, John Houlding, Justin Fennell and
Thomas Bartlett has more than answered Major Johnston's challenge,[2] but, it is to
be feared, the loss of the Dublin Public Records can never truly be made good.
Besides the collections of returns, clothing certificates and routes-of-march so
beloved by the old breed of regimental historian, entire series of papers vital to an
understanding of the army's role in Ireland and to an informed assessment of its
fitness for service, were consumed by flames and a deluge of molten lead.[3] And so
it came about that even the finest military historians, the great C. T. Atkinson, for
example, decided that 'a regiment in Ireland in George I's day made little history',
or that 'Ireland was tranquil enough, and, even if the Irish records of this period
had escaped destruction, there would hardly be much to report of the 39th's
doings.'[4] Another author went far beyond this cautious position by declaring
that 'we know nothing of the life of the [30th Regiment of Foot] in Ireland for ten
years after its return from Gibraltar [in 1728] and it would be of no interest if we
did'.[5]

In reality, above and beyond the fascination of reconstructing the day-to-day
circumstances of military life in Ireland, there are questions of wider importance to
the history of that kingdom, central to the purpose and effectiveness of British
military power in Ireland from the Restoration to the War of American Independence. Was the army in Ireland combat efficient, either as discrete units, or as an
army capable of defending Ireland, England and a growing empire overseas? Were
the king's regiments in Ireland an army of occupation? What was the potential
impact of the Irish army on British politics, and what changes took place in the
religious profile of that army?

On the eve of the rebellion of 1641, the standing army in Ireland numbered 943
horse and 2,297 foot. In Kenneth Ferguson's memorable understatement, it proved

unequal to the multisided conflict which ensued and was expanded beyond recognition by local recruitment and reinforcements from Britain before being swamped by a Commonwealth army 30,000 strong.[6] The Cromwellian garrison of Ireland, it has been argued, systematically suppressed the native population and made that country a proving ground for forceful colonisation and martial government.[7]

The reduction of the bulk of this powerful force in 1661 resulted in an establishment of 2,500 horse and 5,000 foot – three times larger than its early Stuart predecessor and the largest military concentration in the British Isles. As such, it was a not inconsiderable contribution to the military resources of King Charles II and, in theory, was available for military repression elsewhere, although the veteran lord lieutenant, James duke of Ormond, pre-echoed the complaint of many a later Irish viceroy when he lamented that withdrawing soldiers from Ireland undermined the regime and betrayed the loyalists they were there to defend.[8]

With the exception of the 1,200 strong regiment of Irish Foot Guards, raised in England (and thus assumed to be more reliable politically) in 1662 and transported to Dublin, the army in Ireland was 'unregimented' – that is to say it lacked a complement of field officers and regimental staff. The process of regimentation, begun in 1672, was only completed in 1683. This retarded development was largely the result of a dearth of funds, but the Irish army's lack of a corporate identity and its wide dispersal in detachments had political attractions also, for whilst soldiers were a source of strength to government there were continual purges of alleged republicans (who were replaced by men raised in England rather than in Ireland) and nagging doubts about the troops' loyalty. In reality, their grievances focused on the dilatory payment of their wages rather than deep-seated politico-religious discontent.[9] Like many a Tudor and Stuart commander before him, Roger Boyle, earl of Orrery, lord president of Munster, repeatedly dipped into his own pocket to maintain the destitute soldiers under his command. This, he reminded Ormond, with whom he was on increasingly bad terms, was the only way to prevent mutiny. In 1667 the army in Ireland was thirteen months in arrears on its current pay, and there was even an unsettled claim for ten months' 'ancient arrears' from the 1640s. In 1676, the financial situation was so bad that the poverty-stricken army was effectively broken up.[10] As in England and imperial outposts abroad, while some conscientious officers looked after their men, others abused their proprietary status by diverting the soldiers' labour to their own plantations, or pocketing money intended for their clothing and subsistence.[11]

The lingering fear of republican subversion can best be seen in Dublin's handling of the militia issue. After the outbreak of war with France in 1666 fears grew of the threat of invasion via the weakly defended southern ports, but government's chronic inability to pay the regular forces even at their current strength made it necessary to revive the militia. Its role was to keep the country quiet, enabling the regulars to be concentrated at vulnerable points on the coast. Ormond, who feared that a well-disciplined militia might involve itself in matters unrelated to the purpose for which it had been raised, decided to organise it on an *ad hoc* basis rather than by statute, so that he could dispense with its services in times of peace. Its last duty during the reign of Charles II was to assist in the general disarming of Roman Catholics during the Popish Plot. Ironically, as Kenneth Ferguson points out, the militia was shortly to be disarmed itself (together with a large number of other Protestants) as a consequence of Monmouth's Rising in the west of England and the forward policy of King James II's man of business in Ireland, Richard Talbot, earl of Tyrconnell. In the summer of 1689 Tyrconnell distributed the militia's weapons, some of which had been handed in very reluctantly, to his new Roman Catholic militia.[12]

With the process of regimentation completed in 1683, the Restoration standing army in Ireland can be said to have reached its zenith. Around 7,000 strong – still larger, it should be noted, than its English counterpart – it was formed in three regiments of horse and seven of foot, admittedly still dispersed in numerous garrisons and posts. The pageantry of state was maintained by a company of sixty foot, the 'Guard of Battleaxes' formed by Ormond in 1662 and attired like the English Yeomen of the Guard. The welfare of maimed and infirm veterans was catered for by the Royal Hospital at Kilmainham, first mooted in 1675, erected during 1680–4 and pre-dating the Royal Hospital at Chelsea.[13] Shortly however, the Irish military machine was to be overturned in a way which, for a while, transformed its exclusively Protestant character.

Although the remodelling of the Irish army which began in 1685–6 is inextricably linked with the personal histories of James II and Tyrconnell, it originated in a decision taken during Charles II's last weeks to admit Roman Catholic officers. This initiative was vigorously put into effect by Tyrconnell on the assumption that it would make the army more reliable by winkling out what he and King James regarded as the 'old leaven' among the English in Ireland, and correspond with James's intention to give public countenance to his coreligionists. 'You must know my Lord', Tyrconnell informed the earl of Clarendon, whom he was shortly to displace as viceroy, 'the king, who is a Roman Catholic is resolved to employ his subjects of that religion . . . and therefore some must be put out to make room for such as the king likes'.[14] It has been argued that Tyrconnell's remodelling of the Irish army, which soon reached out beyond the officer corps to embrace the rank and file, had little to do with English politics, being instead part of his wider plan to promote the interest of the 'Old English' sector of the Roman Catholic population of Ireland by overturning the Restoration land settlement which had confirmed the dominance of Protestant proprietors. According to this interpretation, the 'Os and Macs' that Tyrconnell brought into the lower ranks of the army were casual beneficiaries only, but there was evidently a cutting edge to the Catholicisation of the army at the lowest level:

———

Whither shall John turn? He has now no red coat on him,
Nor 'Who's there?' on his lips when standing beside the gate.
'You Popish rogue' they won't dare say to us.
But 'Cromwellian dog' is the watchword we have for him.[15]

At the end of the summer of 1686, the nominal strength of the army in Ireland was 7,485 private men, of whom John Miller has computed that 5,043 (67 per cent) were Roman Catholics, as were 166 out of 414 officers (40 per cent) and 251 out of 765 non-commissioned officers (33 per cent). The weeding out of Protestants was virtually complete by the end of 1688, suggesting that whatever doubts there might have been about the military value of the new intake of recruits, Tyrconnell had at least achieved his immediate objective.[16]

The political impact of these changes can best be appreciated from an English perspective, as most of the officers ejected by Tyrconnell had purchased their commissions and in the eyes of military men this was an attack on property rights on a par with King James's ejection of the Fellows of Magdalen. The refusal in September 1688 of the six 'Portsmouth Captains' of the Princess Anne of Denmark's Regiment of Foot to incorporate Irish recruits in their companies, promptly followed by their dismissal from the service, confirmed that the king was well on the way to forfeiting the allegiance of his officers, as did the appearance in the English army of such provocatively titled pressure groups as the 'Association of Protestant Officers' or the 'Treason Club'. Only a tiny minority of James's officers were actually enrolled in an Orangeist conspiracy, but something like two-thirds of the officer corps were to some degree disaffected by the time of Prince William's landing at Torbay in November 1688.[17] The fearsome reputation of Irish troops and reactions to their arrival in England at James's summons brought to mind the alarm caused by Lord Deputy Strafford's Roman Catholic 'new army' of 1639–41, or Charles I's ill-fated call for Irish support against the forces of Parliament in 1643–4. Those Irish soldiers who landed in October 1688 totalled only about 2,500 men, formed in one battalion of guards, two regiments of foot and one of dragoons, but they were inflated by popular rumour and astute Williamite propaganda into a ravening horde of 10,000 – nay, 100,000 – popish fanatics, whose progress was accompanied by every refinement of murder, rapine and arson.[18] This prototype *grande peur* and the hard-fought sectarian war in Ireland which began in 1689, with Tyrconnell's remodelled regiments forming the backbone of the Jacobite army, ensured that with the exception of Lord Forbes's regiment of foot, reformed in England around a rump of about 200 Protestant rank and file (subsequently the Royal Regiment of Ireland, ranking eighteenth in the line) there was scant continuity in Irish soldiering between the reigns of King James and King William.

William's initial armament of 30,000 men for the reconquest of Ireland, in which Protestant officers expelled by Tyrconnell took a prominent part, was supplemented by units raised by Ulster Protestants – disparaged as 'so many Croats' by his

10.1   The Royal Hospital, Kilmainham, built in 1680–1684 to the designs
of Sir William Robinson, to house military veterans. One of the
architectural glories of Ireland, it was a precursor to the Chelsea Royal
Hospital in London. In later years the mastership of the hospital was
combined with the senior British military command in Ireland. Sir Nevil
Macready, the last British commander-in-chief in Ireland, vacated the
premises on 17 December 1922.

general Frederick duke of Schomberg but heralding the penetration of the British
officer corps by Protestant Irish gentry.[19] From July 1690 these locally raised forces
were supplemented by a reconstituted militia – eventually 15,000 strong – which
played an important secondary role in the 1691 campaign and the mopping-up
operations beginning in 1692. Attempts to establish the militia by parliamentary
statute failed both in 1692 and 1697, and was not successfully brought about until
1716, by which time the militia's effectiveness as an instrument of war can be seen

to have declined, notwithstanding later formal arrays in 1719 and 1756 and other mobilisations in 1739–40 and 1745. The government's main commitment in times of crisis was to its regular forces, and militia weapons were kept in store to answer 'some more efficient purpose', which meant that when militiamen gathered in Belfast to repel Thurot's raid in February 1760 they were scantily equipped with muskets and ammunition.[20]

The English Act of Parliament 'for granting an Aid to the Majesty for disbanding the Army and other necessary Occasions', known as the Disbanding Act of 1699 (10 William III cap. 1), can be said to have inaugurated the classic age of the Irish military establishment. It limited the number of the king's 'natural born Subjects, Commission and Non-Commission Officers' under arms in Ireland to 12,000 in time of peace. As before, they were paid for from Irish revenues and the army remained the most expensive item in the Irish budget, yet the Irish parliament had no authority to vary the manpower total as the English Act operated in the sister kingdom by royal proclamation under the Great Seal. There was no Irish Mutiny Act until 1780, when in an implicit denial of the British parliament's right to legislate for Ireland an assertive Irish parliament passed one, although Lord North's government in London insisted on making it permanent rather than annually renewable as in England.[21]

While the English parliamentary vote of men might vary almost from year to year, Irish numbers remained at 12,000 until 1769, except in wartime, when they were increased, albeit with great circumspection, as Charles Yorke, George III's attorney general, indicated in 1762.[22] Thus, for several months during 1756–7 as many as 17,000 men were under arms, and after a vote of credit in 1761 the Irish establishment maintained 24,000 men for a period of two years, 8,000 of them serving overseas.[23] As this demonstrates, the principal role of the Irish army under the Georges was that of a strategic reserve, a policy seen in action as early as June 1701, when 12 battalions, about 5,000 men in all, embarked at Cork for Flanders.

In peacetime, when the quota of 12,000 was scrupulously adhered to, individual battalion strengths were reduced as much as possible. In 1763, for example, there were 30 battalions in Ireland, each with a complement of 328, and including a disproportionately large officer cadre to facilitate rapid wartime expansion to 1,000 rank and file. When units left the kingdom, full of men drafted from the battalions left behind, the supply of trained soldiers available to repel invasion or quell internal unrest was seriously depleted, a fact ever lamented by querulous viceroys. In December 1745, at the height of the Jacobite Rebellion in Britain, only 3 regiments of horse, 3 of dragoons and 4 of infantry remained in Ireland, a reduction of effective strength to less than 7,000. Only that autumn, the generals on the establishment had reported that a minimum of 13,525 men was needed to guarantee the safety of the kingdom.[24] Even the peacetime total of 12,000 concealed a nagging attrition of effective strength, with large numbers of old and infirm serving in the ranks. In 1751, the Irish commander-in-chief calculated that

---

10.2 Richard Talbot, earl of Tyrconnell, 1690.

1,000 men, the equivalent of 3 battalions at Irish peacetime numbers, were thus ineffective, exclusive of deaths, desertion or other vacancies.[25] During the 1760s, the average number of effectives in Ireland was only between 8,000 and 7,000.[26]

As proclaimed on 24 November 1701, the Irish army was once again to be an exclusively Protestant force: 'no Papist or reputed Papist Soldier shall continue or be admitted into any Regiment in the Kingdom'.[27] Not only were Irish Catholics excluded from the ranks, but Irish Protestants also, for it was intended that once a year regiments on the Irish establishment should send recruiting parties to England and Scotland with a view to building up the Protestant interest in Ireland. Some

10.3   The Battle of the Boyne, and flight of King James II from Ireland, 1690.

officers, either through laziness or graft, attempted to hoodwink their field officers by enlisting Irish Catholics;[28] others, despairing of the expense of recruiting in Britain, tried to pass off Irish Protestant recruits as Scotsmen.[29] In times of acute manpower crisis – 1716–17, 1745–7, 1757–63 – restrictions on enlisting Irish Protestants were relaxed, but once any Irishmen were permitted to serve, it became that much more difficult to spot a papist in the ranks and, when peace returned, steps were quickly taken to reduce Irishmen and replace them with recruits from Britain. Officers were excluded from this nationality test, to the extent that by the mid-1770s Protestant Irishmen provided about one-third of the British officer corps as a whole, a number disproportionate to their share of the total population of the British Isles.[30]

The requirement to maintain the Protestant orthodoxy of the army in Ireland prompts the question as to what extent that country should be regarded as occupied territory. Francis Godwin James concluded that 'in the last analysis the Irish state in the early eighteenth century rested upon British military power',[31] but that is not saying a great deal, as a similar situation prevailed in England itself, at least for as long as a credible Jacobite threat existed. The riots in Cork in 1753 which resulted in a civilian being shot by an unknown hand (most likely a soldier's) and which so impressed Lieutenant-Colonel Samuel Bagshawe have a depressingly modern ring,[32] but were no worse than the weavers' and Wilkesite riots in London during 1763, 1765 and 1768, or the 'Boston Massacre' of 1770, and were by no means as destructive of life and property as London's Gordon riots of 1780.[33] Many of the hundred or more barracks that spanned the country from 1698 onwards and which at first sight seem so potent a symbol of military repression were in reality residential buildings, intended to afford the soldiers shelter which could not be provided in public houses as would have been the case in England. They were much different in design from the fortified structures being erected at the same period for the attempted pacification of the Scottish Highlands.[34] As Sean Connolly has persuasively argued, from the time of the suppression of the 'Houghers' in 1711–12 until the outbreak of the 'Whiteboy' disturbances in the 1760s (and which were to disrupt the smooth transfer of reinforcements to America in 1775) Ireland was docile under the rule of justices of the peace and urban magistrates, with armed force deployed only at the behest of the civil power.[35]

This said, the seventeenth-century legacy of religious conflict and the main-tenance of the penal laws created a tension of resentment in the country at large which resulted in some military men, who liked to think themselves above such considerations, scorning Protestant and Catholic communities alike. These soldiers believed that outside Ulster, the Protestants had 'no Pretensions to any Property they enjoy, but what they received from Military Power'.[36] Impatient of the disputes between soldiers and the local labour force typical of any garrison town, they demanded a fraternal reception in Protestant settlements which, we may be sure, they did not always get, and in retaliation they condemned their hosts for lack of public spirit.[37] As for the Roman Catholic population, Lieutenant-Colonel Bagshawe spoke for many when he observed that:

> The common people of this Country are naturally fond of times of Confusion because they have an Oppertunity of indulging some favourite appetites such as Thieving and Cruelty; and if it were not that they stand in Awe of a Sett of Folks in my Neighbourhood We should have had some Instance of both, but we use so little Ceremony with 'em that they do not have any Disputes [where] We are concerned.[38]

Moreover, the continuing difficulty encountered in enforcing the law in the fastnesses of Connacht or the depths of Cork and Kerry, a haunt of smugglers, bandits and, it was alleged, foreign recruiting officers,[39] gave rural Ireland a 'frontier' reputation. The internal security operations carried out by Sir James Caldwell's 'Enniskillen Light Horse' during 1760–3 give some idea of what this meant in practice. In 1760, Caldwell, who was desirous of an Irish peerage, demonstrated his zeal towards government by raising a 200 strong troop of light dragoons in Ulster at his own expense. He was granted the rank of captain-commandant and his new corps appeared in the *Army List* as the 20th Light Dragoons. Inspired by the achievements of British arms in Germany, Caldwell uniformed and equipped his men in the style of the famed Prussian Hussars, but in a poor substitute for European service they were dispatched to Connacht and Munster in support of the revenue commissioners. The dragoons made circuits of 100 miles at a time, traversing mountain and bog and hiring boats to go into 'Islands in the Sea' [Lough Erne] in search of illegal distilleries. Confronting mobs of a hundred or more, they confiscated stills, burned down still-houses and scattered their contents, spilling 'large quantities of Low Wines and Whisky' and 'innumerable Gallons of pot ale'.[40]

For the most part however garrison duty in Georgian Ireland was lacking in such excitement, with little to do 'to divert a high pitch of spleen and melancholy, engend'rd by want of company and ye sulphureous vapours of a boggy situation'.[41] Barracks were often decayed and wretchedly appointed (a public scandal in its own right)[42] with dubious sanitation. Troops quartered in Limerick, for example, were commonly afflicted by a bowel complaint, christened 'the Limericks'.[43] Dublin, the seat of government, with the intermittent splendours of the viceregal court and the largest concentration of troops in the kingdom, attracted every officer who had an excuse to linger there, but the prices of lodgings, provisions and public entertainment were as high as in London.[44] A posting to Ireland therefore was looked upon as a mark of ill-fortune, if not disfavour,[45] and it was believed that only a good interest at court would enable a corps to become a 'compleat English Regiment' once again.[46] The fact that many of the most senior regiments in the service were posted there did nothing to alter the view of Ireland as a place where officers were 'banished from their Friends and Relations and all Hopes of Preferment',[47] a perception which resulted in widespread absenteeism, weakly

10.4 George, fourth Viscount Townshend, lord lieutenant of Ireland, 1767–1772 (mezzotint by T. Jose after Reynolds, *c.* 1775).

counteracted by standing orders and a system of fines for absentees, the notorious 'Country Exchange'.

Underlying this chronic malingering, which afflicted other garrisons during the period, notably Minorca, whose surrender in 1756 elevated officer absenteeism to the level of a national concern, was the suspicion in the English high command that there was a serious malaise afflicting the Irish army. In theory, military arrangements in Ireland were more conducive to good order than in England, for Irish regiments were assigned to their quarters for only a year at a time, the move to new accommodation being made each spring or early summer. Every second or third year a regiment was based in or around a garrison town – Dublin (its concentration of four or five battalions rivalled only by the Mediterranean garrisons of Gibraltar or Minorca), Galway, Limerick, Cork, Waterford and Kinsale. Here regiments could be manoeuvred *en bloc* and brigaded for advanced training. Dublin's Phoenix Park was the largest exercise ground at the British army's disposal.[48] Despite these opportunities however, the combination of wide dispersal, manpower shortages, officer absenteeism and sheer bloody-mindedness led Lord Lieutenant Townshend to conclude at the height of the Falkland Islands Crisis in 1770 that:

> nothing can be more different than an English Regiment is to one in the same Service. There is many a Regiment extremely splendid in its superficial Points of ostensible Merit, and at the same time full of Discontent and habituated to desertion on all Occasions. In such a Situation, should they take the Field the Consequence is obvious.[49]

Specific examples of disarray are not hard to find. In July 1730, Henry Hawley succeeded the earl of Harrington as colonel of what King George II told him was 'the finest Regiment of Dragoons in Ireland [the 13th]'. He soon discovered that his 138 horses, non-commissioned officers and men had been 'farmed out to a Scotch Lieutenant Colonel [Peter Kerr] who had made the most of it and done so many dirty things that he was forced next year to take command of the Regiment from him'.[50] Major-General Philip Bragg's 28th Foot was more notorious. The regiment had attracted favourable attention in Ireland in 1737 and again on active service in 1745, but thereafter performed so badly in France and Flanders that the duke of Cumberland, captain general, decided to disband it. This proposal violated the custom of the army which protected the property rights of the 'old corps' and Bragg, who protested that he had lost touch with his regiment when it left Ireland, rallied his former patrons, notably the duke of Dorset, who as lord lieutenant had placed him in the service and who now pleaded with the king's ministers to persuade Cumberland to reverse his decision. One reason for Dorset's intervention, it was alleged, was to protect the reputation of his son, Lord George Sackville, who had been Bragg's lieutenant-colonel from 1740 to 1746. Once back in Ireland, the regiment continued to misbehave. In July 1750 it quit Limerick in such a drunken state that the drummers were incapable of beating a cadence. Such scenes of indiscipline, Lieutenant-Colonel Caroline Frederick Scott pointedly informed Cumberland, were *quelque chose de règle en Irlande*.[51] In the late 1760s, Bragg's record was perhaps surpassed by Major-General David Graeme's 49th Foot, with its undersized men, poor quality recruits, badly made and ill fitting uniforms and defective accounts. When Townshend drew this to Graeme's attention – the general was living in Perth at the time – he archly replied that he was 'ignorant of what the Regiment can do, and should be astonished to find it expert in anything . . . I ever represented it to be by far the worst in the Service'. He offered to leave for Dublin at once, however, ' . . . and I shall think myself happy if I can fulfil His Majesty's Wishes by performing the Duty of a Sergeant Major, having no Passion so strong as that of yielding to the Royal Pleasure'.[52] In February 1769 these accumulating difficulties resulted in the allegation by the pseudonymous newspaper columnist 'Junius' that the whole army in Ireland was 'absolutely ruined'.[53]

The system of proprietary command which operated in the seventeenth and eighteenth centuries, by which extensive management powers were devolved to officers who had invested in a regiment by purchasing their commissions meant that a unit's efficiency depended to a large extent on the zeal and activity of a few individuals, notably the colonel-proprietor (often an absentee) and more importantly the field officers – the lieutenant-colonel and major – who exercised command on the ground.[54] The poor condition of Hawley's, Bragg's and Graeme's regiments could all be put at the door of ineffective field officers, and this was an affliction that could strike a regiment anywhere. It is noteworthy, however, that the farther away a unit was from the control of the War Office in London or the supervision of an energetic commander-in-chief like Cumberland, who combined the office of captain general with the authority of a prince of the blood, the worse things were likely to be.

Regiments stationed in Ireland were effectively shielded from the reforming activity of Cumberland and his supporters in the army by the viceregal authority of the lord lieutenant.[55] His full title, 'Lord Lieutenant General and General Gouvernour of Ireland' hints at the military power inherent in the office, jealously guarded from the time of Ormond. His progress through the capital was a military event: escorted by a squadron of horse through streets lined with the infantry of the Dublin garrison, he received the sword of state from the lords justices on the Castle steps, the great guns thudding in Phoenix Park to the echo of volleys of musketry from the soldiers drawn up on College Green.[56] His chief secretary, in addition to looking after 'everything that comes under the head of civil affairs',[57] issued all orders relating to the military establishment and was in effect the local equivalent of the secretary at war at the War Office in London. The viceroy had the ascriptive right to nominate officers to the influential staff posts of adjutant and quartermaster-general in Ireland, as well as many lesser appointments. He had a general officer commanding-in-chief under him, plus a staff of two lieutenant-generals, three major-generals and six brigadier-generals. From their ranks he assembled an Irish

Board of General Officers to deliberate and advise him on military problems of all sorts. Besides these senior officers, he had a legion of aides-de-camp, 'gentlemen at large', clerks and commissaries, a master-general of the ordnance in Ireland and principal officers, military engineers, officers of the train, gunners, storekeepers, artisans, matrosses and, from 1755, first one and later four companies of the Royal Irish Artillery.[58]

Since the lord lieutenant freely maintained his prerogatives, it followed that the effectiveness of the Irish army depended to a considerable extent on his military competence, yet it was not usual for Georgian viceroys to possess much military understanding. George Townshend, appointed in 1767, was the first important soldier to hold the office since the duke of Bolton, lord lieutenant from 1717 to 1720, and whose record as colonel of the Royal Regiment of Horse Guards had been highly questionable.[59] Moreover, before Townshend's lieutenancy, it was usual for the viceroy to remain in the kingdom only long enough to secure the passage of the administration's money bills through the Irish Parliament, an average of only eight months in two years. The reputation of the appointment as 'great in itself, but often a step of disgrace to some men who have been or expect to be in the closer parts of the Administration'[60] also meant that even the best lords lieutenant kept their gaze fixed on English politics and delved but little into military business. In this context, the marquess of Hartington's military tour of Ireland in 1755, during which he reviewed a number of regiments, was an unusual event.[61]

It was also rare to find a military man occupying the post of chief secretary. Lord George Sackville, chief secretary to his father the duke of Dorset during his second term as lord lieutenant from 1750 to 1755, was an exception to this rule, and was, moreover, believed to be acting as the duke of Cumberland's 'military man of confidence in Ireland',[62] but he made a host of political enemies for himself and offended the officers by perpetuating the 'Country Exchange', which was all too plainly intended to supplement his income and that of the muster-master general and clerk of the cheque. (Sackville would be reminded of these exactions after his disgrace at the Battle of Minden in 1759.)[63]

Much depended therefore on the capability of the Irish staff, but, in the past, nominations had been sold and reversions granted that still affected the quality of military administration at mid-century. The post of muster-master and clerk of the cheque was held in reversion by the earls of Tullamore, as it had been since the time of George I. Two generations of Butlers had held the post of adjutant-general. Colonel Thomas Butler, who succeeded his father James in 1743, was said to have conducted a review at Kilkenny in 1750 so badly that it 'would make a dog spew'.[64] The marquess of Kildare, master-general of the Ordnance was alleged to have made it 'a monstrous overgrown head to a weak diminutive body'.[65] As for the Irish commander-in-chief, he was subservient to the lord lieutenant, attending Dublin Castle for consultation about twice a week and no more than *primus inter pares*

---

among his fellow generals on the staff. The long line of Irish appointees to this office, none of them notably distinguished in the army's roll of honour, provides further evidence that residence in the sister kingdom was unattractive.[66] Worse, the remaining generals, discouraged by the thought of residing in Ireland and the relatively poor remuneration attached to their posts, were also reluctant to serve unless themselves Irish.[67] It sometimes proved impossible to form a quorum of three for the Board of General Officers. In wartime, and sometimes even during peace, there was a shortage of young, active general officers in Ireland. Those who did serve there, like Major-General Bragg, were more likely to be found busy embarking drafts for foreign service than manoeuvring their battalions.[68]

Irish politics, and what Roy Foster characterises as the 'ancient computations of fees and remuneration, the Byzantine intricacies of jobbery',[69] also intervened to play a dubious role in army affairs. Even those lords lieutenant most inclined to resist the demands of Ireland's aggressive political elite had to make some concessions to the avalanche of requests for patronage showered upon them by Irish MPs and, naturally, they also had clients of their own to satisfy. As a result, regiments posted to Ireland could expect to see their officer corps become more and more Irish every year.[70] Townshend maintained that political pressure had also resulted in a spread of quarters inimical to the defence of the realm and the interior economy of the unfortunate units concerned.[71]

The acid test of the Irish army's efficiency lay in its wartime performance. Among those regiments sent overseas, Blakeney's 27th Foot landed in England in 1739 padded out with boys barely able to hold a musket, but there were, as one might expect, good units as well as bad. Adlercron's 39th Foot, the first royal regiment to serve in India, was hand-picked for its excellence by Cumberland in 1754;[72] Halkett's 44th Regiment and Dunbar's 48th were likewise selected in autumn the same year for service in North America, where that notorious martinet Major-General Edward Braddock placed his greatest faith in them.[73] But as for national defence, it was perhaps fortunate that French invasion plans envisaged operations in Ireland playing a secondary role to a main effort directed against England.[74]

Building on the peacetime practice of encamping troops during the summer months to give them some experience of operating at brigade strength, wartime camps of instruction were regularly established in the south of County Tipperary to cover the possibility of landings at any point on the coast between Shannon and Waterford. During the 'Fifteen', troops were encamped in winter cantonments across Athlone, Limerick and Kilkenny. In 1746 Lord Lieutenant Chesterfield stationed four battalions at Bennetsbridge (near Kilkenny) which he regarded as 'the heart of Ireland', while in 1759 there were summer encampments in Phoenix Park, Thurles and Connacht.[75] But these precautionary arrangements notwithstanding, the one partially successful invasion attempt which took place during this period inspires little confidence in the capability of the overstretched Irish army to respond. Indeed, the story of Commodore François Thurot's capture of Carrickfergus in February 1760 is a quintessentially Georgian mixture of valour and farce.

Thurot's raid was first intended as a diversion in support of major attacks on Essex and the west coast of Scotland, although in the event it was the only operation that went ahead.[76] His little armada of seven frigates and a cutter, carrying 1,110 picked infantry and a small train of artillery slipped out of Dunkirk in October 1759 and cruised indecisively until the new year, reduced by foul weather to only three sail and racked by dissension between the commodore and the officers of the land forces. The attempt on Carrickfergus was Thurot's last throw before abandoning the expedition. At 10 a.m. on 21 February 1760, the refractory squadron anchored off Kilroot, mid-way between Carrickfergus and the entrance to Belfast Lough. A 600 strong assault force was mustered on deck, plied with brandy and put aboard the long-boats for the short journey ashore.

The defence of the castle and town of Carrickfergus had been entrusted to four weak companies of Major-General Strode's 62nd Foot. Only 2 captains were on duty that day, with 2 lieutenants, 3 ensigns, 11 sergeants, 10 corporals, 5 drummers and about 170 private soldiers. At the time the French landed most of them were at drill, about half a mile out of town on the Belfast road. Lieutenant-Colonel John Jennings, their commanding officer, marched them down to the market place and sent a reconnaissance party to the beach; the detachment soon returned, their ammunition spent. Jennings meanwhile had taken the precaution of evacuating 100 French prisoners held in the castle to Belfast, escorted by armed civilians.

The French entered the town in two columns. Jennings and his men, reinforced by a number of local gentry, resisted as long as their cartridges lasted, but soon a 'dreadfull want of Ammunition' obliged them to retreat to the castle. The French attacked the castle gates, forcing the bolts and bursting them open, only to be driven out again by a vigorous counter-attack. Destitute of ammunition, the English pelted their attackers with bricks and stones from the castle walls: some, according to regimental tradition, used their coat-buttons as bullets. The French were badly shaken by this sortie but Jennings quickly saw that his men were by now incapable of further resistance. Not only was their meagre supply of ball entirely used up, but there was a fifty-foot breach in the castle wall on the seaward face that could hardly escape the enemy's notice for much longer. Jennings sued for terms, which allowed the garrison to evacuate Carrickfergus with full honours of war, the officers to be paroled in Ireland, the men also until a like number of Frenchmen were exchanged. The town was preserved from sack in return for a supply of provisions; the gunpowder in the castle was thrown into the sea and the ordnance, dismounted and silent throughout the battle, was spiked. Jennings had lost only three or four men; the French at least thirty-six, with some estimates as high as sixty. It was now about 7 p.m.

Shortly after five that afternoon, word had reached General Strode in Belfast that Carrickfergus had been attacked by 1,000 French. The city was in a state of panic.

10.5 Carrickfergus Castle, begun in the late twelfth century, and an
important strongpoint for 600 years. In 1760 it was captured and held for
several days by a French force under Commodore François Thurot.

Strode sent a courier to the Duke of Bedford in Dublin who ordered three regiments
of dragoons and four of foot to his assistance. At midnight on 27 February, as the
leading British units marched into town, the enemy squadron left Carrickfergus Bay.
Early the next morning they ran into three English frigates, alerted by Bedford.
In the action which followed, Thurot was killed, his ships destroyed and 23 French
officers and 409 soldiers and seamen taken prisoner.

News of the British defeat had been greeted with outrage, but once it became clear
that Jennings's determined resistance had in all likelihood prevented the fall of
Belfast, criticism turned to praise. Senior officers sent to the scene of the action
reported that the men of the 62nd had 'behav'd like Lyons', while Bedford reported
that 'no Man could have made with the small number of Men under his command
a gallanter and better conducted defence of any Place under the Circumstances than
Lieutenant-Colonel Jennings did' and recommended him for promotion. The men
of the 62nd were thanked by a relieved Irish Parliament; the officers were fêted
by the citizens of Carrickfergus and given commemorative silver cups. All was
splendid in retrospect, but the destruction of Thurot's squadron on the high seas
by the Royal Navy was perhaps an indication of how Ireland might have been

227

better defended than by crumbling fortifications, mute artillery and soldiers without ammunition.[77]

At the Peace of Paris in 1763 England was seen to have triumphed so decisively that in the post-war world her former allies and enemies alike remained distinctly unfriendly. With the French apparently planning a garrison of 23,000 for their West Indian possessions, half in the islands and half aboard their fleet, there were more territories to be defended than ever before and, for the first time in peace during the eighteenth century, there were to be more British soldiers serving abroad than at home.[78] In this new 'rationalised' phase of empire the Irish establishment took on a more overtly imperial role and it became necessary both to establish new mechanisms of inspection and to expand the system of regular rotation begun in 1749 for regiments serving in the Mediterranean to embrace the totality of Britain's overseas possessions.

If regiments were to be maintained fit for service in the colonies – itself a far from easy task – it was first necessary that they should go out from home at optimum strength and in good order. In 1763, regiments of foot in Britain, North America and the Mediterranean were reduced to 500 officers and men; in Ireland, where customary arrangements prevailed for the time being, the unit-establishment was as low as 328. The difficulties this would cause were perceived straight away, and when rotation began in 1764, every battalion leaving the country was reinforced by drafts from those left behind. Inevitably, the best men were drafted. The depleted units then awaited the homecoming of regiments relieved abroad in the hope of getting replacements from them when they were reduced to Irish numbers – a doubtful proposition given the weakened state of units returning from foreign service – a 'murdering system of destroying your Regiments' as the English adjutant-general, Edward Hervey, remarked to his Irish counterpart, Lieutenant-Colonel Robert Cunninghame.[79]

The need to augment Irish battalion strengths, and with them the size of the Irish military establishment as a whole for the purposes of imperial defence, lay behind the appointment of a soldier, George, Viscount Townshend as lord lieutenant in August 1767, which in turn led to Townshend's acute political struggle with the 'Undertakers' – the entrenched group of Irish power brokers who steered the Castle's measures through the Irish parliament in return for generous helpings of military and civil patronage.[80] Townshend's difficulties were increased by a rising tide of colonial nationalism which, sometimes in apparent contradiction, depicted military force as a threat to civil liberty (extended in this scenario to include the civil liberties of the Americans). The colonial nationalists insisted, nonetheless, that 12,000 troops should always be kept in Ireland to guarantee the safety of the realm, yet ended by querying the cost of the establishment.

Townshend's struggle to reassert his authority over parliament and regain control of the machinery of Irish patronage was to last for five years, although the augmentation itself was successfully carried in October 1769. The new establishment totalled 15,325 men of all ranks, each battalion being increased to 500 – adjusted to 477 in 1772 to provide funding to add a light company on the British model – but there were strings attached to the deal. Townshend was obliged to convey the king's promise that 12,000 soldiers would remain in Ireland 'except in case of invasion or actual rebellion in Great Britain', a guarantee enshrined in the preamble to the Augmentation Act, and an Irish loan bill was passed to pay for the scheme. These measures gave the Irish parliament a voice in the management of the Irish army it had never enjoyed before, and led to a political storm at the end of 1775 when a clause in an Irish money bill which presumed to sanction the removal of 4,000 men for service in America was deleted by the British Privy Council on the ground that it infringed the royal prerogative, the crown lawyers having concluded, with some relief, that although it might be unbecoming for a royal promise to be broken, it was not illegal.[81] When France entered the American War in 1778 there were only 8,500 troops left in Ireland, although that number was increased by 5,000 at the end of the year, and the following summer almost all the regulars were encamped – an unparalleled achievement which was ominous in its own way, since it was only made possible by the advent of the Volunteers, who took over routine security duties.[82]

A lesser known but equally important feature of Townshend's lord-lieutenancy was the much needed shake-up he administered by personal tours of inspection, accompanied by his old Etonian schoolfriend and director-general of engineers Charles Vallancey, the antiquary and surveyor of Ireland.[83] This must have been a more appealing assignment than grappling with the Undertakers, but Townshend was shocked by 'the deplorable state of His Majesty's military affairs in this Kingdom', with its decaying barracks, mouldering and badly sited fortifications and scattered detachments of soldiers. His solution was to establish strong barracks and magazines at strategic points, quarter his battalions in such a way as to restore their field officers' authority over them and, most importantly, to employ his general officers as district commanders, residing in their localities, with authority to keep regiments under constant inspection and to brigade them and teach them to act like an army. By December 1770 he flattered himself that his influence was helping to transform the 'poor skeleton of an Army' into 'something very respectable'.[84]

Townshend was also responsible for an initiative which once again transformed the religious profile of the Irish army when he responded to a War office proposal to allow regiments on the British establishment to recruit Irish Protestants by recommending the recruitment of Roman Catholics. Cautious approval from London in January 1771 inaugurated widescale Catholic recruitment, underwritten by a statute of 1774 which substituted an oath of allegiance for the former religious test. After March 1775 permission was given for regiments to recruit 'at large' in Ireland.[85] Sixteen of the forty-four battalions serving in America in 1776 had originated in the Irish establishment and had been augmented to combat strength with Roman Catholics, though not, it must be added, without generating considerable unease among Irish Protestants.[86] The way was now open for the massive influx of Irishmen into Wellington's infantry, with its thirteen specifically Irish battalions and an Irish presence of well over 30 per cent in units nominally English in composition.[87]

Chapter 11

The defence of Protestant
Ireland, 1660–1760

S. J. Connolly

On a summer day in 1714 a group of prisoners was conveyed through the streets of
Dublin to Kilmainham jail. They had earlier been taken in the act of enlisting with
agents recruiting for the army of the exiled Stuart pretender. As they passed, one of
the bystanders, a tanner named Cusack, was heard to ask whether anyone would
blame the arrested men 'for endeavouring to get estates if they cou'd, for that
fellows that came over in leathern breeches and wooden shoes, now rides in their
coaches'. Cusack was presented before the grand jury. Yet his remark, though
indiscreet, was hardly new. It recalled, for example, the words spoken in the very
different context of the exclusively Protestant parliament of Charles II, during a
procedural wrangle between the two houses in July 1666. One of the peers involved
complained testily that 'the Commons had a mind all to be Lords', only to hear
Adam Molyneux, MP for County Longford, reply: 'Why not? Another rebellion may
make us Lords, as well as former rebellions have your Lordship's ancestors.'[1]

Behind both of these comments, the licensed insolence of Adam Molyneux the
MP, and the treasonable indiscretion of Cusack the tanner, lay a recognition of
the same central point: that the social and political order of late seventeenth and
eighteenth-century Ireland had its origins in the recent and dramatic restructuring
of society by means of military force.[2] All three kingdoms of the British Isles had
experienced a period of military rule, commencing in December 1648, when
Colonel Thomas Pride's soldiers purged the English parliament in order to clear the
way for the execution the following month of Charles I, and ending in May 1660
with the restoration of Charles II. But the long-term effects of that experience
differed greatly. In England and Scotland the governing classes, alarmed at the
chaos that had threatened to follow the death of Oliver Cromwell in September 1658,
were able to unite around the myth that the restoration of monarchy brought with
it a return to the legal and constitutional position that had obtained before the civil
wars. In Ireland no such pretence was possible.

The main reason why this was so was of course the massive transfer of landed
property that had taken place following the defeat of the royalists and Confederate
Catholics. In 1641 Catholics had owned nearly 60 per cent of the profitable land of

Ireland. By the late 1650s this had fallen to 8 or 9 per cent, most of it concentrated in a few selected counties in the west. The land thus confiscated from Catholics and royalists had been allocated to 'adventurers' who had subscribed towards the cost of the Irish war, or granted in lieu of arrears of pay to soldiers of the parliamentary army. It was the fortunes, large and small, acquired in this manner that were the target of the comments of Molyneux and Cusack. In fact the scale of the influx of new proprietors should not be overstated. Just over 1,000 adventurers and 33,000 soldiers were allocated land in Ireland during the 1650s. Yet only half of these adventurers, and less than a quarter of the soldiers, had their grants confirmed to them under Charles II. The rest had either abandoned, sold or lost their Irish investment. Of 254 men who sat in the House of Commons between 1661 and 1666, only 16 were adventurers and less than 50 soldiers. The image of a ruling elite composed of Cromwellian freebooters was thus a wild exaggeration. At the same time a new and important element had been added to Irish Protestant society.

The influx, both temporary and permanent, of Scottish and English soldiers had also transformed the religious landscape of Ireland, by destroying for ever the monopoly which the Church of Ireland had exercised over Protestant religious life. In Ulster, ministers and elders from Monro's army had encouraged the Scottish settlers of the region, up to then still uneasily accommodated within the established church, to form their own Presbyterian congregations. In the three southern provinces soldiers of the parliamentary armies had brought with them other forms of Protestant dissent: Quaker, Baptist, Independent. The southern dissenting population declined markedly in the decades that followed, as former soldiers returned to England, and social and political pressures promoted adherence to the established church. But the Presbyterians of Ulster, reinforced by further Scottish immigration over the next half century, remained a solid dissenting presence, rivalling the Church of Ireland in numbers and, in the eyes of many, more than matching it in internal discipline and capacity for self-assertion.

If military power was crucial to the mid-century transformation of Irish society, it also played a part, in Ireland as in the other two kingdoms, in the restoration of monarchical rule. In April 1659 the leaders of the army in England deposed Oliver Cromwell's son Richard, who had succeeded his father as Lord Protector six months earlier. The move was not popular in Ireland. Since 1655 the country had been managed by Richard's brother Henry, whose moderate political and religious policies had been more acceptable to established Protestant interests than the radicalism of the early 1650s. Now Quakers and Baptists once again returned to official favour, and there were purges in the army and civilian administration as the commissioners entrusted with the running of the country installed their own men in key positions. In October the army once again disbanded the English parliament, heightening fears of a drift towards anarchy. However it was left to a group of middle-ranking officers, motivated in particular by the recent army purges, to take action. On 13 December some of their number obtained entrance to Dublin Castle

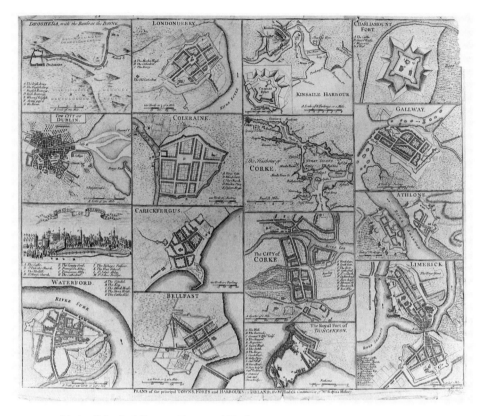

11.1 Principal Towns, Forts and Harbours in Ireland, by Richard William
Seale (fl. 1732–1775). Many Irish towns were still walled in the early
eighteenth century, though the golden age of Irish fortification in the
previous century had culminated with Charles Fort at Kinsale
completed in 1677.

and overpowered the garrison, while others moved through the city securing
control of the streets and arresting key figures in the administration. It was only
after the bloodless coup had succeeded that spokesmen for the local Protestant
landed interest, headed by Lord Broghill and Sir Charles Coote, came forward to join
with the soldiers in demanding a return to parliamentary government.

Once Dublin had been secured, Broghill, Coote and their military allies moved
quickly to establish control of strategic locations elsewhere in the country, and to
displace suspected opponents in the civilian and military administration. They also
organised the election of a Convention, to legitimise their seizure of power and
authorise the raising of taxes. In Great Britain the call for a return to parliamentary
government had already gained the crucial support of General George Monck,
commander of the army in Scotland, who now led his forces south to enforce the
point. Nevertheless there followed several tense months, as supporters of a return to

233

monarchy, and of different forms of republican government, manoeuvred for position. In Ireland, the crisis came on 15 February when Sir Hardress Waller, whose signature on Charles I's death warrant left him no option but to resist the drift towards restoration, attempted to arrest Coote and Broghill. However he was prevented by the soldiers of another military strongman, Colonel Theophilus Jones, a former parliamentary commander now busily making his peace with the emerging new regime. Waller retreated to Dublin Castle, but was surrendered by his own followers after the city authorities had sealed his defeat by turning out the militia against him. With Waller out of the way Coote and Broghill were able to move forward more confidently, though still keeping carefully in step with events in England. Charles II was proclaimed king in London on 8 May and in Dublin six days later.

The reaffirmation of monarchical government did not quite complete the return to political normality. There remained the question of the land settlement. In November 1660 Charles had issued a declaration promising to restore the property of those Catholics and royalists unjustly dispossessed under the Cromwellian regime, while leaving all those who had received land under that settlement (who included the great majority of those now engineering his restoration) undisturbed. The first attempt to reconcile these mutually exclusive commitments promptly reawakened the spectre of armed intervention. A court of claims set up to examine the cases of victims of the Cromwellian confiscations began hearings in January 1663. In May the authorities discovered a plot, led by Captain Thomas Blood, to seize Dublin Castle and stage armed risings in the provinces. In addition to former Cromwellian soldiers like Blood and a couple of Nonconformist ministers, the conspiracy involved no less than ten members of the Dublin parliament. In August the court of claims ended its sessions, although it had heard the cases of only one-seventh of those due to come before it. The question of how far the government was retreating in the face of Protestant disaffection, and how far the king and his ministers were themselves dismayed by the unexpected number of decrees of innocence being awarded to Catholics, continues to be debated. In any event the government next devised a new measure, the act of settlement, requiring Cromwellian grantees to surrender one-third of the land they had received, in order to meet the claims of royalists and of those Catholics who had managed to secure decrees of innocence. This passed through the Irish parliament in December 1665, amid scenes of some tension. MPs faced one another with swords half drawn, 'some being heard to say that the lands they had gotten with the hazard of their lives should not now be lost with Eye's and No's'.[3] By this time, however, the half-drawn swords that had featured in the politics of the last six years at last gave way definitively to the ayes and noes of parliamentary management. The act of settlement was duly passed, and became the basis of the land settlement that was to endure largely unchanged to the end of the nineteenth century.

One further precondition for the establishment of a secure regime under the

---

restored monarchy was the remodelling of the armed forces inherited from Cromwell and his successors. By 1663 the Irish army had been reduced to only 1,500 horse and 3,960 foot, as compared to a force of 15,000 men in the mid-1650s. To these was added a new regiment of 1,200 foot guards, composed of men newly raised in England and so free of both Cromwellian ideology and complicity in the vested interests of the Irish Protestant population. Even with these changes, the lord lieutenant, the duke of Ormond, doubted whether the army could have been counted on if the 1663 conspiracy had gone ahead as planned. Over the next few months there were further reductions in every foot company, with those discharged being replaced by new recruits from England. By the end of the decade, fears of political disaffection in the army had largely faded. In May 1666 Ormond had to put down by force a mutiny by the garrison of Carrickfergus, executing 9 of those involved and sending 100 other men into the navy or to the plantations. But the revolt had been wholly over pay and conditions, with no political dimension.

By the mid-1660s, then, the restored monarchy could feel that it was reasonably safe from further attempts such as Waller's attempted coup of February 1660. It was of course necessary to remain on guard. In Munster, Broghill, now rewarded for his role in the Restoration with the title earl of Orrery, maintained a particularly elaborate network of spies and informers among Dissenters and former Cromwellian soldiers. The belief that many Irish Protestants remained unreconciled was evident in the debates that surrounded the formation of an Irish Militia in 1666. Ormond conceded that there was no shortage of men willing and able to bear arms against an Irish rebellion or foreign invasion, but 'I am not sure that, when that invasion or rebellion shall be suppressed, they will part with those arms or not misemploy them.' Even Orrery, the chief supporter of the new force, believed that only 'old Protestants' – that is those settled in Ireland before 1641 – should be admitted to its ranks.[4] The Presbyterians of Ulster, by now the largest religious denomination in the province, were also the focus of suspicion and hostility, on account of their dissenting principles, their allegiance to the Solemn League and Covenant, and their proximity to their coreligionists in Scotland. Repeatedly during the 1670s and 1680s extra troops were sent into the north to ensure that Scottish religious and political disturbances did not spread to Ireland, and to prevent any contact between the disaffected in the two kingdoms. In general, however, the regime appears to have remained confident that, with these precautions and a remodelled army, it could deal with any threat from either the 'fanatics' and 'sectaries' of the south or the Covenanters of the north. The collapse of Protestant disaffection as a serious threat to the restored regime is confirmed by the absence of any Irish counterpart to the rebellions of Argyll in Scotland and Monmouth in England following the accession of James II in 1685.

At the same time that it kept a careful watch on its enemies to the left, the regime had also to guard against Catholic subversion. The threat here was at first sight formidable. Catholics had lost out badly in the Restoration settlement. They had been left with just over one-fifth of landed property, compared to almost three-fifths in 1641. They were excluded from parliament and local government. Their church was sporadically harassed. At the same time they made up more than three-quarters of the population, and had close links, through what was by now a very substantial body of expatriate soldiers and clergy, with the major Catholic powers of France and Spain. Protestants took it for granted that such discontented elements would if given the opportunity stage a fresh insurrection, and there were recurrent alarms arising out of reports of popish conspiracy or foreign invasion. Most observers, however, saw the risk of a new rebellion overthrowing the social order as relatively remote. Sir William Petty, writing in 1672, went so far as to claim that some Protestants actually longed to see another rising, in order to have an excuse to complete the dispossession of the Catholics. One particularly revealing contrast is between the hysteria generated in England by the wild revelations concerning supposed popish conspiracies propagated by Titus Oates, and the much more muted reaction of Protestant Ireland.

Behind this confidence in the limited potential of any Catholic insurrection lay an assessment of strategic and social realities. Catholics might be numerically strong, but they were impoverished, demoralised, lacking in military experience. The Protestants, Petty argued, included among their number 'far more Soldiers and Soldierlike-men', and they controlled '$3/4$ of all the Lands; $5/6$ of all the Housing; $9/10$ of all the Housing in wall'd Towns, and Places of strength; $2/3$ of the Foreign Trade'. Moreover they could count on the support of the English crown, which would not be distracted by other difficulties as it had been in 1641. Sir Robert Southwell, ten years later, was equally confident 'as things stand, that the Protestants, having the authority of the Government, the garrisons and arms in their hands, could drive the Irish into the sea, if that were fit and thought convenient in such sort to unpeople the land'.[5] Comments of this kind serve to modify the remarks by Molyneux and Cusack with which this discussion began. Military force played a central role in creating a new social order in mid-seventeenth-century Ireland. Once that order had been established, however, it would take more than a military challenge to bring it down.

Such calculations, of course, took no account of the possibility that it might be government itself that would open the doors to a renewed Catholic assault on the social and political order confirmed at the Restoration. Yet this is what happened after 1685. In less than three years James II's Irish servants created an over-whelmingly Catholic army, judiciary and magistracy. The comments of Petty and Southwell were to some extent borne out by the difficulties encountered, after forty years of exclusively Protestant rule, in creating a credible Catholic governing elite. Supporters as well as opponents of James II were alarmed at the calibre of some of the candidates put forward for membership of municipal corporations and other positions of authority. Yet Irish Protestants emerged from the crisis of 1688–9 convinced that they had narrowly escaped the destruction of everything they had

---

The King and the Earl d'Avaux are defeatead by the Protestants att Ineskilling

de Koning en d'Avaux worden geslagen vande protestanten te Ineskilling

11.2   James II and the Earl d'Avaux defeated by the Protestants at
Enniskillen. An imaginative Dutch representation (*c.* 1690) of the battle of
Enniskillen, 1689, with particular stress on the defeat shared by the 'Earl'
(actually Count) d'Avaux, the French ambassador to James II's court, thus
stressing the European, as well as the religious, dimension of the conflict.

gained over the preceding century. They confronted a Catholic population still
further stripped of land and political rights, but as numerous as before, and with
religious and ethnic animosities inflamed by recent memories of civil war. How, in
these new conditions, did the restored Protestant elite provide for its defence?[6]

The nature of the military threat that hung over Protestant Ireland was clear to
all. From 1689 until 1697, and again from 1702 until 1713, England was at war with
France, which continued to recognise the claims of the exiled Stuarts. Irish
Catholics, meanwhile, continued to provide ample confirmation of their political
disaffection, in their flaunting of Jacobite symbols, in the exultation or dejection
that greeted news of victories and defeats on distant battlefields, in the cooperation
which French privateers received from local coastal populations, in the outward
flow of recruits that kept up the numbers serving in the Irish regiments of the French
army. Invasion, insurrection, or any combination of the two, had thus to be seen as

a constant possibility. A French descent on some part of the British Isles seemed likely in 1692, until their fleet was decisively defeated at Barfleur/La Hogue on 19–24 May. A plot by English Jacobites to assassinate William III in February 1696 was followed later the same year by another invasion scare. There was a Jacobite rising in Scotland in 1708, and a much larger insurrection there and in northern England in 1715.

In the early 1690s the possibility of invasion or insurrection caused acute anxiety in Protestant Ireland. In part this was because the country's defences were considered to be in a poor state. But the main reason was a lack of confidence in the willingness of government to take the measures necessary to avert the threat. The Treaty of Limerick, leaving James II's supporters seemingly immune to the penalties of defeat, was seen by most Protestants as a shocking betrayal of their interests. Since then, moreover, the administration had shown what was perceived as excessive zeal in protecting the interests of the defeated Jacobites, in particular by prohibiting searches for arms and horses on the grounds that these might become occasions for plunder and the settling of private scores. Some even claimed that the lord chancellor, Sir Charles Porter, was a secret Jacobite. By the mid-1690s, on the other hand, all this had changed. A new lord deputy of impeccable Protestant credentials, Sir Henry Capel, was appointed in 1695. An act of the same year forbidding Catholics to possess weapons or a horse worth more than £5 had made possible the general disarming that Protestants had been clamouring for since the end of the war. The Militia had been extended. Against this transformed background, the invasion scares of March and November 1696 aroused no great alarm in Ireland.

If factional divisions among Protestants confused responses to the crises of the 1690s, the same was even more true of the next two decades. Within a short time after the accession of Queen Anne in 1702 politics in both England and Ireland had come to be dominated by the opposition of two rival parties, Whig and Tory. Among the issues dividing them were the linked questions of religion and security. Whigs advocated an aggressive anti-French foreign policy and unity among all Protestant denominations in the face of the continuing threat of Catholicism at home and abroad. Tories, on the other hand, argued that popery had now been effectively crushed, and that the real threat to the religious and social order came from an assertive and expansionist Protestant dissent. Jonathan Swift, in 1709, summed up the Tory position in a striking analogy:

> It is agreed, among Naturalists, that a *Lyon* is a larger, a stronger, and more dangerous Enemy than a *Cat*; yet if a Man were to have his Choice, either a *Lyon* at his Foot, bound fast with three or four Chains, his Teeth drawn out, and his claws pared to the Quick, or an angry *Cat* in full Liberty at his Throat, he would take no long Time to determine.[7]

As party animosities intensified during Anne's reign, the defence of Ireland became one of many bitterly debated issues. Whigs pointed to the continued depredations of rapparees in the south-west, the large-scale outbreak of cattle maiming in Connacht in 1711–12, the supposed proliferation of Catholic ecclesiastics, as evidence that the Tory administration was deliberately neglecting the security of the kingdom. More ominously there were claims that the Militia was being deliberately run down, and that the administration was turning a blind eye to the activities of Jacobite propagandists and French recruiting agents. These suspicions form the crucial background to the fears expressed by so many Irish Protestants in the period leading up to the death of Queen Anne.

The extent to which these fears were focused more on the possibility of betrayal from within than on any external threat is evident in the relative calm with which Protestant Ireland reacted to what happened next. When Anne died on 1 August 1714, George Ludwig, prince elector of Hanover, succeeded her unopposed. During the first half of 1715, however, accounts of open demonstrations of Jacobite sentiment in England, and of the flight to France of two Tory leaders, Bolingbroke and Ormond, were followed by reports of an imminent French and Jacobite invasion, and then in early September by the outbreak of rebellion in Scotland and the north of England. All this was more concrete than anything that had happened in the previous four years. And yet, with both Whitehall and Dublin Castle now occupied by staunch Whigs, whose commitment to the Protestant succession was beyond question, there was none of the near panic witnessed on earlier occasions. The Dublin administration took the obvious precautions. Following the first reports of threatened invasion in late July, arms and horses were seized from Catholics and those refusing to take the oath denying the Stuart claim to the throne, and gunpowder stored in shops and warehouses was requisitioned. Commissions were issued for the arraying of the Militia, and the regular army were ordered to assemble at a central cantonment near Athlone, from where they could be dispatched to meet any invader. (Later, following reports that Ormond might lead an expedition to Ireland, the cantonment was shifted to a line running from the old Butler power base in Kilkenny to the River Shannon.) Intelligence reports noted that the Catholic population were watchful and expectant. Yet there is no indication that the possibility of either invasion or insurrection caused serious alarm. In July the government, revealing its true priorities, had returned to Scotland three regiments recently sent from there to Ireland, and there were further transfers once the Scottish and English rebellions began. In all, it was later claimed, Ireland supplied eight regiments for Scotland and four for England. Yet even after these huge reductions the Irish authorities remained confident that they would be able to deal with any likely threat to the security of the kingdom.

The arguments used to justify this confidence were partly those that had earlier been used to dismiss alarmist claims regarding the security of Restoration Ireland. Irish Catholics were numerous, and their disaffection was taken for granted. But they were leaderless, demoralised, and had been carefully deprived of access to arms and military training. In all of these respects, Ireland stood in sharp contrast to the

---

Scottish Highlands, where the traditional social structure that permitted Jacobite clan chiefs to call out their human rent of fighting men in the service of the Pretender was to remain intact for more than three decades more. Hence it was Scotland, not Ireland, that remained up to the middle of the century the weak spot in the defences of the British Isles, the place to which, at the first sign of trouble, troops were transferred from other regions. In 1715, and the years immediately following, Irish Protestants also placed great faith in the Militia, now reorganised and re-equipped after its alleged neglect by the Tories, as a guarantee of the kingdom's safety. In addition, there were important strategic considerations casting doubt on the claim that Ireland was a likely target for either French or Jacobite invasion. Ireland had served as the base for a last ditch resistance to William III's takeover of the English throne. As a springboard for the reconquest of Great Britain, however, it had little to offer. An invading force, aided by the Catholic population, might well overwhelm local resistance. But when it had done so there would still be the invasion of the mainland to be attempted, against an enemy which had now had time to mobilise its land and naval forces. At least some Irish Protestants were also aware of a factor very much in the minds of the Jacobite court itself: that an invasion plan that associated the Stuart cause too closely with Irish Popish rebellion would inflame precisely those fears and prejudices that made Englishmen most reluctant to see the dynasty return.

The thinking behind official responses to the crisis of 1715 continued to shape prevailing attitudes to the defence of the kingdom for half a century or more. In 1719 there was news of a Jacobite invasion force backed by Spain and Sweden. Once again orders were given to seize arms and horses from Catholics, detain disaffected persons, and prevent public gatherings, while four battalions of regular troops were moved to England. However the lord lieutenant expressed confidence in the ability of the remaining troops, along with the militia, to cope with any likely threat. In 1722 six battalions were sent to England following the discovery of a major Jacobite conspiracy. This episode apart, the 1720s and 1730s were relatively quiet, reflecting the detente reached with France following the death of Louis XIV. In 1744, with England again at war with France and Spain, and another Jacobite expedition in preparation, troops were once more shipped from Ireland to Great Britain and continental Europe. The lord lieutenant, the duke of Devonshire, pleaded for time to make the necessary arrangements, but was confident that, as long as the Protestant population of the north were mobilised and armed, they would be able to contain any internal disturbances; as in the past, it was considered unlikely that Ireland would be the target of the invasion.

Matters became more serious the following year, as Prince Charles Edward's Highland army overran Scotland and swept south into England. In Ireland the threat was sufficient to lead government to lift its long-standing ban on local recruitment, enlisting sixteen companies of Protestants to replace the soldiers sent out of the kingdom. But anxiety continued to focus on the outcome of the struggle in Great

---

Britain. Where domestic security was concerned, the most notable feature of the 1745 emergency was that the authorities for the first time held back from forcing a general closure of Catholic places of worship through calls for the strict enforcement of the popery laws. Some observers, indeed, expressed doubts over whether, even in the event of a French or Stuart invasion, Catholics would necessarily rush to offer their support to the enemy. By the time invasion again threatened, in the Seven Years War (1756–63), British Jacobitism had collapsed, while in Ireland representatives of the Catholic propertied classes had begun for the first time to offer unequivocal public declarations of their allegiance to the Hanoverian monarchy. Against this background the debate as to whether Catholics remained uniformly disaffected and untrustworthy intensified, with senior members of the Irish executive offering very different assessments of the likely response to a French invasion. Invasion itself, by contrast, aroused little concern. In February 1760 a force of 600–700 men under François Thurot landed at Carrickfergus. The long awaited French invader had arrived at last; and the inadequacy of the defences available against him were plainly demonstrated in the ease with which he overran the ruined fortress and its ill-equipped garrison. The episode provided the opportunity for a gratifying display of the readiness of the Protestant lower classes of Ulster to rush to the defence of the kingdom. But it was not seen as requiring any radical reassessment of either Catholic policy or military provision.

The defence of the kingdom against invasion and rebellion was of course only part of the army's function. In Ireland as in England the resources available for the direct enforcement of the criminal law were strictly limited. The larger towns maintained forces of watchmen, generally armed with staves or halberds, to patrol the streets. Elsewhere the law provided for the appointment of a high constable in each barony and a petty constable for each parish, but these were part-time officials of limited effectiveness for anything more than routine administrative functions. Instead, law enforcement depended in the first instance on the natural authority of the landed gentry, acting in their capacity as justices of the peace. If authority alone was not enough, the magistrate might recruit a posse of family members, servants and other able-bodied individuals willing to assist. Where such informally recruited forces proved inadequate, the next step was to turn to the military.

The law enforcement functions thus undertaken, in the absence of any police force, by the Irish army were of two main kinds. First, soldiers were routinely used in cases where a preemptive display of armed force was considered necessary: to escort prisoners to and from jail or execution, to guard convoys of cash or valuables, to support revenue officers or tax collectors in the execution of their duties. Secondly, troops were employed where the ordinary machinery of law enforcement had broken down. During 1711–12, for example, soldiers were sent to Connacht to help suppress the campaign of cattle maiming being waged by the Houghers, just as in the 1760s and later they were to be deployed against

Whiteboys, Oakboys and other movements of agrarian protest. Troops were also used, side by side with the Militia and with locally raised armed parties, against the tories and rapparees whose banditry continued up to the 1720s to disturb parts of south Ulster and the south-west, as well as against later bands of highwaymen and housebreakers. In 1749, for example, the notorious James Freney, then at the height of his fame, was being hunted by regular soldiers, members of the Waterford Militia and armed parties – at one point including fifteen disbanded soldiers – raised against him by local gentlemen and merchants. Troops were also regularly deployed against urban riots, irrespective of whether these were political protests, expressions of economic grievance or simply violence for its own sake. In 1748, for example, the mayor of Dublin initiated a campaign to put down the brawls between rival factions of Ormond and Liberty boys in the city by sending out parties of constables and watchmen to patrol the most common flashpoints, but he also had detachments from the city garrison standing by 'ready to march on the first notice, and with direction . . . to fire with ball in case of any opposition'.[8]

All this makes clear that military force was an essential part of the machinery of public order in eighteenth-century Ireland. Yet its employment was neither straightforward nor always effective. A number of considerations combined to reduce both the willingness of authority to use troops, and their usefulness when they were deployed. One of these was the problem of resources. Despite the threat of invasion or rebellion, Ireland in the first half of the eighteenth century appears at times as a society remarkably ill-prepared for the employment of armed force. When the decision was taken in 1712 to provide arms for the use of local Militia engaged in suppressing the Houghers in some western counties, it turned out that there were no supplies any closer than Dublin. A magistrate in County Donegal complained three years later that, although the county could muster 7,000 Militia, he had been unable to find 'thirty men tolerably armed' to pursue a group of tories.[9] The regular army was presumably better equipped. But there too the employment of troops on duties that took them away from their usual quarters was troublesome both to government, which had to pay the extra expenses, and to local householders, who were expected to provide billets, fuel and candles. For this reason alone government did not automatically respond to appeals from magistrates or landowners for the dispatch of troops to deal with local problems of law and order, attempting instead to ensure that military intervention was a last rather than a first resort.

Practical problems of resources and supply were reinforced by constitutional and legal considerations. Opposition in principle to standing armies as a threat to civil liberties was less well developed in Ireland than in England; it was after all for this reason that Ireland was used to house so large a part of the Hanoverian monarchy's defence forces. But some members at least of the establishment did express doubts regarding the use of military force except in cases where all other methods had failed. In all cases, furthermore, military aid to the civil power was governed by strict legal rules. Soldiers could act only with orders from central

11.3   Military parade on Leinster House lawn,
by John James Barralet/Thomas Milton, 1783.

government, and under the direction of a magistrate. Thus in 1737 an inmate of the
Marshalsea prison in Dublin who had stabbed and killed a soldier sent to put him in
irons was acquitted of murder, on the grounds that the soldier's orders had not come
from a duly authorised officer of the prison. To call on the assistance of soldiers who
then resorted to lethal force, equally, could be a risky undertaking. In 1747 the
owner of land adjoining Kilmainham commons had the sub-sheriff come with a
party of constables and soldiers to disperse the crowds assembled for races there.
Fighting broke out, and four civilians were shot dead. The landowner was convicted
of murder, and was eventually pardoned only after a petition on his behalf from 500
leading citizens, and only after he had lain for a month under a sentence of death
twice postponed.[10] Perhaps the memory of his ordeal was one of the considerations
that prompted the mayor of the city, a few months later, to keep soldiers ready but
in reserve, leaving it to his constables and watchmen to take to the streets against
the Ormond and Liberty boys.

   Having said all this it remains clear that the army in early and mid-eighteenth-
century Ireland represented an externally imposed authority. This dimension of
its role was particularly evident in its composition. Irishmen, both Catholic and

Protestant, were excluded from its ranks, the former till the 1770s, the latter till the 1740s. The Irish army was also unusual in that it was housed in barracks, rather than being quartered among the civilian population, from a rather earlier stage than in most European countries. The different potential role of the Irish army was also evident in the way in which its barracks were distributed throughout the interior; in England, by contrast, barracks, when they were built, were located around the coast. On the other hand, Irish barracks, apart from a few fortified redoubts built in trouble spots like south Armagh, were plain residential structures, quite different to the fortified buildings that it was thought necessary to erect in the Scottish highlands. Although the location of some garrisons was undoubtedly influenced by the need to have troops on hand to suppress internal disorder, it was notoriously the case that the siting of most of them was a matter of patronage, eagerly competed for by landowners and other public figures on account of the economic benefits that would follow.

Although members of the Protestant establishment may have been able to accept and even welcome the presence of the army, what of the Catholic population, whose potential disaffection it was one of the tasks of that army to contain? The Munster poet David Ó Bruadair, celebrating the Catholicisation of the army under Tyrconnell, gave vivid expression to the aversion with which he regarded the uniforms, watchwords and general demeanour of the force that had up to recently garrisoned Ireland:

> Whither shall John turn? He has no red coat on him.
>   No 'Who's there?' on his lips when standing beside the gate.
> Seeking on the slightest excuse by provoking me
>   To have me amerced for nocturnal contentiousness.[11]

These, of course, were the sentiments of a traditionally minded member of a disappearing class, expressing ethnic and cultural antagonisms of a kind that were by this time becoming less acute. On the other hand, antagonism towards the army must have been exacerbated, in the short term at least, by the experiences of 1689–91. The tactics of the Williamite army and the reorganised Protestant Militia stopped well short of the standards set by Cromwell's forces half a century before. But even Williamite accounts make clear that there was more than a little rough handling of the civilian population in Jacobite areas. Nor did such conduct end with the conclusion of the war. The executive's disastrous mismanagement of the parliament of 1692 left it without the revenue to provide properly for the hugely increased Irish army, encouraging the soldiers to continue their bad habits. The lord lieutenant complained in April 1693 that the regiments then in Ireland 'have been so used to plunder these four years that it will be almost impossible to bring them into proper order and regularity'.[12] By the end of the decade, however, the worst was over. A resolution of the constitutional impasse regarding financial legislation permitted more regular payment; the military establishment had been reduced to a

11.4   The Rt Hon. Thomas Conolly, MP (1738–1803), of Castletown,
County Kildare, a prominent country gentleman in Volunteer uniform.

more manageable 12,000 men; and the transfer of troops from quarters to barracks was reducing the occasions for plunder and making possible a general tightening of discipline.

Relations between civilians and soldiers after the 1690s appear to have been relatively uncontentious. This is not to say that there was not conflict, and in some cases violence. In 1724, for example, a fight over allegations of cheating at cards initiated a feud between the Cameronian regiment and local citizens. At an earlier posting members of the regiment were alleged to have killed a night watchman as he made his rounds, and soldiers on patrol were now stoned and taunted with calls of 'Who killed the clapperman?', the harassment continuing until an outraged private bayoneted one of his tormentors. In another typical incident, from 1748, a quarrel between a grenadier and one of the coal porters on the Dublin quays escalated into a pitched battle, as soldiers and coal heavers came to the assistance of their respective comrades. But such episodes are by themselves evidence of little more than the interaction of robust plebeian males, conditioned by a culture of aggressive masculinity linked to strong group loyalties, with others of similar instincts and background. Not all of those involved in such brawls were Catholics: a wheelwright prominent in the baiting of the Cameronians, for example, was identified as the son of the keeper of Newgate prison, while in Derry two years earlier it was the members of the corporation, and the Anglican bishop, who complained that they had been manhandled by soldiers who imagined themselves to have been slighted at a recent civic ceremony.[13] Nor is there anything to indicate that the authorities saw such friction between army and civilians as more than a minor nuisance, of the kind likely to arise wherever soldiers were quartered.

The role of the army in Ireland after the 1690s was thus ambiguous. Part of its function was to guard the kingdom against the threat of invasion allied to internal subversion. But in practice this threat was seen as a fairly remote one. Instead the Irish army served primarily as a reserve, to be drawn on wherever the interests of the Hanoverian monarchy required armed protection or defence. The result was a force that was not quite a part of the society in which it was stationed, but could not really be perceived as an army of occupation. This remained the case at least up to the 1760s. Thereafter the growth of popular disaffection, and the collapse of older forms of social control, increasingly brought the military into the front line of law enforcement. By the 1790s Ireland had become a society held down by armed coercion, and this reliance on the army continued until the introduction in the 1820s of a centralised national police force, whose firearms, barracks and parade-style drill all proclaimed a continuity with earlier military traditions. Meanwhile, the composition of the army was also changing, as growing numbers of Irishmen, Catholic and Protestant, were recruited into its ranks. By the early nineteenth century the army in Ireland, for long a familiar yet external presence, was thus becoming at one and the same time a more effective instrument of repression and more clearly a part of the society in which it was based.

Chapter 12

Defence, counter-insurgency and rebellion: Ireland, 1793–1803

Thomas Bartlett

The military history of these ten years cannot be divorced from their politics. These years witnessed the birth both of militant republicanism and of militant loyalism, for the separatist demand would swiftly evoke the response of unionism. Moreover, just as the tradition of armed insurrection in Ireland in association with a foreign power was renewed and invigorated, and carried on into the nineteenth century, and beyond, so too, the tradition of freelance or semi-official resistance to Irish insurgency was reaffirmed as the Orange Order (with the Peep-of-Day Boys) and the United Irishmen (with the Defenders) struggled for supremacy in the south Ulster borderlands, and elsewhere. Fundamental to any consideration of these years is the fact that from 1793 on, Britain and revolutionary France were locked in a titanic struggle for dominance with unprecedented numbers of men, amounts of *matériel* and sums of money being committed to the contest. Ireland – and the Irish – had important, and sometimes central, roles in the tactical, and on occasion, the strategic, thinking of both the French and British governments at this time. Irish recruits were to be vital in the recruitment of the armed forces of the crown, and an earlier reluctance to enlist large numbers of Irish Catholics quickly disappeared as the demands of the British war machine became insatiable. Soon, far-reaching concessions were being offered to Irish Catholics in order to fix their loyalty during the coming trial, and to encourage enlistment. Intensive recruitment took place with possibly as many as one in five of the Irish adult male cohort seeing service of some sort between 1793 and 1815 (see Table 12.1). This had a profound impact on Irish society, for militarisation was conducive to politicisation.[1] Similarly, the crushing expense of the war had major political consequences: by 1799 the war was consuming some 78 per cent of Irish government expenditure (the pre-war level was about 28 per cent) and had brought on the near bankruptcy of Dublin Castle by the time of the Union.[2] Equally, high taxes and wartime inflation seriously hurt the poor and may have made them more receptive to the message of subversives.[3] Furthermore, the likelihood of a French invasion of Ireland forced the British government, with the reluctant support of Dublin Castle, to reassess its long-standing policy of entrusting Protestants alone with the defence of Ireland: and the establishment of the (largely Catholic) Irish Militia in 1793 marked a completely new departure in this area of policy. Finally, mounting evidence of advanced plans for domestic rebellion along with indications of widespread disaffection among the armed forces of the crown in Ireland led Dublin Castle, with the hearty support of London, to adopt draconian counter-insurgency measures which at times amounted to a deliberate policy of counter-terror: the embodiment of the (largely Protestant) Irish Yeomanry in 1796 is central here.[4] It may be suggested that it is in the acute tension between policies designed, on the one hand, to repel foreign invaders and, on the other, those drawn up to crush domestic insurrection that the proximate cause of the military mayhem of the late 1790s can be found. Consideration of the 1798 rebellion reveals a picture of regular military campaigns complete with marches, counter-marches, and a few set-piece battles (in which the Irish on both sides were distinguished for their skill, daring, valour and, occasionally, ineptitude); but it also uncovers a disturbing spectacle of disgusting massacre, religious fury and mindless triumphalism all of which drew deeply from the well of Irish history and which fixed attitudes for generations to come. In short, it was in the decade of the 1790s and the early years of the nineteenth century that the shape of the Irish nation – or nations – was formed: and it was no coincidence that that formation, or formations, had a military cast.

1

At the time of the outbreak of war with revolutionary France (1 February 1793), the Irish army, or army on the establishment of Ireland, consisted of around 9,000 'effective' men, both cavalry and infantry. By the terms of the Augmentation Act of 1769 the army was limited in time of peace to 15,325 men, but some 4,000 soldiers were permitted to serve abroad and there were invariably a large number of regiments on the Irish station 'wanting to complete'. In addition, a high rate of desertion meant that the official targets were never met. The army's purpose in Ireland had barely changed throughout the eighteenth century: it assisted the civil power when called upon, and it defended Ireland against foreign invasion when war, usually with the French, broke out; in addition, regiments came to Ireland in order to recruit as close as possible to their full complement. However, if the army's duties had hardly altered in decades, its composition had, for a growing proportion of the men were Catholics, and there is evidence that Catholics were also being commissioned as officers. This was a comparatively recent development: at one time, Catholics, and indeed all Irish, had been barred from the army, but from the Seven Years War (1756–63) on, recruitment of the Catholic Irish for service abroad, initially in the marines or in the East India Company army, but then for combat during the American War of Independence (1776–83), had proceeded apace. Indeed, as we have seen, the 1780s even witnessed the enrolment of Catholics into some Volunteer regiments. By 1790, recruitment of Irish Catholics was relatively routine,

Table 12.1. *The armed forces of the crown in Ireland,*
1 January 1793 to 1 January 1800

	Cavalry		Infantry				
	Regulars	Fencibles	Regulars	Fencibles	Militia	Yeomanry[a]	Total
Jan. 1793	1,510		8,134				9,644
Jan. 1794	2,331		8,087		9,627		20,155
Jan. 1795	2,715	300	6,126	537	12,847		22,525
Jan. 1796	2,296	508	1,480	10,210	17,162		31,656
Jan. 1797	3,640	664	1,699	9,085	18,188	[–][b]	33,276
Jan. 1798	3,957	1,820	1,812	10,788	22,358	36,854	77,589
Jan. 1799	4,151	3,139	5,572	13,516	32,583	43,221	102,181[c]
Jan. 1800	1,742	3,738	2,657	16,823	25,542	66,082	116,584

[a] Yeomanry figures for October of the previous year
[b] Yeomanry set up in Sept. 1796
[c] Including 1,860 Footguards who arrived and left within the year
Sources: 'Return of the effective men in the British army stationed in Ireland', Jan. 1793–
Jan. 1806 (PRO, HO 100/176/429); 'Numerical Strength of the Yeomanry, 1797–99' (NAI,
Rebellion Papers 620/48/56).

though as before it was assumed that such recruits would ultimately serve abroad, and hence would pose no direct threat to the security of the island. The outbreak of war with France and the speedy realisation that this would be no ordinary struggle brought about a swift appraisal both of the defence needs of Ireland and the role that Ireland would play in the total British war effort.[5]

From the beginning of the war it was assumed that Ireland figured prominently in the plans of revolutionary France. In every war with the French since the 1690s there had been invasion scares: and the large number of invasion plans still extant in the French archives testify that such fears had been by no means groundless.[6] It was the apparent ineptitude of Dublin Castle in dealing with a possible French invasion in 1778 that had prompted the emergence of the Volunteers. This was an unfortunate precedent for both London and Dublin, and both administrations were anxious to guard against a resurgence of this politically suspect, if (thankfully) moribund, force. If only to avoid a Volunteer revival, they simply had to attend to the defence of Ireland. At the same time the problem for the military authorities was that a *possible* French invasion of Ireland required the *certain* presence of a large force of troops there, and with the acute demand for soldiers in the Low Countries, the West Indies and elsewhere, it did not make military sense (at least to the military authorities at the Horse Guards in London) to station an entire army of cavalry and infantry in Ireland merely to repel the French. Moreover, the presence of a British naval fleet cruising off the south coast of Ireland further diminished – in the eyes of some, even seemed to rule out – the threat of a French landing. 'Lord

Howe [the naval commander] will keep us from invasion', declared a confident Edward Cooke, an official in Dublin Castle in December 1793.[7] Nonetheless, it was evident that if regular cavalry and infantry were too valuable to 'waste' on Ireland's defence, some new force (or forces) was needed to defend the country, to head off the threat of a Volunteer revival, and to undertake the customary police work. Initially, it was believed that the embodiment of an Irish Militia would meet these objectives but, in the event this proved insufficient. One of the central military themes of the years 1793 to 1798 is the rapid withdrawal of regular regiments from Ireland and their progressive replacement with, first, Irish Militia (mid-1793), then English and Scottish Fencibles (early 1795) and, eventually, Irish Yeomanry (late 1796).

At various times over the previous decade the question of establishing an Irish Militia had been mooted, usually with a view to striking a blow against the Volunteers. If Irish Protestants could be persuaded to adopt a Militia – as an official outlet for their evident desire to dress up and play at soldiers – then 'some vigorous and coercive step' could be taken against the unofficial Volunteers. Yet it was recognised that there were serious difficulties in the way of establishing a Militia: such an unmistakable attack on Volunteering might perhaps serve only to revive a force that looked like withering away? And, in any case, surely a Militia would damage recruitment to the regular army? By the mid-1780s a new objection was being voiced in London: 'The [proposed] Militia, it is taken for granted, must be a Protestant one', wrote the British home secretary, Lord Sydney in 1786, 'The Roman Catholics cannot but be offended . . . And though it is not advisable to allow the Catholics power, it is extremely unadvisable [*sic*] to give them offence and mortification.'[8] From this point on, it was clear that the establishment of a Militia would depend on Catholics being allowed to participate: and this in turn would depend on the removal of one of the most politically sensitive of all the Penal laws – that against Catholics bearing arms. The defence of Ireland had a political economy of its own.

News of the outbreak of the French Revolution had been enthusiastically welcomed in both Belfast and Dublin by those who favoured parliamentary reform, and in both these cities there was a resurgence of 'political' Volunteering. Dublin Castle regarded this development as potentially if not actually subversive, and Volunteer actions (*feux de joie* on 14 July) and dress (sporting a 'National cockade') were anxiously monitored. By late 1792 so far had the Volunteer revival gone that there were firm plans to set up a 'National Guard' consisting of members of the Volunteers and of a newly formed radical society, the United Irishmen, who would be oathbound not to disband until parliamentary reform and Catholic emancipation had been conceded.[9] Only the establishment of a Militia, coupled with some effective prohibition on the Volunteers, it seemed, could render Ireland secure during the turbulent times that lay ahead.[10]

Other circumstances, too, in the early 1790s conspired to render a Militia more desirable in the eyes of Dublin and London. There had been sectarian disturbances in south Ulster during the winter of 1792–3 – a foretaste of the mayhem that would engulf most of Ireland by the end of the decade – and it had proved difficult to suppress them. Regular troops had been frequently (too frequently in the eyes of the military authorities) called out for duty, and the Castle was bitterly critical of the 'supineness' of local magistrates and gentry who had refused to exert themselves on such occasions. Such disturbances, and the lacklustre response to them of local gentry, demonstrated the need for a properly organised Militia or police force based in the community but mobilised and controlled from Dublin Castle. At Waterford and Cork an attempt had already been made to mobilise the old, pre-1780 Militia, but the machinery for this had proved too rusty to be effective. Equally worrying for the Castle were reports that Volunteering had resumed along the south Ulster borderlands. Unlike their Belfast or Dublin colleagues, these rural Volunteers had little interest in parliamentary reform: they had mobilised in defence of the Protestant Ascendancy which appeared to be under threat nationally (plans for Catholic relief were in the air) and locally (Catholics were engaged in signing petitions and electing delegates to a Dublin Convention). One Volunteer on being asked why he had armed replied succinctly 'that he would not suffer Ireland to become a popish country'; and from counties Down and Monaghan came claims that large numbers of Volunteers were mobilising 'upon the pretext of preserving the peace but they are generally averse to the cause of the Catholics and their real object is to keep them down'. It is no exaggeration to say that Dublin Castle viewed these Protestant Volunteers with almost as much alarm as the radical Volunteers of Belfast and Dublin. With the revival of these Volunteer associations the question of a Militia, to 'render individual armies unnecessary' and thus give the Castle a monopoly of force, took on a new urgency. And yet there were still several 'objections and difficulties' to be overcome. Would the establishment of a Militia hit recruiting for the regular army? What sort of Militia was to be embodied? Most controversially, there was the question of the composition of the new force: would Catholics be admitted or would it be restricted to Protestants?[11]

The first of these objections was dismissed: put simply, recruits were not coming forward in Ireland anyway and, as it was proposed to send large numbers of Irish troops abroad, a substitute defence and police force had to be found. In January 1793, there was a plan to ship Irish regiments abroad and to replace them with British regiments: but this scheme was soon scrapped, for British regiments were too valuable to remain in Ireland. Similarly a proposal to replace Irish regiments with independent companies from Britain who would complete their recruitment in Ireland had to be abandoned as unworkable. Meanwhile, Ireland was being denuded of troops and the lord lieutenant, Westmorland, and his chief secretary, Hobart, grew anxious lest there was uproar in the Irish parliament about Ireland being left defenceless. To head off trouble, they had preliminary soundings taken in Cork and Waterford concerning the expediency of a Militia, and the response had been

---

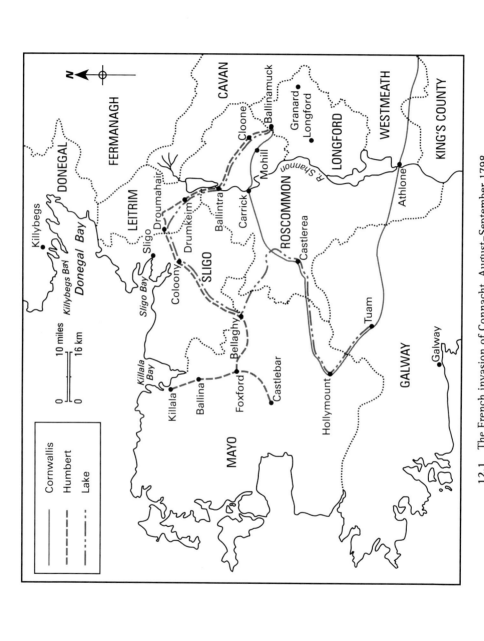

12.1 The French invasion of Connacht, August–September 1798
Source: Elliott, *Partners in revolution*

cautiously favourable. Accordingly they resolved to act. The question remained however: was the 'principle of distinction and separation' between Catholic and Protestant to be maintained where an internal Irish force was concerned?

In arguing the case for an Irish Militia, Westmorland had all along assumed that it would be entirely Protestant. This in fact had constituted a major part of its attraction for him: a Protestant Militia would, he felt, restore Protestant confidence in themselves and in the British government. Such confidence had been severely dented recently as a result of the British government's pressure on the Irish parliament to make far-reaching concessions to Irish Catholics. There had already been one Catholic Relief Act in 1792, and now another, admitting Catholics to the franchise on the same terms as Irish Protestants and, crucially, permitting Catholics to bear arms, was projected. In these circumstances, Westmorland saw a Protestant Militia as helping to reassure Irish Protestants that they had not been abandoned by London. The British prime minister, William Pitt, and his home secretary, Henry Dundas, however, did not see matters in this light: neither could 'see [any] reason why in respect of arms they [Irish Catholics] are to be distinguished from the rest of His Majesty's subjects' and that therefore the proposed Militia force was to be set up with no such distinction. Pitt and Dundas claimed that their purpose was 'to connect all lovers of order and good government in an union of resistors to all the abettors of anarchy and misrule', that they had at heart 'the interests of the Protestants of Ireland and that of the Empire as a whole' and that this meant 'conciliating the Catholics as much as possible . . . the making of them an effectual body of support . . . detaching them from the levellers . . . establishing a strong Militia and . . . putting an end to Volunteer associations'. Their plan of conciliation triumphed and their views prevailed. The Militia Bill and the Catholic Relief Bill went through the Irish parliament and gained royal consent within days of one another. Irish Catholics, having been given the vote on the same terms as Irish Protestants, were now to be charged with defending the state alongside Irish Protestants: within a generation the British state had gone from a policy of firm exclusion of Catholic soldiers to one of reliance on them for the defence of Ireland: it was a revolution almost as startling as anything that France could offer. The Volunteers were speedily outlawed by proclamation, and towards the end of April 1793, Westmorland issued the necessary orders to embody the Irish Militia.

2

The procedure for raising the proposed thirty-eight regiments of militia was quite straightforward and apparently equitable, but in practice it offered ample scope for protest and delay and clearly favoured the towns over rural areas.[12] Each county and county borough was given a figure for the number of men it had to provide, then lists were drawn up of those males eligible to serve, then a ballot was held until the 'quota' assigned to each area was reached. Substitutes were allowed and so too were volunteers. Anyone who refused to serve was liable to a £10 fine and if they would not pay this, could be treated as mutinous.

No trouble had been anticipated at the embodiment of the Irish Militia, and the Militia Bill itself had excited little comment in its passage through the Irish parliament. Speeches in favour were greeted with 'the loud and general cry of Hear! Hear! Hear!' and the main criticism was directed at the speed with which such a long bill (over 60 pages in length and 115 clauses) was being put through the Irish parliament. For the county notables, destined to play an important role in its embodiment, it was the patronage possibilities inherent in the scheme that attracted their attention, and they were also quick to solicit distinctive colours and the adjective 'royal' in their official designation.[13] Petty matters of patronage and costume, however, soon yielded to more pressing issues, for the attempt to embody an Irish Militia triggered off two months of disturbances throughout Ireland.

With days of the announcement of the embodiment of a Militia, reports began reaching Dublin of fierce and unprecedented popular opposition to this measure and throughout May and June there were disturbances in nearly every county in Ireland.[14] The reasons for hostility to the proposed Militia need not detain us. Some people clearly did not understand the act's provisions and hence feared them: for this reason newspapers published frequent reassuring explanations. It was claimed that there were fears that the Militia, contrary to assurances, would in fact be required to serve abroad and the families of Militiamen left unprovided for. In order to head off this fear, further assurances had to be given and steps taken to provide for Militiamen's families. Especially, there was opposition to the Militia because the element of compulsion was generally detested. The only place where the embodiment of the Militia was relatively trouble-free was in Dublin and here the regiment was almost entirely filled with volunteers and substitutes. In this respect, the relative success of the protest against the Militia ballot may be noted: in future, the ballot would be tacitly abandoned when further recruitment was called for. Finally in counties like Wexford, opposition to, and support for, the Militia reflected a pre-existing 'liberal' versus 'hardline' division within the county elite: such divisions had been manifest over earlier issues: but the combination of elite and popular hostility to the Militia Act was both novel and, it may be suggested, ominous for the future.

The most striking aspects of the Militia protests were, however, the near universality of the disturbances, the violence which characterised them and the harsh response elicited from the authorities. In just over eight weeks some 230 people were killed throughout Ireland in violent protest against the embodiment of a militia. This was nearly five times the number of casualties sustained in the previous thirty years of agrarian disturbances in Ireland. In the end, however, despite the violent opposition, the Militia was embodied: by the close of the year 1793 some 9,600 men had been enlisted (out of a target of nearly 15,000); but the violence of the protests had raised a question mark over the reliability of such unwilling recruits and may in fact have made Ireland all the more attractive as the destination of a French invasion fleet. Moreover, the disturbances themselves revealed all too clearly the ready availability of combustible, even insurrectionary, material in Ireland.

3

With an Irish Militia, albeit imperfectly, established, the British government concluded that the defence of Ireland had been secured and, accordingly, began to draw heavily on Ireland for recruits and regiments. However, long before the Militia had been embodied, Ireland had been targeted as a prime source for both. Despite what Westmorland called 'the miserable number of troops unfortunately composing our army', by mid-July 1793 some 4,300 troops had been withdrawn and by mid-1794, 22 battalions, about 6,000 men, had gone.[15] Complicated plans were drawn up to replace Irish regular regiments with British independent companies but little came of these. The fact was, as Hobart pointed out, 'any consideration induces British ministers to weaken us in Ireland';[16] and the so-called replacement companies were always far in arrears. Even during the Militia disturbances in the summer of 1793 it was with very great difficulty that Westmorland was able to secure the retention in Ireland of the four Irish regiments which had been ordered overseas. The Home Office grumbled that this would 'break in materially upon the continental plans' and, when the troubles were over, five regiments, not four, amounting to nearly 2,000 men were speedily sent abroad. A protest from Westmorland was brushed aside with an assurance that there was no danger of invasion and that the troops were urgently needed in Flanders.[17] Similarly, pressing requests from Dublin for large quantities of muskets and munitions for the new Irish armament were turned down on the grounds that there were none to spare.

The opening up of the West Indian theatre led to further demands for Irish troops. In January 1793 the 69th regiment was ordered from Ireland to Dominica and, as the climate there took its deadly toll and insurrections spread to St Lucia and Grenada, more and more Irish regiments were dispatched to the Caribbean.[18] On occasion, it was not possible to recruit in order to bring regiments up to their full complement and numbers of troops were drafted in from other units: in January 1796, for example, men from the 104th, 105th, 106th, 111th and 113th regiments were transferred to the 17th, 32nd, 39th, 56th, 67th, 93rd and 99th regiments of foot which were then sent to the West Indies. The 39th regiment had in fact arrived in Ireland some six months earlier to boost Irish defences but, as had been indignantly pointed out, instead of containing 230 men, as promised, there were only 26 rank and file, most of whom were mere boys who played in the regimental band and the rest were 'worn out men'.[19] Other British regiments that arrived in Ireland during the early years of the war were also very deficient in numbers and it is clear that Ireland was seen as a prime recruiting ground for the armed forces of the crown. In

———————

255

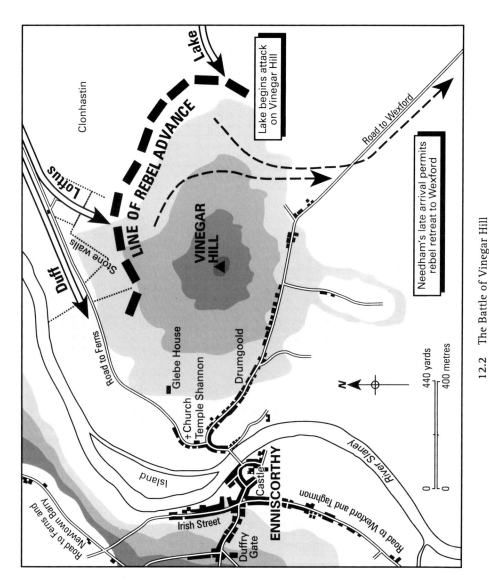

Clonhastin

Lake

Lake begins attack on Vinegar Hill

LINE OF REBEL ADVANCE

Loftus

Duff

Stone walls

VINEGAR HILL

Road to Fems

Road to Wexford

Needham's late arrival permits rebel retreat to Wexford

Glebe House

+ Church

Temple Shannon

Drumgoold

N

440 yards

400 metres

0

0

Island

ENNISCORTHY

Castle

Irish Street

River Slaney

Road to Wexford and Taghmon

Duffry Gate

Road to Fems and Newtown Barry

12.2   The Battle of Vinegar Hill

Source: N. Furlong, *Fr John Murphy of Boocanogue* (Dublin, 1992)

a brief two-month period (December 1793 to January 1794) no fewer than seven British regiments disembarked in Ireland with orders to raise 200 recruits each,[20] and in the months and years that followed, recruiting parties scoured the country, desperate for men to enlist.

In the early years of the war, this ceaseless quest for recruits had led inevitably to abuses.[21] Since recruits had not come forward in anything like the required numbers, extravagant bounties had to be offered and these were of course a standing inducement to desert: John Murphy had the distinction of having deserted from the 56th Foot, the 28th Light Dragoons, the North Cork Militia *and* the South Cork Militia. In any case, offering large sums of money served only to entice (as an army memorandum of 1794 put it) 'the worst sort of recruit . . . ignorant and inexperienced young men'. On the other hand, when recourse was had to crimps, regiments found themselves encumbered with – as an official report had it – 'the refuse of mankind'. Needless to say, with such poor quality recruits desertion rates soared. 'Desertion is terrible at present', wrote Edward Cooke in 1794, 'and we know not how to prevent it', and in early 1795 the new lord lieutenant, Earl Fitzwilliam, echoing his predecessors, remarked that 'there is no keeping Irish troops in Ireland, they desert so abominably'. Evidence for these assertions is not lacking: Colonel E. P. Trench's regiment, when inspected at Granard, County Longford, in May 1794 was found to have lost 233 men (out of a total complement of 1,100) through desertion, and while marching to its port of embarkation, it may have lost more. Trench's regiment was by no means unique.

The solution to the problem of tapping effectively the manpower of Ireland lay ultimately in utilising the Irish Militia as a 'nursery for the regulars'[22] but it would be some time before this conduit would be in place. In the meantime, more and more recruits were enlisted (sometimes illegally) and throughout the 1790s and beyond the 'hibernicisation' of the British regular infantry continued apace. This development held undoubted risks: in 1797 Dundas told the then lord lieutenant, Earl Camden, that he had decided against sending him an available 'English' infantry regiment because its 'recruits have been chiefly got from Ireland' and might therefore be unsuitable for police work: and a year later, in response to Camden's demand for English troops to crush the 1798 rebellion, Portland was forced to admit that he had no really 'English' regiments at all, for 'so large a part of our regular infantry is composed of recruits or men raised in Ireland'.[23] By the early nineteenth century so far had this process gone that Wellington's army in Spain had no fewer than fourteen Irish regiments and he himself reckoned that 30 per cent of the men in the other regiments were Irish.[24]

Towards the end of 1794, English and Scottish Fencible regiments began to be sent to Ireland to make up for, and facilitate, the further massive withdrawals of regular troops that were taking place consequent on the campaigns in the West Indies. On 1 January 1795 there were recorded only 300 Fencible cavalry and 537 Fencible infantry in Ireland but by the end of that year some 10,000 more, almost entirely infantry, had disembarked (see Table 12.1). Fencible regiments were a sort of substitute militia, recruited for service within the British Isles only. There were English Fencible units, but the force was mostly Scottish in composition, frequently comprising the tenantry of a Scottish landlord, and often commanded by him. Following the arrival of these Fencible regiments, Ireland was almost entirely stripped of regular troops. Until the 1798 rebellion provoked a reversal of policy, regulars would form less than 10 per cent of the soldiers available to Dublin Castle for both defence and counter-insurgency duties. Until the embodiment of the Irish Yeomanry in late 1796 the entire burden would fall on the Irish Militia and the Scottish and English Fencibles.

There can be no doubt that in replacing regular troops with Irish Militia and Fencibles, Dublin Castle got the worse of the bargain. The Irish Militia soon proved itself to be a poorly disciplined force, its training was perfunctory, and frequently there were grave doubts as to its reliability in the event of a French invasion. Those who had 'dread[ed] the consequences of teaching all the idlers of the country the use of arms' quickly had their fears confirmed, for the 1790s were studded with numerous examples of interregimental or sectarian brawling, and attacks on civilians. Officers in the Irish Militia were frequently singled out for criticism. Colonel Robert Craufurd dismissed them contemptuously by remarking that 'everyone knows what a brute the uneducated son of an Irish farmer or middleman is', and colonel-commandant Charles Vallancey of the Tyrone Militia complained that his junior officers had no sense of duty but rather only 'a real wish to indulge in walking the streets of Strabane and lounging in the mess room'. In an early comment on London's policy of denuding Ireland of regulars, General Robert Cunninghame, the Irish commander-in-chief, had pointed out the hazards of such a policy. 'You know', he told Hobart, 'there are districts in Ireland quiet only at the point of the bayonet. The militia is experimental. The regular troops [are] your sheet anchor. Your officers are young and inexperienced children, your soldiers raw recruits. The necessities of war have deprived Ireland of the veterans and there are but very, very few sensible military men left.'[25]

The Fencibles that flooded into the country from 1795 on certainly appear to have had a better reputation than the Militia but, on the other hand, their fitness and capacity for duty were frequently questioned. Admittedly, conditions were bad everywhere for the men, and all types of soldier – those in the Militia, the Fencibles and the Regulars, suffered. Barracks were always overcrowded – in Duncannon fort, County Waterford, there were three men to every bed 'and the excessive heat so occasion'd thereby', Major General Fawcett reported in November 1797, 'caused a very bad fever to happen'; and in Cork harbour in 1794, 140 of the soldiers waiting to embark on the transports contracted 'a very malignant and contagious fever'.[26] None the less, there is clear evidence that the physique of the Fencibles made them peculiarly prone to disease and consequently less useful as soldiers. When the Prince of Wales Fencible regiment disembarked at Dublin in May 1795 some 396 out of its total complement of around 500 men were found to be unfit (too old, too fat, too small, too infirm, too young) and had to be sent back to Liverpool and thence to their respective parishes 'whence they were so improperly enlisted'. A few days later Mr Parkyn's Fencible regiment was inspected on disembarking and Camden, despite his wish to oblige the Horse Guards by examining them 'with as little severity as I could', was forced to conclude that the regiment was useless, many of the men having ruptures. Indeed, the death rate from natural causes of soldiers in Fencible regiments was such that the Army Medical Board conducted an inquiry into the grave disparity in mortality between Irish Militiamen and members of British Fencible regiments. The report concluded that whereas the Irish Militia was 'composed of stout men in the prime of life, drawn almost entirely from the Irish peasantry, inured to labour in the fields, to every vicissitude of climate', the Fencibles were all too often 'boys too young for service, or . . . unhealthy old men . . . most of them mechanics from unhealthy parts of Great Britain or from unwholesome sedentary trades'. This difference, it claimed, accounted for a death rate from natural causes among Fencible regiments five times that of the Militia.[27] On occasion, the foibles of the Fencible commanders must have played a part: the Elgin Fencibles were stricken with colds and diarrhoea on account of being forced to wear an unfamiliar garment – a kilt.[28]

These then were the forces which, until the formation of the Yeomanry armament in late 1796, were at the disposal of Dublin Castle. What opposition did they face and how did they perform in the years 1793 to 1796?

4

During the 1790s Dublin Castle faced two problems: that of providing for the defence of Ireland; and that of combatting growing insurgency in the countryside. The central difficulty for the Castle was that no single security policy could accomplish both objectives.[29] The defence of Ireland required the concentration of large numbers of troops who would be garrisoned at, or near, likely invasion sites. These were generally felt to be the south coast, or the north-east coast, of Ireland; Dublin was thought to be out of the question; so too was the west of Ireland – as General Cunninghame wrote: 'In the extent of coast from Galway northward to Lough Swilley [*sic*], it does not seem probable an enemy would attempt to land.'[30] And yet, a policy of concentrating soldiers into large encampments played into the hands of the main disturbers of the public peace, the Defenders, a secret society. These 'midnight insurgents' (as Westmorland dubbed them) had their origins in Armagh in the 1780s, but during the 1790s they spread far beyond that county.[31] In Armagh and in adjacent counties Defenderism had been a response to attacks by Protestant Peep-of-Day Boys; but as the movement spread it shed its defensive character. By 1795 Camden could list thirteen counties in which Defender style depredations such as arms raids on the homes of gentry families, the targeting for assassination of zealous magistrates, the murder of informers, and the swearing in of large numbers were carried out frequently.

Quite what lay behind the spread of Defenderism was something of a mystery. The Defenders paraded their time-honoured grievances over tithes and rents, but they also were self-consciously sectarian, avowedly anti-Protestant; they coupled admiration for the French Revolution – 'the French Defenders will uphold the cause, the Irish Defenders will pull down the British laws' – with strong millenarian expectations of a world turned upsidedown. They also sought to sow disaffection among the soldiers and militiamen in Ireland. What was clear, however, was that the Defenders were a most dangerous and subversive force in rural Ireland; one that despite Camden's harsh counter-measures, including 'speedy execution of offenders' and sending 'suspects' to the Fleet, showed no signs of diminishing. Moreover, the threat posed by Defenderism required the deployment of small garrisons of twenty or thirty men throughout the troubled counties. This was undoubtedly bad for discipline, and it certainly rendered the men more vulnerable to the arguments of seditious emissaries: but worse, the dispersal of soldiers in this way meant inevitably that a French landing might well be unopposed. It could take several days before an adequate force would be mobilised against them, and by that time both Cork and Limerick could have fallen. Westmorland's dilemma and that of his successor Camden was potentially an acute one, but in the event, both gave primacy to a policy of counter-insurgency over that of defence. Not that the latter was altogether neglected: but the British naval blockade of French ports was believed to offer sound security while the establishment of troop concentrations near those areas most at risk (Dublin, Belfast, Cork) was felt to be sufficient to head off the threat of a surprise French descent.

As we have seen, the army in eighteenth-century Ireland had frequently been involved in police work – escorting prisoners, attending executions, on occasion putting down riots, and such like – but in the 1790s it began to pursue a policy of counter-insurgency. The explanation for this stark shift in role, a departure that eventually led the armed forces to advocate and, on occasion, carry out a policy of counter-terror, lies in the nature of the threats posed by the Defenders and (from 1794 on) by the United Irishmen. It cannot be too often stressed that the Defenders, with their subversive objectives, their avowed sectarianism, their millenarian expectations, and their resoluteness in the face of condign punishment – 'they do not fear death' exclaimed one commentator – were an altogether new phenomenon in the history of Irish secret societies.[32] They were insurgents rather than rioters, and they brought about the breakdown of the 'normal' means by which law and order had traditionally been maintained in rural Ireland. The armed forces were constantly deployed against them and the Defenders were quite prepared to fire on soldiers. By law, the soldiers were not permitted to act unless called upon by magistrates, but as successive lords lieutenant and army commanders complained, the magistrates were increasingly reluctant to exert themselves. At one time, it had been almost a point of pride among the leading gentry that they could manage most law and order problems in their county without resort to the army: but in the wake of the anti-Militia riots, the consequent spread of Defenderism, and the perceptible loss of morale among the governing elite, the gentry held back. The Protestant gentry when confronted with disorder in their area, commented Edward Cooke, a Castle official, in 1793, 'no longer rely upon Protestant union and universally run to the army'.[33] By early 1795, so far had this disenchantment gone that the lord lieutenant, Earl Fitzwilliam, was claiming that army officers had to be 'continually employed as civil magistrates in different parts of the Kingdom for I am sorry to say the soldiery is the only magistracy in real authority'.[34]

A few weeks after Fitzwilliam penned these remarks, his successor as lord lieutenant, Camden, acted on them. He dispatched Lord Carhampton the new commander-in-chief, at the head of an army to Connacht to put down disturbances in that area. Camden had warned London that Carhampton might have to employ 'very strong measures' in doing so, and that his soldiers' tactics 'might in some instances be carried on with a warmth which might better have been suppressed', but he claimed that it would be expedient to ignore such enthusiasm.[35] The soldiers had received no training in counter-insurgency, indeed their normal military training was rudimentary in the extreme. Nor were their officers better prepared for what lay ahead. A number of them had seen service in the American War, but the conduct of that conflict offered little guidance to service in Ireland; and few of the Militia officers had any proper military training at all.[36] In so far as there was a coherent counter-insurgency policy, then, it drew its inspiration partly from memories of the '45 in Scotland, but mostly from the contemporary civil war in the Vendée in western France. Carhampton's army resembled nothing so much as one of those *colonnes infernales* with which the Vendée was subdued and his chief tactic on his campaign in the west was the seizure of hundreds of 'suspects' (i.e. vagrants) and 'strangers', and their prompt dispatch to serve in the Royal Navy.[37] Carhampton's campaign in the west was to set a pattern for increasingly harsh counter-insurgency measures over the next few years.

In the borderlands of south Ulster/north Leinster, magistrates also proved most reluctant to exert themselves. In this region, the problem was not so much Defender depredations as those of the Protestant Peep-of-Day Boys, and allied 'Orange' factions, who were intent on waging war on Catholics and who in the course of 1795 and 1796, expelled large numbers of Catholics from their homes in Counties Armagh and Tyrone.[38] Edward Cooke in Dublin Castle denounced the Armagh magistrates for conniving at these expulsions. The army commander in Armagh, Colonel Dalrymple, accused the local magistrates of being reluctant to act lest they damage their electoral prospects; and he claimed that he and the army were powerless to act unless authorised by them. However, Dalrymple himself was elderly and overweight and he shared the lack of zeal of the local authorities. Gosford, a leading local landowner, admitted that the Protestants 'made no scruple of declaring both by words and actions (that could not be misunderstood) a fixed intention to exterminate their opponents', but his remedy for this threat was to join with other magistrates in passing resolutions calling for peace. In fact, the volatile tenantry of south Ulster was beyond the control of their supposed leaders: 'It is impossible', wrote Richard Jephson to Lord Charlemont, the governor of Armagh, 'for the Protestant gentry to keep up the farce of impartiality between the parties or to disavow the absolute necessity of giving a considerable degree of support to the Protestant party.'[39] Eventually, the Protestant gentry in the counties of south Ulster did succeed in imposing a semblance of control over their people, but this was done only by championing the Orange Order. In a sense, in order to preserve their influence they had to abandon their role of leader and settle for that of tribune.

For the military authorities, the religious war in south Ulster was at first a distraction: Captain Benjamin Williamson echoed the official line when he confided to a correspondent in September 1795 'our business is to keep order and we treat both [Defenders and Peep-of-Day Boys] as enemies to the peace of society'.[40] But gradually, as the threat posed by the Defenders showed no sign of diminishing, while that of the United Irishmen began to grow apace, the military authorities, possibly encouraged by Dublin Castle, began to reassess this even-handed approach. Questions of political and military strategy now took precedence. Since the heartland of Orangeism lay across the main communication routes from Dublin to the north-west and from Belfast to Connacht, support for the Orange Order (set up in September 1795) might help block the transmission of subversive ideas and emissaries, both emanating from the United Irishmen, along these routes. General Thomas Knox summed up the new thinking: 'As to the Orangemen, we have rather a difficult card to play. They must not be entirely discountenanced; on the contrary we must in a certain degree uphold them for, with all their licentiousness, on them must we rely for the preservation of our lives and properties should critical times occur.'[41]

In May 1794, following the revelations of treasonable contact between some United Irishmen and the French agent, the Reverend William Jackson, the society was suppressed by proclamation. This had the effect of driving out of its ranks those who might have helped moderate its activities; and when the society was reconstituted eighteen months later, it was secret and oath-bound, and dedicated to the pursuit of an Irish republic to be achieved with the help of French arms. Theobald Wolfe Tone had been implicated in the Jackson affair and had had to leave for the United States. Once there, however, he took ship for France and early in 1796 arrived in Paris determined to obtain an undertaking from the Directory to furnish an army for the invasion of Ireland. Tone's arguments in favour of a French descent on Ireland chimed well with current French military thinking and towards the end of 1796 a French fleet laden with some 20,000 soldiers under the command of General Hoche set sail from Brest, destined for Ireland.[42]

In arguing the case for a French invasion of Ireland, Tone had stressed the large numbers of sworn United Irishmen that would flock to the French standard on landing. The reconstituted United Irishmen had been unremitting in seeking to win adherents: in May 1795 they counted barely 5,000 members, mostly clustered in a 20-mile radius of Belfast: but by October 1796 one United Irish report revealed a strength on paper of some 57,000, the bulk of whom were concentrated in north-east Ulster.[43] A military organisation, by this date, had been engrafted on to the political structure: each local society would elect a sergeant; three such societies would elect a captain and ten captains, representing thirty societies which consti-tuted a regiment, would elect their superior officers. A military committee had been established in Belfast to oversee this paper army. Selection of officers was some-times based on non-military criteria: William Farrell of Carlow later recalled that 'at one time a man that had the greatest number of United Irishmen's songs and could sing them best was chosen [captain]'; and the training of the men was perfunctory: 'The idea is that discipline is not necessary', reported an informer, 'that they need only give one fire and rush out with the bayonet like the French.' Farrell himself recorded that the United Irishmen in his area were told that each captain 'should have a pair of colours and every one of his men that could, should have the same that, in case they were attacked by cavalry, they should all unfurl their colours suddenly at them and by that means aided by shouting, throw them all in confusion'. Farrell concluded sadly: 'I nearly sickened when I heard the story.'[44] Finally, by late 1796, the United Irish leadership in Ulster had formed some sort of informal alliance with the Defender network in the province. At first glance, such an alliance might seem improbable in that the Defenders appeared to be everything that the United Irishmen were not. And yet, such an alliance offered the United Irishmen a ready-made army of rural insurgents with which to take the field or at least reinforce the French army when it would arrive. Viewed in this light, the Defenders' sectarian outlook and millenarian objectives could be dismissed as unimportant, and the middle-class radicals of Belfast reassured themselves that they would be able to 'melt [the Defenders] down' into non-sectarian and enlightened United Irishmen.[45]

The existence of the Defenders, their willingness to fight, their numbers and their extensive catchment area were all powerful arguments in favour of an accommo-dation between them and the United Irishmen: but there was an additional reason that made an alliance militarily vital. The Defenders were widely believed to have infiltrated the Irish Militia: indeed it is more than likely that Defenders were recruited into the Militia and entirely possible that as regiments moved around Ireland, some became unwitting instruments for the diffusion of Defenderism into new, unaffected areas. For their part, the United Irishmen had long targeted soldiers, Irish Militiamen in particular, as prime objects of their attention and they had sought to make converts among them. They had become convinced – and so too had Wolfe Tone – that in the event of a crisis 'the Militia, the great bulk of whom are Catholic, would to a moral certainty abandon their leaders'. By July 1796, it was claimed that the United Irishmen counted 15,000 Irish Militia – 'which they say they are sure of' – among their supporters. In the same month, it was reported that two Belfast United Irishmen had visited allegedly disaffected soldiers at Blaris, a strategic encampment of some 3,000 men, near Lisburn, County Antrim. It was reported that these disaffected soldiers had set aside a room in which to meet: no one was admitted who was not 'Up and Up, that is Defender and United Irishman' and 600 were claimed to be both, while 1,600 were 'simply united'.[46] The explanation for the United Irishmen's neglect of military training in their preparations for rebellion may lie in their confidence that the disaffected Militia would side with them and that the seasoned French troops would discipline their other allies, the Defenders.

Throughout 1796, the depredations of the Defenders, the sectarian war in south Ulster, the spread of the United Irishmen's message and even the sowing of disaffection among the troops showed no signs of abating. Harsh and illegal measures adopted by the military had not had the desired effect; nor indeed had 'the speedy execution of offenders'.[47] An Indemnity Act was put through parliament in early 1796 but Camden's hopes that this evidence of the government's firm resolve to excuse illegal acts committed by the soldiers would remove the need for further 'severer measures' were dashed when Carhampton's chief informant was murdered. An Insurrection Act with 'extremely severe' penalties was rushed through the Irish parliament. Under its terms, the death penalty was prescribed for administering an illegal oath, and transportation for taking one. Moreover, extensive powers were given to local magistrates to search for arms, to impose curfews in disturbed areas and to send 'suspects' to serve in the navy. Clearly, some of the illegal tactics adopted by Carhampton in Connacht a year earlier were now to be enshrined into law. But even this remarkable piece of legislation failed to halt the spread of the Defenders who were by now swearing 'not only to be true to one another but to unite and correspond with the Society of United Irishmen'.[48] In the next few months Habeas Corpus was suspended, large numbers of arrests and transportations were carried out and more Fencible regiments arrived from Britain. Yet the conspiracy spread. Especially alarming was the growing incidence of disaffection in certain regiments: the County Limerick Militia, the City of Limerick Militia, the Queen's County Militia and the Westmeath Militia all aroused anxiety on this score.

For a long time Dublin Castle had persisted in regarding these disturbances in a purely domestic light for its entire military policy had been based on the assumption that '*if no invasion takes place*' they could not seriously challenge the state. But by mid-1796, the Castle's complacency had been severely shaken. In desperation, Camden prepared to listen to those who urged the establishment of a Yeomanry force which would provide both a local police force and, equally important, establish an outlet for loyalist energies hitherto wasted in sectarian feuding in Armagh and elsewhere in the north. In the event, the arrival of the French invasion fleet around Christmas Day 1796 in Bantry Bay, off the south coast of

Ireland, provided an early test of this new force's effectiveness. And, of course, the very fact of the French fleet's presence off the coast of Ireland finally removed any doubts as to the impossibility of invasion. It is not too much to say that these events constituted a turning point in the military history of the 1790s.

5

From time to time during the 1790s there had been suggestions that a Yeomanry force should be embodied in Ireland.[49] Such a part-time force would, it was argued, assist with the policing of the country – this would be its normal task – but it could also be of assistance in the event of an invasion or other emergency when the part-time Yeomanry could be called out on permanent duty and brought under the terms of the Mutiny Act. Unlike the Militia, there was to be no element of compulsion in enlisting in the Yeomanry, and while Militia regiments were positively barred from serving in their home counties, it was understood that the area in which a Yeomanry company was raised would be its primary sphere of operations. A local force raised from those who had a stake in the community (Yeomanry cavalrymen would supply their own horses), commanded by those locals who had social and political authority, and operating locally for the most part, would, it was claimed, play a vital role in the war against crime and subversion. Moreover, a Yeomanry armament had been set up in England and this was frequently adduced as the model for any Irish force.

For various reasons, however, Dublin Castle had not been in favour of a Yeomanry. It was felt that a Yeomanry might damage regular recruitment; that the English model was not at all appropriate to Ireland; and especially that a Yeomanry force might be beyond the control of Dublin Castle. This last consideration alone ensured that proposals for a Yeomanry would meet with a cool reception, for Dublin Castle was terrified at the prospect of creating a force that in any way resembled the old Volunteers. However, during the short-lived viceroyalty of Earl Fitzwilliam (1794–5), the idea of an Irish Yeomanry received a boost. Fitzwilliam was convinced that the divisions within Irish society were at once artificial, anachronistic and dangerous in that they prevented Ireland contributing her full weight to the war effort. In particular he believed that until Catholic Emancipation (by this stage this meant the right of Irish Catholics, if elected, to sit in the Irish parliament) was conceded and the principle of distinction abandoned, then Ireland would constitute a standing invitation to the French to invade and thus remain the weak link in Britain's defences. Should an invasion occur, he explained, 'our means of defence can be no other than those of other countries, namely the co-operation of the mass with the government' and that, he argued, could only be obtained through conciliatory, i.e. pro-Catholic, policies. An Irish Yeomanry – 'an arm'd constabulary compos'd of the better orders of the people', both Catholics and Protestants – could then be embodied and would then have 'the double effect of a defence against an

---

invasion and an additional power in support of magistracy'. The setting-up of a Yeomanry, therefore, 'must not precede the Roman Catholic business'; indeed 'should the Catholic question fail we must think twice' about the establishment of such a force. In the event, as is well known, Fitzwilliam's viceroyalty foundered on the Catholic question and with his recall (February 1795) the question of a Yeomanry was put on the shelf.[50]

The new lord lieutenant, Camden, was for a long time hostile to a Yeomanry, fearful lest it would evoke memories of the disbanded Volunteers and perhaps even seek to emulate that discredited force by involving itself in politics. By the middle of 1796, however, both the security situation in Ireland and the threat of invasion were such that Camden had begun to look carefully once again at the idea of a Yeomanry and to listen to the voices of his advisors calling for one. Disaffection within the Irish Militia had reached such a point that grave doubts were being cast on its reliability in an emergency. Moreover, out of a total force of some 40,000 only 7,000 – so Camden claimed – could be spared to march against an invader for, if the entire army marched against an invading force, there would be no one left to keep an eye on local subversives anxious to make common cause with the French. The earlier objection that a Yeomanry would hit recruitment was brushed aside; and as for the argument that a Yeomanry would inevitably be the Volunteers under another name, Camden now claimed that he was confident he could establish a force 'guarded as much as possible from assuming the appearance of Volunteer'.[51] In late August 1796, the British cabinet reluctantly agreed to the setting up of an Irish Yeomanry, and Camden immediately began to issue commissions to raise companies to local worthies of a particular cast of mind; noted 'Liberals' were frequently passed over while Protestant stalwarts were as frequently distinguished.

There was no significant military difference between the Yeomanry force called for by Fitzwilliam, and that eventually called into being by his successor: what had changed dramatically was the political context in which the Yeomanry armament emerged, and it was this that determined the composition of the force. Fitzwilliam had seen a Yeomanry as part of a package of measures which had to include Catholic Emancipation: in the absence of emancipation, he argued, Catholic leaders would hang back and Catholic alienation increase. However, Camden's brief in Ireland had been in fact to stifle Catholic agitation and 'to rally the Protestants': in these circumstances it was inevitable that the new Yeomanry force should have a strongly Protestant and Orange character, that it would be seen as merely a matter of 'arming the Protestants who can be depended on'. Camden recognised this danger: he admitted that he would be accused of 'arming the Protestants against the Papist', but he claimed that the danger to the state overrode all such considerations.[52]

Following Camden's announcement that a Yeomanry was to be established under strict government control, offers to set up corps began to flood into Dublin Castle. The recruitment to these corps did not go entirely smoothly. In a few areas, fears were expressed that a Yeomanry would be called upon to serve outside its locality or even that it would be drafted into the Irish Militia. In others, there was outright hostility. From Cookstown, County Tyrone, it was reported that James Stewart of Killymoon 'has found the plan of raising Yeomanry so odious to the people that there is no prospect of his succeeding', and Thomas Boyd, attempting to raise Yeomanry near Letterkenny, was met instead with 'expressions of impudent disloyalty'. Predictably, James Brown, the Sovereign of Belfast, had to admit failure for the time being in trying to raise a Yeomanry corps in that city.[53] Perhaps the United Irishmen drew some satisfaction from these rebuffs: 'J.W.' (the informer, Leonard McNally) claimed they laughed at the Yeomanry and 'say it [the Yeomanry] establishes two material facts – the few that *are* in red coats and the multitude that are *not*'.[54] If so, their optimism was entirely misplaced for while there were undoubted difficulties in embodying the Yeomanry these were quickly overcome and by Christmas 1796 over 300 offers to set up corps had been accepted by the Castle and near 20,000 men were drilling in them.[55]

The Yeomanry was not an exclusively Protestant body: Daniel O'Connell was famously a member of a Lawyers' Corps in Dublin, and even that 'red-hot Protestant', Sir Richard Musgrave, had many 'loyal Papists' in his corps at Youghal, County Cork.[56] (On occasion, it was claimed that United Irishmen joined the Yeomanry in order to get military training.)[57] But from the beginning the force was centred disproportionately in the north and had a strong Protestant or Orange character. In Armagh, entire lodges of Orangemen were enlisted into local Yeomanry corps; from County Down came a report that the corps around Newry 'are chiefly Orangemen and all agree in not admitting a Papist however recommended'; and from Omagh, County Tyrone, came word that the Presbyterians there 'declare that if a Catholic should be admitted among their corps they would never assemble'. If the Castle had had its doubts about the merits of a Yeomanry force, these were quickly allayed. 'The wisdom of the measure', wrote John Beresford, 'appears from the confidence that it raises in loyal subjects'; and Cooke claimed that it had awakened 'a real and general spirit among the Protestants'. Chief Secretary Thomas Pelham, had predicted that 'if a standard was once erected', loyalists would flock to it: and he was now fully vindicated.[58]

The speed and, in general, the ease with which the Yeomanry was assembled, a marked contrast to the Irish Militia, requires explanation. It seems clear that it was building on a pre-existing, paramilitary tradition that had its distant origins in the defence requirements of the seventeenth-century plantations, but which had recently been revived by the Volunteers of 1778. As the security situation in mid-Ulster had deteriorated from 1794 on, there is substantial evidence that local 'trained bands' had been set up to answer local defence needs. When forming his Yeoman corps in September 1796, Henry Clements of Fort Henry, near Cavan, recalled how in the winter of 1794, there were Defender depredations nearby but that 'we escaped by having formed an association with the approbation of the late Col. Clements and keeping regular guards for our protection'. Another local association appears to have been set up in Drumahair, County Leitrim, in 1795; and by August 1796 there is evidence that local magistrates in mid-Ulster were proceeding with their own plans for a local defence force which would 'frustrate the hopes of traitors and banditti'.[59] The disbanded Volunteers offered a model for such groups. When Richard Annesley's brother inspected his Yeomen recruits at Castlewellan, County Down, in November 1796, he found to his alarm that 'their intention in proposing to clothe themselves was under the idea of the old Volunteer scheme [but] being informed they could not under that idea be embodied they agreed to accept clothing etc. in the same manner that other corps did'.[60]

In 1793, the award to Catholics of the right to vote on the same terms as Irish Protestants, along with the formation of a largely Catholic Militia entrusted with the defence of Ireland, had appeared to mark a dramatic reversal of a century-old policy of exclusion. By the same token, the collapse of the Fitzwilliam viceroyalty in 1795, the public retreat from Catholic emancipation, and finally the formation a year later of a largely Protestant – indeed, Orange – Yeomanry unmistakably signalled a stark return to that earlier policy. The establishment of a Yeomanry copperfastened the Castle's adherence to a policy of exclusion and reinforced its commitment to the Protestant Ascendancy. In 1793, the threat had been of French invasion and the aspiration had been a united Irish nation resisting foreign subversion; in 1796 there was still a fear of French invasion but the threat of domestic subversion took precedence over it and political calculation now determined that the military response should be a sectarian one. Ironically, the apparently distant danger of a French landing proved now to be only too real. The setting sail of a French invasion fleet in December 1796, and its arrival in Bantry Bay, County Cork around Christmas Day, would provide an early test of the new force and of the Castle's defence plans in general.

6

In the autumn of 1796 there were strong rumours that a French fleet was making ready at Brest and that an attempted invasion of either Britain or Ireland was likely. Camden summoned Admiral Kingsmill to Dublin Castle for consultations and was reassured as to the British fleet's readiness to intercept the enemy: Portland, in London, went so far as to express his hope to Camden that the French force would in fact manage to put to sea 'as it is scarcely possible that it would escape the vigilance and superiority of the squadrons which are stationed to observe its motions'.[61] Such confidence was unwise: at 10 p.m. on 23 December, General Dalrymple reported twenty-five French sail in Bantry Bay. The invasion fleet laden with some 20,000 French soldiers, among them Theobald Wolfe Tone, had taken advantage of some very poor weather, successfully evaded the British fleet positioned to engage them and reached the Cork coast. That, however, was as far as it got for a violent storm blew up, scattered the French ships and sundered lines of communication between them. After a few storm-tossed days, the by now dispersed fleet limped back to France, once again successfully evading her pursuers. The inquest began immediately.

For those religiously minded (or with a sense of history), it was self-evident that, as Lord Clare put it, 'Providence . . . has befriended us' once again, and this was no doubt comforting.[62] Equally pleasing was the spirit evinced by the soldiers and Militiamen as they set off against the French; and the newly formed Yeomanry earned plaudits for the way various corps took over garrisons in order to free regular troops for the expected campaign. Moreover, the 'zeal and loyalty displayed by the inhabitants of the south' during the short-lived emergency was welcome.[63] Dr Moylan, Catholic bishop of Cork, had promptly issued an address enjoining obedience and loyalty on his flock and, as the soldiers and Militiamen marched south in the dead of winter to attack the French, it was reported that 'the peasants in the counties of Cork and Limerick anticipated their wants by preparing potatoes for them on the road' and by clearing snow on their way.[64] These things apart, however, there was precious little else to celebrate. Any lingering doubts about French intentions and, indeed, capability had now been dispelled. The French had come in strength: they could come again; the United Irishmen had had an enormous propaganda coup. In addition, the military response to the crisis had been generally undistinguished, and on occasion chaotic. The army staff was at sixes and sevens in mobilising its forces; Camden reckoned it would take 'a few days' to assemble a force of 9,000 near Cork, and a few days more to increase that number to 14,000. In the meantime, Carhampton, the commander-in-chief, conceded that both Cork and possibly Limerick might fall.[65] Certainly, General Dalrymple in command in Cork admitted he had no plans to defend the city – 'a diversion is all to be expected' from his men. And Colonel Vallancey, commanding the Tyrone Militia in Limerick, had no high opinion of General Smith charged with organising that city's defence: 'I cannot give you any account of the confusion that reigned there', he wrote to a correspondent.[66] Who could say what the consequences would have been if these cities had fallen, and the French had begun to march on Dublin?

This question was particularly apt, for while the south of Ireland had manifested loyalty, this had not been at all the case in the north of Ireland. The abortive French expedition brought home forcefully to Dublin Castle the massive threat posed by the United Irishmen in Ulster. Already by November 1796 large areas of Counties Down and Armagh had been proclaimed under the Insurrection Act: but this had had little effect on the progress of the United Irishmen. Arms raids, communal potato diggings (designed by the disaffected to display numbers and perhaps inculcate some elementary military drill), and murder had continued unabated. The clamour for a policy of 'counter-terror' had grown; but Camden had been reluctant to countenance this, perhaps fearful lest London baulk at such measures.[67] Bantry Bay removed any doubts on this score. On 8 January 1797 Camden revealed to Portland that during the emergency a large body of troops (perhaps 10,000 men) had had to be retained in the north because of the 'very alarming' security situation particularly in Counties Derry and Antrim (including the town of Belfast) and he warned him that additional 'severe steps' would have to be taken in order to crush the conspiracy there. Portland pronounced himself in full agreement: 'There is little distinction to be made between indifference and disaffection'; within a few months he would suggest to Camden an act of parliament 'enabling you to depart for a certain time from the established rule of law'. The north was to be dragooned.[68]

In early spring 1797, Camden ordered General Lake, in command of a mixed force of Militia, Yeomanry and Fencibles, to use all methods to disarm Ulster. 'The general has orders from me', Camden told Portland, 'not to suffer the cause of Justice to be frustrated by the delicacy which might possibly have actuated the magistracy' in implementing the Insurrection Act.[69] Lake's subordinate commanders set to with a will: 'Laws though ever so strict will not do', explained General Knox, 'severe military execution alone will recover the arms from the hands of the rebels . . . I look upon Ulster to be a La Vendée . . . it will not be brought into subjection but by the means adopted by the republicans in power [in France] – namely spreading devastation through the most disaffected parts.'[70] Throughout the remainder of 1797 a wholesale policy of military terror was instituted in Ulster: house burnings, floggings and mass arrests were all carried out in order to recover weapons and to cow the populace. In some areas oaths of loyalty were pressed on the inhabitants: 900 took the oath in Carrickfergus, County Antrim, and nearly 3,000 in Belfast. Capital convictions too were used to enjoin obedience: at the Winter Assizes in 1797 some fifty people were sentenced to death but while some were executed, Camden judged it expedient to postpone sentence on the rest 'from time to time to keep them as hostages for the good behaviour of the neighbour-hood'.[71] Excesses were commonplace for the soldiers were expressly ordered without the modest restraint of a civil magistrate present. 'Many are the military outrages which have been committed in the north,' wrote Dr Haliday to Lord Charlemont, former commander of the Volunteers, 'such as inflictions of military punishments on poor people in no way subject to martial law . . . burglaries, robberies, arsons, murders; and almost every instance passed over without censure or any satisfaction given to the sufferers.'[72] 'It is not to be denied,' wrote Camden, 'that government meant to strike terror', but he justified it by claiming 'that [terror] had been the policy of the rebellious', and could therefore only be countered by greater terror.[73] Inevitably, military discipline went to pieces as the soldiers were turned loose on the populace and, indeed, on each other: at Stewartstown, County Tyrone, in September 1797, an ambush on the Kerry Militia by a mixed group of Tay Fencibles, local Yeomanry and 24th Dragoons left ten dead; and such indiscipline would later cause grave problems for the army command.[74] None-theless, the army's terror tactics got results: the United Irish network in Ulster was thrown into disarray, large quantities of arms (pikes, muskets and even cannon) were lost, and many thousands were terrified – on the United Irishmen's own figures – out of the movement.[75]

While Ulster was being 'pacified', the army authorities had also been concerned with putting their own house in order, and it may be that their success in combatting disaffection among the troops and in sorting out problems of command was in the long run of greater significance than its campaign in Ulster. By common consent the soldiers had behaved well during the Bantry Bay emergency; but that could be no cause for complacency, for it had long been recognised that there was a problem of disaffection in a large number of regiments – particularly in the Irish Militia – and that if the French had landed in strength, the disaffected soldiers might have mutinied. Accordingly throughout 1797 (and after) a close watch was kept on those regiments felt to be at risk and there was a cascade of orders insisting that soldiers wear proper uniform, avoid taverns and remain in their barracks after retreat. The naval mutinies at the Nore and Spithead in April and May 1797, and the strong evidence of United Irish involvement in these, reinforced the army's concern at disaffection among the soldiers. Investigations were launched into allegations of disaffection in various regiments and on foot of these, in the summer of 1797, a series of courts martial was held at army camps throughout Ireland. At places as far apart as Dublin, Bandon (County Cork), Limerick, and Blaris, men from the Louth Militia, the Wexford Militia, the Westmeath Militia, the Kildare Militia, the Leitrim Militia, the Galway Militia, the Meath Militia, the 5th Dragoon Guards, the Clare Militia, the Kerry Militia, the Monaghan Militia and the Tipperary Militia were court-martialled for sedition. Numbers of those convicted were executed, or given severe floggings and ordered to serve abroad for life.

Perhaps the most significant court-martial was that held at the strategically vital Blaris camp, about 10 miles from Belfast. Here, four members of the Monaghan Militia were executed following a public parade on top of a wagon from Belfast to Blaris. Their deaths by firing squad severed the links between the disaffected soldiers of Blaris and the United Irishmen of Belfast, and appears to have been sufficient to being other disaffected soldiers back to their duty. It also brought home to the United Irishmen, already reeling from Lake's *dragonnade*, that they could no longer count on the Irish Militia as some sort of substitute army in case the French did not return.[76]

The Bantry Bay episode had exposed the incompetence of the army command in Ireland and during 1797 steps were taken to bring in effective and efficient generals to command the troops. There was general agreement that there was much negligence and absenteeism among officers: Pelham complained at officers leaving their men on the march south to intercept the French; and Carhampton sent a list of nineteen officers whom he wanted superseded for absenteeism.[77] Some generals had performed lamentably during the Bantry Bay emergency and they were soon got rid of. General Stewart had recently had a stroke and he was retired on grounds of ill-health; and General Amherst was forced to resign because of 'some very questionable language he was in the habit of [uttering?]' Both were pronounced to be 'perfectly useless' by Camden. Others could not be forced out quite so easily and there still remained a number of 'military exotics' (as Lord Clare dubbed them) on the Irish Staff.[78] Camden adjudged Carhampton himself to have performed poorly both during and after the emergency at Bantry Bay. In fact, he had never enjoyed the confidence of Dublin Castle and had only been made commander-in-chief in October 1796 because there was nobody else around. Camden was soon looking for a replacement for him. 'For all his merit', he wrote, 'there is certainly a degree of indiscretion in his character that makes him unfit for the chief commands of the army in times so delicate as the present and the military certainly do not place great confidence in him.'[79] Ironically, the attempted invasion by the French had made a command in Ireland more attractive to ambitious career officers and Camden saw his chance to remove the commander-in-chief, and bring some much-needed talent onto the Irish Staff. An approach was made to Lord Cornwallis who had recovered his military reputation in India after having lost it in the American War: but significantly Cornwallis could not be persuaded to come to Ireland without some political initiative on the Catholic question to accompany him. Camden baulked at that.[80] Sir Ralph Abercromby was then recommended to Camden by the secretary at war, Henry Dundas. 'If you get him . . . ', wrote Dundas, 'you get *entre nous* one of the best, if not on the whole the very best, officers in the King's service.'[81] Abercromby was reluctant to come to Ireland, but in October 1797 he pocketed his misgivings and accepted the post of commander-in-chief. Carhampton retired to Bath. 'The army rejoice at the change', commented Colonel Vallancey.[82] Its joy was not to last.

7

Sir Ralph Abercromby had had some previous experience of Ireland and the Irish and he had already formed certain fairly conventional views on the country and its inhabitants: the Irish people were fine if they were treated well; they made good soldiers if well led; the Irish gentry were contemptible.[83] These earlier impressions were confirmed on arrival in Ireland and from the beginning the new commander-in-chief was on a collision course with the Castle. Abercromby was convinced that the threat of invasion from France must take precedence over the danger (much exaggerated, in his opinion) of domestic insurrection, and he therefore decided to concentrate his troops in large numbers and enforce discipline among them. Moreover, he determined to shift the responsibility for law and order away from the army and on to the Yeomanry and the local gentry. Again, the lack of discipline among the soldiers greatly alarmed him: reports of murder, rape, house-burning, attacks on civilians and pillaging reached him constantly; 'within these twelve months' he told his son, 'every crime, every cruelty that could be committed by Cossacks or Calmucks has been transacted here'. Abercromby attributed these outrages to the scattered deployment of the army into small units: 'the dispersed state of the troops is really ruinous . . . The best regiments in Europe could not long stand such usage,' and he predicted that if nothing were done, 'when the moment for calling forth the Irish army arrives, one half of it will dissolve in a month'.[84]

Neither Abercromby's strictures nor his prescriptions were relished by Camden or his advisors, his 'cabinet' of mostly Irish officeholders that met regularly to review security policy. Throughout 1797, and indeed before then, they had treated the country as being in a state of smothered, if not actual, rebellion and had deployed their forces accordingly. Abercromby now dismissed their fears as exaggerated where they were not groundless, and discounted their advice as worthless. He quickly shut himself off from them. How could the country be in rebellion, he demanded, 'when the orders of his Excellency [Camden] might be carried over the whole kingdom by an orderly dragoon, or a writ executed without any difficulty, a few places in the mountains excepted'?[85] Such scepticism was unwelcome to the members of Camden's 'cabinet'. First, because it was felt to be unwarranted; the reality of incipient insurrection was confirmed to them day and daily by outrages, and the conspiracy had been exposed by various parliamentary inquiries and court cases. Second, because it threatened their hold on the levers of power at Dublin Castle. If the defence of Ireland against the French were taken as the central objective, then inevitably the armchair generals at Dublin Castle would have to defer to the judgement of the vastly experienced commander-in-chief; on the other hand, if domestic insurrection were accorded precedence that would, just as surely, elevate the authority of a 'cabinet' of experts with local knowledge. In a sense, the concentration of the Irish army would consolidate Abercromby's authority just as the dispersal of the troops throughout the country currently diminished it. Finally, there were vital political as well as military issues at stake in this debate. If the threat of invasion were accorded priority then this meant that, as Abercromby put it, the problem of 'the alienation of the minds of the people from government' would have to be addressed by Dublin Castle: the Catholic question might even have to be reopened; this was not at all desired by Camden or his advisors.[86] By contrast, if, as Dublin Castle argued, the primary danger stemmed from the country being in the grip of a jacobin conspiracy pursuing its ends by murder and intimidation then that threat could only be met by a stern repression that left no room for conciliation or concession.

On his arrival in Ireland, Abercromby set out to make himself 'acquainted with the situation and state of the army in Ireland'.[87] He quickly concluded that the armed forces were in a deplorable condition and he soon made his views known. Then, at Christmas 1797, he complained that because he was under the authority of the lord lieutenant, he had not full power to carry out his policies. Camden refused to delegate such power to him and from that point on conflict was inevitable.[88] On 26 February, following the rape by two officers of a witness to a murder, Abercromby issued his famous general orders in which he denounced the Irish armed forces as being in a state of licentiousness 'which must render it formidable to everyone but the enemy'.[89] Surprisingly, little notice was taken of this order (except among the military) in Ireland at the time, and it might have passed by unremarked but for the reaction in England.

By an astonishing coincidence (though some affected to doubt it was anything of the sort), a week earlier in the British House of Lords, Lord Moira, whose seat was at Ballynahinch, County Down had severely criticised the conduct of the army in Ireland but, by common consent, he had been very effectively answered by the Irish Lord Chancellor, the earl of Clare. Abercromby's general orders now proved a powerful counter-weight to Clare's rhetoric: 'They give a great hold to Lord Moira and Co.', wrote Lord Auckland to the archbishop of Cashel; and Pitt was severely embarrassed by them.[90] As a matter of urgency, Portland sought explanations from Camden, and then from Abercromby himself. Why had London not been alerted concerning Abercromby's general orders? Did Camden and Abercromby not realise that Moira and his supporters would see these orders as a complete vindication? Camden claimed that he had felt it best to ignore Abercromby's pronouncements on the grounds that the whole affair was a matter for the military. As for Abercromby, he indignantly rejected the insinuation that he was leagued with Moira, pronounced himself to have lost the confidence of both Camden and his advisors, and determined to resign. Officially, Camden made great efforts to persuade him to stay on, but by the end of March, and in confidence to Pitt, he reported that Abercromby's position had become untenable and that even if he reconsidered 'he would not be attended to' in Ireland.[91] The fact was, if Abercromby's general orders had caused dismay, his subsequent behaviour while campaigning in Leinster had provoked even greater outrage among those who were passionately concerned with security policy in Ireland.

On 14 March 1798, as the furore over his general orders was just beginning, Abercromby was formally ordered to disarm Kildare, Queen's County and King's County. Unlike Lake's campaign in Ulster, however, Abercromby determined that this would be no *dragonnade*. He immediately opened his campaign by issuing a series of commands to his men to maintain strict discipline, to exercise the greatest moderation, and not to go off without an officer. He then sent out thousands of printed proclamations giving the disaffected ten days' notice to bring in their arms or else face free-quarters.[92] This delay was widely criticised: 'There is very general discontent expressed at Abercromby's method of proceeding' wrote Shannon, and Lord Clifden exploded: 'Is Abercrombie [*sic*] turned Jacobin or old woman? I hear the latter!'[93] Moreover, the commander's threat of free-quarters was ridiculed as calculated to hurt the well-to-do more than the disaffected who were poor and had little to lose. In the event, only a small quantity of arms and almost no pikes were recovered.[94] Camden pronounced himself entirely dissatisfied with Abercromby's conduct, though he had to admit that Abercromby's comparatively mild measures had restored order in the counties he visited. By late March, however, Abercromby's

12.1   Operations in County Kildare, 1798. In 1797–1798 the military
authorities in several parts of the country used terror tactics, including
house-burnings, floggings and mass arrests, to quell unrest.

actions were increasingly irrelevant for he had persevered in his determination to
resign his command. A successor was sought. Perhaps Lord Cornwallis, or General
David Dundas or Sir William Howe would take the command? All of these declined
for, following Abercromby's resignation, the Irish command was now out of favour
with the top soldiers. There was nothing for it but to appoint General Gerard Lake,
currently commander in Ulster. Camden had not wanted him for, in his opinion, he
lacked judgement; but Pitt was in a bullish mood. Lake was 'brave, active and, I
believe, popular', he claimed and he argued that his appointment would constitute
the best answer to Abercromby's strictures.[95]

It would be easy to regard Abercromby as the author of his own downfall. He had
issued the general orders without thinking of the consequences on army morale and
regardless of whether they offered encouragement to the enemy to invade or dismay
to those loyalists who were combating insurgency in the countryside. Furthermore,
he had resisted all blandishments to stay and persevered with his initial decision to
quit. When his appointment had been announced, a fellow officer described him
thus: 'He is a soldier and not a politician and I am afraid he will not give

satisfaction. He comes to the country *malgré lui* and [is] in his temper positive and never gives up his own opinion.'[96] So it proved: he could never have seen eye to eye with the Dublin Castle 'junto'; and Camden was glad to see the back of him. 'He leaves Ireland', he wrote, 'having done much mischief here. He has *not* performed the service upon which he was sent to the south with zeal or with ability.' Churlishly, Camden urged that Abercromby be left on ice for a while to teach him a lesson.[97] That said, there are still grounds for arguing that Abercromby's resignation was a tragedy for the country. His scepticism as to the reality of the threat of insurrection could be defended; his concern at the undisciplined state of the Irish forces was entirely justifiable; and his determination to proceed in Ireland as if on a policing operation and not as if he was repressing rebellion was wholly appropriate.

Abercromby's retreat had an effect on the Castle's military policy similar to that brought about in the political sphere by Fitzwilliam's recall three years earlier. Just as the latter's departure meant an end to political concessions so Abercromby's resignation signalled a return to the draconian measures favoured – indeed clamoured for – by Camden's Irish 'cabinet'. 'If we treat rebellion as rebellion, we are safe', wrote Edward Cooke in March 1798, and Lord Clifden reported that he had got Pitt to agree that 'terror could only be repressed by stronger terror'.[98] On 30 March all Ireland was formally proclaimed under the Insurrection Act and the following day Pitt indicated the strategy now to be pursued: Camden was told 'to make a speedy and (as far as circumstances will admit) a well-concerted effort for crushing the rebellion by the most vigorous military exertions in all the disturbed provinces'. Moreover, he was not to concern himself unduly with army discipline.[99] In his turn, General Lake was ordered to abandon free-quarters as a weapon and to 'adopt such *other vigorous and effectual measures* for enforcing the speedy surrender of arms'. Flogging, house-burning and torture were now employed on a large scale. 'We are out every day foraging [i.e. harrying] and burning the houses of known rebels', wrote Lord Clifden on duty with his Yeomanry corps in Kilkenny in early May.[100] Sir Benjamin Chapman later recalled to his correspondent, Lord Shelburne, how he had gone to a cold dinner at a friend's house some 5 miles distant from Trim, County Meath.

> What a dessert had we to our frugal repast! [he wrote] The sudden and shocking exhibition from our windows of the perspective of a conflagration of the surrounding mansions, of farmers and peasants flying for shelter in all directions and unexpectedly involved in this dreadful calamity; a regiment of Scotch Fencibles enjoyed this savage triumph and fired upon the fugitives while thirty wretched houses . . . with every sort of provision, rustic furniture and implements of husbandry were all consumed by the merciless flames before our eyes. I could hear no reason save that a robbery had been attempted without success a few days before on a gentleman in that vicinage.

Flogging especially was employed to elicit confessions and to force the prisoner to divulge where arms were concealed. Even those most in favour of 'firmness', such

---

12.2 The seizing of Lord Edward Fitzgerald, leader of the military
committee of the United Irishmen, in a house in Thomas Street, Dublin, on
19 May 1798. He died on 4 June of wounds sustained during the struggle.

as Lord Shannon (who recommended shooting ten hostages for every loyalist
casualty), conceded that 'the cat is laid on with uncommon severity'; but against
that it was acknowledged that 'by proper flagellation quantities of arms have been
given up'. The bishop of Killaloe on the Clare/Tipperary border claimed that 1,500
pikes had been seized in his area but that now Major Wilford was 'determined to try
what flogging may do' to uncover more.[101]

It seems clear that Dublin Castle viewed with equanimity the possibility of open
rebellion – even welcomed the prospect of a secret conspiracy becoming an
open contest. Convinced as it was that some 200,000 United Irishmen and Defenders
remained sworn into the conspiracy how else could they be crushed save in open
confrontation? As early as May 1797, Camden had told Portland that 'I shall not
lament the attempt at insurrection. It will enable us to act with effect.'[102] A
year later, when news arrived of the seizure of the mail coaches on the night of
23/24 May – the signal for insurrection – swiftly followed by reports of open
fighting in Kildare and elsewhere, the initial reaction of Dublin Castle was far from
alarmist. This rebellion, wrote Cooke, '[is] really the salvation of the country' and
the former lord lieutenant, Westmorland agreed. 'I am glad the explosion has burst',

he told the Archbishop of Cashel, 'and trust you will soon be restored to quiet which could not be expected after the seditious spirit was become so universal without considerable examples.' Camden, however, now struck a cautionary note for the clamour for 'examples' caused him alarm. Already in March 1798 he had drawn attention to the emergence of 'the most extravagant party prejudices . . . calling the present conspiracy a Popish plot'; and within a few days of the outbreak of the rebellion he would report that 'savage cruelties . . . party and religious prejudice has literally made the Protestant part of the country mad'. Ominously, he added, 'the army partake of the fury'.[103]

8

In the circumstances the wonder was that the United Irishmen should have been in a position to stage any sort of insurrection in May 1798. Two years of relentless harrying by government forces had taken its toll on membership, leadership and morale. By May 1798 the prospect of French help seemed forlorn as Bonaparte fixed his gaze on Egypt and directed his forces thither; and that substitute 'army' of disaffected and suborned Irish soldiers which the United Irishmen had counted on, remained entirely notional. In March 1798, moreover, United Irish plans for an insurrection had been dealt a devastating blow by the arrest in Oliver Bond's house in Dublin of almost the entire Leinster leadership. Admittedly, the charismatic Lord Edward Fitzgerald had remained at large, but within a few weeks he too was captured. The United Irishmen were now deprived of his name and, as important, his military leadership and experience. Fitzgerald had served as an officer in the British army and had seen himself as the commander of the insurgent forces. He had clearly dressed for the part: 'Lord Edward's uniform was taken with him', wrote Shannon, 'green cloth, crimson welts down the seams, crimson velvet cap, the cloth and velvet manifestly French, and a green cape.'[104] A further blow to the United Irishmen came with the arrest of John and Henry Sheares who, it appears, following the capture of the old leadership, had taken it upon themselves to organise a rising in Dublin. Aptly described by R. B. MacDowell as 'very energetic, courageous and incompetent conspirators', the Sheares brothers had sought to mobilise the allegedly disaffected troops in the army camp at Loughlinstown. Most unwisely, they took an army officer, Captain John Armstrong of the King's County Militia, into their confidence, and he had delivered them up to the authorities. The Castle was thereby alerted and the capital was quickly made secure.[105] As a result of these early and very disruptive arrests, the Rising when it came was distinguished by a lack of coordination and a lack of focus. Moreover, it tended to be conducted by local leaders with local reputations, rather than by the better known principals, now dead or in prison.

At 10 p.m. on the night of 24 May 1798, Camden, on receipt of the news of open rebellion, wrote excitedly to Portland: 'Martial law is established – the sword is

---

drawn – I have kept it within the scabbard as long as possible – it must not be returned until this most alarming conspiracy is put down'.[106] That night the rebels in County Kildare launched attacks on Prosperous, Naas and Kilcullen bridge and though initially successful they were eventually forced to retreat with heavy casualties. At Naas, where the rebels were led by Michael Reynolds 'whose house we burned some days ago' about 200 of them were killed against military casualties of 6 dead and 12 wounded.[107] The proportion of rebel dead to government casualties was even greater elsewhere. On 24 May, General Lake had issued the order to his commanders to 'take no prisoners' and a day later General Dundas, following the engagement at Kilcullen, reported 'about one hundred and thirty [rebel] dead – no prisoners'; miraculously there were no casualties on the government side, killed or wounded. Ironically, Dundas soon came under strong criticism for permitting rebels to surrender at the Curragh: 'It was the general opinion here,' wrote one commentator that 'they should all have been put to death.' By contrast, his fellow officer, General Duff, with his troops earned the approval of the Dublin Castle 'cabinet' for falling upon rebels who had surrendered at the same place and killing several hundred of them; and there was little criticism of the decision to execute without trial thirty-four allegedly disaffected Yeomen at Dunlavin, or of the massacre of some thirty-eight prisoners at Carnew, both in County Wicklow. As reports came in of rebel atrocities, Camden reported that loyalists 'are so exasperated as scarcely to be satisfied with anything short of extirpation'. By the end of the first week of the fighting Kildare had been secured and Dublin saved from attack. There was a strict curfew in force in the city, and it was reported that 'scarce a cat could steal into this large metropolis at night' because of the ring of troops ('so close . . . that they can almost converse with each other') drawn up around the city.[108]

A few days after the rising in Kildare and adjoining counties, serious disturbances were reported from Wexford. At Oulart in the north of the county a detachment of the North Cork Militia was cut to pieces and this victory electrified the county, tempting many to join in who might otherwise have hung back. On 29 May, the insurgents, gaining strength as they advanced, stormed Enniscorthy and the next day Wexford town fell. But at this point the rebellion in Wexford lost direction; later attacks on New Ross, Newtownbarry and at Arklow were repulsed with much slaughter – perhaps 300 rebel dead at Arklow, 500 at Newtownbarry, and possibly 2,500 at New Ross. This last rebel defeat was a desperately close one. The fall of New Ross could have ignited the entire south-central area of Ireland and would have certainly opened the way for the rebels to move into Waterford and threaten Cork. In years to come, Miles Byrne, a rebel captain and later *Chef de Bataillon* in Bonaparte's army, would bitterly lament the decision to make for Wexford rather than New Ross after the fall of Enniscorthy, for it gave the crown forces a vital few days within which to fortify this gateway to the south.[109] For a time, the result of the battle hung in the balance. The rebels had attacked in force, 'shouting and

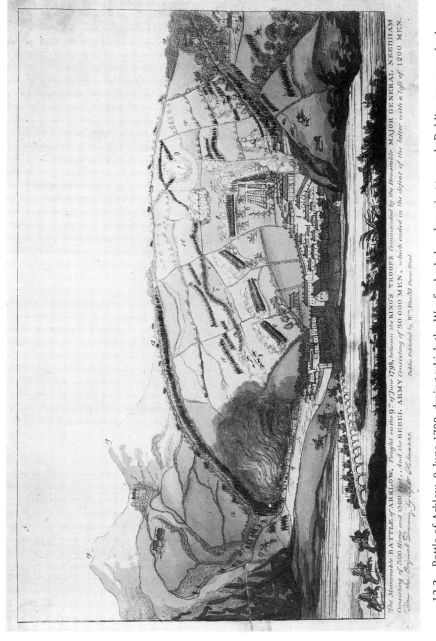

The Memorable BATTLE of ARKLOW, Fought on the 9.th of June 1798, between the KING'S TROOPS Commanded by the Honorable MAJOR GENERAL NEEDHAM Consisting of 300 Horse and 1500 Foot, And the REBEL ARMY Consisting of 30.000 MEN, which ended in the defeat of the latter with a loss of 1200 MEN.

From the Original Drawing of J.P. Salmon 235

Dublin Published by W.m Allen 32 Dame Street.

12.3   Battle of Arklow, 9 June 1798, during which the Wexford rebels, advancing towards Dublin, were repulsed.

driving cattle before them' and forcing the defenders to fall back before the enormous press of rebel pikemen. During the battle, the attackers displayed reckless courage while sustaining grievous casualties. 'I never saw any troops attack with more enthusiasm and bravery than the rebels did on the 5th', wrote Lieutenant-Colonel Robert Craufurd a few days after the battle.[110] The defence of the town had been entrusted to detachments of the Dublin Militia, Midlothian Fencibles, Donegal Militia, Clare Militia, Meath Militia and detachments of artillery and cavalry (mostly 5th Dragoons), all under the command of General Johnson, an Irish officer, and these soldiers fought bravely also. Official returns listed ninety soldiers killed and fifty-seven wounded.[111] In the end, artillery had decided the battle, and the rebels had been forced to retreat. The rebels, however, were by no means routed and a few days later they split into two columns and advanced on Arklow to the north. Once again the insurgents acquitted themselves well: in Byrne's opinion 'our very irregular troops against a regular and disciplined English army' might have carried the day but for some confusion over orders.[112] In the event, after much slaughter, the rebels were forced to withdraw and without clear objectives they fell back to regroup at the vantage point of Vinegar Hill.

While rebellion had been raging in the south-east, the north generally had been quiet. On receipt of news of the fighting in Leinster, there was a stormy meeting of the Ulster Provincial Council of the United Irishmen, at which there were loud protests at the failure to rise in support. The existing leadership was accused (by Henry Joy McCracken and John Hughes, both of Belfast) of having 'completely betrayed the people both of Leinster and Ulster' and it was promptly deposed. McCracken's strictures were largely misplaced. The United Irishmen's plan for insurrection had called for Dublin to be sealed off by risings in the surrounding counties; the city would be taken and reinforcements prevented from reaching it. It was the failure of this strategy that now fuelled demands for a rising in the north of Ireland. What had been hitherto seen as a diversion or sideshow to the main event in the Dublin area was now thrust into prominence.

Following McCracken's outburst the military command of the United Irishmen in Ulster was reorganised and plans were hurriedly made for a rising. Out of twenty-three existing United Irish colonels in Antrim only two had declared for action, 'the other 21 would not act on any plan but on the invasion of the French or success to the efforts of the insurgents about Dublin'.[113] New men, McCracken among them, were now appointed. Word of these stirrings reached Dublin Castle: 'I hear there is a buzz in parts of the north which I like not,' wrote Edward Cooke on 31 May, but it was not until 7 June that General Nugent received word that an attack on Antrim was likely. He moved swiftly and took up many prisoners: none the less, the rebels managed to capture Antrim for a few hours but were then driven out 'with great slaughter' by artillery fire. There were attacks on Larne, Carrickfergus and Glenarm; but none of these amounted to much and the Antrim rebels lost heart and began drifting home.

Meanwhile, the United Irishmen in north Down were attempting to assemble their forces at Saintfield. It was, however, at Ballynahinch a few miles distant on 12–13 June that they were routed by Nugent and several hundred were killed, many of them as they sought to hide in the woods of Lord Moira's estate nearby. General Henry Monroe, the rebel commander, was taken and a few days later hanged outside his front door. Nugent lost only three men and listed some thirty wounded. Much grim amusement was derived from Moira's discomfiture at the number of rebel dead in his pleasure park, for he had been the principal critic of Dublin Castle's counter-insurgency policy. With heavy sarcasm, Cooke reported that 'the countenances of his Lordship's tenants were beaming with loyalty' on the arrival of General Nugent before Moira's gutted mansion.[114]

In the end, very few of the United Irishmen in either Antrim or Down had actually been prepared for combat in 1798 principally, it would seem, because the United Irish military plan had centred on Dublin. In addition, government action in 1796–7 had undoubtedly severely disrupted their organisation; and it is possible that the 'treatment of France to Switzerland and America' had caused a loss of enthusiasm for either a French landing or French principles. Those that did turn out rarely displayed any significant military talent, indeed scarcely appeared to know what to do. One rebel commander of 'The Republican Army of the County Down', from his later exile in the United States, described his campaign in and around north Down thus: 'Instead of the [rebel] forces meeting at any point in collected and organised bodies, they met rather more by accident than design and they were in no better order than a *country mob* . . . when thus assembled, without provisions, without officers and without any military subordination.' It is possible that, as Cooke put it, 'the Popish tinge in the Rebellion' had induced second thoughts among the Presbyterian rebels, causing them to hang back.[115] Certainly, on the night before the battle of Ballynahinch there was a revealing incident when the rebel commanders, the Presbyterian Monroe and the Catholic Magennis disputed the overall command. Monroe finally drew his sword and allegedly 'did declare aloud his intentions was [sic] to establish a presbiterian [sic] independent government after the begun revolution would become compleated'. Magennis was understandably unimpressed with this objective, and he and his men reportedly stole away during the night.[116]

With the rebels scattered in the north, attention shifted once again to those in Wexford and plans were laid to attack their camp at Vinegar Hill. Reinforcements from England had by this time begun arriving in Ireland (9,000 infantry and cavalry by mid-June) and these made easier Lake's plan to assemble the army that would finally crush the rebellion in Wexford and, as the newly appointed chief secretary, Lord Castlereagh, had urged, 'make the rebels there an example to the rest of the kingdom'.[117] Lake was no Bonaparte, but then, he did not need to be; the rebels had played into his hands by their decision to encamp on Vinegar Hill. Years later, Miles Byrne pondered the question: 'How could our leaders for a instant think

---

12.4 'Antient Brittons' (Welsh Fencibles) cut to pieces near Carnew, County Wicklow, by the Insurgents, 1798 (Sadler, 1868).

that Vinegar Hill was a military position susceptible of defence for any time without provisions, military stores or great guns?'[118] By 20 June, Lake had assembled an army of some 20,000 and a vast array of artillery before the rebel encampment. This had not been easy; Lake's subordinate commanders had frequent cause for complaint about his 'extraordinary and contradictory orders' and the indiscipline of the soldiers also hampered his plans.[119] General Francis Needham, fresh from his triumph at Arklow, reported that his troops were too exhausted to go to Vinegar Hill for they had wasted their energies in killing 'above 100 fugitives on their way here [about six miles from Vinegar Hill] this day whom they found conceal'd in ditches'. Ironically, Needham's failure to close the ring around Vinegar Hill was to allow the rebels to retreat in tolerable order after the battle.[120]

On 21 June, General Lake attempted to surround Vinegar Hill with four columns of soldiers in order to prevent a rebel breakout. Battle was then joined. It lasted about two hours: the rebels were mercilessly shelled; once again artillery carried the day. 'The rebels made a tolerable good fight of it', wrote Lake, and then pronounced the 'carnage . . . dreadful' among them; hundreds may have fallen on the field of battle, many of them camp followers. In his dispatch announcing his victory, Lake singled out the commander of the Mid-Lothian Fencibles, Lord Ancram, for special praise for his conduct during the battle and his men soon found themselves singing a new regimental song:

12.5   Queen's Own Royal Dublin Militia going into action at Vinegar Hill,
near Enniscorthy, County Wicklow (Sadler, 1879).

Ye croppies of Wexford, I'd have ye be wise
and go not to meddle with Mid-Lothian Boys
For the Mid-Lothian Boys they vow and declare
They'll crop off your head as well as your hair
derry, down down
Remember at Ross and at Vinegar Hill
How your heads flew about like chaff in a mill
For the Mid-Lothian Boys when a croppy they see
they blow out his daylights and tip him cut three
derry, down down[121]

The rebels fought until their ammunition ran out, and then began their retreat –
northwards towards Wicklow or, first southwards to Wexford via 'Needham's gap',
and then westwards into Kilkenny. As they retreated, rebel discipline collapsed in
some places. Already, after the reverse at New Ross, about 100 civilians (almost
all Protestant) had been burnt to death in a barn at Scullabogue; and now after
the defeat at Vinegar Hill about 70 Protestant prisoners were piked to death on the
bridge at Wexford town. The army repaid these atrocities with interest: a makeshift
rebel hospital with some 80 wounded inside was set on fire by the troops and all
inside perished. In general, the mopping up operations after Vinegar Hill resembled,

12.6   Vinegar Hill: charge of the 5th Dragoon Guards (Sadler, 1879).

to the fury of the new lord lieutenant, Lord Cornwallis, universal rape, plunder and murder. These punitive operations continued for some weeks and there were occasional ferocious skirmishes, notably at Baltinglass (thirty carloads of rebel dead carried away) and Kilconnel Hill in Wicklow (General Asgill claimed 1,000 rebels killed), and at Kilbeggan in Meath (30–40 rebel casualties): but the first act of the 'open' rebellion was over.

The second act opened with the arrival of a French force of some 1,100 men under the command of General Humbert in late August.[122] Camden had long forecast that disturbances in Ireland 'would probably tempt even a small force from France', but as the summer passed and the rebellion was crushed, the threat of invasion seemed to recede. Humbert's successful landing therefore came as a shock, but an even greater one lay in store. The French quickly secured Ballina and then, picking up local allies, they advanced on Castlebar, routing their march through the mountains instead of, as anticipated by Lake, along the Foxford road. Very rashly, Lake with his mixed force of mostly Irish Militia, but with English and Scottish Fencibles and some regulars in support, offered battle and opened fire with his artillery. Those Irish who had joined the French promptly ran, but French veterans of Italy and the Vendée were not so easily intimidated and, forming themselves into two columns, they bayonet-charged the Irish force. This time the Irish (and the Scots and the English) in Lake's army broke in panic and fled the field.

Those who had long doubted the reliability of the Irish Militia in an emergency had their doubts confirmed. The defeat at Castlebar proved to be a turning point in the deployment of the Irish Militia for they were never really trusted by Dublin Castle thereafter. But there is no need to choose disaffection as the explanation for the defeat and flight of Lake's force; and there are mitigating circumstances which help set the defeat in an appropriate context. It is true that the Irish army out-numbered the French by over two to one (1,700 to 800) but Lake's forces were mostly 'half soldiers' who were probably half-trained as well. With a force thus composed it was most unwise of Lake to risk a pitched battle with French veterans. Moreover, while Lord Auckland may have ranked the 'Castlebar catastrophe' with Burgoyne's disgrace at Saratoga, twenty years earlier, in the amount of shock and surprise it caused, other commentators took a more dispassionate view. William Wickham at the Foreign Office, an experienced observer of the military revolution of the 1790s consoled Castlereagh in Dublin Castle by pointing out that better troops had fled before the French:

> I have seen so much of the enemy you have to deal with and know so well all the tricks he has in store to terrify those who are not acquainted with them that I shall not wonder if some of your best regiments should be a little *astonished* at this new kind of warfare.[123]

It is also true that a number of Militiamen who fled the field in panic subsequently joined the French. Lake reported a figure of some 278 men missing after the battle of whom 158 were from the Longford Militia, 44 from the Kilkenny Militia and 33 from the Galway Volunteers. A small proportion of these (probably no more than 60) appear to have gone over to the French but some of them claimed later that they had joined Humbert under duress, and certainly some deserted from the French soon after. But the remainder – the large majority – seem simply to have fled in terror and to have taken advantage of the confusion to desert. Almost certainly, many more joined one of the bands of robbers abounding at that time than marched with Humbert.[124] Finally, the aftermath of the battle offered the Castle some further cause for consolation. According to every prediction 'the races of Castlebar', for so the battle was dubbed by the wags, ought to have ignited the whole of Ireland into insurrection, but this did not happen and the signal victory in the end turned out to be rather an empty triumph.

In the days following the defeat of Lake at Castlebar, a large force of perhaps 20,000 men converged on Humbert's army. General George Nugent moved his men to Enniskillen, County Fermanagh, to block any move into Ulster: and Adjutant-General Hewett oversaw the assembling of an impressive army from the south and south-east at Portumna, County Galway. A large 'hospital squad' consisting of seven covered wagons with 'hospital bedding, medecines, instruments etc., etc.' left Dublin under escort for Athlone. In the west, Colonel Craufurd, later the distinguished commander of the Light Brigade in the Peninsular War, dogged

Humbert's footsteps and harried his rear while, off the western coast, British frigates patrolled constantly in order to see off any French attempt at reinforcing the French expeditionary force.[125] Finally, Cornwallis, the commander-in-chief, made his way 'with extraordinary, perhaps with excess of caution' to Tuam, County Galway to take command.[126] His unlucky predecessor, General Abercromby, at this time preparing for military adventures in Egypt, was mildly critical of all this: 'It is mortifying to military pride to see the lord lieutenant and the first officer in our service marching in person against 1,500 men, and yet', he conceded, 'I believe it was necessary'.[127] Castlebar had delivered a salutary lesson: the rebels and their French allies were to be denied a second victory. Starved of reinforcements and well aware that Cornwallis's force was closing in, Humbert moved north, then east, then ran out of steam. With his Irish allies becoming impossible to control, his own soldiers growing daily more mutinous, with no hope of reinforcements and with little expectation of any significant insurrection in support, surrender was the only option available to him. On 8 September at Ballinamuck, County Longford, the French force laid down its arms. Honourable terms had been offered to Humbert and his men – indeed the French officers were fêted on their arrival in Dublin – but no such terms were offered to their Irish allies and they were scattered 'with much slaughter'.

The rebellion appeared to be finally over. The rebels had failed because they lacked coordination and because, with one or two exceptions, their leaders had had no time to instil even a modicum of military discipline and training into the numbers that flocked to them. They generally lacked both a leadership structure and a coherent strategy with the result that it was often difficult or impossible, so Miles Byrne claimed, to know who had given which order and for what reason.[128] The failure to take Dublin and then the staggered outbreak of the rebellion played into the government's hands: 'We may be thankful', wrote Lord Auckland, 'that the insurgents have acted so little in unison and have presented us with the means of [beating?] them seriatim and separately.'[129] Dublin Castle had thus ridden out the storm and it derived some consolation from the fact that the rebellion had been crushed by Irish troops before substantial English reinforcements had arrived. But there was little else to rejoice about. Perhaps 25,000 rebels (including a high proportion of non-combatants) and some hundreds of soldiers had been slain and large areas of the country had been effectively laid waste. Such destruction and ruination were, wrote one traveller, 'the joint labours of rebellion and loyalty, soldiers and insurgents making a common cause of devastation'.[130]

It was understandable that in the aftermath of the rebellion there was much talk of providence and good fortune, lessons and examples. Lord Shannon hoped that the 'examples made . . . will give the gentry [i.e. rebels] a surfeit of rebellion and quiet us for 100 years to come', and Sir John Hort, active in a military capacity in the north-west of Ireland, reckoned that 'as the former lesson to rebels held by my computation about 110 years', he was certain, he told his correspondent, that 'that to which you and other gentlemen have so nobly contributed will I trust serve them for the whole of the century which is to finish with A.D. 2000'.[131] Others were not so confident of lessons having been learnt. 'The people of Ireland are, and *will long continue* to be ripe for general insurrection', wrote Colonel Craufurd, adding 'it is not in the nature of things that men's minds should become less influenced in consequence of the chastisement inflicted on them by the successful part in a civil war.' The former lord lieutenant, Westmorland, also had his doubts: rebellion had been put down 'for the present in Ireland, but unless we can root out the spirit, I fear', he told the archbishop of Cashel, 'you will always be suspect upon a favourable opportunity to these explosions'. Even Cornwallis concluded reluctantly that Britain should for strategic purposes consider 'the majority of the Irish people as enemies and employ a large proportion of the force which ought to act against a foreign invader to keep our own countrymen in subjection'.[132]

The 1798 rebellion, and its aftermath, shattered existing relationships within Ireland, awakening atavistic fears and evoking memories of 1641. The very fact that a rebellion had occurred at all also called into question the future of the Irish political structure. In a notable departure from precedent that revealed clearly the close connection between military and political affairs, Camden's successor, Cornwallis, had been appointed both commander-in-chief *and* lord lieutenant, and he had been charged not only with crushing the rebellion but also with seizing the opportunity the crisis offered to put through a legislative union between Ireland and England. The Irish parliament was to be another casualty of the 1798 rebellion, part innocent victim but also part conspirator. Union was duly accomplished in January 1801.

The rebellion may have been crushed but disturbances continued in the years after 1798, notably in County Wicklow where Michael Dwyer and his band remained 'masters of the mountains' defying all efforts to capture them or make them surrender.[133] Moreover, despite the failure of 1798 there remained in place (more accurately, in prison, at Fort George in Scotland) a United Irish leadership which sought to draw appropriate lessons from the experiences of 1798. Robert Emmet, a brother of one of the leaders of the rebellion, was the leader of those revolutionaries who urged that an insurrection centring on Dublin could have a chance of success. Great secrecy was enjoined on the few who were privy to Emmet's plans: stores of explosives, including rockets, were acquired; and emissaries, among them Thomas Russell, were sent off to make preparations in their own areas.[134] In the end ill-luck as much as anything contrived to foil Emmet. An explosion in one of his munition dumps in Dublin in July 1803 forced Emmet and his men to rise up prematurely and they were easily crushed; but Dublin Castle was shocked at its intelligence failure.[135] Shortly after Emmet's execution, Dwyer who had been heavily involved in his schemes, surrendered and was subsequently transported to Australia. The 1798 rebellion, it may be said, was now finally over.

———

12.7 'Hunted Down – '98', J. F. O'Hea (1885). A dramatic representation of heroic Irish resistance in the face of overwhelming odds.

12.8   1798 Centenary Certificate, showing the escape of Michael Dwyer,
who remained at liberty until surrendering in December 1803. The
document certifies that the holder is a member of the 1798 Commemoration
Committee in County Wicklow, and adds 'Remember 1798'.

9

It only remains for us to consider the military lessons that were drawn from the experience of the 1790s. Insurgency between 1798 and 1803 prompted a vital change in the composition of the force which would garrison and police Ireland in the future. Put simply, whereas in the 1790s the Irish Militia had been in the vanguard of the Irish defence forces, after 1800, and especially after 1803, this position was taken by the Irish Yeomanry. This shift was of great political significance.

As previously noted, the formation of a largely Catholic Militia in 1793 had represented an act of faith on the part of Pitt and his advisers, over the serious misgivings of Dublin Castle, that such a force could be trusted to protect Ireland against both invaders and insurgents. That faith had been justified in the main: the Militia's record in the field was a fairly creditable one. But their notorious indiscipline, their reputed disaffection (however exaggerated), their disgrace at Castlebar (however unmerited) and perhaps more influential than anything, their overwhelming Catholic composition had forced a reappraisal of their role. No

12.9 'A scout of '98' (*Weekly Freeman*, 19 December 1891). A late-
nineteenth-century vision of the passionate commitment offered by Irish
patriots – women as well as men – to the national cause in 1798.

formal decision was taken regarding them: instead one emerged in the aftermath of the rebellion. In July 1799, in reviewing the future defence needs of Ireland, Cornwallis effectively dismissed the Irish Militia as worthless. 'I need not tell you', he informed Dundas, 'how little dependence is to be placed on the Irish Militia serving in their own country.'[136] From this point on the role of the Irish Militia in the defence of Ireland appears to have been brought to a close. In 1807, Sir Arthur Wellesley, then chief secretary, reported that from the point of view of defence, the Irish Militia was more of an embarrassment than anything else. In a long memorandum reviewing the defence needs of Ireland, Wellesley envisaged a mixed force of regulars and yeomanry dealing with a possible invasion. Nowhere was there mention of a role for the Irish Militia. 'In respect to the Militia', he wrote, 'the general opinion is that they are disaffected and that they ought to be disbanded or removed from the country.'[137] This latter suggestion had already been taken up by government and from 1800 on the Irish Militia's primary role had been as 'a nursery for the regulars'. Bounties were offered to encourage Militiamen to enter the regular service and by 1805 some 3,000 a year were passing into the line regiments.[138] In 1811 the Militia Interchange Act authorised the removal from Ireland of up to one third (around 10,000 men) of the Irish Militia on an annual basis to serve in Great Britain and their replacement with English and Scottish militia regiments.[139]

Military exigencies were the ostensible reason for this act, and indeed for the whole policy of recruiting from the Irish Militia: but there were also important political considerations which though rarely openly avowed, carried great weight. Once Catholic Emancipation had been denied in 1800, a denial reaffirmed throughout the war years and after, then there was no alternative but for the Irish government to become exclusively committed, as Edward Cooke put it, to Protestant principles, and in this scheme of things the Irish Militia, a largely Catholic force, was an anomaly, at best an embarrassment in Ireland, at worst a standing threat. The avowedly Protestant state created by the Union could not feel at ease so long as its protection lay largely in the hands of a Catholic force. Inevitably that state came to rely on the Yeomanry. This force may have been as undisciplined as the Irish Militia, and it certainly had had some cases of disaffection during the 1798 rebellion, but such blemishes could be ignored, for the Yeomanry, unlike the Militia, were perceived to be indisputably loyal. By 1800, and largely as a result of the rebellion, loyal had become synonymous with Protestant, and disaffected with Catholic. There had been 'Catholic' Yeomanry corps during the late 1790s but the trend had been unmistakably to protestantise the force and after 1800 it seemed to be almost a settled principle to exclude Catholics. As the Yeomanry became more Protestant, its size increased from an initial establishment of about 30,000 in 1797 to nearly 60,000 in 1805. Over the same period its function also changed: it became more like a fencible force, that is, light troops on permanent duty for the duration of the war and not limited to their own immediate area for service. Moreover, brigade-majors for each county were appointed by Dublin Castle, and through them the whole yeomanry establishment was controlled at national level, making it a flexible instrument in the event of invasion or rebellion. Certainly during the abortive rising in Dublin and other places planned and led by Emmet in 1803, the Yeomanry proved its worth. Those who had predicted on the formation of the Yeomanry in 1796 that loyalists would flock into it were vindicated, for the force embodied the spirit of the Protestant state of the early nineteenth century. In 1807, Lord Castlereagh pointed with great satisfaction to 'the great increase of determined and zealous loyalists since the commencement of the Yeomanry armament', and he very astutely ascribed this increase 'to no cause more decidedly than . . . the influence of that institution itself'.[140] Moreover, if the Yeomanry can be regarded as the military expression of the Protestant nation, then so too can the Irish Militia be seen as that of the Catholic nation. Catholic leaders certainly regarded the Irish Militia as 'their' army in pointed contrast to the 'Protestant' Yeomanry. Daniel O'Connell, for example, bitterly opposed the Militia Interchange Act of 1811, on the grounds that by transferring large numbers of the 'Catholic' Militia to England, it would undoubtedly weaken the Catholic cause in Ireland.[141] Equally, Dublin Castle, alarmed at reports that priests were urging the Militiamen to sign Catholic petitions, was glad to see the departure for England on an annual basis of a large proportion of the 'Catholic' Irish Militia.[142] None of these developments augured well for the future of the Union. In 1795 Edmund Burke had poured scorn on those who prattled on about the merits of the Irish constitution: in the absence of 'a prudent and enlightened policy' he thundered, 'you may call your constitution what you will; in effect it will consist of three parts (orders, if you please) – cavalry, infantry and artillery'.[143] Post-rebellion Ireland and post-Union (and post-Emmet) Ireland bade fair to have a similar military constitution.

Chapter 13

Irish soldiers abroad,
1600-1800

Harman Murtagh

D'imthigh Clanna Néill thar sáile
'S ta Éire cráidhte ó d'imthigh siad
Acht déanfaidh uibheacha iolair iolraidh
Cibé an áit i ngorthar iad.[1]

Contingents of soldiers from Ireland occasionally served overseas in the Middle Ages. They included the hobelars and other forces of Edward I's wars against the Scots, various groups in the Hundred Years War and the kerne employed in France by Henry VIII.[2] In the nineteenth and twentieth centuries Irish military involvement abroad has largely been with the regular armies of the English-speaking world. A sustained process of large-scale military migration to mainland Europe only occurred in the seventeenth and eighteenth centuries. Soldiers were not the sole migrants of that period, but they were the most significant group in terms of numbers and repute. The diaspora was predominantly of Roman Catholics, impelled by their military defeats in Ireland, the ensuing social and economic deprivation of the plantations, and related political and religious repression. The endemic warfare of late Tudor Ireland and the two major upheavals of the seventeenth century furnished a pool of military manpower in need of redeployment which was recruited by officers of local Catholic gentry background. Initially the process was encouraged by a government concerned to rid the country of 'idle swordsmen'. Ireland became a major source of mercenaries to serve on the Continent and in the burgeoning European colonies in North America, India and North Africa. Irish Protestants served to some extent in the armies of European powers and in British India, but especially in the military formations of the American colonies where, for mainly economic reasons, they settled in large numbers during the eighteenth century. The establishment abroad of a network of Irish families, settlements and permanent military units generated its own supply of military personnel, as well as facilitating further migration from Ireland.

The scale of European warfare was transformed in the seventeenth 'century of crisis', and out of the harsh experience of the Thirty Years War there was a shift from dependency on the rabbles furnished by venal military contractors to 'standing' armies, raised by 'absolutist' rulers who developed the financial and material resources to maintain such forces on a permanent basis. The standing armies were refined and improved in the eighteenth century, and in many cases substantially expanded to give the soldier and his officer greatly increased and more secure employment, as well as better discipline and professional competence. It has been estimated, for example, that although a new man made a passable soldier within twelve months, it took six years to mould a really steady infantryman.[3]

The migration commenced with the exodus of significant numbers of Munster Irish to Spain and Portugal after the crushing of the Desmond rebellion in 1583. Some entered Spanish military service and at least 200 participated in the great Armada of 1588.[4] About the same time 600 'idle Irish' were recruited to serve in Flanders with the Dutch against the king of Spain. Sir William Stanley, their commander, was an English Catholic who changed sides with his regiment in 1587.[5] The unit was disbanded in 1600 following tension between English officers and their Irish rank and file who served thereafter in independent companies under Irish captains. Another wave of migration followed the defeat at Kinsale. In 1605 the groups of Irish soldiers in Spanish Flanders were consolidated in an Irish regiment under Colonel Henry O'Neill, the Salamanca educated second son of the earl of Tyrone.[6] Throughout its existence Tyrone's, as it became, was always under the command of an O'Neill. In 1649 it was claimed that this regiment had suffered more than 12,000 casualties in Spanish service 'most of them at the point of the sword'.[7] The demands of the Thirty Years War on Spanish manpower caused at least five further Hispano-Irish regiments to be formed between 1632 and 1646. These were the earl of Tyrconnell's, Owen Roe O'Neill's, Thomas Preston's, Patrick FitzGerald's and John Murphy's. Further Irish regiments entered the Spanish service from the private armies of the prince de Condé and the duke of Lorraine. The Irish soldiers brought to Flanders their ancient antipathies: an O'Donnell would not serve under an O'Neill, and there was feuding and antagonism between Old English and Old Irish personified in the bitter rivalry of their leading protagonists, Colonel Thomas Preston, the defender of Louvain and Genappe, and Colonel Owen Roe O'Neill, the hero of the defence of Arras. Colonel Garret Barry's lengthy *Discourse of military discipline*, published in Brussels in 1634, is the earliest significant contribution by an Irishman to military thought.

The Cromwellian conquest of Ireland precipitated a fresh migration of Irish soldiers to the Continent in the 1650s. Once again, the exodus occurred with government authorisation as part of the process of pacification. Over 30,000 fighting men left in a score or more of regiments, commanded by prominent ex-Confederate officers. France and Spain were still at war and competed for their services. True to the mercenary tradition, the Irish sometimes responded to a better offer by changing sides. The most notorious example occurred in 1653 when Colonel Richard Grace, who had been a leading figure in the final phase of the Irish war, passed over with his regiment from the Spanish to the French service in Catalonia during the siege of Gerona. This embarrassing defection moved the remaining Irish colonels in Spain to protest strongly their loyalty to King Philip IV, apparently with success.[8] Employment for most of the Irish soldiers ended with the peace of 1659 and Charles II's restoration the following year enabled many to return to Ireland. The sole Irish regiments then retained by Spain were those of Tyrone, commanded for a time by a grandson of Owen Roe O'Neill, and of Hugh Balldearg O'Donnell, whom the Spaniards recognised as earl of Tyrconnell. Both were disbanded in the 1680s.

The Succession war reintroduced Irish units into the Spanish army from France. The dragoon regiments of Daniel O'Mahony and Henry Crofton dated, respectively, from 1703 and 1705.[9] Four Irish infantry regiments taken on to the Spanish establishment in 1709, and a fifth (formerly Bourke's) which transferred from the French service in 1715, were given the titles Hibernia, Ultonia (Ulster), Limerick, Waterford and Irlanda.[10] For a time there was also a short-lived Momonia (Munster) regiment. Waterford became the second battalion of Irlanda in 1733. Limerick transferred to the Neapolitan service in 1735 where it continued as the Regimiento del Rey.[11] Irlanda, Ultonia and Hibernia remained in Spanish service throughout the eighteenth century during which they bore the harp on their colours and continued to wear the red uniforms of the Stuart tradition. From 1802 they were dressed in light blue.

Spain, even in decline, remained the centre of a great empire. The eighteenth-century Hispano-Irish regiments fought not only on the Peninsula, but in Flanders, Italy, Sicily, Minorca, North Africa and Spanish America. Amongst their best-known engagements were the bloody battles of Campo Santo and Velletri in Italy in the 1740s after which they were granted the proud motto *In omnes terras exivit sonitus eorum* (Their sound hath gone forth into all the earth).[12] Ultonia's steadfast defence of Gerona in 1808–9 is still commemorated in that city. The Spanish military orders enrolled almost 200 knights of Irish origin.[13] A number of Irish officers had careers of distinction and rose to high rank in Spain. Count Daniel O'Mahony won renown at the battle of Almanza (1707) and became a lieutenant general. The romantic Jacobite hero, Charles Wogan, distinguished himself against the Moors in North Africa at the relief of Santa Cruz and ended his career as governor of La Mancha. Earlier, while an officer in France, he had organised the rescue of Clementina Sobieski, the Old Pretender's bride, from captivity in Innsbruck.[14] He was a man of letters who corresponded with Swift and Pope. Alexander O'Reilly, born in Meath, joined Hibernia as a teenager in 1737.[15] By the end of the Seven Years War he was a general, and was sent to the Caribbean, where he was responsible for revamping the fortifications of Havana and Puerto Rico. Later he imposed Spain's authority on Louisiana. He became a knight of Calatrava, a count, inspector general of infantry and military governor of New Castile. Unfortunately, in 1775, his 20,000-strong expedition against Algiers ended in disaster. His

13.1   Irish kerne or mercenaries, and peasants, by Albrech Dürer (1521).
The inscription on the left reads: 'Here go the warriors in Ireland beyond
England'; and on the right: 'Here go the peasants in Ireland'.

reputation was slow to recover, but he had just been appointed commander in Catalonia for the coming offensive against France at the time of his death in 1794. The spread of French revolutionary ideals divided the Irish in Spain: at one point during the Peninsular War General Juan O'Donoju headed the royalist war department at Cadiz while General Gonzalo O'Farrell served King Joseph Bonaparte as war minister in Madrid.[16] Irlanda, Hibernia and Ultonia retained little of their Irish identity by the time of their final disbandment in 1818.

Irish regiments in France date from 1635.[17] Seven were raised by Irish colonels over the next few years, involving – with replacements – the recruitment of at least 10,000 men. A leading role was played by the Wall brothers of Coolnamuck, County Waterford, of whom four eventually died in French service.[18] Numbers declined in the 1640s, but rose again to eight regiments during the next decade in the wake of the Catholic defeat in Ireland. The Wall regiment survived longest, passing in 1652 to the exiled James Stuart, Duke of York and, as *Royal Irlandais*, only finally disbanding in 1664. The involvement of Louis XIV in the Jacobite war brought a fresh migration of Irish soldiers to France. In 1690, in exchange for a French brigade sent to Ireland, Louis received over 5,000 Irish infantry, commanded by

Justin MacCarthy, Lord Mountcashel. They formed three regiments which were incorporated into the French army;[19] 200 Irish soldiers left over from a British force which had served in France in the 1670s were distributed amongst them. On their first campaign in Savoy the Irish troops performed well and it became a French objective to secure more. The opportunity arose in 1691 when the articles of Limerick permitted 16,000 soldiers of the defeated Irish army to go to France where they were formed into a small French-paid army for King James, composed of ten regiments of infantry, two of cavalry and two troops of Horse Guards.[20] After the Treaty of Ryswick (1697), this force was reduced to a single cavalry regiment and five of infantry, and became part of the French army like the Mountcashel Brigade. All eight Irish infantry regiments were simultaneously reduced to single battalions, giving a total strength of about 7,000 officers and men.

Sheldon's cavalry regiment became Nugent's and then FitzJames's until it was disbanded in 1762, after its virtual annihilation in the Seven Years War. Albemarle's was successively Nugent's and O'Donnell's until its disbandment, with Galmoy's, in 1715. Walter Bourke's passed into the Spanish service the same year. A new Irish regiment of Lally, formed in 1744, was disbanded in 1762 after being involved in the French defeat in India. Mountcashel's became Lee's and then Bulkeley's until the reorganisation of 1775 which incorporated it into Dillon's, and O'Brien/Clare's into Berwick/FitzJames's. The revolutionary regime abolished the distinctive Irish identity of the three extant regiments in 1791 and they were allotted French regimental numbers. Dillon's and Berwick/FitzJames's, which throughout the eighteenth century had retained their original names under a succession of family colonels, became, respectively, the 87th and 88th. Walsh's, previously the Footguards/Dorrington's/Rothe's/Roscommon's, was henceforth the 92nd.

Up to the end the brigade proudly proclaimed its roots in the old Irish Jacobite army. Regimental colours carried the cross of St George and (with the exception of Walsh's) the motto of Constantine, *In hoc signo vinces* (In this sign – i.e. of the cross – thou shalt conquer), which had been employed in Ireland.[21] The troops wore the traditional red uniform coats of their Stuart allegiance, which (under the 1762 regulations) were faced black for Dillon's, red for Berwick's, yellow for Clare's, white for Rothe's and green for Bulkeley's. An account of Dillon's by the Chevalier Gaydon, a veteran of more than forty years' service, portrays a unit constantly on the move in wartime, heavily and frequently engaged, and suffering severe casualties from both combat and disease.[22] Gaydon estimated that by 1738 the regiment's losses had been 6,000 soldiers and a proportionate number of officers. The experience of the other Franco-Irish regiments cannot have been dissimilar.

In Louis XIV's wars the best-known engagement of the Irish was the defence of Cremona in 1702 where they foiled a surprise attack by Prince Eugene and the imperial army. They also fought with distinction at such famous battles as Steenkirk, Landen, Marsaglia, Luzzara, Blenheim and Almansa. At Ramillies, Clare's took the only colours captured from the allies. Malplaquet, in 1709, witnessed an epic

13.2 'Remember Fontenoy!' The role of the Irish Brigade at the Battle of
Fontenoy, 30 April 1745, where the French army won a notable victory
over the British and Dutch, has been regarded as the greatest of Irish battle
honours. In this supplement to the *Weekly Nation* for Christmas 1898, Irish
soldiers are seen displaying captured British standards.

musquetry duel between the British Royal Regiment of Ireland and the Franco-Irish
regiment commanded on the day by Michael Rothe, a Kilkenny officer who had
served through the Jacobite War in Ireland and rose to the rank of lieutenant-
general in France.[23] Rothe subsequently became colonel proprietor of the regiment,
in which he was succeeded by his son, also a lieutenant-general. The most famous
action of the Franco-Irish Brigade was the battle of Fontenoy, fought in Flanders in
1745 during the War of the Austrian Succession. The six Irish infantry regiments
were brigaded together on the left of the front line under Charles O'Brien, sixth
Viscount Clare, later to be a marshal of France. FitzJames's cavalry was also
present. Victory was gained for the French by the charge of their left wing in which
the Irish Brigade played the leading part, to the cry, it is said, of *Cuimhnigí ar
Luimneach agus feall na Sasanach!* (remember Limerick and English treachery!).[24]
In the Seven Years War the Irish regiments campaigned for the most part in
western Germany. Individual Irishmen also served in Canada, where the French
forces in 1755–7 included an Irish company formed from British prisoners-of-war.[25]

The credit for using close-range artillery to halt the initial British attack at

Fontenoy belonged to Thomas Arthur Lally de Tollendal, colonel of one of the Irish regiments and the son of a County Galway exile related to the Dillons.[26] He also played a leading role in the storming of the Dutch fortress of Bergen-op-Zoom in 1747. The highpoint of Lally's career came in 1756 with his promotion to lieutenant-general and appointment to command the French expedition to India. Unfortunately, his forces, which included his own Irish regiment, were totally inadequate to retrieve French fortunes against the British, and despite his valiant efforts the venture inevitably ended in disaster. Lally's impatience with corruption had antagonised French officials; he was made the scapegoat for the French defeat and beheaded in Paris in 1766. His treatment was one of the major scandals of the *ancien régime*, and deeply resented in the Irish Brigade. He was partially vindicated in 1778 through the efforts of his son, the marquis de Lally Tollendal, but it was not until 1929 that the process was completed with the solemn erasure of his degradation and restoration of his name and rank to the rolls of the French army.

After the revolution many Franco-Irish officers with royalist sympathies became *émigrés*, and furnished the colonels and senior officers of six Hiberno-British regiments formed in 1795. A leading part was taken by Count Daniel O'Connell, uncle of the Liberator, who had commanded the German Salm-Salm regiment in France. This new Irish Brigade was devastated by fever in the West Indies and soon disbanded. Of the officers who remained in France, several of the more prominent were victims of the revolution.[27] General Theobald Dillon was murdered by mutinous troops in Lille; Brigadiers James O'Moran of Roscommon and Thomas Ward of Dublin, together with Colonel Arthur Dillon who was the last proprietor of the family regiment and one of the heroes of the French victory at Valmy, were all guillotined during the Terror. Former Irish Brigade officers who had successful careers in the revolutionary and Napoleonic armies included Generals Oliver Harty, Charles Jennings Kilmaine and Henry Clarke, who on three occasions was French war minister. An Irish Legion, formed by Napoleon in 1803, subsequently became the 3rd Foreign Regiment, Irish.[28] It wore green uniforms and at one stage comprised five battalions. Its officers were mostly exiled United Irishmen, although some were former members of the Irish Brigade or their descendants. The rank and file were of many nationalities, including Irish deserters from the British army and a party of 1798 prisoners, liberated by the French from the mines of Prussia, where they had been sent by the British. The 1st Battalion notably distinguished itself in 1809 at the defence of Walcheren and Flushing under William Lawless, a former anatomy professor at the Royal College of Surgeons in Dublin. The regiment, which was the last distinctive Franco-Irish unit, was disbanded in 1815.

The Habsburg monarchy was the principal employer of the Irish in Central Europe. Its multinational character was peculiarly favourable to the advancement of gifted foreigners, and altogether over 100 Irishmen were Austrian field marshals, generals or admirals, with correspondingly greater numbers in the lower commissioned ranks.[29] The earliest of note was Colonel Richard Walsh (Wallis) of

Carrickmines, County Dublin, who came to Germany in 1612, and was mortally wounded at the battle of Lützen. His son, Oliver, also served the emperor, becoming a major-general and proprietor of a regiment of foot, as well as a baron and an estate owner in Bohemia. The Walshs had the longest military tradition of any of the Austro-Irish families; eleven were field marshals or generals, the last of whom died only in 1895.[30] Many Irish served with the Catholic imperial forces throughout the Thirty Years War, including a detachment at the battle of the White Mountain which marked the commencement of hostilities in 1620.[31] The earliest identifiable Irish *inhaber* (colonel proprietor) was Jacob Butler who raised a regiment of foot in 1630 which was wiped out by the Swedes a year later. Colonel Walter Butler from Roscrea, a dragoon *inhaber*, came to prominence for his defence of Frankfurt-on-Oder against Gustavus Adolphus. In 1634 he won honour and reward from Ferdinand II, and international notoriety for Irish mercenaries, by organising the assassination, at Cheb in Bohemia, of the controversial imperial general, Albrecht von Wallenstein.[32] An Irish priest wrote from Prague: 'this deed made our country and nation, otherwise quite unheard of here, most famous and well-known'.[33]

A leading role in the imperial campaigns of the 1680s against the Turks was played by Sligo born Francis Taaffe, subsequently 4th Earl of Carlingford.[34] His career benefited from a lifelong friendship he formed with the young duke of Lorraine, the future imperial general, while they both attended the Jesuit college at Olmütz in Moravia. Taaffe joined the imperial army and played a prominent part in the celebrated relief of Vienna in 1683, and the subsequent successful offensive against the Turks in Hungary. His letters from the front were published in England and did much to spread the fame of the imperial victories. King James II placed his gifts of a Turkish tent and weapons on public display in London and several officers from the English and Irish armies attended the siege of Buda with him in 1686–7. Taaffe became a field marshal, a knight of the Golden Fleece and eventually prime minister of the restored Duchy of Lorraine.

Irish involvement in Austria was at its height in the mid-eighteenth-century wars of the Empress Maria Theresa. Her army was said to 'swarm with the offspring of the best Roman Catholic families of that kingdom [of Ireland] – high spirited, intrepid, nervous youth – retaining a hankering desire after their country, [and] feeling themselves worthy of it'.[35] The most outstanding figure was Field Marshal Maximilian Ulysses Browne.[36] Although born on the Continent, he was from a Limerick family, and evidently returned to Ireland for his education, before entering the imperial regiment commanded by his uncle. By the age of thirty he was a major-general and a seasoned veteran of the Turkish wars. He proved an extremely enterprising and capable general in a succession of increasingly important wartime commands in Bohemia, the Rhineland, Italy and the south of France. He died in action at Prague in 1757 while leading the Austrian army in Bohemia against Frederick the Great. Browne encouraged the early career of his kinsman, Field Marshal Francis Maurice Lacy – a son of Field Marshal Peter

13.3   Count Maximilian Ulysses Browne, field marshal in the Austrian
service, mortally wounded at the Battle of Prague, 1757.

Lacy of Russia – who was subsequently president of the *Hofkriegsrath*, or imperial
war council, and the leading reformer of the army under the demanding Emperor
Joseph II.[37] Over a score of high-ranking, Irish-born officers were knights of the
prestigious Imperial Military Order of Maria Theresa.[38] They included General
William O'Kelly of Galway for his conduct at the battles of Breslau (1757) and
Torgau (1760), General John Sigismund Maguire of Kerry for his capture of Dresden
(1758), General Karl O'Donnell of Leitrim for his conduct at Torgau, Colonel Hume

13.4   Field Marshal Francis Maurice Lacy, who also achieved high rank
in the Austrian service, came from a distinguished 'Wild Geese' family.
His father, also a field marshal, served in the Austrian and Russian armies.

Caldwell of Fermanagh – exceptionally, of Protestant planter stock – for his courage
against the Prussians at Breslau and Olmütz (1758), and Field Marshal Laval Nugent
of Westmeath for his service in Italy (1800). Lacy received the Grand Cross for his
conduct at the battle of Hochkirch (1758) and was the order's chancellor in his final
years. During the Revolutionary and Napoleonic wars at least 200 Irish officers were

still serving in the Austrian army which continued to attract a trickle of Irishmen in the nineteenth century. After the Thirty Years War rank and file soldiers from Ireland were a rarity in Austria and there were no permanent Irish units, as such. Cadres of Irish officers would gather for a time in regiments with Irish colonel-proprietors only to melt away again on the appointment of non-Irish successors. William III sent two parties of ex-Irish Jacobites to the emperor via Hamburg.[39] They suffered heavily from hardship, disease and the peculation of their officers. The survivors proved reluctant to fight for an ally of William of Orange and were eventually distributed amongst other units of the imperial army. A short-lived battalion of Irishmen, recruited from French prisoners of war, served the emperor in Italy from 1702 to 1705.

Elsewhere in Germany, Irishmen, mainly from Tipperary, formed 8 per cent of the Bavarian officer corps in the War of the Spanish Succession.[40] The elector nominated others to commands in Walloon regiments in the Spanish Netherlands of which he was governor. In Protestant Saxony, the O'Byrns and Bourks were prominent military families. In Italy, the Bourbons of eighteenth-century Parma employed a company of Irish guards in scarlet uniforms with blue facings. In Portugal, Hugh O'Kelly and Hugh Beatty were colonels of native infantry regiments. Sweden, in the opening decades of the seventeenth century, employed at least 6,000 swordsmen from Gaelic Ulster, who were rounded up and shipped off by the Irish government for the security of the new plantation.[41] Unhappy under a Protestant power, these soldiers were encouraged to desert to Poland and Germany by Irish friars who went among them, dressed as soldiers. Gustavus Adolphus in 1631 declined to accept any more recruits from Ireland as he considered them too untrustworthy. However, a trickle of Irish soldiers continued to go to Scandinavia. The most prominent were the Hamiltons, descendants of a Scot who was Protestant archbishop of Cashel. Hugh Hamilton, one of several brothers in the Swedish army, was master-general of the Swedish artillery by 1662, when he retired to Ballygawley, County Tyrone. His nephews, Hugh and Malcolm, also entered the Swedish service. Young Hugh interrupted his career to fight on the Williamite side in the Irish Jacobite war, but subsequently returned to Sweden where both brothers became generals and were ennobled.

A score of Irish officers are known to have served the Russian court in the eighteenth century.[42] The most outstanding was undoubtedly Peter Lacy of Bruff, County Limerick, dubbed 'the Prince Eugene of Muscovy' by Frederick the Great. Lacy commenced his spectacular military career as a thirteen-year-old ensign in the Irish Jacobite army. In 1691 he moved to France, but was demobilised after the Treaty of Ryswick and subsequently recruited by Peter the Great who depended on foreign officers to professionalise his army. Lacy fought with distinction against the Swedes in the Great Northern War and contributed to the Russian victory at Poltava in 1709. He later campaigned in Poland and Finland, and against the Turks, rising steadily in rank to become a field marshal in 1736. A succession of Russian rulers

---

relied on him for military expertise and leadership, particularly the Empress Elizabeth. Lacy died a wealthy man in 1751 as governor of Livonia. Several other Lacys in Russian service were evidently his kinsmen and his daughter married George Browne of County Limerick, another Hiberno-Russian general. Count John O'Rourke, one of two County Leitrim brothers who served Catherine the Great, wrote a treatise on warfare. His nephew, Count Iosiph Kornilovich O'Rourke, served with distinction in the Russian cavalry against Napoleon and was promoted major general.

There were obvious difficulties about the employment of Irish Catholic soldiers on mainland Britain; 10,000 troops sent by the Kilkenny Confederacy to reinforce the royalists in England and Wales in 1643–4 excited intense antagonism, while undoubtedly contributing in a major way to the prolongation of Charles I's resistance to 1646.[43] The parliamentary response was the uncompromising 1644 'Ordinance of no quarter to the Irish'. The Confederacy also sent 2,000 men in three regiments under the famous warrior, Alasdair MacColla, to Scotland, where they formed the backbone of the earl of Montrose's royalist army which won a string of victories in 1644–5.[44] A generation later, in 1688, the Irish army was seriously weakened on the eve of the Jacobite war when almost half its strength was squandered in England in a vain attempt to prop up James II on the eve of the Glorious Revolution.[45] The Irish presence excited intense public hostility and exacerbated James's domestic problems by giving his opponents a propaganda victory. An Irish dragoon regiment sent to the aid of the Scottish Jacobites in 1689 disintegrated after the battle of Killiekrankie.

The use of Irish Catholics in British forces overseas presented fewer problems. In 1627 a newly raised Irish regiment, under Sir Piers Crosby, participated in the duke of Buckingham's ill-fated invasion of the Isle de Rhé in support of the Huguenots of La Rochelle.[46] During Charles II's reign Irishmen were employed in the Tangier garrison, including two regiments in the first force sent there in 1662.[47] At least 1,000 Irish recruits were sent to reinforce the British brigade in Portugal in 1664 and other Irish soldiers served in the British West Indies. In Holland, a 500-strong Irish regiment formed part of the Anglo-Dutch brigade from 1674 to 1688 when its officers were recalled to England to provide the nucleus of Colonel Roger MacElligott's short-lived Irish regiment. The British force sent to aid Louis XIV against the Dutch in 1671 included a 1,500-strong regiment raised in Ireland by Sir George Hamilton, a Catholic nephew of the duke of Ormond.[48] It served on the Rhine under Turenne and was the nursery of most of the Irish-born general officers of the later Irish Jacobite army, including Patrick Sarsfield, Richard and Anthony Hamilton, brothers to the colonel, and their cousin, Justin MacCarthy. After George Hamilton's death in action, Thomas Dongan of Kildare succeeded to the colonelcy while MacCarthy became commander of the duke of Monmouth's Royal English regiment, which appears to have contained numerous Irishmen. Both units were recalled to Britain in 1677 when Charles II changed sides in the war; the

---

following year they formed part of his expeditionary force to aid the Dutch in Flanders. Dongan held the rank of major-general for this short campaign, but resigned on being made deputy governor of Tangier. He later became a distinguished governor of New York. MacCarthy succeeded him as commander of the Irish regiment, but the Popish Plot dashed any hopes the Catholic officers had of being taken on to the permanent establishment. The Irish regiment was disbanded on its return in 1679 and MacCarthy, after a brief period of imprisonment, took service in Denmark.

James II had permitted the British East India Company to raise a small number of troops in Ireland in the 1680s.[49] The recruitment of Catholics by the company resumed in the 1770s;[50] 500 Irish recruits were sent to India in 1777 and within a few years a third to a half of the company's European soldiers were Irish by birth or extraction. Prominent Anglo-Irish officers in the company's army included Major Randfurlie Knox of Sligo (d. 1764) and Colonel John Carnac of a Dublin Huguenot family, who commanded the troops in Bengal in 1761. Lieutenant-Colonel Joseph Nelley, who entered the service in 1781, was evidently a Catholic as he left £1,000 to build a chapel in County Galway. Sir Eyre Coote from Limerick was Lally's conqueror at the battle of Wandewash and commander-in-chief from 1779 to 1783. Amongst many other Anglo-Irish officers in the king's service in India were Thomas Russell, the future United Irishman, and the youthful Arthur Wellesley, later duke of Wellington. Several Irish adventurers also served with the armies of Indian princes. They included William Tone, who had originally been in the company's service, but was a colonel with the Mahrattas at the time of his death in action in 1802. He was a brother of Wolfe Tone who in 1788 had himself briefly contemplated a career in India.[51]

There was a steady stream of Irish emigration to America in the eighteenth century. It has been calculated that by 1790 almost 450,000 Americans were of Irish stock.[52] Two-thirds were Ulster Scots who were most heavily concentrated in the Middle Colonies and the Carolinas, providing up to half the continental army's manpower in states such as Pennsylvania during the revolution. Seven of Washington's generals were Irish-born, three being Trinity College Dublin graduates: Richard Montgomery, William Irvine and Edward Hand.[53] Montgomery, a major-general, was the first significant hero of the revolution, killed at the head of his troops in the unsuccessful assault on Quebec in 1775. Irvine commanded the Western Department. Hand, a former surgeon's mate with the 18th Royal Irish regiment, became adjutant general in 1781. William Maxwell, who commanded the New Jersey brigade, was a veteran of the French and Indian wars. James Hogan commanded the North Carolina Brigade until his capture at Charleston in 1780. Most Irish Catholics in America had come as indentured servants. From this lowly status, enlistment in the armed forces offered an escape and they were recruited in disproportionate numbers for the frontier campaigns of the Seven Years War and again for the continental army, but served mainly in the lower ranks. The highest ranking were the Kerry-born Major-General Thomas Conway, for a time the continental army's inspector general and a former Irish Brigade officer in France to which he returned in 1779, and Colonel Stephen Moylan, a brother of the bishop of Cork. Leading officers of Irish descent in the continental army included Henry Knox, Anthony Wayne and John Sullivan.

The continental army contained no specifically Irish units, but detachments of Dillon's and Walsh's regiments from the Irish Brigade in France participated in the unsuccessful siege of Savannah in 1779, and the Spanish Hibernia regiment was prominent in the capture of Pensacola, the capital of British West Florida, in 1781. Contrary to what is sometimes believed, the Dillon regiment was *not* at Yorktown. However, Rochambeau's expedition to America did include three Dillon brothers from the Bordeaux wine family and – in the rank of captain – the future General Kilmaine. On the British side, it may be added, sixteen of the forty-four battalions serving in America in 1776 originated in Ireland which continued to provide recruits, mainly Catholics, throughout the war. Amongst the Irish officers serving with the British army in America were General Charles O'Hara of County Sligo, who led the surrender party at Yorktown, and Lord Edward Fitzgerald, afterwards the leading military figure in the United Irishmen.

The Irish soldiers abroad were a factor in the domestic politics of Ireland and Britain. Initially, the Irish administration regarded the military migration as a contribution to internal peace and security, and Lord Mountjoy wrote sanguinely 'it hath ever been seen that more than three parts of the four of these countrymen do never return, being once engaged in any such voyage'.[54] But this view disregarded the concomitant risks inherent in the presence overseas of large numbers of disaffected Irishmen, proficient in the techniques of contemporary warfare. The fraction of the migrants that did return to Ireland furnished military leadership when the opportunity arose in 1641–53, 1689–91 and 1798. In Spanish Flanders the leading Irish soldiers kept in close touch with affairs at home. Their numerical contribution to the Confederacy after the 1641 Rising was small, but Preston, O'Neill and Barry returned with some other officers to lead, respectively, the Leinster, Ulster and Munster armies, and John Bourke, another Flanders veteran, was the commander in Connacht. By then all were elderly men and O'Neill's return was the culmination of a lifetime's plotting and ambition. A generation later the Irish Jacobite army, during the war of 1689–90, depended heavily on the expertise of approximately 200 Irish officers with continental experience.

The ethos of the Irish Brigades, which subsequently served in France and Spain, was strongly Jacobite. They were in a sense the public manifestation of the Jacobite shadowlife of early-eighteenth-century Catholic Ireland. Their existence and reputation lent credibility to the exiled Stuart 'pretenders' and they featured prominently in the recurrent schemes for a Jacobite restoration, especially when England and France were at war. In 1692 a planned invasion of England involving most of the Irish regiments, which were assembled in readiness on the Cherbourg peninsula, was thwarted by the French naval defeat off La Hogue. Four years later the Irish were brought to Calais to support an abortive scheme for a Jacobite rising in England. Irish Brigade officers were involved in the Jacobite projects of 1708 and 1715. On the latter occasion it was planned that detachments from each of the five infantry regiments should go to Scotland, although in the event they never sailed. Prince Charles on his expedition to Scotland in 1745 was heavily dependent on Franco-Irish bankers for finance and shipping. His principal adviser was the controversial Irish soldier, John William O'Sullivan, who combined the offices of quartermaster and adjutant general.[55] About 400 men from the Irish Brigade regiments in France, who managed to get through the British naval blockade, formed the most professional part of the Jacobite army and fought with distinction at Falkirk and Culloden. Others captured in transit and those who surrendered after the Jacobite defeat were treated as prisoners-of-war and allowed to return to France. Captain Felix O'Neill, who had taken leave from Hibernia to accompany the prince, was also released after Culloden to resume his military career in Spain where he eventually rose to be captain general of Aragon.

In the mid-eighteenth century commanders of the calibre of Lally, O'Reilly and Marshal Lord Clare all individually cherished plans for a military intervention in Ireland. Irish regiments were included in a French force for a projected invasion of England in 1759 and about the same time several Irish soldiers in the service of France put forward proposals for a descent on Ireland. There were French plans for a landing in Ireland during the American War of Independence, including three prepared by Major-General Patrick Wall, a Carlow-born veteran of the Forty-five.[56] Some specifically envisaged a role for the Irish Brigade. The French expeditions to Ireland in the revolutionary period were in a military sense the continuation of this earlier strategy. Colonel Arthur Dillon spoke of the enslaved condition of Ireland at a Paris meeting in 1792 and expressed his hope that the time was near when he would give his sword to the service of his own land.[57] Tone was taken aback to learn in 1796 that the French were still thinking in terms of a Stuart restoration. Napoleon's Irish Legion was formed to provide officers to command the native Irish in a projected French invasion of the British Isles.[58] As late as 1811 a legion officer paid a clandestine visit to Dublin to investigate the likely reaction to a French descent on Ireland.

In the eighteenth century Irish Protestants were concerned at the military potential and professed Jacobitism of Irish soldiers on the Continent. In 1728 a hostile Dublin pamphleteer wrote:

> As long as there is a body of Irish Roman Catholic troops abroad the chevalier [i.e., the Old Pretender] will always make some figure in Europe by the credit they give him, and be considered as a prince that has a brave and well-disciplined army of veterans at his disposal, though he wants the opportunity to employ them at present which he expects time and fortune will favour him with . . . They are British subjects, they speak the same language with us, and are consequently the fittest

13.5 A sentimental representation of an Irish soldier fighting abroad:
'I fought for my country far, far from my true love,
Savoureen deelish Eileen oge.'

troops to invade us with. They are seasoned to dangers, and so perfected in the art of war, that not only the sergeants and corporals, but even the private men, can make very good officers upon occasion.[59]

In the 1690s over 1,000 Jacobite exiles were attainted for treason 'committed in parts beyond the seas', a euphemism for service in France. The Irish parliament subsequently enacted a series of statutes banning unlicensed recruiting for foreign service (1722), prohibiting those serving in the French or Spanish armies from holding property in Ireland (1746), and making service abroad treasonable (1756). The penal laws and the traitorous imputations of overseas military service were particularly resented by the Irish in Austria, which was normally a British ally. Generals Richard and James Dalton saw no conflict of loyalties in the obelisk erected beside their new country house in Westmeath in the 1780s, which honoured their imperial employers, Maria Theresa and Joseph II, together with their sovereign, George III. A dignified plea for the more generous treatment of Irish Catholics was published in 1766 by Nicholas, the sixth Viscount Taaffe, who was an Austrian lieutenant general.[60]

Military men on their return to Ireland strongly resented the social and political discrimination they experienced, after the equality they had known abroad. Some were influenced by the radical politics they encountered on the Continent and in America in the last quarter of the eighteenth century, and this contributed to their dissemination in Ireland. Edward Sweetman of County Wexford and James Plunkett of Roscommon, both former French officers, were prominent United Irishmen in the early 1790s. Other Irish officers, who seem originally to have been involved in the organisation's military plans, had resumed their careers abroad on the outbreak of the Revolutionary War and so were absent from the scene in 1798. However, Hervey Morres, 'commandant' of the Westmeath insurgents, had served in Austria; as had Mathew Bellew and James O'Dowd, who emerged from retirement in north Mayo to take commissions from Humbert, only to be hanged after his defeat at Ballinamuck.[61] Other insurgent leaders of 1798, such as Lord Edward FitzGerald and Matthew Keogh of Wexford, were possibly imbued with radical ideas while serving with the British army in America.

Officers of Irish regiments overseas were normally Irish by birth or extraction, and there were also many instances of Irish officers serving states which had no specifically Irish units, or in non-Irish units of those that had. In Spanish Flanders, troops always served under officers of their own nationality; it was only in the 1790s that significant numbers of non-Irish names began to appear in the commission lists of the Hispano-Irish infantry regiments.[62] In 1803 Irlanda had only twenty-nine officers with Irish names and the number continued to dwindle up to its disbandment in 1818. English, as well as Spanish, was still spoken by the officers of Ultonia in 1808. In France, Irish officers were dominant in the Irish Brigade up to the end, and the words of command continued to be given in English.

The officer corps of the regiment of Limerick was largely Irish at the time of its transfer to the Neapolitan service in 1736. Seventeenth-century commissions were generally issued to officers who could supply soldiers. Such men emerged from the Irish wars, or were inducted into military life as youthful gentlemen volunteers. With the establishment of standing armies the normal avenue to a commission became an officer cadetship with a regiment. Family connections and relationships were of the greatest importance in securing this, the desired commission and subsequent promotion – especially where money was short. The impoverished Catholic gentry, particularly in the south and west of Ireland, made repeated use of their Irish kinship network on the Continent to secure military careers for their younger sons in France, Spain and Austria. Many surnames constantly recur, such as O'Neill and MacDonnell in Spain, and Taaffe, Lacy and Browne in Central Europe. Commissions in the aristocratic French army were immensely prestigious and normally acquired by purchase. The existence of their own regiments gave the Irish a niche in this privileged system. Several of the Shees of County Limerick, for example, served in the Franco-Irish Brigade over three generations, commencing with the entry of William Shee and his three sons to Clare's in 1725.[63] The Shees brought their young kinsman, Oliver Harty, over from Ireland in 1762 to a cadet-ship in Berwick's. Colonel Henry Shee, military secretary to the duke of Orleans, promoted the early career of his nephew, Henry Clarke, a graduate of the École Militaire in Paris who was commissioned into Berwick's regiment in 1782. Clarke, in turn, subsequently assisted in placing two of his Irish Shee cousins in the brigade. The Irish preoccupation with genealogy was useful in furnishing the pedigrees needed to satisfy the requirements of European monarchs for officers of noble birth.

As time went on, although a growing number of officers were continental-born, many still originated in Ireland. Some were ex-students of the Irish colleges on the Continent, notably Paris, which maintained close contact with the Irish Brigade. In France and Austria, from the mid-eighteenth century, a proportion of commissions went to graduates of the new military academies. Numbers fluctuated, but for most of the eighteenth century as many as 500 Irishmen would have held commissions on the Continent at any one time, more than compensating for their exclusion from the small British army of the period. Economic difficulties resulting from a contraction of military employment abroad may have been a radicalising factor for the Irish Catholic gentry in the 1780s.

Major movements abroad of Irish soldiers occurred in the wake of each of the late Tudor and seventeenth-century Irish wars. At other times officers came to Ireland to raise men for existing or projected units, for which they held contracts. The numbers involved could be considerable. For example, three new Irish regiments established in Spanish Flanders in 1632–4 required 9,000 men. Seventeenth-century recruiting normally took place with English and Irish government approval and even active support. Sometimes the soldiers were pressed. They either caused commotion by marching through England, or sailed directly to the Continent on packed vessels hired in the Irish ports. After the Jacobite war the shipping to transport the Irish army to France was supplied by the victorious Williamites. Thereafter, although occasional foreign recruitment took place in Ireland under licence, the replenishment of Irish units abroad was generally a more clandestine affair which, for some recruiting officers and their associates, ended on the scaffold. The earliest reference to the migrating soldiers as 'those persons commonly called wild geese' was in 1726.[64] Recruiting was often concentrated on different groups or localities. Thus the bulk of the rank and file initially furnished to Sweden and Flanders was drawn from the Gaelic populations of Munster and Ulster, although the government favoured Old English officers to command them. The Confederate defeat brought regiments from the midlands and south to the Continent. Mountcashel's Brigade was supplied by the southern half of the island, while the exodus at the end of the Jacobite war seems to have been from all four provinces. Subsequently the Bourbon Irish regiments recruited most successfully in the south, south-west and midlands. The Protestant migrants to America were largely Ulster Scots, while the East India Company's recruits were mostly from the Dublin region.

Irish recruiting for the Franco-Irish Brigade peaked in the 1720s. In 1729, for example, while Dillon's was stationed at Sedan, it received more than 800 recruits from Ireland. Information on prisoners captured in the Jacobite rebellion of 1745 suggests that up to that time the rank and file of the Irish Brigade was still overwhelmingly Irish-born (with virtually every county represented).[65] Within a generation the proportion of Irish rankers declined to less than 10 per cent. Inevitably, this led to a contraction in the number of Irish regiments; the Irish content of those that remained was diluted by a mixture of nationalities that included Flemings, Walloons, Germans, Swiss and even former French deserters who enlisted as a means of returning home. Eighteenth-century Spain was not an attractive destination, and the rank and file of the Hispano-Irish Brigade was never exclusively Irish. As early as 1731 only a few of Irlanda's sergeants bore Irish names, implying that even at that stage, except for the commissioned officers, the regiment was largely non-Irish, and probably even less so after the heavy losses incurred by it and Hibernia in Italy in 1743-4. Ultonia still retained a handful of non-commissioned officers and other ranks with Irish names when it was stationed in Mexico in 1769. However, in 1808 it was observed that none of its privates or non-commissioned officers could speak a word of English or Irish.

At first the Irish soldiers on mainland Europe were noted for their wild appearance and behaviour. They were regarded as 'naked savages' who were 'strangers to both humanity and civility'. On arrival, they were normally destitute, dispirited by defeat and the prospect of exile, and ill and exhausted after the sea voyage. The French commissary at Brest reported in 1690 that the soldiers of the newly disembarked Mountcashel Brigade were without shirts, shoes and hats, dreadfully dirty and eaten by vermin.[66] So many were ill that there were fears of an epidemic in the Breton towns where they were first quartered. The demobilisations

---

in France that followed the Treaty of Ryswick in 1697 left the disbanded soldiers with no means of support. For a time gangs of Irish highwaymen infested the road between Paris and St-Germain. Others sought civilian employment or continued their military careers elsewhere. Those who entered the Bavarian service were alleged to have introduced 'a spirit of brutality, gambling, drunkenness and pugnacity which had never before been known in that army'.[67] Nevertheless, a number of factors made the Irish attractive as mercenaries. The ordinary soldiers were available in good supply and noted to be physically fit and strong. The comte d'Avaux observed that in the Irish Jacobite army none of the musketeers was less than 5' 6" in height, and the grenadiers and pikemen were even taller.[68] With training and experience they could be depended upon to respond loyally to good leadership and to show courage and resolution in battle. Their background of extreme poverty prepared them to bear hardship and the rigours of military service with remarkable equanimity.

Some impression of life in the ranks may be gleaned from the lively memoirs of 'Captain' Peter Drake of Meath, an adventurer who sailed to France with Sarsfield in 1691 and afterwards served in the French, Dutch, Spanish and English armies.[69] More typical, probably, was the career of Darby Quinan.[70] He was a native of Limerick who had joined the Jacobite army in 1689 at eighteen years of age and in France enlisted in Dillon's regiment. He was wounded by a bayonet thrust in the side at the battle of Cassano and by a bullet in the leg at Malplaquet. By 1729 he held the rank of corporal, but at fifty-eight and disabled by constant chest trouble, he was then considered unfit for further service. Major Gaydon discharged him from the regiment at Sedan and it was hoped he would secure admission to Les Invalides, the soldiers' hospital in Paris.

Irish soldiers frequently travelled abroad in family groups with their wives, children and other relatives.[71] In Spanish Flanders women often went with their menfolk to war; if widowed, the well-born could hope for a pension from the king of Spain, while those of humble origin might be given a licence to beg. Women and children accompanied the Jacobite army to France in 1691, although there were harrowing scenes at the embarkation ports as some dependants were left behind. Irish quarters appear to have developed in Flemish towns such as Brussels and Bruges. St Germain-en-Laye became a centre for Irish exiles in France because of the presence there of the Jacobite court. This grouping together at certain locations facilitated marriages within the Irish community, and the children of these unions frequently continued the military tradition of their fathers. In France, General Edward Rothe's only daughter, Lucy, married her cousin, Colonel Arthur Dillon. His military career kept him abroad for long periods during which he left his wife and daughter to reside at the Paris home of his uncle. In Spain, few officers could afford to marry until they were captains. Some officers returned to Ireland to marry, settle or retire. Others spent the rest of their lives abroad. In 1770 a number of retired officers were noted as living at Cambrai 'for cheapness and the convenience of being near their countrymen, who were and usually are stationed in Flanders'.[72] In Austria, where many of the Irish remained bachelors, provincial centres such as Graz and Prague were popular places of retirement.

There were several reasons for the decline in Irish military migration to the Continent. Official hostility discouraged foreign recruiting in Ireland. America became increasingly available as an alternative destination for the poorest elements of the Irish Catholic community. Ideological motivation was lessened by the failure of Jacobitism, the shabby fate of Lally and the easing of Catholic disabilities in Ireland. Irish Catholics were recruited into the British marines from 1758 and into the regular and East India Company armies in the 1770s. From 1793 they could hold commissions in the British army. Finally, the French Revolution divided the Irish abroad, ruptured the network of family ties that had underlain so many military careers and destroyed the identity of the remaining Irish units.

Chapter 14

Non-professional soldiery,
c. 1600–1800

David W. Miller

An important reason for investigating military forces in the past is to understand their role in the formation of the state. Max Weber's definition of the state as an ideal type – 'a human community that (successfully) claims the monopoly of the legitimate use of physical force within a given territory' – rightly focuses on the centrality of force to our understanding of the state.[1] In the twentieth century, however, we understand legitimacy as deriving from consent: a state is fully legitimate if, paradoxically, it does not generally have to deploy armed force to obtain compliance with its basic political laws. Sir John Davies, writing in 1612, identified the same issue when he reflected on the problem of the sixteenth-century monarch who in much of Ireland could not 'punish treasons, murders, or thefts unless he send an army to do it'.[2] Thus both in the present, and in early modern times, legitimacy derives from some mechanism which extends the polity's power beyond what can be achieved by direct government coercion. In the twentieth century that mechanism is often the semi-automatic consent which derives from nationalism; prior to the growth of democracy it is more likely to be non-professional soldiery, by which I mean forces deployable on behalf of the *polity*, but not composed of full-time, permanent employees of the *government*.

By 'polity' – a term which avoids begging the question of the existence of a state – I mean that subset of the population in which 'politics' take place, i.e. among whom there is regular contention for power, including power to dispose of the resources of the government.[3] The government is a subset of the polity (even if it is not part of the population) which controls the concentrated means of coercion (though not necessarily all such means). In times of crisis members of a polity often seek alliances with groups outside that polity, either within the population of the society or elsewhere, which, depending upon the outcome, may alter the social boundary between the polity and the rest of the population. We are accustomed to think of the polity in the form of the modern democratic state, within which contention for power is supposed to take place without physical coercion. In a feudal monarchy, on the other hand, it is assumed that some use of violence by members of the polity, the feudal lords, against one another is normal. By 1600 the

Irish polity was already at several removes from the feudal model, but it was a long way also from the modern democratic model. Since 1541, when Henry VIII assumed the title of king (rather than lord) of Ireland, the government had been extending the area of its effective jurisdiction. By around 1600 none of Ireland lay outside the geographic bounds of the polity, and the use of force in contention for power within the polity carried with it the risk of loss of one's membership in the polity.

Thus the period of this chapter – from the time that the kingdom of Ireland completed its conquest of the island until the time it was replaced by the United Kingdom of Great Britain and Ireland – has a certain unity as a period when there was a polity coterminous with the island, with the important exception that the government was extra-territorial. One consequence of slicing time this way is to place an important body of non-professional soldiery, the Volunteer Movement, in a different context from the one in which they are often treated, the history of Irish nationalism. In this chapter they and their allies in the Patriot party are seen as part of the (ultimately unsuccessful) process of state-formation within the Irish polity which they knew, not as part of the process by which the successor to that polity was delegitimated.

Conquest by professional military forces had been an important part of the process by which the government extended the polity's territory in the sixteenth century. However, since no government could afford a permanent army large enough to enforce its will everywhere in Ireland, in the long run the government would have to consolidate conquests by ensuring that there were local elites in the newly conquered territories who would place their own resources for the maintenance of order at the disposal of the polity. In the sixteenth century the most obvious way to attain that goal was to incorporate the existing defeated or submissive elites, whether Gaelic chieftains or Anglo-Irish magnates, into the polity by the familiar rituals of feudalism. This option usually involved 'surrender and regrant' procedures by which local leaders would acknowledge the king's lordship in return for secure title to their traditional territories. A second option for attaining the goal was to add new members to the polity who would have an interest in advancing the government's interest. This option was pursued by formal plantations of new elites with their retainers and by other means. Around 1600 the second option was replacing the first as the government's primary strategy. Each plantation was intended to supplant recalcitrant members of some specific local elite whose successful incorporation into the polity seemed hopeless to the government. In addition, the planters, as Protestants, were cast in the role of allies of the government in its contention with the Catholic components of the whole polity, both Gaelic and 'Old English'. It was not yet clear, however, that the result would be a redrawing of the polity's social boundary to exclude all of its Catholic members.

As long as the Old English aristocracy, as well as some Gaelic Irish leaders, were being treated as part of the polity (e.g. by their inclusion in Irish parliaments), feudal arrangements for the mobilisation of non-professional soldiery might

---

theoretically have been invoked. In fact, a general hosting of the Pale in 1618 miscarried because those involved successfully invoked a technicality which made the whole exercise impractical. It seemed obvious that this anachronistic system should be replaced by one based not on feudal obligation but on a more modern type of civic duty such as the English system of 'trained bands'. However, a government agreement with Catholic Palesmen in 1625 to establish such a system fell afoul of the suspicion of Protestants and the scheme was dropped.[4] This episode should be seen not only as foreshadowing the exclusion of Catholics from the polity, but also as an instance of the government's need for an alternative to feudal obligation to supplement permanent professional military forces.

In legal form, the alternative to feudalism which was evolving in Ireland was essentially that which emerged in England (but not, for example, in France). At the local level, members of the polity took on responsibility for maintenance of public order, normally in the role of magistrates. Such physical force as they required in the execution of that role might be provided by constables (who were probably quite rare), by a posse which they assembled, or by the army. Another alternative which had been available to their counterparts in England since Elizabethan times, the militia, did not come into existence until 1666, when the duke of Ormond, the lord lieutenant, was prompted both by war with France and by an upsurge of attacks on settlers in the countryside to constitute one, not by statute but by royal prerogative. It was deployed on at least three occasions before it was disarmed in 1685.[5]

Apparently the term 'militia' was also used loosely to refer to any non-professional forces the magistrates had authority to call upon. Sir William Petty, writing around 1672, refers to two 'militias'. The first consisted of the sheriffs and justices of the peace together with their constables, bailiffs and servants as well as the *Posse Comitatus* 'upon extraordinary occasions'. Petty estimated the numbers of this 'militia' as 'near 3,000'. Its deployment was restricted to the locality in which it was raised, and, in some counties its efficacy on behalf of the polity after the confiscations of the 1650s was compromised by the fact that it included '*Irish-Papists*, devested and discontented Persons'.[6] Second, according to Petty there was 'a Protestant Militia, of about 24000 Men, *viz.* about ten thousand Horse, and the rest Foot'. By 'Protestant militia' Petty probably meant the militia officially established in 1666. The discrepancy between his estimate of its composition – 10,000 horse and 14,000 foot – and the government's original plan to raise 4,000 horse and 16,000 foot, along with the ambiguity over the usage of the very term 'militia', alerts us to a difference between official concept and social reality.

In January of 1667, when a rumour of 'a party of Irish drawn together in the co. Cavan, and a new oath of secrecy given amongst them' was passed from constable to constable to Sir George Rawdon at Lisburn, he reported that 'about Lurgan, Magheralin, and all the way the English inhabitants were drawn together by 40 or 50 in a company, with pitchforks and such arms as they had, for their own defence'.[7] Another four days elapsed before army officers and militia captains for County

---

Antrim and Carrickfergus met in Belfast and made arrangements to coordinate their efforts with the militia of Down and Armagh two days later in a meeting at Newry with captains and commissioners of array of those counties.[8] Were the men who initially turned out a posse being raised by the constables, and therefore part of Petty's first 'militia'? Or were they about to be embodied as units of the newly created official militia? Or both? Or neither? The reality was that Protestant communities were used to making *ad hoc* defence arrangements like these whenever necessary, whether the government sanctioned them or not.

Indeed the government had encouraged such arrangements when it established plantations. The plantations seemed to preserve some of the forms of feudalism, but in substance they came to represent a new order. The allotments to landlords in the Munster plantation of the 1580s had, in feudal fashion, been called 'seignories' and each landlord ('undertaker') undertook to provide a certain number of soldiers as needed. In the plans for the Ulster plantation two decades later, however, the term 'seignory' was dropped and, whereas the Munster seignories had been intended to contain up to 12,000 acres, the 'proportions' allotted to the Ulster undertakers were to be limited to 3,000 acres, probably in hopes of avoiding the creation of such overmighty subjects[9] as had been the legacy both of feudalism and, beyond the Pale, of the Gaelic social system. The government had no interest in promoting the use of force in contention for power within the polity as had often happened under feudal arrangements. Indeed, the government acknowledged the anachronistic character of specifically feudal defence arrangements by dropping a proposal to require the undertakers of larger proportions to hold them by the burdensome feudal tenure known as knight service *in capite*.[10] The Ulster undertakers were obliged to build fortifications, to ensure that a certain number of their tenants were able to bear arms, and to provide such arms. In addition, some sections of the land to be planted were reserved for 'servitors' – former government officials who might be civilians, but often were military veterans. Did the soldiery resulting from these arrangements constitute an organised military force? The 1618 muster list for the Ulster plantation accounts for 6,215 'Men with Arms', but, apart from enumerating them with their landlords, does not seem to reflect any military organisation of companies, regiments, etc., or any system of military ranks or functions.[11]

How well did the plantation defence arrangements work? The example of the Munster plantation in the late sixteenth century was not encouraging. When a rebellion broke out in October 1598, it should theoretically have been possible for the planters to muster a force of 1,200 foot and 375 horse, but only about 200 men could be found. Though government control of the port towns and disarray among the rebels themselves ensured the ultimate failure of the rebellion, the plantation was completely overthrown and had to be reconstituted over the next several decades.[12]

On the whole, settler response to the rebellion which broke out in Ulster on 22 October 1641 was more successful. To be sure, the Irish forces under Sir Phelim

---

O'Neill achieved surprise and by the end of the month controlled nearly all significant settlements in mid and south Ulster. Both north-east and north-west of this area, however, the British settler community had enough time to organise resistance. The Protestant gentry of the area around Belfast and Carrickfergus managed to assemble some 1,500 men at Lisburn and, on 28 November, were able to stop O'Neill's drive eastward. In the hinterland of the fortified town of Derry two professional soldiers, Sir William and Sir Robert Stewart, organised a settler army which became known as the Laggan forces.[13] No doubt these 'British forces', as the settler armies were described, would have had difficulty holding their districts but for the arrival of a Scottish army under Major-General Robert Monro in April 1642. However, the settlers had turned out in sufficient strength and order to stabilise the situation until this professional force could arrive. In Munster, to which the rebellion had spread by early 1642, a similar settler army was organised after considerable early losses. The British forces continued to be active throughout the protracted troubles of the 1640s, but for the purposes of this chapter our main interest is in their first year or so; presumably after several years in the field they came to resemble professional forces in many respects.[14]

The other important seventeenth-century test of the Protestant community's self-defence capabilities occurred in 1688–9 when James II sought to maintain his regime in Ireland after being forced off the English throne by William of Orange and the governing classes of England. There were important differences between the resistance in east and west Ulster. In the west, both the walled city of Derry and the island town of Enniskillen faced official demands in December 1688 that they admit Catholic garrisons. In both cases certain townsmen prevented their social betters from acceding to the demands; and in Enniskillen a local gentleman, Gustavus Hamilton, allowed himself to be elected governor by the townsmen and assumed leadership of Protestant forces which began to be formed in the surrounding countryside and came to be known as the 'Inniskilling Men'. In the east, somewhat protracted discussions led eventually to formation in January of an armed 'Association' headed by the earl of Mountalexander with its headquarters at Hillsborough. After considerable delay, indecision and ineptitude, the association found itself unable to halt the expedition of a Catholic army sent to subdue the north. Mountalexander's forces were routed at Dromore on 14 March 1689, and Protestants retreated to Derry, which was shortly besieged by Catholic forces. The Inniskilling Men were not strong enough to lift the siege, but they did manage to harass the besiegers and prevent the Jacobite government from consolidating its hold on the west of Ulster. Defeated Protestant forces from the east of the province who had taken refuge in Derry did improve their tactical skills in skirmishes outside the walls during the long months before the relief of Derry at the end of July.[15]

How did the *ad hoc* settler armies differ from regular professional armies? To George Story, chaplain to the recently arrived Williamite army of the duke of Schomberg in September 1689, three regiments of Inniskilling Men who were serving as an advance guard presented an appearance somewhat different from that of the professional soldiers to which he was accustomed: 'most of the Troopers and Dragoons had their Waiting-men mounted upon *Garrons* (those are small *Irish Horses*, but very hardy); some of them had Holsters, and others their Pistols hung at their Sword-Belts'. More revealing, they had caught sight of enemy scouts on a nearby hill and wished that they might attack them, but had orders to proceed no further. They told Story that 'They should never thrive, so long as they were under Orders.'[16]

It does seem that discipline tended to be laxer and command structures less rigidly hierarchical in non-professional forces. One symptom of this in the early 1640s was a continuing cycle of revenge killings in Ulster until professional armies arrived and imposed discipline on their local British and Irish allies respectively.[17] In some cases the process of embodying a force involved a written undertaking which established some sort of collective authority. In Derry a 'League of Captains' was entered into in 1641.[18] The enthusiasm with which the Solemn League and Covenant was taken in Ulster in 1644 may have owed something to a perception that it placed the military regime under a sort of popular authority. Gustavus Hamilton, as governor of Enniskillen, took an oath 'that I shall not act nor do any thing contrary to the Consent and General Advice of the Officers under my Command', and indeed there were specific instances in which crucial decisions were made collectively by the officers. In one case the officers decided to call the soldiers together and consult them on the decision whether to engage the enemy.[19] We can gain perspective on the meaning of this seemingly democratic impulse in the culture of non-professional soldiery by comparing their efforts in 1641–2 and 1688–9.

A major difference between 1641 and 1688 was that in 1641 most Protestants at all social levels recognised only two alternatives – resistance or flight – whereas in 1688 some Protestants entertained a third option, accommodation. Of course, the immediacy of the danger in 1641 helps to account for this difference, but it does not account for the apparent relationship between social class and readiness to seek accommodation in 1688–9. It was, significantly, the *apprentice* boys who barred Derry's gates to the Catholic army outside while the city's elite debated whether to admit them. Although the townsmen of the little frontier town of Enniskillen did gain early support from Gustavus Hamilton and some of his gentry neighbours in the barony of Magheraboy in their determination to prevent Catholic soldiers from entering the town, the majority in a meeting of gentlemen from the east side of Lough Erne favoured admitting them.[20] In the weeks immediately after James's Christmas Eve flight, his lord deputy in Dublin, Tyrconnell, deliberately allowed the impression to get abroad that he might make terms with William. The landed elite of Down and Antrim were at least willing to send a representative so that they might be courted by Tyrconnell, and even as late as the middle of January Lord Massarene and several Antrim gentlemen were arguing against too public a declaration of an armed association.[21]

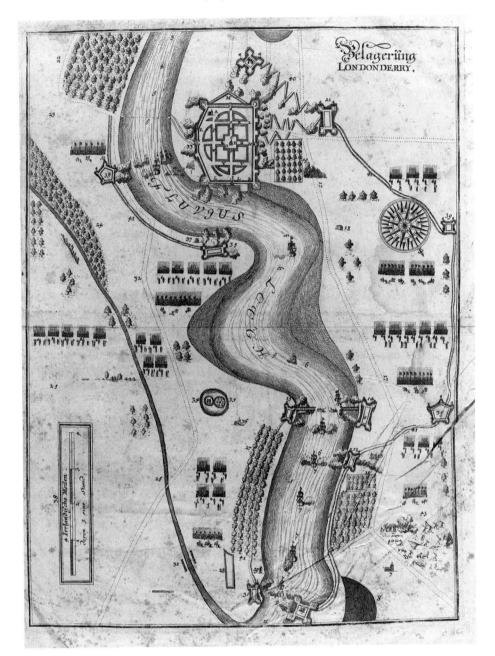

14.1 Aerial view of the siege of Londonderry, 1689, the engagement
which remains a powerful inspiration for 'unofficial soldiery' in
contemporary loyalist Ulster.

To understand this difference in attitudes toward possible accommodation we should reflect on what was at stake for members of different social classes in times of crisis. For the governing classes what was fundamentally at stake was their right to govern; to play the game of contending for power by means of force was to risk one's membership in the polity. The usual mechanism by which losers in this game were expelled from the polity was the confiscation of their land, and indeed the events of 1688–91 turned out to be the last roll of the dice by the Catholic aristocracy and gentry. But in the early days of this crisis, Protestant landlords did not know that that would be the outcome. James might conceivably have succeeded, given the backing of Louis XIV, in retaining his kingdom of Ireland. For a Protestant gentleman, therefore, it might well make sense not to rush precipitately into armed opposition.

The situation was entirely different for ordinary Protestants. Not being members of the polity, they did not risk being expelled from it. What they stood to lose was their lives, and many perceived their lives to be as much at risk from not taking up arms as from doing so. To the extent that they lived in isolated thatched farmhouses their lives were no doubt more at risk than those of the gentry if they did not organise resistance. But military service itself also carried significantly more risk for the lower orders than for their betters. The author of a contemporary account of the exploits of the Inniskilling Men describes an engagement near Newtownbutler in which a body of defeated Irish foot soldiers mistakenly chose an escape route which led through a bog directly into Lough Erne. The Inniskilling foot followed them 'through the Bog into a Wood near *Loghearn*, and gave Quarter that day to few or none that they met with, unless Officers'.[22] It is the matter-of-fact tone of the passage which chills us today: of course the enlisted men were slaughtered, only officers who might command ransom being worth taking prisoner. It is in this context that we should evaluate any suggestions of democracy within seventeenth-century settlers' defence forces. The Protestant community in Ireland remained a stratified and deferential society in which ordinary military service did not yet confer membership in the polity.

The Williamite settlement of the 1690s marks the definitive exclusion of the Catholic aristocracy and gentry from the Irish polity. While Protestant determination to enforce effectively those parts of the penal code directed against Catholic clergy and religious practice might flag, the provisions designed to prevent Catholics from accumulating the sort of property from which political power derived, i.e. land, and of course to deny them access to military force, were taken very seriously indeed. This decisive shift in the social boundary of the polity had important consequences for the ways in which non-professional military force was deployed.

Both an official militia and *ad hoc* local defence arrangements were employed both before and after the 1690s. However, after the Williamite settlement the militia became a regular feature of Irish political life. By contrast, between 1600 and

1689 the militia existed for only nineteen years (1666–85), and it did not exist at the outbreak of either of the two principal crises of the century in 1641 and 1688. Why had an official militia been so neglected as a means for supplementing professional military force? Why, for example, did the government not impose some more centralised and permanent structure on the plantation defence arrangements prior to 1641? Probably the reasons had to do not only with expense, but also with an aversion to creating any armed force formidable enough to pose a potential threat to the government itself. Better to rely on local bands of armed settlers to defend the polity by simply following their own self-interest when an emergency arose than to create in advance a structure which might encourage their leaders to use force to contend for power within the polity. Because the composition of the polity was itself a prime subject of contention, the polity lacked a consensus interest which could provide the mission for a militia. When Ormond did establish the militia in 1666, he had to overcome his own fears that a 'well-trained, armed and cohesive militia' might involve itself in politics.[23]

The problem was complicated by the fact that the government itself was not unreservedly committed to any one contending party within the Irish polity. This is why, paradoxically, nearly all parties to the complicated conflicts of the 1640s in Ireland could satisfy themselves that they were acting in the king's name. In 1666, when the earl of Orrery, lord president of Munster, urged that only 'old' Protestants be admitted to the new militia – i.e. that not only Catholics but 'fanatics' be excluded – he reflected official uncertainty over the reliability of Cromwellian settlers[24] despite the fact that, at the Restoration, Cromwellians in possession of large tracts of land had essentially been accepted into the polity. Significantly, it was Monmouth's rebellion, i.e. a revolt of English 'fanatics' against a Catholic king, which occasioned the disarming of this Irish militia nineteen years later.

From 1691 the monarchy would be as firmly in Protestant hands as would the Irish polity. For that reason, as well as the fact that the polity was still limited to members of the landed class, there was now little cause for concern that a militia might be turned against the government. As for 'fanatics', in Ireland as in England such remnants of the Cromwellian elite as might still exist were probably absorbed into the Whig consensus which was the basis of the new regime. The northern Presbyterian community did compromise the homogeneity of Irish Protestantism, but except for a brief interval under Queen Anne the Ulster Presbyterian clergy were in receipt of salaries from the crown which could easily be understood to mean that their particularism was as legitimate as that of the established church in Scotland. Relatively few Presbyterians owned enough land to have qualified for membership in the polity anyway, but some who probably did took out officers' commissions in defiance of the law, but with apparent official connivance, when the militia was arrayed for the Jacobite invasion scare of 1715.

There were four potential elements outside the polity against which it might be necessary to mobilise non-professional soldiery between 1691 and 1789: (1) the

---

dispossessed Catholic elite; (2) tories and rapparees; (3) France (and the Pretender); and (4) the lower orders. There was a tendency among some Protestants to conflate the first of these with the other three, though in fact the dispossessed Catholics turned out to pose no serious security problem. In the mid-seventeenth century some tories had no doubt been former Catholic landowners. This identification of toryism with the dispossessed elite ended well before the turn of the century, and, as Connolly argues, they are best understood as bandits whose existence reflects the opportunities for plunder which present themselves when a central government extends the forms of law more rapidly than it provides the means to enforce the law's penalties.[25] Some parts of the country suffered depredations by gangs as large as thirty, and these dangers continued until the 1750s or so.

French and/or Jacobite forces actually landed in the British Isles three times in this period – expeditionary forces in 1715 and 1745 in Scotland, and a landing party in 1760 in Ireland. In each case, non-professional soldiery in Ireland were mobilised, as they were on several other occasions when there was a Jacobite rebellion in Scotland which did not spread to Ireland (1708) or when hostilities with France were anticipated but no invasion in fact occurred (1756, 1778). Of course many members of Catholic elite families had made careers in French military service, and no doubt news of French or Jacobite successes sent an expectant thrill through many hearts. Perhaps if Commodore Thurot had chosen a more propitious harbour than Belfast Lough for his landing in 1760 he might even have found a few supporters. But whatever their private wishes, throughout this period Catholic gentlemen in Ireland were on their good behaviour whenever the French were on the sea.

The lower orders were remarkably quiet between the 1690s and 1760; the only large-scale outbreak of agrarian violence, the Hougher movement in Connacht, occurred in 1711–12.[26] After 1760, however, the situation changed dramatically. There were widespread disorders in the south of Ireland in 1761–5 (Whiteboys), 1769–76 (Whiteboys) and 1785–8 (Rightboys), and in the north in 1763 (Hearts of Oak) and 1769–72 (Hearts of Steel). Locally raised forces, which might or might not be militia units were a normal part of the machinery for putting down these disturbances. Better off Catholics were often the victims of these disturbances, and might even lend a hand in suppressing them.[27]

So invasion scares occurred throughout the period 1691–1789, at sufficiently regular intervals to seem a constant threat. Banditry was concentrated largely in the first half of the period, and violent agrarian protest became endemic only after 1760s. Government decisions actually to array the militia and to take other steps to make it effective seem to have been prompted more by concerns over events outside Ireland than by intestine commotions. Militia arrays were held in 1708, 1715, 1719, 1727, 1745 and 1756, but none was held in the periods of widespread domestic unrest of the 1760s and 1770s. Though this turned out to have been very unwise on the government's part, we should see it as a continuation of a

14.2 Kerry Legion Volunteer badge, showing the English lion both
toppling an Irish harp and being struck by a strong Volunteer arm.

long-standing tendency to devolve local peacekeeping functions upon the local
Protestant elite. In contrast to the seventeenth century, it reflects the virtual
consensus of the polity (including the government) on serious questions of security.
If the force which the magistrates mounted to deal with a particular disturbance
happened to have been officially constituted a militia unit, that was a tidy arrangement, but the authorities do not seem to have been obsessed with such niceties.
'[S]end out privately by night a number of stout fellows, well armed under a bold
leader', was how a Dublin Castle official advised a local magistrate to carry out arms
searches during the Hougher troubles.[28]

At least as early as 1715, units described as 'independent' or 'volunteer'
companies or troops appeared in the militia arrays.[29] These were units raised by
particular gentlemen and equipped at their expense. Perhaps some were created at
the time of an array to gratify the vanity of a landlord, but we should probably see
them more generally as in the tradition of the *ad hoc* defence forces which we noted
in the seventeenth century. When Charles Coote set out mounted and armed from
his seat at County Cavan with fourteen of his tenants in July of 1763 to harry the
Hearts of Oak who were rioting in the neighbourhood, he described the little party
as his 'Light Horse'.[30] We should perhaps read this application of formal military
nomenclature to a somewhat irregular unit as a joke to keep up spirits in a very
dangerous situation, but had a militia array occurred in the subsequent months, a
'Cootehill Light Horse' might very well have appeared on its return. What is
significant is that the authorities were apparently comfortable including such units
in militia arrays alongside units created at official initiative. The irregularity of such

formations was more troubling to later historians than it seems to have been to contemporaries.

In the early decades of the eighteenth century it was nearly inconceivable that members of the polity would use any force at their disposal for contention within the polity (rather than for defence against those outside the polity, such as rapparees, Houghers and the French). This was so because the polity's ordinary members, the landed Protestant elite, manifestly had overriding interests in common, and their only plausible adversary within the polity, the government, was, as the representative of British military power, their saviour. Of course there was non-violent contention within the polity, and it took place primarily in the well-defined context of biennial sessions of the Irish parliament. From the 1690s there was dissatisfaction with the continued application of Poynings' Law, a fifteenth-century enactment designed to protect the king's interest in Ireland by granting to his English Privy Council a revising power over legislation of the Irish parliament. In the eighteenth century, with the growth of cabinet government in England, it came increasingly to be seen as giving a set of politicians in London control of the Irish government while denying to their Irish counterparts the very benefits of constitutional monarchy which had brought them to power. Until around 1750 the London government usually was able to keep matters under control by co-opting a small group of Irish politicians who would use the crown's patronage to manage the Irish parliament in the British interest. During the 1750s, however, 'patriots' in the Irish parliament began to have some successes, and serious contention between what might be called court and country parties dominated politics in the 1760s and 1770s.

These developments are of importance for our topic because in thirteen of the sixteen years from 1761 to 1776 at least one region of Ireland was wracked by popular disturbances of a scope which had previously occurred in only a single two-year interval since the Williamite settlement. During the 1760s and 1770s independent 'volunteer' units were frequently formed in various localities to supplement the regular army in efforts to repress the disturbances. At the same time there was not a single militia array in these years. In one sense, this neglect of the militia is not surprising. As we have seen, the government had typically attended to the militia only out of concern over external threats, not over internal matters like the Whiteboys. However, the government did have security concerns in these years both about the vulnerability of Ireland during the Seven Years War which ended in 1763 and about the growing difficulties in North America. The government's proposal was 'augmentation' of the regular army; patriot spokesmen preferred a reconstituted militia in keeping with Old Whiggish suspicion of standing armies. After considerable difficulty the government did manage to get an augmentation bill passed in 1769 to increase the regular establishment from 12,000 to 15,235, of whom 3,235 would be sent to America. However, the militia having become a rallying cry of the Patriot party, the government found it embarrassing to accept even sensible militia reforms. In 1776 the Irish parliament and the government were unable to agree on a new Militia Act. Authority for a militia under the 1715 Act was allowed to lapse, and that force, which had been neglected since 1760, legally ceased to exist.[31]

Further depletion of the regular army stationed in Ireland once the American War was under way seems to be what led the Irish House of Commons in the spring of 1778 to bring forward new militia legislation. The course of the debates indicated a preference for independent companies over compulsory militia service, and there was some effort to embody this alternative formally in the legislation. However, the house turned conciliatory and set aside this potentially controversial issue. With some amendments by the English Privy Council, the Militia Bill was returned in June and became law, but considerable ambivalence in official circles remained, and the act was not implemented during 1778. Meanwhile, the process of forming volunteer units, which had been prompted by agrarian disturbance in recent years, quickened in response to recurrent worries over invasion, especially in light of the entry of France into the war on the American side. In the north some of these units committed themselves in writing to a democratic form of decision-making, and rejected in advance any commission from the government. Nevertheless, Smyth has persuasively argued that, as late as the spring of 1779, if the government had implemented the Militia Act at least the gentlemen commanding the more conservative southern volunteer units would have accepted commissions, and what we know as the Volunteer Movement would have been absorbed into the militia.[32]

The point of no return may have been 4 June 1779 when news of the sighting of a French fleet in Bantry Bay arrived in Cork during celebrations of the king's birthday featuring both local volunteer companies and the garrison troops. As the professionals marched off to guard the coast, the volunteers were left to police and defend the city. In a wave of excitement many new companies were organised. Where, as in Cork itself, Catholic gentlemen volunteered and were accepted, another obstacle was placed in the way of simply incorporating the volunteer units into an official militia. By late July the government accepted the situation and began distributing arms which had been in storage since the 1756 militia array to the volunteer units.[33] Thus from the middle of 1779 there are not just *ad hoc* local volunteer security forces; there is a Volunteer Movement. To understand that movement we need to look at what it actually did; its activities fall into three main categories: (1) policing; (2) advocacy and (3) ceremonial.

Policing was the original purpose of volunteering. Some twenty units which existed in 1784 and traced their origins to dates prior to 1778 were clearly created specifically for police purposes. But this figure no doubt understates the number of *ad hoc* forces formed initially to deal with Whiteboyism, for on one occasion in 1775 the gentry of County Wexford alone were able to muster 'some 4000 armed followers, most of them regularly formed into light-horse or foot militias'.[34] Even after the Volunteers had clearly become a 'movement', policing continued to be a

---

major activity. In the period after 1778 examples have been found of Volunteer units not only repressing Whiteboyism, but making arrests, escorting arms, pursuing robbers, conducting criminals to whippings or hangings or from one gaol to another, preventing the landing of a privateer, guarding a shipwreck, arresting a counterfeiter, maintaining order at a labour demonstration, enforcing laws against 'combination', carrying out an eviction, preventing an abduction, forcing out a party in illegal possession of certain buildings, searching for pirates, protecting houses threatened with mob attack, protecting victims at a criminal trial, protecting soldiers from a crowd, protecting Quakers from mob violence and confiscating arms.[35] One of the objections in the English Privy Council to constituting a militia in 1776 had been that in the north it might have to be composed of people who were themselves inclined to the very sorts of agrarian protest which it would be their chief duty to suppress.[36] We do not know how impartially the Volunteers carried out their policing functions, but the Belfast Volunteers, one of the most radical units, were very proud of the fact that on one occasion they assisted the sheriff in carrying out an eviction for an absentee landlord even though they believed the latter to be in the wrong.[37]

It was in their role as advocates of political change between 1779 and 1784 that the Volunteers received most attention in traditional nationalist historiography. Initially this took the form of seconding the programme of the Patriot party. The celebrated demonstration by Dublin volunteers outside the Parliament House on 4 November 1779, with cannon labelled 'Free Trade – or this' no doubt augmented the Patriot majority to which the British government yielded within a few weeks, granting Ireland open access to British and imperial markets. Volunteer resolutions might also outrun parliamentary opinion however. The resolutions of a February 1782 meeting of Ulster Volunteer corps at Dungannon in favour of legislative independence did not produce such a demand from parliament itself until it was seconded by numerous county grand juries and meetings of constituents and the fall of Lord North's government in London presented a favourable opportunity for extracting concession. Once Poynings' Law had been drastically amended during 1782, the Volunteers began to drift toward advocating parliamentary reform and the admission of Catholics to the franchise. By 1784 it was clear that political leaders were not going to respond to such appeals and the Volunteers' advocacy role at the national level ended.[38] Nevertheless, the achievement of legislative independence would now be seen as an important increment of state-formation if the Irish polity had survived long enough to build upon it.

Perhaps the activity which made the Volunteers most visible to contemporaries was their continual public celebration, display and festivity. Reviews at which each unit could sport the finery of its elegant and distinctive uniforms, as well as complicated exercises and mock battles at which they could rehearse the military arts, became a familiar sight throughout the country. Festivals of the cult of Williamite deliverance which had developed during the eighteenth century –

14.3   The Dublin Volunteers on College Green, 1784.

especially the Boyne anniversary and William's birthday – were observed with special enthusiasm, including manoeuvres, evolutions and, of course, the drinking of loyal toasts. The Belfast Volunteers even went to the somewhat recondite length of commissioning a special performance of Rowe's *Tamerlane*, which Irish Protestants construed as an allegory of the victory of William (Tamerlane) over James (Bajazet, emperor of the Turks).[39] It is instructive to compare these elaborately accoutred companies striving to impress the public with the professional exactness of their performance on the parade ground with the seventeenth-century *ad hoc* defence forces like the Inniskilling Men whose frontier dishabille as well as their contempt for command structures had set them apart from Schomberg's professionals. The entire Volunteer episode in Irish history – advocacy and policing as well as ceremony – should be understood as ritual performance whose meaning was both an affirmation of the polity and an effort to redefine it.

In the twentieth century we expect legitimacy to be conferred upon a polity's disposition of coercive force by nationalism's answer to the question posed by our modern reverence for majority rule: a majority *of whom*? It is misleading to suppose that anyone in the 1780s had come up with the answer to a question whose premise had not yet even been stated. For the Volunteers, the polity's use of force was legitimated not by the imagined community which nationalism offers in the impersonal world of our times, but by a combination of personalistic ties of

14.4 James Caulfield, first earl of Charlemont at the provincial Volunteer
reviews in Phoenix Park, Dublin, 3 June 1782.

deference to traditional leaders and actual participation in the deployment of that
force. The elaborate and exaggerated armed celebrations of the polity's defining
experience affirmed both the polity's claim to deploy force and the individual
participant's claim to membership in the polity by virtue of his landlord's musket
on his shoulder – indeed after the summer of 1779 it might be the government's
musket. The rituals of the Volunteers thus had a very different purpose from those
of their twentieth-century namesakes (depicted in Figures 14.5 and 14.6). Virtually
all of the latter, as individuals, were already assured in 1914 of membership as voters in some democratic polity or other. They were engaged in an elaborate game,

14.5   The Protestant volunteering tradition expressed in the twentieth century by the Ulster Volunteer Force in North Down, on parade in 1914.

under the new rules of 'nationality', to influence the geographic boundaries of the polity within which their respective votes would be counted.

In a deferential society, both the franchise and the right to bear arms were necessary but not sufficient conditions for membership in the polity. By their frequent adoption of democratic decision-making within their units, by their advocacy role in general and by their specific demand in 1783 for parliamentary reforms which might have made the franchise truly effective for non-elite Protestants, however, the Volunteers were claiming membership in the polity for rank and file citizen-soldiers. On a seventeenth-century battlefield, attention might be paid at a vital moment to the opinions of the none-too-serried ranks of the rank and file; when a Catholic army was at the gates, humbler Protestants might even be able to force the hand of their betters. But the reality had been that ordinary soldiers were cannon fodder, struggling to preserve their lives while their betters fought to maintain their membership in the polity. Any rough-and-ready democracy fostered by emergency conditions was set aside when normality was restored in 1691. Conditions after 1760, however, made plain the exposed position of the Protestant landed elite. In face of widespread threats to their security, they found they could not count on an overextended government; nor, in light of the Oakboy and Steelboy troubles, could they automatically count on all their Protestant retainers. The Volunteers were acting out a new reality – that the social boundary of the polity was shifting to include more than the Protestant landed elite.

There ensued a period of two decades in which the composition of the Irish polity was itself in contention again. Should membership in the polity be limited to the landed? Should it be limited to Protestants? Most explosive of all, should a certain group of persons who were not even part of the population of Ireland – namely those politicians who constituted the government of the day in London – continue to hold *ex officio* membership in the Irish polity by virtue of that government's control of the Irish government. All these questions came into play in the period from 1779 to 1800. The mere fact that the social boundary of the polity was in motion impelled members of the polity to seek alliances across it.

One such alliance, between opposition politicians and a hitherto excluded group, the northern Presbyterians, was consummated during the Volunteer heyday of 1779–84, when the 'volunteer sermon' was a common exercise on the part of Presbyterian clergy. The Test Act which had prevented Protestant Dissenters from holding municipal office was repealed in 1779. The radicalism of the Volunteer resolutions in these years reflected the thinking of the nascent non-landed, mostly Presbyterian, elite of the north composed of linen entrepreneurs and Belfast merchants. A second excluded group which was courted by members of the polity was Catholics; indeed from about 1782 what Speaker Foster called 'the race for the Catholic' was on.[40] Not only certain Ascendancy politicians, but also the government and the northern radicals, could see that Catholics were in the process of being readmitted to the polity – the mere fact that many had served in the Volunteers without let or hindrance made that plain. Therefore each of these groups sought at one time or another to be perceived as the vehicle by which that change was effected. In 1793, it was the government which 'won' the race by forcing the Irish parliament to grant the franchise to Catholics on the same basis as Protestants. Respectable Protestant tenants had generally made their way into the polity via the Volunteer movement, as already indicated, but especially in the north there were significant numbers of poor Protestants who in 1779 would not have been considered fit material for Volunteer units. The formation of the Orange Order in 1795 can be seen, therefore, as a means by which this third excluded group was invited into the polity, in this case by conservative Protestant landlords who were alarmed by the countryside's descent into violence and the increasingly inflammatory rhetoric of the United Irishmen.

Could an Irish polity with these new social boundaries attain legitimacy? To answer that question we need to attend to how the polity's need for non-professional soldiery was addressed in the turbulent 1790s. The 1778 Militia Act had never been implemented, and the Volunteer movement was finally suppressed in 1793 (indeed it had been inactive in many parts of Ireland since 1784). In 1793 also, a new Militia Bill was enacted, and this time, in keeping with current government policy which also produced the Catholic Relief Act, the force was to be drawn (by lot) from the entire able-bodied male population aged 18 to 45, without respect to religion, and to serve four-year enlistments within Ireland but outside their home counties. The result was a force which tended to mirror the sectarian division of the

14.6   The nationalist response to the UVF: John Redmond inspecting
Irish Volunteers, August 1914.

population; perhaps 75 per cent of the militia was Catholic, though the officers were
mainly Protestants.[41]

By the time this militia was formed many rural areas were disturbed by the
Defenders, a Catholic peasant organisation which had originated in a bitter conflict
with Protestant 'Peep o'Day Boys' in County Armagh during the 1780s. As the
United Irish movement, whose bases were among Presbyterians in Belfast and urban
radicals in Dublin, moved in the mid-1790s from reformist to revolutionary politics,
many Protestants suspected, rightly, that they would try to co-opt Defender cells
and seduce to their cause Catholic members of the militia. Accordingly a movement
arose in 1796, initially among gentry in Counties Tyrone and Armagh, to form a
yeoman cavalry to oppose the United Irishmen and defend established property
rights. Government officials, despite concern over the appearance of setting
Protestant against Catholic, condoned the movement. Indeed, within a few months
the yeomanry were placed under commissions from the crown and armed and
equipped by the government.[42] Both militia and yeomanry were used in the
measures to disarm the north in 1797 and in the suppression of the rebellion in
1798. Whereas the yeomanry went about their work with enthusiasm, a few
executions were required to keep some militia units up to the mark.

The fact that the Irish polity included only a very small proportion of the
population between 1600 and the 1770s did not impede the statebuilding process.

Many European countries during this very period were taking important steps towards the modern state without yet drastically expanding the polity beyond a narrow elite. Such elites could attain consensus on the use of the polity's coercive resources fairly easily if they had a clear common economic interest. This was the case in Ireland once the confiscation-reconfiscation cycle was broken by the exclusion of one party to that contest in the 1690s. However, between 1789 and 1914 the central question in European politics would be how polities could be expanded to include groups with sharply conflicting economic interests without losing legitimacy. As I have suggested, the answer to that question in most cases was provided by nationalism.

The conventional reading of the Volunteer movement as part of an early stage in the development of Irish nationalism is wrongheaded not only because it misreads Volunteer and Patriotic rhetoric, but because it misconceives the historical situation of the Volunteers. Volunteering arose to defend the polity against some of those outside it: insurgent peasants; it was sustained by ritual which partly demanded, partly requested, partly demonstrated the inclusion of others: respectable non-elite Protestants and respectable Catholics. It is possible to conceive of an Irish polity which would include those who were already members around 1780 plus those groups who were respectfully knocking at the door seeking admission, but still exclude those who threatened to break the door down. It is considerably more difficult to imagine a process by which that end might have been achieved.

As the key to legitimacy in the pre-nationalist polity is trust among those who bear arms in the polity's name, the very rationale for a separate yeomanry force after the new militia had been formed testifies to the hopelessness of the Irish polity attaining legitimacy within the expanded social boundaries which were being drawn in the last two decades of the eighteenth century. It was precisely to address that problem that the government took steps to abolish the Irish polity in the Act of Union of 1800. Statebuilding had manifestly failed, and Ireland was swept into a new polity, the United Kingdom of Great Britain and Ireland, in whose subsequent failure we must seek the origins of modern Irish nationalism.

Chapter 15

Army organisation and society in the nineteenth century

E. M. Spiers

Irish military participation was particularly prominent in the nineteenth century. Whether serving in the British army or the army of the East India Company or in a myriad of foreign battalions, brigades and legions, Irishmen readily volunteered for military service. Much of this service required acceptance of fierce discipline, spartan conditions of service and minimal rewards. Much of it involved lengthy commitments, extensive tours of duty overseas, and adaptation to the routine, rigours and risks of military life. Nevertheless, Irishmen became a conspicuous element within numerous armies, displaying not only an enthusiasm for martial adventure but also a distinctive comradeship and spirit in peace and war.

Although Irish recruiting plummeted before and immediately after the rebellion of 1798, it had flourished at the outset of the French Revolutionary War. By 1 November 1796, it had produced over 50,000 soldiers and had ensured a sizeable Irish presence in the British army, consolidated by the removal of the separate Irish establishment under the Act of Union (1800). In the first fifteen years of the century, the British authorities deployed forces involving Irish soldiers around the globe in the Second Mahratta War (1803–6), the ill-advised intervention in South America (1806), the Nepal War (1814–15) and in meeting the world-wide challenge from France, especially once Holland had become a French province. Irish soldiers saw active service in Egypt, the Mediterranean, the Cape of Good Hope, Mauritius, the West Indies and the Dutch East Indies, quite apart from the major engagements of the Peninsular War (1808–14), Waterloo (18 June 1815) and the war with the United States (1812–14).[1]

Irishmen (and boys) responded to the many different recruiting campaigns; they enlisted in the 'Army of Reserve' (1803), in the 'Permanent Additional Force' (1804) and in the four levies raised from 1803 to 1805. Some 3,000 to 4,000 enlisted annually as regular recruits, comprising about one-third of the total intake, and many thousands of militiamen enlisted whenever parliament passed the necessary legislation. Irish recruiting exceeded 90,000 in the fifteen years before Waterloo, boosted by 28,499 militiamen from September 1806 to January 1813, and remained substantial after 1815 when the army was nearly halved in size.[2] By 1830, when the

15.1   A group of the 27th Foot (Inniskillings) during the battle of
Waterloo (18 June 1815).

Irish comprised some 32.2 per cent of the population of the United Kingdom, there were more Irishmen than Englishmen in the British army. The Irish proportion declined marginally before the Famine of 1846 and the subsequent crop failures, but it fell more sharply as mortality and migration took its toll of the population. As the Irish population slumped to a mere 11 per cent of the United Kingdom total by 1900, the rate of enlistment fell too, sharply reducing the proportion of Irish soldiers (table 15.1).

Ireland also contributed far more soldiers than her population warranted to the European armies of the East India Company. The company, which had never imposed restrictions upon Catholic military service, profited from the reduction in the king's forces and opened recruiting offices in Ireland. Out of the 7,620 recruits taken by the Bengal army from 1825 to 1850, 3,639 were Irish or 47.9 per cent and some of the 307 born outside the United Kingdom, often soldiers' sons born in India, were almost certainly Irish. Even *ad hoc* military formations, like the British legion sent to fight in Spain (1835–7), attracted large numbers of Irishmen (2,800 out of the first batch of 7,800 recruits). As the Irish came primarily from agricultural trades, they generally impressed the legion's medical examiner, Rutherford Alcock, who deplored the condition of at least one-eighth of the force, mainly English and

Table 15.1. *The Irish proportion of the British army in the nineteenth century*

Year	Irish NCOs and other ranks[a]	Irish proportion of the UK army %	Proportion of Roman Catholics in the UK army %
1830	40,979	42.2	n.a.
1840	39,193	37.2	n.a.
1868	55,583	30.8	28.7
1873	42,284	23.7	23.0
1878	39,121	21.9	23.2
1883	36,297	20.0	23.1
1888	31,335	15.7	19.7
1893	27,143	13.4	18.0
1898	26,376	12.9	17.7

[a]These statistics may understate the Irish contribution inasmuch as some Irishmen were probably among those classified as born in India or the colonies (about 2 per cent of the annual totals). The less steep decline in the proportion of Roman Catholics may also mean that some English or Scots-born soldiers were the offspring of Irish Catholic immigrants or of former Irish Catholic soldiers who had settled in England or Scotland.
Sources: Return of the Number of English, Scotch, and Irish Non-Commissioned Officers and Privates in the British Army, in each of the years on the 1st January 1830 and 1840, HC 1841 (307), xiiv; *General Annual Returns of the British Army* . . . , p. 65 [C. 3,083], HC 1881, lviii, 56 and p. 94 [C. 9,426], HC 1899, liii, 428; B. R. Mitchell and P. Deane, *Abstract of British Historical Statistics* (Cambridge, 1962), pp. 8–14.

Scots lured from the ranks of the unemployed in cities like Glasgow, London, Liverpool and Bristol. The Irish, he reckoned, would prove hardier and less susceptible to disease; they 'were physically and morally the best adapted for the service'.[3]

Irishmen served in all branches of the army but were most numerous in the infantry of the line and the Royal Artillery, comprising 28 per cent and 18.5 per cent of these arms in 1874, with the proportions falling to 14.2 per cent and 14.7 per cent respectively by 1899.[4] Relatively few served in the Household Cavalry and the Guards (indeed the first companies of the Irish Guards were not raised until 1900), and they were much less prominent in Irish cavalry regiments than in their infantry counterparts (in 1822, the 8th King's Royal Irish Hussars numbered 484 men of whom 192, barely 40 per cent, were Irish). By 1872 only the 5th Royal Irish Lancers had an Irish component which exceeded 30 per cent (and its 202 Irish troopers, or 42 per cent, contrasted sharply with the eighty-three Irishmen, or only 17 per cent, in the 6th Inniskilling Dragoons); by 1878, no cavalry regiment had an Irish component in excess of 30 per cent: all were overwhelmingly English in composition.[5]

Irishmen were much more conspicuous in the infantry. They filled the ranks of

337

15.2 *Listed for the Connaught Rangers*, by Lady Butler. Elizabeth Butler (1846–1933) was the English wife of General Sir William Butler, an Irish Catholic soldier with strong nationalist sympathies. The painting was exhibited at the Royal Academy in 1879.

most Irish regiments (in 1840, Irishmen accounted for 205 out of the 217 privates in the 87th (later 1st Battalion Royal Irish Fusiliers)), and filled second and, in the case of the 27th (later 1st Battalion Royal Inniskilling Fusiliers), third battalions during the Napoleonic War. They also served in large numbers in Scots and English regiments, comprising a majority in several non-Irish regiments, including the 74th (later 2nd Battalion Highland Light Infantry) in 1820 and the 67th (later 2nd Battalion Hampshire regiment) in 1843. They were so noticeable in the 33rd (later 1st Battalion Duke of Wellington's) that it was known as an 'Irish' regiment during the Abyssinian expedition (1867–8).[6] As late as 1872, two English county regiments – the 2nd Battalion of the 10th (the Lincolnshire regiment) and the 1st Battalion of the 16th (the Bedfordshire regiment) – had a majority of Irishmen in their ranks. This pattern rapidly changed partly on account of the dwindling number of Irish recruits, but even more on account of the reforms of Edward Cardwell (secretary of state for war, 1868–74). By linking battalions in pairs and localising them in specific territorial areas, Cardwell hoped that the battalions would develop local identities and recruit more thoroughly within their own areas. Although the scheme did not work as effectively as he envisaged, even when the battalions were converted into double battalions in 1881, it transformed the composition of the English battalions. By 1878, none of the non-Irish battalions had an Irish composition in excess of 40 per cent. Conversely, it consolidated an Irish predominance in excess of 65 per cent within well-established Irish battalions, like the 88th (Connaught Rangers), 86th (Royal Irish Rifles), the 27th, the 87th and the two battalions of the 18th (Royal Irish). It also enabled the six former Indian battalions, which had recently been based in Ireland after their transfer into the British army, to acquire more Irish recruits.[7]

Why Irishmen chose to sustain this tradition of military service throughout the century remains a matter of debate. Professor Hanham has questioned whether there was anything special about the Irish which made them prone to enlist. 'Ireland,' he claims, 'was simply like good recruiting districts in England, where men were encouraged to enlist by want of alternative employment.'[8] Undoubtedly army life had a low esteem throughout the United Kingdom and possibly less appeal than service in the East India Company, where soldiers had better promotion and pension prospects and more opportunities for civil employment. The army often attracted men in desperate circumstances, especially among those who frequented 'haunts of dissipation and inebriation' where much of the recruiting was conducted.[9] Some recruits looked to the army as a means of escape either from amatory indiscretions or from the rigours of the law (twenty lads, known as 'thrashers' – a violent agrarian group from Sligo and Mayo – preferred enlistment in 1807 to punishment under the Insurrection Act). Some enlisted on impulse, like Sergeant J. MacMullen who gave up the chance of clerical employment in Dublin for a life of travel and adventure. Some had positive military predilections, either enlisting from the militia or following in a family tradition, often as boy soldiers. When Patrick

Connors joined the 87th in 1839, at the age of thirteen, he followed in the footsteps of his father and grandfather. He served alongside his two brothers and was followed into the same regiment by one of his sons. The Royal Hibernian Military School, Dublin, sustained a supply of boy soldiers, providing 550 from 1815 to 1830 and about 110 per annum by the end of the century.[10]

Ireland was also distinctive as a recruiting area. It had more potential than many areas of England and Scotland in the early nineteenth century, partly because it was less industrialised and partly because conditions were so dire. Recruiting was likely to flourish amidst a burgeoning population, considerable poverty, and average rates of pay for agricultural labourers which were not only worse than those in England and Scotland but were also lower – at 7s 1¹/₄d a week in 1863 – than the nominal pay in the army (actual army pay was probably less on account of the various stoppages but it had the further appeal of being regular). As many Irish recruits came from rural areas, they tended to be healthier and hardier than those drawn from the urban slums of England and Scotland (over the years from 1837 to 1840, medical inspectors in Glasgow rejected 34.7 per cent of those who offered themselves for enlistment, whereas their counterparts in Cork rejected only 17.6 per cent).[11]

However, this pattern was not destined to endure. As the Irish population slumped after the Famine, and many young men emigrated, the rural basis of recruiting sharply declined. By 1861, the medical rejection rates for prospective Irish recruits were broadly comparable with those in the rest of the United Kingdom. By the 1870s, officers were frankly bemoaning, and somewhat exaggerating, the scale of the social change. In his 'Plea for a Peasant' Lieutenant-Colonel William Butler, who was prone to hyperbole, deplored the 'disappearance of the peasant soldier' from the ranks of the Irish and Highland regiments, while, in an official report, Lord Sandhurst, the commander-in-chief of Ireland (1870–5), confirmed the same phenomenon. Although he applauded the quality of men still coming from the Irish Militia, he deprecated the tendency of recruiting sergeants to bring in only the 'riffraff . . . of Cork and Dublin'. He added that 'The decent men who want to better their condition do not now think of entering the Army, as was the case before the famine of 1846 and 47–48. This class now emigrates *en masse* to England, the United States, and the British Colonies, in search of work and high wages.'[12]

Cardwell's reforms only partially alleviated this problem. Although territorial localisation enabled the Irish battalions to recruit more intensively within their separate districts,[13] the concomitant introduction of short service (eventually prescribed as seven years with the colours followed by five years in the reserve) increased the turnover of men. The army required larger annual recruiting intakes, while at the same time returning reservists to Ireland, many of whom were unemployed and so hardly added to the appeal of service life. Overcoming this new deterrent and meeting higher recruiting targets from a diminishing base proved an insoluble problem, despite the energetic efforts of some recruiting officers, especially those in Tralee in the early 1890s. The Irish proportion of the annual recruiting intake slipped from 15 per cent in 1880 to 10.7 per cent in 1898, and not even the outbreak of the Second Boer War boosted recruiting as much in Ireland as it did elsewhere in the United Kingdom. The anti-recruiting drives of Maude Gonne and her pro-Boer ladies may have had some effect, but they did not bring Irish enlistment to 'a virtual standstill' as her biographer claims. In fact, Irish recruiting marginally increased to 4,040 in 1900, but the underlying decline as a proportion of the annual intake simply continued during and after the war.[14]

If Irish recruiting had its peculiar aspects, the contribution of Irish officers was fairly distinctive, too. By producing so many distinguished commanders, including the duke of Wellington, Viscount Wolseley, Lord Roberts, Viscount Gough, Sir William and Sir Charles Napier, John Nicholson, Sir Henry Lawrence and Sir Henry Wilson, they achieved a prominence out of all proportion to their numbers. Irish officers accounted for about 17.5 per cent of British officers in 1878, which compares with similar estimates of the Irish proportion of senior officers in 1854, 1868 and 1899. They were more noticeable in the cavalry (20.2 per cent) and infantry (20.1 per cent) than in the Household Cavalry (11.6 per cent), Royal Engineers (10.4 per cent) and the Guards (6.7 per cent). In 1878, they did not comprise a majority in any regiment, leaving all Irish cavalry and infantry regiments with an overwhelming majority of English officers (indeed fourteen of the sixteen infantry battalions had proportions of English officers in excess of 65 per cent).[15]

What limited the scale of the Irish contribution was the large dependence upon the services of the Anglo-Irish gentry. There were some distinguished officers from outside this source, such as Lieutenant-General Sir George de Lacy Evans and General Sir Richard Kelly, but their forefathers had converted to Protestantism. Roman Catholics felt more inhibited as the formal disabilities preventing Catholics from holding commissions outside Ireland were not removed until 1817. Admittedly some Catholics had evaded these restrictions and gained commissions in the eighteenth century; they had also been allowed to hold commissions (if not staff appointments) in Ireland since an act passed in 1793. The anomaly of Irish Catholic officers either having to break the law or of having to resign whenever they came to England or Scotland underpinned the drive for repeal, but, even after repeal, the perception of a lingering prejudice against Catholic officers persisted. As Butler recalled, he had to struggle to overcome parental reticence about his choice of career: 'My father was not keen that his son should enter a profession in which the disadvantage of the absence of money could only be overcome by the surrender of one's religion – for that at least was the lesson which the cases of his relatives in the army had taught him.'[16]

The Anglo-Irish links were underpinned in many cases by illustrious military traditions and a strong affinity with the army in Ireland. Several officers, such as Gough, Lawrence, Roberts and Wolseley, followed in the footsteps of military fathers and forefathers; indeed Wolseley could trace his military connections back

---

341

to a brigadier-general who had served in the army of King William III. Others remembered the respect and affection with which the army was regarded within the Anglo-Irish community. Lieutenant-Colonel Charles Head, recalling memories of his youth, reflected

> Nothing I enjoyed more, when driving into Birr, than seeing the red-coated soldiers walking along the road in or out of the town. They looked such gentlemen compared with the local inhabitants. And the officers I came into contact with always appeared to me to be veritable gods from Olympus.[17]

The military presence was ever present and highly visible, as large numbers of soldiers were regularly stationed in Ireland (about 25,000 per annum during the last quarter of the century). Deployed in small barracks across the country, these detachments were often welcomed locally as a boost to trade, as socially desirable (especially eligible young officers from the more prestigious English regiments) and, above all, as a bulwark for Loyalism. Nora Robertson, the daughter of an Anglo-Irish officer, perceptively recalled that 'the close association of the officer class with the civilians of like mind created and encouraged a Loyalist standpoint which no other influence could have created'. She added, too, that this was not merely a political link:

> The Anglo-Irish country gentlemen of my day took their colour absolutely from the garrison, not only the patriotic orientation of the latter but their social and mental angle. It had become obligatory to look and speak like an English public school man . . . [18]

Accordingly, many better-off Anglo-Irish families sent their sons to English public schools, partly to lose any Irish brogue, and thence into the armed services. Quite apart from following in a family tradition or of confirming social status, this choice seemed prudent as the career opportunities for scions of the Anglo-Irish gentry were much more limited than those of their English counterparts. They lacked coal, railways and industrial sites to exploit on their land and there were relatively few appointments to be gained in Dublin Castle. Moreover, in the army they had plenty of time to indulge their passion for field sports – a passion shared, and fondly recalled, by many officers who served in Ireland. Whether Anglo-Irishmen became less university-minded than their English contemporaries, as Nora Robertson claimed, cannot be proven, but Sir Hugh McCalmont exemplified her point. An old Etonian destined for Oxford, he abandoned any thought of a university career after spending some months hunting and socialising with the 9th Lancers, when the latter were quartered in Dublin. McCalmont purchased a cornetcy in the regiment.[19]

Less affluent Irishmen had to enter the army by a more circuitous route. Under the purchase system, which was not abolished until 1871, the purchase costs in the 5th Royal Irish Lancers ranged from £450 for a cornetcy to £4,500 for a lieutenant-

15.3 Major-General Frederick S. Roberts (1832–1914) – Earl Roberts of
Kandahar, Pretoria and Waterford – encompassing in his titles the British
imperial service of many Irish soldiers.

colonelcy (and the over-regulation prices of £750 for a lieutenancy rising to £8,700
for a lieutenant-colonelcy), so ensuring that only the well endowed, like the duke
of Montrose, could gain a commission. Aspirants whose fathers were yeomen or
gentlemen farmers, like Maurice Griffin Dennis and de Lacy Evans, sought

commissions without purchase by volunteering initially for service in the Colonial Corps or in India, and thereafter by gaining promotions to the regular army. Another possible route was through the Militia, and, in the post-purchase army, this was still favoured by a large number whose parents could not afford the fees of Sandhurst or Woolwich, or who, like Henry Wilson, failed the entrance examinations. Even in the post-purchase army, officers could not live on their pay and required private means to provide their own uniform, cases, furniture, mufti, servant's outfit and incoming mess contribution (about £200 for an infantry officer or £600 to £1,000 for a cavalry officer). Thereafter the expenses of dining in the mess, sport, social entertainment and the constant moving of army life required an annual private income of about £100 to £150 for an infantry officer, and of £600 to £700 for a cavalry officer. In these circumstances, the least well-off undertook service in India where the costs of military life were considerably less, or sought commissions in the least expensive infantry regiments which included most of the Irish regiments. The latter had a somewhat lowly status as a consequence, not only within the army but also in the perceptions of the Anglo-Irish gentry.[20]

How then should the Irish contribution to the British army be assessed? It was highly visible and, alongside the Scots and to a much lesser extent the Welsh, it made the army seem less English than it might otherwise have been. It added a culturally different element to the army, reflecting the presence of Irish-speaking soldiers (particularly in the early part of the century), the prominence of Roman Catholicism, and the pervasiveness of Irish humour and forms of camaraderie. John Shipp, writing in the 1820s, reckoned that the effects were wholly positive:

> I must confess that I do love to be on duty on any kind of service with the Irish. There is a promptness to obey, a hilarity, a cheerful obedience, and willingness to act ... [and] in the corps (I mean the 87th Regiment) a degree of liberality amongst the men I have never seen in any other corps – a willingness to share their crust and drop on service with their comrades ... In that corps there was a unity I have never seen in any other; and as for fighting, they were the very devils.[21]

Such comments have to be placed in perspective. Many British officers extolled the *esprit de corps* of their own regiment, and Shipp's observations, like other assessments of Irish fighting qualities, whether positive or negative,[22] were essentially impressionistic. Even so, they testified to a recognition of the army's cultural diversity about which the authorities had somewhat ambivalent feelings. During the Peninsular War, Sir Arthur Wellesley, though fiercely opposed to any interference by the priesthood, was willing to let Catholic soldiers attend mass locally (at a time when, legally, they could only do so in Ireland). He was confident that the soldiers, if left to their own devices, would probably not bother, and this pragmatic attitude persisted after the war. Although the authorities expanded the rights of Catholic soldiers to attend mass, they feared any subversive influence by the priesthood, particularly during the Emancipation crisis, and subsequently created their own establishment of Roman Catholic chaplains in 1836. If fairly nominal, like the rest of the religious provision before the Crimean War (when a mere seven chaplains comprised the department in March 1854), the number of chaplains grew thereafter. Fifteen commissions were given to Roman Catholic chaplains on 18 January 1859, and many of them became closely associated with Irish regiments. Father Robert Brindle, DSO, did much to boost the spirits of the Royal Irish during the ill-fated Gordon relief expedition (1884–5). When several soldiers fell out on the line of march, Colonel Percival Marling recalled that 'Dear old Father Brindle borrowed the Adjutant's pony and went out and hauled in 17 of his flock. I believe he said he would excommunicate them if they wouldn't come in.'[23] On 7 September 1886, a Roman Catholic priest was allowed for the first time to consecrate the new Colours of the 1st Battalion Royal Irish.

The authorities, nonetheless, remained concerned lest any semblance of sectarianism manifest itself within the ranks. When evidence of an Orange lodge came to light in 1822 among the soldiers of the 55th Foot (later 2nd Battalion Border Regiment) after a tour of duty in Ireland, the duke of York, the commander in chief, formally proscribed such organisations. Lord Hill, his successor, had to reissue the order in 1829 and 1835 as sectarianism resurfaced among regiments based in Ireland. It was particularly evident during 1826–8 as the emancipation crisis worsened. Reports reached the authorities of priests haranguing soldiers, some of whom were contributing to the Catholic rent, of regiments split into Orange and Green factions, and of soldiers taking part in Orange celebrations or wearing Orange lilies while on guard duty at Dublin Castle. Commanding officers were required not only to suppress all signs of factionalism, but to curb any signs of disloyalty among Irish Catholic soldiers.[24]

In Newry, on 10 October 1830, the Catholic soldiers in six companies of the 87th initially disobeyed orders and refused to march to chapel, without the customary accompaniment of their fifes and drums. As Roman Catholics comprised five-sixths of the regiment, they had been permitted to march to chapel with their band in England, but this practice had been revoked in Newry lest it provoke local Orangemen (and some of these soldiers had already fought with Protestants in Armagh on 4 October). Considered as far more serious than the 'little unrest' described by the regimental historian, the initial refusal to obey orders in front of watching townsfolk prompted a flurry of correspondence between the authorities in Dublin and London. Sir Henry Hardinge, the chief secretary of Ireland, considered the regiment as 'worse than useless' and recommended its immediate dispatch to the West Indies. Retaining the regiment, he feared, would be

> worse than having no 87th Regiment here, because one or two tried Regiments must be employed in watching its conduct – besides the example might be contagious, or the defection at a crisis fatal, and the hope of treasonable assistance in a Catholic armed force would give confidence to the People, the only ingredient wanting to make a large mass rush into insurrection.[25]

Deeply concerned about the influence of Daniel O'Connell in Ireland, Sir Robert Peel, the home secretary, and the duke of Wellington, then prime minister, endorsed these sentiments. The duke only demurred at the removal of the regiment to the West Indies in case such service became considered as a disgrace and punishment. Having mooted Botany Bay as an alternative, the duke accepted the prompt removal of the 87th to Plymouth! The incident remained a lingering source of anxiety for the political and military authorities. Although they regularly dispatched Irish regiments on long tours of overseas duty, sometimes in excess of twenty years (as they did with non-Irish regiments), they had to rotate these units and felt that they had to thwart any subversive influences. Hence in Ireland, commanding officers were required to exercise 'dire attention and vigilance' in this matter, regiments were frequently moved from barrack to barrack (to avoid undue fraternisation with civilians), and concern was voiced about soldiers reading seditious literature or hearing speeches by radicals or priests. Hardinge was appalled to learn that a party of the 45th Foot had been deployed to preserve public order at a meeting addressed by O'Connell in May 1843, as the speaker had the effrontery to propose three cheers for the military![26]

These anxieties paled by comparison with those which arose in the mid-1860s, when Fenians infiltrated British regiments, seeking recruits among trained soldiers with access to arms and ammunition, and so hoping to maximise their impact, and the enemy's demoralisation, come the day of insurrection. Over the period from 1863 or early 1864 to February 1866, the Fenians launched determined recruiting drives within the army under the leadership of 'Pagan' O'Leary, then William Francis Roantree and finally, John Devoy. Concentrating upon Irish Catholic soldiers, they recruited substantial numbers in Ireland and England, possibly several thousands but probably not the 15,000 claimed by Devoy in his memoirs. The British authorities never knew the exact number and initially Sir George Brown, the ailing commander-in-chief in Ireland (1860–5), grossly underestimated the extent and seriousness of the problem. His successor, Sir Hugh Rose (later Lord Strathnairn) did not, and he worked vigorously with the civil authorities in Ireland to pre-empt the rebellion. By close surveillance and intelligence gathering, the authorities prepared their major strike on the Brotherhood on the night of 15 September 1865. Thereafter they gradually tightened their security controls, suspending the Habeas Corpus Act in February 1866 and arresting many of the Fenian agents, including Devoy. Even so, Rose recognised the persistent 'spirit of disaffection and hostility to British rule'; he remained on the alert, and when the Fenians staged their abortive rising (March 1867), dispatched flying columns of cavalry, infantry and engineers to capture or disperse the remaining insurgents.[27]

In their subsequent writings, Fenians claimed that the British authorities dealt with 'crack Fenian regiments' by the simple expedient of sending them overseas. A. J. Semple rightly states that the roster was not altered, and that two of the supposedly 'crack' regiments – the 5th Dragoon Guards and the 10th Hussars – were

15.4 5th Dragoon Guards and 2nd Battalion Connaught Rangers
returning from the garrison church, Nasiribad, India, 1898.

employed in the flying columns. Rose, nonetheless, had repeatedly pressed for a
change of the roster and for the removal of coreligionists from southern Ireland. He
claimed that there were precedents in the 1830s and 1840s when Scots regiments
were sent out of turn to Ireland, and, as Fenianism had become so pervasive among
Irish Roman Catholic soldiers, he desperately wanted more of his fellow Scots in
Ireland. The duke of Cambridge, the commander-in-chief, refused, arguing that,
'It would never do to show the slightest want of confidence in any particular
Regiment.'[28] Compelled to rely upon the forces under his command, Rose persevered
and, in June 1867, paid a handsome tribute to the discipline of his men. He reported
that

> There is no present danger to be apprehended from disaffection in the Army. Very
> bad, and far too many cases of individual, but not collective, treason have occurred
> amongst the Irish Roman Catholic soldiers. But discipline has been vindicated . . .
> Not a single order I ever gave for the suppression of Fenianism or apprehended
> outbreaks has been, in the slightest degree, disobeyed by any soldier, or soldiers.[29]

Although there were no further incidents in the last quarter of the century, the military authorities remained vigilant, particularly in view of the agrarian disturbances in Ireland during the 1870s and 1880s. In 1886, W. H. Smith, the secretary of state for war, proposed that the chief secretary should seek to improve the employment prospects for army reservists in Ireland. 'They are probably disposed to be loyal,' he surmised, but it would 'be just as well to make it worth their while to remain so.'[30] If this reasonably constructive suggestion failed to elicit a positive response, so did the alarmist reports from Wolseley when he was commander-in-chief in Ireland (1890–5). He fiercely deprecated any Irish indiscretion, whether by individuals or groups (including the sixty Munster Fusiliers who ran amok on a train in November 1893), and, in April 1893, recommended that 'it would be well to get *all* the Irish Regts. out of Ireland as soon as possible & not to send any more until Mr Gladstone dies or is turned out of office. I would not trust them in a riot here.'[31] His successor Lord Roberts, another Anglo-Irishman but one with more temperate views, reported after three and a half years that the 25,000 men under his command had all 'been remarkably well behaved'.[32]

In fact, Irish regiments generally proved disciplined, loyal and ready to do their duty. Even in the arduous task of providing aid to the civil power, when they were often split into small detachments and quartered in private billets, mills and other unsatisfactory premises, and where their sympathies, like those of some Irish commanders (notably Sir Charles Napier), may have been divided, they proved reliable. They served in all parts of the United Kingdom but were a useful substitute for English regiments in the north of England during the Chartist disturbances and for Scottish regiments during the outbreaks of disorder in Scotland. Occasionally their discipline could be stretched, as when the 87th was quartered in the Lowlands near gangs of Irish railway navvies in 1843–4 (whereupon the number of court-martials and desertions soared), but Irish units were frequently praised for their forbearance and discipline in maintaining public order.[33]

Organised, drilled and deployed on the same lines as other British regiments, Irish units took their turn in garrisoning some unhealthy stations, suffering losses from disease and dissipation (the two battalions of the 18th lost 52 officers and 1,777 other ranks during their service in the West Indies from 1805 to 1817). They also endured privations on active service. William Grattan graphically described how the spirit of the 88th survived some appalling conditions in the Peninsular War, especially when officers and men were reduced to rags, lacked shoes, tents and coats, and found their pay far in arrears during the retreat from Burgos in the winter of 1812. Despite firm leadership, discipline periodically wavered as soldiers indulged a penchant for plundering and, if they could find it, drink. Nevertheless Irish soldiers, like their counterparts throughout the British army, appear to have had strong desire for action. They chafed at underemployment, sometimes felt that others were preferred for active service (as the Highlanders almost certainly were), and responded with wild enthusiasm when the chance of action occurred (for example, the 18th on the eve of the assault on Redan, 18 June 1855).[34]

When actively engaged, Irish infantry repeatedly confirmed their value as assault troops (the 88th at Busaco, 27 September 1810, the 87th at Barrosa, 5 March 1811, 101st in the storming of Delhi, 14 September 1857, and 86th in the attack upon Jhansi, 3 April 1858). They displayed, too, considerable stoicism under attack (the 87th in the defence of Tarifa, 31 December 1811, and the 27th at Waterloo), and proficiency in handling their weapons (in 1870–1, the 27th attained the highest shooting standard of any regiment in the army). Irish cavalry were also fully involved in the major wars (the 8th Hussars in the Mahratta and Nepalese Wars and in the charge of the Light Brigade, 25 October 1854; the Inniskilling Dragoons in the charge of the Union Brigade at Waterloo and, with the 4th and 5th Dragoon Guards, in the charge of the Heavy Brigade at Balaklava). Finally Irish soldiers, including those in the artillery, engineers and support services, found their stamina, courage, health and adaptability frequently tested in the plethora of small colonial campaigns.[35]

Ultimately nearly all the Irish regiments were involved in the Second Boer War (1899–1902). Despite the pro-Boer agitation, regiments such as the 8th Hussars, the 2nd Royal Irish Rifles and the 1st Royal Inniskilling Fusiliers left Ireland amidst scenes of great enthusiasm. They earned considerable acclaim for their fortitude and resolve, especially as some battalions suffered from appalling generalship and staffwork in the early battles. During the retreat from Stormberg (10 December 1899) 4 officers and 216 other ranks of the Royal Irish Rifles were left behind, and in Natal the Irish Brigade, including 2nd Battalion Dublin Fusiliers, 1st Battalion Inniskillings and 1st Battalion Connaught Rangers, incurred heavy casualties at Colenso (15 December 1899) and Hart's Hill (23–4 February 1900). When the tide of battle turned, Irish forces proved that they could adapt to the new conditions of war, dictated by the use of smokeless magazine rifles, and to the rigours of campaigning for nearly two and a half years in South Africa. They were fully engaged in the harassment and pursuit of the Boers, and in the tedious work of escorting convoys, outpost duty, manning blockhouses and garrison work generally. Queen Victoria marked the valour of the Irish in Natal by ordering that all ranks of the Irish regiments should wear a shamrock on St Patrick's Day.[36]

Foreign military service was another facet of the Irish military tradition. Throughout the nineteenth century, Irishmen served in foreign armies, fought in distinctively 'Irish' formations, and periodically challenged the forces of the crown. Irishmen served in South America, Europe, South Africa, and most prominently in the American Civil War. In the attacks against the Stone Wall at Marye's Heights,

15.5   Camp of the 18th (Royal Irish) Regiment at Sebastopol, May 1856.

Fredericksburg (13 December 1862), the charge at Antietam (17 September 1862) and in rescuing abandoned cannon during the battle of Chancellorsville (2–6 May 1863), Irish soldiers added mightily to their fighting reputation. However tangible these specific achievements, the broader phenomenon of Irish foreign military service has all too often been embellished in subsequent descriptions, becoming wrapped at times in romantic mythology.

Underpinning this mythology is the assumption that this form of military service, often characterised as fighting for a cause, readily attracted Irishmen. In his account of the Irish Brigade, Captain David P. Conyngham maintained that 'The Irish people in New York, and throughout the Northern States, were not slow in declaring for the Union and volunteering for its defence.'[37] Some certainly did so. Thomas Francis Meagher, the fervent Irish nationalist who later commanded the brigade, was quick to respond. By raising an Irish Zouave company to fight for the Union in 1861, he argued that Irishmen should show their patriotic support for their adopted country, seek to preserve the republic without whose moral and material aid Ireland could never be free, and gain military experience which could later be employed 'in a fight for Ireland's freedom'. In such circumstances, argues Thomas J. Mullen, Irishmen were willing to set aside their political preferences and rally to the republic. 'Besides,' he adds, 'what Irishman could keep out of the war, especially when it was reported that England favoured the South.'[38]

In fact, the war aroused mixed emotions among Irish–Americans, the largest immigrant group, in the North. Although some promptly answered the call to arms, and left for the front amid euphoric scenes in their local communities (notably in New York city), the Irish as a whole were possibly 'the most under-represented group in proportion to population'.[39] Many did not set aside their political attachments. Overwhelmingly Democratic, they were not enamoured of the Republican war aims, especially emancipation. Having competed with free blacks at the bottom of the social order, many Irish–Americans were fiercely anti-Negro. They had frequently rioted against black people in northern cities, and continued to do so during the war (notably in Cincinnati and Brooklyn in the summer of 1862). Admittedly, as the war dragged on, more and more Irishmen joined the Union ranks; some of those who had not filed for citizenship (or claimed that they had not done so), furnished a large number of the substitutes and bounty men in the last year of the war. Yet Irish–Americans also participated in the anti-draft riots in the coalfields of eastern Pennsylvania, in Boston and in New York city. As James McPherson observed, the Irish, 'working in low-skill jobs for marginal wages, fearful of competition from black workers, hostile toward the Protestant middle and upper classes who often disdained or exploited them . . . were ripe for revolt against this war waged by Yankee Protestants for black freedom'.[40]

Even so, some 144,000 Irishmen eventually served in the Federal armies and facilitated the formation of several regiments and brigades which were predominantly Irish in composition. This was not the case in many other wars, where the units which were described as Irish, or were raised by Irishmen to fight under specially designed Irish colours, were often largely dependent on non-Irishmen to become remotely credible as fighting formations. Napoleon's Irish Legion found it impossible to maintain an establishment of Irish officers up to the rank of captain, and filled its ranks primarily with German and Polish prisoners-of-war. The Anglo-Irish Legion raised in 1818–20 to fight for South American independence had a much larger Irish proportion, comprising more than half of its 5,500 officers and men, but the Saint Patrick's Battalion, formed during the American–Mexican War (1846–8) had a smaller Irish contingent. Despite the leadership of John Riley, an Irish-born deserter from the American army, and his exploitation of Irish Catholic symbolism (an emerald green ensign with an image of Saint Patrick emblazoned on one side and with a shamrock and the harp of Erin on the other), only two-fifths of the San Patricios were Irish. The two Irish brigades which fought for the Boers in the Second Boer War were also heavily dependent on non-Irishmen, especially the second brigade raised by the linguistically fluent Arthur Lynch.[41]

If the presence of non-Irishmen did not necessarily detract from the distinctively Irish character of these formations, it underlined certain aspects of them. Many of the units were grossly under strength or soon became so, as in the case of the three Irish regiments (Hibernia, Ultonia and Irlanda) which fought for Spain against Napoleon. In addition to the normal campaign losses, part of the Hibernia regiment was captured while covering the British evacuation at Corunna (January 1809) and the 250 survivors of the 800 strong Ultonia regiment surrendered after the third siege of Gerona (May–December 1809). Some Irish brigades or battalions had a strength which was little more than that of a company (in British parlance a battalion of some 1,100 men had 8 companies). The San Patricios were never much of a force; they grew from a 'company' of 48 to a 'battalion' of over 200 by July 1847. Irishmen may have been deterred from desertion by the threat of severe punishment, just as those living in Britain may have been deterred from foreign service by the penalties of the Foreign Enlistment Act (1819). Imposed to contain volunteering for South America, the Act may also have ensured that the brigade of 10,000 Irishmen sought by Pope Pius IX in 1860 never materialised. Only 1,400 men served in the Saint Patrick Battalion, and they were split with one half acting as a garrison at Spoleto while the other four companies fought in the disastrous battle of Castelfidardo (18 September 1860) and in the abortive defence of Ancona (29 September 1860). Even less formidable (at least in numerical terms) were the Irish company which served in the French *Regiment Etranger* (1870–1) and the two Irish brigades of the Boer War. The 100 strong Irish company lost about one-third of its number at the battle of Montbeliard (16 January 1871), and by the armistice (2 February 1871) had only forty-five rifles remaining. The first brigade in South Africa, commanded by Colonel John Blake, possibly numbered about 200 men, the second about 150, and the Irish–American reinforcements from Chicago and Massachusetts, predicted to number 1,000, totalled a mere 58.[42]

The paucity of numbers also meant that the units had little choice about whom to accept. Those corps formed from prisoners-of-war or deserters, or raised in the wake of the Napoleonic War, at least had a nucleus of trained men and officers. Neither the papal battalion, commanded by a militia officer and gentleman farmer from County Louth, nor the brigades raised from the Rand Irish could draw on much military experience. Blake, a former lieutenant in the US cavalry, had at least fought the Apaches, but Lynch gained the colonelcy of the Second Brigade without any military experience whatsoever.

Simon Bolivar undoubtedly benefited from his ability to recruit experienced men from among the Anglo-Irish veterans of the Napoleonic War. He gained the services of some 5,500 officers and men, who were lured by the promises of Lopez Mendez and the appeals of John D'Evereux, an Irish adventurer. These legionaries assisted in the training and in the tactical instruction of Bolivar's forces, particularly in mixed formations. They also served valiantly, even in relatively small units, at the battles of Pantano de Vargas (24 July 1819), Boyaca (7 August 1819) and Carabobo (24 June 1821) which led to the liberation of Venezuela. Yet the legion never served *en masse*; the men arrived in batches in South America over a period of two and a half years. The legion also suffered, as similar formations did, from an inability to replace its wastage of manpower. The legion's numbers dwindled rapidly from the effects of desertion and disease (both typhus brought from Britain and the malaria, small-pox and yellow fever contracted locally). It incurred losses on the line of march (one quarter of those who crossed the Andes and the Paramo desert – at 13,500 feet – died from exposure and lack of oxygen) and suffered heavy casualties in combat (11 officers and 95 men died out of the 350 legionaries who fought at Carabobo). The Europeans, nonetheless, had rendered crucial assistance in the liberation struggle; Bolivar recognised this, even claiming once that Mendez was the real liberator of South America, as he had raised and dispatched the legion.[43]

Irishmen from virtually every walk of life volunteered to serve in foreign military armies. They cannot all be described as mercenaries or as men committed to particular causes. There were certainly some who were tempted to leave their state of destitution by promises of regular pay, rations, uniforms, and, in some cases, the prospect of land grants or return passages. There were others who abandoned paid employment to volunteer for foreign service, and, in the Boer War, volunteers who agreed to fight for the Boers without any pay. Some half-pay officers and officers who had sold out of the British army saw attractions in the prospect of promotions, higher rates of pay, active service, and, in particular cases, field command. Some were simply itinerant soldiers like Captain Myles Keogh, who served in the Papal army, the Union army, and finally the US cavalry (he was killed with General Custer at the battle of the Little Bighorn river, 24 June 1876). Alfred Aylward moved from cause to cause, fighting first for Guiseppi Garibaldi before serving as second-in-command of the 'European Corps' – a handful of Uitlanders who supported the Boers in the First Boer War (1880–1). Finally, some were simply discontented with their life at home; they were either stirred by the thought of foreign adventure or they wished to 'prove' themselves in combat. As Arthur Lynch recollected, 'I was resolved to show that I, a thinker, could ride with the boldest horsemen in the world and, pitted with the "men of action", would set them a pace which would test their nerve and call forth every ounce of energy.'[44]

The Saint Patrick's Battalion which fought for Mexico was unique inasmuch as it was composed entirely of deserters. They did not desert *en bloc* to fight for a cause, but left the American ranks for a myriad of personal reasons. These included dislike of the brutal military discipline and harassment by native born officers in the American army, disorientation on account of sickness or lack of food, religious sentiments, the charms of Mexican senoritas, drunkenness which sometimes led to capture by the enemy, and the enticements of promised promotion, bounties and land bonuses. Yet the Irish-born renegades constituted only 'a minute percentage of the total number of Irishmen who served in the American army'.[45] In effect, they ended up – as many others did – simply fighting fellow Irishmen. This pattern had happened in the Peninsular War where Napoleon's legion fought not only Irishmen in the British army but also the Irish regiments in the Spanish army. It recurred in the American Civil War, where a smaller, but highly conspicuous, number of the Irishmen fought for the Confederacy in units such as the 'Louisiana Tigers', the Emerald Guards of Alabama and the Irish Jasper Greens of Georgia. Indeed at the battle of Fredericksburg, Confederate Irish in Colonel Robert McMillan's 24th Georgia infantry were defending part of Marye's Heights while it was under attack from Meagher's Irish Brigade. During the Second Boer War, the Irish Brigades fought not only the Irishmen in the British regiments but also fellow Rand-Irish, who had volunteered to fight for Britain, and the enmity between these groups, particularly between the former miners in Blake's Irish and the Imperial Light Horse, was intense.[46]

The achievements of the legionaries are commemorated in the medals, plaques and monuments of their host countries, but these are often retrospective memorials. Contemporaries were not always so appreciative of the Irish involvement. Whenever legionaries found that the promises of regular pay, rations, uniforms and land grants were largely bogus, they often protested vigorously and/or lapsed into drunkenness, indiscipline, desertion or mutiny. Inevitably such behaviour simply made the Irish seem more trouble than they worth to the host army, at least when they were not actively engaged. Bolivar was unusual in his staunch support of the legion, and in his dependence upon the advice of trusted *aides-de-camp* like James Rooke and Daniel Francis O'Leary. Some of his generals were much less well disposed; indeed, General Urdaneta reportedly said that he would prefer to fight ten battles than to make another march with the legionaries.[47] The Brazilian authorities were even more severe upon the Irish regiment which Colonel Cotter had raised to serve in Brazil in 1826. When 200 Irishmen mutinied in the wake of appalling local treatment, the Brazilians promptly ordered the whole body of 2,400 settlers to leave the country. In the United States the formation of Irish volunteer companies in the 1840s and 1850s simply fuelled the resentment of American nativists and Know Nothings. Several Irish companies had to be disbanded and the anti-Irish sentiment reached a crescendo in 1860 when Colonel Michael Corcoran refused to parade the Irish 69th Regiment to welcome the prince of Wales on his visit to New York. Corcoran would probably have been court-martialled had not the Civil War intervened. *Harper's Weekly* castigated the Irish:

> As militiamen and soldiers they have not infrequently been an absolute nuisance. It is not worth while to repeat the story . . . of the Irishmen who deserted from our army and constituted the battalion of San Patricio in the Mexican War . . . The spectacle of the ignominious surrender of the Irishmen in Lamoricere's army, who had volunteered to assist the Pope in keeping down his Italian subjects, has not been forgotten. Before our Irishmen thrust themselves anew under the public nostril they should allow the effluvia of this transaction to pass away.[48]

Even on active service there was relatively little that small bodies of Irishmen could accomplish. Unless composed largely of veterans, their tactical impact was always likely to prove marginal, however valiantly they fought. Depleted units were employed in garrison duties (like the single-battalion Hibernia Regiment from 1812 to 1814), in support roles (like protecting the Boer long-range artillery) and in performing specialist tasks (like dynamiting bridges, culverts and buildings to cover the Boer retreats). Irish commanders, if well connected locally, could act more effectively. Bernardo O'Higgins, the illegitimate son of an Irishman who became governor of Chile, commanded rebel armies and secured the vital services of Admiral Lord Cochrane in the struggle for Chilean independence. He later fought for Bolivar in the liberation of Peru.[49]

The larger bodies of Irish soldiers were more useful. If the full strength Spanish regiments and Bolivar's legion made important contributions on the battlefield, the Irish forces in the American Civil War were even more effective. In the Federal and Confederate armies, Irish soldiers were remembered as resolute, enthusiastic and remarkably healthy. If often characterised as improvident with their kit, prone to drink and sometimes to recklessness, they were also considered as loyal, courageous (with some exceptions), and more useful in offensive spurts than in protracted defensive operations. Their presence brightened camp life, prompting B. Irvin Wiley to conclude that 'all in all their influence and example both in battle and in garrison was an immense asset to the Union cause'.[50]

In several wars, though, Irish volunteers were valued as much for their political symbolism as for their military contribution. Bolivar appreciated that the presence of European volunteers in his army gave the struggle for Venezuelan independence a measure of international support and external credibility. Where the Irish were willing to fight against the British, they had a double propaganda value. They served as a possible focus for further dissent both at home and on the battlefield. During

15.6   Bernardo O'Higgins (1778–1842), president of Chile.

the Napoleonic War, the Irish legion underscored the continuing concern about political stability in Ireland (after the rising of 1798), and encouraged the defection of further prisoners of war. In the Second Boer War, the Irish brigades reflected both the depth of pro-Boer sentiment in Britain and of the international hostility to the British war aims in 1899.[51]

Irishmen, in sum, sustained their military reputation by an immense range and diversity of service. Their military participation, like their emigration overseas, reflected elements of 'push' and 'pull': the 'push' coming from attempts to escape the poverty, the lack of prospects and the restricted confines of life in Ireland; the 'pull' deriving from the attractions of regular pay and provisions, the sense of community and comradeship in regimental life, and the appeal of action and adventure, often in distant locations. The Anglo-Irish had further inducements to reaffirm their patriotism, their affinity with the English and Scots gentry, and their long-standing traditions of serving the crown or the East India Company. Finally, there were Irishmen willing to fight for a cause, or to fight against Britain (or prepare to do so), or to fight for a mixture of motives. If only a small minority of Irishmen ever volunteered for military service, they always proved a conspicuous element in regimental life, and, if properly drilled, equipped and organised, they regularly served with distinction.

Chapter 16

The army and law and order in the nineteenth century

Virginia Crossman

'I have no patience with playing police in this unsociable country.'[1] The cry uttered by Major-General G. C. Mundy of the 43rd Foot when stationed in Cork in the summer of 1834 struck a chord which was to echo down the remaining decades of the nineteenth century. Assisting the civil power to preserve the peace was an accepted function of the army second only to the defence of the realm. But whereas in Britain troops were called on to perform such duties comparatively rarely, in Ireland applications for assistance were far more common and in times of widespread disturbance placed considerable strain on army resources and discipline. Soldiers in Ireland found further cause for complaint in being stationed in remote districts in barracks which provided few comforts and fewer social amenities. The potential hazards of a tour of duty in Ireland thus included not only harassing activity in the form of night patrols and riot duty but also the boredom of enforced idleness unrelieved, outside Dublin, by the distractions of polite society. The presence of substantial numbers of troops in Ireland (the amount of force fluctuated between 15,000 and 30,000 men) reflected the weak hold of civil government. Despite the establishment of professional police forces in 1822 and their reorganisation on a national basis in 1836, the army retained a vital role in law enforcement. It acted not so much as an arm of government, that function being performed by the police, but as a staff to be grasped when occasion required. This was a distinction which commanding officers were anxious to maintain. Writing to the commander of the southern district, Major-General Sir Charles Doyle, in 1825, the assistant military secretary at Kilmainham warned that 'the magistrates are generally very ready to transfer the duties of the police to the military, if it be possible, but these attempts have always been resisted. Where the civil authorities are not strong enough, and require assistance it should undoubtedly be given them, but if they demand it unnecessarily, a representation is generally made to Government.'[2] Representations of this nature were still being made in the closing decades of the century,[3] suggesting a degree of continuity not only in the way in which the Irish command perceived its task but also in the nature of the task itself.

The duties most commonly performed by military parties furnished in aid of the

civil power were providing escorts for prisoners and witnesses and military guards at gaols and executions, protecting sheriffs, bailiffs and other functionaries, and attending public gatherings such as fairs, markets and political meetings at which breaches of the peace might be expected. Troops were extensively deployed during elections throughout the century both as a riot control force and as escorts for voters and poll books.[4] It was widely believed that they were more efficacious than the constabulary on such occasions, being deployed in larger numbers and with greater deterrent effect. Most military authorities stressed the importance of ensuring that detachments comprised both cavalry and infantry. According to one commander of the forces in Ireland, Sir Richard Hussey Vivian, cavalry could keep the people at arm's length, preventing them from pressing on the infantry and if trouble occurred could more easily capture the ring-leaders.[5] Much of the effect of cavalry was psychological rather than practical. When an application for cavalry to attend a fair at Muff in August 1839, was objected to by the local commanding officer on the grounds that cavalry were unsuited to the ground, the requisitioning magistrate responded that cavalry were a 'valuable and necessary *prevention* to disturbance' at the fair.[6] Cavalry were not trained for the conditions which prevailed in Ireland. They could not manoeuvre in narrow streets and were unused to operating across cultivated land. Belief in the 'moral effect' of cavalry nevertheless remained strong until the end of the century.[7]

The terms of the relationship between the civil and military authorities, central and local, which form the subject matter of this chapter, were clearly laid down in army regulations and in Dublin Castle circulars. But while the line between the respective duties of the police and the military could be preserved with fairly little difficulty under ordinary circumstances, in periods of disturbance it was far harder to maintain.[8] The stresses and strains imposed on the forces of law and order by the land war, for example, have been explored by a number of historians.[9] The general consensus emerging from such studies is that the period saw a change in the basis on which the army acted in aid of the civil power. But the events of the land war must be seen in the context of the century as a whole and specifically in comparison with those of the tithe war of the 1830s which had presented the army with similar problems and had called forth a similar response. As a consequence of the tithe war army regulations were redrawn in an attempt to define more clearly the manner and the occasions on which troops should be deployed. That these proved incapable of preventing the army being drawn into the political maelstrom of the 1880s was a reflection of the predominance of political over purely military considerations.

In determining the amount of force stationed in Ireland the military authorities had to balance the need to guard against the possibility of insurrection, a possibility which was always taken more seriously if events abroad assumed a threatening aspect, with competing demands from other quarters for both financial and man-power resources. Commanders of the forces in Ireland rarely felt that the correct balance had been struck. Their anxiety on this score related not merely to the number of men available but also to their fitness for the duties required. In the early years of the century when Britain was at war with France and the home army was consequently depleted, auxiliary forces were mobilised, the most important of these being the militia and the yeomanry. Problems of ill-discipline and inadequate training plagued both these forces and it was with some relief that the Irish authorities dispensed with their services after the conclusion of the war. Some regular troops also gave cause for concern. A frequent complaint concerned the relative numbers of depot troops and battalions of the line. As Sir Hugh Rose (commander of the forces 1865–70) explained to the lord lieutenant, Lord Wodehouse, in 1865, the depots were made up of young soldiers recruited to supply regiments in foreign service, old soldiers nearing retirement and recovered invalids. They were not qualified for the peculiar service in Ireland 'which is that at any moment a battalion may, in detachments or pickets, have to give active assistance to the civil power under commanders of inferior grade in remote parts of the country at a distance from head quarters'.[10] Not only was a large proportion of the depot battalions Catholic, but they were recruited in areas, such as the south-west, prone to disaffection. Using such troops to police their own countrymen seemed to be asking for trouble and in times of political excitement or popular disturbance steps were taken where possible to replace Irish troops by English or Scottish regiments. During the Fenian disturbances of the 1860s, Rose reverted to the policy that he had adopted in the 1830s when he had been a junior officer in Ireland. 'It was for the sake of avoiding the embarrassments which so generally ensue from controlling popular agitation with soldiers, coreligionist friends and relatives of the agitators', he informed the duke of Cambridge (commander-in-chief) in 1865,

> that I ventured to see that as much as possible soldiers *without* these sympathies should be so employed in the South of Ireland. This system was adopted with the *best effects* from 1830 to 1838 for the repression of the monster or tithe meetings as I know from experience, my old regiment, the 92nd, having been stationed, because non-sympathetic, in the scenes of those meetings.[11]

In fact Irish soldiers seem to have performed even the most harassing duties as reliably as those recruited from other parts of the United Kingdom. A resident magistrate's warning in 1881 concerning the doubtful loyalty of the locally recruited 18th Royal Irish regiment stationed at Clonmel, was repudiated by the local police inspector who reported that the officers of the regiment had no difficulties with their men who performed duties such as protecting sheriffs at evictions 'cheerfully . . . and with alacrity'.[12] Allegiance to any body outside the army was officially discouraged. Sir Edward Blakeney (commander of the forces 1836–55) disliked soldiers joining even temperance societies, observing that he would rather that the men 'got drunk occasionally than see them acknowledge any

16.1   Sub-Sheriff Gabriel Whistler, with military assistance, attempting to
enforce a rent demand in 1840 (sketch by Sadler). 'The woman in the
window is discharging a bucket on my bold Sub-Sheriff; a soldier "out of
sport is leveling [*sic*] his musket".'

authority, good or bad, that is not founded on their profession'.[13] But there was a
reluctance to countenance the possibility of any serious threat to internal discipline.
Both Vivian and Blakeney played down cases of soldiers being sworn as Ribbonmen
claiming these were isolated instances, a response which Rose was later to hold
partially responsible for the spread of Fenianism in the army in the 1860s.[14]
Disapproval of Orange societies expressed in confidential circulars issued in 1822
and 1829 failed to permeate the lower ranks as officers assumed any prohibition to
be unnecessary. This was rectified in 1835 by a general order to be read to troops
on parade forbidding attendance at all party meetings.[15]

    Much of the anxiety felt by those responsible for the conduct of the army lay not
simply in the duties the troops were required to perform but in the fact that they
were frequently operating in small detachments. This caused practical problems in
terms of accommodation and discipline, as well as dissipating the army's strength.
A contemporary map of military stations in Ireland in 1822 clearly illustrates the
extent to which the force sent to the south-west to repress agrarian disorder was
scattered over the disturbed districts.[16] Summarising the position in 1838, Blakeney
concluded that 'in point of fact, the army in Ireland may be said to be an army of

IRELAND
Divided into
Provinces and Counties
Shewing also
the Distribution of the TROOPS in each

Qr Mr Generals Office 1st July
1822

W. Duncan
Assist Draftsman

Lithographic Press
Qr Mr Generals Office

31

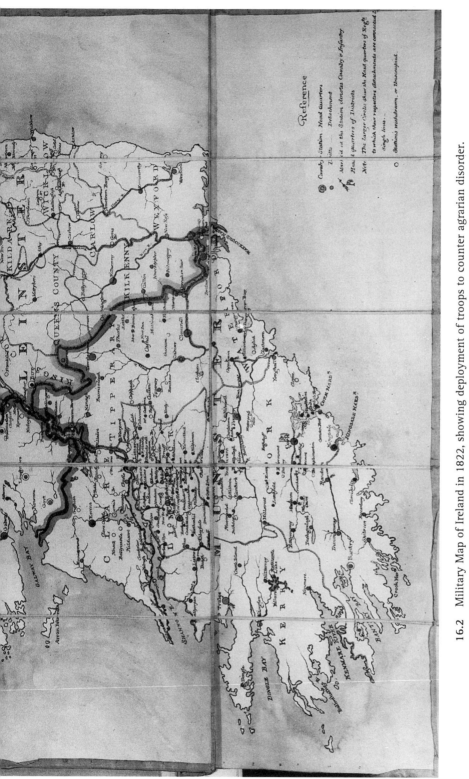

16.2   Military Map of Ireland in 1822, showing deployment of troops to counter agrarian disorder.

THE ILLUSTRATED LONDON NEWS

PURSUIT OF THE FENIANS IN TIPPERARY.

CONSTABULARY BARRACKS AT ROS-KEENE, BURNT BY THE FENIANS.

THE TIPPERARY FLYING COLUMN CROSSING THE HOLLYFORD MOUNTAIN.

16.3   Pursuit of the Fenians in Tipperary. Two illustrations from the *Illustrated London News*, 30 March 1867.

detachments in aid of the civil power with a disposable force greatly disproportionate to its numerical strength'. With garrison duties tying down troops in
Dublin, Cork, Limerick and other major centres, the force available in the event of
a sudden emergency was, he argued, severely restricted. Any such emergency
would, moreover, inevitably increase the demand for detachments at a time when
army procedure demanded that the troops be concentrated in defensible positions.[17]

Confronted with this problem in 1865, Rose alerted the government to the need
to resist the pressure for

> numerous and small detachments [which] weaken the means of *General Protection*,
> of concentrated bodies, so placed as to convey assistance to detached and isolated
> points by short lines, and the most rapid means of communication. There is, I
> believe, hardly a gentleman, or community, well-affected, who does not require
> troops. If all these demands were acceded to the Force would, in very numerous
> cases, be needlessly frittered away in small and unconnected detachments,
> affording no general or mutual help and from their weakness almost inviting
> attack. I say nothing as to the relaxation of discipline and other unfavourable
> results.[18]

Senior officers found themselves engaged in a long-running battle with local
magistrates, as their efforts to reduce the number of detachments came into conflict
with the anxiety of magistrates, often motivated by the economic benefits to be
gained by the presence of troops as well as their own personal security, to retain
a military station in their neighbourhoods. Attempts to withdraw detachments
frequently prompted memorials to government from local inhabitants[19] as well as
agitated letters from resident landowners, and as Vivian had pointed out in a
letter to the Horse Guards in 1833 justifying the distribution of troops under his
command, if a detachment was withdrawn and the law was then broken, the
government and Vivian himself would be held responsible.[20]

Improved communications did ease the situation somewhat. The advent of steam
ships meant that troops could be moved across the Irish Sea much more quickly. In
1834 William Gosset, the under-secretary at Dublin Castle, triumphantly informed
the chief secretary, Edward Littleton, of an incident in which troops landed in
England from Ireland less than twenty hours after the order for embarkation was
received. He cited this as an instance of the celerity with which 'thanks to steam and
the alacrity of the troops' men could be moved from one country to another. It
showed that it was of little moment whether the disposable force was in England or
Ireland.[21] The growth of the rail network later in the century also had implications
for troop movements although this could be overestimated. Writing to a colleague
in 1867, Rose, now elevated to the peerage as Lord Strathnairn, admitted that he,
like others, had attributed greater capabilities to rail than it merited. The rapidity of
the railway, he cautioned, was deceptive since there were so many places where it
did not go.[22]

One way of achieving greater flexibility within limited resources was to deploy 'movable' columns of troops to traverse the countryside. This tactic was resorted to on a number of occasions. In 1831 when the government was faced with a growing number of agrarian outrages combined with an increasingly vigorous anti-tithe agitation, the lord lieutenant, Lord Anglesey, directed Sir John Byng (commander of the forces 1828–31) to send movable columns of cavalry and infantry to the disturbed areas. Each column was to keep well connected and to proceed to the most disturbed parts halting wherever there were serious outrages and remaining there until quiet was restored, when it was to proceed to the next scene of disturbance. This, he informed his chief secretary, Edward Stanley, was the best way to act with a very small force.[23] The columns seem to have been effective. The arrival of one column in Cork the following summer was welcomed by the GOC of the district, Sir George Bingham, who commented that the known zeal of the commander of the column and 'the means he possesses of showing a force at once on distant points cannot fail to be of service'.[24] Bingham's superior, Vivian, who had replaced Byng in 1831, was, however, reluctant to make extensive use of movable columns believing that this was more harassing for the troops than being posted in temporary stations in disturbed districts, and more uncomfortable.[25] Flying columns, which were a later variation on movable columns, were deployed during the Fenian outbreak of 1867, the Ribbon disturbances of 1869–70 and during the land war. A memorandum drawn up in 1867 following the disbandment of the columns described how the rapid traversing of the most disturbed districts with troops demonstrated 'their mastery of and the undisputed right of the Government to the country, whilst the insurgents there who had asserted so continually that it would and must be theirs were compelled to seek humiliating concealment and flight'. Where the flying columns deployed in 1867 differed from the movable columns of the 1830s was in being accompanied by a resident magistrate. This was an important difference. Movable columns could only arrest people who were actually committing an offence, flying columns could stop people on suspicion as well as being able to enter houses to search for arms. 'In some cases', the memorandum noted, 'these columns, marching from one town to another, in the worst affected districts, divided into numerous small parties, and searched all the houses for arms, intervening ground, etc., arresting suspected persons'.[26]

Movable/flying columns acted as both a deterrent and a response to disorder. In this respect they served a similar function (and suffered from similar disadvantages) as patrols. Regular patrols through disturbed areas were felt to be one of the best methods of preventing outrages and of giving visible expression to the determination of government to impose its authority. The problem with patrols was that people simply refrained from outrage while the patrol was in the neighbourhood. The only possible advantage to be gained from patrolling opined the chief secretary, Francis Leveson Gower, in 1829, was the proof it afforded of the intention of the government to do its utmost.[27] Despite Gower's scepticism, patrols introduced in Tipperary in 1829 were believed to have restored the county to order.

Writing to Anglesey the following year, Byng remarked that the disturbances in Tipperary had been remedied by frequent nightly patrols of military and police united and an occasional and extensive search for arms.[28] Joint patrolling with the police became the routine response to disorder. Problems relating to the size and mobility of patrols continued to hamper their effectiveness and in 1882 it was decided to relax the rules governing their employment in order to provide a more flexible response to disorder. A circular memorandum issued in 1882 directed that where patrols had been authorised by government they should be provided at the requisition of the local police authorities (the power of requisition having previously been reserved to magistrates and sheriffs), the details to be decided by the officer in command in consultation with the police. Patrols could be broken up into sections to be assigned different routes, regrouping at a fixed point. The minimum strength of patrols was also reduced from twenty to six. The new regulations meant that detachments were able to furnish a larger number of patrols whose movements were less easily detected. It was stressed that each party should be accompanied by a member of the constabulary.[29]

The presence of the police was necessary to invest patrols with the authority to arrest people on suspicion. Soldiers could arrest anyone found actually committing an offence (and, as the authorities sometimes found it necessary to remind them, it was their duty to do so),[30] but their powers went no further than this. Outlining the position in 1870, the under-secretary at Dublin Castle explained that although lawful arrests could be made, the necessity which the law imposed on the person making such an arrest 'to justify it by proof of the actual commission of an offence renders it imprudent and as a general rule unsafe for persons who are not constables or peace officers to take upon themselves the responsibility of arresting'. Burke passed on the recommendation of the Castle's law adviser that in cases of suspicion the constabulary should be left to deal with suspected persons, and that the military should refrain from interfering 'except when duly called on to aid the civil power'.[31] Commanding officers were insistent that the troops should be accompanied by a magistrate or peace officer at all times. A general order issued in 1831 directed that troops were not to act in aid of the civil power except under the 'express orders of a magistrate, or in absolute self-defence or in the protection of persons or property directly endangered'. Under these circumstances the troops were to do their duty always bearing in mind that 'Humanity is the brightest gem in the character of a British soldier.'[32] However tightly army regulations attempted to embrace the soldier, some element of discretion had to remain, and it was accepted that in an emergency regulations were often better honoured in the breach than in the observance. The problem of establishing clear guidelines which would be adaptable enough to be useful was never satisfactorily solved. A parliamentary committee appointed in 1908 to investigate the employment of the military in cases of disturbance acknowledged the onerous responsibility of officers commanding troops on such occasions but confessed itself unable to define their duty any more precisely. This was always a conundrum which caused greater headaches at head-quarters than in the field. Complaints from soldiers serving in Ireland concerned the harassing nature of patrol and escort duties, not the danger of finding themselves before the courts,[33] and in actual fact the likelihood of this happening was much exaggerated. As one senior officer rather pompously explained to members of the 1908 committee:

> an officer accepts, and has the honour of bearing, the King's Commission, and he must accept the responsibilities attaching to it. I do not think he has anything to fear from the civil or military powers if he fearlessly does his duty. I can certainly find no trial in my researches where anyone either a civil magistrate or a military officer, has suffered from doing his duty.[34]

Dislike of the tasks the troops were required to perform in aid of the civil power was heightened by the feeling that magistrates, as the local representatives of that power, were failing to play their part in maintaining the authority of law and government. The relationship between army officers and civil magistrates was by its very nature a difficult one. By calling on military assistance magistrates were admitting their own incapacity. Thus the military came most frequently into contact with magistrates when the latter were at their weakest and least effective. Many soldiers were also convinced that, as local landowners, magistrates bore at least some of the responsibility for the disturbed state of the country. Lord John Russell summed up the general tone of Guards officers stationed in Dublin in 1833 as 'pity for the peasantry, dislike of the gentry, complaints concerning want of truth',[35] a comment that could have been made at almost any point during the century. It would be wrong, however, to suggest that irritation with the activities of some Irish landowners was translated into a disinclination to protect the rights and property of landowners in general.[36] District commanders were expected to make themselves known to local landowners and to comply with their wishes whenever possible. Major-General Sir Hugh Gough felt it necessary to write to the military secretary in 1822 to assure him that his remarks on the want of exertion on the part of magistrates in Cork should not be taken to suggest that he did not draw well with them. In fact he had regular meetings with the magistrates in his district, including the 'most respectable'.[37] There were also practical reasons for maintaining good relations with local dignitaries. Outlining his recommendations for action in response to the Ribbon disturbances of 1870, Strathnairn advised that advantage should be taken of the assistance of lieutenants of counties and local magistrates: 'of course some are insufficient by age or other causes, but their body comprises a large number of energetic, intelligent men, with great local experience, and in possession of the best sources of information which, communicated to the Government, would greatly strengthen their hands'.[38]

On a number of occasions over the course of the century the inactivity of local magistrates coupled with doubts about their efficiency and reliability led to the

16.4   Troops camped at the workhouse at Kells, from the *Illustrated
London News*, 9 April 1870.

appointment of military officers to the commission. This was done in counties
placed under emergency powers in 1822 and 1833, and during the Fenian outbreak.
It was also extensively used by Anglesey's government in 1831–2, when military
officers attended petty sessions and performed 'all manner of duties which in many
parts of the country local magistrates shrink from'.[39] It was an expedient with which
neither central government nor the military authorities felt entirely happy since it
implied an uncomfortably close connection between civil and military responsibilities, and it was generally regarded as appropriate only under exceptional
circumstances. When Strathnairn urged the appointment of military magistrates to
take command of troops during the 1868 elections, citing earlier precedents, the
suggestion was firmly rejected by the lord chancellor, Lord Chelmsford, who ruled
that such appointments would be inexpedient if not unconstitutional and that there
were sufficient magistrates and stipendiary magistrates to ensure that the troops
would not be required to act without a magistrate present.[40] The position of
stipendiary magistrates in relation to their ordinary colleagues was not formally
defined, but the former were normally considered by military personnel to be the
senior and more responsible authority in the district.[41] In most cases stipendiaries,
many of whom had military experience, worked in close concert with officers
commanding detachments but problems could arise if they attempted to direct
the manner as well as the occasion of troop deployment. A report from

Lieutenant-Colonel Greave that the resident magistrate at Clonmel, Colonel Carew, had dispensed with the services of dismounted artillery during an election in 1869, prompted a pained letter from the assistant military secretary to the under-secretary protesting that Carew's action had been 'contrary to all custom and much to the detriment of the public service'. Resident magistrates should not interfere with the interior arrangement of troops, 'the sole responsibility for the disposition of which rests after consultation with the Resident Magistrate upon the officer in command of the troops'.[42] Stipendiary magistrates tended to regard the police and the troops as virtually interchangeable. This was to some degree inevitable in the early decades of the nineteenth century when the constabulary was still in its infancy and the number of men available for duty relatively small. During the Rockite disturbances of the 1820s troops were stationed in private houses as protection parties and the army took primary responsibility for patrolling disturbed districts and searching for arms with the peace preservation police acting almost as auxiliaries. Once the emergency was over, however, the commander of the forces, Sir George Murray, issued instructions that his officers were to direct their attention 'solely to the discipline of the army' and not to interfere with the police 'further than is absolutely necessary, in giving the assistance of the military to the civil power, when properly called upon for that purpose'. If officers took upon themselves the role of inspector of the magistracy and police, he warned, 'I fear you will only involve yourself in endless trouble and hostility with the country gentlemen, and receive the thanks of no party for your interference.'[43]

Senior constabulary officers were divided over the extent to which the duties of the two forces could be kept separate. The provincial inspector of the Munster force, Major Miller, was firmly of the opinion that the government should endeavour to enforce submission to the law through the constabulary alone. He vigorously opposed a proposal put forward in 1827 by Major Carter, a stipendiary magistrate stationed in Tipperary, that the police should be able to summon military assistance directly, asserting that in ordinary circumstances the police could cope unassisted and in the event of any unexpected emergency the assistance of the troops could be obtained on the requisition of a magistrate. Any arrangement which would make the troops 'liable to be called into activity under the conduct of less responsible functionaries' would, he opined, have lamentable consequences.[44] George Warburton, on the other hand, provincial inspector for Connaught and a former brigade-major in the yeomanry, was inclined to advocate a more flexible role for the troops. When acting as a stipendiary magistrate in Limerick in 1821 in charge of a force of peace preservation police, he had urged on government the necessity of sending a powerful force of infantry and cavalry to the county to ensure that every gentleman's house might be occupied, patrols kept up and houses searched for arms. He attempted to revert to this policy in response to the Whitefeet outrages in the south-western counties in 1831 only to come into conflict with the GOC, Sir Thomas Arbuthnot, who informed him that placing protection parties in

16.5   Lancers clearing the street at Granard at the Longford election, from the *Illustrated London News*, 28 May 1870.

private houses was inappropriate.[45] It is clear from other correspondence that Arbuthnot and Warburton did not find it easy to work together harmoniously.[46] The importance of personal relations in these matters should not be underestimated. Clifford Lloyd's initiative as a special resident magistrate in the early 1880s which resulted in soldiers being detached on special service in disturbed districts, could not have got off the ground had he not enjoyed the good opinion of both the commander of the forces, Sir Thomas Steele, and the GOC, Henry Torrens. The daughter of the chief secretary, Florence Arnold-Forster, recorded in her diary a meeting at the vice-regal lodge between Steele and Lloyd, observing that the two men seemed to have hit it off very well, Steele being much impressed with the younger man's vigour and capacity, and that he had willingly given Lloyd the men he asked for.[47] Lloyd appreciated the value of this cooperation, commenting in his memoirs that there could easily have been friction with the military authorities over the use of troops on special duties, but that this was not the case.[48] The War Office had been distinctly unenthusiastic about the plan, eventually agreeing to its execution on the condition that the men assigned to each district were to be accompanied by a commissioned officer and NCOs and that each post should be under the military charge of an NCO or acting NCO. The experiment, which lasted until the end of 1882 and involved a total of 700 men drawn from the guards regiments, was deemed a success. A memorandum drawn up shortly afterwards by the Castle's military adviser noted its good effects but concluded that it was unlikely to be repeated since the military authorities 'could never approve of employing soldiers in this manner'.[49]

As such unorthodox arrangements indicate, ordinary methods of law enforcement were found to be inadequate when the popular distrust of government moved from passive to active mode. This was not simply a matter of individuals defying the law but of whole communities doing so. Army officers were confident that they would emerge victorious from any purely military encounter and were generally dismissive of rumours of armed uprisings, believing that Irish insurgents did not have either arms in sufficient quantities or leaders of sufficient quality to pose any real threat to government.[50] The task of putting down armed rebellion held few terrors for the army. Opposing the mass of the population combined in defiance of the law was a very different matter. The political landscape of Ireland in the 1880s was not the same as that of the 1830s but the field of battle on which the land war was conducted bore striking similarities to that on which the tithe war had been waged fifty years earlier. In both instances the army was called upon to enforce laws which were admitted to require amendment, caught between property owners demanding that their legal rights be vindicated, and the rural populace mobilised in a national campaign against the law under leaders who could pursue the issue in parliament in the full glare of media attention. Both periods also provided an opportunity for the settling of old scores under the cloak of wider political activity. The resulting combination of agrarian outrages, mass meetings and civil disobedience caused a virtual paralysis of the operation of the ordinary law. In a situation in which the civil authorities manifestly could not cope, the army found itself performing tasks to which under other circumstances most strenuous objections would have been made. Military force, Anglesey informed the prime minister, Lord Grey, in July 1832, was necessary for the twofold purpose of checking disturbances and reaping crops, adding, 'You know that Troops are constantly so employed.'[51] Faced with the prospect of a bruising confrontation with tenants every time an attempt was made to collect tithe or to seize goods in default of payment, magistrates and sheriffs in increasing numbers demanded military assistance. By December 1832 the popular excitement over tithes was such that 'the collection of them requires in almost every instance the support and countenance of the military, whose exertions however, with few exceptions, have been attended with success'.[52]

Vivian had expressed strong reservations to Anglesey about using troops to enforce the payment of tithes, given that 'the feelings of the whole people' were opposed to them. In Vivian's opinion the situation presented the government with two alternatives: 'concession or rebellion'.[53] Ministers, however, were adamant that the law had to be enforced before any concession could be granted or reform introduced. Vivian acquiesced but remained sceptical of the wisdom of government policy, reporting to Horse Guards early in 1833 that 'Ireland has never been in such a state as it is in consequence of the collection of tithes under the late law, nor were the Government or the troops ever placed in so difficult a situation.'[54] Anglesey left Ireland in 1833 as did his hard-line chief secretary, Stanley. The new Irish administration adopted a more relaxed approach to tithe payments in anticipation of legislative reform, allowing the troops to take a less active role in their collection. In September 1834, Vivian wrote to Arbuthnot, informing him that the lord lieutenant, Lord Wellesley, had agreed with Vivian that

> neither police nor troops should in any way whatever be employed in matters relating to tithes, farther than to be on hand to preserve the peace when a breach is expected, that expectation having according to law been verified by affidavit . . . on no account giving that active interference we did last year in assisting to serve notices or in some instances even assisting in driving and employing stipendiary or military magistrates.[55]

Anxious to prevent a repetition of such scenes in the future, Vivian's successor, Sir Edward Blakeney, who had witnessed the tithe war first hand as commander of the eastern district, sought government sanction for the introduction of a rule that 'military aid shall be granted in the protection of persons serving civil bill processes and decrees on the requisition of the sheriff and his deputy *only* and not on that of a magistrate except in case of actual, not previous breach of the peace'.[56] This was in line with government policy and a general order was issued on 23 January. A new version of the book of general orders for the guidance of troops affording aid to the civil power, amended accordingly, was issued in April.[57] Blakeney did his best to ensure that these rules were observed and was vigilant in guarding against violations. He was quick to object to applications for aid which required the troops to become mere agents of the civil power. In 1849 he approved the action of an officer in Mayo who had refused to comply with a requisition to protect poor-rate collectors. The officer maintained that this was a duty that belonged to the police: 'he considers he does *their duties* instead of merely *aiding* the Civil Power.'[58] So strict an interpretation of the rules was not always practicable. In this instance the inspector-general of the constabulary explained that it would be impossible to meet the requisitions referred to 'without denuding a large district of the country of police, where duties are required that can only be performed by the civil power', and pleaded exceptional circumstances: 'in no other part of the country, and at no former period, has it been so necessary as at present in the west of Ireland to protect the collectors of poor rates'.[59]

The restraints imposed by the new rules on those authorised to requisition military aid operated with some success over the following decades, but they were unable to stem the tide of applications for protection from sheriffs and their deputies that flooded in to military stations during the land war. In January 1882,

---

373

16.6   Victoria Barracks, Belfast, a posting from which troops were frequently employed in aid of the civil power during sectarian rioting in the industrial districts of the city.

Steele wrote to the chief secretary, William Forster, urging that the power of requisitioning the military should be placed on a more systematic footing. Unless this was done, he warned, there would soon be a complete breakdown and troops would be unable to attend when their presence was required 'owing to the short notice and inconsiderate manner in which their services are applied for'.[60] The solution adopted, that requisitions should go through the local constabulary inspector, made practical sense in terms of coordinating the activities of the police and the troops and making the most effective use of manpower resources, but caused further headaches at Kilmainham as county inspectors took the new arrangements to mean that they could summon troops on their own initiative. It had been agreed that requisitions might pass through the inspectors, the assistant military secretary protested in February 1882, in order not to throw difficulties in the way of the civil authorities during the present crisis, 'but it was never intended save in cases of emergency that county inspectors should demand troops except on the requisition of a magistrate or sheriff'.[61] In order to clarify the position subsequent circulars stressed that demands from county inspectors for troops to protect sheriffs should be accompanied by the sheriff's requisition. Where protection parties were required for other purposes, the arrangements were to be made by a resident magistrate. In urgent cases the police could summon immediate assistance but officers commanding were instructed to use their discretion as to the necessity of complying with the request and to the number and composition of any party that was sent. Each party was to be accompanied by a few police who were to be responsible for making any arrests.[62] As the Castle's military adviser, Ross of Bladensburg, later noted, the military were 'in fact . . . considered to be police escorts'.[63] Despite the 'crisis' conditions, the military authorities succeeded in preserving the separate spheres of police and army responsibilities. But the appointment of officers such as special resident magistrates to coordinate the activities of police and army detachments signalled a growing belief amongst ministers and Castle officials that military procedures would have to be sacrificed on the altar of operational efficiency. As we have seen, Clifford Lloyd deployed the force available to him in a way which paid scant attention to separate spheres. In 1886 a new post of special commissioner of police was created, the holder being given direct command of both police and troops in his district. Sir Alfred Turner, who replaced the first appointee, Sir Redvers Buller, in 1887, recalled in his memoirs that he was given a free hand in requisitioning troops. He took full advantage of this even in cases when police alone would have sufficed, seeing it as a way of preventing resistance or bloodshed, outcomes which he regarded not only as deplorable in themselves but as potentially embarrassing to the government.[64]

That such arrangements were adopted as temporary expedients in particular districts no doubt helped to make them less unpalatable to the military. Senior officers were unwilling to stand in the way of any expedient which would help to restore order without forcing them to resort to overtly oppressive tactics. This was a primary concern throughout the century. Vivian had warned one of his district commanders, in 1834, to take care when dealing with a magistrate whose proposals for enforcing tithe payments, 'such as the billeting of soldiers on the houses of those who refuse payment', made him a 'most dangerous person to have to act with'.[65] Every effort was made to avoid associating the army with any faction or party in Ireland. 'Beyond our professional duties', Murray declared in 1827, 'all we have to attend to as military men is to support the civil authorities when they need our assistance and to conduct ourselves upon such occasions with the strictest impartiality and freedom from party feeling, by any participation in which we should only increase the evil and bring discredit upon ourselves'.[66] Even when entitled to vote in the district in which they were stationed officers rarely availed themselves of this, believing, as Sir Montagu McMurdo told the 1869 select committee on parliamentary and municipal elections, that it was not proper for an officer in command to interfere in political matters. Appearing before the same committee, Strathnairn vigorously denied a suggestion that Tory administrations used the troops for party political purposes. Military aid, he insisted, was granted to magistrates irrespective of their political views,[67] though his comments to Lord de Vesci in 1868, concerning the conduct of radically disposed stipendiary magistrates at elections would suggest that he was rather regretful that this was so.[68] Whilst endeavouring to keep the army out of party politics, commanders of the forces kept themselves abreast of political developments. Florence Arnold-Forster's assessment of Steele as a vigorous clear-headed man 'preferring to deal with things from a military point of view, but quite capable at the same time of taking in the political bearing of the situation',[69] would have been applicable to almost all the men appointed to the Irish command in the nineteenth century. This capacity was essential if the commander was to fit smoothly into the administrative machine. Arnold-Forster observed with satisfaction that Steele and her father got on very well together, 'which considering there are so many military arrangements to be made now-a-days at the Ch. Sec's office, is very fortunate'.[70] Relations between the senior representatives of the civil and military authorities in Ireland were much closer than those between their counterparts in England. This reflected not only the size of the country and of Irish social circles which brought politicians, members of the landed classes and senior officers into regular contact, but also the nature of the Irish command. Objecting to a reduction in his table allowance in 1865, Rose pointed out that the Irish commander was a privy councillor and a 'member of the Government' and was expected to return the hospitality offered to him.[71] It is clear from Arnold-Forster's diary that Steele was a frequent guest at the vice-regal lodge. Conflict between the commander of the forces and the Irish government was not unknown – Sir David Baird's biographer refers to the frequent collisions that took place between Baird (commander of the forces 1820–2) and Lord Wellesley following the latter's appointment as lord lieutenant at the end of 1821[72] – but commanders largely accepted the view expressed by Robert Peel when home secretary in 1822,

16.7 *Military Manoeuvres* (1891) by Richard T. Moynan. The soldier,
dressed in the uniform of the 4th (Royal Irish) Dragoon Guards appears to
represent no more than a decorative and desirable addition to the social life
of this unidentified Irish town.

that it was essential to the public service that the commander should act 'cordially with and in friendly subordination to the Lord Lieutenant'.[73]

For most of the nineteenth century the army retained a considerable degree of popular support. A Scottish recruit serving in Ireland in the early decades of the century noted a decided aversion among the people to the police who were considered as being 'selected from the ranks of sectarian oppressors', but claimed that this was not the case with the military who were 'welcomed until they proved themselves unfriendly'.[74] References to the popularity of the army were part of ministerial vocabulary. Lord Ebrington's remark, as lord lieutenant in 1839, that there was no part of the Queen's dominions where there was more cordial feeling towards the troops than in Ireland was typical in this respect.[75] Cordiality could rapidly turn to bitterness, however, in the event of bloodshed. An incident at Sixmilebridge during the Clare election in 1852 when six rioters were shot by the army was still causing popular hostility towards the regiment involved in the 1860s,[76] and a spate of verbal and physical attacks on soldiers stationed in Mitchelstown in 1867 was linked to the death in a collision with the military of the Fenian, Peter Crowley. The parish priest of Mitchelstown was alleged to have referred to the troops responsible as 'those blackguard soldiers' to whom no respectable person should be seen speaking.[77] The deeper the army was sucked into the political morass of the land war and the plan of campaign the more difficult it was to preserve the impartial image upon which army personnel so prided themselves. An officer commanding a detachment at Maryborough, in 1881, reported growing hostility to the troops amongst the townspeople and attributed this to the operation of the Coercion Act: 'since the passing of the act the landlords have begun to press for their rents, and the military have been so frequently called upon to aid the civil power that they are now in almost as bad odour with the mob as the constabulary, who are looked on with feelings of intense hatred all through this district'. He added that everyone connected with the maintenance of law and order in the neighbourhood was regarded with hatred.[78] It was exactly this situation that Vivian and his officers had feared would result from their involvement in the tithe war. That it did not was largely due to the political decision to reform the tithe system. By the time the land question had been resolved the initiative had passed to nationalist politicians, and, as the national question replaced the land question as the major political issue in Ireland, government replaced the landlords as the focus of popular hostility. So long as the conflict in the Irish countryside had pitted the Catholic population against the Protestant landlord class, the army and the government had been able to assume the mantle of impartial arbitrators. Once the landlords retired from the field, the government found itself under direct rather than indirect attack and with the government's authority gradually slipping away, the army was forced into the role of combatant as opposed to mere auxiliary in the conflict. The consequences of this were only to become fully apparent during the war of independence.

Chapter 17

Militarism in Ireland, 1900–1922

David Fitzpatrick

The common rhetoric of militarism transcended political divisions in Ireland throughout the turmoil of the period between the Anglo–Boer War of 1899–1902 and the Anglo–Irish 'settlement' of 1921–2.[1] For unionists, nationalists and republicans alike, soldiery was an ideal to be extolled rather than a menace to be confronted. The ideal soldier was both courageous and disciplined, not only a personal hero but part of a team. Despite the latent antagonism between these images, they were smoothly blended in the militarist vision. It was a commonplace that bravery was an inherent attribute of the Irish, whereas obedience required inculcation. While the political aims of disciplined behaviour were hotly contested, the need for submission to an appropriate authority was almost universally acknowledged. The wild courage of the Celtic type had only to be harnessed in order to turn a stampede into a cavalry charge. As a diehard rector of Limerick reflected in 'The Magnificent Irish Soldier':[2]

> He asks no question as to wrong or right in [sic]
>> No qualm of conscience e'er assails his manly breast.
> For Queen and country he must do the fighting,
>> And wiser heads than his may settle all the rest.
> No Scot or Saxon e'er shall march before him,
>> Nor are his equals to be found to bear the battle's brunt.
> Far-famed for fighting was the land that bore him,
>> And Erin's sons were always to the foremost front.

Likewise John Redmond, the leader of the Irish Parliamentary Party, affirmed in a recruiting tract that 'the Irish people . . . have been endowed in a distinguished degree with a genuine military spirit, a natural genius and gift for war which produces born soldiers and commanders, and which is the very reverse of the brute appetite for slaughter'.[3] Militarism was one of the few Irish stereotypes which evoked almost universal approbation in a bellicose era.

South Africa provided the focus for Irish militarism between 1899 and 1902. Despite emphatic opposition to Irish involvement from almost every nationalist faction, about 30,000 Irishmen are thought to have served against the Boers, suffering 3,000 casualties. In addition to Irish soldiers in the regular army, there were enough volunteers in all but three of the Irish militia battalions to enable them to be embodied for active service. On occasion, the Irish regiments found themselves in combat with members of the two so-called 'Irish Transvaal Brigades', whose combined membership never exceeded 300 men. These pro-Boer brigades, commanded by John Blake and Arthur Lynch (natives of the USA and Australia respectively), included a bizarre medley of adventurers and 'uitlanders' of Irish, British and continental origin, as well as a sprinkling of recent emigrants from Ireland such as John MacBride. According to Lynch, only about a dozen 'from Ireland direct found their way to the fighting line'.[4] At Talana Hill (October 1899), the Blake–MacBride brigade found itself defending Boer positions against the Royal Dublin Fusiliers, so generating the ballad ''Twas an Irish Fight':[5]

> Dicey took a lad named Walsh; Dooley got McGurk;
>   Gilligan turned in Fahey's boy – for his father he used to work.
> They had marched to fight the English – but Irish were all they could see –
>   That's how the 'English fought the Dutch' at the Battle of Dundee.

Confrontation was resumed during the relief of Ladysmith (February 1900), where the casualties included Corporal James Flynn and Volunteer Michael Flynn, enrolled respectively with the Royal Inniskilling Fusiliers and Blake's brigade. They were brothers, from County Longford.[6] Despite such droll coincidences, the disproportion between Irish involvement for and against the Boers was so obvious that unionists purred with approval and saw hope for Ireland yet. After Ladysmith, Queen Victoria ordained that all Irish regiments would henceforth wear shamrock on St Patrick's Day, and created a new regiment with headquarters at Buckingham Gate, London, to be known as the Irish Guards.

The prominence of Irish troops in the war against the Boers reflected the continuing importance of Irish recruitment. Though the Irish-born component in the British army had fallen sharply during the later nineteenth century, it remained well in excess of the declining Irish share in the population of the British Isles. By March 1901 the wartime army had expanded to 440,000 officers and men, including more than 50,000 Irishmen. Natives of Ireland comprised only 12.0 per cent of the overall population, but 13.5 per cent of soldiers and non-commissioned officers.[7] Irish overrepresentation was entirely attributable to the very high intake of emigrants, particularly those resident in British industrial cities.[8] This is revealed by the annual returns of army enlistment, which indicate that only 9.6 per cent of those accepted between 1896 and 1905 were raised in Ireland itself, a proportion which fell to 8.7 per cent between 1905 and 1913. In each period Ireland was marginally underrepresented, the decline being attributable to depopulation rather than the impact of Sinn Féin's virulent campaign against recruiting.[9] Within Ireland, enlistment was heaviest in the major towns and their hinterlands. While the Belfast district was only slightly overrepresented, Dublin regularly raised more than double its fair share of recruits. The Mullingar district also provided an excess of recruits, especially militiamen. By contrast, enlistment ratios were very low in mid-Ulster as well as in Connacht.[10] Whether in Dublin, Liverpool or Glasgow, the urban Irish found military life particularly enticing.

Irish recruits, like their British counterparts, were typically unemployed lads in their late 'teens for whom the risks entailed by soldiery (casual violence, venereal disease, oppressive discipline, active service) were outweighed by its benefits (long-term employment, bed and board, camaraderie, adventure). In 1909, less than one recruit in ten had a job at the time of enlistment;[11] and the attestation of 'corner-boys' or loungers was notoriously brisk in the vicinity of public houses. Between 1905 and 1913, half of the recruits accepted in Ireland thought of themselves as unskilled urban workers such as porters, carters, servants or casual labourers. One-sixth were skilled workers, while the proportion with professional or clerical experience was negligible. Rural labourers accounted for one recruit in three, a far higher proportion than in Britain. The Irish were less likely than the British to be rejected as unfit, though in both countries urban manual workers were less healthy than rural labourers.[12] There is little direct evidence concerning the religion of recruits, which must often have been as exiguous as their civil occupation. The Catholic component in the British army (18.3 per cent in 1899) was swollen by British residents of Irish Catholic descent, who undoubtedly outnumbered Catholics enlisted in Ireland itself. The 1911 census indicates that about two-thirds of military and naval pensioners living in Ireland were Catholics, a proportion which presumably mirrors the religious distribution of those enlisting around 1880. This proportion remained stable until the outbreak of the Great War.[13] By contrast, the influential Irish minority in the officer class was drawn largely from the Protestant landed gentry, contributing an abundance of strategists, heroes, gallants and ne'er-do-wells to regimental messes throughout the empire.[14]

For the forces of the crown, Ireland was a theatre of operations as well as a source of recruitment. The forces posted in Ireland had multiple functions, ranging from basic training to defence against invasion and suppression of civil 'disturbances'. In 1901, the census recorded the presence of 21,000 soldiers and officers, nearly 4,000 militiamen and yeomanry, and over 2,000 members of the Royal Navy and Royal Marines. Most of the forces posted in Ireland were of British origin, as suggested by the fact that less than 30 per cent of each group of servicemen were Catholics.[15] The preference for posting British troops in Ireland (and Irish troops in Britain) reflected the widespread belief that the loyalty displayed by Irish servicemen in peacetime was likely to crack under communal pressure, in case of invasion, war or even civil commotion. From 1895 to 1909, the War Office adopted the advice of Field Marshal Viscount Wolseley that, in the event of mobilisation, all Irish battalions of regulars, reservists and militiamen (except for a few Ulster units) should be withdrawn from Ireland. Even in peacetime, a system of rotation was applied which ensured that most Irish battalions were displaced by British units. In 1909, however, another commander-in-chief in Ireland (General Sir Neville Lyttelton, a Home Ruler) gained acceptance of the principle that 'the time has now come when the Irish soldiers can be safely entrusted with the local defence of Ireland'.[16] In case of mobilisation, this duty would fall to the Special Reserve, the force created by Haldane's reforms of 1908 to replace the cumbersome county militia. Ireland had no Territorial Army to match that constructed out of the yeomanry and county volunteer units in Britain; while attempts to create a National Veterans' Reserve generated nothing more formidable than Dublin's 'Gorgeous Wrecks' (whose armbands bore the legend 'Georgius Rex'). But Ireland did participate in the Officers' Training Corps (1908) which spawned thriving units in several schools and universities including Trinity College, Dublin.[17] The presence of these forces in more than eighty barracks, with their parades, drills and ceremonies, provided Ireland with reiterated reminders of the military presence and power of the state.

Since the forces were not mobilised between 1902 and 1914, their main functions at home were precautionary and intimidatory. During the land war of the 1880s, the role of the army in 'aid of the civil power' had been extended to include private protection, as well as 'flying columns' and escorts for magistrates or officials. As shown in chapter 16, the relationship between the army and the police was always edgy, since the theoretical subordination of military parties to the civil power was difficult to apply in practice. The Royal Irish Constabulary (RIC) was itself an armed paramilitary force under central command, but its use of arms was largely ceremonial rather than lethal. The RIC was supported in Dublin by the unarmed Metropolitan Police, their combined manpower exceeding 12,000 in 1902. The religious composition of the police mirrored that of Irishmen in the army, the officers being mainly Protestants whereas three-quarters of the constables were Catholics. The continuing prevalence of 'outrages' and other 'disturbances of the peace' ensured that, even in peacetime, the police were more military and the military more police-like than in Britain. Military parties were called out to suppress industrial unrest (as on Belfast's Falls Road in August 1907, when two rioters were shot dead), to protect property (as during the Dublin lock-out of 1913–14), and to assist police actions against nationalist paramilitaries (as in July 1914, when ineffectual attempts were made to disarm those running guns from Howth). Military frustration arising from the last incident led to the killing of three civilians on Bachelor's Walk, Dublin, and consequently to the censure of the King's Own Scottish Borderers for firing on civilians without authorisation. The uneasy relationship between civil and military agencies for maintaining 'the peace' was to be strained beyond endurance over the following decade.

The use of armed force by the state against its Irish citizens became ever likelier as militarism spread and private armies multiplied. The growing menace of European war doubtless contributed to the cult of discipline, training and mastery of arms which swept Ireland, and indeed the world, in the last years of peace. Its most benign manifestation was the development of pseudo-military youth groups such as the Church Lads' Brigade and the Boys' Brigade (both Protestant), and the Catholic Boys' Brigade, all of which were active in Ireland by the turn of the century. These British-based bodies aimed to inculcate 'manly' virtues such as obedience, discipline, reverence and self-respect, using military organisation as their model.[18] The same applied to Baden-Powell's Boy Scouts, active in Ireland from their inception in 1908. The first Irish commissioner was the twelfth earl of Meath, a forceful proponent of 'duty and discipline', compulsory national service and Empire Day. The republican counterpart was the Fianna Éireann (established in Belfast by Bulmer Hobson in 1902). Like its exemplars, The Fianna inculcated 'discipline and obedience', urging the boys to become 'strong and self-reliant', 'manly and independent'. Despite the formidable presence of Countess Constance Markievicz as vice-president of the Fianna after its revival in 1909, Irish youth movements were almost exclusively masculine in composition as well as ethos. Even the Girl Guides seem to have had only a single company in pre-war Ireland, formed at Belfast in 1910.[19] The construction of 'manliness' espoused by youth groups was shared by a host of sporting clubs, of which the most overtly militarist was the Gaelic Athletic Association (1884).

Among adults, the militarist spirit first became manifest in the growth of gun clubs, which could be formed with the permission of two magistrates. Access to weaponry was facilitated in 1907 by the lapsing of the Peace Preservation (Ireland) Act of 1881, although the importation of arms was prohibited between December 1913 and the outbreak of war. During 1913 and 1914, through an extraordinary outburst of mimetic militarism, a large proportion of Irish adult males began to train, dress and strut about in the manner of soldiers. Among the earliest paramilitary forces was the ostensibly 'non-sectarian and non-political' Young Citizen Volunteers of Ireland, established at a meeting of 2,000 people at Belfast's City Hall in September 1912. This force aimed to apply the scouting model to middle-class youths rather than boys, 'to develop the spirit of responsible citizenship and municipal patriotism', and 'to cultivate, by means of modified military and political drill, a manly physique, with habits of self-control, self-respect and chivalry'.[20] When the government declined their request for recognition, and expenses, the Young Citizens transferred their energies to the service of a far larger body created by the Ulster Unionist Council in January 1913. This was the Ulster Volunteer Force, an outgrowth from the numerous drilling parties which had lately been gathering at Orange halls to prepare for defence against Home Rule. The Ulster Volunteers were restricted to male signatories of Ulster's Solemn League and Covenant, and soon approached their limit of 100,000 members despite relatively low recruitment in Belfast and Donegal. One Protestant Ulsterman in every three enrolled in the force.[21] It had the appearance of an efficient fighting unit, with a distinguished array of retired army officers headed by Lieutenant-General Sir George Richardson, backed by the Irishman and former commander-in-chief, Field Marshal Earl Roberts.

Practical soldiery was inculcated by thousands of army veterans acting as drill-instructors or members of the mobile Special Service Force.

While the Ulster Volunteers were never recognised by the War Office and were discountenanced by Asquith's Liberal government, they received support from a staggering range of politicians, staff officers and military personnel in Ireland. Despite their avowed readiness to use force to prevent the application of Home Rule to Ulster, and their contingency plans for cutting communications and seizing arms and supplies from the crown forces, the Ulster Volunteers were left undisturbed. In March 1914, after an ill-judged and superfluous ultimatum from the army commander in Ireland (General Sir Arthur Paget), Brigadier-General Hubert Gough and most of his officers in the 3rd Cavalry Brigade resolved to resign and face dismissal rather than to obey any order to act against 'loyal' Ulstermen. In the subsequent confusion two senior general staff officers and the responsible minister were forced to resign, whereas the 'mutineers' were reinstated and the government's attempts to intimidate Ulster Unionists were subverted. In April, the Ulster Volunteers were able to import 25,000 German, Austrian and Italian rifles supplied with over 2,000,000 rounds, thus providing them with armament to match their sophisticated apparatus.[22] No military or police attempt was made to interfere with this spectacular and illegal 'gun-running' through Larne and other coastal sites near Belfast. A private army ruled in Ulster with the acquiescence of the state.

The Ulster Volunteers served as the model for several less businesslike forces created by their political opponents. In mid-November 1913, James Connolly called upon his fellow trade unionists to form a vigilante force to protect workers in the Dublin lock-out: 'Why should we not drill and train our men in Dublin as they are doing in Ulster?'[23] Connolly had himself served for almost seven years in the Royal Scots, before deserting in order to evade overseas service in 1889.[24] The outcome of his proposal was the Irish Citizen Army, a band of perhaps 200 members who were mainly, but not exclusively, male trades unionists. Countess Markievicz, as so often, was an active exception. The force was briefly commanded by Captain J. R. White, DSO, an idiosyncratic Gordon Highlander who had left the army shortly after his marriage, perceiving that 'marriage decreases mobility and increases the exposed front'.[25] Other private militias included the Hibernian Rifles, serving a dissident faction of the Ancient Order of Hibernians with strong republican connections, and the Midland Volunteer Force, reportedly convened at Athlone in October 1913.[26]

These organisations were dwarfed by the Irish Volunteers (Óglaigh na hÉireann), formed in Dublin in late November 1913 under the titular control of Eoin MacNeill, an historian prominent in the Gaelic League. Military organisation soon passed to Colonel Maurice Moore, another Gaelic Leaguer, formerly of the Connaught Rangers, who became inspector-general. In 'The North Began', published in the League's journal *An Claidheamh Soluis* on 1 November 1913, MacNeill inferred from the success of the Ulster Volunteers that 'all Irish people, Unionist as well as Nationalist, are determined to have their own way in Ireland'. His joy was shared by

---

17.1   North Down 1st battalion of the Ulster Volunteer Force, illustrating
the conjunction of religion and politics in a paramilitary organisation.

his fellow Gaelic Leaguer Patrick Pearse, who wrote in the following issue that it
was 'a goodly thing to see arms in Irish hands' – even in the hands of the unionist
Ulster Volunteers. For Pearse, the creation of an army promised 'bloodshed', while
bloodshed seemed 'a cleansing and a sanctifying thing'.[27] The creation of the
'National Army of Defence' was however largely the work of the Irish Republican
Brotherhood (IRB), a recently revived secret society dedicated to the use of armed
force but so far unarmed. The organisers were careful to avoid specifying whom the
Irish Volunteers might fight; though it seemed increasingly likely that they might
be deployed against the Ulster Volunteers once Home Rule had been applied.
According to its original manifesto, this 'defensive and protective' force was
destined to become 'a prominent element in the national life under a National
Government'. Membership was open 'to all able-bodied Irishmen without
distinction of creed, politics or social grade'.[28] Women were relegated to Cumann na
mBan, an auxiliary created in April 1914, which could not match the activity of the
female signallers, motor cyclists and nurses associated with the Ulster Volunteers.
So long as the Irish Volunteers remained an offshoot of the Gaelic League and the
IRB, enrolment was sluggish: about 20,000 by March 1914, compared with 85,000
Ulster Volunteers.[29]

It was at this point that organisers of the Irish Parliamentary Party determined to
take control of the Irish Volunteers (otherwise Irish National Volunteers), in order
to reinforce their demand for Home Rule with the latent menace of force. Hibernian
halls were made available for drill, local politicians took over the supervisory
committees, and in June the central Provisional Committee was itself packed with

followers of John Redmond. Membership reached 50,000 in late May 1914, 100,000 by mid-June and 150,000 a month later. At its peak, the movement enrolled about one-sixth of all Catholic adult males, as well as a scattering of Protestants. Participation was most intensive in mid-Ulster, where the promise of conflict with the Ulster Volunteers was most pronounced. The attachment of the Irish Volunteers to mainstream nationalism encouraged many army veterans to join up as drill sergeants, and a growing parade of Protestant ex-officers offered their services in leadership. A few days before the outbreak of war, the nationalists followed Ulster's example by running guns to Howth and then Kilcoole, though only 1,500 German rifles and perhaps 30,000 rounds were landed. Once again the security forces failed to intercept the weapons, despite a more vigorous response than in the case of Larne three months earlier. By comparison with the Ulstermen, the Irish Volunteers seemed ill-trained, under-armed and incompetent, notwithstanding energetic attempts to add military substance to their nominal strength. Even so, the existence of private armies with over a quarter of a million members posed a daunting potential challenge to the forces of the crown, outnumbered by at least six to one. On the eve of mobilisation, the spread of militarism had generated the nightmare of uncontrollable civil conflict.

The immediate impact of the outbreak of war in August 1914 was to intensify militarism in every sector, while reducing the risk of collision within Ireland. Some 58,000 Irish servicemen were mobilised at once, including 21,000 regulars, 18,000 reservists, 12,000 members of the Special Reserve, 5,000 naval ratings and a couple of thousand officers. Although mobilisation entailed the removal of many of the drill sergeants who had trained both the Ulster and Irish Volunteers, enlistment in the latter force did not reach its peak at 191,000 until mid-September. The political mentors of both volunteer forces (Sir Edward Carson and John Redmond) found common cause with the Allies in a fight which each expected to bring political benefits. For Redmond, despite his earlier opposition to intervention in South Africa, Irish participation in the war promised the reward of early Home Rule; while Carson saw an opportunity to strengthen Ulster's case for exclusion by demonstrating that Ulster loyalism was more than a rhetorical figment. Both leaders expected their volunteer forces to be embodied as divisions of the new army, and bargained strenuously with the War Office and the government before urging unqualified participation in the war effort. Redmond's initial suggestion that both forces should be recognised as Territorial units for home defence was not adopted, partly because the Territorials themselves were soon being drafted into overseas service. His subsequent attempt to form an Irish Brigade with officers vetted by the Volunteer leadership was subverted by Kitchener and his senior staff at the War Office, who remained sceptical of nationalist motives and contemptuous of nationalist soldiery. Even so, police estimates suggest that the Irish Volunteers eventually yielded at least 24,000 men to the army, in addition to losing over 7,500 reservists.

———————

17.2 Young citizens: these sprightly images of the Ulster Division's training camp at Finner, County Donegal, were sketched by the American Jim Maultsaid. He had enlisted in Belfast's Young Citizen Volunteers in September 1914.

The Ulster Volunteers secured a more sympathetic official response, and in early September their command was given effective control over the organisation and officering of the new 36th (Ulster) Division. Over 26,000 recruits and 4,000 reservists were transferred from the Ulster Volunteers, representing one-third of peak membership compared with one-sixth for the Irish Volunteers. In addition to the 50,000 enlistments supplied by volunteer forces, about 80,000 men without recorded paramilitary experience joined the wartime army in Ireland. The best estimate for recruitment in Ireland after mobilisation suggests that the army secured about 134,000 men, the navy and naval reserve over 6,000, and the air force about 4,000. Some 3,700 officers had obtained direct commissions in the army and navy by early 1916, suggesting that Ireland's aggregate male contribution to the wartime forces was about 210,000. An unknown but substantial number of Irishwomen also participated, mainly as nurses in auxiliary units.[30] Though military historians have sometimes estimated 'Irish' participation at 400,000 or even 500,000, such totals could only be justified by admission of non-Irish members of 'Irish' regiments as well as natives of Ireland who joined units in Britain, the colonies and the USA.[31] The proportion of eligible men who volunteered was well below that in Britain before the introduction of conscription, after due allowance for the concentration in Ireland of agricultural producers doing 'essential' work on the 'home front'.[32] Even so, the participation of over 200,000 Irishmen was proportionately the greatest deployment of armed manpower in the history of Irish militarism.

Who joined the army – when, where and why? While the collation of personal records has scarcely begun, and the motives of recruits will always be uncertain, the basic statistics of enlistment gathered by the Irish authorities provide an unusually rich background.[33] The rapidity of enlistment naturally declined during the war, as the pool of prospective recruits was drained and the fate of former recruits became known. About 44,000 men joined the army in the five wartime months of 1914, 46,000 in 1915, 19,000 in 1916, 14,000 in 1917 and fewer than 11,000 in 1918.[34] Until early 1916, when conscription was applied to Britain but not Ireland, the daily rate of enlistments in Ireland followed almost the same curve as that for the army overall. After the initial flurry in August and September 1914, recruiting subsided before recovering in the second quarter of 1915 – partly in response to vigorous marketing under the professional guidance of Hedley le Bas, exploiting posters, pamphlets and public meetings. As in Britain this surge gave way to a lull during summer and autumn, followed in winter by a brief recovery attributable to more effective cooperation between the Irish Parliamentary Party, the Irish Executive (under Lord Wimborne), and the new Department of Recruiting for Ireland. Terminal decline ensued in early 1916, and by April the daily rate of enlistment had fallen below sixty. It is significant that these fluctuations applied in both Ulster and the southern provinces, as well as in Britain. The factors determining fluctuations in enlistment evidently transcended local influences such as loyalism or nationalism.

The regional origins of recruits conformed to no simple pattern, although Ulster consistently provided the highest provincial ratio of enlistment. The Belfast district supplanted Dublin as Ireland's busiest recruiting field, and just over half of all wartime Irish enlistments occurred in Ulster. Apart from Dublin and the north-east, the counties with heaviest recruitment were clustered in the midland belt stretching from Longford southwards to Tipperary and Carlow. Few recruits came from the Atlantic seaboard (except Sligo), with particularly low ratios for Kerry, Mayo and Donegal. Despite Ulster's pre-eminence in the intensity of enlistment, only about 43 per cent of all Irish recruits were Protestants.[35] In the Belfast–Antrim area, during 1915, Catholics were actually more likely to join the forces than their Protestant neighbours. It thus seems likely that the propensity to enlist was primarily a function of economic and social context, rather than religion or politics. Cities and towns continued, as before the war, to supply the army with their surplus manhood.[36] By 1916 Connolly's Irish Transport and General Workers' Union, parent of the Irish Citizen Army, had lost almost as many men to the trenches as it retained in the union.[37] Yet the heaviest enlistment of urban workers seems to have affected relatively prosperous and stable sectors such as engineering and shipbuilding, where guarantees of post-war re-employment facilitated recruitment of a class of worker hitherto deaf to the army's appeal.[38] Workers in 'soft' trades such as printing, clothing and bootmaking were less forthcoming, while recruiters complained repeatedly about the recalcitrance of clerks and shop-assistants as well as farm workers. The sons of small farmers without alternative resources of labour were under especially strong pressure to serve the collective interest, by remaining at home.

Variation in economic circumstances, though influencing the degree to which men were *reluctant* to fight, cannot explain why so many nevertheless took that dangerous, uncomfortable and ultimately 'irrational' decision. Whereas peacetime soldiery might actually better the living conditions of an unemployed slum-dweller, the risks and horrors of war made the balance of economic costs and benefits highly unfavourable. The vast increase in enlistment after August 1914 must therefore be ascribed to deeper motives, reflecting powerful loyalties or commitments. The appeal to 'patriotism', in the abstract sense of defending the 'freedom or rights' of one's country, was of course the foundation of most recruiting rhetoric from official, unionist and nationalist sources alike. Yet the available reminiscences of veterans suggest that the personal decision to enlist was seldom constructed in terms of ideology. Family precedent provided a strong impulse, and those having fathers or brothers with military experience often emulated them as a matter of course. Such, however, was the flood of enlistment after August 1914 that only a small proportion of recruits could have followed the family path.[39] Other soldiers remembered the influence and example of peer groups: workmates, friends and neighbours.[40] For personal well-being, camaraderie was often more important than income or security. For many recruits, the army offered the promise of an

---

adventure whose dangers were outweighed by the pleasure of being with one's mates.

Those belonging to militias, fraternities or sporting clubs were particularly susceptible to collective pressure. The prominence of Irish and Ulster Volunteers in recruitment reflected not only their prior interest in militarism, but also their desire to maintain the bonds of friendship forged in peacetime. Fraternities such as the Ancient Order of Hibernians, the Freemasons and the Orange Order may also have fostered group movements into the army. The Orange and Protestant Friendly Society had over 16,000 members in uniform by late 1914; while veterans of the Boys' Brigade accounted for nearly half of all Protestant recruits in Dublin.[41] Orange and masonic lodges, in which the 'worshipful master' might be a common soldier and the candidate a captain, flourished among the forces awaiting action in France. Since fighting was easily pictured as a team sport, it is not surprising that sportsmen were enticed into units such as the 'Pals' Company' of the 7th Royal Dublin Fusiliers, initiated by the Irish Rugby Football Union. Though emphatically middle class, the 'Pals' were remarkable for their diversity in terms of birthplace, occupation, schooling and religion: their common interest was games, as experienced at school or university.[42] The influence of a peer group depended in part on the ability of organisers to persuade key members to enlist and so guide the group towards 'take-off' – as a coach might coax a team onto a muddy field to confront brutal opponents. Recruiting strategists were well aware of the power of the sporting motif, and their stories of football in no-man's-land lent glamour, and the illusion of fair play, to trench warfare.[43] Such images of the masculine culture of soldiery provided recruits with reassurance of continuity between civilian and military life.

The army's induction procedures seemed to confirm that military organisation was built upon fraternal loyalties. Those enlisting in Ireland enrolled in regiments bearing 'Irish' titles redolent of past campaigns (the Royal Irish, Dublin, Munster and Inniskilling Fusiliers; the Royal Irish Regiment and Rifles; the Connaught Rangers, Leinster Regiment, and Irish Guards). Friends could join battalions with a strong local flavour, and receive training at camps full of familiar faces. Ethnic loyalties were also recognised in the allocation of the newly raised Irish battalions to three divisions with Irishmen prominent as senior officers. The 10th (Irish) Division, initially under Lieutenant-General Sir Bryan Mahon, was an original element of Kitchener's New Army formed in August 1914. The 16th (Irish) Division, commanded by Lieutenant-General Sir Lawrence Parsons during its prolonged training but by Major-General William Hickie in the field, was part of the Second New Army created in the following month. The 36th (Ulster) Division, though formed slightly later than the 16th, left for France a few months earlier under Major-General Charles Powell. Mahon, Parsons and Hickie were of the Irish gentry, Hickie having the added qualification of Catholicism. Though Powell himself was not an Ulsterman, his division was unique in being organised and largely officered by an Irish

---

18.5   German Heinkel HE 111H, photographed at Bonmahon, County
Waterford, 1 April 1941. During the period of the Emergency there
were over 160 forced landings and crashes on or close to Ireland
involving belligerents.

relatively better prepared for war. Her defence effort is proportionately many times
greater than the Irish . . . and is directed to protection against attack by Russia.' By
contrast, NATO powers knew full well that 'Irish defences are inadequate' to meet
a Soviet attack on Ireland aimed at securing her ports and principal airports:
'Following from this, they must also conclude that Irish Defences are a danger to the
Atlantic Pact Defence System because of their inadequacy.' At a time of crisis, NATO
might simply 'provide in their plans for the establishment by their forces of defences
in Ireland on the outbreak of war', whether the Irish liked it or not. The document
pointed out that the Americans, who dominated NATO, had shown far less respect
during the Second World War for the sovereignty of small nations, including
Ireland, than had Britain.[31] Predictably, these unwelcome arguments fell on deaf
ears, although post-war governments did allow liaison on related security problems
between army intelligence and British and American security agencies. Successive
governments have managed ever since to have their cake and to eat it: Ireland
remained outside NATO, a policy increasingly invested with an aura of high moral
principle, while nothing was done to make the country a militarily credible neutral
state. The decision to stay out of NATO also accentuated the army's chronic
equipment problems. In 1952 the British dissuaded the Americans from supplying
arms sought by Ireland, and, a year later, while one Commonwealth Office official

thought it 'a good time to feed them with a little material', another argued that Irish 'acquisition of arms . . . so far from contributing to the security of NATO, would merely have an unsettling effect on Northern Ireland'.[32]

The first serious post-war call on the army came in 1957, after the IRA had begun a campaign of cross-border attacks into Northern Ireland. Under pressure from Britain, the government introduced internment for republican suspects, who were kept under military custody. They also deployed troops along the border. This placed some strain on the undermanned army, though it at least varied the peacetime diet of activities. The army's border role was to deter republican activities – at that time there was no danger of corresponding attacks southwards by loyalists, although there were minor incursions by Northern security forces. In 1958, the army also became involved in United Nations duties, when a number of officers volunteered for observer missions. This was the start of what soon became an important and some would say redeeming feature of army life – overseas service with the UN.

In July 1960 Ireland sent a composite battalion of troops for UN service in the Congo. The UN aim was to help the Congolese government to restore order, and to assert its authority in the secessionist province of Katanga. The first Irish battalion, equipped and trained for wet weather along the border rather than for tropical heat, endured great discomfort but performed its mission without loss. Its successors had a more difficult time. In November 1960 nine soldiers died in an engagement at Niemba, a tragedy met with a combination of sorrow and intense national pride in Ireland. Further deaths followed after a UN resolution authorised the use of force to restore order. For the first time since the end of the civil war in 1923 Irish soldiers took part in serious fighting, in combination with other UN troops. This continued fitfully until the autumn of 1963, to the great benefit of army experience and morale.

UN service has since become an important dimension of Irish military life. The horizons of new recruits are no longer bound by the twenty-six counties of independent Ireland. At the very least such service provides a change from the tedium of peacetime soldiering, as well as travel, some extra money and frequently some danger. It also enables the army to sharpen up its troops in a manner not possible at home, it facilitates contact with other armies, and it allows officers to broaden their knowledge of military affairs and their experience of military operations. Irish officers served as UN force commanders in the Congo and in the Lebanon, and from the early 1970s a succession of officers held a senior advisory post at UN headquarters. From the government's point of view, the army's contribution to UN operations has enhanced the country's international standing, though a cynic might argue that the state would do better to develop its own defence capacity through a greater investment in equipment and training than to dilute its forces for overseas service. There is also a certain irony in the likelihood that Irish officers are better briefed on, say, the strength and activities of the opposing forces in southern Lebanon than anyone in the Department of Defence is on submarine

---

18.6   Soldier on checkpoint duty in Irish area of operations,
South Lebanon, 1990.

movements in Irish territorial waters. But the benefits of UN service seem to out-
weigh enormously the costs and, despite occasional fatalities, it remains popular
with both the army and the public. Whether attitudes would change should Irish
troops be asked to assist directly with peace enforcement, a doctrine increasingly
invoked by the UN, is another matter.

The army in contemporary Ireland

In 1969 there was extensive rioting in Derry and Belfast. Thousands of refugees
came south to escape attacks on Catholic districts. The initial Irish response was one
of shock and outrage at the treatment meted out to Northern nationalists by the
Stormont government, whose security forces seemed more interested in assaulting
Catholics than in protecting them. What was the state to do? Some ministers saw
military intervention in Northern Ireland as a plausible response. Though that idea
was dismissed, the crisis was to bring the army back into the centre of political
controversy.

425

Whatever individual officers may have anticipated, it is clear that the Northern outbreak took the army unawares. There was no pool of knowledge and experience about Northern Ireland – apart from the period of the Emergency, army intelligence had not studied it systematically since 1926. Had senior officers been more familiar with the intricacies of northern nationalist politics, the imbroglio that followed might have been avoided. Instead, a relatively junior army intelligence officer with good personal contacts in Northern Ireland, Captain James Kelly, became a key intermediary between some Northern republicans and some government ministers. In circumstances which are still controversial and obscure – the then minister for defence and the then minister for finance later gave directly conflicting evidence on events under oath – he appears to have been accorded a very free hand by his army superiors, who were perhaps preoccupied with straightforward military problems. Covert steps were taken to import weapons into Ireland for distribution to 'citizens' defence committees' in Catholic enclaves in Northern Ireland, while a handful of Northerners were given firearms training at an army camp. When the arms importation came to light, apparently through police surveillance, two government ministers were sacked and, together with Captain Kelly and two civilians, were charged with various offences.[33] All were acquitted, though the episode ended Captain Kelly's army career. It had very serious implications for the army, once more caught up and once more the loser in an intra-government intrigue. The main beneficiary of the affair was the newly formed Provisional IRA, which apparently got its hands on some weapons and government money.

This disaster left its mark on the army. In contrast to the pattern in the early 1920s and again during the Emergency, it has since chosen – or been confined to – a supporting part in coping with subversion and disorder. The army has also eschewed an active counter terrorism role (although it does have a special forces unit). Instead it has been content to act entirely in support of the police. The Northern troubles have imposed considerable demands, reflected partly in a 50 per cent increase in numbers. Cooperation with the security forces in Northern Ireland has intensified since the early 1970s, though British sources remain critical of the army's border performance, arguing that it should have adopted a more aggressive approach to patrolling. By and large, however, republicans on cross-border raids did not attempt to engage the Southern security forces. The army's view has been that it will mind its side of the border, and that the British should mind theirs – one experienced officer commented in 1992 that there was nowhere safer for an IRA unit than south Armagh. While republican and loyalist violence has not spilled over into the South to any great extent, the army's other internal security functions are considerable. Troops routinely escort cash and explosives shipments, they guard the country's maximum security prison at Portlaoise, and they support the police in anti-terrorist operations. Very occasionally the defence forces steal the limelight: the gun runners *Claudia* and *Marita Ann* were intercepted at sea by the naval service, while the

---

notorious gunman Dessie O'Hare was wounded and his companion killed in 1987 in an exchange of fire with troops covering police at a roadblock.

The army today finds itself in a familiar plight. Defence policy continues to consist mainly in maintaining the form, not the substance, of an army organised to defend the state unaided from external aggression. In reality, to quote an authoritative report, 'most of the day-to-day activities . . . are concerned with matters other than the stated primary role of defence of the State against external aggression'. The 'operational focus' is a familiar miscellany: UN service, fisheries protection, air-sea rescue and air ambulance duties, flying government ministers about, and 'aid to the civil power', a phrase that embraces everything from border security to the collection of rubbish during bin strikes and, most recently, to running temporary hostels for homeless people in Dublin.[34] All this reflects the reality that successive Irish governments, too embarrassed, too negligent or too worldly wise to worry about national defence, have instead treated the defence forces as an enormously useful, docile and obedient reservoir of ancillary manpower and skills. There have, however, been some positive developments: since 1983 the army has been represented at the Conference on Security and Cooperation in Europe, a belated acknowledgement by the Department of Foreign Affairs that military expertise is sometimes useful in the foreign policy process. Through membership of the European Union Ireland is now involved in the formulation of policy on difficult political issues, such as the break up of the Soviet Union and civil war in the former Yugoslavia, which require military as well as diplomatic analysis. But attitudes are slow to change. A Foreign Affairs official recently scoffed at reports that, because of the increasing complexities of UN military interventions, the army hoped to second an officer to the Irish UN diplomatic mission: the army coveted the post only 'for the [subsistence] allowances . . . We've been blocking it for years!'

Border duties and internal security apart, the last two decades have seen a continuation of the difficulties which have beset the army since its foundation. Defence spending remains overwhelmingly on 14,000 men – and, in the last decade, also on a handful of women soldiers – rather than on weapons and equipment, although both the air corps and the naval service have benefited from considerable European Union funding for fisheries protection aircraft and ships. In 1987 the government began a major defence review 'with the particular objective of developing the most realistic and cost-effective defence arrangements',[35] a remit which appeared to duck the fundamental issue of what national defence policy was and should be. Shortly thereafter the Department of Defence embarked on a belated programme of disposal of a few of the decaying assets inherited from the British in 1922. Unrest amongst officers and men about pay, conditions of service and archaic methods of administration led in 1989 to the formation of representative bodies in the defence forces, and to the Gleeson commission of inquiry into pay and career structures. Its illuminating report produced swift action: in addition to pay rises, a new selection process for senior officers was introduced to counter the political and personal cabals which, so it is said, previously influenced the process.

These reforms did not address the underlying issue of what the proper role of the army is. In 1994, however, a study by the management consultants Price Waterhouse supported the view that the contemporary army is not only small and underequipped, but also militarily ineffective even in proportion to its actual strength, its personnel largely embroiled in administration and housekeeping, and its operational capacity impaired by the extraordinarily complicated, inflexible and wasteful system of military management deplored by the Devlin report as long ago as 1969. The Price Waterhouse recommendations were, in the words of their principal author, the distinguished Canadian General Lewis MacKenzie, based on the assumption that 'you want an army that can fight'.[36] They reportedly envisaged an army just 40 per cent below existing strength, properly equipped and trained and with adequate support services, and organised by brigade rather than by geographic command. The air corps would concentrate on helicopter duties and on maritime reconnaissance, while the operational role of the naval service would be expanded. The report's most contentious suggestion was the closure of seventeen of the army's forty or so barracks and posts, many of which serve no useful military purpose. Such action would facilitate the concentration of personnel for training and operational purposes, and would greatly reduce the time and money spent on barracks administration, maintenance, security and supply. It is, therefore, ironic that despite the compelling military logic for rationalisation and concentration the army appears to have come out *against* the idea, with the enthusiastic support of local interests. Its reasoning is clear enough: public awareness of the army and support for defence spending is largely linked to a visible military presence throughout the country, not to an informed appraisal of how well organised and equipped the military are to do their primary job. If closures did take place, consequently, the army assumes that the government would be far more likely simply to cut defence spending than to finance the development of a modern fighting force. While the minister for defence was quick to say that closures were not on the government's agenda, army relief at this precipitate announcement may be lessened by apprehension that the Department of Finance will have its way by other means.[37] The dismal history of defence procurement suggests that, even if numbers are not drastically cut, the army may be left even worse off than at present in equipment, weapons, transport and ordnance.

The army's difficulty in justifying its existence in its present form has been increased by recent developments in Northern Ireland. If the Northern crisis fades away, and if anti-state organisations finally embrace strictly constitutional politics, what real military role will remain for the army? Many of the tasks now thrust upon it under the rubric 'aid to the civil power' could just as easily be discharged by civilian organisations. Even the lifeline of UN service may be attenuated, if it does not go altogether, if the recent shift from peace keeping to peace enforcement

18.7   Army–Garda co-operation near the border with
Northern Ireland in the 1990s.

gathers pace. Only the possibility of Irish involvement in a new European defence
community after 1996 offers much hope for professional soldiers, and this prospect
is threatened by the public's attachment, however ill-informed, to the traditional
policy of military neutrality. By a curious irony, the naval service, for decades the
object of well merited ridicule – for some months in 1970 it had *no* operational craft
– is the one defence arm certain to prosper even without a clear shift in policy,
because of its job of protecting European Union fisheries. Despite renewed hints that

429

Ireland might consider eventual participation in a European Union defence system, ministers have been unwilling either to say publicly what this might entail, or to elaborate on alternative approaches. Until they do so, a national defence policy which is both militarily credible and publicly acceptable will remain as elusive as it has been since 1922.

Chapter 19

The British army and
Ireland since 1922

Keith Jeffery

The Anglo-Irish settlement of the early 1920s, which formally partitioned Ireland, had two main military consequences regarding the new 'province' (or 'statelet', as it was contemptuously called by nationalists) of Northern Ireland. These concerned recruitment to the British army and the politically very contentious issue of continued military aid to the (new) civil power in the province.

Although the end of hostilities in the Anglo-Irish war certainly relieved the British army of many onerous and unpleasant duties, the treaty of 6 December 1921 by which the Irish Free State was to be established as an independent dominion within the British empire was not regarded by the military authorities in London as a wholly unmixed blessing. The Irish settlement coincided with a period of severe government retrenchment in Britain, and it was recognised that the agreement had given enormous relief to the military budget. 'If there had been no Irish settlement', reported a Cabinet committee in February 1922, 'not only no reduction of the army would have been possible, but, on the contrary, a very large increase would have been necessary to bring the rebellion to an end.' It was also noted, however, that 'compared with the pre-war situation, the evacuation of Ireland affords no relief'. Before the war Ireland had been a military asset, not a liability and 'the 30,000 troops maintained there more cheaply than in Great Britain' had always been regarded as part of the general reserve of forces for both the United Kingdom and the empire.[1]

But Ireland had not been merely an economical location for barrack accommodation; it had also been a major British recruiting ground. In 1920 there were nearly 22,000 Irish soldiers in the British army, comprising 7.8 per cent of the total. This meant that Ireland as a whole, with approximately 9 per cent of the United Kingdom population, was proportionately underrepresented in the army's ranks. It was, however, a better showing than for either Scotland (7.5 per cent of soldiers to 10 per cent of the population) or Wales (2.5 per cent soldiers and 6 per cent population). In the immediate post-war period, moreover, Irish recruitment held up very well indeed at 9 per cent of all enlistments – Scotland managed 8 per cent and Wales 3 per cent[2] – and there is no evidence to indicate that the Anglo-Irish conflict of 1919–21 had any significant effect on recruitment. But the political changes which followed the conflict were accompanied by an alteration in recruiting arrangements and the disbandment of five southern Irish infantry regiments.[3] There was, too, a financial aspect to the changes. At the time of the Anglo-Irish truce of 11 July 1921 senior policymakers in the War Office in London were engaged in a difficult series of meetings to decide on cuts in the army estimates. On 14 July the Irish-born chief of the Imperial General Staff (CIGS), Sir Henry Wilson, raised the question of the future of the Irish regiments and was told by the secretary for war that the prime minister, Lloyd George, 'was going to agree with Valera having an Army or Militia or whatever he liked'. The following day Wilson and his colleagues unhappily came to the conclusion that all eight Irish infantry regiments[4] could be disbanded at an annual saving of £3 million.[5]

The government, however, had not entirely given up the cause of Irish recruitment. When Lloyd George presented his 'proposals for an Irish settlement' to the Cabinet on 20 July 1921, he included a stipulation that recruitment in Ireland would be permitted in the future. But, at the insistence of H. A. L. Fisher, the Liberal president of the Board of Education, this condition was significantly weakened. 'It is . . . assumed', read the final document, 'that voluntary recruitment for these [British] forces will be permitted throughout Ireland, particularly for those famous Irish Regiments which have so long and so gallantly served His Majesty in all parts of the world.'[6] Despite this provision, in the sometimes hard negotiations over defence matters which preceded the signing of the Treaty, the matter of recruitment was not raised again, nor was it mentioned in the final agreement of 6 December. A couple of English Unionist MPs raised the matter during the Commons' debates on the Treaty,[7] but no government statement was made. In fact the assumption seems to have been that the regiments would be disbanded. On 19 December recruitment was suspended for all the Irish infantry regiments except the Irish Guards.[8]

Sir Henry Wilson, however, was keen to save the three 'Ulster' regiments – the Royal Ulster Rifles (of which he was colonel), the Royal Inniskilling Fusiliers and the Royal Irish Fusiliers – and in January 1922 he encouraged Sir James Craig, the prime minister of Northern Ireland, to lobby Lloyd George directly in their favour.[9] This was successful and the three northern regiments were reprieved when the disbandment of the southern ones was announced in February and implemented five months later. But the northern units did not escape completely unscathed. The government decided that four battalions could only be raised in Northern Ireland and for a while the future of the Irish Fusiliers, with a traditional recruiting area which straddled the new Irish border (County Armagh in Northern Ireland and Counties Monaghan, Cavan and Louth in the Irish Free State), remained uncertain. Although its disbandment had actually been announced with that of the five southern regiments, the Fusiliers survived with just one battalion, thanks to a vigorous campaign opposing disbandment and, crucially, the willingness of the Inniskilling Fusiliers to sacrifice one of their battalions.[10]

One of the arguments marshalled in favour of retaining the Irish Fusiliers was that in recent years the regiment had drawn some 85 per cent of its recruits from County Armagh. But all the remaining Irish infantry regiments – especially the Irish Guards – continued to accept men from the Irish Free State after 1922. An Irish Fusiliers 'regimental census' published in January 1933 showed that 69 per cent of the soldiers came from Northern Ireland, 20 per cent from the Free State and 11 per cent from Great Britain. A further census, taken in the autumn of 1938, a year after the regiment's second battalion had been restored (with that of the Inniskillings), suggested that most of the additional men had been drawn from outside Northern Ireland. Now 34 per cent of the regiment came from the Free State and 21 per cent from Great Britain. The Inniskillings also drew a significant number of men from outside Northern Ireland. In 1926–7, 117 recruits (27 per cent of the total) came from the Free State. Recruiting for the Ulster Rifles was more concentrated in Northern Ireland. In 1923–4 only 7 per cent of recruits came from the South. Recruitment, even in Northern Ireland, was drawn from across the communal religious divide. In the mid-1920s, 25 per cent of the Ulster Rifles recruits and 61 per cent of those for the Inniskillings were Catholic.[11]

It is important to stress that people from all parts of Ireland continued to join the British army even after partition. As had been the case during the First World War, in the inter-war years many recruits with a Catholic background – both North and South – joined up (and have continued to do so). As has already been noted in this volume, there may have been nothing specifically *political* about this; men enlist for complex reasons. Family tradition, a love of the military life, or even desperation for any job whatsoever, might count for more than any party political preference or religious affiliation. But the point is worth making since in Northern Ireland a not inconsiderable segment of loyalist Protestant opinion began to equate Catholicism exclusively with militant Irish nationalism, and hence with political unreliability and 'disloyalty'. Much of this suspicion of their Irish fellow-countrymen stemmed from the violence of the campaign for Irish independence, but it drew strength from a fierce determination to secure and maintain Northern Ireland as an integral part of the United Kingdom. Whatever its source, the shadow of Irish politics, both unionist and nationalist, fell across military affairs in Northern Ireland after 1922.

This can be seen in the various attempts – ultimately successful – to establish some Territorial Army formation in the province between the wars. Ireland had been omitted from the pre-First World War Territorial Force organisation, and Northern Ireland was equally neglected when the force was re-established as the Territorial Army in 1921. In 1923, however, the secretary for war, Lord Derby, visited the province. After inspecting units of the 10,000 strong full-time 'C1 Special Constabulary', he expressed regret that these men did not have the opportunity to enter the Territorial Army. Sir James Craig, who greatly favoured the establishment of an 'Ulster Territorial Division', sprang upon Derby's observation and amplified it into a definite promise, which he pressed both Derby and, in 1924, his Labour successor, Stephen Walsh, to implement. But London was not so enthusiastic. While the War Office agreed that Territorial units could legally be raised in Northern Ireland, concerns were raised that so doing might prejudice relations with the Free State and also that the Northern Ireland government might expect to use Territorials for employment in the event of civil disturbance. After consulting Derby, who grumbled that 'it just shows how careful one ought to be not to make any casual remark which can be construed into a definite statement of policy', Walsh bluntly informed Craig that it was not possible to raise a Territorial Division from the C1 Constabulary.[12]

By the end of the 1920s the Belfast government was less wholeheartedly behind the extension of the Territorial Army to Northern Ireland. Prompted by Lord Craigavon (the title taken by Sir James Craig in 1927) London had agreed to review defence questions concerning the province, and a 'Northern Ireland Defence Committee' was set up in 1929. Once again the possibility of transforming special constables (by this time the 'B-Specials') into Territorial soldiers was raised, this time by the director of Military Operations in the War Office. But now it was the Northern Ireland representatives who demurred. Sir Charles Wickham (inspector-general of the Royal Ulster Constabulary) observed that the B-Specials were all of one religion (Protestant), many of them were over military age, and they were generally engaged 'in the protection of their own homes'. In the case of the Territorials, 'no religious discrimination would be possible, and the different elements might not mix. Further, a Territorial Force [*sic*] would not be under the control of the Northern Ireland Government.'[13] When the matter was referred back for further consideration, Belfast agreed that Territorial artillery units could certainly be raised to man coast defences (as was the case elsewhere in the United Kingdom), but felt that 'a local territorial infantry force' should not be raised. While the government did not fear the *collective* partiality or unreliability of prospective territorial battalions, it was

> considered that it would be unwise at the present time to afford training facilities to men – more especially in bomb-throwing and machine gun practice – who might use the knowledge which they had acquired for subversive purposes. For some years, at any rate, it is thought inadvisable that there should be in Northern Ireland a territorial infantry organization.[14]

The committee accepted these views and left the final decision to the War Office. At last, in 1937, a 'Territorial Army and Air Force Association' for County Antrim was set up to oversee the raising of units for coast defence. But the political implications of this move were not entirely forgotten. It was laid down that for recruiting the new body should take into account: '(i) the social position of the recruit; (ii) his political aspect; (iii) his ability to attain the rank of NCO'.[15]

As had been the case in Ireland throughout the nineteenth century, and up to partition, politically the most contentious aspect of the British army's role after 1921

19.1   Ulster Special Constabulary platoon at the Rectory, Garrison, County
Fermanagh, c. 1921. Although a reserve police force, they demonstrate here
a decidedly military character.

was its duties in aid of the civil power. During the 1919–21 hostilities relations
between the military, the police and the civil authority had never been clearly
defined and were at times quite acrimonious. The new Northern Ireland government,
while anxious that London should continue to help foot the bill for maintaining
internal security (always a lively concern for economically minded Unionist
ministers), were less keen to share control of security policy. One of the more
unpalatable pieces of advice which Sir Henry Wilson, as military adviser to the
Northern Ireland government, had offered to James Craig was that any auxiliary
force which was created in the North should both be organised along military lines
and remain under strict British military command. Only thus could the dangers
of bias and indiscipline so grievously demonstrated by the Black and Tans and
the Auxiliary Division of the RIC be avoided. Craig and his colleagues, however,
realistically feeling that London's security priorities might not always coincide with
their own, preferred to reinforce the police with both full and part-time special
constables, a process described by one historian as 'arming the Protestants'.[16]

   The raising of supplementary personnel to back up what became the Royal Ulster

---

435

Constabulary (RUC) – in early 1923 there were nearly 41,000 full and part-time policemen – together with the very wide-ranging 1922 Civil Authorities (Special Powers) Act, and a general decline in anti-state violence, meant that the Belfast government was able to maintain order without much recourse to army help. The only major military operation of the 1920s in Northern Ireland was the 'battle of Beleek'. Between 28 May and 4 June 1922, Northern Specials, Free State forces, IRA and British troops fought over the isolated Beleek–Pettigo triangle on the County Fermanagh frontier with the Free State. The British army commander in Ireland, Sir Nevil Macready, who was still based in Dublin, was not inclined to take the matter very seriously: 'except for some sniping across the border line, and the presence of a few armed scallywags in the Pettigo Triangle, the situation was in reality but little worse than its normal condition'.[17] But there was a clear political imperative in defending the Northern Ireland enclave around Beleek. Several hundred British troops were brought in and the area was secured after artillery had been used. Following this the War Office were able to reduce the British garrison in the province to five, and, in the late 1920s, just four infantry battalions.

It was, however, recognised in London that the position of these troops was significantly different to those in other parts of the United Kingdom and special instructions were issued to the 'General Officer Commanding [GOC], Northern Ireland District' at the end of 1922. It was laid down that the troops under his command were 'responsible for the defence of Northern Ireland, which is to be taken as meaning defence against external aggression or internal organised attack on a large scale involving military operations beyond the capacity of the Ulster Special Constabulary'. Border security was generally to be left to the local police and it was 'not considered possible or desirable that . . . you should attempt to protect the whole border of Ulster [*sic*] from incursion by small raiding parties'. In the event of regular troops being involved in any border incident, 'no advance into the territory of the Free State [was] to be made without the approval of the Army council being first obtained'. While close liaison was to be maintained with the Northern Ireland authorities, the War Office specifically instructed that the Belfast government had no power to issue orders to the army commander 'regarding the disposition or employment of British forces'. The GOC, moreover, was to deal only with the prime minister of Northern Ireland, or the Cabinet secretary, and not with any subordinate minister.[18] Only in the gravest of emergencies was the GOC to deploy troops in aid of the civil power without reference to London. In 1932 these instructions were broadly confirmed by the War Office, which once more emphasised that there could be 'no question, under any circumstances, of the responsibility for the use of troops for this purpose being placed upon the Government of Northern Ireland'.[19]

Bearing in mind the recent history of civil-military relations in Ireland, the care with which the War Office laid down the GOC's responsibilities was very understandable. In the event, there was little call for military assistance to the civil power. Although troops were readied for deployment during both the 1926 British general strike and the (uniquely) non-sectarian riots against the Belfast poor relief system in October 1932, they were only actually used in July 1935, following serious Protestant–Catholic violence, which eventually claimed ten lives. At midnight on 13 July the army were called out for the first time since 1922 and remained on duty for the following eleven days. The use of the military in 1935 raised issues which were to recur some thirty-odd years later when troops were once more called out in aid of the civil power in Belfast. The historian of the 1935 riots argues that the army 'should have been called out earlier' on the night of 13 July, 'and no doubt would have been but for the political implications'. There was concern in Westminster about who was actually in charge of the soldiers. A Liberal MP, Edward Mallalieu, asked that the imperial troops be withdrawn from Northern Ireland because 'no Minister is responsible to this House'. By the time the request was made, however, the troops had returned to barracks.[20] But in the early 1970s the protracted deployment of troops in Northern Ireland proved to have very serious constitutional implications indeed.

The experience of the surviving Irish regiments in the British army between the wars mirrored that of the army in general. The defence cuts following the Great War not only robbed the Inniskillings and the Irish Fusiliers of their second battalions, but also cut the Irish Guards back to a single battalion and forced Irish cavalry regiments into amalgamations. Reflecting the very wide range of British military commitments, Irish units were deployed throughout the world. The Royal Inniskilling Fusiliers, for example, served in Iraq, China (Shanghai) and Singapore, as well as in the United Kingdom (including a spell in Northern Ireland in the late 1920s). The 1st battalion, Royal Ulster Rifles, served in the occupation forces in Germany, and later went to Aldershot, Belfast, Cairo, Jerusalem and Hong Kong. In the mid-1930s, with the worsening international situation, the post-war reductions began to be reversed. Recruitment of Irishmen into the army, too, started to recover, though not dramatically. In 1924–5 the proportion of Irish-born in the army fell to its lowest inter-war level of 4.8 per cent. By 1938 this had risen to 5.7 per cent.[21] In March 1936 the adjutant-general observed that the annual average of infantry recruits from Northern Ireland (over 690 men) was sufficient to sustain six infantry battalions as against the current four,[22] and this contributed to the decision to restore the Inniskillings' and Irish Fusiliers' second battalions in 1937. In 1939 the second battalion of the Irish Guards was restored.

The period immediately before the Second World War also saw the raising of additional part-time military units in Northern Ireland.[23] In April 1939 recruitment was opened for a complete anti-aircraft brigade of the Supplementary Reserve. Women – who evidently posed less of a security risk than men – had already begun enlisting in a Northern Ireland Group of the Auxiliary Territorial Service (ATS) after it was first organised throughout the United Kingdom in September 1938, and they began training for a variety of manual, clerical and motor-driving tasks. In the summer of 1939 the government began recruiting a 'Home Guard', and after the

---

outbreak of war 6th and 7th battalions of the Ulster Rifles and a 5th battalion of the Irish Fusiliers were embodied for home defence.[24] In May 1940, when the Local Defence Volunteers – later the Home Guard – was set up in Great Britain, a parallel force was raised in Northern Ireland within the existing Special Constabulary organisation. But this led to uncertainty as to the precise status – civil or military? – of the new body. The matter was not cleared up until March 1942 when the volunteers were required to reattest, making themselves liable for military service as 'Ulster Home Guards' in the event of an emergency requiring their employment in military operations.[25] Although enlistment in Northern Ireland for overseas service naturally picked up after September 1939, it never reached the levels attained during the First World War. An 8th battalion of the Ulster Rifles served mostly as an anti-aircraft regiment and in 1940 the Inniskilling Fusiliers raised a 6th battalion which from 1942 formed part of the 38th (Irish) Brigade.

In general, recruitment from Northern Ireland during the Second World War was disappointing. There was an initial spurt at the beginning of the war and a further surge after Dunkirk. During 1941 and 1942, however, 'the average monthly figure was relatively low', exceeding the 1,000 mark only three times. The numbers increased in 1943, with over 1,500 joining in June and September, but they fell away thereafter. The nationalist writer Denis Ireland mordantly reflected on the spectacle in Belfast of 'streets, cinemas and cafés packed with "loyal Ulstermen" loyally staying at home'.[26] In all, an estimated 38,000 people, of whom 7,000 were woman, joined up between 1939 and 1945.[27] A significant number also enlisted from Southern Ireland. In 1946 the Dominions Office calculated that over 43,000 men and women 'born in Eire' had joined the British services during the war, of whom 32,778 were serving in the army at the end of 1944.[28] As always, the motives for enlistment were mixed. For some the reason was purely economic. Chris Byrne, an unemployed Dublin plasterer, felt he had 'no other alternative but to join the [British] army . . . I'd a family. I had to go.' Jimmy Tallon from Whitehall in Dublin left the Irish army, which paid him 13 shillings a week, for the British which paid 22 shillings. 'It was', he said, 'nothing to do with being anti-Hitler.' William Shorten, from Dundrum, County Dublin, was driven by 'a desire for adventure which was not about to be satisfied in the army of neutral Ireland'. Others were certainly concerned about the issues at stake, and the combination of this with the prospect of excitement often proved irresistible. Romie Ryan, a middle-class Dublin Catholic who enlisted in the ATS, decided after the Battle of Britain that she did not 'want to be left out of war shaking events'. 'I do want to be in uniform', she wrote at the time, 'and driving all sorts of exciting people about instead of being cooped up in a ghastly boring office behind the Four Courts.'[29]

While Irish recruitment for the Allied cause may have fallen below some expectations, that for the Axis powers was negligible. Echoing Roger Casement's scheme in 1914–15, an attempt was made to recruit Irish-born prisoners-of-war into an anti-Allied 'Irish Brigade'. But this was a dismal failure. After the fall of France

19.2   Northern Ireland vehicle maintenance class, 18 March 1942,
showing women sharing in the war effort.

in the summer of 1940 the German authorities decided to approach all Irish prisoners with the offer of detention at a special camp with improved living conditions. By the spring of 1941 about eighty men had taken up the offer. The majority refused to serve the Germans save in the event of a British invasion of Southern Ireland and in the end the proposed brigade amounted to only some ten individuals, none of whom were ever actually employed. It emerged, too, that the senior Irish officer involved was a British agent.[30]

As in the First World War, conscription was not applied in any part of Ireland, though the matter was considered on a number of occasions. In early 1939 the British government contemplated including provision for the future application of conscription to Northern Ireland in the legislation introducing it to Great Britain. Lord Craigavon felt that it should immediately be extended to the province, but the suggestion provoked strong opposition. In Dublin de Valera declared that the conscripting of any Irishmen for service in British forces would constitute 'an act of aggression'; Cardinal MacRory, the Catholic Primate of All Ireland, asserted that the people had a 'moral right' to resist compulsion; and Irish–American groups pressed President Roosevelt to use his influence against the proposal.[31] London dropped the relevant clause from the bill, overriding Ulster Unionist protests. Two years later, following further representations from Belfast and in the context of a general manpower review, the British government reconsidered the issue. This time the opposition was even greater: apart from the Irish government and nationalists in Northern Ireland, objections came from some Protestant and Labour groups in the province, the United States minister in Dublin, and the prime ministers of Australia and Canada. Most telling, perhaps, was a sombre warning of widespread disorder from the inspector-general of the RUC. Finally, even the authorities in Belfast abandoned their hitherto unqualified support. Neatly passing the buck back to London, the prime minister, John M. Andrews (who had succeeded Craigavon in November 1940), informed the British home secretary that 'the strength of opposition would be more widespread than had been realised. While, speaking for themselves, the Government of Northern Ireland would like to see conscription applied, the real test, in their view, must be whether it would be for the good of the Empire.' Accordingly, the Cabinet in London concluded that 'it would be more trouble than it was worth to apply conscription to Northern Ireland'.[32]

In military terms Northern Ireland was not directly affected by the war, though a plan was drawn up in 1940 for joint British and Irish action against any possible German invasion of the island. This 'W Plan' also appears to have been the basis for a possible British invasion of independent Ireland. Apart from supplying recruits for the armed services, Northern Ireland's main contribution to the war effort lay in the provision of base facilities – for land, sea and air forces – and in food production and the manufacture of various war materials, especially in Belfast's aircraft factory and shipyard. Derry became a major base for North Atlantic convoy protection vessels and ten RAF Coastal Command squadrons operated from local airfields. After the USA entered the war in December 1941, American naval and air units joined the existing British and Allied forces.

Between 1942 and 1945 some 300,000 American soldiers passed through the province. The presence, however brief, of such large numbers of American servicemen was both reassuring and and unsettling. The use of Northern Ireland as an American military staging-post both amplified the province's contribution to the Allied war effort and also, from a unionist perspective, pleasingly strained relations between Dublin and Washington. Shortly after the first American troops had landed

———————

19.3   Armoured cars on exercise near the Giant's Causeway,
County Antrim, 28 January 1941.

at Belfast, de Valera asserted that the United States had thereby 'recognised a
Quisling government in Northern Ireland'. Cardinal MacRory also complained about
'our country being overrun by British and United States soldiers against the will of
the nation'. The wartime garrison – both American and British – had, moreover, a
disturbing impact on the province's very conservative society. As one local woman
put it: 'If nothing else, they gave Irishmen something of a jolt! Changes were on the
way!' Despite strong pressure from the military authorities, the Belfast City Council
refused to take the apparently dangerous step of allowing cinemas to operate on
Sundays, and in 1942 the army eventually commandeered the Hippodrome cinema
and ran it themselves on the Sabbath. There were also tensions arising from the
exploits of youthful GIs with plenty of money to spend and little to spend it on apart
from drink and women. The presence of black American troops added a further
social complication. A system of unofficial segregation was operated in towns near
American bases west of Lough Neagh, though this was more to protect the soldiers
from each other than from local feeling. Magherafelt was open to each race on
alternate nights, while Moneymore was reserved for black personnel and Cookstown
for white. Some individuals found the province oppressive. On being asked by a
priest if he were a Catholic, one black GI replied: 'Holy Snakes, no . . . it's bad
enough being a negro in Ulster.' Yet for most servicemen Northern Ireland was no
worse than other parts of the United Kingdom; social antagonisms were matched by
much local generosity and hospitality. Many of the Americans, indeed, responded
warmly to this, resulting, among other things, in several thousand war brides and
several hundred illegitimate children.[33]

441

In 1941 Belfast suffered two major German air raids, the first of these, on 15–16 April, when at least 900 people were killed, was one of the United Kingdom's most costly single bombing attacks of the war outside London. After the second raid on 4–5 May it was calculated that some 56,000 houses had been damaged – over half the city's total housing stock; 15,000 people lost their homes altogether and 100,000 were temporarily left homeless while repairs were being carried out. The high casualty rate can be put down to several causes: the bombs, in April at least, fell principally on densely populated working-class districts, containing shoddily built terrace houses; official preparations, moreover, were woefully inadequate. Labouring under the misapprehension that Northern Ireland was too remote from enemy airfields to be much at threat, there were few anti-aircraft installations, only patchy provision of shelters had been made, and little had been done in the way of evacuating families from the city. After the attacks widespread panic powerfully helped to alter this, and over 220,000 people fled Belfast. The suffering during the blitz, nevertheless, provided a sacrifice to match that of the Ulster Division on the Somme twenty-five years earlier. In 1943 Churchill affirmed that 'the bonds of affection between Great Britain and the people of Northern Ireland have been tempered by fire' and were now, he believed, 'unbreakable'.[34]

Irish units served in all the major theatres of war. The 1st battalion of the Irish Guards took part in the brief, ill-fated Norwegian campaign in the late spring of 1940, and battalions from all three Ulster infantry regiments served in the British Expeditionary Force in France, and were evacuated from Dunkirk in May–June 1940. One of these units, the 2nd Inniskillings, sailed east in 1942, briefly served in Madagascar, and subsequently in India, Syria, Egypt and Italy. The 1st Inniskillings fought in Burma during the 1942 retreat to India, and again in 1942–3. A regiment recruited in Derry (another was raised in Belfast) for the Supplementary Reserve Anti-Aircraft Brigade formed in the spring of 1939 served in North Africa between 1939 and 1943, and with the Eighth Army in Italy in 1943–4. A section of the Belfast regiment was captured at Tobruk in 1942, while the remainder served in England during the Battle of Britain and later went to the Far East. In North-West Europe, both regular battalions of the Ulster Rifles participated in the Normandy landings, the second reaching the beaches at 1000 hours on 'D' Day, 6 June 1944, while the first, which had been converted to a glider battalion, came over by air later that day. Both units then took part in the steady Allied advance through the Low Countries into Germany.

Both of the Ulster Rifles battalions survived the war intact. Other units were not so fortunate. One of the gravest reverses suffered by an Irish formation during the war occurred with the 2nd Irish Fusiliers, part of a small force occupying the Aegean island of Leros, were completely overrun by the enemy in November 1943. Virtually all the battalion were killed (including the commanding officer) or captured. At Anzio in January 1944, the 1st Irish Guards were so badly knocked about that they ceased to exist as a fighting force. The fact that these two units were

19.4   US troops arriving at Derry, 13 May 1942.

not reformed, and the disbandment of the 6th Inniskillings and its absorption into
the 2nd battalion of the regiment in the summer of 1944, reflected in part the
comparatively small reservoir of available Irish recruits. The Irish Guards, too, which
had had three battalions by 1940, became progressively less 'Irish' as the war went
on (as had been the case in the '14–'18 conflict). The Irish cavalry regiments, too,
were by and large just nominally Irish. Only the North Irish Horse, a Supplementary
reserve tank regiment which fought in North Africa and Italy, was primarily
composed of Irishmen.

   One of the most significant Irish formations in the Second World War was the
'Irish Brigade', which was the specific brainchild of Winston Churchill.[35] Inevitably
the Belfast government complained about the use of the title 'Irish', but their
objections were ignored and in January 1942 the 38th (Irish) Brigade officially came
into being. The historic title was well appreciated within the formation, and The

O'Donovan, who was its first brigadier, 'felt the mantle of Sarsfield had fallen on his shoulders'.[36] It comprised one regular battalion (1st Royal Irish Fusiliers), one wartime (6th Royal Inniskilling Fusiliers) and one Territorial Army (2nd London Irish Rifles, which was associated with the Royal Ulster Rifles). The brigade landed at Algiers in November 1942 and served successively in North Africa, Sicily, Italy and Austria. The formation was unequivocally Irish: there was a specially printed brigade song-book full of Irish songs; each battalion had a pipe band; that distinctively Irish head gear, the caubeen, was adopted for use throughout the brigade; St Patrick's Day was celebrated appropriately. In 1944 telegrams of greeting were sent, among others, to King George VI, Eamon de Valera and both the Protestant Church of Ireland Primate, Archbishop Gregg, and Cardinal MacRory. In Rome in June 1944 men from the brigade – Protestants as well as Catholics – were granted an audience with Pope Pius XII, following which the brigade pipes played 'The Wearing of the Green' and 'The Minstrel Boy'. Reflecting at about the time they were in Rome on the fact that a significant number of his men came from neutral Ireland, the brigade commander hoped that 'all the magnificent deeds wrought by the sons of Éire in this war, against the barbarisms of Germany and her Allies, may be remembered to her credit', and would be balanced against the fact that 'Éire' had been neutral.[37]

It may be that the most visible Irish contribution to the Allied war effort lay in the strikingly high number of Irishmen in senior British military positions. Four wartime field marshals had an Ulster background: Sir John Dill, CIGS 1940–1, and later head of the British Joint Staff Mission to the United States; Sir Alan Brooke (later Lord Alanbrooke; also uncle of the Northern Ireland prime minister, Sir Basil Brooke), CIGS 1941–6; Sir Harold Alexander (Earl Alexander of Tunis), C-in-C Middle East and subsequently supreme allied commander, Mediterranean; and Sir Bernard Montgomery – 'Monty' (Viscount Montgomery of Alamein) – who commanded the Eighth Army in North Africa, and the British and Allied Groups of Armies in North-West Europe, 1944–5. Alexander's predecessor as C-in-C Middle East was Sir Claude Auchinleck, another Ulsterman, who was appointed field marshal in 1946. Other Irish generals played significant roles during the war: Richard O'Connor in North Africa; Tom Pile, who commanded the United Kingdom anti-aircraft defences; The O'Donovan, Nelson Russell and Pat Scott, who successively led the Irish Brigade; and 'Chink' Dorman-Smith, a controversial soldier who was sacked by Alexander in 1942. After the war he changed his name to O'Gowan, returned to the family home in County Monaghan and in the 1950s became an active supporter of the IRA.[38]

The Second World War had a considerable impact on Northern Ireland in both a social and a political sense. The shared experience of the conflict undoubtedly brought the divided community of the province closer together. One Belfast civil servant recalled that 'religion in fact played little part in the wartime administrative story. All were at risk and all played their part in the processes of survival, aid,

19.5 Victoria Barracks, Belfast, after the air raid of 15–16 April 1941. The soldiers are clearing the magazine which was hit but did not explode.

neighbourliness and defence in general.'[39] The demands of the war economy reduced the very high levels of unemployment which the province had suffered between the wars (from over 25 per cent in the mid-1930s, the unemployment rate fell to under 5 per cent by the end of the war), and the relative prosperity of the war years certainly helped to ease communal tensions. The Unionist government, however, was unwilling – or unable – to exploit the opportunity to draw the minority community more fully into the whole life of the province. Indeed, the neutrality of southern Ireland did much to confirm the partition of the island and for unionists merely emphasised the perceived disloyalty of all Irish nationalists, north or south of the border. Yet Irish neutrality had been clearly benevolent towards the Allied war effort: no restriction had been placed on Irish people wishing to enlist in the British forces; there was very close cooperation between Irish military intelligence and the British security authorities, especially regarding enemy aliens in southern Ireland; Allied planes based in County Fermanagh were permitted to use an air corridor over southern County Donegal; German servicemen who landed in Ireland were interned, while Allied personnel were returned to the United Kingdom, albeit after some delay.[40] Despite evidence of this having been circulated to the British Cabinet before the end of the war, Churchill himself in his victory broadcast sharply criticised the southern Irish stance. He singled out 'the action of Mr de Valera, so much at variance with the temper and instinct of thousands of southern Irishmen, who hastened to the battlefront to prove their ancient valour,' for having denied British use of Irish ports and airfields for the protection of the Western Approaches. 'This was indeed a deadly moment in our life,' he continued, 'and if it had not been for the loyalty and friendship of Northern Ireland, we should have been forced to come to close quarters with Mr de Valera, or perish for ever from the earth.'[41] The speech provoked a strong response from de Valera, for whom, in fact, neutrality had been the only practical political option.

The end of the Second World War brought little respite for the Irish units in the British army. In the 1940s and 1950s they saw service in 'peacekeeping' and counter-insurgency operations in India, Palestine, Kenya, Cyprus and Malaya, and regular operations during the Korean War, in which the 2nd battalion of the Ulster Rifles lost over 180 men killed, wounded and captured at the Battle of Imjin River in April 1951 where they withdrew in the face of numerically superior communist forces under covering fire provided by the King's Royal Irish Hussars.

During 1947 there was a major reorganisation of the British infantry of the line: each regiment was reduced to one battalion and the units were grouped into brigades. It was decided to combine the three Northern Ireland regiments into an 'Irish Brigade', but the proposed new title was not universally welcomed. Arguing that the designation 'Irish' had been used during the war 'to give recognition to the part being played in the Army by men enlisted from Eire', Sir Basil Brooke (who became Lord Brookeborough in 1962) told London that his government felt 'very strongly that nothing should be done now which would blur the distinction between this part of the United Kingdom and a State which was neutral in the last war'. Clearly well briefed by his civil servants, he further asserted that the proposed name

> would inevitably be associated with the Irish who fought against England in the days of Marlborough; the Irish Brigade which fought against Britain in the Boer War; Sir Roger Casement's effort in the First World War and also with the body of 'Blueshirts' organised in Eire to fight with Franco in the Spanish Civil War.

Brooke proposed that the title 'Ulster' or 'Northern Ireland' be used, the former being particularly suitable since the principal local Territorial Army unit, which for the first time would cover the whole province, was to be called '107 (Ulster) Independent Infantry Brigade'.[42]

Brooke's proposal, however, did not commend itself to the War Office, chiefly because the commanding officers of the three regiments themselves objected to any title which might identify their units solely with Northern Ireland. Their chief concern was with recruitment. While Brooke believed that an 'Irish Brigade' might be a serious deterrent to enlistment in the province, for their part the colonels wished to avoid anything which would discourage men from Eire – who comprised half of all the recruits – from joining up. A further consideration was 'the importance of avoiding any title which would encourage political feeling within Regiments between men drawn from Ulster and those from Eire'. After Brooke had rejected a further War Office proposal to use the title 'Royal Irish Brigade' ('The association of that term [Royal] with the word "Irish" seems to me particularly unfortunate, implying as it would the existence of a united Ireland owing allegiance to the Crown.'), a compromise was reached with 'The North Irish Brigade'. It did not completely satisfy the regiments, but they agreed to it 'in order to get a settlement', and they were 'prepared to meet the recruiting risk involved'.[43] The argument over the title of the new brigade stemmed from the political sensitivities of the Northern Ireland government, powerfully coloured by the experience of Irish neutrality during the war. They were also concerned to entrench the province's position within the United Kingdom. There was, moreover, the added complication that Irishmen from both sides of the border continued to enlist in significant numbers into the British army.

The position of servicemen from Ireland arose again after southern Ireland formally became a republic and finally left the British Commonwealth in 1949. In fact, the Admiralty first raised the problem, since two Irish naval airmen had subsequently applied to leave the service on political grounds. The War Office felt that there was no need to make any special concessions. No-one had any idea how many southern Irishmen there were in the British forces, and in any case it was suggested that most of those who would take any discharge offered 'would do so not because they were Southern Irish but for other reasons, e.g. an offer of a good civil job, dislike of their Sergeant Major etc.'. The army director of personnel services, however, felt that 'any coercion exercised to retain Southern Irishmen who wished to be released might have unfortunate results . . . Past history', he solemnly warned, 'shows that an Irishman who considers himself to be suffering under an injustice is potentially a very dangerous person.' Despite this caution, a joint meeting of all three services eventually decided that no particular provisions needed to be made for Irish service personnel: 'It was felt that citizens of the Irish Republic should continue to be treated in exactly the same way as U.K. citizens.'[44]

The island of Ireland remained a significant source of men, at least for the Irish infantry regiments. In the late 1950s, for example, one quarter of the officers in the Royal Irish Fusiliers, and over 40 per cent of the men, had home addresses in the Republic.[45] Family tradition has certainly sustained enlistment from Ireland, but also for those Irishmen who simply desired to pursue a military career, the British army, still with world-wide commitments in the 1950s and 1960s, offered more exciting opportunities than the Irish army. Besides, the pay and conditions of service were substantially better. Although citizens of the Irish Republic still join the British army, Britain's shrinking overseas military responsibilities, improvements in Irish pay and conditions, and, since the 1960s, Irish service with the United Nations, providing opportunities for foreign travel, have eroded the attractions of service in the British forces. In 1989, nevertheless, about 20 per cent of the 2nd Royal Irish Rangers came from the Republic. Such service has understandably always been regarded with suspicion by extreme Irish nationalists, and the emergence of violent conflict in Northern Ireland from the late 1960s onwards, with the deployment of regular troops in the province, also clearly exposed the political ambiguities which might have to be faced by Irishmen in the British army. Irish soldiers from the Republic, for example, when home on leave 'tell no one what they do, and pretend to be working in England'. One officer, a Dubliner, who enlisted as a private soldier in the late 1950s, reported in the late 1980s that 'as far as anyone at home knows, I'm still on the buildings at Swindon'.[46] In recent years a trickle of recruits has gone the other way. Between 1974 and 1984 an average of just under 2 per cent of all Irish army enlistments were from Northern Ireland. In the latter year out of 14,000 personnel in the Irish armed force some 270 came from Northern Ireland.[47]

As had been the case before the Second World War, even the raising of volunteer part-time military units had a political dimension. As part of a general post-war reorganisation of the Territorial Army, in 1946 it was agreed to establish Territorial infantry units and TA Associations throughout the province. In Great Britain, nominations to the associations were made by various representative bodies, such as local government, trade unions and employers' federations, and the War Office intended to follow the same procedure in Northern Ireland. But the Belfast government, while appreciating that they could not demand any formal consultation (under the 1921 Treaty military matters were exclusively the preserve of London), were concerned 'lest unreliable elements should gain admission to TA Associations and misuse the information obtained there'. Although it was suggested that they might be able to liaise unofficially, Belfast in the end did not 'wish to bring any direct pressure to bear on the nominating authorities', and was content merely to keep a watching brief on the associations.[48] As it happened, the new Territorial organisation worked well – there was never any security problem with the associations – and a peak strength of over 7,000 men and women was attained in 1954. Numbers stayed at about 6,000 until the mid-1960s when under a further national reorganisation they were cut by about half, at which level they remained until the early 1990s.

The military authorities in Northern Ireland were always aware of the needs of internal security, although in the immediate post-war years it was never a very serious problem. The province's difference from the rest of the United Kingdom, however, may be illustrated by a quotation from one of the GOC, Northern Ireland's periodic reports. 'Outwardly the situation remains quiet,' he wrote in March 1950, 'notwithstanding two bomb incidents in Belfast.'[49] There was a resurgence of IRA activity in the mid-1950s. Among other attacks on military targets there was a dramatically successful arms raid in June 1954 on the Irish Fusiliers' depot at Gough Barracks in Armagh, when 60 machine guns and 340 rifles were seized. In October the same year eight IRA volunteers were caught during an abortive attack on the Inniskillings' depot at Omagh.

In December 1956 the IRA began a sustained campaign of violence which lasted until 1962. Three principal tactics were adopted: the bombing of fixed targets, such as government buildings, police barracks and economic and communications infrastructure close to the border; attacks on individual security force personnel, especially those recruited locally; and large-scale sustained efforts against the security forces, either through ambushes or against police barracks. Each of these classic guerrilla tactics, which can be mounted with comparatively few people and simple equipment, had been adopted during the 1919–21 hostilities, and the first two were to be taken up again after 1970. The IRA planners also decided to exclude Belfast from active operations. The leading republican organiser in the city was arrested shortly before the campaign was due to begin, and it was also felt that the movement was not strong enough to defend Belfast Catholics against the anticipated Protestant attacks. This decision, however, fatally undermined an already under-resourced campaign and confirmed its essential peripherality.[50] The RUC, and the B-Specials, were able to cope adequately with the IRA challenge, and apart from static guard duties the army took little active part in the campaign. There were in any case very few regular troops stationed in the province at the time. In February 1955, for example, there was only one infantry battalion (about 750 men), although the garrison was later increased to brigade strength (three battalions).

During the 1960s the Irish infantry regiments continued to serve in exotic trouble spots, as well as carry out routine tours in Germany and at home. The Inniskillings went to Kenya, Kuwait and Cyprus; the Ulster Rifles to Sarawak; and in 1966 the Irish Fusiliers were deployed in Swaziland, Bechuanaland (Botswana) and Basutoland (Lesotho), where political tension was running high following Rhodesia's Unilateral Declaration of Independence in November 1965. It is said that since this required movement over land through the Republic of South Africa the army authorities checked specially to see that the troops possessed correct travel documents. When it was discovered that some two-fifths of the men were citizens of the Irish Republic, they were hurriedly issued with British passports.[51] A company of Fusiliers afterwards went to Aden, where the Irish Guards – at this stage nearly 80 per cent Irish – also served in 1966–7. Aden's independence in 1967 marked a stage in Britain's strategic withdrawal from East of Suez. The consequent scaling-down of overseas military responsibilities brought reductions in the army, and in 1967 it was announced that the three regiments of the North Irish Brigade would be re-formed into one, new, regiment, to be called the Royal Irish Rangers, which came into existence on 1 July 1968.

Nineteen sixty-eight also marked the beginnings of large-scale civil rights agitation in Northern Ireland.[52] Demands for reform centred particularly on local government where gerrymandering had ensured Unionist control even in boroughs like the city of Derry with a Catholic majority. Catholics were sharply discriminated against in the allocation of local authority jobs and housing, and even the local franchise, following a British model abandoned in the 1940s, gave businessmen (who were usually Protestant) additional votes according to the value of their property. In calling for the establishment of a properly democratic system in the province, the reformers also demanded abolition of the coercive pillars of the Northern Ireland state, notably the Special Powers Act and the wholly Protestant B-Specials. The movement attracted support from students, Catholic and nationalist groups, as well as liberal Protestants. Inevitably more conservative elements in the unionist community identified the protests, which certainly challenged the political status quo in Northern Ireland, as subversive, and some (wrongly) believed that the whole campaign had been fomented by the IRA. In fact, by the late 1960s the IRA had virtually ceased to exist as a fighting force. Indeed, the avowedly Marxist leadership of the organisation was considering abandoning the use of violence as a political weapon altogether. In the autumn of 1968 civil rights marchers clashed violently with counter-demonstrators, led by the funda- mentalist Protestant preacher Ian Paisley. The liberal-minded Unionist prime minister, Captain Terence O'Neill (who had served with the Irish Guards in the 1939–45 war), responded with a package of political and administrative reforms, which, while they did not go far enough to satisfy the civil rights activists, gravely unsettled many in the majority unionist community. In April 1969 bombs were set off by Protestant extremists hoping to drive O'Neill from power. Under heavy political pressure from within his own party O'Neill resigned and was replaced by another Irish Guardsman, Major James Chichester-Clarke.

It is noteworthy that four of the six prime ministers of Northern Ireland served in the British army. Apart from the two guardsmen (O'Neill and his successor), Craigavon served in the South African War and with the 36th (Ulster) Division in the Great War, and Brookeborough, who joined up in 1908, served both at Gallipoli and on the Western Front. O'Neill's father, a captain in the Life Guards, was the first British MP to be killed during the First World War. The predilection for army titles, which survived in Northern Ireland much longer than in other parts of the United Kingdom, is an indication of how military tradition was valued in the province. Indeed, there were several 'captains' in the Northern Ireland parliament. Clearly Ulster Unionists were proud to use titles which explicitly marked service under, and loyalty to, the British crown.

The civil rights marches and counter-demonstrations continued on into 1969. The more momentum the reform campaign gathered, the more hard-line unionists feared for the security of the state itself. Orange marches, which traditionally had been occasions when Protestant and loyalist power could be proclaimed, became infused with an anxious and belligerent determination to resist the civil rights challenge.

During the summer 'marching season' of 1969 very serious violence broke out in both Derry and Belfast. By the middle of August it was evident that the RUC and the B-Specials could not cope with the disorder, especially the sharp rise in communal conflict. The Northern Ireland government requested military assistance and on 15 August British army units were deployed on riot control duties. The GOC, Northern Ireland, was 'instructed to take all steps . . . to restore law and order', and the public was assured that 'troops will be withdrawn as soon as this is accomplished'.[53] The use of the army was officially described as 'a limited operation' and clearly the authorities hoped that they would be able to withdraw the soldiers very quickly, perhaps even within days, as in 1935. This assumption no doubt explains the absence of any coherent plans whatsoever regarding the overall command and control of the security forces in the province after the army had been deployed. In retrospect, too, it is clear that this development had very serious implications for the Unionist government. Once the army was used for peace-keeping, London would inevitably play an increasing role in the administration of the province and the British government's final assertion of control over law and order three years later led to the suspension of the Northern Ireland parliament and the imposition of 'direct rule' from Westminster.

By the end of 1969 there were over 8,000 regular soldiers in Northern Ireland, compared with about 2,000 when the 'Troubles' had begun. The number of troops reached a peak of 21,800 in July 1972 at the time of 'Operation Motorman', when the security forces entered 'No-Go' areas which had been established in nationalist parts of Belfast and Derry. Thereafter the numbers fell back to about the 11,000 mark which was the total in the early 1990s. During 1970 the military forces available for aid to the civil power in Northern Ireland were reinforced by the formation of the Ulster Defence Regiment (UDR), which was created to replace the B-Specials as a locally raised, largely part-time force. As originally conceived, and in marked contrast to the Specials, it was hoped that the regiment would provide an opportunity for Catholics as well as Protestants to participate in the security forces. At first quite a number of Catholics did enlist and by the beginning of 1971 some 20 per cent of the unit came from the minority community. But a combination of republican intimidation, a loss of sympathy among Catholics for the government's security policy, and a reaction against the Protestant and unionist ethos which apparently existed within at least part of the regiment – many other recruits were, after all, former B-Specials – steadily reduced the proportion of Catholics to 8 per cent in November 1971 and less than 3 per cent in the 1980s.[54] The UDR, which reached a maximum strength of over 9,000 men and women in the autumn of 1972 (a number which subsequently fell to just over 6,000, including 700 female 'Greenfinches'), were never used for riot control duties, but relieved the regular army by patrolling, manning vehicle check points and guarding vulnerable installations.

The UDR had an anomalous existence as part of the British army, since no other unit was territorially limited within the United Kingdom. The status of the regiment owed much to political considerations: it was formed at a time when London wished to keep ultimate responsibility for security out of local Northern Ireland hands as much as possible. In the opinion of some regular officers the UDR was simply a device to provide a *legal* outlet for Protestants to defend themselves. For nationalists it increasingly came to be regarded as no more than a revived – and more heavily armed – version of the hated B-Specials. The involvement of some UDR personnel in loyalist organisations and sectarian murders merely served to confirm this view. On the other hand, the regiment itself worked hard to maintain high standards of enlistment and discipline. Its locally recruited personnel, living in the community and vulnerable to attack from terrorists (over 240 past and serving members were killed between 1970 and 1991), themselves displayed courage of a very high order. There is no doubt that the vast majority of the 40,000 or so people who served in the UDR did so from an honourable sense of duty to the community (or communities) of Northern Ireland, if not also in keeping with some perceived longstanding tradition of Irish soldiering.

Such a tradition has certainly been utilised to sustain support on the republican side in the Northern Ireland conflict. Styling itself an 'army', the IRA has drawn inspiration, and asserted legitimacy, both from more recent anti-colonial wars of national liberation, and an older, Irish tradition of armed resistance to British rule. The split in the IRA which occurred late in 1969 largely stemmed from the conflicting priorities of these two sources of inspiration. One group, which was Marxist, and as concerned with social and economic liberation as with national freedom, became the 'Official IRA', which subsequently ceased active military operations in 1972. The other, larger, group, which held that national freedom must precede all other matters, was the 'Provisional IRA', whose title recalled the 'Provisional Government of the Irish Republic' proclaimed at Easter 1916. The 'Provos', along with smaller splinter-groups such as the Irish National Liberation Army, constitute the armed wing of the republican movement.

In its early days the Provisional IRA emerged as quite a large and loosely organised body, with an active strength estimated at up to 2,000 in 1972. Its original primary function was to protect urban Catholics from attack by Protestant mobs,[55] and much of its support since has been based in the Catholic working-class districts of Belfast and Derry. The Provisionals modelled themselves on the command structure of the Officials, with a military hierarchy of brigades, battalions and companies. At its head was an Army Council, whose first chief of staff was Seán Mac Stiofáin, an English-born Irish nationalist, who had served in the RAF in the 1940s. On the military side the Provisionals pursued three main lines of attack. In the beginning their role as protectors of the Catholic community soon developed into one of mobilising mass demonstrations, both violent and peaceful. Large-scale street disorder – in both Protestant and Catholic parts of the province – was characteristic of the early days of the 'Troubles'. Although for the most part these riots were not 'organised' in any systematic sense, paramilitaries from both sides

19.6   Troops facing rioters in Derry, 10 April 1971. Note the military shields and batons. CS gas, rubber and plastic bullets – intended to be non-lethal weapons though they were not always so – were also used in crowd control duties.

certainly sought to capitalise on the disorder and opportunistically use it to promote their own ends. By the 1980s, however, the incidence of street violence had dropped considerably. One reason for this was the development of a strong political side to the republican movement, and the belief that peaceful mass demonstrations might pay more political dividends than violent ones.

The second main strand in the Provisionals' military campaign consisted mainly of bomb attacks on government, security and economic targets with the intention of destabilising the community and fatally undermining the (British) state in Northern Ireland. Mac Stiofáin is credited with developing the car bomb as a major weapon. The 'strategic aim' of using such devices, he argued, 'was to make the government and administration of the occupied North as difficult as possible, simultaneously striking at its colonial economic structure'. The 'tactical reason' for introducing the car bomb was that it 'tied down large numbers of British troops in the centre of Belfast and other large towns'.[56]

The use of bombing attacks, which has not been confined to Northern Ireland, picked up a tactic used in the 1956–62 campaign. So, too, did the third strand, which constituted attacks on those who were regarded as servants of British imperialism, a category which encompassed a large range of people, including security force personnel, judges, magistrates, prison officers, civilian employees of the security forces, and even shopkeepers and traders supplying any goods at all to the army or police. But the chief targets remained soldiers and police. Over the period from 1969 to the Provisionals' ceasefire of 31 August 1994, 944 members of the security forces were killed, of whom 445 were from the regular army.[57] One of these deaths in particular, that of 19-year old Ranger William Best in May 1972, illustrates the tragic complexities of Irish soldiering. Best, a Catholic from the Creggan district of Derry, had joined the Royal Irish Rangers. While home on leave from Germany, he was shot by the Official IRA 'in retaliation for murders committed by the British Army'. The killing provoked anti-IRA demonstrations by local women which directly contributed to the Officials' decision to call a unilateral ceasefire on 19 May that year.[58]

The Provisionals' strategy of the early 1970s, which aimed at a complete breakdown of government, depended on a large body of active IRA volunteers. This arrangement proved to be highly insecure and easily penetrated by the security and intelligence agencies. In the mid-1970s there was a review of policy driven by a new, younger leadership which contained men like Martin McGuinness and Gerry Adams who had emerged as important figures since 1969. A semi-autonomous 'Northern Command' was established and the organisation was reformed into a smaller active core based on a system of cells. Compact 'active service units' were to be responsible for carrying out military operations. This structure proved to be more secure than the previous organisation and it accorded with the Provisionals' strategy of a 'long war', in which a continued campaign of attrition against the security forces and the 'British state' in general was combined with the development of an overt political organisation. This approach has been called the 'bullet and ballot box' strategy, following a speech by Danny Morrison, the publicity officer of Provisional Sinn Féin (the movement's political wing), at their 1981 annual conference in which he dramatically spoke of taking power in Ireland 'with a ballot paper in this hand and an Armalite [rifle] in this'.[59] Yet, until the August 1994 ceasefire the active armed struggle – the 'military dimension' of Irish nationalism – remained the Provisionals' *raison d'être*. 'We are not going to stop fighting till we get our rights', remarked a west Belfast republican in 1976. 'And our rights are to rule over this country . . . We're soldiers fighting for our own country.'[60]

Symbiotically linked to the IRA are loyalist paramilitary groups which also claim historical legitimacy. The Ulster Volunteer Force (UVF), for example, which emerged in 1966 took its title from the Ulster resistance to Irish Home Rule before the First World War. The new UVF was the creation of 'Gusty' Spence, an ex-Royal Ulster Rifleman and fervent loyalist who was sentenced to life imprisonment for the killing of a young Catholic barman in May 1966. He became leader of the UVF in prison

19.7   A British soldier on patrol in west Belfast in the 1990s, posed in
front of a mural noting the military honour bestowed on an Irish
republican casualty.

and was a legendary hero among Belfast loyalists. 'I am a soldier', he said, 'and I
have been motivated purely by patriotism.'[61] During the mid-1970s the UVF carried
out a large number of sectarian assassinations, a policy which it resumed in the
early 1990s. The largest Protestant paramilitary organisation in the 1970s and 1980s
was the Ulster Defence Association (UDA), which acted as an umbrella organisation
for other loyalist groups, most notably the Ulster Freedom Fighters, a comparatively
well-equipped terrorist group which specialised in sectarian attacks. Like the
Provisionals, the loyalist paramilitaries – who declared a ceasefire on 13 October
1994 – have been sustained by military organisation and discipline. Parts of the ora-
tion of an east Belfast UVF man, Bobby 'Squeak' Seymour, who was shot by the IRA
in the summer of 1988, could have been spoken at the graveside of *any* Irish
soldier: 'A young man who dedicated his life to his country has given all that any
Soldier could give . . . At the going down of the sun and in the morning / We will
remember them.'[62]

455

Appeals to a unique quality of *Irish* soldiering have consistently characterised British army attitudes towards Ireland. This can clearly be seen in material used for recruiting purposes. 'Join an *Irish* regiment of the Regular Army', called a news-paper advertisement of 1955, in which the carefully named Lance Corporal 'Terry McQuaid' is seen learning skills, playing sport, travelling overseas and generally enjoying his 'new life in an Irish regiment that has such a proud history'. Twenty years on a recruiting brochure jointly sponsored by four units (the 5th Royal Inniskilling Dragoon Guards, the Queen's Royal Irish Hussars, the Irish Guards and the Royal Irish Rangers) appealed: 'If you are Irish, come join us, we're Irish too . . . There is a special atmosphere about an Irish regiment which is different.'[63]

In the 1970s a possible advantage of enlisting in an Irish regiment was the fact that the one place Irish units were not sent was Northern Ireland. In the mid-1980s, however, it was decided to change this policy, and subsequently both the Royal Irish Rangers and the Irish Guards did so. The decision had both practical and political merits: the availability of these units relieved pressure on the other infantry regiments which had to supply troops for the province, and the change (though no public announcement was made) also allowed the military authorities to assert a measure of 'normalisation' with regard to duties in Northern Ireland. Increasingly close security cooperation between the British and Irish governments also meant that the deployment of units which partly recruited in the Republic was much less politically contentious than it would have been in the early 1970s.

One quality of the regular army's Irish units which British politicians have found attractive is their non-sectarian nature. In 1969, indeed, Denis Healy, the minister for defence, went so far as to commend them as instruments of 'social integration'. He told the House of Commons that 'for many years, our Irish regiments have included both Protestants and Catholics . . . But while the Catholics and Protestants in these regiments remain equally proud of their faith and their special traditions, this is never a source of conflict in their daily work, and still less in battle.'[64] It seems that attitudes such as this may have played a role in the decision, announced in July 1991, that the Ulster Defence Regiment would be merged with the Royal Irish Rangers (which was about 30 per cent Catholic) to form a new unit called the Royal Irish Regiment, the name of the senior Irish infantry regiment of the line (18th of Foot) disbanded in 1922. It was hoped that the Rangers' tradition of recruiting in the Republic would be continued, and that Catholics would not be discouraged from joining the new regiment. There were also hopes that the new arrangement might allow locally raised and part-time soldiers to be employed free from the opprobrium associated in the nationalist community with the UDR, though clearly only time would tell if the exercise was more than cosmetic.

As in 1941 and again in 1947–8, the title of the new Irish formation proved contentious. One proposal, which, apparently, was very nearly adopted, was the 'Royal Regiment of Ireland' – following the style of the existing Royal Regiment of Wales. But well-founded fears that the proposed use of 'Ireland' in the title would

---

19.8 Recruiting advertisement for Irish Regiments, from the *Belfast News-Letter*, 22 March 1955. The acquisition of new skills, travel, sport and education are all mentioned; fighting is not.

be regarded widely as offensive in the Republic vetoed the suggestion and 'Royal Irish Regiment' was adopted instead. When an Ulster Unionist MP complained about the name – 'Irish' was not thought to be an acceptable substitute for 'Ulster' – a government minister told him the name had been agreed by the colonels of the regiment. 'It is important', he continued, 'to take into account the bi-partisan nature of the new regiment, which will recruit from the Catholic as well as the Protestant community. That will be one of its strengths in the future.'[65] So the UDR and the Royal Irish Rangers were disbanded, and from 1 July 1992 their personnel subsumed in a formation bearing the name of a regiment which seventy years before had been raised entirely in what is now the Irish Republic.[66] Thus was the 'Irish military tradition' sustained.

Notes

---

1 An Irish military tradition

1. Deane (ed.), *Field Day Anthology*, i, 10–14 (extract translated by Cecille O'Rahilly).
2. Sabatino Moscati *et al.* (eds.), *The Celts*: 'The Celtic image', p. 683; and see also, 'The Art of War', p. 684.
3. For all this, see Sheehy, *Rediscovery of Ireland's Past*; see also, Williams, 'Ancient mythology and revolutionary ideology'. Turpin, 'Cuchulainn lives on' offers a detailed examination of the visual history of the myth.
4. Hobsbawm & Ranger, *The Invention of Tradition*: the witty essay by H. R. Trevor-Roper, 'The Highland tradition of Scotland' (pp. 5–41) is perhaps most appropriate to our purposes.
5. Harrison, *Irish Anti-War Movements*.
6. 'The Irish whom we have seen to be such good soldiers in France and Spain have always fought badly at home' (editor's transl.), Masson & Prothero, *Histoire du Siècle de Louis XIV*, part II, p. 20. There is a good discussion of Voltaire's 'Irish' writings in Gargett, 'Voltaire and Irish history'.
7. Mathew O'Conor, *Military History of the Irish Nation*. Significantly, O'Conor translated *mal combattu* as 'fought shamefully' and later commentators have followed this considerably harsher judgement.
8. Ibid., pp. 2, 4, 97, 369.
9. Hayes-McCoy, *The Irish at War*.
10. Hayes-McCoy, 'Militant Ireland', in *The Irish at War*, pp. 97–108 (quotations at pp. 100, 105).
11. Hayes-McCoy, *Irish Battles* (pbk edn), p. 314.
12. Belfast, 1990. Hayes-McCoy took a great interest in those Irishmen who went off to join the British army in the nineteenth century. In particular, he admired the Connaught Rangers and was instrumental in having a commemorative window to this regiment installed in the Catholic cathedral in Galway.
13. Hayes-McCoy, *The Irish at War*, p. 106.
14. Hayes-McCoy, *Irish Battles*, p. 1.
15. See the chapters below by Thomas Charles Edwards, Marie Therese Flanagan, Robin Frame and Katharine Simms covering the periods *c.* 600 to *c.* 1550.
16. Bradshaw *et al.*, *Representing Ireland*, p. 3.
17. Connolly, *Religion, Law and Power*, p. 264; Hayes-McCoy, *Irish Battles*, p. 1.
18. Discussed below by Sean Connolly and Virginia Crossman respectively.

---

19. See David Fitzpatrick below.
20. See the respective chapters of Eunan O'Halpin and Keith Jeffery below.
21. As argued by Fitzpatrick below.
22. See Edward Spiers below, pp. 341–2.
23. Johnston, *Great Britain and Ireland*, p. 51: 'The Irish Ascendancy was essentially a military class.'
24. See A. J. Guy, p. 219 and Spiers, p. 341 below; see also Jeffery, 'Irish military tradition'.
25. Quoted in Lord Dunboyne (ed.), 'Happiest they; letters mainly from America written 1784–1799' (unpublished mss in private possession).
26. Harries-Jenkins, *The Army in Victorian Society*, pp. 42 3. See also the revealing table 'Regional background of senior officers in 1854, 1899, and 1914 [in the British Army] expressed in percentage terms' in Spiers, *Army and Society*, p. 297: in 1899, fully 21 per cent of all colonels and 16 per cent of all generals were Irish-born, the corresponding percentages for Scots-born being 12 per cent colonels, and 12 per cent generals.
27. See the chapters by S. G. Ellis, Ciaran Brady and Jane Ohlmeyer below.
28. See John Childs below, pp. 188–210.
29. On the police, see Palmer, *Police and Protest*.
30. See the chapters by Connolly, Crossman, Jeffery and O'Halpin.
31. Fitzpatrick below pp. 383–6.
32. Lady Moira to Lady Granard (her daughter), 7 Apr. 1802 (PRONI, T. 3765/J/9/2/39).
33. Connolly, below, p. 236, citing William Petty.
34. Katharine Simms, below pp. 99–115.
35. O'Dowd, *Power, Politics and Land*, p. 61.
36. Johnston, *Great Britain and Ireland*, pp. 240–1; Namier & Brooke, *The House of Commons*, i, p. 138.
37. Connolly below pp. 241–2; O'Donovan, 'The Militia in Munster, 1715–78'; Power, *Land, Politics and Society*, chapter 5, 'Rural Unrest'.
38. Miller, *Queen's Rebels*.
39. Below, p. 104.
40. Anon., *The Case of Count O'Rourke, Presented to His Majesty in June 1784* (London, 1784), p. 8; O'Rourke claimed that his forebears had been unlawfully deprived of lands and titles by Cromwell.
41. The journal, the *Irish Sword* (1949–) contains a very large number of articles on Irish soldiers abroad.
42. See Harman Murtagh below pp. 294–314.
43. Henry, *The Irish Military Community in Spanish Flanders*, p. 72. The earlier work edited by Brendan Jennings, *Wild Geese in Spanish Flanders*, is still of great value.
44. Stradling, *The Spanish Monarchy and Irish Mercenaries*.
45. Maurice O'Connell, Daniel O'Connell's uncle and benefactor, claimed in 1785 that there were 'three Kerry people in the Irish regiments for one of any other county in Ireland' (quoted by Cullen, 'Catholic social classes', p. 73). For the O'Connell military service abroad, see O'Connell, *The Last Colonel*.
46. Archives de la Guerre, Château de Vincennes, France, Berwick contrôle, 14 YC 127.
47. Ibid., 'Memoire pour obtenir la retraite du Sieur de Comerford', Dillon's Regt., 1776, Dillon contrôle. 'His grandfather was a major in the regiment of Bulkeley when it entered France; his granduncle, a former captain in this regiment was killed at Malplaquet; his father, a former captain of the same regiment died of his wounds in Scotland in 1746. He has today two uncles Chevalier de St Louis who are retiring and

his son is an officer in the regiment of Dillon which makes the fourth generation of father and son in the service of the King' [editor's translation].

48. Cullen, 'The Irish diaspora'.
49. Bartlett, 'A weapon of war yet untried'.
50. Spiers, below p. 337. There were very few Irish Catholics in the officer corps of the British army during the nineteenth century – less than 5 per cent, by some estimates. Some Irishmen (for example, Richard O'Dogherty) who sought a commission would change their names to avoid religious identification (Spiers, *Army and Society*, p. 298).
51. Jeffery, 'Irish military tradition'.
52. O'Callaghan, *Irish Brigades*, p. 157.
53. Ibid., p. 158.
54. See the chapters by Murtagh, Jeffery, Fitzpatrick and Spiers; see also Henry, *Irish Military Community*; Cullen, 'Irish Diaspora'. There is a useful survey of the Irish soldier abroad in McGurk, 'Wild Geese'.
55. O'Connell, *The Last Colonel*, p. 223 quotes extensively a letter written in 1779 by Lieutenant Rickard O'Connell in the French Service in which he denounces in no uncertain terms 'the rascally spawn of Cromwell' and wishes that he were in Ireland with 200,000 men. But M. J. O'Connell comments that the 'bitter anti-English tone in this [letter] . . . [is] . . . wanting in all the other Irish Brigade letters I have seen' (p. 223).
56. Quoted in Henry, *Irish Military Community*, p. 23.
57. Ohlmeyer below p. 173; and Murtagh below pp. 312–13. See also Stradling, *Spanish Monarchy and Irish Mercenaries*; see also Beresford, 'Ireland in French strategy 1691–1798'. Perhaps the best known 'Wild Goose' was Patrick Sarsfield, on whom see Wauchope, *Patrick Sarsfield*. For a contrasting picture see the racy autobiography of another Irish soldier abroad: *The Memoirs of Captain Peter Drake*. Drake is discussed below by Murtagh, p. 313.
58. 'Observations on the Diseases of the militia and Fencible regiments on the Irish establishment', Apr. 1796 (NAM, MS 6807/174/123–41).
59. Spiers, below, pp. 336–7.
60. Ó Gráda & Mokyr, 'The height of Irishmen and Englishmen'.
61. See Spiers, below pp. 335–57; for further discussion of the 'Irish soldier' see Jeffery, 'Irish military tradition'.
62. Johnstone, *Orange, Green and Khaki*. In the 1640s, it is recorded that when an Irish soldier on Montrose's campaign had his leg smashed by a cannonball, he used his knife to cut off the remnants and then remarked, he hoped Montrose 'will make me a trooper now I am no good for the foot' (Carlton, *Going to the Wars*, p. 221).
63. Denman, 'The Catholic Irish soldier', p. 363. See also the comments of the historian of the Connaught Rangers, Lt.-Col. H. F. N. Jourdain, in Jourdain & Fraser, *The Connaught Rangers*, i, 432, 434, 437–8.
64. Orr, *Road to the Somme*, p. 57.
65. Jourdain & Fraser, *Connaught Rangers*, i, 42–3.
66. Bartlett below p. 271; the appalling massacre at Dunlavin, Co. Wicklow, in 1798 in which thirty-four Catholic Yeomanry were summarily executed had no legal basis whatsoever.
67. Leonard, 'Getting them at last'.
68. Campbell, *Emergency Law in Ireland*, appendix 2: National Army executions, pp. 361–71. For the mutiny in India, see Babington, *The Devil to Pay*. It appears that Daly's execution had as much, and probably more, to do with the maintenance of British authority in India than with military or Irish reasons.

69. Wheatley, 'I hear the Irish are naturally brave'.
70. O'Callaghan, *Irish Brigades*, p. 188.
71. Bartlett, ch. 12 this volume, p. 281.
72. See Conyngham, *The Irish Brigade and its Campaigns*.
73. McWhiney & Jamieson, *Attack and Die*, pp. 178, 180 & passim.
74. Denman, 'Catholic Irish soldier', p. 355.
75. Denman, *Ireland's Unknown Soldiers*, p. 75; Hall, *Sacrifice on the Somme*, pp. 14, 21.
76. Johnstone, *Orange, Green and Khaki*, p. 241.
77. Denman, 'Catholic Irish soldier', p. 355. On war as a 'game' see Fitzpatrick below.
78. Gunner, *Front of the Line* (emphasis added).
79. See Jeffery, 'Irish military tradition'. Ironically, during the Second World War, Munster met the Maghreb when soldiers of the Irish Brigade and France's Moroccan soldiers joined together in the assault on Monte Cassino (Gunner, *Front of the Line*, p. 78).
80. Orr, *Road to the Somme*, pp. 165–6.
81. Denman, 'Irish Catholic soldier', p. 355.
82. 'Remember Limerick and English treachery.'
83. McDowell (ed.) *Memoirs of Miles Byrne*, p. 109.
84. Wright, *The Irish Brigade*, p. 2. The 69th regiment of the Union army bore a banner with the legend 'Sixty-Ninth, remember Fontenoy!' (Conyngham, *Irish Brigade* (1867 edn), p. 21).
85. J. Keating, 'The Tyneside Irish Brigade', in Lavery (ed.), *Irish Heroes*, p. 111.
86. The Irish Guards were only formed in 1900 as a reward for Irish service in the South African wars; see Denman, 'Politics and the army list'.
87. 'The Irish Guards' in *Definitive Edition of Rudyard Kipling's Verse*, pp. 196–8.
88. Gwynn, 'Irish Soldiers', p. 739. For a less enthusiastic look at Irish Brigades see Spiers, ch. 15 this volume.
89. The 'Irish Brigade' of the French monarchy transferred to the British Establishment in the 1790s following the Revolution: but the experiment did not prove a success and the Brigade was destroyed by disease on overseas service. We have taken the liberty of bracketing Bonaparte's 'Irish Legion' with the other Irish Brigades.
90. The story is told in Doherty, *Clear the Way!*, pp. 6–7.
91. The words of a hostile critic of Irish soldiers enlisting abroad in the early seventeenth century, quoted in Henry, *Irish Military Community*, pp. 33–4.
92. Gwynn, 'Irish soldiers', p. 744.
93. Jeffery, below, p. 454.
94. See Fitzpatrick below p. 380.
95. Dillon's speech of 11 May 1916 is conveniently reprinted in Dudley Edwards & Pyle, *1916: The Easter Rising*, pp. 62–78 (quotation at p. 74).
96. Hayes-McCoy, 'Military History of the 1916 Rising', p. 255. But see Fitzpatrick below pp. 393–5 for a 'reckless' verdict.
97. Dillon's speech, 11 May 1916 in Edwards & Pyle, *Easter Rising*, pp. 74, 78.
98. See Jeffery, 'The Great War in modern Irish memory'.
99. Duggan, *History of the Irish Army*.
100. O'Halpin, below, p. 407.
101. For some of their stories see Dungan, *Distant Drums*.
102. Ibid., pp. 6–7. The Volunteers of 1913 made use of this iconography also.
103. Hayes-McCoy, *Irish at War*, p. 106.

2 Irish warfare before 1100

1. Forms of names in this chapter are standardised to late Old Irish. I use Connacht for the territory, but Connachta for the ruling dynasties of the province. Dated information taken from the annals comes, unless there is an indication to the contrary, from the *Annals of Ulster (to A.D. 1131)* (henceforward *AU*).

2. See *Cath Almaine*, p. 7, line 88, on Fergal mac Maíle Dúin's *amuis*.

3. The civilian status of women and children was the particular concern of the Law of Adomnán, abbot of Iona, promulgated at a great assembly at Birr in 697. The text survives, prefaced by later material, in *Cáin Adamnáin*.

4. *Togail Bruidne Dá Derga*, lines 236–44. The political conditions implied by this story seem to be those of the late eighth or early ninth century (especially the position of the Uí Briúin Cualann).

5. *De Excidio Britanniae*, c. 19, in Gildas, *The Ruin of Britain*. I have used the translation of Professor Winterbottom, but with the substitution of 'Irish' in place of 'Scots'.

6. *AU* 913.5: an Ulster fleet on the coast of England; 955.3: Domnall ua Néill, king of Cenél nÉogain, uses inland waterways; 1022.4: the Ulstermen defeat a fleet from the Vikings of Dublin in a naval engagement.

7. Cf. Mallory & McNeill, *Archaeology of Ulster*, pp. 167–8, on the evidence of the sagas.

8. *Gaisced: Táin Bó Cúailnge*, pp. 19–20, transl. pp. 142–3. Use of swords is suggested by the formulaic descriptions in the sagas, e.g. *Táin Bó Cúailnge, Recension I*, pp. 109–16, transl. pp. 221–9 (see also *AU* 738.4, where a sword is used on the battlefield to decapitate an enemy king). The helmets mentioned in *Táin Bó Cúailnge, Recension I*, pp. 67–8 (lines 2196 & 2238) transl. pp. 185–6, come from the section of the text entitled *In Carpat Serda* ₇ *in Breslech Mór Maige Muirthemne*, which is agreed to be a later insertion, probably of the eleventh century. It has some obvious references to antiquity (Simon Magus and Darius king of the Romans, as well as the scythed chariot), but there are elements, in addition to the helmets, which may be indicative of post-Viking practice: leather jerkins, lines 2190–2 (Lóeg) and 2219–3 (Cú Chulainn); waxed shirts as a form of body-armour, line 2216.

9. Sawyer, *Age of the Vikings*, pp. 66–85.

10. The Old Irish saga of 'The Three Collas', speaking of a period then centuries in the past, declares that 'it was the practice at that time that the king himself did not go into the battle, but rather his "enforcer of rule" in his place', thus emphasising a fact clear from the annals, that in the seventh and eighth centuries kings very much did go into battle: *Corpus Genealogiarum Hiberniæ* (henceforward *CGH*), p. 148.

11. *Bethu Phátraic*, lines 1752–3 (cf. *CGH*, p. 179 (146 c 21 ff.)).

12. The Cloitech of the *bellum Cloitigi* of *AU* 789.12 has been identified with Clady (grid ref.: H 29 94), 4 miles south of Lifford (Hogan, *Onomasticon Goidelicum*, p. 253).

13. The evidence for the kings killed at the battle of Allen is conveniently assembled and discussed by P. Ó Riain in his edition of *Cath Almaine*, pp. 66–70, and in the notes to the text on pp. 52–7.

14. O Daly, 'A Poem on the Airgialla', stanzas 23-4 (transl. p. 186).

15. Compare, however, Mac Eoin, 'The mysterious death of Leogaire mac Néill', who rejects the historicity of the reference to an imposition of the *bórama* in *AU* 721.8 on the grounds, plausible but not conclusive, that the entry is in Irish.

16. Compare *AU* 743.4 where they are all of Airgialla.

17. *AU* 771.10; followed in the next year by an expedition to Cnocc Báne, probably near Clogher and thus within Airgiallan territory.

---

18. For example, the North Riding of Yorkshire in Darby & Maxwell, *Domesday Geography*, pp. 139–50.
19. Hudson, 'The family of Harold Godwinson', pp. 92–100; and Flanagan, *Irish Society*, pp. 58–60.
20. *Togail Bruidne Dá Derga*, lines 236–41; Binchy, 'A text on the forms of distraint', p. 80, § 12.
21. *Chronicum Scotorum* (henceforward *CS*), 929; *AU* 930.1. Gothfrith is given his unflattering epithet at *AU* 934.1.
22. *Críth Gablach*, lines 511–12.
23. At this meeting, according to a secondary entry in the Annals of Ulster, the clergy of Ireland were freed by Áed Oirdnide from the obligation to go on expeditions and hostings.
24. *AU* 756.3 (cf. 819.2).
25. *AU* 809.7. This Tulach Léis is Tullylish, County Down (J 08 48), not Tulach Léis na Sachsan (Tullylease on the border of County Cork and County Limerick at R 34 18).
26. Byrne, *Irish Kings and High-kings*, p. 148.
27. *AU* 770.8.
28. *CGH*, i, 147 (142 a 10–11), 151–2 (142 b 20 ff.; the Fir Ol nÉcmacht are the Connachta); Ailill Molt of the Connachta is no. 12 in the late seventh-century king-list in *Baile Chuind*, p. 146 (transl. p. 148).
29. *AU* 603.2; 683.2.
30. The early medieval Corann may have been of wider extent than the later barony: see Hogan, *Onomasticon*, p. 291.
31. *AU* 707.2.
32. *AU* 715.4. For such expeditions to royal ceremonial sites, compare *AU* 770.8, 840.4, 841.5, 856.2, 908.1; and, on a lesser scale, 733.7. An ecclesiastical counterpart is *AU* 817.8, where the community of Columba go to Tara in order to excommunicate Áed Oirdnide.
33. *AU* 713.6. Glendamnach is represented by the modern village of Glanworth, County Cork.
34. The problem is the entry under 738 on the hosting by Cathal mac Finnguine to Leinster, which is not merely misplaced but, exceptionally for this period, entirely in Irish. I think it likely that the Chronicle of Ireland (c. 913) took it from another source, perhaps favourable to Munster.
35. Thurneysen, *Die Bürgschaft im irischen Recht*, pp. 32–3. The *aire échta*, for whom see *Críth Gablach*, legal glossary s.v., and McCone, 'Werewolves, Cyclops, *Díberga*, and *Fíanna*', pp. 7–8, seems only to have operated in the first months of a new *cairde*.
36. *Bethu Phátraic*, lines 2545–57; Birr was *in confino Fer Cell ⁊ hÉli* (*Félire Óengusso Céli Dé* Nov. 29, Notes (*R¹*)); similarly Kinnitty (N 18 05) was *i cocrích Éle ⁊ Fer Cell* (*CGSH*, no. 665.3).
37. Byrne, *Irish Kings and High-kings*, p. 225.
38. Hughes, *Church in Early Irish Society*, pp. 186–9, 217.
39. N 68 34.
40. Smyth, *Celtic Leinster*, p. 153, plate XII, shows the early road from Dún Cuair (Rathcore) to Cláenad (Clane).
41. Charles-Edwards, *Early Irish and Welsh Kinship*, pp. 60–1, 473–6.
42. The settlement belonged to the realm of legend; cf. Bannerman, *Studies in the History of Dalriada*, p. 73, who thinks that the ruling dynasty of Dál Riata moved to Scotland c. 500; whether peripatetic Irish kings ever settled permanently in one part of their dominions is open to doubt.

43. *Admiralty Tidal Stream Atlas*, the maps for 4 hours before high water and 3 hours after high water at Dover. Cormac's Glossary in 'Sanas Cormaic' (ed. Kuno Meyer) no. 323, shows a remarkable understanding of the tidal flows off the north coast of Ireland.

44. Bede, *Historia Ecclesiastica*, ii, 5 ([*Bede's Ecclesiastical History*], ed. Colgrave & Mynors, p. 148).

45. Stein, *Histoire du Bas-Empire*, i, 389, 391–2.

46. Patrick, *Epistola ad Coroticum*, c. 2.

47. The principal discussions are Smyth, *Scandinavian Kings*; *Scandinavian York and Dublin*; Ó Corráin, 'High-kings'; Sawyer, 'The Vikings and Ireland'. The best general account of Ireland in the period is Ó Corráin, *Ireland before the Normans*.

48. Buckley & Sweetman, *Archaeological Survey of County Louth*, no. 259 (Linns), O 08 94.

49. *AU* 757.6, 763.4, 790.2; ibid., no. 259. The *longphort* of the ninth and tenth centuries was a fortified camp with facilities for ships. It might be occupied only briefly, but the word is applied to the permanent settlement at Dublin (*AU* 841.4, 902.2). The other examples in the Annals of Ulster are: Lind Duachaill (841.4), apparently abandoned in 927; Cenn Fuait (possibly near St Mullin's on the Barrow (917.3); Rubae Mena (later Shane's Castle, at the mouth of the R. Main on the north side of Lough Neagh) (930.3). By the twelfth century, *longphort* was employed for any military camp, not merely one which was established by a fleet, and it is in this later sense that the word is used in chapter 3.

50. As argued by Smyth, *Scandinavian Kings*, pp. 24–6, 113–17, but see Ó Corráin, 'High-kings', p. 296.

51. For Waterford see *AU* 914.5 (but I take *nochoblach mar* to be, not 'great new fleet' but simply 'great fleet' with *no-* being a compositional form of *naue* not *nue*); CS 913. Vikings from Limerick are first mentioned at *AU* 845.1; the next mention in *AU* is not until 922.3.

52. On this period, see Ó Corráin, *Ireland before the Normans*, pp. 101–4; Smyth, *Scandinavian York and Dublin*, ii, 1–61.

53. Ó Corráin, *Ireland before the Normans*, pp. 128–31.

54. Kelleher, 'Rise of the Dál Cais', pp. 230–4.

55. There is a good discussion of some aspects of his reign in Ó Corráin, 'High-kings', pp. 301–11.

56. Smyth, *Scandinavian York and Dublin*, ii, 297–313, discusses the parallels.

57. Anglo-Saxon Chronicle, s.a. 913 (transl. Whitelock, *English Historical Documents*, p. 194).

58. *AU* 922.3.

59. *AU* 853.2; CS 853.1.

60. Gerriets, 'Kingship', pp. 39–52.

61. *AU* 856.3; CS 856.4.

62. CS 858.

63. Professor F. J. Byrne has given strong reasons (in an unpublished paper) for thinking that *airrí* always means 'viceroy' or 'deputy for a king'.

64. *AU* 1014.2 notes that the 1,000 warriors who came from Lochlann were protected with mail-shirts.

65. *AU* 1013.11.

3 Irish and Anglo-Norman warfare in twelfth-century Ireland

1. Hayes-McCoy, *Irish Battles*, pp. 22–34; Otway-Ruthven, *History of Medieval Ireland*, pp. 44–5, 59; Frame, *Colonial Ireland*, pp. 9–10.

2. The failure of Ruaidrí Ua Conchobair, king of Connacht, and claimant to the high-kingship of Ireland, to eject the Anglo-Normans from Ireland has been attributed to the fact that 'Strongbow arrived without cows', with the implication that Irish warfare did not go beyond cattle-raiding (Simms, 'Warfare in the medieval Gaelic lordships', p. 108).

3. Giraldus, 'Topographia', in *Giraldi Cambrensis Opera*, v, 101, 107; *Expugnatio*, pp. 33–4, 48–9, 50–1, 76–7, 176–7, 230–1. On Giraldus see Bartlett, *Gerald of Wales*; Stewart, 'Topographia Hiberniae'.

4. An additional difficulty is the incomplete coverage in some of the major twelfth-century annals: *AU* are lacking from 1132 to 1155; *Ann. Inisf.* from 1131 to 1159; *ALC* from 1139 to 1169; *CS* ends at 1150; *Ann. Tig.* at 1178.

5. The earliest ms of Cogad Gaedel re Gallaib (CGG) is the twelfth-century Book of Leinster, which contains chapters 1–28 of the text as printed in *Cog. Gaedhel*, with the loss of the remainder due to a lacuna in the manuscript. Interpolations of post twelfth-century date occur in late manuscripts of fourteenth and seventeenth-century date. This might be said to limit its value as evidence for pre-Norman warfare, but that a well-developed version of CGG already existed in the early decades of the twelfth century may be inferred from Caithréim Cellacháin Chaisil (CCC) (a title coined by Eugene O'Curry), and from Giraldus's account in his 'Topographia', of the super Viking Turgesius which must have drawn on a twelfth-century recension of CGG. On the twelfth-century date, see further Ní Mhaonaigh, 'Bréifne bias in Cogad Gáedel re Gallaib'. CCC also survives in elaborated versions, but the original date of compilation has been assigned by Ó Corráin on historical grounds to 1127–34 (Ó Corráin, 'Caithréim Chellacháin Chaisil').

6. For raids see *Cog. Gaedhel*, pp. 60–1, 70–1, 82–5, 103, 106–9, 148–51; pitched battles, pp. 76–7, 155–211; the taking of Limerick, pp. 78–81; siege of Dublin, pp. 110–11, 116–17, 118–19, 150–1, 154–5.

7. Ibid., pp. 104–5, 110–11.

8. Ibid., pp. 74–5, 76–7, 190–1.

9. *Ann. Inisf.* state that Brian was attacking the foreigners in Osraige and Leinster from September until Christmas without bringing about a peace; *AU* that the men of Leinster and the foreigners began warring against Brian who encamped at Sliab Mairce and plundered Leinster as far as Dublin. It is the twelfth-century author of CGG who depicted this campaign as a siege of Dublin.

10. *Cog. Gaedhel*, pp. 108–9. Cf. the mention of the *coblach mór* in *Ann. Inisf.*, 983.

11. *Cog. Gaedhel*, pp. 132–3. The annalistic entries do not specifically mention the involvement of a fleet (*Ann. Inisf.*, AU, AFM, s.a. 1101).

12. *Cog. Gaedhel*, pp. 134–5.

13. Ibid., pp. 153, 162–3, 181.

14. *Caithréim Chellacháin Chaisil*, pp. 7, 64.

15. *Bk Rights*, ed. Dillon, l. 856, and *passim*. Dillon variously translated *lúirecha* as breast-places, coats of mail and corselets.

16. Ó Corráin, 'Brian Boru', pp. 31–40.

17. *Caithréim Chellacháin Chaisil*, pp. 2, 59.

18. Ibid., pp. 31, 88.

19. Ibid., pp. 42–100.

20. In 1101 Ua hIndredháin, *toísech teglaig* of Ua Máel Sechlainn, king of Mide, was slain along with 200 men (*AFM*). In 1143 Gilla Brenainn Ua Flainn, *taisech loctha tighe* of Toirdelbach Ua Conchobair, king of Connacht, was unhorsed and killed when attacked

by Toirdelbach Ua Briain, king of Thomond, and a Munster army raiding in Connacht (*Ann. Tig.*).

21. Apparent in the emergence at the Synod of Kells, 1152, of the diocese of Kilfenora to correspond to the kingdom of Corcu Mruad, and the claims advanced by Inis Cathaig (Scattery) to be the cathedral church of a diocese coterminous with Corcu Baiscinn, and of Roscrea to be the cathedral church of a diocese coterminous with the kingdom of Éile. The assumption of the abbacy of Terryglass by the Leinster ecclesiastic, Áed mac Crimthainn, may be presumed to result from Dairmait Mac Murchada's participation at Móin Mór. Móin Mór also facilitated the re-emergence and reconsolidation of Desmond under Diarmait Mac Carthaig (1143–85), which had been greatly weakened by the slaying of Cormac Mac Carthaig in 1138.

22. *Cog. Gaedhel*, pp. 49–50 (cf. *Caithréim Chellacháin Chaisil*, pp. 1–2, 58).

23. *Notatiae as Leabhar Cheanannais*, pp. 10, 34; *Registrum prioratus omnium sanctorum*, p. 50.

24. *Cog. Gaedhel*, pp. 60–1.

25. Ibid., 140–1 (cf. the list of strongholds of the king of Cashel in *Bk Rights*, pp. 42–7).

26. Ó Corráin, 'Aspects of early Irish history', pp. 64–75.

27. Sweetman, 'Archaeological investigations at Ferns castle', p. 224.

28. Dillon, 'The inauguration of O'Conor', pp. 190, 196, 198, 202; Simms, 'Gabh umad a Fheidhlimidh', pp. 132–45.

29. *Bk Rights*, ll. 810–11, 834, 2088, 2147.

30. Gillmor, 'War on the rivers'; Dearden, 'Charles the Bald's fortified bridge at Pitres'; Dearden & Clark, 'Pont-de-l'Arche or Pitres?'

31. *Bk Rights* = 'steeds of the road' (*each don ród*, l. 87); 'swift horses to mount' (*eich luatha fora ling*, l. 847); 'horses that are fast away' (*eich luatha re lecon*, l. 1454); 'horses for racing' (*gabra glantreasa*, l. 1303); 'horses for keen pursuit' (*eich bus triúin re togroim*, l. 1197); 'horses used to hosting' (*gabra gnáth-shluagaid*, l. 1283); 'cavalry horses' (*eochu marc-shluaig*, l. 1000, *gabra marc-shluaig*, l. 1044); 'horses from over the sea', 'horses from abroad' (*gabra tar glasmuir*, l. 445, *eich tar crícha*, l. 1016); 'horses brought in well-laden ships' (*eich a longaib lána*, l. 1459); 'horses from Scotland' (*eich a hAlbain*, l. 1434); and a 'French horse' (*each frangcach*, l. 1935). Some are preferred with harness, bridles and saddles (for *sadall* an Old Norse loan word, see l. 1571; for 'sheltering cloth', l. 1542).

32. Dillon, 'The inauguration of O'Conor', pp. 190, 195, 198, 201.

33. *Caithréim Chellacháin Chaisil*, pp. 29, 86. Giraldus in his Topography and *Expugnatio* defined a cantred as an area of territory sufficient to support 100 *villae* or settlements (*Gir. Camb. op.*, v, 145; *Expugnatio*, pp. 185, 337).

34. Service in the host, and work on bridges and fortresses is described in Anglo-Saxon charters from the late eighth century onwards as the 'common burdens' from which no one might be excused' (Stenton, *Anglo-Saxon England*, pp. 289–90).

35. *Song of Dermot*, ll. 1748–60.

36. Hayes-McCoy, *Irish Battles*, pp. 22–34.

37. *Song of Dermot*, ll. 3222–3303.

38. A point made by Rogers, 'Aspects of the military history'.

39. 'Associatus sibi Hyberniensibus illis qui parti eorum favebant' (Roger of Howden, *Gesta Regis*, i, 137). F. J. Byrne in *New Hist. Ire.*, ii, 16, has suggested Murchad Ua Cerbaill, king of Airgialla, as an ally of John de Courcy.

40. Roger of Howden stated that Henry II was met at Waterford by William fitz Audelin, his steward, and Robert fitz Bernard, 'and others of his household whom he had sent ahead

of him from England, and was honorably received by them as well as by the Irish who were with them' (*Gesta Regis*, i, 25).

41. Roger of Howden, *Gesta Regis*, i, 25. Gervase of Canterbury, who probably drew on Roger's *Gesta*, recorded that 'it was said' that Henry II had 400 ships (*Historical Works*, i, 235). William the Conqueror's fleet in 1066 is estimated to have comprised about 770 ships (Gillmor, 'Naval logistics').
42. *Radulphi de Diceto Opera Historica*, i, 350.
43. *The Whole Works of Rev. James Ussher*, iv, 502.
44. Gwynn, 'The Irish missal of Corpus Christi College', pp. 56–8, 61–4.
45. *Bk Rights*, l. 1776.
46. Gillingham, 'Richard I and the science of war'.
47. Smail, *Crusading Warfare*, pp. 140–89.
48. Gillingham, 'War and chivalry'. On intentional devastation as a key part of medieval strategy, see also Bennett, 'Wace and warfare'.
49. Gillingham, 'War and chivalry', p. 12.
50. *Bk Rights*, l. 1462.
51. See Brooks, 'Arms, status and warfare'.
52. Keating, *Foras Feasa*, i, 4–7.
53. See Ryan (ed.), *Illustrated Archaeology of Ireland*, pp. 152, 512. I wish to thank Dr Raghnall Ó Floinn, Irish Antiquities Division, National Museum of Ireland, for providing me with information on this sword.
54. *Song of Dermot*, ll. 2011–14.
55. Flanagan, 'Anglo-Norman change and continuity'.
56. Flanagan, 'Mac Dalbaig'.
57. McNeill, 'Early castles in Leinster'.
58. Stalley, 'The Anglo-Norman keep at Trim'.
59. Gervase of Canterbury, *Historical Works*, i, 235; ii, 79–80.
60. Davies, *Domination and Conquest*, p. 3.
61. Ibid., p. 24.

4 The defence of the English lordship, 1250–1450

1. Otway-Ruthven, 'Ireland in the 1350s', pp. 58–9.
2. The fullest account of political and military events in this period remains Otway-Ruthven, *Medieval Ireland*. Briefer outlines are in the chapters by J. F. Lydon, J. A. Watt and Art Cosgrove in *New Hist. Ire.*, ii.
3. See Frame, 'Power and society', pp. 5–18.
4. Otway-Ruthven, 'Knight service in Ireland'; 'Royal service in Ireland'; Ellis, 'Taxation and defence'.
5. *Stat. Ire., John–Hen. V*, pp. 194–213 (1297), 258–77 (1310), 280–91 (1320), 374–97 (1351), 430–69 (1366). See Frame, 'Judicial powers'; 'Military service', pp. 105–14.
6. *Stat. Ire., John–Hen. V*, pp. 200–1, 244–57.
7. *Calendar of the Gormanston Register*, pp. 10, 182.
8. *Stat. Ire., John–Hen. V*, pp. 382–5, 454–5.
9. Frame, 'Commissions of the peace', pp. 36–7.
10. *A Roll of the Proceedings of the King's Council . . . 1392–3*, pp. 6–8.
11. *Stat. Ire., John–Hen V.*, pp. 200–1 (cf. pp. 204–5, 206–7, 270–3, 378–81, 450–1).
12. *Calendar of the Justiciary Rolls . . . 1308–14*, pp. 209–10.
13. NAI, R.C. 8/16, pp. 377–8.

14. *Rot. Pat. Hib.*, p. 56 no. 31.
15. *Statute Rolls . . . Henry VI*, pp. 32–5.
16. *Calendar of Ormond Deeds, 1413–1509*, no. 38. See P. Connolly. 'The financing of English expeditions'.
17. Frame, 'Military service', pp. 114–22.
18. *Thirty-eighth Report of the Deputy Keeper of the Public Records of Ireland*, pp. 68, 87; *Calendar of the Justiciary Rolls . . . 1295–1303*, p. 4.
19. NAI, R.C. 8/26, pp. 349–53 (cf. Frame, 'Military service', p. 116).
20. Cf. Prince, 'The strength of English armies'.
21. NLI, MS 760, pp. 276–7.
22. PRO, E 101/243/3. See Richardson & Sayles, 'Irish revenue', pp. 99–100.
23. PRO, C 81/194/5817.
24. Sayles, *Documents*, p. 193.
25. Gilbert, *Viceroys*, p. 561.
26. *Calendar of the Patent Rolls, 1340–3*, p. 9; NAI, R.C. 8/22, pp. 15–17 & R.C. 8/24, pp. 243–5; *Rot. Pat. Hib.*, p. 39, no. 79.
27. *Chartularies of St Mary's Abbey*, ii, 382.
28. Cambridge University Library, MS 3104, fol. 89.
29. *Annals of Ireland by Friar John Clyn*, p. 30.
30. Sayles, *Documents*, no. 202.
31. Hewitt, *Organization of War*, pp. 93–139; Gillingham, 'Richard I and the science of war', pp. 78–91.
32. Cf. Hayes-McCoy, *Irish Battles*, pp. 35–47; Simms, 'The Battle of Disert O'Dea', pp. 64–5.
33. PRO, C 49/47/4.
34. PRO, E 101/244/2.
35. *Three Prose Versions of the Secreta Secretorum*, p. 129. The earl lived until 1382 and it is possible that Yonge had some other occasion in mind.
36. *Rot. Pat. Hib.*, p. 55 no. 29; p. 56 nos. 30–1, 35, 62; p. 57 nos. 132–3; p. 60 no. 41; p. 62 nos. 108, 112, 116–17.
37. NAI, R.C. 8/27, pp. 185–95, 343–51, 385–6.
38. E.g. O'Keeffe, 'Rathnageeragh and Ballyloo'; 'Medieval frontiers'.
39. Lydon, 'Richard II's expeditions to Ireland'.
40. Curtis, 'Unpublished letters from Richard II', pp. 292–3.
41. Johnston, 'The interim years', pp. 176–7.
42. See Frame, 'English officials and Irish chiefs'; 'Military service', pp. 120–6.
43. *Calendar of the Justiciary Rolls . . . 1305–7*, p. 354.
44. NLI, MS 760, pp. 289–90.
45. *Original Letters Illustrative of English History*, i, 59.
46. Genealogical Office, Dublin Castle, MS 191, pp. 57–8.
47. Ibid., MS 192, pp. 53–5.
48. *Facsimiles of the National Manuscripts*, iii, plate XIV.
49. Sayles, *Documents*, pp. 207–8.
50. PRO, E 101/242/11, 14; E 101/243/3.
51. PRO, E 101/242/11.
52. Curtis, 'The clan system', pp. 116–20; Simms, *From Kings to Warlords*, pp. 37–8.
53. PRO, E 101/244/1.
54. Curtis, 'Unpublished letters from Richard II', p. 286.
55. See Frame, 'Power and society'; and 'War and peace', pp. 133–40.
56. Davies, 'Kings, lords and liberties'.

57. Cambridge University Library, MS 3104, fol. 61d; Frame, 'War and peace', pp. 138–40.
58. *Calendar of the Gormanston Register*, pp. 9–10, 181–2.
59. PRO, E 101/244/3.
60. *Calendar of Ormond Deeds, 1350–1413*, nos. 33, 35–7, 39.
61. Matthew, 'The financing of the lordship of Ireland'.
62. Frame, 'Ralph Ufford'; *English Lordship in Ireland*, ch. 7.
63. Frame, 'Ralph Ufford', pp. 45–6.
64. Empey & Simms, 'Ordinances of the White Earl', p. 186.
65. Lydon, 'An Irish army'; 'Irish levies'; 'Edward I, Ireland and the war in Scotland'; Nicholson, 'An Irish expedition'; Frame, *English Lordship in Ireland*, ch. 4.
66. Lydon, 'The hobelar'; Morris, 'Mounted infantry'.
67. Frame, 'The Bruces in Ireland'; Duffy, 'The Bruce brothers'.
68. Sayles, 'The siege of Carrickfergus castle'.
69. Frame, 'The campaign against the Scots'.
70. Smith, 'Gruffydd Llywd'.

5 Gaelic warfare in the Middle Ages

 1. Simms, *From Kings to Warlords*, pp. 82, 86, 94, 140; Ó Doibhlín, *Domhnach Mór*, pp. 43–62.
 2. Carpenter, 'The pilgrim', p. 110.
 3. *Holinshed's Irish Chronicle*, p. 114.
 4. *Calendar of Justiciary Rolls, 1305–7*, p. 176; see Simms, 'Nomadry', pp. 385–7.
 5. Meyer, 'Sanas Cormaic', p. 295.
 6. Harrison, 'The shower of hell'.
 7. McCone, 'Werewolves'; *Pagan Past*, pp. 203–12; Sharpe, 'Hiberno-Latin *Laicus*'.
 8. McCone, 'Aided Cheltchair', pp. 28–9; Plummer, *Bethada*, i, 38; ii, 37; Meyer, *Fianaigecht*, pp. xi–xii; O'Grady, *Silva Gadelica*, i, 92–3.
 9. *Statutes and Ordinances . . . John to Henry V*, i, 210–11.
10. E.g. Curtis, *History of Medieval Ireland*, p. 190; Frame, *Colonial Ireland*, p. 106.
11. Meyer, *Fianaigecht*, pp. ix–xxxi.
12. Thurneysen, 'Tochmarc Ailbe'.
13. O'Grady, *Silva Gadelica*, i, 90; see also Meyer, *Fianaigecht*, pp. xxvi–vii.
14. Duby, *The Chivalrous Society*, pp. 120–1.
15. De Pontfarcy, 'Le Tractatus', p. 460; Picard & de Pontfarcy, *St Patrick's Purgatory*, pp. 50–3, 72–3.
16. Picard & de Pontfarcy, *The Vision*, pp. 111–12.
17. Thurneysen, 'Tochmarc Ailbe', pp. 258, 276; see McCone, 'Werewolves', pp. 16–19.
18. Murphy, *Dunaire Finn*, ii, 132.
19. Duby, *The Three Orders*, pp. 23, 41.
20. Cowdrey, 'The Peace'; Duby, *The Chivalrous Society*, ch. 8.
21. Loomis, 'The oral diffusion'; Nitze, 'Perlesvaus', p. 265; Frappier, 'The Vulgate Cycle', p. 306.
22. Mac Cana, '*Fianaigecht*', p. 89; see Herbert, 'The preface to *Amra Coluim Cille*', pp. 71–3, on the date of this text.
23. McCone, 'Werewolves', pp. 1–2; Ó Fiannachta, 'The development of the debate', pp. 185–8. See Mac Cana, *The Learned Tales*, p. 105; Herbert, 'Múineadh', p. 45.
24. Murphy, *The Ossianic Lore*, pp. 30–9; Carney, 'Literature in Irish', p. 698.
25. McCone, 'Werewolves', p. 4.

26. O'Grady, *Silva Gadelica*, i, 92 (my italics: see Sjoestedt, *Gods and Heroes*, ch. 6).
27. Simms, 'Images', pp. 608–10; 'Guesting', pp. 68, 90–2.
28. McCone, 'Werewolves', p. 13; Sharpe, 'Hiberno-Latin *Laicus*', p. 85.
29. Williams, *The Poems*, p. 143.
30. *Annála Connacht*, entries for the years 1225 (§§ 12, 14, 25, 27); 1228 (§ 16); 1230 (§ 8); 1233 (§ 2); 1235 (§§ 8, 14, 16, 18); 1236 (§§ 4, 12, 14, 16); see O'Dwyer, 'The Annals', pp. 89–101.
31. Sharpe, 'Hiberno-Latin *Laicus*', pp. 82 n. 35, 87.
32. Watt, *The Church*, pp. 76–7; Simms, *From Kings to Warlords*, pp. 15, 27–8.
33. O'Grady, *Caithréim*, i, 12; ii, 13–14; cf. ibid., i, 79; ii, 71–2.
34. Ibid., i, 75; ii, 68.
35. Ibid., i, 40–1, 212–13; ii, 39–40, 228–9.
36. Ibid., i, 111; ii, 98; cf. *Annála Connacht*, pp. 10, 226.
37. O'Grady, *Caithréim*, i, 21, 41, 63, 107; ii, 23, 40, 58, 62–3, 95–6; see Harbison, 'Native Irish arms'.
38. O'Grady, *Caithréim*, i, 40, 68; ii, 39, 63; see Kavanagh, 'The horse', p. 97.
39. O'Grady, *Caithréim*, i, 19; ii, 20–1; see also ibid., i, 14, 80, 82–3; ii, 15, 72, 74–5; Simms, 'Warfare', pp. 103–5.
40. Simms, *From Kings to Warlords*, pp. 119–20.
41. O'Grady, *Caithréim*, i, 61; ii, 57.
42. NLI, MS 760, p. 290.
43. Curtis, 'The MacQuillan or Mandeville Lords'; see Otway-Ruthven, *History of Medieval Ireland*, pp. 216–17 and McNeill, *Anglo-Norman Ulster*, p. 70.
44. Simms, *From Kings to Warlords*, pp. 138–9.
45. Curtis, *Richard II*, pp. 89–90, 140–3; McNeill, *Anglo-Norman Ulster*, pp. 120–1.
46. Simms, *From Kings to Warlords*, pp. 80, 117–18.
47. Orpen, *Ireland*, ii, 290–1.
48. Simms, *From Kings to Warlords*, pp. 121–3.
49. Hayes-McCoy, *Scots Mercenary Forces*, p. 26.
50. Walsh, *Leabhar Chlainne Suibhne*, p. 45.
51. Simms, *From Kings to Warlords*, pp. 87, 94–5, 123–4, 139, 143; Hayes-McCoy, *Scots Mercenary Forces*, pp. 33, 36–7.
52. *Holinshed's Irish Chronicle*, p. 114.
53. Hunt, *Irish Medieval Figure Sculpture*, ii, plates 248–51.
54. *Annála Connacht*, p. 429; cf. O'Grady, *Caithréim*, i, 79; ii, 71.
55. *Annála Connacht*, p. 447; Simms, 'Warfare', pp. 106–7. The Four Masters (*Annala Rioghachta Eireann*, v, 1278) record the suicidal tenacity of Clanrickard's galloglasses at the Battle of Knocktoe (1504).
56. Simms, 'Niall Garbh II'.
57. Brewer & Bullen, *Carew Manuscripts*, ii, 364. See Simms, *From Kings to Warlords*, p. 128; Hayes-McCoy, *Scots Mercenary Forces*, pp. 44–5.
58. Dineen, *Foclóir*, p. 182; see Williams, *Pairlement*, pp. 30, 89.
59. Ibid., pp. 3, 66–7; see above, note 6.

6 The Tudors and the origins of the modern Irish states: a standing army

1. F. W. Maitland, quoted in Frame, 'Power and society', p. 8. Most of the secondary literature on which I have relied in this chapter is listed in the bibliography of my *Tudor*

Ireland: Crown, Community and the Conflict of Cultures, particularly the works by Robin Frame, James Lydon and Kenneth Nicholls.

2. Frame, 'Power and society', p. 32.
3. NAI, Ferguson coll., iv, ff. 52–2v.
4. Some of the commissions are transcribed in NAI, Lodge MSS, 'Articles', i, f. 221. See also *Rot. Pat. Hib.*, p. 272.
5. Parliament roll, 38 Hen. VI c. 7 (*Statute Rolls . . . Henry VI*, pp. 646–8).
6. NAI, Lodge MSS, 'Articles', i, f. 221; *Rot. Pat. Hib.*, p. 272.
7. *Calendar of the Carew Manuscripts*, Book of Howth, pp. 181–4.
8. Quoted in Ellis, *Tudor Ireland*, pp. 30, 70.
9. BL, Caligula MS B. I, ff. 141–1v (*L. & P. Hen. VIII*, xv, 570) (cf. *Calendar of Documents Relating to Scotland*, iv, no. 1542).
10. *Calendar of Ancient Records*, i, 381.
11. *S.P. Hen. VIII*, ii, 78.
12. PRO, E 101/71, file 5/949.
13. See especially *L. & P. Hen. VIII*, vi, 1381–2; vii, 420.
14. Ibid., vii, 980, 1682; PRO, E 101/421/6, nos. 35, 36, 39.
15. PRO, C 113/236, box 51 (I am grateful to Dr Margaret Condon of the PRO for bringing this document to my attention); *L. & P. Hen. VIII*, vii, 1013–14, 1019, 1064; *Cal. S.P. Spain, 1534–8*, pt. i, no. 84.
16. PRO, PRO 31/18/3/1, f. 127 (*Cal. S.P. Spain, 1534–8*, pt. i, no. 86); ibid., no. 84 (quotation); *L. & P. Hen. VIII*, vii, 1014 (quotation).
17. *Cal. S.P. Spain, 1534–8*, pt. i, nos. 86–7, 90; *L. & P. Hen. VIII*, vii, 1019, 1161; *S.P. Hen. VIII*, ii, 201–2.
18. PRO, E 101/421/6, no. 46; *Cal. S.P. Spain, 1534–8*, pt. i, nos. 75, 84.
19. PRO, SP 65/1 (*L. & P. Hen. VIII*, xi, 934) (cf. ibid., vi, 196(8), 1481 (5, 29); vii, 1026 (26), 1455). Kelway stayed on in Ireland after the rebellion, but was killed by the O'Tooles in 1538.
20. *L. & P. Hen. VIII*, vii, 1181, 1186; xiv (ii), 194; *Cal. S.P. Spain, 1534–8*, pt. i, nos. 75, 86, 90, 102; PRO, E 101/421/6, no. 43; *S.P. Hen. VIII*, ii, 202–3, 219–20, 227.
21. PRO, SP 65/1, no. 1 (*L. & P. Hen. VIII*, xi, 934); *S.P. Hen. VIII*, ii, 221, 233, 267 (cf. PRO E 101/421/6, no. 43; *L. & P. Hen. VIII*, vi, 615, 1379; vii, 674, 679, 895, 1498 (30); x, 1045; xii (ii), 249–50, 696 (2), 712).
22. *S.P. Hen. VIII*, ii, 32–3, 48, 61; *L. & P. Hen. VIII*, v, 398 (p. 318); vii, 1498 (30).
23. Cumbria Record Office (CRO), Carlisle, MS D/Ay/1/180; *L. & P. Hen. VIII*, iv, 2374.
24. CRO, Carlisle, MS D/Ay/2/24; *L. & P. Hen. VIII*, vii, 895.
25. PRO, SP 65/1, no. 1 (*L. & P. Hen. VIII*, xi, 934). Thomas Dacre later founded a junior branch of the Dacre family through his purchase of the priory of Lanercost.
26. Ibid.; PRO, SP 60/3, f. 6 (*L. & P. Hen. VIII*, x, 30); SP 1/112, ff. 153–4 (*L. & P. Hen. VIII*, xi, 332); SP 1/104, ff. 158, 160–5 (*L. & P. Hen. VIII*, x, 1102–4); Bain, *Hamilton Papers*, i, no. 289.
27. PRO, SP 65/1, no. 1; *L. & P. Hen. VIII*, vii, 380 (i–iii).
28. PRO, SP 65/1, no. 1; SP 60/2, ff. 100–01 (*L. & P. Hen. VIII*, viii, 449); *L. & P. Hen. VIII*, vii, 1366; xii (ii), 537.
29. *L. & P. Hen. VIII*, xii (ii), 537; *S.P. Hen. VIII*, ii, 32–3, 48, 61; *L. & P. Hen. VIII*, v, 398 (p. 318).
30. PRO, SP 65/1, no. 1; *S. P. Hen. VIII*, ii, 38, 48, 223, 293; *L. & P. Hen. VIII*, vii, 1574.
31. *L. & P. Hen. VIII*, vii, 1574, 1019, 1102, 1186; *Cal. S.P. Spain, 1534–8*, pt. i, no. 87; PRO, SP 65/1, no. 1.

---

32. *L. & P. Hen. VIII*, vii, 1068 (12), 1291, 1368; PRO, E 101/421/6, no. 41; *Cal. S.P. Spain, 1534–8*, pt. i, nos. 86–7.
33. PRO, SP 60/2, f. 59 (*L. & P. Hen. VIII*, vii, 1186); *S.P. Hen. VIII*, ii, 202; *Cal. S.P. Spain, 1534–8*, pt. i, nos. 87, 257.
34. *Cal. S.P. Spain, 1534–8*, pt. i, nos. 84, 90; *S.P. Hen. VIII*, ii, 228; Holinshed, *Chronicles*, vi, 299.
35. PRO E 101/421/6, nos. 45–6; *L. & P. Hen. VIII*, vii, 1161, 1168; xiv (ii), 194; *Cal. S.P. Spain, 1534–8*, pt. i, no. 102 (cf. *S.P. Hen. VIII*, ii, 205, 225; *L. & P. Hen. VIII*, viii, 193, 263).
36. *L. & P. Hen. VIII*, vii, 1186; PRO, E 101/421/6, no. 43.
37. PRO, SP 65/1, no. 1; *S.P. Hen. VIII*, ii, 202–3.
38. *Cal. S.P. Spain, 1534–8*, pt. i, nos. 102, 257; PRO, E 101/421/6, no. 45.
39. *S.P. Hen. VIII*, ii, 203–5; PRO, SP 60/2, f. 100 (*L. & P. Hen. VIII*, viii, 449).
40. *L. & P. Hen. VIII*, vii, 1019, 1064, 1161, 1165, 1167–8, 1186.
41. *S.P. Hen. VIII*, ii, 228 (where 'towne' should read 'towre' (of London)); *L. & P. Hen. VIII*, viii, 226, 267.
42. *L. & P. Hen. VIII*, viii, 287, 345.
43. *S.P. Hen. VIII*, ii, 202, 206.
44. Ibid., 228.
45. PRO, SP 2/Q, f. 163 (*L. & P. Hen. VIII*, vii, 1682); *L. & P. Hen. VIII*, vii, 1681, Add. 936.
46. *S.P. Hen. VIII*, ii, 221.
47. *L. & P. Hen. VIII*, vii, 1497 (cf. ibid., vii, 1437; viii, 529 (an army supply ship impounded at Cardiff)).
48. *S.P. Hen. VIII*, ii, 37–9, 232–3, 262, 280; *L. & P. Hen. VIII*, viii, 449.
49. *S.P. Hen. VIII*, ii, 266–7, 302–3.
50. PRO, SP 60/2, ff. 81–2 (*L. & P. Hen. VIII*, vii, 1574); *S.P. Hen. VIII*, ii, 227, 231, 233.
51. *S.P. Hen. VIII*, ii, 225–6, 227.
52. PRO, E 101/421/6, nos. 35–6, 41–3, 45–6.
53. *S.P. Hen. VIII*, ii, 219–20, 225, 227; *L. & P. Hen. VIII*, viii, 449.
54. PRO, SP 60/2, f. 87 (*L. & P. Hen. VIII*, viii, 193); E 101/421/6, no. 33; *L. & P. Hen VIII*, ix, 234.
55. *L. & P. Hen. VIII*, viii, 653; ix, 217, 513; *S.P. Hen. VIII*, ii, 243, 268.
56. PRO, SP 60/3, ff. 99–100 (*L. & P. Hen. VIII*, x, 1224).
57. *S.P. Hen. VIII*, ii, 219–24, 227.
58. Ibid., 223, 225, 229, 242, 261–2, 291–2 (cf. *L. & P. Hen. VIII*, iii, 1285 (p. 498), 1379 (25); v, 1715; vii, 1167).
59. *S.P. Hen. VIII*, ii, 223, 225.
60. Ibid., ii, 222–3, 229, 242–3.
61. Ibid., 237–8, 240–1; *L. & P. Hen. VIII*, vii, 45, 287.
62. *S.P. Hen. VIII*, ii, 225, 227, 230n, 235, 237–8, 241–3; *L. & P. Hen. VIII*, viii, 287, 449, 574–5.
63. PRO, SP 60/2, f. 136 (*L. & P. Hen. VIII*, viii, 914); SP 65/1, no. 2 (*L. & P. Hen. VIII*, xii (ii), 1310); *S.P. Hen. VIII*, ii, 260–1, 267–8, 272; *L. & P. Hen. VIII*, Add., i, 982.
64. *S.P. Hen. VIII*, ii, 261, 264, 266–8; *L. & P. Hen. VIII*, viii, 1019; ix, 357; PRO, SP 65/1, no. 1.
65. Archbishop Marsh's Library, Dublin, MS Z4 2 7, f. 410; PRO, SP 60/2, f. 109 (*L. & P. Hen. VIII*, viii, 695); TCD, MS 543/2, s.a. 1534; Holinshed, *Chronicles*, vi, 289–92; Ware, *Histories and Antiquities*, p. 89; Dowling, *Annales Breves Hiberniae*, s.a. 1534; Lambeth Palace Library, MS 602, f. 138 (*Calendar of the Carew Manuscripts . . . 1515–74*, no. 84).

---

66. *Calendar of the Carew Manuscripts*, Book of Howth, p. 193; *S.P. Hen. VIII*, ii, 200; Lambeth Palace Library, MS 602, f. 138; Ware, *Histories and Antiquities*, p. 89; Holinshed, *Chronicles*, vi, 294; *AU*, s.a. 1534; *Annála Connacht*, s.a. 1534; *AFM*, s.a. 1535; *ALC*, s.a. 1534.
67. PRO, SP 3/14, f. 41 (*L. & P. Hen. VIII*, vii, 1064); *Annála Connacht*, s.a. 1534.
68. TCD, MS 591, ff. 12v–13; Holinshed, *Chronicles*, vi, 293–5; Ware, *Histories and Antiquities*, p. 89; Lambeth Palace Library, MS 602, f. 138; *AFM*, s.a. 1656; Dowling, *Annales Breves Hiberniae*, s.a. 1534.
69. Holinshed, *Chronicles*, vi, 293–6; *S.P. Hen. VIII*, ii, 250–1; *Statutes of Ireland*, 28 Henry VIII c. 1; *Cal. S.P. Spain, 1534–8*, pt. i, no. 87; Dowling, *Annales Breves Hiberniae*, s.a. 1534.
70. *S.P. Hen VIII*, ii, 202.
71. BL, Sloane MS 1449, f. 154; Cherbury, *Life . . . of King Henry VIII*, p. 387; Holinshed, *Chronicles*, vi, 297–8; *S.P. Hen. VIII*, ii, 203–4; PRO, SP 65/1, no. 2; SP 60/2, f. 109 (*L. & P. Hen. VIII*, viii, 695).
72. *S.P. Hen. VIII*, ii, 203–5; PRO, SP 60/2, ff. 100–1 (*L. & P. Hen. VIII*, viii, 449); PRO, SP 1/86, f. 160 (*L. & P. Hen. VIII*, vii, 1366); Holinshed, *Chronicles*, vi, 298–9; Lambeth Palace Library, MS 602, f. 138; *Calendar of the Carew Manuscripts*, Book of Howth, p. 194.
73. *S.P. Hen. VIII*, ii, 226.
74. Ibid., 220–1, 234.
75. Ibid., 236–8; *L. & P. Hen. VIII*, viii, 397, 449, 487; *AU*, s.a. 1535.
76. *S.P. Hen. VIII*, ii, 247–8, 256, 262, 272.
77. White, 'Henry VIII's Irish kerne', p. 223.
78. PRO, SP 65/1, no. 1; SP 60/3, f. 25 (*L. & P. Hen. VIII*, x, 402); SP 60/10, f. 177 (*L. & P. Hen. VIII*, xvi, 393).
79. See Jackson, 'Violence and assimilation'.
80. PRO, SP 60/3, f. 77 (*L. & P. Hen. VIII*, x, 1082).
81. PRO, SP 60/5, f. 1v (*L. & P. Hen. VIII*, xii (ii), 468, 472); *Fiants Ire., Edw. VI*, no. 84, *Eliz.*, no. 1801.
82. Edwards, *Church and State*, p. 141; *Fiants Ire., Hen. VIII*, nos. 389, 418, 449.
83. PRO, SP 60/12, ff. 9–9v (*L. & P. Hen. VIII*, xx, 274).
84. PRO, SP 60/2, ff. 100–1 (*L. & P. Hen. VIII*, viii, 449); SP 65/1, no. 1; *L. & P. Hen. VIII*, vii, 1366, 1498 (30).
85. PRO, SP 60/3, f. 4 (*L. & P. Hen. VIII*, ix, 332; an undated letter which appears to date from Sept. 1535); SP 65/1, no. 1.
86. PRO, SP 60/3, f. 6 (*L. & P. Hen. VIII*, x, 30); SP 1/112, ff. 153–4 (*L. & P. Hen. VIII*, xi, 1249); SP 1/104, ff. 158, 160–5 (*L. & P. Hen. VIII*, x, 1102–4).
87. PRO, SP 60/3, ff. 99–100 (*L. & P. Hen. VIII*, x, 1224).
88. *L. & P. Hen. VIII*, xi, 993, 1228, 1236, 1331.
89. Ibid., xii (ii), 249 (3ii, 6), 250; xiii (i), 646 (41); xvii, 362 (28); xxi (ii), 472.
90. *S.P. Hen. VIII*, iii, 276.

7 The captains' games: army and society in Elizabethan Ireland

1. Falls, *Elizabeth's Irish Wars*; *New Hist. Ire.*, iii, *Early Modern Ireland, 1534–1691*, chs. 2–4.
2. On O'Neill, see Falls, *Elizabeth's Irish Wars*, ch. 6, and Hayes-McCoy, *Irish Battles*, ch. 6; on Fitzmaurice, see Falls, ch. 7 and Piveronus, 'Sir Warham St Leger'. A popular

account of these events, which draws heavily on older secondary sources, is Berleth, *The Twilight Lords.*

3. Contrasting interpretations of Bingham's conduct in Connacht are supplied by Bagwell, *Ireland under the Tudors*, iii, 151–7, and Knox, *History of Mayo*, pp. 220–45. On the threat of the Armada, see Bagwell, iii, ch. 42 *passim*, and Fallon, *The Armada in Ireland.*

4. There is a substantial literature on the military history of the Nine Years War: in addition to Falls, *Elizabeth's Irish Wars* and Hayes-McCoy, *Irish Battles*, chs. 7–8, see Hayes-McCoy, 'Strategy and tactics'; 'The tide of victory and defeat'; 'The army of Ulster'; Ó Domhnaill, 'Warfare in sixteenth-century Ireland'; Silke, *Kinsale.*

5. On the restricted nature of the war in Ulster before 1598, see Morgan, *Tyrone's Rebellion*, chs. 7–9.

6. Hayes-McCoy, *Irish Battles*, ch. 6; Brady, 'The killing of Shane O'Neill'.

7. Hughes, 'Sir Edmund Butler'; Edwards, 'The Butler revolt'.

8. O'Rahilly, *The Massacre at Smerwick*; Petrie, 'The Hispano-Papal landing at Smerwick'.

9. More than 3,000 men were disbanded between Nov. 1581 and Jan. 1582 (PRO, SP 63/88/36, 40; 89/9; 90/29).

10. For a recent account see Sheehan, 'The killing of the Earl of Desmond'.

11. Morgan, *Tyrone's Rebellion*, ch. 9; Moryson, *An Itinerary*, pt. ii, ch. 1; Lord Deputy Russell's 'Journal', *Calendar of the Carew Manuscripts, 1589–1600*, pp. 220–60; for the abortive 1597 peace with Ormond, see ibid., pp. 274–8; for Essex's truce with Tyrone, see ibid., pp. 321–7.

12. Such shadowy outlaw figures as Piers Grace and 'the Keating kerne', each of whom were capable at times of raising bands of 100 men or more, have yet to receive serious study; glimpses of their activity can, however, be obtained in occasional government reports. For Grace see, for instance, PRO, SP 63/15/15, 47/16; and for the Keatings, SP 63/51/42. For representative complaints by northern lords against raids from the Pale see SP 63/9/17, and for appeals for arbitration from Munster and Connacht lords such as MacCarthy More, O'Sullivan Beare and O'Shaughnessy, see SP 63 14/6, 16 and 21/37. The most frequent result of the government's intervention in such conflicts can be seen in the innumerable grants of pardon which are a feature of the Elizabethan Fiants, see *Fiants Ire., Eliz., passim.*

13. See, for instance, Robert Cowley's tracts in 1536–7, printed in *S.P. Hen. VIII*, ii, pp. 323–9, 445–7.

14. Dowdall's proposal written in 1558 (TCD, KS 842, ff. 75–82) was probably merely rhetorical, designed to assure his readers that the more moderate suggestions he was about to make were not his preferred solution; whatever his own views, the fact that he believed it necessary to make such a profession is indicative of the popularity of the idea in certain quarters. Raleigh's call was more straightforward (Raleigh to Walsingham, 23 Feb. 1581, PRO, SP 63/80/74).

15. Churchyard, *Generall Rehearsall*; Rawlinson, *Sir John Perrot*; John Ward to Cecil, 18 Oct. 1569 (PRO, SP 63/29/68); Perrot's 'memorial of service', 1572/3 (SP 63/43/27).

16. Bingham to Walsingham, 20 Sept. 1580 (SP 63/76/49).

17. Malby's 'Discourse of service', 8 Apr. 1580 (SP 63/72/39); Bingham's 'Answer to charges', Nov. 1589 (SP 63/48/39); Dowcra, 'A relation of services'; the quotation is from O'Flaherty, *Chorographical Description of West . . . Connaught*, p. 186.

18. Fitzwilliam to Burghley & Walsingham, 19 June 1589 (PRO, SP 63/145/12–13).

19. Morgan, *Tyrone's Rebellion*, ch. 3; Perrot's complaints against Bingham, July 1587 (PRO, SP 65/12/ff. 56–8).

---

20. Quinn, 'Renaissance influences'.
21. For the mid-century drive to refortify and increase the royal forts, see *inter alia*, PRO, SP 61/2/3, 12, 30, 57; 61/3/32, 38; 61/4/4, 48.
22. For the midlands forts, see SP 62/1/20, 21, 24; for Athlone, SP 63/20/41 & 22/1; for Carrickfergus, SP 62/2/22, enclosure (ii) and SP 63/16/69.
23. Randolf to Cecil, 27 Oct. 1566; Cecil to Leicester, 9 May 1567 (SP 63/19/29, 20/77).
24. SP 63/207/pt. iii, no. 57.
25. MacCarthy, 'The "jorney" of the Blackwater', provides a convenient collection of relevant documents with commentary.
26. 'Petition of the undertakers', 29 Jan. 1589 (PRO, SP 63/128/22).
27. Lascelles, *Liber Munerum*, pt. ii, pp. 119–24.
28. See, for example, the arguments advanced by Humphry Gilbert in his 'Discourse on Ireland, 1574' (BL Add. MSS 48015, ff. 136–43), and by Sir William Herbert in his *Croftus*.
29. Rich, *Pathway to Military Practice*; Dawtrey, 'A book of questions and answers' (Petworth House Archives, HMC 90), I am grateful to Dr Hiram Morgan for a copy of his unpublished edition of this important text.
30. Sussex to Cecil, 31 July 1561 (PRO, SP 63/4/25).
31. Nicholas Malby & William Stanley to Walsingham, 31 Aug. 1580 (SP 63/75/82, 83).
32. For a detailed account, see Falls, *Elizabeth's Irish Wars*, ch. 15, and Hayes-McCoy, *Irish Battles*, ch. 8.
33. These figures have been estimated from the detailed accounts provided in Sheehan, 'Irish revenues'.
34. On the recruitment, mustering and general financial administration of the Elizabethan army, see Cruickshank, *Elizabeth's Army*, chs. 2, 8, 9; Falls, *Elizabeth's Irish Wars*, chs. 2, 3.
35. These figures have been derived from the comprehensive tables drawn up by Anthony Sheehan from the treasurer at war accounts surviving in the State Papers and other sources. I am most grateful to Mr Sheehan for his generosity in allowing me access to his unpublished work.
36. 'A treatise on Ireland', NLI, MS 669.
37. These were the numbers which both men were able to field during their feud in the early 1560s (PRO, SP 63/12/28, 30, 31; 13/4, 6).
38. Sidney to Leicester, 1 Mar. 1566 (SP 63/16/35); Bagenal to Piers, 25 May 1580 (SP 63/73/54, enclosure 9 (i)).
39. Among several estimates of the numbers of MacDonnells in arms in the period, see SP 63/29/38; 63/75/40; 63/82/52; 63/111/67.
40. 'A treatise on Ireland', NLI, MS 669.
41. Ibid.
42. Lascelles, *Liber Munerum*, pt. ii, pp. 110–11.
43. Gilbert to Cecil, 18 Oct. 1569 (SP 63/29/67); Falls, *Elizabeth's Irish Wars*, p. 36.
44. Lascelles, *Liber Munerum*, pt. ii, p. 110; Sidney to Privy Council, 27 Apr. 1576 (SP 63/55/34); *Fiants Ire., Eliz.*, no. 2905.
45. On the Bagenals in general, see Bagenal, *Vicissitudes of an Anglo-Irish Family*; 'Sir Nicholas Bagenal'.
46. Cruikshank, *Elizabeth's Army*, ch. 2; Falls, *Elizabeth's Irish Wars*, ch. 3. For a detailed administrative study of the levying and recruitment of troops, see McGurk, 'A survey of the demands'.

47. This for instance was Sidney's experience during his first months as viceroy in 1566; see Brady, *Chief Governors*, pp. 120–1.
48. Lascelles, *Liber Munerum*, pt. ii, p. 108.
49. Ibid.; Edward Denny to Burghley, 17 Feb. 1587 (PRO, SP 63/128/47).
50. Lascelles, *Liber Munerum*, pt. ii, p. 104; 'Information . . . touching abuses in the office of Ordnance', Jan. 1589 (PRO, SP 63/140/26); 'Allegations against Richard Hopwood', 17 June 1589 (SP 63/145/10).
51. Lascelles, *Liber Munerum*, pt. ii, p. 102.
52. Ibid., p. 107. On Eliot's service and pursuit of private interests, see PRO, SP 63/1/63; 63/8/8; 63/20/15, 16; 63/34/45; 63/38/8; *Fiants Ire., Eliz.*, nos. 312, 1242.
53. 'Book of the garrison', 31 Mar. 1586 (PRO, SP 63/123/21).
54. *Fiants Ire., Eliz.*, no. 4268; 'Beverley's report on the state of the victuals', July 1582 (PRO, SP 63/94/30, enclosure (i)).
55. For a contemporary account of the risks involved, see Henry Sackford's memorandum of 20 June 1575 (SP 63/52/31); and on the failure of earlier contract victuallers, see Brady, *Chief Governors*, pp. 231–3.
56. Ibid., ch. 6.
57. Longfield, *Fitzwilliam Accounts*; PRO, SP 63/210/70, enclosure (a).
58. The procedures are lucidly described in Cruikshank, *Elizabeth's Army*, ch. 9; for the abuses to which they gave rise in Ireland, see PRO, SP 63/7/38; 63/9/19, 45.
59. Lascelles, *Liber Munerum*, pt. ii, p. 108.
60. Ibid., p. 99; Cruikshank, *Elizabeth's Army*, pp. 144–5.
61. 'Articles' against King and his 'Replys', Sept. 1563 (PRO, SP 63/9/1–5).
62. King to Cecil & Leicester, 2, 3 Mar. 1566 (SP 63/16/39, 40); Lascelles, *Liber Munerum*, pt. ii, p. 99.
63. More to Walsingham, 14 Dec. 1575 (PRO, SP 63/54/16 & enclosure (i)). For other signs of early reforms, see SP 53/55/10, enclosure (i), and SP 63/55/37, enclosure (ii); Mynne to Sir Henry Wallop, 3 July 1581 (SP 63/84/16, enclosure (i)): also SP 63/96/25, enclosures (i), (ii).
64. Lascelles, *Liber Munerum*, pt. ii, p. 99.
65. Brady, *Chief Governors*, ch. 6; 'Conservative subversives'. The abuses of the captains featured regularly in the state correspondence of the period, but for a representative summary from a source by no means unsympathetic to the army, see the several reports compiled by Burghley's agent Maurice Kyffin in the later 1590s (PRO, SP 63/96/29; 97/89, 91; 99/39, 98; 202/pt. 2, 108; 202/pt. 3, 55).
66. On the close links between the viceroys and a select group of captains, see Brady, *Chief Governors*, chs. 3–4.
67. Buckley, 'Viceregal progress'; Perrot's 'Declaration of services', 14 Dec. 1588 (PRO, SP 63/139/7).
68. Baker, 'Off the map'.
69. On Agard's service in Munster in 1574, see PRO, SP 63/47/57, 48/6, 12.
70. On Davell's mission in 1579, see SP 63/66/28; 67/30, 52; 68/6; 70/5, 6.
71. See the terms of appointment printed in Lascelles, *Liber Munerum*, pt. ii, pp. 119–24, and the commissions entered in the register of the Irish Council (HMC, *Fifteenth Report, appendix iii: Haliday MSS* (London, 1897), pp. 20–2); Sidney's 'Ordinances for seneschals', 15 Apr. 1556 (PRO, SP 63/17/13, enclosure (i)).
72. Brady, *Chief Governors*, pp. 258–9; for Piers's views on the reform of Ulster through the cultivation of local alliances, see his 'Plot' in HMC, *MSS of Lord De Lisle and Dudley* (6 vols., London 1925–66), ii, 87–91.

73. Sussex's 'Opinion . . . touching the reform of Ireland', c. June 1562, *Calendar of the Carew Manuscripts, 1515–74*, pp. 330–44; Sidney's 'Ordinances', 15 June 1566 (PRO, SP 63/17/13, enclosure (i)); *Fiants Ire., Eliz.*, nos. 1409, 1564.
74. Brady, *Chief Governors*, pp. 137–41.
75. Ibid., 141–5.
76. Ibid., pp. 144–8, 271–89; Morgan, *Tyrone's Rebellion*, ch. 3.
77. Sidney to Elizabeth, 20 Apr. 1578 (PRO, SP 63/60/42); Loftus to Burghley, 4 Dec. 1586 (SP 63/127/4); Perrot to Walsingham, 12 May 1588 (SP 63/125/22).
78. For details of Rory Oge O'More, see O'Hanlon & O'Leary, *History of the Queen's County*, i, ch. 16. For an account of the atrocity committed by the captains at Mullaghmast in the aftermath of the rebellion, see O'Donovan, *Annals*, s.a. 1578, and O'Donovan's extensive commentary on the affair.
79. Morgan, *Tyrone's Rebellion*, chs. 3–4. For a case-study, see Brady, 'The O'Reillys of East Briefne', esp. pp. 258–61.
80. Knox, *History of Mayo*, pp. 220–45; Bingham's commission to John Browne, 13 Jan. 1589 (PRO, SP 63/140/20); Fitzwilliam to Burghley, 9, 30 Apr. 1589 (SP 63/143/12, 48 and the enclosed reports).
81. Capt. Merbury's collection of reports, 1 Aug., 27 Sept. 1589 (SP 63/146/2, 57); Bishop Jones to Burghley, 13 May 1589 (SP 63/44/30); Fitzwilliam to Burghley, 7 Aug., 2 Sept., 8 Oct., 19 Dec. 1589 (SP 63/146/5, 28; 147/11 (for the specific allegation of George Bingham's use of torture); 149/43).
82. 'Examination of Capt William Mostyn', June 1589 (SP 63/145/46).
83. 'Note of oppressions in Tirconnell', Dec. 1594 (SP 63/177/48); Ó Cleirigh, *Aodh Ruadh O'Domhnaill*, i, pp. 37–57; Morgan, *Tyrone's Rebellion*, chs. 4, 6, 7; Brady, 'The O'Reillys of East Briefne', pp. 259–62; also McCaffrey, *Elizabeth I*, chs. 16–17.
84. Compare the different views in Morgan, 'The end of Gaelic Ulster"; Brady, 'Ulster and the failure of Tudor reform'; and Canny, *From Reformation to Restoration*, pp. 138–43.
85. Hayes-McCoy, 'Army of Ulster'; Canny, 'Hugh O'Neill'.
86. On Lee, see Morgan, 'Tom Lee'; on Warren's negotiations with Tyrone in the late 1590s, PRO, SP 63/198/128, enclosure (i) and 201/132; on Mostyn's defection, Arthur Savage to Sir Robert Cecil, 26 Nov. 1600 (SP 63/207/pt. 6, 33).
87. Mostyn's 'Plot for Ireland', Nov. 1598 (PRO, SP 63/202/pt. 3, 185).
88. For an overview of the emergence of such hard-line views, see Canny, 'Edmund Spenser'.

8 The wars of religion, 1603–1660

I would like to thank the following for reading earlier drafts of this chapter and for their helpful and incisive comments: Aidan Clarke, Tom Connors, Barbara Donagan, Ian Gentles, Raymond Gillespie, Rolf Loeber, John Lynn and Geoffrey Parker.

1. *Franciscan MSS*, p. 113.
2. Cited in *New Hist. Ire.*, iii, 233.
3. For further details see Parker, *The Military Revolution*. Parker's thesis and conclusions have, however, been subjected to criticism by a number of scholars. For instance Black, *A Military Revolution?* argues that the critical precondition was enhanced state power; while Lynn, 'The *trace italienne*', suggests that army size was the key development. The impact of 'military revolution' on Ireland is discussed at length in Loeber & Parker, 'The military revolution'.

4. Estimate of the charge for the fortifications of Derry and Coleraine, *c.* 1627 (Huntington Library, Ellesmere MSS, 7056).

5. *Ormonde MSS*, ii, 33.

6. *Cal. S.P. Ire. 1625–32*, p. 293.

7. Knowler, *Earl of Strafforde's Letters*, ii, 300 and 358. This is discussed in detail in Ohlmeyer, *Civil War and Restoration*, pp. 77–94.

8. St Leger to [Ormond], 21 July & 17 Aug. 1640 (Bodl., Carte MSS 1, ff. 214, 231).

9. Recently the origins and course of the rebellion have attracted historical attention. See especially Mac Cuarta, *Ulster 1641* and Canny, 'What really happened in 1641'.

10. *An exact relation of all such occurences . . .* (London, 1642), p. 1. The main outlines of the conspiracy which resulted in the rising are reasonably well defined though the details remain obscure, but the origins are the subject of historical debate. Clarke, *The Old English in Ireland*, pp. 230–4 has suggested that particular circumstances in 1641 forced the Irish to rebel and that their objectives were limited; Gillespie, 'The end of an era', pp. 19, 193–204, has modified Clarke's argument and suggested that the rebellion had more complex social, economic and political origins; while Russell in his *Causes of the English Civil War*, pp. 18–19, 129–30, and *Fall of the British Monarchies 1637–1642*, pp. 375, 379–80, and Perceval-Maxwell, 'Ireland and Scotland', p. 198, have stressed its British context.

11. *An exact relation of all such occurences . . .* (London, 1642), p. 1.

12. Cregan, 'The Confederation of Kilkenny', p. 102.

13. For further details see Ohlmeyer, 'Ireland independent'.

14. Ohlmeyer, *Civil War and Restoration*, pp. 127–48.

15. Wheeler, 'Four armies'; Gentles, *New Model Army*, pp. 350–84.

16. *Franciscan MSS*, p. 239.

17. Bernard, *Siege of Drogheda*, p. 18.

18. Wheeler, 'Four armies in Ireland', p. 65.

19. The population of France at this point numbered *c.* 19 million; while the size of Louis XIV's army stood at *c.* 333,000. For details see Lynn, 'Recalculating French army growth'. I am grateful to John Lynn for sharing his expertise on this issue with me.

20. The musters, upon which these conclusions are based, are printed in Gilbert, *Irish Confederation*, vi, 78–81; vii, 282–9, 348; Gilbert, *Contemporary History*, ii, 496–500, 502–7; Stevenson, *Scottish Covenanters*, appendix 3; HMC, *Fourteenth Report, appendix vii: The Manuscripts of the Marquis of Ormonde, Preserved at the Castle, Kilkenny* (2 vols., London, 1895, 1899), i, 129–30, 132–7, 160–78, 185–6, 200–20.

21. HMC, *Fourteenth Report, appendix vii*, p. 429.

22. Gilbert, *Contemporary History*, ii, xxxviii.

23. Gilbert, *Irish Confederation*, vi, 66.

24. Brown to [ ], 18/28 Feb. 1642 (BL, Add. MSS 12,184 f. 63).

25. Gilbert, *Irish Confederation*, iv, 284.

26. Ibid., i, 74.

27. Gilbert, *Contemporary History*, i, 30.

28. Jennings, *Wild Geese*, pp. 507–8.

29. Turner, *Memoirs*, p. 26.

30. Hayes-McCoy, *Irish Battles*, p. 184.

31. Gilbert, *Irish Confederation*, iv, 284.

32. 'State of the kingdom of Ireland, 10 December 1646' by [Arthur] Annesley and Sir William Parsons (BL, Egerton MSS 917, ff. 25–7).

33. *Lawes and orders of warre . . . established for the good conduct of the service of Ireland* (Dublin, 1641); Gilbert, *Irish Confederation*, ii, 94–5; iii, 74–85.
34. *A Bloody Fight at Balrvd-Derry in Ireland . . .* (London, 1647), p. 4.
35. Gilbert, *Irish Confederation*, vii, 149.
36. Ibid., vi, 216–17, 221–2, 223.
37. *Ormonde MSS*, i, 147.
38. Gillespie, 'The Irish economy', p. 169.
39. Gilbert, *Irish Confederation*, ii, 262; see also *Franciscan MSS*, p. 139.
40. Hazlett, 'The financing of the British armies'.
41. Lowe, *Clanricarde Letter-book*, p. 354.
42. Gilbert, *Irish Confederation*, iv, 36.
43. PRONI, D. 2977/5/1/1.
44. Bodl., Carte MSS 24, f. 158.
45. Gilbert, *Irish Confederation*, vi, 81–2.
46. Ibid., 271.
47. Gilbert, *Contemporary History*, ii, 350.
48. Conway to the committee of Irish affairs at Derby House [1646–7] (Huntington Library, Hastings MSS, Irish papers, box 9/14345).
49. *Ormonde MSS*, ii, 86.
50. Bernard, *Siege of Drogheda*, p. 50.
51. Gilbert, *Irish Confederation*, iv, 187.
52. *Ormonde MSS*, ii, 121; see also pp. 155–6, 195–6, 327.
53. Logan, 'Medical services', pp. 225–7.
54. *Ormonde MSS*, ii, 327.
55. Wheeler, 'Logistics and supply', pp. 44–7.
56. Hazlett, 'The financing of the British armies', p. 41.
57. Hugh Peter, *A Word for the Army and Two Words to the Kingdome* (1647), cited in Kishlansky, 'The case of the army truly stated', p. 51.
58. Darcy to Muskerry, 6 Nov. 1647 (Bodl., Carte MSS 21, f. 517).
59. Quoted in Dionysius Massari, 'My Irish campaign', *The Catholic Bulletin*, 6: 4 (Apr. 1916), p. 221.
60. McNeill, *Tanner Letters*, pp. 201–2.
61. *Another extract of more letters sent out of Ireland . . .* (London, 1643) (Cambridge University Library, HIB. 7.643.3).
62. Jennings, *Wild Geese*, p. 507.
63. McNeill, *Tanner Letters*, p. 361.
64. *Ormonde MSS*, i, 89. Those received between 18 Apr. and 15 May 1647 hardly totalled £50 (ibid., 115).
65. Gilbert, *Irish Confederation*, ii, 205.
66. Gillespie, *Transformation of the Irish Economy*, p. 39.
67. Foissotte to Rosas, 14/24 Oct. 1644 (Archivo General, Simancas, Guerra Antigua 1570 unfol.).
68. *Franciscan MSS*, p. 196.
69. HMC, *Thirteenth report, app., part I. The Manuscripts of His Grace the Duke of Portland, preserved at Welbeck Abbey* (London, 1891), i, 510.
70. Gilbert, *Irish Confederation*, vi, 270–1.
71. Gilbert, *Contemporary History*, iii, 266–7.
72. McNeill, *Tanner Letters*, p. 371.
73. Petty, *Political Anatomy of Ireland*, pp. 18–19.

74. Parker, *Thirty Years' War*, pp. 210-12.
75. Gilbert, *Contemporary History*, iii, 195-6.
76. Gilbert, *Irish Confederation*, iv, 93-5.
77. Ibid., i, 265-6.
78. Quoted in *New Hist. Ire.*, iii, 317.
79. *Worse and worse newes from Ireland . . .* (London, 1641), pp. 1-2.
80. *The Lord Balmerino's Speech in the High Court of Parliament in Scotland . . .* (London, 1641), p. 3.
81. Hill, *The Stewarts of Ballintoy*, pp. 14-15.
82. Jennings, *Wild Geese*, p. 507.
83. *Speciall Good News from Ireland . . .* (London, 1643[-4]), pp. 2-3.
84. *A Letter from Sr Lewis Dyve to the Lord Marquis of Newcastle . . .* (Hague, 1650), p. 5.
85. Bellièvre to Brienne, 3/13 Nov. 1648 (Archives du Ministère des Affaires Etrangères [Paris], Correspondance politique, Angleterre, Côte 57, ff. 314-15).

9 The Williamite war, 1689–1691

1. Childs, *Nine Years' War*, pp. 1-29.
2. Childs, *The Army, James II, and the Glorious Revolution*, pp. 4-5; *British Army of William III*, pp. 9-14.
3. Much of this chapter has been based on three main sources: Simms, *Jacobite Ireland*; Murtagh & Murtagh, 'The Irish Jacobite army'; and Ferguson, 'The organisation of King William's army'.
4. de Cavelli, *Les Derniers Stuarts*, ii, 447-8.
5. BL, Add. MSS 61,318, ff. 1-2; *Cal. S.P. Dom., 1689-90*, pp. 5-6, 16-17; BL, Add. MSS 15,897, f. 106.
6. BL, Add. MSS 15,897, ff. 88-9; *Cal. S.P. Dom., 1689-90*, p. 48.
7. *Cal. S.P. Dom., 1689-90*, p. 265.
8. *Diary of Abraham de la Pryme*, p. 16; Danaher & Simms, *The Danish Force in Ireland*, pp. 5-14.
9. *Cal. S.P. Dom., 1689-90*, p. 441.
10. *Correspondentie van Willem III*, ii, 27-8.
11. Henning, *House of Commons*, ii, 488.
12. *Commons' Jn.*, x, 295-6; Grey, *Debates*, ix, 451-3.
13. Establishment, Ireland, 1690 (Dorset County Record Office, Ilchester MSS, D. 124); *Cal. S.P. Dom., 1690-91*, p. 7; PRO, WO 24/10, f. 19.
14. Steele, *Bibliography of Royal Proclamations*, ii, 133, 140, 144, 149.
15. Danaher & Simms, *The Danish Force in Ireland*, p. 20.
16. *Correspondence of Sir John Lowther*, pp. xxxiv-xxxix, xli-xliii.
17. Walton, *History of the British Standing Army*, p. 849; *Cal. S.P. Dom., 1690-91*, pp. 356-7.
18. *English Army Lists*, iii, 105-23; Childs, 'For God and for Honour', p. 48.
19. O'Callaghan, *Irish Brigades*, pp. 8, 28.
20. Hayes-McCoy, *Irish Battles*, pp. 214-37; O'Carroll, 'An indifferent good post'; Harrington, 'Images of the Boyne'.
21. Hayes-McCoy, *Irish Battles*, pp. 238-72.
22. O'Callaghan, *Irish Brigades*, pp. 28-9, 61.
23. Simms, *The Treaty of Limerick*.
24. See Guy, 'A whole army absolutely ruined'; Bartlett, 'Army and society'.

10 The Irish military establishment, 1660–1776

1. Johnston, 'The Irish establishment'.
2. The principal studies referred to are: Childs, *Army of Charles II*; *The Army, James II, and the Glorious Revolution*; Ferguson, 'The army in Ireland'; Houlding, *Fit for Service*; Fennell, 'The army in Ireland'; Bartlett, 'Army and society'.
3. Wood, *Guide to the Records*; Ratcliff, 'Destruction of the public records'; Ferguson, 'Military manuscripts'.
4. Atkinson, *Royal Hampshire Regiment*, i, 49; *Dorsetshire Regiment*, i, 31.
5. Bannatyne, *History of the XXXth Regiment*, p. 116.
6. Ferguson, 'The army in Ireland', p. 8.
7. Webb, *The Governors-General*, pp. 39–49.
8. Ferguson, 'The army in Ireland', p. 9; Webb, *The Governors-General*, pp. 44–5.
9. Ferguson, 'The army in Ireland', pp. 9–10; Childs, *Army of Charles II*, pp. 203–6; Connolly, *Religion, Law and Power*, pp. 24–5.
10. Irwin, 'Earl of Orrery', pp. 10–11; Childs, *Army of Charles II*, p. 206.
11. Webb, *The Governors-General*, p. 39.
12. Ferguson, 'The army in Ireland', pp. 11–14; Irwin, 'Earl of Orrery', pp. 13–14; Miller, 'Earl of Tyrconnell'.
13. Ferguson, 'The army in Ireland', pp. 16–18.
14. Miller, 'Earl of Tyrconnell', pp. 817–18.
15. David Ó Brudair, quoted in Connolly, *Religion, Law and Power*, p. 34.
16. Miller, 'Earl of Tyrconnell', pp. 818–19.
17. Childs, *The Army, James II, and the Glorious Revolution*, pp. 56–82 & *passim*; Priestley, 'The Portsmouth captains'.
18. Melvin, 'The Irish army'; 'Irish troop movements'; Jones, 'The Irish fright'. In addition to the recently landed Irish regiments, there was another, Roger MacElligott's, based at Portsmouth, substantially Irish in composition (Ferguson, 'The army in Ireland', p. 21; Garland, 'Regiment of MacElligott').
19. Ferguson, 'The army in Ireland', p. 28.
20. Ibid., pp. 45–53; Fennell, 'The army in Ireland', pp. 59–60; Connolly, *Religion, Law and Power*, pp. 201–2.
21. *New Hist. Ire.*, iv, *Eighteenth-Century Ireland*, p. 227.
22. Yorke to the king, 27 Dec. 1762 (PRO, SP 63/420/26).
23. Ferguson, 'The army in Ireland', p. 60.
24. McLynn, 'Ireland and the Jacobite Rising', p. 340.
25. RA, Cumberland papers, box 44, no. 145.
26. Account of the numbers of commissioned officers and men in Ireland, 1763–7 (PRO, SP 63/420/139).
27. BL, Ellis papers, Add. MSS 28,945.
28. Guy, *Samuel Bagshawe*, pp. 218–20; Ferguson, 'The army in Ireland', p. 73.
29. Fennell, 'The army in Ireland', pp. 42–3; Leask & McCance, *Royal Scots*, p. 120.
30. Ferguson, 'The army in Ireland', pp. 70–2; Odintz, 'British officer corps', pp. 209–11.
31. James, *Ireland in the Empire*, p. 181.
32. Guy, *Samuel Bagshawe*, pp. 117–19.
33. Hayter, *Army and Crowd*, pp. 129–59; Zobel, *Boston Massacre, passim*.
34. Ferguson, 'The army in Ireland', pp. 78–80.
35. Connolly, *Religion, Law and Power*, p. 47; Burns, 'Ireland and British military preparations', *passim*.

---

36. Guy, *Samuel Bagshawe*, pp. 18-19.

37. Webb, *The Governors-General*, p. 47.

38. Guy, *Samuel Bagshawe*, p. 18.

39. Townshend to the earl of Rochford, 16 Oct. 1770 (NAM, Townshend papers, NAM 6806-41-7-5).

40. *A Proposal for increasing His Majesty's Revenue of Ireland, with the* [Revenue] *Commissioners' Attestation of the Service of the Inniskillen Light Horse*, 1763 (John Rylands University Library of Manchester, Bagshawe papers, B3/21/1). For Caldwell's military career, see Bagshawe, *The Bagshawes of Ford*; Cunningham, *Castle Caldwell*.

41. Ensign John Mackenzie to his brother William, 6 Apr. 1739 (BL, Mackenzie of Suddie papers, Add. MSS 39,189, f. 216).

42. Fennell, 'The army in Ireland', pp. 24–8.

43. Ensign Nicholas Delacherois to his brother Daniel, 22 May 1757 (NAM, Delacherois papers, NAM 7805-63).

44. Guy, *Samuel Bagshawe*, pp. 39–40, 94–6.

45. 'Some Thoughts, Observations and Remarks . . . Touchant le Militaire', *c.* 1725 (NAM, Hawley papers, NAM 7411-24-16); Col. Joseph Yorke to the earl of Hardwicke, 4 Mar. 1757 (BL, Hardwicke papers, Add. MSS 35,357, f. 102).

46. John Calcraft, army agent, to to Maj. Gen. Edward Pole, 23 Dec. 1758 (BL, Calcraft papers, Add. MSS 17,494, f. 56).

47. Hawley's 'Remarks' (NAM 7411-24-16).

48. Houlding, *Fit for Service*, pp. 46–55.

49. Townshend to the earl of Rochford, 16 Oct. 1770 (NAM, Townshend papers, NAM 6806-41-7-5); and to the earl of Weymouth, 20 Dec. 1770 (PRO, SP 63/432/262).

50. Manuscript Life of Gen. Hawley, *c.* 1756 (NAM 7411-24-15).

51. Guy, *Oeconomy and Discipline*, pp. 40–1.

52. Graeme to Townshend, 7 Oct. 1767 (PRO, SP 63/425/233).

53. Letter III, 'To Sir William Draper, Knight of the Bath', 7 Feb. 1767 (Cannon, *Letters of Junius*, p. 42). Junius's attack on the marquess of Granby, the English commander-in-chief, was part of his general assault on the duke of Grafton's administration. 'Junius' was furnished with inside information from the War Office, which is not surprising if, as seems to be the case, he was Philip Francis, first clerk in the Office from 1763 to 1772 (ibid., pp. 539–72; Hayter, *The Papers of William, Viscount Barrington*, pp. 11–13).

54. Guy, *Oeconomy and Discipline*, pp. 12–15.

55. Ibid., pp. 36–7.

56. Account of the arrival of the duke of Northumberland, 22 Sept. 1763 (PRO, SP 63/432/21).

57. The words are those of George Macartney, Townshend's chief secretary (Bartlett, *Macartney in Ireland*, p. xiv).

58. 'An Establishment [of] Our Army, Ordinance [sic] and Other Officers . . . for Military Affairs . . . for Our Kingdom of Ireland, to commence from yᵉ. 24ᵗʰ. of August, 1717' (NAM 7406-50-47); Forde, 'The Royal Irish Artillery', pp. 32–8.

59. Guy, *Oeconomy and Discipline*, p. 21.

60. This was the opinion of Arthur Onslow, speaker of the British House of Commons, 1728-61 ('An account of his Family', HMC, *Fortieth Report Appendix, part IX* (1895), 'Onslow MSS', p. 508).

61. Hartington to Fox, 23 May 1755 (Ilchester, *Letters to Henry Fox*, pp. 65–6).

62. Chesterfield to Maj. John Irwin, 1 Sept. 1751 (Bradshaw, *Letters of Philip Dormer Stanhope*, p. 993).

63. 'Military Memorandum of Irish Affairs, picked up by a Lover of Truth [Col. Caroline Frederick Scott?] from one and another', c. 1749–50 (RA, Cumberland papers, box 61); Maj. Thomas Gage to Charles Hotham, 13 Feb. 1750 (Brynmor Jones Library, University of Hull, Hotham-Thompson papers, DDH04/4); *Consolatory Letter to a Noble Lord*, pp. 35–6.

64. 'Observations concerning Military Affairs', in Ireland by 'Mr Lovetruth', enc. in no. 98, Col. Caroline Frederick Scott to Col. Robert Napier, adjutant-general, 29 July 1750 (RA, Cumberland papers, box 44, no. 99).

65. Memorial by Lt.-Col. Eyre, 30 Aug. 1765 (PRO, SP 63/421/71).

66. Ferguson, 'The army in Ireland', pp. 85–7.

67. Maj.-Gen. Edward Hervey, adjutant-general, to Lt.-Col. Robert Cunninghame, adjutant-general of Ireland, 24 May 1772 (PRO, WO 3/3/35).

68. Fennell, 'The army in Ireland', pp. 7–10.

69. Foster, *Modern Ireland*, p. 229.

70. Fennell, 'The army in Ireland', pp. 3–6; Guy, *Samuel Bagshawe*, p. 201; Odintz, 'British officer corps', pp. 290–2.

71. Townshend to Weymouth, 13 Sept. 1769, 3 Mar., 16 Oct. 1770 (PRO, SP 63/430/27, 431/103 & 432/876).

72. Harding, *Amphibious Warfare*, p. 70; Guy, *Samuel Bagshawe*, p. 122.

73. Koppermann, *Braddock at the Monogahela*, pp. 14–16; Fennell, 'The army in Ireland', pp. 46–7.

74. Connolly, *Religion, Law and Power*, p. 245.

75. Ferguson, 'The army in Ireland', pp. 100–1.

76. Middleton, *The Bells of Victory*, pp. 107–29.

77. This account of the fall of Carrickfergus is based on Richard Rigby, chief secretary, to the duke of Newcastle, 23 Feb. 1760 (BL, Newcastle papers, Add. MSS 32,902, f. 40); Lt Patterson RN to John Cleveland, secretary to the Admiralty, 24 Feb. (ibid., f. 76); Strode to Bedford, 22 Feb. (ibid., f. 344); Bedford to William Pitt, 23 Feb. (PRO, SP 63/418); Rigby to Newcastle, 3 p.m. & 10 p.m., 24 Feb. (BL, Add. MSS 32,902, ff. 358, 362); report by Maj.-Gen. Strode, 23 Feb. (ibid., f. 364); Newcastle's 'Memoranda for the King', 27 Feb. (ibid., f. 430); Strode to Bedford, 26 Feb. (ibid., f. 434); Lt.-Col. Cunninghame to Bedford, 26 Feb. (ibid., 436); Newcastle to Rigby, 27 Feb. (ibid., f. 466); Return of Officers and Men made Prisoners of War, etc. (BL, Add. MSS 32,903, f. 37); Bedford to Newcastle, 4 Mar. (ibid., f. 79); Col. Edward Sandford to Rigby (ibid., f. 89); Bedford to Pitt, 26 Mar. (PRO, SP 63/418); *The London Gazette*, 26 Feb.–1 Mar. 1760; Guy, *Samuel Bagshawe*, pp. 213–25; Beresford, 'François Thurot'; Kenrick, *Wiltshire Regiment*, pp. 14–19; Young & Foster, *Thurot*, *passim*.

78. Maj.-Gen. Edward Hervey, adjutant-general, to Viscount Barrington, 8 Dec. 1767 (PRO, WO 3/1/129); Bullion, 'Securing the peace'.

79. Hervey to Cunninghame, 28 Jul. 1768 (PRO, WO 3/3/14).

80. The revisionist accounts of Townshend's lord lieutenancy are by Bartlett, 'Augmentation of the army in Ireland'; 'The Townshend viceroyalty'. For the growing assertiveness of Irish public opinion, see 'Army and society', pp. 181–2.

81. Bartlett, 'Augmentation', pp. 558–9; *New Hist. Ire.*, iv, *Eighteenth-Century Ireland*, pp. 216–17; Burns, 'Ireland and British military preparations', pp. 54–8.

82. Ferguson, 'The army in Ireland', pp. 101–2.

---

83. Andrews, 'Charles Vallancey'.
84. Townshend to Weymouth, 2 Mar., 5 May, 16 Oct., 20 Dec. 1770 (PRO, SP 63/431/102, 431/216, 432/76, 432/262); to Rochford, Sept. 1771 (434/70). For persistent doubts about the effectiveness and morale of some units of the Irish army in 1775, however, see Burns, 'Ireland and British military preparations', pp. 49–52.
85. Ferguson, 'The army in Ireland', pp. 73–5.
86. Ibid., p. 100; Burns, 'Ireland and British military preparations', pp. 48–9, 54–5.
87. Glover, *Wellington's Army*, p. 25.

11 The defence of Protestant Ireland, 1660–1760

1. Brady, *Catholics and Catholicism*, p. 311; *Commons' Jn., Ireland* (2nd edn, Dublin, 1763), 17 July 1666.
2. Except where otherwise indicated, full documentation for the discussion that follows will be found in Connolly, *Religion, Law and Power*, chs. 1, 6. For the armed forces of the Restoration period, see also Beckett, 'The Irish armed forces'; and Irwin, 'Earl of Orrery'.
3. *Cal. S.P. Ire., 1663–5*, p. 699.
4. *Cal. S.P. Ire., 1666–9*, pp. 113, 157.
5. Petty, *Political Anatomy of Ireland*, pp. 27–8; HMC, *Papers of the Earl of Egmont* (2 vols., London, 1905–9), ii, 112.
6. For fuller documentation on what follows, see Connolly, *Religion, Law and Power*, ch. 6; 'Law, order and popular protest'; 'Albion's fatal twigs'. There are useful general discussions of the role of the army in James, *Ireland in the Empire*, pp. 174–81; Palmer, *Police and Protest*, ch. 2; and especially, Bartlett, 'Army and society'.
7. 'A letter . . . concerning the sacramental test' (1709), in *Prose Works of Jonathan Swift*, ii, 122.
8. McEvoy, *James Freney*, pp. 33–4, 52, 56–7; *Dublin Courant*, 1–4 Oct. 1748.
9. Connolly, 'Law, order and popular protest', pp. 58–9; Frederick Hamilton to Archbishop William King, 9 Aug. 1715 (TCD, MSS 1995-2008/1700).
10. Judgment in the King *v.* Thomas Corr, 12 Feb. 1739 (Dublin Municipal Library, Gilbert MSS 32, pp. 3–9; 39, pp. 91–115); *Dublin Courant*, 4–8 Aug., 31 Oct.–3 Nov., 14–16 Nov., 17–21 Nov., 1–5 Dec., 15–19 Dec. 1747.
11. *Poems of David Ó Bruadair*, iii, 97.
12. *Cal. S.P. Dom. 1693*, p. 109.
13. PRO, SP 63/384/119–20, 123–8; *Dublin Courant*, 15–19 Mar. 1748; William Nicolson, bishop of Derry, to William Wake, archbishop of Canterbury, 4 Mar. 1722 (Dublin Municipal Library, Gilbert MSS 27, pp. 316–17).

12 Defence, counter-insurgency and rebellion: Ireland, 1793–1803

1. Bartlett, 'Militarisation and politicisation'.
2. Fitzpatrick, 'The economic effects'.
3. Dickson, 'Taxation and disaffection'.
4. It should be noted that whereas the rank and file of the Militia were mostly Catholic, the officers were almost entirely Protestant. By contrast, the officers and most of the rank and file of the Yeomanry were Protestants.

5. Bartlett, 'A weapon of war yet untried'.

6. Beresford, 'Ireland in French strategy 1691–1798'.

7. Edward Cooke to Evan Nepean, 4 Dec. 1793 (PRO, HO 100/41/287).

8. Sydney to Rutland, 7 Jan. 1786 (HMC, *Fourteenth Report, appendix : the Manuscripts of the 4th Duke of Rutland* (4 vols., London, 1888–1905), iii, p. 273).

9. For the United Irishmen see, Curtin, *The United Irishmen*.

10. McDowell, *Ireland in the Age of Imperialism and Revolution*, ch. 12, 'Radicalism and reaction'.

11. Bartlett, 'An end to moral economy'. Unless otherwise stated, my discussion of the establishment of the Irish Militia is taken from this article.

12. The classic history of the Irish Militia is McAnally, *The Irish Militia 1793–1816*.

13. Westmorland to Dundas, 12 (*bis*), 25, 26 Apr., 6, 15 May 1793 (PRO, HO 100/39, 282, 286, 317, 387, 343, 381).

14. There is a full discussion of the Militia disturbances and their significance in Bartlett, 'An end to moral economy'.

15. Westmorland to [Pitt?], 30 Dec. 1793 (PRO, HO 100/41/367); 'State of the forces sent to Great Britain and received from thence', July 1793 (ibid., 100/40/105).

16. Hobart to Nepean, 1 Jan. 1793 (ibid., 100/42/31–2).

17. Nepean to Hobart, 6 June 1793; Dundas to Westmorland, 21 Sept. 1793, 13 Feb. 1794 (ibid., 100/44/89–90, 40/340, 47/183–6).

18. Westmorland to –, 3 Jan. 1793 (ibid., 100/39/1); see Duffy, 'War, Revolution', for the demands of the West Indian theatre.

19. Camden to Portland, 27 Jan. 1796; 1 Oct. 1795 (PRO, HO 100/60/38, 55/248).

20. See papers in PRO, HO 100/47/9, 11, 13, 15, 17, 91, 167.

21. For discussions of the shortcomings of the Irish army in the 1790s, see Bartlett, 'Indiscipline and disaffection'; and 'Reflections on indiscipline and disaffection in the French and Irish armies'. Unless otherwise stated this paragraph is based on these papers.

22. Col. T. H. Foster to John Foster, 4 Apr. 1804 (PRONI, D. 207/11/46).

23. Dundas to Camden, 22 Apr. 1797; Portland to Camden, late May 1798 (PRO, HO 100/69/218–9, 76/311).

24. Above, pp. 000–00. At its peak the British army in the Peninsular War numbered nearly 60,000 men: Napier, *History of the War in the Peninsula*, iv, pp. 456–7.

25. Gen. Robt. Cunninghame to Hobart, 17 Oct. 1793 (PRONI, T. 2627/1/7); see also sources listed in note 17.

26. Cooke to Nepean, 14 Jan. 1794 (PRO, HO 100/47/69); Maj.-Gen. Fawcett to –, 17 Nov. 1797 (ibid., 100/70/304).

27. Camden to Portland, 24, 29 July 1795 (ibid., 100/55/70, 58/165–6); The Irish Army Medical Board, Apr. 1796, 'Observations on the diseases of the Militia and Fencible Regts. on the Irish Establishment' (NAM, MS 6807/174/123–41). The general good health of the Irish recruit in the eighteenth century has been confirmed by modern research: see Ó Gráda & Mokyr, 'The height of Irishmen and Englishmen'.

28. 'Report of sick in Army', 1 June 1796 (NAI, Official Papers/23/23).

29. On this difficulty see Stoddard, 'Counter-insurgency and defence'.

30. Cunninghame to Camden, 16 Aug. 1796 (PRO, HO 100/62/171).

31. The literature on the Defenders is now quite substantial: preliminary surveys are in Elliott, *Partners in Revolution*, pp. 15–20, 39–46; and Bartlett, 'Defenders and Defenderism'. See also Smyth, *Men of No Property*.

32. Ibid.
33. Cooke to Nepean, 5 July 1793 (PRO, HO 100/40/102–4).
34. Fitzwilliam to Portland, 31 Jan. 1795 (PRO, HO 100/46/271).
35. Camden to Portland, 30 May 1795 (PRO, HO 100/69/345–40).
36. Gruber, 'On the road to Poonamalle', has a little information on the Irish officers who served in the American War.
37. Bartlett, 'Religious rivalries', explores some similarities and contrasts between the religious feuding in these countries at this time.
38. See Miller, *Peep of Day Boys*; and 'The Armagh troubles'.
39. Cooke to Gosford, 7 July 1796 (PRONI D. 1606/1/1/185a); Gosford to Pelham, 29 Feb. 1796 (NAI, Rebellion Papers 620/23/33); Richard Jephson to Charlemont, 9 Oct. 1795 (HMC, *Twelfth Report, appendix x* and *Thirteenth Report, appendix vii: the Manuscripts and Correspondence of James, first earl of Charlemont* (2 vols., London, 1891–4), ii, pp. 265–6).
40. Williamson to James Horne, 27 Sept. 1795 (PRONI T. 3513).
41. Knox to Cooke, 13 Aug. 1796 (NAI, Rebellion Papers 620/24/106).
42. Elliott, *Partners in Revolution*, chs. 3 & 4: see also *Theobald Wolfe Tone*.
43. Curtin, *The United Irishmen*, ch. 3; Spy's report on United Irishmen in Belfast, Oct. 1796 (PRO, HO 100/62/333).
44. Curtin, *United Irishmen*, ch. 4; McHugh, *Carlow in '98*, pp. 50, 63.
45. Bartlett, *Fall and Rise of the Irish Nation*, p. 212.
46. Bartlett, 'Defenders and Defenderism', p. 375; Tone, *Life of Theobald Wolfe Tone*, i, p. 290; 'Report on United Irishmen', Oct. 1796 (PRO, HO 100/62/333); Bartlett, *Fall and Rise of the Irish Nation*, p. 213.
47. Camden's remedy: Camden to Portland, 25 Sept. 1795 (PRO, HO 100/58/334–43).
48. Camden to Portland, 22 Jan. 1796 (PRO, HO 100/62/15–20).
49. Morton, 'Rise of the Yeomanry', is still useful, but see also Blackstock, 'The Yeomanry'.
50. Bartlett, 'A weapon of war yet untried'.
51. Camden to Portland, 28 June 1796 (PRO, HO 100/64/129–35); 24 Aug. 1796 (ibid., 100/62/190–4).
52. Bartlett, *Fall and Rise of the Irish Nation*, pp. 221-2.
53. John Walsh to –, 3 Nov. 1796; Thos. Boyd to Justice R. Boyd, 5 Oct. 1796 (NAI, Rebellion Papers, 620/25/14, 148); James Brown to –, 28 Dec. 1796 (ibid., 620/26/177). Significantly, a Belfast Yeomanry was formed in 1798.
54. 'JW' to –, 4 Feb. 1797 (ibid., 620/10/121/49).
55. Cooke to Auckland, 26 Nov. 1796 (PRONI, T. 3229/2/10).
56. Richd. Musgrave to Cooke, 4 Oct. 1796 (ibid., 620/25/145).
57. Thirty-four Yeomen from the Narraghmore and Saunderson corps in Wicklow were executed at Dunlavin as suspected United Irishmen in 1798 (Furlong, *Fr. John Murphy*, p. 48).
58. Bartlett, *Fall and Rise of the Irish Nation*, p. 222.
59. Henry Clements, 'Forthill, near Cavan', to Cooke, 20 Sept. 1796 (NAI, Rebellion Papers, 620/25/102); Jones to Cooke, 4 Sept. 1796 (ibid., 620/25/133); Morton, 'Rise of the Yeomanry', p. 59.
60. Richard Annesley, to Cooke, 9 Nov. 1796 (NAI, Rebellion Papers 620/26/37).
61. Camden to Portland, 10 Dec. 1796; Portland to Camden, 29 Nov. 1796 (PRO, HO 100/62/362–3, 348–9).
62. Clare to Auckland, 2 Jan. 1797 (PRONI, T. 3229/1/11).
63. Westmorland to Archbishop of Cashel, 13 Jan. 1797 (PRONI, T. 3719/c31/1).

64. Camden to Portland, 3 Jan. 1797 (PRO, HO 100/69/23–4).
65. Camden to Portland, 26 Dec. 1796 (PRO, HO 62/409–10); Carhampton to Camden, 18 Jan. 1797 (ibid., 61/45–56).
66. Dalrymple to Pelham, 10 p.m. 23 Dec. 1796 (PRO, HO 62/385); Vallancey to Abercorn, 6 Apr. 1797 (PRONI, T. 2541/1C5/17).
67. Henry Alexander to –, 24 Dec. 1796 (NAI, Rebellion Papers, 620/26/150).
68. Camden to Portland, 8 Jan. 1796 (PRO, HO 100/69/7–9); Portland to Camden (ibid., 100/71/3–4); Pelham to Lake, 3 Mar. 1797 (NAM, MS 6807/174/230–4).
69. Camden to Portland, 9 Mar. 1797 (PRO, HO 100/69/132–8).
70. Knox to Abercorn, 21 Mar. 1797 (PRONI, T. 2542/1B3/6/10).
71. Camden to Portland, 12 June 1797 (PRO, HO 100/69/387–90); ibid., 6 Oct. 1797 (HO 100/72/283–6).
72. Haliday to Charlemont, 6 Oct. 1797 (HMC, *Charlemont* (cited n. 39), ii, p. 306).
73. Camden to Portland, 3 Nov. 1797 (PRO, HO 100/70/191–8).
74. Camden to Portland, 17 July 1797 (PRO, HO 100/72/109). This incident can scarcely be compared to the serious 'friendly fire' mishap at Borris, County Carlow, when detachments of the Meath and Donegal Militias and the Mid-Lothian Fencibles opened fire on one another leaving twelve dead (Clifden to Cashel, 4 June 1798, PRONI, T. 3719/C32/70); but both illustrate the lack of discipline among the troops.
75. Curtin, *The United Irishmen*, ch. 3.
76. Bartlett, 'Indiscipline and disaffection', pp. 125–7.
77. Pelham to Duke of York, 4 Jan. 1797, in Gilbert, *Documents*, pp. 101–3; Carhampton to Pelham, 19 Oct. 1797 (PRO, HO 100/68/221–2).
78. Camden to Portland, 8 Mar., 18 May 1797 (PRO, HO 100/69/128–30, 305); Clare to Auckland, 14 Jan. 1797 (PRONI, T. 3229/1/12): Clare denounced Lt.-Gen. Edw. Smith as 'a mad methodist' and claimed that Maj.-Gen. Amherst 'utters more treason than any United Irishman'.
79. Camden to Portland, 28 Apr. 1797 (PRO, HO 100/69/233–4).
80. Portland to Camden, 10 June 1797 (PRO, HO 100/69/379–82).
81. Dundas to Camden, 2 Oct. 1797 (PRONI, T. 2627/4/80).
82. Vallancey to Abercorn, 12 Oct. 1797 (PRONI, T. 2541/1C5/17).
83. Dunfermline, *Abercromby*.
84. Quoted in ibid., pp. 79–80, 84, 85–6.
85. Ibid., p. 110.
86. Abercromby to Camden, 15 Mar. 1798 (PRO, HO 100/75/229–30).
87. Camden to Portland, 14 Dec. 1797 (PRO, HO 73/67–8).
88. Abercromby to Elliot, 25 Dec. 1797; Camden to Abercromby, post 25 Dec. 1797 (PRO, HO 75/315–18).
89. Copy of Abercromby's 'General Orders' (BL, Fox MSS 47569/77).
90. *The speech of . . . John, Earl of Clare* [19 Feb. 1798] . . . *on a motion made by the Earl of Moira* (Dublin, 1798); Auckland to Cashel, 11 Mar. 1798 (PRONI, T. 3719/C32/21); Pitt to Camden, 13 Mar. 1798 (PRO, PRO 30/8/325/5–8).
91. Camden to Portland, 15 Mar. 1798 (PRO, HO 100/75/225); Camden to Pitt, 30 Mar. 1798 (PRO, PRO 30/8/326/282/3).
92. Adj.-Gen. Hewett to Lieut.-Gen. Dundas, 16 Mar. 1798 (PRO, HO 100/75/247–50); Abercromby's orders, 3 Apr. 1798 (ibid., 80/178).
93. Shannon to Boyle, 7 Apr. [1798] (PRONI, D. 2707/A3/3/51); Clifden to Cashel, 12 Mar. 1798 (ibid., T. 3719/C32/22).

---

94. The figures were as follows

Returns of arms and ammunition delivered or taken in Cos. Kildare,
Queen's, King's, 26–30 Mar. 1798

	Muskets	Bayonets	Pistols	Swords	Pikes
Kildare	626	52	148	122	12
King's	1,040	128	200	147	13
Queen's	447	55	88	68	8

(There is a note appended to this return to the effect that most of the arms were returned to the owners who were well-affected).
Source: PRO, HO 100/80/175

95. Pitt to Camden, 31 Mar. 1789 (PRONI, T. 2627/4/217).
96. Vallancey to Abercorn, 12 Oct. 1797 (PRONI, T. 2541/1C5/17).
97. Camden to Pitt, 25 Apr. 1798 (PRONI, T. 2627/4/219).
98. Cooke to Auckland, 24 Mar. 1798 (PRONI, T. 3229/2/32); Clifden to Cashel, 12 Mar. 1798 (ibid., T. 3719/C32/22).
99. Pitt to Camden, 31 Mar. 1798 (PRONI, T. 2627/4/217).
100. Bartlett, *Fall and Rise of the Irish Nation*, p. 231.
101. Benj. Chapman to Shelburne, 13 Oct. 1798 (Clements Library (Ann Arbor, Michigan), Shelburne MSS); Bartlett, *Fall and Rise of the Irish Nation*, p. 231.
102. Camden to Portland, 10 May 1797 (PRO, HO 100/69/291–2).
103. Bartlett, *Fall and Rise of the Irish Nation*, pp. 231-2.
104. Shannon to Boyle, 21 May [1798] (PRONI, D. 2707/A/3/3/70).
105. McDowell, *Ireland in the Age of Imperialism and Revolution*, pp. 601–2.
106. Unless otherwise stated I have drawn on my account of the rebellion published in *Fall and Rise of the Irish Nation*, pp. 232–44.
107. Col. Gosford to Lake, 24 May 1798 (PRO, HO 100/76/267).
108. Jas Arbuckle to Patk Heron, 3 June 1798 (PRONI, T. 3162/1/2).
109. McDowell, *Memoirs of Miles Byrne*, pp. 63–4.
110. Craufurd to Maj.-Gen Craddock, 7 June 1798 (PRO, HO 100/77/126–7); extract of letter from Maj. Vesey of Dublin County Militia, 8 June (ibid., 77/82).
111. Maj.-Gen. Johnston's report, 7 June 1798 (PRO, HO 100/77/108–10).
112. Gen. Needham to Camden, 10 June 1798 (PRO, HO 100/77/120–3); McDowell, *Memoirs of Miles Byrne*, pp. 132–8. Over sixty years later, Byrne's memory of the Arklow pikemen commanded by Mathew Doyle was still fresh: 'I could not help admiring the clever military manner he kept his men manoeuvring, marching, counter-marching in the presence of the enemy. Doyle was stript, in his shirt, a red girdle or sash round his waist, an immense drawn sabre in his hand. He was at the head of about two hundred fine fellows, all keeping their ranks as if they had been trained soldiers and strictly executing his command.' (*Memoirs of Miles Byrne*, p. 155.)
113. 'Ulster provincial meeting', 29 May 1798 (PRO, HO 100/77/44).
114. Cooke to Wickham, 16 June 1798 (PRO, HO 100/77/157).
115. Cooke to Wickham, 2 June 1798 (PRO, HO 100/79/21–2); William Fox, 'A Narrative of the Principal Proceedings of the Republican Army of the county Down during the late Insurrection' n.d. [pre May 1799] (PRO, HO 100/86/327–35).
116. 'Information of Felix Conroy or Convery of Townland of Achantorack, parish of

Ballymore, near Poyntzpass, Co. Armagh', 29 Sept. 1798 (Scottish Record Office, GD 26/9/527/1/19).

117. Castlereagh to Nugent, 6 June 1798 (NAM, MS 6807/174/457).
118. McDowell, *Memoirs of Miles Byrne*, p. 165.
119. General Fredk. St Johnston to Gen. Stewart, 9 June 1798 (PRONI, Lake papers, Mic. 67).
120. Maj.-Gen. Needham to Lake, 21 June 1798 (ibid.).
121. Regimental song, n.d. [*c.* summer of 1798] (National Library of Scotland, Ancram Papers, MS 5750 f. 121).
122. Unless otherwise stated this account of the French expedition is based on my 'General Humbert takes his leave'.
123. Wickham to Castlereagh, 1 Sept. 1798 (PRO, HO 100/78/244–5).
124. Bartlett, 'General Humbert', p. 99.
125. These preparations can be followed in General Lake's letterbook (PRONI, Mic 67).
126. Quoted in McDowell, *Ireland in the Age of Imperialism and Revolution*, p. 649.
127. Abercromby to Dundas, 5 Sept. 1798 (Clements Library, Melville papers).
128. *Memoirs of Miles Byrne*, pp. 138, 140.
129. Auckland to Cashel, 14 June 1798 (PRONI, T. 3719/C32/83).
130. P. Lattin to Lansdowne, 11 Nov. 1799 (Clements Library, Shelburne papers).
131. Shannon to Henry Boyle [18 June 1798] (PRONI, D. 2707/A3/3/89); Sir John Hort to Sir John Caldwell, 21 Dec. 1798 (ibid., D. 1634/2/94).
132. Craufurd to Wickham, 28 July 1798 (PRO, HO 100/66/198–203); Westmorland to Cashel, 28 July 1798 (PRONI, T. 3719/C32/107); quoted in Bartlett, *Fall and Rise of the Irish Nation*, p. 267.
133. See Bartlett, 'Masters of the Mountains'.
134. On Russell see Woods, *Journals and Memoirs of Thomas Russell*.
135. Robert Emmet's rebellion still awaits the attention of a modern historian, but see the brief but reliable account in Elliott, *Partners in Revolution*.
136. Cornwallis to Dundas, 17 July 1799, in Ross, *Correspondence of Cornwallis*, iii, pp. 117–19.
137. Wellesley to Hawkesbury, 7 May 1807 in Wellington, *Supplementary Dispatches*, v, 28–36.
138. Col. Foster to John Foster, 4 Apr. 1804 (PRONI, D. 207/11/46); Bartlett, 'Indiscipline and disaffection', p. 130.
139. Bartlett, 'Militarisation and Politicisation', p. 135.
140. Castlereagh to Wellesley, 28 Dec. 1807 in Wellington, *Supplementary Dispatches*, v, 279–83.
141. Bartlett, 'Militarisation and Politicisation', p. 135.
142. During the Catholic Emancipation crisis of 1826–8, Dublin Castle was frequently taunted with the large numbers of Catholic Irish in the British army, even in supposedly English regiments: Bartlett, 'Militarisation and Politicisation', p. 127. The implication here was that if ordered against their co-religionists they might prove unreliable. The fact that they had proved reliable in 1798 was ignored.
143. Burke to Langrishe, 26 May 1795 (*Burke Correspondence*, viii, 252–7).

13 Irish soldiers abroad, 1600–1800

1. The O'Neill families went overseas / and Ireland is miserable since they went / But eagles' eggs bring forth eagles / In whatever place they are hatched (Hyde, *Amhráin Chúige Chonnacht*, p. 22).
2. Lydon, 'The hobelar'; 'Irish levies'; White, 'Henry VIII's Irish kerne'.

3. Childs, *Armies and Warfare*, p. 105.

4. Fallon, *The Armada in Ireland*, pp. 221-2.

5. Jennings, *Wild Geese, passim*.

6. Casway, 'Henry O'Neill'.

7. Quoted in Walsh, 'The wild goose tradition', p. 5.

8. *Manifesto que hizieron los maestros de campo Irlandeses, que estan siruiendo a su magestad . . . in el principado de Cataluna* (Barcelona, 1653).

9. MacSwiney, 'Notes on the formation'.

10. Oman, 'Irish troops in the service of Spain'.

11. MacSwiney, 'Notes on some Irish regiments'.

12. Mullen, 'Campo Santo'; Hayes-McCoy, *History of Irish Flags*, p. 71.

13. Walsh, *Spanish Knights of Irish Origin*.

14. His account of the episode is in Gilbert, *Narratives*, pp. 31–108.

15. Beerman, 'Alexander O'Reilly'; Ireland, 'General Alexander O'Reilly'.

16. Griffin, 'Irish generals and Spanish politics'.

17. Hayes, 'Earliest Irish troops'; Gouhier, 'Mercenaires'.

18. Gallwey, *The Wall Family*.

19. Simms, *Jacobite Ireland*, pp. 138–9; Murphy, *Justin MacCarthy*.

20. O'Callaghan, *Irish Brigades*, p. 61.

21. Hayes-McCoy, *History of Irish Flags*, pp. 66–8.

22. Ó Briain, 'The Chevalier Gaydon's memoir'.

23. *Memoirs of Captain Robert Parker*, pp. 138–9.

24. O'Callaghan, *Irish Brigades*, pp. 350–67.

25. Guerin, 'Irish soldiers'.

26. Hayes, *Irish Swordsmen*, pp. 233–56; MacCauley, 'Lally-Tollendal in India'.

27. Hayes, *Biographical Dictionary of Irishmen in France, passim*.

28. Clark & Thompson, 'Napoleon's Irish Legion'.

29. Murphy, 'Irish units', p. 75.

30. Walsh, 'Further notes', pp. 169–70; Fitzsimon, 'A further note'.

31. Fitzsimon, 'Irish swordsmen'.

32. Mann, *Wallenstein*, pp. 813–44.

33. Quoted in Jennings, 'Irish Franciscans in Prague', p. 214.

34. Murtagh, 'Two Irish officers'.

35. Duffy, 'The Irish in the Imperial service'.

36. Duffy, *The Wild Goose and the Eagle*.

37. O'Neill & Thompson, 'Field Marshal Lacy'.

38. Cavenagh, 'Irish knights'.

39. O'Neill, 'Conflicting loyalties'.

40. Garland, 'Irish officers'.

41. Jordan, 'Wild Geese in the north'.

42. O'Meara, 'Irishmen in eighteenth-century Russian service'.

43. Malcolm, 'All the king's men'.

44. Ó Danachair, 'Montrose's Irish regiments'; Stevenson, *Alasdair MacColla*.

45. Melvin, 'The Irish army'.

46. Clarke, 'Sir Piers Crosby', p. 152.

47. Childs, *Army of Charles II*, pp. 115–95, 237–53; *Nobles, Gentlemen and the Profession of Arms*.

48. Atkinson, 'Charles II's regiments in France'.

49. *Cal. S.P. Dom, 1687–9*, p. 49.

50. Gilbert, 'Recruitment and reform'; Cadell, 'Irish soldiers'.
51. *Autobiography of Theobald Wolfe Tone*, i, 2–4, 19–20.
52. Doyle, *Ireland, Irishmen and Revolutionary America*, p. 73 & *passim*.
53. Collins, 'Irish participation at Yorktown'.
54. *Calendar of the Carew MSS, 1601–3*, pp. 50-1.
55. Hayes-McCoy, 'Irish soldiers of the '45'.
56. Beresford, 'Ireland in French strategy'.
57. Hayes, *Irish Swordsmen*, pp. 143-4.
58. Elliott, *Partners in Revolution*, pp. 331 ff.
59. Forman, *A Letter*.
60. *Observations on Affairs in Ireland* (Dublin, 1766).
61. Hayes, *The Last Invasion of Ireland, passim*; Van Brock, 'Morres's memorial'.
62. Wall, Gallwey & Garland, 'Irish officers'.
63. Hayes, *Biographical Dictionary of Irishmen in France, passim*.
64. Quoted in Simms, 'The Irish on the Continent', p. 637. The explanation of the term is said to have been that recruits were entered as wild geese in the ships' manifests.
65. McDonnell, 'Some documents'.
66. *Franco-Irish Correspondence*, i, 294–5, 304–5.
67. Quoted in Garland, 'Irish officers', p. 241.
68. *Négociations de M. le comte d'Avaux*, p. 29.
69. *The Memoirs of Captain Peter Drake*.
70. Murtagh, 'Corporal Darby Quinan'.
71. Walsh, 'Some notes'; Henry, '"Wild geese" in Spanish Flanders'; de la Tour du Pin, *Recollections*.
72. Burney, *An Eighteenth-century Tour*, p. 9.

14 Non-professional soldiery, c. 1600–1800

1. Finer, 'State- and nation-building'; Weber, *From Max Weber*, p. 78 (italics omitted).
2. Davies, *Discovery of the True Causes*, p. 72.
3. This framework is based loosely on the polity model presented in Tilly, *From Mobilization to Revolution*, pp. 52–4.
4. Clarke, *Old English in Ireland*, pp. 29–38.
5. Beckett, 'The Irish armed forces', pp. 50–1; Irwin, 'Earl of Orrery'; *Cal. S.P. Ire., 1666–9*, pp. 56, 62, 81–2.
6. Petty, *Economic Writings*, i, 166–70.
7. *Cal. S.P. Ire., 1666–9*, p. 274.
8. Ibid., p. 278.
9. In practice these guidelines were sometimes exceeded: MacCarthy-Morrogh, *Munster Plantation*, pp. 62, 291–2; Robinson, *Plantation of Ulster*, pp. 72–80, 85–6, 196–209; Davies, *Discovery of the True Causes*, pp. 145-57.
10. Hill, *Historical Account*, pp. 81, 89.
11. The text is reprinted in ibid., pp. 451–590.
12. MacCarthy-Morrogh, *Munster Plantation*, pp. 134–5; Sheehan, 'Overthrow of the plantation of Munster'.
13. Reid, *Presbyterian Church in Ireland*, i, 313–24, 343–8; Bagwell, *Stuarts*, i, 348; ii, 17.
14. Canny, *From Reform to Restoration*, p. 214; Stevenson, *Scottish Covenanters*, pp. 96–9.
15. Simms, *Jacobite Ireland*, pp. 56–7, 95–119; *Faithful History of the Northern Affairs*.
16. [Story], *True and Impartial History*, p. 12.

---

17. Perceval-Maxwell, *Outbreak of Irish Rebellion*, pp. 240–60.
18. Reid, *Presbyterian Church in Ireland*, i, 349–50n.
19. McCarmick, *Further Impartial Account*, p. 38; Hamilton, *True Relation*, pp. 25, 39–40, 46.
20. McCarmick, *Further Impartial Account*, p. 5.
21. Simms, *Jacobite Ireland*, pp. 48–52; *Faithful History of the Northern Affairs*, pp. 10–17.
22. Hamilton, *True Relation*, pp. 42-4.
23. Irwin, 'The earl of Orrery', p. 13.
24. *Cal. S.P. Ire., 1666–9*, p. 157.
25. Connolly, 'Violence and order'.
26. Connolly, 'Law, order and popular protest'.
27. Donnelly, 'Irish agrarian rebellion', pp. 306–7.
28. Connolly, 'Law, order and popular protest', p. 54.
29. O'Donovan, 'Militia in Munster', p. 34.
30. [Coote], *Genuine Account*, p. 6.
31. O'Donovan, 'Militia in Munster', pp. 39–43; McDowell, 'Colonial nationalism', pp. 204–7; Smyth, 'Volunteer Movement', pp. 40–2.
32. Ferguson, 'Volunteer movement and government', pp. 208–12; Smyth, 'Our cloud-cap't grenadiers', pp. 190–3.
33. Smith, 'Our cloud-cap't grenadiers', pp. 194–6; Ferguson, 'Volunteer movement and government', pp. 212–13; McDowell, *Ireland in the Age of Imperialism and Revolution*, p. 257.
34. Donnelly, 'Irish agrarian rebellion', p. 330.
35. Ó Snodaigh, 'Police and military aspects of the Volunteers'.
36. Ferguson, 'Volunteer movement and government', p. 209.
37. Ó Snodaigh, 'Class and the Volunteers', pp. 183–4.
38. Smyth, 'The Volunteers and parliament'.
39. Simms, 'Remembering 1690'; *Belfast News-Letter*, 30 Oct.–3 Nov. 1778.
40. Quoted in Bartlett, *Fall and Rise of the Irish Nation*, p. 121.
41. Bartlett, 'An end to moral economy', pp. 45–50; McAnally, *Irish Militia*, pp. 58, 126.
42. Morton, 'Rise of the Yeomanry'; Richardson, *History of Irish Yeomanry*, pp. 15–18, 25–6.

15 Army organisation and society in the nineteenth century

1. Chart, 'Irish levies'; Ferguson, 'The army and the 1798 rebellion', p. 88; Bredin, *History of the Irish Soldier*, pp. 220–2, 229–82.
2. Chart, 'Irish levies', pp. 510–16; Fortescue, *The County Lieutenancies and the Army*, p. 235; 'Weekly recruiting by extra recruiting parties' (PRO, WO 1/904).
3. Alcock, *Notes on the Medical History*, pp. 4, 6–7; Cadell, 'Irish soldiers'.
4. *General Annual Return[s] of the British Army*, p. 54 [C. 1323], HC 1875, xliii, 442; p. 91 [C. 9426], HC 1899, liii, 425.
5. Murray, *King's Royal Irish Hussars*, i, 382; *Return of the Number of English, Scotch, and Irish Non-Commissioned Officers, Corporals and Privates in each Regiment*, p. 2, HC 1872 (171), xxxvii, 428; and p. 2 1878–9 (15), xliii, 502.
6. Webb-Carter, 'A subaltern in Abyssinia'; Henderson, *Highland Soldier*, p. 10; Atkinson, 'Irish regiments of the line'.
7. The former Indian battalions were the 101st (Royal Bengal Fusiliers), 102nd (Royal Madras Fusiliers), 103rd (Royal Bombay Fusiliers), 104th (Bengal Fusiliers), 108th

(Madras Infantry) and 109th (Bombay Infantry). *Return of the Number of English, Scotch, and Irish Non-Commissioned Officers* . . . , pp. 3–5, HC 1872 (171), 429–31; pp. 4–5, HC 1878–9 (15), 504–5.

8. Hanham, 'Religion and nationality', p. 162; see also Karsten, 'Irish soldiers'.

9. Macdonald, *Personal Narrative*, p. 296; Somerville, *Autobiography*, p. 114; MacMullen, *Camp and Barrack-Room*, p. 13; Edmondson, *Is a Soldier's Life Worth Living?*, p. 5; Stanley, 'White mutiny', pp. 19–24.

10. Longford, *Wellington*, p. 132; MacMullen, *Camp and Barrack-Room*, p. 1; Cunliffe, *Royal Irish Fusiliers*, p. 231; 'The army 1815–54', p. 93; 'Royal Hibernian Military School, Dublin', *The Navy and Army Illustrated* (14 Jan. 1899), pp. 421–3.

11. 'Recruiting service' & 'General Correspondence', *United Service Magazine*, pt. iii (Oct., Nov. 1841), pp. 273 & 390; Lt.-Col. A. C. Cooke, 'Statement of the relative pecuniary position of the soldier and town labourer (August 1867)' (PRO, WO 33/18); Karsten, 'Irish soldiers', pp. 38–9.

12. Lord Sandhurst, 'Memorandum on recruiting in 1874 by the General Commanding the Forces in Ireland' (PRO, WO 33/27); Butler, *Far Out*, pp. 308–10; *Report of the Army Medical Department for 1861*, p. 29 [C. 3233], HC 1863, xxxiv.

13. The district headquarters were Clonmel (East Munster (Royal Irish) Regiment, formerly 1st & 2nd Bns. 18th); Omagh (Royal Inniskilling Fusiliers, formerly 27th & 108th); Belfast (Royal Irish Rifles, formerly 83rd & 86th); Armagh (Princess Victoria's Royal Irish Fusiliers, formerly 87th & 89th); Galway (Connaught Rangers, formerly 88th & 94th); Birr (Leinster Regiment, formerly 100th & 109th); Tralee (Royal Munster Fusiliers, formerly 101st & 104th); Naas (Royal Dublin Fusiliers, formerly 102nd & 103rd).

14. Cardozo, *Maud Gonne*, pp. 183–4; *Annual Report of the Inspector-General of Recruiting for the Year 1900*, pp. 25, 29 [Cd. 519], HC 1901, ix, 323, 327; Viscount Wolseley (q. 8798) and Maj.-Gen. J. K. Fraser (q. 12967), evidence before the *Committee appointed by the Secretary of State for War to consider the terms and conditions of service in the Army*, pp. 286, 449 [C. 6582], HC 1892, xix, 508, 671; *General Annual Return of the British Army for the Year 1898* . . . , p. 31 [C. 9426], HC 1899, liii, 365.

15. *Return of the Number of English, Scotch and Irish Commissioned Officers* . . . , pp. 2–7, HC 1878–9 (15), xliii, 502–7; Spiers, *Army and Society*, p. 297; *Late Victorian Army*, p. 98; Muenger, 'British Army in Ireland', pp. 102–3.

16. Butler, *Autobiography*, p. 13; Western, 'Roman Catholics', pp. 428–32; Melvin, 'Sir R. D. Kelly'; Spiers, *Radical General*, pp. 2–3.

17. Head, *No Great Shakes*, pp. 24–5; Wolseley, *Story of a Soldier's Life*, i, 2.

18. Robertson, *Crowned Harp*, pp. 24–5. 101.

19. Callwell, *Sir Hugh McCalmont*, pp. 27–8; Robertson, *Crowned Harp*, pp. 20, 101–2; on sporting memories of Ireland, see Marling, *Rifleman and Hussar*, p. 168; May, *Changes and Chances*, pp. 71–2, 84, 89; Head, *No Great Shakes*, pp. 78–9.

20. Head, *No Great Shakes*, p. 25; Harvey, *History of 5th Royal Irish Lancers*, p. 149; Spiers, *Radical General*, p. 3; Melvin, 'Maurice Griffin Dennis'; Cadell, 'Irish soldiers', p. 77; *Report of the Select Committee appointed by the Secretary of State to enquire into the nature of the expenses incurred by officers of the army*, pp. 7–8 [Cd. 1421], HC 1903, x, 541–2.

21. [Shipp], *Memoirs*, ii, 78–9.

22. Barrow, *Fire of Life*, p. 7; Willcocks, *From Kabul to Kumasi*, pp. 7–8, 101–2; for a critical view, see Montgomery-Cuninghame, *Dusty Measure*, p. 29.

23. Marling, *Rifleman and Hussar*, p. 147; Sir Arthur Wellesley to J. Villiers, 8 Sept. 1809 (Gurwood, *Wellington Dispatches*, v, 135); Gretton, *Royal Irish Regiment*, pp. 285, 305;

Smyth, *In This Sign Conquer*, pp. 55, 70, 113; Lord Anglesey to Sir Robert Peel, 20 & 26 July 1828 ([Peel], *Memoirs*, i, 158, 164).

24. Ibid.; Wellington to Peel, 31 July 1828 (BL, Peel MSS, MS 40307, f. 170); Col. A. Wedderburn to Col. Hancox, 19 July 1826, & to Maj.-Gen. Taylor, 9 Mar. 1827 (PRO, Murray MSS, WO 80/6). On the suppression of the Orange lodges, see J. Hume to Lord Howick, 25 July 1835; Howick to Lord Hill, 27 July 1835; Hill to Howick, and general order, 31 Aug. 1835 (PRO, WO 43/649).
25. Sir H. Hardinge to Peel, 12 & 13 Oct. 1830 (Hardinge MSS, McGill University, Montréal); Cunliffe, *Royal Irish Fusiliers*, p. 186.
26. Cunliffe, *Royal Irish Fusiliers*, p. 186; Peel to Hardinge, 15 Oct. 1830; Hardinge to Sir J. Graham, 23 May 1843; Col. Taylor to Hardinge, 1 Oct. 1836 (Hardinge MSS).
27. Sir G. Brown to duke of Cambridge, 11 Mar. 1865; Sir H. Rose to duke of Cambridge, 30 Aug. 1865; Aug. 1865; 27 Mar. 1866 (RA, Cambridge MSS, Add. E/1/4657, 4829, 4832, 5029); Lord Strathnairn to Sir R. Napier, 30 Sept. 1866 (BL, Rose MSS, Add MSS. 42822, f. 134); Devoy, *Recollections*, p. 130; Semple, 'Fenian infiltration'.
28. Semple, 'Fenian infiltration', pp. 159–60; Pomeroy, *Story of a Regiment*, i, 197; duke of Cambridge to Lord de Grey & to Rose, 23 Jan. 1866; Rose to Cambridge, Aug. 1865 & 26 Sept. 1865, 1 Feb. & 4 May 1866 (RA, Cambridge MSS, Add. E/1/4936, 4937, 4832, 4856, 4954, 5092); Devoy, *Recollections*, pp. 62, 185.
29. Lord Strathnairn, annual report, June 1867 (PRO, WO 32/6000, pp. 22–3).
30. W. H. Smith to Sir M. Hicks Beach, 15 Nov. 1886 (PRO, Smith MSS, WO 110/15, f. 849).
31. Viscount Wolseley to duke of Cambridge, 2 Feb., 23 Apr., 17 Nov. 1893 (RA, Cambridge MSS, Add. E/1/12918, 12945, 12996).
32. Lord Roberts to Rev. W. J. Mathans, 23 May 1899 (NAM, Roberts MSS, 7101-23-110-1).
33. Pomeroy, *Story of a Regiment*, i, 195, 199–200; Gretton, *Royal Irish Regiment*, p. 120; Cunliffe, *The Royal Irish Fusiliers*, pp. 186, 194; Laurie, *Royal Irish Rifles*, p. 312; *Royal Inniskilling Fusiliers*, p. 312; Palmer, 'Sir Charles Napier'.
34. Grattan, *Adventures with the Connaught Rangers*, pp. 87, 305–11; Rait, *Hugh, First Viscount Gough*, i, 102–3; Bredin, *History of the Irish Soldier*, pp. 248, 257; Gretton, *Royal Irish Regiment*, pp. 119, 178; Jourdain, *Ranging Memories*, p. 25.
35. McCance, *Royal Munster Fusiliers*, i, 148–53; see also Bredin, *History of the Irish Soldier*, pp. 292–8, 300–22, 332–70.
36. Bredin, *History of the Irish Soldier*, pp. 370–7; Laurie, *Royal Irish Rifles*, pp. 369, 374; Jourdain, *Connaught Rangers*, i, 253–4, 293; *Royal Inniskilling Fusiliers*, pp. 383, 396–409, 436–47, 478–85; Murray, *King's Royal Irish Hussars*, i, 512, 530, 534; Romer & Mainwaring, *Second Battalion Royal Dublin Fusiliers*, pp. 36–9, 193.
37. Conyngham, *The Irish Brigade* (1869 edn), p. 5.
38. Mullen, 'Irish Brigades'; Cavanagh, *Thomas Francis Meagher*, p. 369.
39. McPherson, *Battle Cry of Freedom*, p. 606.
40. Ibid., pp. 137, 493, 507, 609–10; Lonn, *Foreigners in the Union Army and Navy*, pp. 578, 584.
41. Lonn, *Foreigners in the Union Army and Navy*, p. 578; Clark & Thompson, 'Napoleon's Irish Legion'; Lambert, 'Irish soldiers in South America'; Miller, *Shamrock and Sword*, pp. 32–3, 174–5; Pottinger, *The Foreign Volunteers*, pp. 45, 161; McCracken, *Irish Pro-Boers*, pp. 141–5.
42. Miller, *Shamrock and Sword*, p. 32; Crean, 'Irish battalion of St Patrick'; Davitt, *Boer Fight for Freedom*, p. 322; Pottinger, *The Foreign Volunteers*, pp. 141, 257; Bredin, *History of the Irish Soldier*, pp. 387–8, 397; Mullen, 'The Hibernia Regiment'.

43. Masur, *Simon Bolivar*, pp. 333–4, 339, 379, 432; Lambert, 'Irish soldiers in South America', pp. 27–30.
44. Lynch, *My Life Story*, p. 161; Crean, 'Irish battalion of St Patrick', p. 54; Lambert, 'Irish soldiers in South America', p. 32; Pottinger, *The Foreign Volunteers*, pp. 44–5, 296–9; Allendorfer, 'An Irish regiment in Brazil'; Hayes-McCoy, 'Captain Myles Walter Keogh'.
45. Miller, *Shamrock and Sword*, p. 174.
46. Pottinger, *The Foreign Volunteers*, pp. 152, 316; Lonn, *Foreigners in the Confederacy*, pp. 496–502; Garland, 'Irish soldiers of the American Confederacy'; Mullen, 'The Hibernia Regiment', p. 225.
47. Masur, *Simon Bolivar*, p. 338. On commemorations, see Pottinger, *The Foreign Volunteers*, p. 270; Lambert, 'Irish soldiers in South America', p. 31; Miller, *Shamrock and Sword*, pp. 180–1.
48. *Harper's Weekly*, 20 Oct. 1860, p. 658; Cunliffe, *Soldiers and Citizens*, pp. 227–9; Allendorfer, 'An Irish regiment in Brazil', pp. 28–31.
49. Pottinger, *The Foreign Volunteers*, pp. 44, 141, 145, 151, 262, 318–19; Mullen, 'The Hibernia Regiment', p. 225; Black, 'John Tennent'; Mehegan, *O'Higgins of Chile*, pp. 13, 59, 120, 201–2.
50. Wiley, *The Life of Billy Yank*, p. 309; Lonn, *Foreigners in the Union Army and Navy*, pp. 645–7; *Foreigners in the Confederacy*, pp. 229–34.
51. Masur, *Simon Bolivar*, p. 340; Clark & Thompson, 'Napoleon's Irish Legion', pp. 165, 168; Pottinger, *The Foreign Volunteers*, pp. 53, 56, 318.

16 The army and law and order in the nineteenth century

1. Mundy to his father, 9 Aug. 1834 (NAM, Mundy papers, MS 8409/32, f. 7).
2. Wedderburn to Doyle, 7 Sept. 1825 (PRO, WO 80/6, f. 18).
3. See, for example, Steele to Forster, 10 Jan. 1882 (NLI, Kilmainham papers, MS 1073, p. 165).
4. For a discussion of the use of troops at elections, see Hoppen, *Elections, Politics and Society*, pp. 415–23.
5. Vivian to Somerset, 24 July 1832 (NAM, Vivian papers, MS 7709/6/10, f. 363). Vivian served as commander of the forces in Ireland, 1831–5. Cf. Wedderburn to Thornton, 14 June 1826 (PRO, WO 80/6, f. 53).
6. Reports from Capt. Croker, 13 Aug. 1839, and Mr Little, 19 Aug. 1839 (NLI, Kilmainham papers, MS 1051, p. 439).
7. Strathnairn to Abercorn, 3 May 1867 (BL, Strathnairn papers, Add. MSS 42824, f. 27); Strathnairn to de Ros, 12 Aug. 1868 (ibid., 42825, f. 65).
8. Evidence of Maj.-Gen. Montgomery Moore, *Report of the Commission of Enquiry, 1886, respecting the origin and circumstances of the riots in Belfast* [C. 4925], HC 1887, xviii, 206.
9. Hawkins, 'An army on police work'; Haire, 'In aid of the civil power'; Townshend, *Political Violence in Ireland*.
10. Rose to Wodehouse, 18 Dec. 1865 (BL, Strathnairn papers, Add. MSS 42821, f. 141). Cf. Murray to Taylor, 23 Aug. 1826 (PRO, WO 80/6, f. 81); Taylor to Murray, 28 Aug. 1826 (Surrey Record Office, Goulburn papers, Ac. 319/38).
11. Rose to Cambridge, 20 Sept. 1865 (BL, Strathnairn papers, Add. MSS 42821, f. 49). Cf. Anglesey to Byng, 14 Mar. 1831 (PRONI, Anglesey papers, D. 619/32G, f. 46); Vivian to Macdonald, 19 Oct. 1834 (NAM, Vivian papers, MS 7709/6/12, f. 248).
12. Ireland to Hillier, 25 Oct. 1881 (NAI, Registered papers, 1881/38371).

13. Blakeney to Macdonald, 5 Dec. 1839 (PRO, WO 35/28, f. 38).
14. Rose to Cambridge, 3 Jan. 1866 (BL, Strathnairn papers, Add. MSS 42821, f. 168).
15. General order no. 522, 31 Aug. 1835 (PRO, WO 43/649, ff. 326–61).
16. Military map of Ireland 1822 (NLI, Miscellaneous maps, MS 16B6/31).
17. Blakeney to Somerset, 15 Sept. 1838 (NLI, Kilmainham papers, MS 1237, p. 201).
18. Strathnairn to Wodehouse, 14 Sept. 1865 (BL, Strathnairn papers, Add. MSS 42821, f. 39).
19. Arbuthnot to Blakeney, 18 Aug. 1836 (NLI, Kilmainham papers, MS 1051, p. 75); Tully to Blakeney, 3 June 1840 (ibid., p. 506).
20. Vivian to Taylor, 20 Jan. 1833 (NAM, Vivian papers, MS 7709/6/11, f. 125). Cf. Strathnairn to Abercorn, 27 Mar. 1867 (BL, Strathnairn papers, Add. MSS 42823, f. 170).
21. Gosset to Littleton, 22 Apr. 1834 (Staffordshire Record Office, Hatherton papers, D. 260/M/01/11, f. 83).
22. Strathnairn to Grant, 24 Mar. 1867 (BL, Strathnairn papers, Add. MSS 42823, f. 166).
23. Anglesey to Stanley, 19 Feb. 1831 (PRONI, Anglesey papers, D. 619/31T, f. 7).
24. Bingham to Anglesey, 25 July 1832 (PRONI, D. 619/32A/6/303).
25. Vivian to Taylor, 20 Jan. 1833 (NAM, Vivian papers, MS 7709/6/11, f. 120).
26. Memo, 4 Apr. 1867 (NLI, Kilmainham papers, MS 1059, p. 371).
27. Gower to Byng, 31 Oct. 1829 (NAI, Gower letter books, MS 737, p. 177).
28. Byng to Anglesey, 22 Nov. 1830 (PRONI, Anglesey papers, D. 619/32F, f. 6).
29. Circular memo, 6 Apr. 1882 (NLI, Kilmainham papers, MS 1073, p. 270).
30. Wedderburn to Macintosh, 29 June 1826 (PRO, WO 80/6, f. 56).
31. Burke to Smyth, 4 Jan. 1870 (NLI, Kilmainham papers, MS 1063, p. 237).
32. General order, 11 July 1831 (NAM, Vivian papers, MS 7709/6/10, p. 1).
33. See, for example [Calladine], *Diary*; and Journal of James Bailie, King's Royal Rifles, 1844 (PRONI, D. 3524/1/1).
34. *Report of the Select Committee on the Employment of the Military in Cases of Disturbances*, HC 1908 (236), vii, 395.
35. Journal of a visit to Ireland, 6 Sept. 1833 (University College London, Ogden papers, MS 84).
36. A number of army officers were themselves landowners in Ireland. Strathnairn's military secretary, Colonel Smyth, for example, married an Irish heiress.
37. Gough to Sorrell, 10 Nov. 1822 (NAI, State of the country papers, 2347/31).
38. Smyth to Burke, 1 Mar. 1870 (NLI, Kilmainham papers, MS 1063, p. 317).
39. Gosset to Stanley, 7 Jan. 1833 (NAI, Registered papers, 1833/1087).
40. Strathnairn to Chelmsford, 1 Nov. 1868 (BL, Strathnairn papers, Add. MSS 42825, f. 82).
41. Evidence of Lord Strathnairn, *Report from the select committee on parliamentary and municipal elections*, HC 1869 (352), viii, q. 111757–8.
42. Smyth to Larcom, 25 Nov. 1869 (NLI, Kilmainham papers, MS 1063, p. 177).
43. Wedderburn to Doyle, 1 Nov. 1825 (PRO, WO 80/6, f. 25).
44. Miller to Lamb, 14 Dec. 1827 (PRO, HO 100/220, f. 128). Murray had vetoed a similar suggestion the previous year (Murray to Goulburn, 9 Nov. 1826 (PRO, WO 80/6, f. 95)).
45. Précis of information relating to the disturbed state of County Limerick and its neighbourhood from 13 Oct. to 20 Dec. 1821 (PRO, HO 100/200, f. 14); Warburton to Gosset, 31 Mar. 1831 (ibid., 100/237, f. 371).
46. Anglesey to Arbuthnot, 26 May 1831 (PRONI, Anglesey papers, D. 619/32G, f. 77); Vivian to Arbuthnot, 26 Aug. 1831 (NAM, Vivian papers, MS 7709/6/10, f. 31).

47. [Arnold-Foster], *Journal*, p. 344 (6 Jan. 1882). A later entry in the diary suggests relations between another of the special resident magistrates, Henry Blake, and the military were not so cordial (ibid., p. 452 (17 Apr. 1882)).
48. Lloyd, *Ireland under the Land League*, p. 236.
49. Ross of Bladensburg's memo, 11 Dec. 1882, quoted in Hawkins, 'An army on police work', p. 97.
50. Vivian to Somerset, 12 Jan. 1832 (NAM, Vivian papers, MS 7709/6/10, f. 144); Rose to Bessborough, 28 Oct. 1865 (BL, Strathnairn papers, Add. MSS 42821, f. 108).
51. Anglesey to Grey, 6 July 1832 (PRONI, Anglesey papers, D. 619/28C, f. 258).
52. Blakeney to Somerset, 5 Dec. 1832 (NLI, Kilmainham papers, MS 1236, p. 451).
53. Vivian to Anglesey, 9 July 1832 (NAM, Vivian papers, MS 7709/6/10, f. 181).
54. Vivian to Taylor, 20 Jan. 1833 (NAM, Vivian papers, MS 7709/6/11, f. 119).
55. Vivian to Arbuthnot, 16 Sept. 1834 (NAM, Vivian papers, MS 7709/6/12, f. 203).
56. Blakeney to Drummond, 8 Jan. 1836, and General order, 23 Jan. 1836 (NLI, Kilmainham papers, MS 1051, p. 12).
57. *General Orders for the Guidance of Troops in Affording Aid to the Civil Power and to the Revenue Department in Ireland*, 4 Apr. 1836 (NAI, Official papers, unregistered miscellaneous papers, 1836/354).
58. Greaves to Redington, 22 Jan. 1849 (NLI, Kilmainham papers, MS 1055, p. 102).
59. McGregor to Redington, 25 Jan. 1849 (NLI, Kilmainham papers, MS 1055, p. 102).
60. Steele to Forster, 10 Jan. 1882 (NLI, Kilmainham papers, MS 1073, p. 165).
61. Maclean to Burke, 8 Feb. 1882 (ibid., p. 190).
62. Circular memo, 6 Apr. 1882 (ibid., p. 270).
63. Ross of Bladensburg's memo, 11 Dec. 1882, quoted in Hawkins, 'An army on police work', p. 88.
64. Turner, *Sixty Years of a Soldier's Life*, p. 230.
65. Vivian to Arbuthnot, 16 Sept. 1834 (NAM, Vivian papers, MS 7709/6/12, f. 205).
66. Murray to Thornton, 19 Mar. 1827 (PRO, WO 80/6, f. 118).
67. *Report from the select committee on parliamentary and municipal elections*, HC 1869 (352), viii, q. 7699 (McMurdo), qq 11753 & 11758 (Strathnairn).
68. Strathnairn to de Vesci, 4 Nov. 1868 (BL, Strathnairn papers, Add. MSS 42828, f. 17).
69. [Arnold-Foster], *Journal*, p. 34 (9 Dec. 1880).
70. Ibid., p. 161 (30 May 1881).
71. Rose to Forster, 6 July 1865 (BL, Strathnairn papers, Add. MSS 42819, f. 68).
72. Hook, *Sir David Baird*, p. 359.
73. Peel to Wellesley, 16 Aug. 1822 (BL, Peel papers, Add. MSS 40324, f. 72).
74. Anton, *Retrospect of a Military Life*, p. 278.
75. Ebrington to Russell, 26 June 1839 (PRO, Russell papers, PRO 30/20/3C, f. 357).
76. Smyth to Larcom, 10 Feb. 1867 (NLI, Kilmainham papers, MS 1059, p. 184).
77. Smyth to Larcom, 30 May, 1 June 1867 (NLI, Kilmainham papers, MS 1060, pp. 114 & 119).
78. Collingwood to Smyth, 16 May 1881 (NLI, Kilmainham papers, MS 1072, p. 255).

17 Militarism in Ireland, 1900–1922

1. The term 'militarism' is here used in the first two senses recognised by the *OED*: 'the spirit and tendencies characteristic of the professional soldier; the prevalence of military sentiments or ideals among a people'.
2. [Ross-Lewin], *Poems*, pp. 30–1.

3. John Redmond's introduction to MacDonagh, *The Irish at the Front*, pp. 2–3.
4. McCracken, *The Irish Pro-Boers*, pp. 123–4; Lynch, *Ireland: Vital Hour*, p. 71.
5. McCracken, *The Irish Pro-Boers*, p. 146.
6. NAI, RIC, Crime Special Branch [CSB], Carton 16 (21831S).
7. Census of England and Wales, *General Report*, p. 304, HC 1904 [Cd 2174], cviii. Proportions refer only to those whose birthplace was specified, and in the United Kingdom. Among those serving *abroad* in the navy and marines, natives of Ireland comprised only 8.2 and 2.1 per cent respectively.
8. This complication has been ignored in two major studies of the nationality of recruits: see Hanham, 'Religion and nationality'; Karsten, 'Irish soldiers'.
9. Ireland contained 10.7 per cent of the population of the British Isles in 1901 and 9.7 per cent in 1911.
10. The number of recruits raised in each regimental area in 1898, 1902, and 1909–13, was compared with the number of unmarried men aged 15–19, in corresponding counties in 1901 or 1911: *General Annual Reports of the British Army* [GAR], in House of Commons papers.
11. Spiers, 'The regular army in 1914', p. 44.
12. This analysis is based on annual occupational returns for soldiers (aged 17 or more) accepted for the regular army after medical examination, in *GAR*.
13. In 1911, Catholics comprised 68.8 per cent of army pensioners, 70.3 per cent of navy pensioners, and 73.9 per cent of the Irish population. Other returns (in the NAI), show that on 1 Oct. 1913, Catholics comprised 68.3 per cent of Irishmen in both the regular army and Special Reserve; while 68.1 per cent of ordinary reservists mobilised in Aug. 1914 were Catholics.
14. In 1901, Irishmen constituted 14.4 per cent of regular army officers whose birthplaces were recorded as in Britain or Ireland. The Protestant population of Ireland represented only 2.8 per cent of the population of the United Kingdom in 1901.
15. Catholic percentages were 13.9 for army officers, 27.2 for other ranks, 22.5 for militiamen and yeomanry, 23.1 for naval officers, 29.8 for ratings, and 6.4 for marines.
16. Muenger, *British Military Dilemma*, pp. 146–7.
17. Dooney, 'Trinity College and the war'.
18. Springhall, *Youth, Empire and Society*; [Williams], *Dublin Charities*, pp. 247–8.
19. Na Fianna Éireann, *Fianna Handbook* (Dublin, 1914), pp. 23–4; Springhall, *Youth, Empire and Society*, pp. 130–3; Girl Guides, 'Records of active companies and packs, brought up to date (October 1929), registered at Ulster headquarters' (PRONI, D. 3875/5/1).
20. Orr, *Road to the Somme*, p. 31.
21. Peak membership probably exceeded the 85,000 reported by the police in May 1914. In 1911, Ulster contained 348,000 non-Catholic males aged 9 or more, of whom about 250,000 would have fallen within the prescribed age-band for Ulster Volunteers (17–65).
22. Stewart, *The Ulster Crisis*, pp. 244–9. The imported weapons comprised at least half of all rifles and carbines in the force by July 1914.
23. Nevin, 'The Irish Citizen Army', p. 120.
24. Levenson, *James Connolly*, p. 24. For a conflicting account, see Greaves, *James Connolly*, pp. 20–5.
25. White, *Misfit*, p. 98. White's father, Field Marshal Sir George White, had led the defence of Ladysmith.

26. Sean MacEoin, 'The lone patriot', in *Easter Commemoration Digest*, viii (1966), pp. 189–90; Snoddy, 'The midland volunteer force'. Others have dismissed this force as a journalist's fabrication: Martin, 'MacNeill and the foundation of the Irish Volunteers', pp. 123–9.

27. Martin, *Irish Volunteers*, p. 61; Pearse, *Political Writings and Speeches*, pp. 98–9.

28. Martin, *Irish Volunteers*, pp. 99–100.

29. Maurice Moore, 'History of the Irish Volunteers' (NLI, ILB 94109 (newspaper cutting, 8 Jan. 1938)); Mac Giolla Choille, *Intelligence Notes*, p. 37.

30. This figure includes the 58,000 Irish-born servicemen who were mobilised in Aug. 1914, not all of whom had joined the services in Ireland itself. My estimates are derived from a wide variety of official police and military returns in the PRO and the NAI.

31. These vital qualifications are seldom made, giving a misleading impression of Ireland's participation. See Harris, *Irish Regiments in the First World War*, p. 32; Duggan, *History of the Irish Army*, p. 328.

32. The ratio of enlistments in Ireland to the number of men with occupations *other than agriculture* (in 1911), was 6.3 per cent in 1914 and 6.7 per cent in 1915, compared with 10.3 per cent and 11.1 per cent for the entire United Kingdom. The same index is used below, in comparisons of enlistment ratios according to region and religion.

33. See also Callan, 'Recruiting for the British army'; 'Voluntary recruiting'; and Staunton's outstanding, 'The Royal Munster Fusiliers in the Great War', esp. ch. 3.

34. These statistics refer solely to army recruitment reported in Ireland, excluding officers.

35. Denominations were not tabulated by the police for enlistments after mid-Jan. 1918.

36. Analysis of the addresses of dead Royal Munster Fusiliers shows that almost three-quarters of those from Clare, Cork, Kerry and Limerick had been townsmen, compared with only one-quarter of the regional population: Staunton, 'Royal Munster Fusiliers', pp. 12–13.

37. By Apr. 1916, membership of the union had shrunk to 5,000. Union officials stated that the number of members who had joined the army was 2,700 by May 1915, and 5,000 by Mar. 1917 (an exaggeration designed to elicit sympathy from Arthur Henderson). See [O'Shannon], *Fifty Years of Liberty Hall*, p. 70; CSB, Précis for Cork East Riding, May 1915 (PRO, CO 904/97); Irish Trades Union Congress, *Report of the Twenty-Third Annual Meeting* (Londonderry, 1917), p. 29.

38. This analysis is based upon 'Z8' returns from a sample of Irish employers for August–October 1914, tabulated in *Report of the Board of Trade on the State of Employment in the United Kingdom in October, 1914*, in HC 1914–16 [Cd 7703], xxi, 25.

39. Recorded recruitment to the regular army in Ireland in the 50 years between 1864 and 1913 was barely 150,000, little more than the number raised in the 51 months of war.

40. Gardiner S. Mitchell's *'Three Cheers for the Derrys!'*, makes moving use of oral testimony, following the example of Orr, *Road to the Somme*.

41. *Belfast News-Letter*, 15 Dec. 1914 (NLI, chief secretary's Office [CSO], Newspaper Cuttings, vol. xlvii); *Church of Ireland Gazette*, lviii (20 Oct. 1916), p. 747.

42. Hanna, *The Pals of Suvla Bay*. This analysis is based on Hanna's brief biographies of 316 'Pals'.

43. The charge of the London Irish at Loos (Sept. 1915) was celebrated for the football which was kicked from man to man before scoring a 'goal' in the first line of German trenches: MacDonagh, *The Irish at the Front*, ch. 10.

44. Among these were Thomas Kettle (a former MP) and John Redmond's brother William, both of whom were killed in action.

45. Cooper, *The Tenth (Irish) Division*; Hanna, *The Pals of Suvla Bay*.

———

46. Mitchell, *'Three Cheers for the Derrys!'*, p. 111 (from *Londonderry Sentinel*, 15 July 1916).

47. Denman, *Ireland's Unknown Soldiers*, pp. 183–5. These 44 days of combat accounted for 57 per cent of the division's wartime casualties.

48. Sullivan, *Old Ireland*, p. 174; Macardle, *The Irish Republic*, p. 261; Harris, *Irish Regiments in the First World War*, p. 31; Duggan, *History of the Irish Army*, p. 328; Johnstone, *Orange, Green and Khaki*, p. 428.

49. Denman, *Ireland's Unknown Soldiers*, p. 185, evidently using data for Irish battalions in the series *Soldiers Died in the Great War* (80 parts, London, 1921).

50. Saorstát Éireann, Census of Population 1926, vol. x, *General Report* (Dublin, 1934), p. 12. This figure refers to soldiers (except officers) from all 32 counties of Ireland, and is restricted to deaths on active service outside the British Isles (1914–18). The source of the conventional estimate, *Ireland's Memorial Records, 1914–1918* (8 vols., Dublin, 1923), provides birthplace and place of enlistment for most victims. Sample analysis suggests that only about 25,000 of those recorded were both born and enlisted in Ireland.

51. Friend to Kitchener, 16 Nov. 1914 (PRO, PRO 30/57/60, WK 12). Friend had replaced Paget as general-officer-commanding in Ireland just after mobilisation.

52. Police returns for Apr. 1916 referred to 15,000 opponents of Redmond, including 4,000 'National Volunteers' following MacNeill (Mac Giolla Choille, *Intelligence Notes*, p. 176).

53. Pearse, *Political Writings and Speeches*, p. 216.

54. Dudley Edwards, *James Connolly*, p. 133; 'Notes on the front', *Workers' Republic*, 1: 27 (27 Nov. 1915); Fox, *Irish Citizen Army*, p. 128.

55. Brennan, *The War in Clare*, p. 14. A recently published version of Plunkett's 'plan' for a provincial rising suggests that Brennan should have been keeping people out (Duggan, '1916').

56. Duggan, *History of the Irish Army*, pp. 11-12. McNeill had cancelled mobilisation after news of Casement's capture, so further splitting the Volunteers and reducing participation.

57. Fitzpatrick, 'De Valera in 1917', p. 104.

58. The National Volunteers split during 1917 over whether to drill illegally, one faction declining to do so but maintaining its existence 'as the nucleus of a future National Citizen force' (report of conventions in PRO, CO 904/23/5).

59. Police returns indicate that 1,125 men enlisted in the calendar month ending 15 May 1916, compared with 1,736 in the previous month and 1,568 in the following month. Corresponding figures for the Dublin district were 197, 422 and 499.

60. Cabinet minutes for 10 June 1918 (PRO, CAB 23/6/429(18)).

61. Blythe's unsigned article appeared in *An tÓglach*, 1:4 (14 Oct. 1918).

62. According to the War Office's *Statistics of the Military Effort of the British Empire during the Great War, 1914–1920* (London, 1922), p. 708, 4,335 officers and 82,699 other ranks were demobilised in Ireland between the armistice and 12 May 1920. After adjustment for cases in which the 'dispersal' area was unspecified, we may estimate Irish dispersal as 5,700 officers and 92,900 men. Since Ireland's contribution to the wartime army was about 200,000, of whom 25,000 died, there remains a residue of 75,000 who were either re-enlisted, demobilised elsewhere, or invalided out of the army before the armistice. For a wild over-estimate of demobilisation, see Harris, *The Irish Regiments in the First World War*, p. 30.

63. *Parliamentary Debates*, 5th ser., cxxi (10 Nov. 1919), col. 77.

64. This analysis is based on the number of ex-servicemen registered in each Irish exchange

during the week ending 14 Jan. 1921 (NAI, CSO, RP 1921/2195). Figures have been aggregated by county, and divided by the number of reservists and recruits returned by the police for the period Aug. 1914 to Oct. 1916. By this yardstick, Cork ranked highest among the 32 counties with a ratio of 54 per cent, Carlow ranking lowest with 6 per cent. The provincial figures for Munster, Connacht, Leinster, and Ulster were 39, 23, 17, and 12 per cent respectively.

65. In Oct. 1921, Irishmen accounted for 8.2 per cent of all soldiers born in the United Kingdom. Tables in *GAR* show that 9.1 per cent of recruits over the two preceding years had been enlisted in Ireland. See also Jeffery, 'The post-war army'.

66. See Dallas & Gill, *The Unknown Army*, ch. 5; Babington, *The Devil to Pay*, ch. 5; cf. Pollock, *Mutiny for the Cause*, pp. 94–6.

67. Jeffery, *British Army and the Crisis of Empire*, pp. 268–9.

68. RIC Registers in PRO, HO 184/36; Fitzpatrick, *Politics and Irish Life*, pp. 22, 44.

69. Monthly Confidential Report by inspector-general, RIC, July 1919 (PRO, CO 904/109); Townshend, *Political Violence in Ireland*, p. 341.

70. Farrell, *Arming the Protestants*, chs 1, 2; Buckland, *Irish Unionism*, pp. 445–50; Macready, *Annals of an Active Life*, ii, 487–90; *Constabulary Gazette* (4 Dec. 1920), p. 166.

71. Leonard, 'Getting them at last'.

72. Barry, *Guerrilla Days*, p. 8.

73. *Saturday Record* (Ennis), 29 Apr. 1916; conversation with author (2 Feb. 1974). Paddy Mulcahy eventually followed Richard's example by becoming chief of staff of the National Army (1955–9).

74. Byrne, 'An Irish soldier remembered', pp. 31–3.

75. Townshend, 'The Irish Republican Army'. For a more positive account, see Valiulis, *Portrait of a Revolutionary*, p. 53.

76. Ibid., p. 257. Another 51 guns and 313 rifles arrived over the following five months, too late to be used against their intended targets.

77. O'Donoghue, *No Other Law*, ch. 5.

78. Townshend, *The British Campaign in Ireland*, pp. 100–1, 120.

79. These statistics are based on a return in the Ministry of Defence Papers, A/0396 (microfilm copy in NLI). They vary considerably from the police returns, which however relate only to 'Sinn Féin outrages' and exclude killings by the Crown forces and 'anti-Sinn Féin gangs'. Both sources exclude deaths attributed to sectarian conflict in Ulster, which claimed over 80 deaths in 1920 and another 350 by mid-1922.

80. This undated census of munitions also enumerated 61 machine guns, 6,000 revolvers and automatics, and 15,000 shotguns. The rifles were supplied with only 150,000 rounds, less than one-tenth of the quantity smuggled in by the Ulster Volunteers in Apr. 1914 (see UCDA, Mulcahy papers, P7/A/15).

81. Although up to 40,000 troops were stationed in Ireland during early 1921, fewer than 300 in each of the 51 battalions were available for 'offensive action', according to the official 'Record of the Rebellion in Ireland in 1920–21', vol. i, p. 33 (copy in IWM, Jeudwine papers). Many of the 17,000 policemen (including the residue of the 'old RIC', special constables and temporary cadets, but excluding the Ulster Special Constabulary) would also have been unavailable for combat.

18 The army in independent Ireland

1. The only sustained account of the Irish army's origins and development is Duggan, *History of the Irish Army*.

2. O'Donoghue, *No Other Law*, pp. 195, 231 (at pp. 208–46 he deals with the background to the IRA split in Apr. 1922); Hopkinson, *Green Against Green*, pp. 58–69, 72–6.
3. Hopkinson, *Green Against Green*, pp. 221–7.
4. 'Memo on Demobilisation and Reorganisation of the Army', July 1923 (MA); report by General Sean McMahon, 14 Aug. 1923 (NAI, DT, S.587); O'Higgins to W. T. Cosgrave (president of the executive council), 5 Apr. 1923 (NAI, DT, S.582).
5. Chief of staff to minister for defence, 24 Nov. 1923 (NAI, DT, S.3442A); O'Halpin, 'Army, politics and society', pp. 161–8.
6. Office of director of intelligence to command intelligence officer, Athlone, 1 Oct. 1923 (MA, in file on 'Demobilization of National Forces').
7. Quoted in de Vere White, *O'Higgins*, p. 160; interview with Col. Dan Bryan, Jan. 1983. As an intelligence officer Col. Bryan was involved in the interception in Crown Alley telephone exchange of the mutineers' telephone conversation, and informed his superior, Col. Costello, that the plotters were meeting in Devlin's. See also Valiulis, *Portrait of a Revolutionary*, pp. 209–22; Lee, *Ireland 1912–85*, pp. 100–4; de Vere White, *O'Higgins*, pp. 155–8.
8. Lee, *Ireland 1912–1985*, pp. 175–6; Brady, *Guardians of the Peace*, pp. 167–9. The date of O'Duffy's resignation is given in NAI, DT, S.6483.
9. 'Articles of agreement for a treaty between Great Britain and Ireland', reproduced in Kohn, *Constitution of the Irish Free State*, pp. 413–18.
10. Department of Defence memo, 22 July 1925 (NAI, DT, S.4541).
11. Memo approved by executive council, 13 Nov. 1925 (ibid.).
12. 'Fundamental factors affecting Irish defence policy', marked 'G2/0057, dated May 1936', with private secretary, minister for defence, to private secretary, minister for finance, 23 Dec. 1937 (UCDA, MacEntee papers, P67/191, pp. 54–5). Col. Dan Bryan maintained that this paper was 'at least 90% my own effort'. Dan Bryan transcripts, p. 2 (in the writer's possession). Col. Bryan took part in the 1927 discussions with the British.
13. TS 'Notes on attached memo', n.d. [1929] (NAI, DT, S.4541).
14. O'Halpin, 'Army, politics and society', p. 168; memo by Capt. S. Rooney, n.d. [1927?] (MA, G2 1920s/1930s records); director of intelligence to chief of staff, 20 Feb. 1936 (copy in UCDA, MacEntee papers, P67/191(3)).
15. 'Army Confidential Report for half year ended 31/3/29' (UCDA, Blythe papers, P24/223); O'Halpin, 'Intelligence and security', p. 64; NAI, DT, S.6091A.
16. 'Memorandum on the necessity for Provision in the Army Estimates for expenditure on Experimental work and Research and on the purchase for training and General Staff purposes of contemporary inventions', 3 Feb. 1926 (MA, G2 1920s/1930s records).
17. It is difficult to be accurate about army numbers. Duggan, *History of the Irish Army*, pp. 155–6, 159, 162, gives a number of different sets of figures but does not attempt a consistent chronological account. Precise figures are given for Oct. 1926 in NAI, DT, S.5170, and for 1928, 1929 and 1930 in the half-yearly 'Army confidential reports' in UCDA, Blythe papers, P24/223 & 224.
18. G-2 report no. 6000, by Lieut. J. C. MacArthur, n.d. [1928], with F. A. Sterling [US consul-general in Dublin] to J. T. Marriner [State Department], 11 May 1928 (USNA, State Department, 841d.20/1).
19. Archer to Brennan, 2 Feb. 1936, with Brennan to minister for defence, 22 Sept. 1936 (UCDA, MacEntee papers, P67/191/(3)): 'Fundamental factors', p. 16 (ibid., P67/191). NAI, DT, S.9183; S.8202 & S.9183 contain papers on censorship and on the defence committee respectively.

20. Brennan to minister for defence, 22 Sept. 1936 (as n. 19 above); Department of Defence memo submitted on 19 Dec. 1936 (NAI, DT, S.9452); Brennan to minister for defence, 21 May 1938 (UCDA, MacEntee papers, P67/193). Defence spending questions are covered in various documents in this collection in P67/191–3 & 195.

21. 'General report on the army for the year 1st April 1940 to 31st March 1941', p. 10 (MA). This annual series is cited hereafter as 'General report', followed by the relevant year.

22. O'Halpin, 'Intelligence and security', p. 66; Dan Bryan transcripts, p. 20.

23. The decision to replace Maj.-Gen. Brennan had been taken before the Magazine Fort raid. In May 1940 he won a libel action against the *Daily Telegraph* for suggesting otherwise. Papers on this are in NAI, DT, S.11607.

24. 'General report', 1940–1, p. 2; Department of Defence memo, 3 June 1940 (NAI, DT, S.11101); 'General report', 1942–3, p. 4; 'General report', 1943–4, p. 3; and 1944–5, p. 10.

25. Interviews and conversations with various former army officers, including Mr Gageby and a one-time intelligence officer who described himself as 'West British' by background. Campbell, 'Sean Tar joins up', in his *Come Here Till I Tell You*, pp. 220–33, gives an hilarious account of his service in the Maritime Inscription.

26. Fisk, *In Time of War*, pp. 265–7; memo by director of naval intelligence for chiefs of staff, 16 Aug. 1941, and minutes of meetings of chiefs of staff committee, 5 Sept. & 28 Nov. 1941 (PRO, CAB 79/14).

27. 'General report', 1942–3, p. 15.

28. Minutes of the defence conference are in NAI, DT, S.11896 & 11896B.

29. Memo by director of naval intelligence, 16 Aug. 1941 (as in n. 26 above).

30. 'General report', 1944–5, p. 44.

31. Undated memo [1949?] (NAI, Department of Foreign Affairs, DFA, A89).

32. Fraser (Commonwealth Relations Office) to Le Tocq (British Embassy, Dublin), 20 July 1953 (PRO, DO 130/122).

33. O'Halpin, 'Anglo-Irish security co-operation', p. 11.

34. *Report of the Commission on Remuneration and Conditions of Service in the Defence Forces* [Gleeson Report] (Dublin, 1990), p. 17.

35. Gleeson Report, p. 23.

36. Interviewed on RTE's *Prime Time*, 8 Nov. 1994; *Report of Public Services Organisation Review Group 1966–1969* [Devlin Report] (Dublin, 1969), p. 247.

37. *Irish Times*, 15 Nov., and *Sunday Tribune*, 20 Nov. 1994.

19 The British army and Ireland since 1922

1. Report of committee appointed to examine Part I of the Report of the Geddes Committee on National Expenditure, Feb. 1922 (PRO, CAB 24/132, C.P. 3692). The general circumstances are discussed in Jeffery, *British Army and the Crisis of Empire*.

2. Sept. 1919–Sept. 1920. Figures drawn from the *General Annual Report of the British Army for year ending 30 Sept. 1920* (1922, Cmd 1610). See also Jeffery, 'The post-war army'.

3. The Royal Irish Regiment, the Connaught Rangers, the Leinster Regiment, the Royal Munster Fusiliers and the Royal Dublin Fusiliers.

4. The five named above together with the Royal Inniskilling Fusiliers, the Royal Ulster Rifles (Royal Irish Rifles until January 1921) and the Royal Irish Fusiliers.

5. Diary of Sir Henry Wilson, 14, 15 July 1921 (IWM, Wilson MSS).

6. Proposals of the British government for an Irish Settlement, 20 July 1921 (PRO, CAB

24/126 C.P. 3149). See also Cabinet minutes, 20 July 1921 (CAB 23/26/60(21)) and diary of H. A. L. Fisher, 20 July 1921 (Bodl., Fisher MS Box 8A).

7. Sir William Davison and Col. Charles Burn, *Hansard* (House of Commons), 14 Dec. 1921, 5 ser., vol. 149, col. 107, 118–19.

8. Maj. G. White (Royal Irish Fusiliers) to Col. W. Spender, 19 Dec. 1921, enclosed in Spender to Sir Henry Wilson, 22 Dec. 1921 (IWM Wilson MSS, HHW 2/63/8).

9. Wilson diary, 4 Jan. 1922; Wilson to Craig and reply, 4 & 7 Jan. 1922 (IWM Wilson MSS, HHW 2/63/9 & 10).

10. Cunliffe, *Royal Irish Fusiliers*, pp. 370–1. Other regimental histories are: Corbally, *Royal Ulster Rifles*; Graves, *Royal Ulster Rifles*; Fox, *Royal Inniskilling Fusiliers*; Verney, *The Micks*. Bredin, *History of the Irish Soldier*, provides a good resumé of military operations.

11. *Faugh-a-Ballagh* (regimental journal of the Royal Irish Fusiliers) 28:132 (Jan. 1933), 38:149 (Jan. 1939); Royal Inniskilling Fusiliers Recruiting Register, 1 Oct. 1926–30 Sept. 1927 (Regimental Museum, Enniskillen, County Fermanagh); Royal Ulster Rifles Recruits Register, 1 Oct. 1923–30 Sept. 1924 (Regimental Museum, Belfast).

12. See papers (Nov. 1923–Mar. 1924) in PRO, WO 32/5309 (copies in PRO, HO 45/18349).

13. Minutes of first meeting of Northern Ireland Defence Committee, 20 Feb. 1929. The only other meetings of this committee were on 6 June 1929 and 23 Jan. 1935 (PRO, HO 45/18349).

14. Spender (permanent secretary, Northern Ireland Ministry of Finance) to C. G. Markbrieter (Home Office), 1 May 1929 (ibid.).

15. Gailey, *et al.*, *The Territorials in Northern Ireland*, p. 77.

16. See Farrell, *Arming the Protestants*.

17. Macready, *Annals of an Active Life*, ii, p. 645.

18. This provision was significant in that the minister of home affairs, Richard Dawson Bates, was widely regarded as unreliably extreme in his political opinions.

19. War Office to GOC, NI, Dec. 1922 (Bonar Law papers, House of Lords Record Office, 114/1/31); ditto, 30 June 1932 (Cambridge University Library, Baldwin papers, vol. 101, fol. 263–4).

20. See Hepburn, 'The Belfast riots of 1935'.

21. *General Annual Report of the British Army, 1938* (1939 Cmd 5950).

22. Memo by adjutant-general, 3 Mar. 1936 (PRO, WO 32/4622).

23. The best sources for Northern Ireland before and during the Second World War are Fisk, *In Time of War*; Bardon, *History of Ulster*; and the rather uncritical official history: Blake, *Northern Ireland in the Second World War*.

24. The 3rd, 4th and 5th battalions of all three Irish infantry of the line regiments continued to exist on paper as part of the more-or-less defunct Militia.

25. Blake, *Northern Ireland in the Second World War*, pp. 178–84.

26. Ireland, *Six Counties*, p. 21.

27. Blake, *Northern Ireland in the Second World War*, pp. 199–200

28. 28,645 men and 4,133 women. *Hansard* (House of Lords), 19 Mar. 1946, 5 ser., vol. 140, col. 241.

29. Dungan, *Distant Drums*, pp. 145–6, 95; Lambkin, *My Time in the War*, p. 7.

30. Stephan, *Spies in Ireland*, pp. 215–20; Fisk, *In Time of War*, p. 453.

31. Fisk, *In Time of War*, p. 80.

32. The British Cabinet discussions, 12–27 May 1941, are in PRO, CAB 65/18, W.M. 51–4.

33. Swift, 'Americans in Ulster', *passim*.

34. Barton, *The Blitz, passim*.

35. Doherty, *Clear the Way!*, provides an excellent account of the brigade.
36. Ibid., p. 7.
37. Brigadier Pat Scott, quoted in ibid., p. 160.
38. See Doherty, *Irish Generals*, and Greacen, *Chink*.
39. Oliver, *Working at Stormont*, p. 67.
40. Fanning, *Independent Ireland*, pp. 124–5.
41. Mitchell & Ó Snodaigh, *Irish Political Documents*, p. 239.
42. Brooke to home secretary, 24 Mar. & 28 July 1947 (PRO WO 32/12380, nos. 1B & 12B).
43. See War Office minutes, Nov. 1947–May 1948; and Gen. Sir James Steele to under sec. of state for war, 2 Mar. 1948 (ibid., nos. 19A–45A & 25B).
44. Minutes of meeting regarding citizens of the Irish Republic in the Regular Forces, 31 May; and War Office notes, 19–31 May 1949 (PRO, WO 32/13259 nos. 6A & 1–5).
45. *Faugh-a-Ballagh*, 43:196 (Autumn 1959).
46. *Irish Times*, 22 July 1989.
47. *Irish News*, 9 Jan. 1986.
48. Note of interview with Home Office officials, 30 Oct. 1946; and letter from GOC, NI, 6 Jan. 1947 (PRO, WO 32/11827, nos. 1B & 17C).
49. Lt.-Gen. Sir R. Denning (GOC, NI) to Lt.-Gen. N. Brownjohn (vice-CIGS), 24 Mar. 1950 (PRO, WO 216/706, no. 1A).
50. Coogan, *The I.R.A.*, ch. 14.
51. Private information.
52. The account of contemporary Northern Ireland is drawn substantially from Arthur & Jeffery, *Northern Ireland since 1968*; Jeffery (ed.), *The Divided Province*; and Jeffery, 'The security forces'.
53. Official statement quoted in Callaghan, *A House Divided*, pp. 43–4.
54. Information on the UDR from Ryder, *The Ulster Defence Regiment*.
55. As also was that of the 'Catholic Ex-Servicemen's Association', which was briefly active in the early 1970s.
56. Mac Stiofáin, *Revolutionary in Ireland*, p. 243.
57. Over the same period 2,225 civilians died as a result of the security situation.
58. *Fortnight*, no. 41, 8 June 1972.
59. Bishop & Mallie, *The Provisional IRA*, p. 378.
60. Murphy, *A Place Apart*, p. 241.
61. Bruce, *The Red Hand*, p. 112.
62. Ibid., p. 114.
63. *Belfast News-Letter*, 22 Mar. 1955; Ministry of Defence (Army) & Central Office of Information Pamphlet APS Code 0769 (Mar. 1976).
64. *Hansard* (House of Commons), 19 Nov. 1969, 5 ser., vol. 791, col. 1340.
65. Ibid., 15 Oct. 1991, 6 ser., vol. 196, col. 137 (Mr Archie Hamilton).
66. The recruiting district for the regiment comprised Counties Tipperary, Waterford, Kilkenny and Wexford.

Bibliography

Admiralty Tidal Stream Atlas: North Coast of Ireland and West Coast of Scotland (Taunton, 1983).

Alcock, Rutherford, *Notes on the Medical History and Statistics of the British Legion in Spain* (London, 1909).

Allendorfer, Frederic von, 'An Irish regiment in Brazil, 1826–1828', *Irish Sword*, 3 (1957–8), pp. 28–31.

Almqvist, Bo, Ó Catháin, Séamus, Ó hÉalaí, Pádraig (eds.), *The Heroic Process: Form, Function and Fantasy in Folk Epic* (Dun Laoghaire, Co. Dublin, 1987).

Andrews, J. H., 'Charles Vallancey and the map of Ireland', *Geographical Journal*, 132 (1966), pp. 48–61.

Annála Connacht. The Annals of Connacht (A.D. 1224–1544), ed. & transl. A. Martin Freeman (Dublin, 1944).

Annala Rioghachta Eireann; Annals of the Kingdom of Ireland by the Four Masters from the Earliest period to the Year 1616, ed. & transl. John O'Donovan (7 vols., Dublin, 1851; reprint, New York, 1966).

The Annals of Inisfallen (MS. Rawlinson B.503), ed. & transl. Seán Mac Airt (Dublin, 1951).

Annals of Ireland by Friar John Clyn, ed. Richard Butler (Dublin, 1849).

The Annals of Loch Cé: a Chronicle of Irish Affairs, 1014–1690, ed. W. M. Hennessey (2 vols., London, 1871; reflex facsimile, Dublin, 1939).

'The Annals of Tigernach', ed. Whitley Stokes, *Revue Celtique*, 16–18 (1895–7).

Annals of Ulster (to A.D. 1131), ed. Seán Mac Airt & Gearóid Mac Niocaill (Dublin, 1983).

Anton, James, *Retrospect of a Military Life* (Edinburgh, 1841).

[Arnold-Foster], *Florence Arnold-Foster's Irish Journal*, ed. T. W. Moody & R. A. J. Hawkins (Oxford, 1988).

Arthur, Paul & Jeffery, Keith, *Northern Ireland since 1968* (Oxford, 1988).

Atkinson, C. T., 'Charles II's regiments in France, 1672–78', *Journal of the Society for Army Historical Research*, 24 (1946), pp. 53–64, 128–36, 161–71.

    The Dorsetshire Regiment (2 vols., Oxford, 1947).

    'The Irish regiments of the line in the British army', *Irish Sword*, 1 (1949–53), pp. 20–3.

    The Royal Hampshire Regiment (3 vols., Glasgow & Aldershot, 1947–55).

Babington, Anthony, *The Devil to Pay, The Mutiny of the Connaught Rangers, India, July 1920* (London, 1991).

Bagenal, P. H. D., *Vicissitudes of an Anglo-Irish Family* (London, 1925).

'Sir Nicholas Bagenal, Knight Marshall', *Journal of the Royal Society of Antiquaries of Ireland*, 6th ser., 5 (1915), pp. 5–26.

Bagshawe, W. H. G., *The Bagshawes of Ford: A Biographical Pedigree* (London, 1886).

Bagwell, Richard, *Ireland under the Stuarts and During the Interregnum* (3 vols., London, 1909–16; reprinted London, 1963).

Ireland under the Tudors (3 vols., London, 1885–90).

Baile Chuind, ed. Gerard Murphy, 'On the dates of two sources used in Thyrnyesen's Heldensage', *Ériu*, 16 (1952), pp. 145–55.

Bain, Joseph (ed.), *The Hamilton Papers: Letters and Papers Illustrating the Political Relations of England and Scotland in the XVIth Century* (2 vols., Edinburgh, 1890–2).

Baker, David J., 'Off the map: charting uncertainty in Renaissance Ireland', in Bradshaw, *Representing Ireland*, pp. 76–92.

Bannatyne, Neil, *History of the XXXth Regiment, 1689–1881* (Liverpool, 1923).

Bannerman, John, *Studies in the History of Dalriada* (Edinburgh, 1974).

Bardon, Jonathan, *A History of Ulster* (Belfast, 1992).

Barrow, Gen. Sir George de S., *The Fire of Life* (London, 1941).

Barry, Tom, *Guerilla Days in Ireland* (Dublin, 1962 edn).

Bartlett, Robert, *Gerald of Wales, 1146–1223* (Oxford, 1982).

Bartlett, Thomas, 'Army and society in eighteenth-century Ireland', in W. A. Maguire (ed.), *Kings in Conflict: the Revolutionary War in Ireland and its Aftermath, 1689–1750* (Belfast, 1990), pp. 173–82.

'The augmentation of the army in Ireland in 1769', *English Historical Review*, 96 (1981), pp. 540–59.

'Defenders and Defenderism in 1795', *Irish Historical Studies*, 24 (1984–5), pp. 373–94.

'An end to moral economy: the Irish Militia disturbances of 1793', *Past and Present*, 99 (May 1983), pp. 41–64.

The Fall and Rise of the Irish Nation: the Catholic Question, 1690–1830 (Dublin, 1992).

'General Humbert takes his leave', *Cathair na Mart: Journal of the Westport Historical Society*, 11 (1991), pp. 98–104.

'Indiscipline and disaffection in the armed forces in Ireland in the 1790s', in Corish, *Radicals, Rebels and Establishments*, pp. 115–34.

Macartney in Ireland, 1768–72: a Calendar of the Chief Secretaryship Papers of Sir George Macartney (Belfast, 1978).

'"Masters of the Mountains": The insurgent careers of Joseph Holt and Michael Dwyer, County Wicklow, 1798–1803', in K. Hannigan (ed.), *Wicklow County History* (Dublin 1994), pp. 379–410.

'Militarisation and politicisation in Ireland, 1780–1820', in L. M. Cullen and Louis Bergeron (eds.), *Culture et pratiques politiques en France et en Irlande, xvi–xviii siècle* (Paris, 1990), pp. 125–36.

'Reflections on indiscipline and disaffection in the French and Irish armies in the revolutionary period', in David Dickson and Hugh Gough (eds.), *Ireland and the French Revolution* (Dublin, 1991), pp. 179–201.

'Religious rivalries in France and Ireland in the age of the French revolution', *Eighteenth-Century Ireland*, 6 (1991), pp. 57–76.

'The Townshend viceroyalty, 1767–72', in Thomas Bartlett & David Hayton (eds.), *Penal Era and Golden Age* (Belfast, 1979), pp. 88–112.

'"A weapon of war yet untried": Irish Catholics and the armed forces of the crown', in Fraser & Jeffery, *Men, Women and War*, pp. 66–85.

Barton, Brian, *The Blitz: Belfast in the War Years* (Belfast, 1989).

Béaslaí, Piaras, *Michael Collins and the Making of a New Ireland* (2 vols., London, 1926).

Beckett, Ian F. W. (ed.), *The Army and the Curragh Incident* (London, 1986).

Beckett, Ian F. W., & Simpson, Keith (eds.), *A Nation in Arms* (Manchester, 1985; rev. edn, London, 1990).

Beckett, J. C., 'The Irish armed forces 1660–1685', in John Bossy & Peter Jupp (eds.), *Essays Presented to Michael Roberts* (Belfast, 1976), pp. 41–53.

Bede, *Historia Ecclesiastica [Bede's Ecclesiastical History]*, ed. Bertram Colgrave & R. A. B. Mynors (2 vols., Oxford, 1969).

Beerman, Eric, 'Alexander O'Reilly, an Irish soldier in the service of Spain', *Irish Sword*, 15 (1982–3), pp. 101–14.

Bennett, M., 'Wace and warfare', in *Anglo-Norman Studies xi: Proceedings of the Battle Conference* 1988, ed. R. A. Brown (Woodbridge, 1989), pp. 37–57.

Beresford, Marcus de la Poer, 'François Thurot and the French attack at Carrickfergus, 1759–60', *Irish Sword*, 10 (1971–2), pp. 255–74.

   'Ireland in French strategy 1691–1798' (M.Litt. thesis, University of Dublin, 1975).

   'Ireland in French strategy during the American War of Independence, 1776–83', *Irish Sword*, 12 (1975–6), pp. 285–97; 13 (1977–9), pp. 20–9.

Berleth, Richard, *The Twilight Lords* (London, 1978).

Bernard, Nicholas, *The Whole Proceedings of the Siege of Drogheda* . . . (London, 1642).

Bethu Phátraic, ed. Kathleen Mulchrone (Dublin, 1939).

Binchy, D. A. (ed.), 'A text on the forms of distraint', *Celtica*, 10 (1973), pp. 72–86.

Bishop, Patrick, & Mallie, Eamonn, *The Provisional IRA* (pbk edn, London, 1988).

Black, Eileen, 'John Tennent, 1777–1813, United Irishman and Chevalier de la Legion d'Honneur', *Irish Sword*, 13 (1977–9), pp. 157–9.

Black, Jeremy, *A Military Revolution? Military Change and European Society, 1550–1800* (London, 1991).

Blackstock, Alan, 'The origin and development of the Irish Yeomanry, 1796–c. 1807' (Ph.D. thesis, Queen's University, Belfast, 1993).

Blake, John W., *Northern Ireland in the Second World War* (Belfast, 1956).

Boulger, D. C., *The Battle of the Boyne* (London, 1911).

Bradshaw, Brendan, Hadfield, Andrew & Maley, Willy (eds.), *Representing Ireland: Literature and the Origins of Conflict, 1534–1660* (Cambridge, 1993).

Bradshaw, John (ed.), *Letters of Philip Dormer Stanhope, Earl of Chesterfield* (3 vols., London, 1892).

Brady, Ciaran, *The Chief Governors: the Rise and Fall of Reform Government in Tudor Ireland, 1536–1588* (Cambridge, 1994).

   'Conservative subversives: the community of the Pale and the Dublin administration, 1556–86', in Corish, *Radicals, Rebels and Establishments*, pp. 11–32.

   'The killing of Shane O'Neill: some new evidence', *Irish Sword*, 15 (1982), pp. 116–23.

   'The O'Reillys of East Bréifne and the problem of surrender and regrant', *Bréifne: Journal of Cumann Seanchais Bréifne*, 6 (1985), pp. 233–62, esp. pp. 258–61.

   'Ulster and the failure of Tudor reform', in Brady, Ciaran, O'Dowd, Mary & Walker, B. M. (eds.), *Ulster: an Illustrated History* (London, 1989), pp. 77–103.

Brady, Conor, *Guardians of the Peace* (Dublin, 1974).

Brady, John, *Catholics and Catholicism in the Seventeenth-century Press* (Maynooth, 1965).

Bredin, A. E. C., *A History of the Irish Soldier* (Belfast, 1987).

Brennan, Michael, *The War in Clare, 1911–1921* (Dublin, 1980).

Brewer, J. W., & Bullen, William (eds.), *Calendar of the Carew Manuscripts Preserved in the Archiepiscopal Library at Lambeth* (6 vols., London, 1867–73).

Brooks, N. P., 'Arms, status and warfare in late-Saxon England', in D. Hill (ed.), *Ethelred the Unready* (BAR British series, 59 (Oxford), 1978), pp. 81–103.

Bruce, Steve, *The Red Hand: Protestant Paramilitaries in Northern Ireland* (Oxford, 1992).

Buckland, Patrick (ed.), *Irish Unionism, 1885–1923: a Documentary History* (Belfast, 1973).

Buckley, James, 'A viceregal progress through the south-west of Ireland in 1567', *Journal of the Waterford and South-East of Ireland Archaeological Society*, 12 (1909), pp. 61–76, 132–46, 174–84.

Buckley, V. M., & Sweetman, P. D., *Archaeological Survey of County Louth/Suirbhé Seandálaíochta Chontae Lú* (Dublin, 1991).

Bullion, John L., 'Securing the peace: Lord Bute, the plan for the army and the origins of the American "Revolution"', in Karl W. Schweizer (ed.), *Lord Bute: Essays in Reinterpretation* (Leicester, 1988), pp. 17–39.

[Burke], *Correspondence of the Rt Hon. Edmund Burke . . .* [1744–97], ed. Charles William, Earl Fitzwilliam & Sir Richard Bourke (4 vols., London, 1844).

Burney, Charles, *An Eighteenth-century Tour in France and Italy*, ed. Percy Scholes (London, 1959).

Burns, R. E., 'Ireland and British military preparations for war in 1775', *Ciathara*, 2 (1963), pp. 42–61.

Butler, Sir William, *An Autobiography* (London, 1911).

Butler, Lt.-Col. W. F., *Far Out: Rovings Retold* (London, 1880).

Byrne, F. J., *Irish Kings and High-kings* (London, 1973).

Byrne, Liam, 'An Irish soldier remembered', *An Cosantóir*, 51: 4 (Apr. 1991), pp. 31–3.

Cadell, Sir Patrick, 'Irish soldiers in India', *Irish Sword*, 1 (1949–53), pp. 75–9.

Cáin Adamnáin, ed. Kuno Meyer, Anecdota Oxoniensia, 12 (Oxford, 1905).

Caithréim Cellachain Caisil, ed. Alexander Bugge (Christiania [Oslo], 1905).

Calendar of Ancient Records of Dublin, ed. J. T. Gilbert [etc.] (18 vols., Dublin, 1889–1922).

Calendar of the Carew Manuscripts Preserved in the Archiepiscopal Library at Lambeth (6 vols., London, 1867–73).

Calendar of Documents Relating to Scotland . . . in the Public Record Office, ed. Joseph Bain (4 vols., London, 1881–8).

'Calendar to fiants of King Edward VI', in *Report of the Deputy Keeper of the Public Records in Ireland*, 8 (Dublin, 1876), app. ix, pp. 26–230.

'Calendar to fiants of Queen Elizabeth', in *Report of the Deputy Keeper of the Public Records in Ireland*, 11 (Dublin, 1879), app, iii, pp. 31–242; 12 (1880), app. v, pp. 17–194; 13 (1881), app. iv, pp. 16–220; 15 (1883), app. i, pp. 15–174; 17 (1885), app. iv, pp. 29–276; 18 (1886), app. vi, pp. 27–150; 21 (1889), app. iii, pp. 29–254; 22 (1890), app. vi, pp. 255–862.

'Calendar of fiants of Henry VIII', in *Report of the Deputy Keeper of the Public Records in Ireland*, 7 (Dublin, 1875), app. x, pp. 27–110; 18 (1886), app. vi, pp. 147–8.

Calendar of the Gormanston Register, ed. James Mills & M. J. McEnery (Dublin, 1916).

Calendar of the Justiciary Rolls . . . of Ireland: Edward I [1295–1307], ed. James Mills (2 vols., Dublin, 1905–14).

Calendar of the Justiciary Rolls . . . of Ireland: I to VIII Years of Edward II [1308–14], ed. Herbert Wood & A. E. Langman; revised by M. C. Griffith (Dublin, [1956]).

Calendar of Letters, Despatches, and State Papers Relating to the Negotiations between England and Spain, Preserved in the Archives at Simancas and Elsewhere, 1458–1509 [etc.] (London, 1862–).

Calendar of Ormond Deeds . . . [1172–1603], ed. Edmund Curtis (6 vols., Dublin, 1932–43).

Calendar of the Patent Rolls . . . 1232–[1509] (53 vols., London, 1891–1971).

Calendar of State Papers, Domestic Series, 1547–80 [etc.] (London, 1856–).

Calendar of the State Papers relating to Ireland, 1509–[1603] (11 vols., London, 1860–1912).

[Calladine], *The Diary of Colour-Sergeant George Calladine, 19th Foot, 1793–1837*, ed. M. L. Ferrar (London, 1922).

Callaghan, James, *A House Divided: the Dilemma of Northern Ireland* (London, 1973).

Callan, Patrick, 'Recruiting for the British army in Ireland during the First World War', *Irish Sword*, 17 (1987–90), pp. 42–56.

'Voluntary recruiting for the British army in Ireland during the First World War' (Ph.D. thesis, University College, Dublin, 1984).

Callwell, Sir C. E. (ed.), *The Memoirs of Sir Hugh McCalmont* (London, 1924).

Campbell, Colm, *Emergency Law in Ireland, 1918–1925* (Oxford, 1994).

Campbell Patrick, *Come Here Till I Tell You* (London, 1960).

Cannon, John (ed.), *The Letters of Junius* (Oxford, 1978).

Canny, Nicholas, 'Edmund Spenser and the development of an Anglo-Irish identity', in *The Yearbook of English Studies*, 13 (1983), pp. 1–19.

From Reformation to Restoration, Ireland 1534–1600 (Dublin, 1987).

'Hugh O'Neill, Earl of Tyrone and the changing face of Gaelic Ulster', *Studia Hibernica*, 10 (1970), pp. 7–35.

'What really happened in 1641', in Ohlmeyer, *Independence to Occupation*.

Cardozo, Nancy, *Maude Gonne: Lucky Eyes and a High Heart* (London, 1979).

Carlton, Charles, *Going to the Wars: the Experience of the British Civil Wars 1638–51* (London, 1992).

Carney, James, 'Literature in Irish, 1168–1534', in *New History of Ireland*, ii, *Medieval Ireland 1169–1534* (Oxford, 1987), pp. 688–707.

Carpenter, Dorothy M., 'The pilgrim from Catalonia/Aragon: Ramon de Perellós, 1397', in Michael Haren & Yolande de Pontfarcy (eds.), *The Medieval Pilgrimage to St Patrick's Purgatory: Lough Derg and the European Tradition* (Enniskillen, Co. Fermanagh, 1988), pp. 99–119.

Casway, Jerrold, 'Henry O'Neill and the formation of the Irish regiment in the Netherlands, 1605', *Irish Historical Studies*, 17 (1972–3), pp. 481–8.

Cath Almaine, ed. Pádraig Ó Riain (Dublin, 1978).

Cavanagh, Michael, *Memoirs of General Thomas Francis Meagher* (Worcester, Mass., 1892).

Cavenagh, Lieut.Col., 'Irish knights of the Imperial Military Order of Maria Theresa', *Journal of the Royal Society of Antiquaries of Ireland*, 56 (1926), pp. 95–105.

Charles-Edwards, T. M., *Early Irish and Welsh Kinship* (Oxford, 1993).

Chart, D. A., 'The Irish levies during the Great French War', *English Historical Review*, 32 (1917), pp. 497–516.

Chartularies of St Mary's Abbey, Dublin, . . . and Annals of Ireland, 1162–1370, ed. J. T. Gilbert (2 vols., Dublin, 1884–6).

Cherbury, Edward, Lord, *The Life and Raigne of King Henry the Eighth* (London, 1649).

Childs, John, *Armies and Warfare in Europe, 1648–1789* (Manchester, 1982).

    The Army of Charles II (London, 1976).

    The Army, James II, and the Glorious Revolution (Manchester, 1980).

    The British Army of William III (Manchester, 1987).

    '"For God and for Honour": Marshal Schomberg', *History Today*, 38 (July, 1988), pp. 46–52.

    The Nine Years' War and the British Army, 1688–97: the Operations in the Low Countries (Manchester, 1991).

    Nobles, Gentlemen and the Profession of Arms in Restoration Britain, 1660–1688: a Biographical Dictionary of British Army Officers on Foreign Service (London, 1987).

Chronicum Scotorum: a Chronicle of Irish Affairs . . . to 1135, with a Supplement . . . 1141–1150, ed. W. M. Hennessy (London, 1866).

Churchyard, Thomas, *A Generall Rehearsall of the Warres* (London, 1579).

Clark, Brian, & Thompson, F. Glenn, 'Napoleon's Irish Legion, 1803–15: the historical record', *Irish Sword*, 12 (1975–6), pp. 165–72.

Clark, Samuel & Donnelly, Jr, J. S. (eds.), *Irish Peasants: Violence and Political Unrest, 1780–1914* (Manchester, 1983).

Clarke, Aidan, *The Old English in Ireland 1625–1642* (Worcester & London, 1966).

    'Sir Piers Crosby, 1590–1646: Wentworth's "tawney ribbon"', *Irish Historical Studies*, 26 (1988–9), pp. 142–60.

Cogadh Gaedhel re Gallaibh [*War of the Gaidhil with the Gaill*], ed. J. H. Todd (Rolls series, London, 1867).

Collins, James L., 'Irish participation at Yorktown', *Irish Sword*, 15 (1982–3), pp. 3–10.

Connolly, Philomena, 'The financing of English expeditions to Ireland, 1361–76', in Lydon, *England and Ireland in the Later Middle Ages*, pp. 104–21.

Connolly, S. J., 'Albion's fatal twigs: justice and law in the eighteenth century', in Rosalind Mitchinson & Peter Roebuck (eds.), *Economy and Society in Scotland and Ireland 1500–1939* (Edinburgh, 1988), pp. 117–25.

    'Law, order and popular protest in early eighteenth-century Ireland: the case of the Houghers', in Corish, *Radicals, Rebels and Establishments*, pp. 51–68.

    Religion, Law and Power: the Making of Protestant Ireland, 1660–1760 (Oxford, 1992).

    'Violence and order in the eighteenth century', in Patrick Flanagan, Paul Ferguson & Kevin Whelan (eds.), *Rural Ireland 1600–1900: Modernisation and Change* (Cork, 1987), pp. 42–61.

Consolatory Letter to a Noble Lord (London, 1760).

Conyngham, Capt. D. P., *The Irish Brigade and Its Campaigns* (New York, 1867 (reprint edition n.d.); Boston, 1869).

Coogan, Tim Pat, *The I.R.A.* (London, 1970).

Cooper, Bryan, *The Tenth (Irish) Division in Gallipoli* (London, 1918).

[Coote], *A Genuine Account of the Progress of Charles Coote, Esq., in pursuing and defeating the Oakboys in the counties of Monaghan, Cavan and Fermanagh* (Dublin, 1763).

Corbally, M. J. P. M., *The Royal Ulster Rifles 1793–1960* (Glasgow, 1960).

Corish, P. J. (ed.), *Radicals, Rebels and Establishments (Historical Studies XV)* (Belfast, 1985).

Corpus Genealogiarum Hiberniæ, vol. i, ed. M. A. O'Brien (Dublin, 1962).

The Correspondence of Sir John Lowther of Whitehaven, 1693–1698, ed. D. R. Hainsworth (London, 1983).

Correspondentie van Willem III en van Hans Willem Bentinck, ed. Nicolas Japikse (5 vols., The Hague, 1927–37).

Cowdrey, H. E. J., 'The peace and the truce of God in the eleventh century', *Past & Present*, 46 (1970), pp. 42–67.

Crean, C. P., 'The Irish battalion of St Patrick at the defence of Spoleto, September 1860', *Irish Sword*, 4 (1959–60), pp. 52–60.

Cregan, Donal F., 'The confederation of Kilkenny', in Brian Farrell (ed.), *The Irish Parliamentary Tradition* (Dublin, 1973), pp. 102–15.

Críth Gablach, ed. D. A. Binchy (Dublin, 1941).

Cruickshank, C. G., *Elizabeth's Army* (2nd edn, Oxford, 1966).

Cullen, Louis M., 'Catholic social classes under the Penal laws', in Thomas Power and Kevin Whelan (eds.), *Endurance and Emergence: Catholics in Ireland in the Eighteenth Century* (Dublin, 1990), pp. 57–84.

'The Irish diaspora of the seventeenth and eighteenth centuries', in N. P. Canny (ed.), *Migration in Early Modern Europe* (Oxford, 1994), pp. 113–49.

Cunliffe, Marcus, 'The army 1815–54 as an institution' (B.Litt. thesis, University of Oxford, 1947).

The Royal Irish Fusiliers 1793–1968 (Oxford, 2nd edn, 1970).

Soldiers and Citizens: the Martial Spirit in America, 1775–1865 (New York, 1968).

Cunningham, J. B., *Castle Caldwell and its Families* (Beleek, 1980).

Curtin, Nancy J., *The United Irishmen: Popular Politics in Ulster and Dublin, 1791–1798* (Oxford, 1994).

Curtis, Edmund, 'The clan system among English settlers in Ireland', *English Historical Review*, 25 (1910), pp. 116–20.

A History of Medieval Ireland (London, 1923).

'The MacQuillan or Mandeville Lords of the Route', *Proceedings of the Royal Irish Academy*, sect. C, 44 (1938), pp. 99–113.

'Unpublished letters from Richard II in Ireland, 1394–5', *Proceedings of the Royal Irish Academy*, sect. C, 37 (1924–7), pp. 276–303.

Curtis, Edmund (ed. & transl.), *Richard II in Ireland 1394–5 and Submissions of the Irish Chiefs* (Oxford, 1927).

Dallas, Gloden, & Gill, Douglas, *The Unknown Army: Mutinies in the British Army in World War I* (London, 1985).

Danaher, Kevin, & Simms, J. G. (eds.), *The Danish Force in Ireland, 1690–91* (Dublin, 1962).

Darby, H. C., & Maxwell, I. S., *The Domesday Geography of Northern England* (Cambridge, 1962).

Davies, Sir John, *A Discovery of the True Causes Why Ireland was Never Entirely Subdued . . . until . . . His Majesty's Happy Reign* (London, 1612), ed. James P. Myers, Jr (Washington, DC, 1988).

Davies, R. R., *Domination and Conquest: the Experience of Ireland, Scotland and Wales, 1100–1300* (Cambridge, 1990).

'Kings, lords and liberties in the March of Wales, 1066–1272', *Transactions of the Royal Historical Society*, 5th ser., 39 (1979), pp. 41–61.

Davitt, Michael, *The Boer Fight for Freedom* (New York, 1902; reprint Melville, 1988).

Deane, Seamus (ed.), *The Field Day Anthology of Irish Literature* (3 vols., Derry, 1991).

Dearden, Brian, 'Charles the Bald's fortified bridge at Pitres (Seine): recent archaeological investigations', in R. Allen Brown (ed.), *Anglo-Norman Studies* 11 (1988), pp. 107–21.

Dearden, Brian, & Clark, Anthony, 'Pont-de-l'Arche or Pitres? A location and achaeo-magnetic dating for Charles the Bald's fortifications on the Seine', *Antiquity*, 64 (1990), pp. 567–71.

de Cavelli, Campana, *Les derniers Stuarts à Saint-Germain-en-Laye* (2 vols., Paris, 1871).

de la Tour du Pin, La Marquise, *Recollections of the Revolution and the Empire*, ed. Walter Greer (London, 1933).

Denman, Terence, 'The Catholic Irish soldier in the First World War: the "racial environment"', *Irish Historical Studies*, 27 (1990–1), pp. 352–65.

    Ireland's Unknown Soldiers: the 16th (Irish) Division in the Great War (Dublin, 1991).

    'Politics and the army list: the formation of the Irish Guards', *Irish Sword* (forthcoming).

    '"The red livery of shame": the campaign against army recruitment in Ireland, 1899–1914', *Irish Historical Studies*, 29 (1994–5), pp. 208–33.

De Pontfarcy, Yolande, 'Le *Tractatus de Purgatorio Sancti Patricii* de H. de Saltry: sa date et ses sources', *Peritia*, 3 (1984), pp. 460–80.

Devoy, John, *Recollections of an Irish Rebel* (New York, 1929).

The Diary of Abraham de la Pryme, ed. Charles Jackson (Surtees Society, Durham, 1870).

Dickson, David, 'Taxation and disaffection in late eighteenth-century Ireland', in Clark & Donnelly, *Irish Peasants*, pp. 37–63.

Dillon, Myles, 'The inauguration of O'Conor', in J. A. Watt, J. B. Morrall and F. X. Martin (eds.), *Medieval Studies Presented to Aubrey Gwynn, S.J.* (Dublin, 1961), pp. 186–202.

Dinneen, Patrick S., *Foclóir Gaedhilge agus Béarla, an Irish-English Dictionary* (Dublin, 1927).

Doherty, Richard, *Clear the Way! A History of the 38th (Irish) Brigade, 1941–47* (Blackrock, Co. Dublin, 1993).

    Irish Generals: Irish Generals in the British Army in the Second World War (Belfast, 1993).

Donnelly, James S., 'Irish agrarian rebellion: the Whiteboys of 1769–76', *Proceedings of the Royal Irish Academy*, sect. C, 83 (1983), pp. 293–331.

Dooney, Laura, 'Trinity College and the war', in David Fitzpatrick (ed.), *Ireland and the First World War* (Dublin, 1988 edn), pp. 38–46.

Dowcra, Sir Henry, 'A relation of services done in Ireland', in John O'Donovan (ed.), *Miscellany of the Celtic Society* (Dublin, 1849).

Dowling, Thaddaeus, *Annales Breves Hiberniae: Annals of Ireland*, ed. Richard Butler (Dublin, 1849).

Doyle, David Noel, *Ireland, Irishmen and Revolutionary America* (Cork, 1981).

[Drake], *Amiable Renegade: the Memoirs of Captain Peter Drake, 1671–1753*, ed. S. A. Burrell & Paul Jordan-Smith (London & Stanford, 1960).

Duby, Georges, *The Chivalrous Society*, transl. C. Postan (London, 1977).

    The Three Orders: Feudal Society Imagined, transl. A. Goldhammer (Chicago & London, 1982).

Dudley Edwards, Owen & Pyle, Fergus (eds.), *1916: The Easter Rising* (London, 1968).

Dudley Edwards, Ruth, *James Connolly* (Dublin, 1981).

Duffy, Christopher, 'The Irish in the Imperial service; an Englishman's comment', *Irish Sword*, 7 (1965–6), pp. 76–7.

    The Wild Goose and the Eagle: a Life of Field Marshal von Browne, 1705–1757 (London, 1964).

Duffy, Michael, 'War, revolution and the crisis of the British empire', in Mark Philp (ed.), *The French Revolution and British Popular Politics* (Cambridge, 1992), pp. 118–45.

Duffy, Sean, 'The Bruce brothers and the Irish Sea world, 1306–29', *Cambridge Medieval Celtic Studies*, 21 (1991), pp. 55–86.

Duggan, J. P., *A History of the Irish Army* (Dublin, 1990).

'1916. Overall plan: a concept of operations', *An Cosantóir*, 51: 4 (Apr. 1991), pp. 23–9.

Dunfermline, Lord, *Sir Ralph Abercromby, K.B., a Memoir by his Son* (Edinburgh, 1861).

Dungan, Myles, *Distant Drums: Irish Soldiers in Foreign Armies* (Belfast, 1993).

Edmondson, Robert, *Is a Soldier's Life Worth Living?* (London, 1902).

Edwards, David, 'The Butler revolt of 1569', *Irish Historical Studies*, 28 (1992–3), pp. 228–55.

Elliott, Marianne, *Partners in Revolution: the United Irishmen and France* (New Haven & London, 1982).

Theobald Wolfe Tone: Prophet of Irish Independence (New Haven & London, 1989).

Ellis, P. B., *The Boyne Water* (London, 1976).

Ellis, S. G., 'Taxation and defence in late medieval Ireland: the survival of scutage', *Journal of the Royal Society of Antiquaries of Ireland*, 107 (1977), pp. 5–28.

Tudor Frontiers and Noble Power: the Making of the British State (Oxford, 1995).

Tudor Ireland: Crown, Community and the Conflict of Cultures, 1470–1603 (London, 1985).

Empey, C. A. & Simms, Katharine, 'The ordinances of the White Earl and the problem of coign in the later middle ages', *Proceedings of the Royal Irish Academy*, sect. C, 75 (1975), pp. 161–87.

English Army Lists and Commission Registers, 1660–1714, ed. Charles Dalton (6 vols., London, 1892–1904).

Facsimiles of the National Manuscripts of Ireland, ed J. T. Gilbert (4 vols., Dublin, 1874–84).

A Faithful History of the Northern Affairs of Ireland: from the late K. James' accession to the Crown, to the siege of Londonderry (London, 1689).

Fallon, Niall, *The Armada in Ireland* (London, 1978).

Falls, Cyril, *Elizabeth's Irish Wars* (London, 1950).

Fanning, Ronan, *Independent Ireland* (Dublin, 1983).

Farrell, Michael, *Arming the Protestants: the Formation of the Ulster Special Constabulary and the Royal Ulster Constabulary, 1920–27* (London & Dingle, 1983).

Félire Óengusso Céli Dé, ed. Whitley Stokes (Henry Bradshaw Society, xxix, London, 1905).

Fennell, Justin, 'The army in Ireland at the time of the Seven Years' War' (MA thesis, University College, Dublin, 1983).

Ferguson, Kenneth P., 'The army in Ireland from the Restoration to the Act of Union' (Ph.D. thesis, Trinity College, Dublin, 1980).

'The army and the Irish rebellion of 1798', in A. J. Guy (ed.), *The Road to Waterloo* (Stroud, 1990), pp. 88–100.

'Military manuscripts in the Public Record Office of Ireland', *Irish Sword*, 15 (1982), pp. 112–13.

'The organisation of King William's army in Ireland, 1689–92', *Irish Sword*, 18 (1990), pp. 62–79.

'The Volunteer movement and the government, 1778–1793', *Irish Sword*, 13 (1977–9), pp. 208–16.

Finer, Samuel E., 'State- and nation-building in Europe: the role of the military', in Charles Tilly (ed.), *The Formation of National States in Western Europe* (Princeton, 1975), pp. 84–163.

Fisk, Robert, *In Time of War: Ireland, Ulster and the Price of Neutrality* (London, 1983).

Fitzpatrick, A. J., 'The economic effects of the French Revolutionary and Napoleonic war on Ireland' (Ph.D. thesis, Manchester University, 1983).

Fitzpatrick, David, 'De Valera in 1917: the undoing of the Easter Rising', in John P. O'Carroll & John A. Murphy (eds.), *De Valera and his Times* (Cork, 1983), pp. 101–12.

Politics and Irish Life, 1913–21 (Dublin, 1977).

Fitzsimon, Robert Daley, 'A further note on the Walsh/Wallis family in the Imperial service', *Irish Sword*, 3 (1957–8), p. 75.

'Irish swordsmen in Imperial service in the Thirty Years' War' *Irish Sword*, 9 (1969–70), pp. 22–31.

Flanagan, Marie Therese, 'Anglo-Norman change and continuity: the castle of Telach Cail in Delbna', *Irish Historical Studies*, 28 (Nov. 1993), pp. 385–9.

Irish Society, Anglo-Norman Settlers, Angevin Kingship (Oxford, 1989).

'Mac Dalbaig, a Leinster chieftain', *Journal of the Royal Society of Antiquaries of Ireland* 111 (1981), pp. 5–13.

Forde, Frank, 'The Royal Irish Artillery, 1755–1801', *Irish Sword*, 11 (1973–4), pp. 32–9.

Forman, Charles, *A Letter . . . for Disbanding the Irish Regiments in the Service of France and Spain* (Dublin, 1728).

Fortescue, Hon. J. W., *The County Lieutenancies and the Army, 1803–1814* (London, 1909).

Foster, R. F., *Modern Ireland, 1600–1972* (London, 1988).

Fox, Sir Frank, *The Royal Inniskilling Fusiliers in the Second World War, 1939–45* (Aldershot, 1951).

Fox, R. M., *The History of the Irish Citizen Army* (Dublin, 1943).

Frame, Robin, 'The Bruces in Ireland, 1315–18', *Irish Historical Studies*, 19 (1974–5), pp. 3–37.

'The campaign against the Scots in Munster, 1317', *Irish Historical Studies*, 24 (1984–5), pp. 361–72.

Colonial Ireland, 1169–1369 (Dublin, 1981).

'Commissions of the peace in Ireland, 1302–1461', *Analecta Hibernica*, 35 (1992), pp. 1–43.

English Lordship in Ireland, 1318–1361 (Oxford, 1982).

'English officials and Irish chiefs in the fourteenth century', *English Historical Review*, 90 (1975), pp. 748–77.

'The judicial powers of the medieval Irish keepers of the peace', *The Irish Jurist*, new ser., 2 (1967), pp. 308–26.

'The justiciarship of Ralph Ufford: warfare and politics in fourteenth-century Ireland', *Studia Hibernica*, 13 (1973), pp. 7–47.

'Military service in the lordship of Ireland, 1290–1360: institutions and society on the Anglo-Gaelic frontier', in R. A. Bartlett & A. MacKay (eds.), *Medieval Frontier Societies* (Oxford, 1989), pp. 101–26.

'Power and society in the lordship of Ireland, 1272–1377', *Past & Present*, 76 (1977), pp. 3–33.

'War and peace in the medieval lordship of Ireland', in J. F. Lydon (ed.), *The English in Medieval Ireland*, pp. 118–41.

Franco-Irish Correspondence, December 1688–February 1692, ed. Sheila Mulloy (3 vols., Dublin, 1983).

Frappier, Jean, 'The Vulgate Cycle', in Loomis, *Arthurian Literature*, pp. 295–318.

Fraser, T. G. & Jeffery, Keith (eds.), *Men, Women and War (Historical Studies XVIII)* (Dublin, 1993).

Furlong, Nicholas, *Fr. John Murphy of Boolavogue, 1753-1798* (Dublin, 1991).

Gailey, I. B., Gillespie, W. F. & Hasset, J., *An Account of the Territorials in Northern Ireland 1947-1978* (Belfast, 1979).

Gaisced: Táin Bó Cúailnge, ed. Cecile O'Rahilly (Dublin, 1976).

Gallwey, Hubert, *The Wall Family in Ireland, 1170-1970* (Naas, 1970).

Gargett, Graham, 'Voltaire and Irish history', *Eighteenth-Century Ireland*, 5 (1990), pp. 117-41.

Garland, John L., 'Irish officers in the Bavarian service during the War of the Spanish Succession', *Irish Sword*, 15 (1982-3), pp. 240-55.

'Irish soldiers of the American Confederacy', *Irish Sword*, 1 (1949-53), pp. 174-80.

'The regiment of MacElligott, 1688-1689', *Irish Sword*, 1 (1949-53), pp. 121-7.

Garvin, Tom, *Nationalist Revolutionaries in Ireland, 1858-1928* (Oxford, 1987).

Gentles, Ian, *The New Model Army in England, Ireland and Scotland 1645-1653* (Oxford, 1992).

Gerriets, Marilyn, 'Kingship and exchange in pre-Viking Ireland', *Cambridge Medieval Celtic Studies*, 13 (Summer 1987), pp. 39-52.

Gervase of Canterbury, *Historical Works* (Rolls series, 2 vols., London, 1879-80).

Gilbert, Arthur N., 'Recruitment and reform in the East India Company army, 1760-1800', *Journal of British Studies*, xv (1975), pp. 89-111.

Gilbert, J. T., *History of the Viceroys of Ireland* (Dublin, 1865).

History of the Irish Confederation and the War in Ireland, 1641-3 (7 vols., Dublin, 1882-91).

Narratives of the Detention, Liberation and Marriage of Maria Clementine Stuart (Dublin, 1894).

Gilbert, J. T. (ed.), *A Contemporary History of Affairs in Ireland, from A.D. 1641 to 1652* (3 vols., Dublin, 1879).

Documents Relating to Ireland, 1795-1804 (Dublin, 1893).

Gildas, *The Ruin of Britain and Other Works*, ed. & transl. Michael Winterbottom (London, 1978).

Gillespie, Raymond, 'The end of an era: Ulster and the outbreak of the 1641 rising', in Ciaran Brady and Raymond Gillespie (eds.), *Natives and Newcomers. Essays on the Making of Irish Colonial Society 1534-1641* (Dublin, 1986), pp. 191-213.

'The Irish economy at war, 1641-52', in Ohlmeyer, *Independence to Occupation, pp. 160-80*.

The Transformation of the Irish Economy (Dublin, 1991).

Gillingham, John, 'Richard I and the science of war in the Middle Ages', in Gillingham, J. & Holt, J. C. (eds.), *War and Government in the Middle Ages: Essays in Honour of J. O. Prestwich* (Woodbridge, 1984); reprinted in Strickland (ed.), *Anglo-Norman Warfare*, pp. 194-207.

'War and chivalry in the *History of William the Marshal*', in *Thirteenth-Century England: Proceedings of the Newcastle-upon-Tyne Conference*, ii (1987), pp. 1-13; reprinted in Strickland (ed.), *Anglo-Norman Warfare*, pp. 251-63.

Gillmor, C. M., 'Naval logistics of the cross-channel operation, 1066', *Anglo-Norman Studies*, 1 (1985), pp. 105-31.

'War on the rivers: Viking numbers and mobility on the Seine and Loire, 841-886', *Viator*, 19 (1988), pp. 79-109.

Giraldi Cambrensis Opera, ed. J. S. Brewer, J. F. Dimock & G. F. Warner (8 vols., London, 1861-91).

Giraldus, *Expugnatio Hibernica*, ed. & transl. A. B. Scott & F. X. Martin (Dublin, 1978).

Glover, Michael, *Wellington's Army in the Peninsula, 1808–1814* (Newton Abbot & London, 1977).

Gouhier, Pierre, 'Mercenaires Irlandais au service de la France (1635–1664)', *Irish Sword*, 7 (1965–6), pp. 58–75.

Grattan, William, *Adventures with the Connaught Rangers 1809–14*, ed. Charles Oman (London, 1989, reprint of 1903 edn).

Graves, Charles, *The Royal Ulster Rifles*, iii, *1919–48* (Belfast, 1950).

Greacen, Lavinia, *Chink: a Biography* (London, 1989).

Greaves, C. Desmond, *The Life and Times of James Connolly* (Dublin, 1972 edn).

Gretton, Lt.-Col. G. le M., *The Campaigns and History of the Royal Irish Regiment from 1684 to 1902* (Edinburgh, 1911).

Grey, Anchitel, *Debates of the House of Commons, 1667–1694* (10 vols., London, 1769).

Griffin, William D., 'Irish generals and Spanish politics under Fernando VII', *Irish Sword*, 10 (1971–2), pp. 1–9.

Gruber, Ira D., '"On the road to Poonamalle" an Irish officer's view of the war for American independence', *The American Magazine*, 4 (Spring/Summer 1988), pp. 1–12.

Guerin, Thomas, 'Irish soldiers of the old regime in Canada', *Irish Sword*, 2 (1954–6), pp. 57–61.

Gunner, Colin, *Front of the Line: Adventures with the Irish Brigade* (Antrim, 1991).

Gurwood, Lt.-Col. John (ed.), *The Dispatches of Field Marshal The Duke of Wellington* (13 vols., London, 1834–9).

Guy, Alan J., 'A whole army absolutely ruined in Ireland: aspects of the Irish Establishment', in *Annual Report of the National Army Museum* (1978–9) (London, 1979), pp. 30–43.
  Oeconomy and Discipline: Officership and Administration in the British Army, 1714–63 (Manchester, 1985).

Guy, Alan (ed.), *Colonel Samuel Bagshawe and the Army of George II* (London, 1990).

Gwynn, Aubrey, 'The Irish missal of Corpus Christi College, Oxford', *Studies in Church History*, 1 (1964), pp. 47–68.

Gwynn, Stephen, 'Irish Soldiers and Irish Brigades', *Cornhill Magazine*, n.s., 53 (1922), pp. 737–49.

Haire, D. N., 'In aid of the civil power, 1868–90', in F. S. L. Lyons & R. A. J. Hawkins (eds.), *Ireland under the Union: Varieties of Tension* (Oxford, 1980), pp. 115–47.

Hall, Michael, *Sacrifice on the Somme* (Belfast, 1993).

Hamilton, Andrew, *A True Relation of the Actions of the Inniskilling-Men, from their first taking up of arms in December, 1688* (London, 1690).

Hanham, H. J., 'Religion and nationality in the mid-Victorian army', in M. R. D. Foot (ed.), *War and Society* (London, 1973), pp. 159–81.

Hanna, Henry, *The Pals of Suvla Bay* (Dublin, 1916).

Harbison, Peter, 'Native Irish arms and armour in medieval Gaelic literature, 1170–1600', *Irish Sword*, 12 (1975/6), pp. 173–99, 270–84.

Harding, Richard, *Amphibious Warfare in the Eighteenth Century: the British Expedition to the West Indies, 1740–1742* (London, 1991).

Harling, Col. Sir P., *Rifleman and Hussar* (London, 1931).

Harries-Jenkins, Gwynn, *The Army in Victorian Society* (London, 1979).

Harrington, Peter, 'Images of the Boyne', *Irish Sword*, 18 (1990), pp. 57–61.

Harris, Henry, *The Irish Regiments in the First World War* (Cork, 1968).

Harris, R. G., *The Irish Regiments: a Pictorial History, 1683–1987* (Tunbridge Wells, 1989).

Harrison, Alan, 'The shower of Hell', *Éigse*, 18, pt. II (1981), p. 304.

Harrison, Richard S., *Irish Anti-War Movements, 1824–1974* (Dublin, 1986).

Harvey, Col. J. R., *History of 5th (Royal Irish) Regiment of Dragoons from 1689 to 1799, afterwards the 5th Royal Irish Lancers from 1858 to 1921* (Aldershot, 1923).

Hawkins, R. A. J., 'An army on police work, 1881–2. Ross of Bladensburg's memorandum', *Irish Sword*, 11 (1973–4), pp. 75–117.

Hayes, Richard, *Biographical Dictionary of Irishmen in France* (Dublin, 1949).

'Earliest Irish troops in the French service', *Irish Sword*, 1 (1949–53), pp. 231–3.

Irish Swordsmen of France (Dublin, 1934).

The Last Invasion of Ireland: When Connacht Rose (Dublin, 1937).

Hayes-McCoy, G. A., 'The army of Ulster, 1593–1601', *Irish Sword*, 1 (1949–53), pp. 105–17.

'Captain Myles Walter Keogh', *Irish Sword*, 1 (1949–53), pp. 210–13.

A History of Irish Flags from Earliest Times (Dublin, 1979).

Irish Battles: a Military History of Ireland (London, 1969; pbk edn, Belfast, 1990).

'Irish soldiers of the '45', in Etienne Rynne (ed.), *North Munster Studies* (Limerick, 1967).

'A military history of the 1916 Rising', in Kevin B. Nowlan (ed.), *The Making of 1916: Studies in the History of the Rising* (Dublin, 1969), pp. 255–338.

Scots Mercenary Forces in Ireland (1565–1603) (Dublin & London, 1937).

'Strategy and tactics in Irish warfare, 1593–1601', *Irish Historical Studies*, 2 (1940–1), pp. 255–79.

'The tide of victory and defeat: Clontibret, 1595', *Studies*, 38 (June 1949), pp. 158–68.

Hayes-McCoy, G. A. (ed.), *The Irish at War* (Cork, 1964).

Hayter, Tony, *The Army and the Crowd in mid-Georgian England* (London, 1978).

An Eighteenth-Century Secretary at War: the Papers of William, Viscount Barrington (London, 1988).

Hazlett, Hugh, 'The financing of the British armies in Ireland, 1641–9', *Irish Historical Studies*, 1 (1938–9), pp. 21–41.

Head, Lt.-Col. C. O., *No Great Shakes: an Autobiography* (London, 1943).

Henderson, D. M., *Highland Soldier 1820–1920* (Edinburgh, 1989).

Henning, B. D. (ed.), *The House of Commons, 1660–1690* (3 vols., London, 1983).

Henry, Gráinne, *The Irish Military Community in Spanish Flanders, 1586–1621* (Dublin, 1992).

'"Wild geese" in Spanish Flanders: the first generation, 1586–1610', *Irish Sword*, 17 (1987–90), pp. 189–201.

Hepburn, A. C., 'The Belfast riots of 1935', *Social History*, 10: 1 (Jan. 1990), pp. 75–96.

Herbert, Máire, 'Múineadh na Fiannaíochta', in *Léachtaí Cholm Cille*, 9 (1978), pp. 44–57.

'The preface to *Amra Coluim Cille*', in Donnchadh Ó Corráin, Liam Breatnach & Kim McCone (eds.), *Sages, Saints and Storytellers: Celtic Studies in Honour of Professor James Carney* (Maynooth, 1989), pp. 67–75.

Herbert, Sir William, *Croftus: Sive de Hibernia Liber*, ed. Arthur Keaveney & J. A. Madden (Dublin, 1992).

Hewitt, H. J., *The Organization of War under Edward III* (Manchester, 1966).

Hill, George, *An Historical Account of the Plantation in Ulster at the Commencement of the Seventeenth Century, 1608–1620* (Belfast, 1877; reprinted Shannon, 1970).

The Stewarts of Ballintoy: with notices of other families of the district in the seventeenth century (Coleraine, 1865; reprinted Ballycastle, 1976).

Hobsbawm, Eric & Ranger, Terence, *The Invention of Tradition* (Cambridge, 1983).

Hogan, Edmund, *Onomasticon Goidelicum* (Dublin, 1910).

Holinshed, Raphael, *Chronicles of England, Scotland and Ireland* (6 vols., London, 1807–8).

Holinshed's Irish Chronicle, ed. Liam Miller & Eileen Power ([Dublin], 1979).

Hook, T. E., *The Life of the Rt Hon. Sir David Baird* (London, 1832).

Hopkinson, Michael, *Green Against Green: the Irish Civil War* (Dublin, 1988).

Hoppen, K. T., *Elections, Politics and Society in Ireland, 1832–1885* (Oxford, 1984).

Houlding, J. A., *Fit for Service: the Training of the British Army, 1715–1795* (Oxford, 1980).

Hudson, B. T., 'The family of Harold Godwinson and the Irish Sea province', *Journal of the Royal Society of Antiquaries of Ireland*, 109 (1979), pp. 92–100.

Hughes, James, 'Sir Edmund Butler of the Dullough, Knt', *Journal of the Royal Historical & Archaeological Society of Ireland*, 4th ser., 1 (1870–1), pp. 153–92, 211–31.

Hughes, Kathleen, *The Church in Early Irish Society* (London, 1966).

Hunt, John, *Irish Medieval Figure Sculpture 1200–1600* (2 vols., Dublin & London, 1974).

Hyde, Douglas, *Amhráin Chúige Chonnacht – an leath-rann* (Dublin, n.d.).

Ilchester, The earl of (ed.), *Letters to Henry Fox* (The Roxburghe Club, London, 1915).

Ireland, Denis, *Six Counties in Search of a Nation* (Belfast, 1947).

Ireland, John De Courcy, 'General Alexander O'Reilly and the Spanish attack on Algiers, 1775', *Irish Sword*, 12 (1975–6), pp. 131–8.

Irwin, Liam, 'The Earl of Orrery and the military problems of Restoration Munster', *Irish Sword*, 13 (1977–9), pp. 10–19.

Jackson, Donald, 'Violence and assimilation in Tudor Ireland', in Eoin O'Brien (ed.), *Essays in Honour of J. D. H. Widdess* (Dublin, 1978), pp. 113–26.

James, F. G., *Ireland in the Empire, 1688–1770: a History of Ireland from the Williamite Wars to the Eve of the American Revolution* (Cambridge, Mass., 1972).

Jeffery, Keith, *The British Army and the Crisis of Empire 1918–22* (Manchester, 1984).

'The Great War in modern Irish memory', in Fraser & Jeffery, *Men, Women and War*, pp. 136–57.

'The Irish military tradition and the British empire', in Jeffery (ed.), *'An Irish Empire'? Aspects of Ireland and the British Empire* (Manchester, forthcoming).

'The post-war army', in Beckett & Simpson, *Nation in Arms*, pp. 210–34.

'The security forces', in 'The Northern Ireland question 1968–88', special issue of *Revue Française de Civilisation Britannique*, 5: 2 (1989), pp. 131–44.

Jeffery, Keith (ed.), *The Divided Province: the Troubles In Northern Ireland 1969–1985* (London, 1985).

Jennings, Brendan, 'Irish Franciscans in Prague', *Studies*, 28 (1939), pp. 210–22.

Jennings, Brendan (ed.), *Wild Geese in Spanish Flanders, 1582–1700* (Dublin, 1964).

Johnston, Dorothy, 'The interim years: Richard II and Ireland, 1395–9', in Lydon (ed.), *England and Ireland*, pp. 175–95.

Johnston, E. M., *Great Britain and Ireland: a Study in Political Administration* (Edinburgh, 1962).

Johnston, S. H. F., 'The Irish establishment', *Irish Sword*, 1 (1949–53), pp. 33–6.

Johnstone, Tom, *Orange, Green and Khaki: the Story of the Irish Regiments in the Great War, 1914–18* (Dublin, 1992).

Jones, George Hilton, 'The Irish fright of 1688: real violence and imagined massacre', in *Bulletin of the Institute of Historical Research*, 55 (1982), pp. 148–57.

Jordan, John, 'Wild Geese in the north', *An Cosantóir*, 15 (1954), pp. 77–82, 147–50, 192–6.

Jourdain, H. F. N. & Fraser, E., *The Connaught Rangers* (3 vols., London, 1924–8).
Ranging Memories (Oxford, 1934).

Karsten, Peter, 'Irish soldiers in the British army, 1792–1922: suborned or subordinate?', *Journal of Social History*, 17 (1983), pp. 31–64.

Kavanagh, Rhoda, 'The horse in Viking Ireland: some observations', in John Bradley (ed.), *Settlement and Society in Medieval Ireland* (Kilkenny, 1988), pp. 89–121.

Keating, Geoffrey, *Foras feasa ar Éirinn; The History of Ireland*, ed. David Comyn & P. S. Dinneen (4 vols., London, 1902–14).

Keating, Joseph, 'The Tyneside Irish Brigade', in Felix Lavery (ed.), *Irish Heroes in the War* (London, 1917).

Kelleher, J. V., 'The rise of the Dál Cais', in Etienne Rynne (ed.), *North Munster Studies* (Limerick, 1967).

Kenrick, N. C. E., *The Story of the Wiltshire Regiment* (Aldershot, 1963).

[Kipling], *The Definitive Edition of Rudyard Kipling's Verse* (London, 1973 edn).

Kishlansky, Mark, 'The case of the army truly stated: the creation of the New Model Army', *Past and Present*, 81 (1978), pp. 51–74.

Knowler, William (ed.), *The Earl of Strafforde's Letters and Despatches with an Essay Towards his Life by Sir George Radcliffe* (2 vols., London, 1739).

Knox, H. T., *The History of the County of Mayo* (Dublin, 1908).

Kohn, Leo, *The Constitution of the Irish Free State* (London, 1932).

Koppermann, Paul E., *Braddock at the Monogahela* (Pittsburgh, 1977).

Lambert, Eric T. D., 'Irish soldiers in South America, 1818–30', *Irish Sword*, 16 (1984–6), pp. 22–35.

Lambkin, Romie, *My Time in the War: an Irishwoman's Diary* (Dublin, 1992).

Lascelles, Rowley (ed.), *Liber Munerum Publicorum Hiberniae; or the Establishments of Ireland* (2 vols., London, 1852).

Laurie, Lt.-Col. G. B., *History of the Royal Irish Rifles* (Aldershot, 1914).

Leask, J. C. & McCance, H. M., *The Regimental Records of the Royal Scots* (Dublin, 1915).

Lebor na Cert; The Book of Rights, ed. Myles Dillon (Dublin, 1962).

Lee, J. J., *Ireland 1912–1985: Politics and Society* (Cambridge, 1989).

Le Fevre, 'The battle of Bantry Bay, 1 May 1689', *Irish Sword*, 15 (1990), pp. 1–16.

Leonard, Jane, 'Getting them at last: the I.R.A. and ex-servicemen', in David Fitzpatrick (ed.), *Revolution? Ireland 1917–1923* (Dublin, 1990), pp. 118–29.

Levenson, Samuel, *James Connolly: a Biography* (London, 1973).

Lloyd, Clifford, *Ireland under the Land League: a Narrative of Personal Experiences* (Edinburgh, 1892).

Loeber, Rolf & Parker, Geoffrey, 'The military revolution in seventeenth century Ireland', in Ohlmeyer, *Independence to Occupation*, pp. 66–88.

Logan, Patrick, 'Medical services in the armies of the confederate wars (1641–52)', *Irish Sword*, 4 (1959–60), pp. 217–27.

Longfield, A. K. (ed.), *Fitzwilliam Accounts, 1560–65 (Annesley Collection)* (Irish Manuscripts Commission, Dublin, 1960).

Longford, Elizabeth, *Wellington: the Years of the Sword* (London, 1969).

Lonn, Ella, *Foreigners in the Confederacy* (Gloucester, Mass., 1965).
Foreigners in the Union Army and Navy (Baton Rouge, 1951; repr. edn, New York, 1969).

Loomis, R. S., 'The oral diffusion of the Arthurian legend', in Loomis, *Arthurian Literature*, pp. 52–63.

521

Loomis, R. S. (ed.), *Arthurian Literature in the Middle Ages: a Collaborative History* (Oxford, 1959).

Lowe, John (ed.), *Letter-book of the Earl of Clanricarde 1643–47* (Irish Manuscripts Commission, Dublin, 1983).

Lydon, J. F., 'Edward I, Ireland and the war in Scotland, 1303–4', in Lydon (ed.), *England and Ireland*, pp. 43–61.

    'The hobelar: an Irish contribution to medieval warfare', *Irish Sword*, 2 (1954–6), pp. 12–16.

    'An Irish army in Scotland, 1296', *Irish Sword*, 5 (1961–2), pp. 184–90.

    'Irish levies in the Scottish wars, 1296–1302', *Irish Sword*, 5 (1961–2), pp. 207–17.

    'Richard II's expeditions to Ireland', *Journal of the Royal Society of Antiquaries of Ireland*, 93 (1963), pp. 135–49.

Lydon, J. F. (ed.), *England and Ireland in the Later Middle Ages* (Blackrock, 1981).

Lynch, Arthur, *Ireland: Vital Hour* (London, 1915).

    My Life Story (London, 1924).

Lynn, John A., 'Recalculating French army growth during the *Grand Siècle*, 1610–1715', *French Historical Studies* (Fall, 1994).

    'The *trace italienne* and the growth of armies: the French case', *Journal of Military History*, 55 (1991), pp. 297–330.

Macardle, Dorothy, *The Irish Republic* (Dublin, 1951 edn).

Mac Cana, Proinsias, '*Fiannaigecht* in the pre-Norman period', in Almqvist *et al.*, *The Heroic Process*.

    The Learned Tales of Medieval Ireland (Dublin, 1980).

MacCarthy, Daniel (ed.), 'The "jorney" of the Blackwater from the State Papers of Queen Elizabeth', *Journal of the Kilkenny & South-East of Ireland Archaeological Society*, 2nd ser., 1: 2 (1857), pp. 256–62.

MacCarthy-Morrogh, Michael, *The Munster Plantation: English Migration to Southern Ireland, 1583–1641* (Oxford, 1986).

MacCauley, J. A., 'Lally-Tollendal in India, 1758–1761', *Irish Sword*, 5 (1961–2), pp. 81–7.

Mac Cuarta, Brian (ed.), *Ulster 1641. Aspects of the Rising* (Belfast, 1993).

MacDonagh, Michael, *The Irish at the Front* (London, 1916).

Macdonald, Robert, *Personal Narrative of Military Travel and Adventure in Turkey and Persia* (Edinburgh, 1859).

Mac Eoin, Gearóid S., 'The mysterious death of Leogaire mac Néill', *Studia Hibernica*, 8 (1968), pp. 21–48.

Mac Giolla Choille, Breandán (ed.), *Intelligence Notes, 1913–16* (Dublin, 1966).

Mackenzie, J., *A Narrative of the Siege of Londonderry* (London, 1690).

MacMullen, J. M., *Camp and Barrack-Room; or the British Army as it is* (London, 1846).

Macready, Sir Nevil, *Annals of an Active Life* (2 vols., London, 1924).

Macrory, Patrick, *The Siege of Derry* (London, 1980).

Mac Stiofáin, Seán, *Revolutionary in Ireland* (Farnborough, 1974).

MacSwiney of Mashanaglass, The Marquess, 'Notes on the formation of the first two Irish regiments in the service of Spain in the eighteenth century', *Journal of the Royal Society of Antiquaries of Ireland*, 57 (1927), pp. 3–16.

    'Notes on some Irish regiments in the service of Spain and Naples in the eighteenth century', *Proceedings of the Royal Irish Academy*, sect. C, 37 (1925–7), pp. 158–74.

Malcolm, Joyce Lee, 'All the king's men: the impact of the crown's Irish soldiers on the English Civil War', *Irish Historical Studies*, 21 (1978–9), pp. 239–64.

Mallory, J. P. & McNeill, T. E., *The Archaeology of Ulster from Colonization to Plantation* (Belfast, 1991).

Mann, Golo, *Wallenstein* (London, 1976).

Marling, Sir Percival, *Rifleman and Hussar* (London, 1931).

Martin, F. X., 'MacNeill and the foundation of the Irish Volunteers', in F. X. Martin and F. J. Byrne (eds.), *The Scholar Revolutionary: Eoin MacNeill* (Shannon, 1973), pp. 99–179.

Martin, F. X. (ed.), *The Irish Volunteers, 1913–1915* (Dublin, 1963).

Masson, Gustave, & Prothero, G. W. (eds.), *Histoire du siècle de Louis XIV par Voltaire*, pt. II (Cambridge, 1889).

Masur, Gerhard, *Simon Bolivar* (Albuquerque, 1948).

Matthew, E. A., 'The financing of the lordship of Ireland', in A. J. Pollard (ed.), *Property and Politics: Essays in Later Medieval History* (Gloucester, 1984), pp. 97–115.

May, Maj.-Gen. Sir E. S., *Changes and Chances of a Soldier's Life* (London, 1925).

McAnally, Sir Henry, *The Irish Militia 1793–1816: a Social and Military Study* (Dublin, 1949).

McCaffrey, Wallace T., *Elizabeth I: War and Politics, 1588–1603* (Princeton, 1992).

McCance, Capt. Stouppe, *History of the Royal Munster Fusiliers* (2 vols., Aldershot, 1927).

McCarmick, William, *A Farther Impartial Account of the Actions of the Inniskilling-men . . .* (London, 1691).

McCone, Kim R., 'Aided Chelchair Maic Uthechair: hounds, heroes and hospitallers in early Irish myth and story', *Ériu*, 35 (1984), pp. 1–30.

    Pagan Past and Christian Present in Early Irish Literature (Maynooth, 1990).

    'Werewolves, Cyclopes, *Díberga*, and *Fíanna*: juvenile delinquency in early Ireland', *Cambridge Medieval Celtic Studies*, 12 (1986), pp. 1–22.

McCracken, Donal P., *The Irish Pro-Boers, 1877–1902* (Johannesburg & Cape Town, 1989).

McDonnell, Hector, 'Some documents relating to the involvement of the Irish Brigade in the rebellion of 1745', *Irish Sword*, 16 (1984–6), pp. 3–21.

McDowell, R. B., 'Colonial nationalism and the winning of parliamentary independence, 1760–82', in *New History of Ireland*, iv, *Eighteenth-Century Ireland* (Oxford, 1986), pp. 196–235.

    Ireland in the Age of Imperialism and Revolution, 1760–1801 (Oxford, 1979).

McDowell, R. B. (ed.), *Memoirs of Miles Byrne* (facsimile reprint of 1863 edn, Shannon, 1972).

McEvoy, Frank (ed.), *Life and Adventures of James Freney, Written by Himself* (Kilkenny, 1988).

McGurk, John, 'A survey of the demands made on the Welsh shires to supply soldiers for the Irish war, 1594–1602', *Transactions of the Honourable Society of Cymmrodorion* (1983), pp. 56–68.

    'Wild Geese: the Irish in European armies (sixteenth to eighteenth centuries)', in Patrick O'Sullivan (ed.), *The Irish World Wide*, i, *Patterns of Migration* (Leicester, 1992), pp. 36–62.

McHugh, R. J. (ed.), *Carlow in '98: The Autobiography of William Farrell of Carlow* (Dublin, 1949).

McLynn, F. J., 'Ireland and the Jacobite Rising of 1745', *Irish Sword*, 13 (1979), pp. 339–52.

McNeill, Charles (ed.), *The Tanner Letters. Documents of Irish Affairs in the Sixteenth and Seventeenth Centuries Extracted from the Thomas Tanner Collection in the Bodleian Library, Oxford* (Irish Manuscripts Commission, Dublin, 1943).

McNeill, T. E., *Anglo-Norman Ulster. The History and Archeology of an Irish Barony, 1177–1400* (Edinburgh, 1980).

'Early castles in Leinster', *Journal of Irish Archeology*, 5 (1989/90), pp. 57–64.

McPherson, J. M., *Battle Cry of Freedom: the Civil War Era* (Oxford, 1988).

McWhiney, Grady & Jamieson, Perry D., *Attack and Die: Civil War Military Tactics and the Southern Heritage* (University, Alabama, 1982).

Mehegan, J. J., *O'Higgins of Chile* (London, 1913).

Melvin, Patrick G., 'Colonel Maurice Griffin Dennis, 1805–63', *Irish Sword*, 13 (1977–9), pp. 45–59.

'General Sir R. D. Kelly', *Irish Sword*, 12 (1975–6), pp. 252–4.

'The Irish army and the Revolution of 1688', *Irish Sword*, 9 (1969–70), pp. 288–307.

'Irish troop movements and King James' army in 1688', *Irish Sword*, 10 (1971–2), pp. 87–105.

Meyer, Kuno, 'Sanas Cormac. An Old-Irish Glossary compiled by Cormac úa Cuilennáin, King-Bishop of Cashel in the ninth century. Edited from the copy in the Yellow Book of Lecan', in *Anecdota from Irish Manuscripts*, ed. O. J. Bergin, R. I. Best, Kuno Meyer & J. G. O'Keeffe (Halle, 1912).

Meyer, Kuno (ed. & transl.), *Fiannaigecht, being a Collection of Hitherto Unedited Irish Poems and Tales Relating to Finn and His Fianna, with an English Translation* (Dublin, 1910).

Middleton, Richard, *The Bells of Victory: the Pitt-Newcastle Ministry and the Conduct of the Seven Years' War* (Cambridge, 1985).

Miller, David, 'The Armagh troubles', in Clark & Donnelly, *Irish Peasants*, pp. 155–91.

Peep of Day Boys and Defenders: Selected Documents on the County Armagh Disturbances, 1784–96 (Belfast, 1990).

Queen's Rebels: Ulster Loyalism in Historical Perspective (Dublin, 1978).

Miller, John, 'The Earl of Tyrconnell and James II's Irish policy, 1685–1688', *Historical Journal*, 20 (1977), pp. 803–23.

Miller, R. R., *Shamrock and Sword: the Saint Patrick's Battalion in the U.S.–Mexican War* (Norman, Okla., & London, 1989).

Mitchell, Arthur, & Ó Snodaigh, Pádraig, *Irish Political Documents 1916–1949* (Blackrock, Co. Dublin, 1985).

Mitchell, Gardiner S., *'Three Cheers for the Derrys!' A History of the 10th Royal Inniskilling Fusiliers in the 1914–18 War* (Derry, 1991).

Montgomery-Cuninghame, Col. Sir Thomas, *Dusty Measure: a Record of Troubled Times* (London, 1939).

Morgan, Hiram, 'The end of Gaelic Ulster: a thematic interpretation of events between 1534 and 1610', *Irish Historical Studies*, 26 (1988–9), pp. 8–32.

'Tom Lee: posing peacemaker', in Bradshaw, *Representing Ireland*, pp. 132–65.

Tyrone's Rebellion: the Outbreak of the Nine Years War in Tudor Ireland (Woodbridge, 1993).

Morris, J. E., 'Mounted infantry in medieval warfare', *Transactions of the Royal Historical Society*, 3rd ser., 8 (1914), pp. 77–102.

Morton, R. Grenfell, 'The rise of the Yeomanry', *Irish Sword*, 8 (1967–8), pp. 58–64.

Moryson, Fynes, *An Itinerary* (3 parts, London, 1617).

Moscati, Sabatino, Frey, O. H., Kurta, V., Raftery, B. and Szabó, M. (eds.), *The Celts* (London, 1991).

Muenger, Elizabeth A., 'The British Army in Ireland, 1886–1914' (Ph.D. thesis, University of Michigan, 1981).
  The British Military Dilemma in Ireland: Occupation Politics 1886–1914 (Lawrence, Kan., & Dublin, 1991).
Mullen, Thomas J., 'Campo Santo – the darkling plain, 1743', *Irish Sword*, 11 (1973–4), pp. 222–5.
  'The Hibernia Regiment of the Spanish army', *Irish Sword*, 8 (1967–8), pp. 218–25.
  'The Irish Brigades in the Union Army, 1861–65', *Irish Sword*, 9 (1969–70), pp. 50–8.
Mulloy, Sheila, 'The French navy and the Jacobite War in Ireland, 1689–91', *Irish Sword*, 18 (1990), pp. 17–31.
Murphy, Dervla, *A Place Apart* (Harmondsworth, 1979).
Murphy, Gerard, *The Ossianic Lore and Romantic Tales of Medieval Ireland* (Dublin, 1955).
Murphy, Gerard (ed. & transl.), *Duanaire Finn: the Book of the Lays of Fionn*, pt. II (London, 1933).
Murphy, John A., *Justin MacCarthy, Lord Mountcashel, Commander of the First Irish Brigade in France* (Cork, 1959).
Murphy, W. S., 'Irish units in Imperial service', *Irish Sword*, 3 (1957–8), pp. 74–5.
Murray, Rev. R. H., *History of the VIII King's Royal Irish Hussars, 1693–1927* (2 vols., Cambridge, 1928).
Murtagh, Diarmuid & Murtagh, Harman, 'The Irish Jacobite army, 1689–91', *Irish Sword*, 18 (1990), pp. 62–79.
Murtagh, Harman, 'Corporal Darby Quinan', *Irish Sword*, 15 (1982–3), p. 32.
  'Two Irish officers and the campaign to relieve Vienna, 1683', *Irish Sword*, 15 (1982–3), pp. 255–7.
Namier, Sir Lewis & Brooke, John, *The House of Commons, 1754–1790* (3 vols., London, 1985).
Napier, Sir W. F. P., *History of the War in the Peninsula* (6 vols., London, 1856).
Négociations de M. le Comte d'Avaux en Irlande, 1689–90, ed. John Hogan (Dublin, 1934).
Nevin, Donal, 'The Irish Citizen Army', in Dudley Edwards & Pyle, *1916*, pp. 119–31.
New History of Ireland (10 vols., Oxford, 1976–).
Nicholson, Ranald, 'An Irish expedition to Scotland in 1335', *Irish Historical Studies*, 13 (1962–3), pp. 197–211.
Ní Mhaonaigh, Máire, 'Bréifne bias in Cogad Gáedel re Gallaib', *Ériu*, 43 (1992), pp. 135–58.
Nitze, W. A., 'Perlesvaus', in Loomis, *Arthurian Literature*, pp. 263–73.
Notitiae as Leabhar Cheanannais [The Book of Kells], ed. Gearóid Mac Niocaill (Dublin, 1961).
Nowlan, Kevin B. (ed.), *The Making of 1916: Studies in the History of the Rising* (Dublin, 1969).
Ó Briain, Liam (ed.), 'The Chevalier Gaydon's memoir of the regiment of Dillon, 1738', *Irish Sword*, 3 (1957–8), pp. 98–106, 194–202, 273–81; 4 (1959–60), pp. 29–39, 212–6, 157–62, 257–63; 5 (1961–2), pp. 88–93, 175–8, 218–22; 6 (1963–4), pp. 34–41, 88–93, 180–91.
[Ó Bruadair], *Poems of David Ó Bruadair: Duanaire Dháibhidh Uí Bhruadair*, ed. J. C. McErlean (3 vols., London, 1910–17).
O'Callaghan, J. C., *History of the Irish Brigades in the Service of France* (Glasgow, 1870; repr. Shannon, 1969).
O'Carroll, Donal, 'An indifferent good post: the battlefield of the Boyne', *Irish Sword*, 18 (1990–2), pp. 49–56.

Ó Cléirigh, Lughaidh, *The Life of Aodh Ruadh O Domhnaill*, ed. and transl. Paul Walsh (2 parts, Dublin, 1948, 1957).

O'Connell, M. J., *The Last Colonel of the Irish Brigade* (2 vols., London, 1892).

O'Conor, Mathew, *Military History of the Irish Nation, Comprising a Memoir of the Irish Brigade in the Service of France* (Dublin, 1845).

Ó Corráin, Donnchadh, 'Aspects of early Irish history', in B. G. Scott (ed.), *Perspectives in Irish Archeology* (Belfast, 1974), pp. 64–75.

    'Brian Boru and the battle of Clontarf', in Liam De Paor (ed.), *Milestones in Irish History* (Dublin, 1986), pp. 31–40.

    'Caithréim Chellacháin Chaisil: history or propaganda?', *Ériu*, 25 (1974)1–69.

    'High-kings, Vikings and other kings', *Irish Historical Studies*, 21: 83 (Mar. 1979), pp. 283–323.

    Ireland before the Normans (Dublin, 1972).

O Daly, Mary, 'A Poem on the Airgialla', *Ériu*, 16 (1952), pp. 179–88.

Ó Danachair, Caoimhin, 'Montrose's Irish regiments', *Irish Sword*, 4 (1959–60), pp. 61–7.

Odintz, M. F., 'The British officer corps 1754–1783' (Ph.D. thesis, University of Michigan, 1988).

Ó Doibhlín, Éamon, *Domhnach Mór (Donaghmore), an Outline of Parish History* (Omagh, Co. Tyrone, 1969).

Ó Domhnaill, Seán, 'Warfare in sixteenth-century Ireland', *Irish Historical Studies*, 5 (1946–7), pp. 29–54.

O'Donoghue, Florence, *No Other Law (the Story of Liam Lynch and the Irish Republican Army, 1916–1923)* (Dublin, 1954).

O'Donovan, Jim, 'The Militia in Munster, 1715–78', in M. G. R. O'Brien (ed.), *Parliament, Politics and People: Essays in Eighteenth-Century Irish History* (Dublin, 1989), pp. 31–47.

O'Donovan, John (ed. & transl.), *Annals of the Kingdom of Ireland* (7 vols., Dublin, 1851).

O'Dowd, Mary, *Power, Politics and Land: Early Modern Sligo, 1568–1688* (Belfast, 1991).

O'Dwyer, Barry W., 'The annals of Connacht and Lugh Cé and the monasteries of Boyle and Holy Trinity', *Proceedings of the Royal Irish Academy*, sect. C, 72 (1972), pp. 83–101.

Ó Fiannachta, Pádraig, 'The development of the debate between Pádraig and Oisín', in Almqvist, *et al.*, *The Heroic Process*.

O'Flaherty, Roderick, *Chorographical Description of West or h-Iar Connaught*, ed. James Hardiman (Dublin, 1846).

Ó Gráda, Cormac & Mokyr, Joel. 'The height of Irishmen and Englishmen in the 1770s; some evidence from the East India Company [Army] records', *Eighteenth Century Ireland*, 4 (1989), pp. 83–93.

O'Grady, Standish Hayes (ed. & transl.), *Caithréim Thoirdhealbhaigh: The Triumphs of Turlough*, text vol. i, transl. vol. ii (London, 1929).

    Silva Gadelica (I–XXXI). A Collection of Tales in Irish with Extracts Illustrating Persons and Places (2 vols., London, 1892).

O'Halpin, Eunan, 'Anglo-Irish security co-operation: a Dublin perspective', *Conflict Quarterly*, 10 (1990), pp. 5–24.

    'Army, politics and society in independent Ireland, 1923–1945', in Fraser & Jeffery, *Men, Women and War*, pp. 158–74.

    'Intelligence and security in Ireland, 1922–45', *Intelligence and National Security*, 5 (1990), pp. 50–83.

O'Hanlon, John, & O'Leary, Edward, *History of the Queen's County* (2 vols., Dublin, 1907, 1914).

Ohlmeyer, Jane H., *Civil War and Restoration in the Three Stuart Kingdoms: the Career of Randal MacDonnell, Marquis of Antrim, 1609–1683* (Cambridge, 1993).

'Ireland independent: confederate foreign policy and international relations', in Ohlmeyer, *Independence to Occupation*, pp. 89–111.

Ohlmeyer, Jane H. (ed.), *Independence to Occupation: Ireland 1641–1660* (Cambridge, 1994).

O'Keeffe, Tadhg, 'Rathnageeragh and Ballyloo: a study of stone castles of probable 14th to early 15th century date in County Carlow', *Journal of the Royal Society of Antiquaries of Ireland*, 117 (1987), pp. 35–9.

'Medieval frontiers and fortification: the Pale and its evolution', in F. H. A. Aalen & Kevin Whelan (eds.), *Dublin City and County from Prehistory to Present* (Dublin, 1992), pp. 57–77.

Oliver, John A., *Working at Stormont* (Dublin, 1978).

O'Malley, Ernie, *On Another Man's Wound* (London, 1936).

Oman, Charles, 'Irish troops in the service of Spain, 1709–1818', *Journal of the Royal United Services Institution*, 63 (1918), pp. 1–7, 193–9, 450–63.

O'Meara, Patrick, 'Irishmen in eighteenth-century Russian service', *Irish Slavonic Studies*, 5 (1984), pp. 13–25.

O'Neill, James, 'Conflicting loyalties: Irish regiments in the imperial service, 1689–1710', *Irish Sword*, 17 (1987–90), pp. 116–19.

O'Neill, James & Thompson, F. Glenn, 'Field Marshal Francis Maurice Lacy (1725–1801), *Irish Sword*, 17 (1987–90), pp. 1–3.

O'Rahilly, Alfred, *The Massacre at Smerwick, 1580* (Cork, 1938).

Original Letters Illustrative of English History, ed. Henry Ellis, 2nd ser. (4 vols., London, 1827).

Orpen, Goddard Henry, *Ireland under the Normans* (4 vols., Oxford, 1911–20).

Orr, Philip, *The Road to the Somme: Men of the Ulster Division Tell Their Story* (Belfast, 1987).

[O'Shannon, Cathal], *Fifty Years of Liberty Hall* (Dublin, 1959).

Ó Snodaigh, Padraig, 'Class and the Irish Volunteers', *Irish Sword*, 16 (1984–6), pp. 165–84.

'Some police and military aspects of the Irish Volunteers', *Irish Sword*, 13 (1978–9), pp. 217–29.

Otway-Ruthven, A. J., *A History of Medieval Ireland* (London, 1968).

'Ireland in the 1350s: Sir Thomas de Rokeby and his successors', *Journal of the Royal Society of Antiquaries of Ireland*, 97 (1967), pp. 47–59.

'Knight service in Ireland', *Journal of the Royal Society of Antiquaries of Ireland*, 89 (1959), pp. 1–15.

'Royal service in Ireland', *Journal of the Royal Society of Antiquaries of Ireland*, 98 (1968), pp. 37–46.

Palmer, Stanley H., 'Major-General Sir Charles Napier: Irishman, Chartist and commander of the northern district in England 1830–41', *Irish Sword*, 15 (1982–3), pp. 89–100.

Police and Protest in England and Ireland 1780–1850 (Cambridge, 1988).

Parker, Geoffrey, *The Military Revolution. Military Innovation and the Rise of the West, 1500–1800* (Cambridge, 1988; 2nd edn, 1989).

The Thirty Years' War (London, 1984).

[Parker], *Memoirs of Captain Robert Parker, late of the Royal Regiment of Foot* (London, 1747).

Patrick, *Epistola ad Coroticum*, in Ludwig Bieler (ed.), *Libri Epistolarum Sancti Patricii Episcopi* (Dublin, 1952; repr. 1993).

Pearse, Pádraic H., *Collected Works: Political Writings and Speeches* (Dublin, 1924).

[Peel], *Memoirs of The Right Honourable Sir Robert Peel* (2 vols., London, 1857).

Perceval-Maxwell, Michael, 'Ireland and Scotland 1638–1648', in John S. Morrill (ed.), *The Scottish National Covenant in its British Context 1638–51* (Edinburgh, 1990), pp. 193–211.

The Outbreak of the Irish Rebellion of 1641 (Montreal & Kingston, 1994).

Perry, Nicholas, 'Nationality in the Irish infantry regiments in the First World War', *War and Society*, 12 (1994), pp. 65–95.

Petrie, Sir Charles, 'The Hispano-Papal landing at Smerwick', *Irish Sword*, 9 (1969–70), pp. 82–94.

Petty, William, Sir, *The Economic Writings of Sir William Petty, together with the Observations upon the Bills of Mortality more probably by John Graunt*, ed. Charles Henry Hull (2 vols., Cambridge, 1899; reprint 1986).

The Political Anatomy of Ireland, with the Establishment for that Kingdom when the late Duke of Ormond was Lord Lieutenant (London, 1691; reprinted Shannon, 1970).

Picard, Jean-Michel & de Pontfarcy, Yolande (ed. & transl.), *Saint Patrick's Purgatory: a Twelfth-century Tale of a Journey to the Other World* (Blackrock, Co. Dublin, 1985).

The Vision of Tnugdal (Blackrock, Co. Dublin, 1989).

Piveronus, P. J., 'Sir Warham St Leger and the first Munster plantation, 1568–9', *Éire-Ireland* (Summer 1979), pp. 15–36.

Plummer, Charles (ed. & transl.), *Bethada Náem nÉrenn. Lives of Irish Saints* (2 vols., Oxford, 1922; rev. imp., 1968).

Pollock, Sam, *Mutiny for the Cause* (London, 1969).

Pomeroy, Hon. R. L., *The Story of a Regiment of Horse, being the Regimental History from 1685 to 1922 of the 5th Princess Charlotte of Wales' Dragoon Guards* (2 vols., Edinburgh, 1924).

Pottinger, B., *The Foreign Volunteers: They Fought for the Boers (1899–1902)* (Melville, 1986).

Power, Thomas, *Land, Politics and Society in Eighteenth-Century Tipperary* (Oxford, 1994).

Priestley, E. J., 'The Portsmouth captains', *Journal of the Society for Army Historical Research*, 55 (1977), pp. 153–64.

Prince, A. E., 'The strength of English armies in the reign of Edward III', *English Historical Review*, 46 (1931), pp. 353–71.

Quinn. D. B., 'Renaissance influences in English colonisation', *Transactions of the Royal Historical Society*, 5th ser., 25 (1976), pp. 73–93.

Radulphi de Diceto Opera Historica (Rolls series, 2 vols., London, 1876).

Rait, R. S., *The Life and Campaigns of Hugh, First Viscount Gough, Field Marshal* (2 vols., London, 1903).

Ratcliff, S. C., 'Destruction of the public records in Dublin', *Bulletin of the Institute of Historical Research*, 2 (1924), pp. 8–9.

Rawlinson, Richard (ed.), *The History of the Most Eminent Statesman, Sir John Perrot* (London, 1727).

Registrum prioratus omnium sanctorum, ed. Richard Butler (Dublin, 1845).

Reid, J. S., *History of the Presbyterian Church in Ireland*, ed. W. D. Killen (3 vols., Belfast, 1867).

Rich, Barnaby, *A Pathway to Military Practice* (London, 1587).

Richardson, H. G. & Sayles, G. O., 'Irish revenue, 1278–1384', *Proceedings of the Royal Irish Academy*, sect. C, 62 (1962), pp. 87–100.

Richardson, W., *History of the Origin of the Irish Yeomanry* (Dublin, 1801).

Robertson, Nora, *Crowned Harp* (Dublin, 1960).

Robinson, Philip S., *The Plantation of Ulster: British Settlement in an Irish Landscape, 1600–1670* (Dublin, 1984).

Roger of Howden, *Gesta Secundi Benedicti Abbatis*, ed. William Stubbs (Rolls series, 2 vols., London, 1867).

Rogers, Randall, 'Aspects of the military history of the Anglo-Norman invasion of Ireland, 1169–1225', *Irish Sword*, 16 (1986), pp. 135–46.

A Roll of the Proceedings of the King's Council in Ireland for a Portion of the Sixteenth Year of the Reign of Richard II, 1392–93, ed. J. Graves (London, 1877).

Romer, Maj. C. F. & Mainwaring, Maj. A. E., *The Second Battalion Royal Dublin Fusiliers in the South African War* (London, 1908).

Ross, Charles (ed.), *Correspondence of Charles, first Marquis Cornwallis* (3 vols., London, 1859).

[Ross-Lewin, R. S.], *Poems by a County of Clare West Briton* (Limerick, 1907).

Rotulorum Patentium et Clausorum Cancellariae Hiberniae Caldarium (Dublin, 1828).

The Royal Inniskilling Fusiliers, compiled by the Regimental Historical Records Committee (London, 1928).

Russell, Conrad, *The Causes of the English Civil War* (Oxford, 1990).

The Fall of the British Monarchies 1637–1642 (Oxford, 1991).

Ryan, Michael (ed.), *The Illustrated Archaeology of Ireland* (Dublin, 1991).

Ryder, Chris, *The Ulster Defence Regiment: an Instrument of Peace?* (London, 1991).

'Sanas Cormaic, An Old-Irish glossary compiled by Cormac úa Cuilennáin, King-Bishop of Cashel in the ninth century. Edited from the copy in the Yellow Book of Lecan', *Anecdota from Irish Manuscripts*, iv. ed. O. J. Bergin, R. I. Best, Kuno Meyer & J. G. O'Keeffe (Halle, 1912).

Sayles, G. O., *Documents on the Affairs of Ireland before the King's Council* (Dublin, 1979).

'The siege of Carrickfergus castle, 1315–16', *Irish Historical Studies*, 10 (1956–7), pp. 94–100.

Sawyer, P. H., *The Age of the Vikings* (2nd edn, London, 1971).

'The Vikings and Ireland', in Dorothy Whitelock *et al.* (eds.), *Ireland in Early Medieval Europe*, pp. 345–61.

Semple, A. J., 'The Fenian infiltration of the British army', *Journal of the Society for Army Historical Research*, 52 (1974), pp. 135–60.

Sharpe, Richard, 'Hiberno-Latin *Laicus*, Irish *Láech* and the Devil's Men', *Ériu*, 30 (1979), pp. 75–92.

Sheehan, Anthony, 'Irish revenues and English subventions, 1559–1622', in *Proceedings of the Royal Irish Academy*, sect. V, 90: 2 (1990), pp. 1–64.

'The killing of the Earl of Desmond, November 1583', *Journal of the Cork Historical & Archeological Society*, 88 (1983), pp. 106–10.

'The overthrow of the plantation of Munster in October 1598', *Irish Sword*, 15 (1982–3), pp. 11–22.

Sheehy, Jeanne, *The Rediscovery of Ireland's Past: the Celtic Revival, 1830–1930* (London, 1980).

[Shipp], *Memoirs of the Extraordinary Military Career of John Shipp, late a Lieutenant in His Majesty's 87th Regiment Written by Himself* (3 vols., London, 1829).

Silke, J. J., *Kinsale* (Liverpool, 1970).

Simms, J. G., 'The Irish on the Continent, 1691–1800', in *New History of Ireland*, iv, *Eighteenth-Century Ireland* (Oxford, 1986), pp. 629–56.

  Jacobite Ireland, 1685–91 (London, 1969).

  'Remembering 1690', *Studies*, 63 (1974), pp. 231–42.

  The Treaty of Limerick (Dundalk, 1961).

  War and Politics in Ireland, 1649–1730 (London, 1986).

Simms, Katharine, 'The Battle of Dysert O'Dea and the Gaelic resurgence in Thomond', *Dál gCais*, 5 (1979), pp. 59–66.

  'Gabh umad Fheidhlimidh: a fifteenth-century inauguration ode?', *Ériu*, 31 (1980), pp. 132–45.

  From Kings to Warlords: the Changing Political Structure of Gaelic Ireland in the Later Middle Ages, Studies in Celtic History VII, gen. ed. David Dumville (Woodbridge, 1987).

  'Guesting and feasting in Gaelic Ireland', *Journal of the Royal Society of Antiquaries of Ireland*, 108 (1978), pp. 67–100.

  'Images of warfare in Bardic poetry', *Celtica*, 31 (1990), pp. 608–19.

  'Niall Garbh II ODonnell, king of Tír Conaill 1422–39', *Donegal Annual*, 12 (1977), pp. 7–21.

  'Nomadry in medieval Ireland: the origins of the creaght or *coaraigheacht*', *Peritia*, 5 (1986), pp. 379–91.

  'Warfare in the medieval Gaelic lordships', *Irish Sword*, 12 (1975–6), pp. 98–108.

Sjoestedt, Marie-Louise, *Gods and Heroes of the Celts*, transl. by Myles Dillon (London, 1949).

Smail, R. C., *Crusading Warfare (1097–1193)* (Cambridge, 1956).

Smith, J. B., 'Gruffydd Llwyd and the Celtic alliance, 1315–16', *Bulletin of the Board of Celtic Studies*, 26 (1974–6), pp. 463–78.

Smyth, Alfred P., *Celtic Leinster* (Blackrock, 1982).

  Scandinavian Kings in the British Isles, 850–880 (Oxford, 1977).

  Scandinavian York and Dublin (2 vols., New Jersey & Dublin, 1975–9).

Smyth, James, *Men of No Property: Popular Politicisation in Ireland in the 1790s* (London, 1992).

Smyth, Sir John, *In This Sign Conquer: the Story of the Army Chaplains* (London, 1968).

Smyth, P. D. H., '"Our cloud-cap't grenadiers": the Volunteers as a military force', *Irish Sword*, 12 (1978–9), pp. 185–207.

  'The Volunteer movement in Ulster: background and development, 1745–85' (Ph.D. thesis, Queen's University, Belfast, 1974).

  'The Volunteers and parliament, 1779–84', in Thomas Bartlett & David W. Hayton (eds.), *Penal Era and Golden Age: Essays in Irish History, 1690–1800* (Belfast, 1979), pp. 113–36.

Snoddy, Oliver, 'The midland volunteer force, 1913', *Journal of the Old Athlone Society*, 1: 1 (1969), pp. 38–44.

Somerville, Andrew, *The Autobiography of a Working Man*, ed. John Carswell (London, 1951).

Song of Dermot and the Earl, ed. Goddard H. Orpen (Oxford, 1892).

Spiers, Edward M., *The Army and Society, 1815–1914* (London, 1980).

  The Late Victorian Army 1868–1902 (Manchester, 1992).

  Radical General: Sir George de Lacy Evans 1787–1870 (Manchester, 1983).

  'The regular army in 1914', in Beckett & Simpson, *Nation in Arms*, pp. 36–61.

Springhall, John, *Youth, Empire and Society: British Youth Movements, 1883–1940* (London, 1977).

Stalley, Roger, 'The Anglo-Norman keep at Trim: its architectural implications', *Archaeology Ireland*, 6: 4, 22 (1992), pp. 16–19.

Stanley, P. A., 'White mutiny: the Bengal Europeans, 1825–75, a study in military social history' (Ph.D. thesis, Australian National University, 1993).

State Papers, Henry VIII (11 vols., London, 1830–52).

Statute Rolls of the Parliament of Ireland, Reign of King Henry VI, ed. Henry F. Berry (Dublin, 1910).

Statutes and Ordinances, and Acts of the Parliament of Ireland, King John to Henry V, ed. Henry F. Berry (Dublin, 1907).

Staunton, Martin, 'The Royal Munster Fusiliers in the Great War, 1914–19' (M.A. thesis, University College, Dublin, 1986).

Steele, Robert, *A Bibliography of Royal Proclamations of the Tudor and Stuart Sovereigns, 1485–1714* (2 vols., Oxford, 1910).

Stein, Ernst, *Histoire du Bas-Empire*, transl. J.-R. Palanque (2 vols., Paris, 1949–59).

Stenton, F. M., *Anglo-Saxon England* (3rd edn, Oxford, 1971).

Stephan, Eno, *Spies in Ireland* (pbk edn, London, 1965).

Stevenson, David, *Alasdair MacColla and the Highland Problem in the Seventeenth Century* (Edinburgh, 1980).

   Scottish Covenanters and Irish Confederates: Scottish-Irish relations in the mid-seventeenth century (Belfast, 1981).

Stewart, A. T. Q., *The Ulster Crisis* (London, 1967).

Stewart, J., 'Topographia Hiberniae', *Celtica*, 21 (1990), pp. 642–57.

Stoddard, P. M., 'Counter-insurgency and defence in Ireland, 1790–1805' (D.Phil. thesis, Oxford University, 1972).

[Story, George], *A True and Impartial History of the Most Material Occurrences in the Kingdom of Ireland during the Two Last Years* (London, 1691).

Stradling, R. A., *The Spanish Monarchy and Irish Mercenaries: the Wild Geese in Spain 1618 to 1688* (Dublin, 1994).

Strickland, Matthew (ed.), *Anglo-Norman Warfare: Studies in Late Anglo-Saxon and Anglo-Norman Military Organization and Warfare* (Woodbridge, 1992).

Sullivan, A. M., *Old Ireland* (London, 1927).

Sweetman, P. D., 'Archaeological investigations at Ferns castle', *Proceedings of the Royal Irish Academy*, sect. C, 79 (1979), pp. 217–45.

Swift, John, 'Americans in Ulster: the Anglo-American Garrison. 1942–45' (M.A. thesis, University of Lancaster, 1992).

[Swift], *The Prose Works of Jonathan Swift*, ed. Herbert Davis (14 vols., Oxford, 1939–68).

Thirty-eighth Report of the Deputy Keeper of the Public Records of Ireland (Dublin, 1906).

Three Prose Versions of the Secreta Secretorum, ed. R. Steele (Early English Texts Soc., 74, London, 1898).

Thurneysen, Rudolf, *Die Bürgschaft im irischen Recht* (Berlin, 1928).

   'Tochmarc Ailbe, "Das Werben um Ailbe"', *Zeitschrift für Celtische Philologie*, 13 (1919), pp. 251–82.

Tilly, Charles, *From Mobilization to Revolution* (Reading, Mass., 1978).

Togail Bruidne Dá Derga, ed. Eleanor Knott (Dublin, 1936).

531

[Tone], *Autobiography of Theobald Wolfe Tone, 1763–1798*, ed. R. Barry O'Brien (London, 1893).

Tone, W. T. W. (ed.), *Life of Theobald Wolfe Tone* (2 vols., Washington, DC, 1826).

Townshend, Charles, *The British Campaign in Ireland, 1919–1921: the Development of Political and Military Policies* (Oxford, 1975).

'The Irish Republican Army and the development of guerrilla warfare, 1916–1921', *English Historical Review*, 94: 371 (1979), pp. 318–45.

Political Violence in Ireland: Government and Resistance since 1848 (Oxford, 1983).

Turner, Sir Alfred, *Sixty Years of a Soldier's Life* (London, 1912).

Turner, Sir James, *Memoirs of His Own Life and Times*, ed. Thomas Thomson (Bannatyne Club, vol. xxviii, Edinburgh, 1829).

Turpin, John, 'Cuchulainn lives on', *Circa*, 69 (Autumn, 1994), pp. 26–31.

[Ussher], *The Whole Works of the Most Rev. James Ussher*, ed. C. R. Elrington & J. H. Todd (17 vols., Dublin, 1847–64).

Valiulis, Maryann Gialanella, *Portrait of a Revolutionary: General Richard Mulcahy and the Founding of the Irish Free State* (Dublin, 1992).

Van Brock, F. W., 'Morres's memorial, 1798', *Irish Sword*, 15 (1982–3), pp. 36–44.

Verney, Peter, *The Micks: the Story of the Irish Guards* (London, 1970).

Walker, George A., *A True Account of the Siege of Londonderry* (London, 1689).

Wall, Richard, Gallwey, Hubert & Garland, John L., 'Irish officers in the Spanish service', *Irish Genealogist*, 5 (1974–9), pp. 431–4, 601–5; 6 (1980–5), pp. 18–21, 204–11, 328–33, 461–8, 601–6.

Walsh, Micheline Kerney, 'Further notes on some Irishmen in the Imperial service', *Irish Sword*, 6 (1963–4), pp. 46–51, 70–5, 166–70.

'Some notes towards a history of the womenfolk of the wild geese', *Irish Sword*, 5 (1961–2), pp. 98–106, 133–45.

Spanish Knights of Irish Origin (4 vols., Dublin, 1960–78).

'The wild goose tradition', *Irish Sword*, 17 (1987–90), pp. 4–15.

Walsh, Paul (ed. & transl.), *Leabhar Chlainne Suibhne. An Account of the MacSweeny Families in Ireland with Pedigrees* (Dublin, 1920).

Walton, Clifford, *A History of the British Standing Army, 1660–1700* (London, 1894).

Ware, Sir James, *The Histories and Antiquities of Ireland*, ed. Robert Ware (Dublin, 1704).

Watt, John, *The Church in Medieval Ireland* (Dublin, 1972).

Wauchope, Piers, *Patrick Sarsfield and the Williamite Wars* (Dublin, 1992).

Webb, Stephen Saunders, *The Governors-General: the English Army and the Definition of the Empire, 1569–1681* (Chapel Hill, 1979).

Webb-Carter, Brig. B. W., 'A subaltern in Abyssinia', *Journal of the Society for Army Historical Research*, 38 (1960), pp. 144–9.

Weber, Max, *From Max Weber: Essays in Sociology*, ed. & transl. H. H. Gerth & C. Wright Mills (New York, 1946).

Wellington, Duke of (ed.), *Supplementary Dispatches and Memoranda of Field Marshal Arthur Wellesley, Duke of Wellington. India 1797–1805* (15 vols., London, 1858–72).

Western, J. R., 'Roman Catholics holding military commissions in 1798', *English Historical Review*, 70 (1955), pp. 428–32.

Wheatley, C. J., '"I hear the Irish are naturally brave": dramatic portrayals of the Irish soldier in the seventeenth and eighteenth centuries' (seminar paper, University College Galway, 1994).

Wheeler, Scott, 'Four armies in Ireland', in Ohlmeyer, *Independence to Occupation*.
 'Logistics and supply in Cromwell's conquest of Ireland', in Mark Charles Fissel (ed.), *War and Government in Britain, 1598-1650* (Manchester, 1991), pp. 38-56.

White, Dean Gunter, 'Henry VIII's Irish kerne in France and Scotland, 1544-45', *Irish Sword*, 3 (1957-8), pp. 213-25.

White, J. R., *Misfit: an Autobiography* (London, 1930).

White, Terence de Vere, *Kevin O'Higgins* (London, 1948).

Whitelock, Dorothy (ed.), *English Historical Documents c. 500-1042* (London, 1955).

Whitelock, Dorothy *et al.* (eds.), *Ireland in Early Medieval Europe* (Cambridge, 1982).

Wiley, B. Irvin, *The Life of Billy Yank: the Common Soldier of the Union* (New York, 1971).

Willcocks, Brig.-Gen. Sir James, *From Kabul to Kumasi: Twenty-four Years of Soldiering and Sport* (London, 1904).

[Williams], G. D. W[illiams] (ed.), *Dublin Charities* (Dublin, 1902).

Williams, Martin, 'Ancient mythology and revolutionary ideology in Ireland, 1878-1916', *Historical Journal*, 26 (1983), pp. 307-28.

Williams, N. J. A. (ed.), *Pairlement Chloinne Tomáis* (Dublin, 1981).

Williams, N. J. A. (ed. & transl.), *The Poems of Giolla Brighde Mac Con Midh* (London, 1980).

Wolseley, Field Marshal Viscount, *The Story of a Soldier's Life* (2 vols., London, 1903).

Wood, Herbert, *A Guide to the Records Deposited in the Public Record Office in Ireland* (Dublin, 1919).

Woods, C. J. (ed.), *The Journals and Memoirs of Thomas Russell* (Dublin, 1992).

Wright, Steven, J., *The Irish Brigade* (Springfield, Pa., 1992).

Young, G. V. C. & Foster, Caroline, *Captain François Thurot* (Peel, Isle of Man, 1986).

Zobel, Miller B., *The Boston Massacre* (New York & London, 1970).

Index